THE LIFE AND TIMES OF
G.D. Birla

Ghanshyamdas Birla was a complex public figure, businessman, merchant, philanthropist, political figure, and builder of magnificent temples. He was deeply involved in the affairs of the Indian National Congress and was its most important benefactor. He challenged the colonial domination of the Indian economy and was an industrial pioneer whose initiatives helped create a climate in which Indian enterprise could flourish.

Kudaisya's biography explores all the aspects of this legendary figure. Elegantly written, it reconstructs Birla's eventful public and private life drawing upon the rich historical evidence available in his private papers. Kudaisya was the first to have access to these papers.

Born in Victorian times, Birla lived through two World Wars, an epic struggle for freedom, the Nehru era of economic planning, and the beginning of India's experiment with economic liberalization. The book also provides a window on the transformation that India had witnessed in the twentieth century. It portrays how Birla's life was marked by a complex interplay of profit, power, and piety. By interweaving these elements, Birla was able to make a unique and enduring contribution to the making of contemporary India, in which many of his seminal ideas seem to be coming of age.

Medha M. Kudaisya is Assistant Professor, Department of History and the University Scholars Programme, The National University of Singapore.

'This is a work of meticulous scholarship and also very readable. It illuminates the times in which the man lived, as much as the man himself. The book is a "must" for serious students of twentieth-century India, whether their concerns are economic, political or cultural.'

— *Judith Brown, University of Oxford*

'The importance of Birla as one of India's major private industrialists and business politicians and the richness of the archival base used make this an important book for anyone who wishes to understand 20th century.'

—*Thomas A Timberg, senior economist*

'*The Life and Times of G.D. Birla* by Medha M. Kudaisya is useful in understanding the contributions and impact made by this man.'

—*Business Line*

'The book on G.D. Birla originated as a Ph.D thesis, but it has transcended the academic straightjacket to give readers the story of a man who had a large say in both the industrial world and the political arena.'

—*Business India*

'Medha M. Kudaisya's *The Life and Times of G.D. Birla* distinguishes itself from the fare that passes for corporate biography today.'

—*Business World*

'...this [is] an important book for anyone who wishes to understand 20th century India. ...the insights in the book will help us all understand a person and an epoch which were critical in the formation of the modern Indian state and economy.'

—*Economic and Political Weekly*

'Kudaisya has researched extensively... Her style is crisp and readable. If Birla were alive he would have had no complaints.'

—*Indian Express*

'The book apart from being eminently readable, tells us much not only about an industrialist with a vision but also philanthropist and a patriot.'

—*The Hindu*

'At one level, the book is the story of the life of a man; at another, it provides a window to the changes the country saw in the 20th century.'

—*The Telegraph*

'*The Life and Times of G.D. Birla* by Medha M. Kudaisya is the first definitive biography of Birla. Elegantly written it reconstructs Birla's eventful private and public life...'

—*Sunday Navhind Times*

THE LIFE AND TIMES OF
G.D. Birla

Medha M. Kudaisya

OXFORD
UNIVERSITY PRESS

OXFORD

UNIVERSITY PRESS

Oxford University Press is a department of the University of Oxford.
It furthers the University's objective of excellence in research, scholarship,
and education by publishing worldwide. Oxford is a registered trademark of
Oxford University Press in the UK and in certain other countries

Published in India by
Oxford University Press
22 Workspace, 2nd Floor, 1/22 Asaf Ali Road, New Delhi 110 002

First Edition published in 2003
Oxford India Paperbacks 2006
Digitally Printed in 2024

ISBN-13: 978-0-19-568332-5
ISBN-10: 0-19-568332-3

Typeset in AGaramond 10.5/12
by InoSoft Systems, New Delhi 110 092
Printed in India by Manipal Technologies Limited, Manipal

Contents

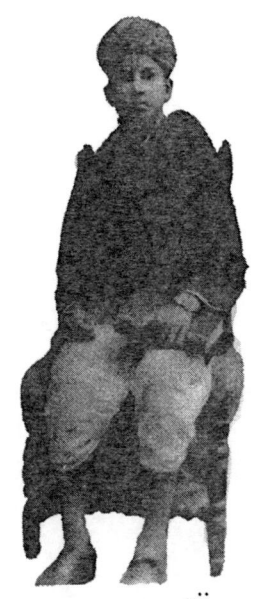

vi   Contents

Preface

'Mill-owner, Merchant and Zemindar' is how the *Indian Year Book and Who's Who of 1941–2* described Ghanshyamdas (G.D.) Birla. To most Indians and those familiar with India, Ghanshyamdas Birla, as a public figure, needs no introduction. He is perhaps best remembered as a builder of magnificent temples, as a philanthropist whose charities ran into millions, as the man who sheltered Gandhiji and at whose house the Mahatma was assassinated. While most Indians at some stage of their lives come across the name of Birla and the name itself remains pervasive, the figure behind the name—that of G.D. Birla—is becoming somewhat obscure. To an extent this is due to the passage of time but it is also because G.D. Birla as a historical figure was amazingly complex and few of his contemporaries really understood his persona. This book is an attempt to provide a narrative of his life and to place him in the context of the historical forces which shaped his life and the manner in which he, in turn, tried to influence them.

Birla's complexity as a historical figure arises in part from his amazing ability to function in several spheres of public life at the same time while, of course, never losing grip over his business interests. Among other things Birla was a zealous reformer within his mercantile community of the Marwaris; throughout his life he freely gave his patronage and money to Hindu causes; he was the single most important benefactor of the Indian National Congress before independence and generously financed its many causes and campaigns against the British Raj. For over two decades between 1927 and the 1950s, he remained one of the most influential spokesmen of Indian big business as well as its chief strategist. He led a dogged fight against foreign capital and was responsible for forging much of the solidarity that Indian big business displayed against the British before 1947. For decades he remained a powerful critic of the fiscal and industrial policies of the colonial state: at the same time he conducted one of the most successful Indian private enterprises of his time—reaping huge profits during the inter-war years. His triumphs often lay in his varied roles as a lobbyist—in establishing what he called 'the personal touch'—in England, pleading for great concessions for India;

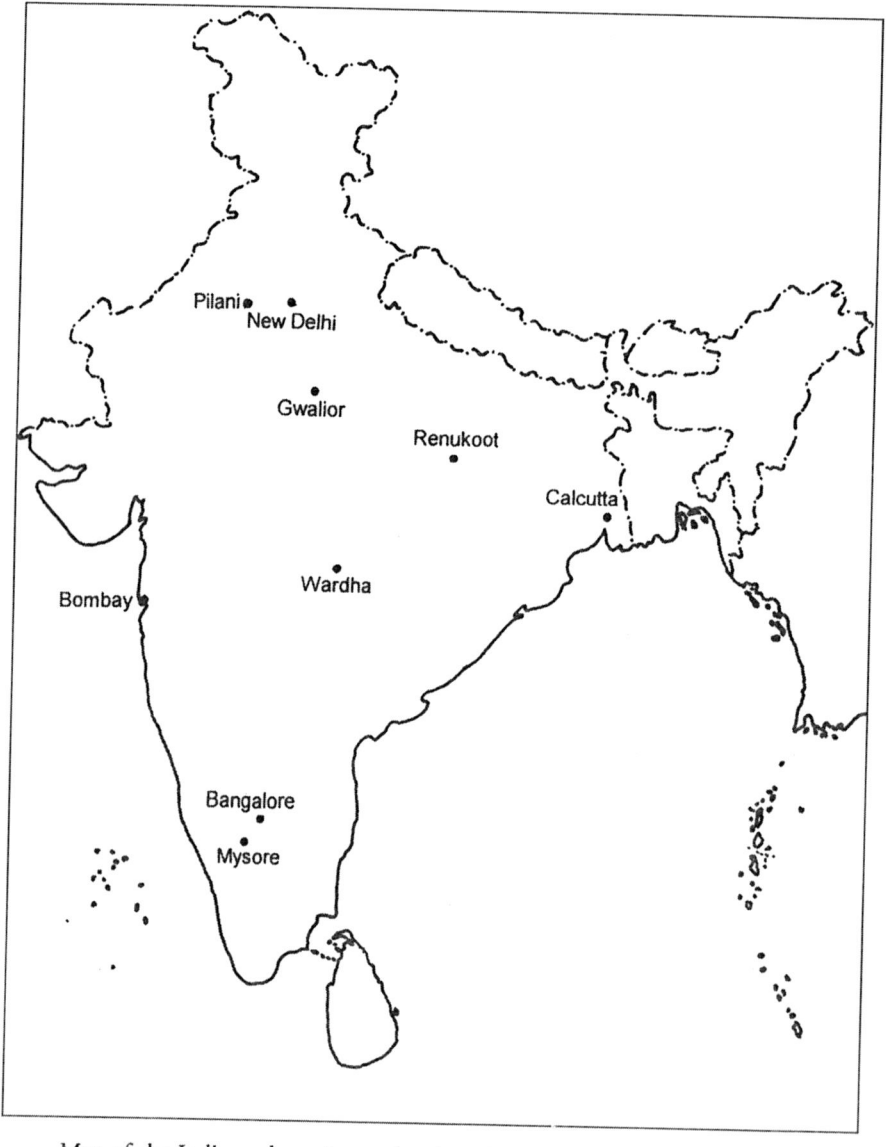

Map of the Indian subcontinent, showing places associated with Birla's life

within Congress organizational circles, working for right-wing ascendancy; within wider nationalist politics, promoting the Constitutionalist viewpoint; and in corporate circles, quietly lobbying for solidarity and closer understanding with the political establishment.

The question may well be asked: why write about Birla now that we are well into the twenty-first century? The man has, after all, been dead for nearly two decades and, in any case, the peak of his public career lay more than half a century ago. The answer lies in two parts. In many ways Birla was a pioneer and a study of his life and experiences can provide insights into important facets of public life such as the interface between business and politics, philanthropy and religion. The second part of the answer lies in the fact that a historical assessment of Birla, who was by any reckoning one of the pre-eminent Indians of the twentieth century, remains to be done.

Although Birla published his memoirs in 1953, they mainly highlighted his close relationship with Gandhi and did not provide a full account of his own life. During his lifetime and especially when Gandhi was alive, he liked to call himself the Mahatma's follower: hence he titled his memoirs *In the Shadow of the Mahatma*. The memoirs were published following the death of Birla's powerful patron, Vallabhbhai Patel. These years also marked the heyday of Nehru's socialist rhetoric which put private enterprise on the defensive. Moreover, the controversy surrounding Birla's reluctance to hand over his New Delhi residence to be converted into a national memorial for Gandhi had seriously annoyed Nehru and the relations between the two men were at their lowest ebb. These circumstances compelled Birla to publish selections of letters exchanged with Gandhi which established his proximity to the 'Father of the Nation' and showed him as a benefactor of the Congress. The publication was timely and through the 350 pages of text, Birla set out to portray the image which he wanted to cast for himself—that of someone who had always remained 'in the shadow of the Mahatma'. Then, in 1977, Birla published *Bapu: A Unique Association*—four volumes of his correspondence with Gandhi, which provided further details of his relationship with the Mahatma. The timing of the publication was again significant. Just a few months earlier Birla had defended Indira Gandhi's 'Emergency' and, when the first non-Congress government came to power at the centre, the Birla fortunes seemed to be under a cloud and the need to reinforce his Gandhian credentials seemed imperative.

This image which Birla carefully crafted in these publications revealed only one facet of his personality and masked the many paradoxes and ambiguities which featured in his life. His biographers picked up and reinforced this image. Soon after his death in 1983, Alan Ross, a British journalist well known for his writings on cricket, was encouraged by a section of the Birla family to produce a biography. The result was *The Emissary*, which provided a readable account of his life but did not break out of the mould which Birla himself had cast. It did not illuminate the historical context which produced Birla, nor did it raise any questions about the man.[1]

A historical appraisal of Birla thus remains to be done, and this study is a step in that direction. Ironically, it attempts to narrate the story of a man who did not want his biography to be written. 'Certainly no Indian can write my biography because biography isn't an Indian skill,' he remarked in 1978 to Ian Jack, a correspondent of the *Times*. He was concerned that accounts of his life were likely to be hagiographic, given the fact that biography is not a strong genre in contemporary Indian writing.

Birla makes a difficult, even formidable, biographical subject. His origins were relatively unpretentious and his orthodox Hindu background emphasized values of self-effacement. Further, Marwari mercantile practices prescribed secrecy in everyday transactions and encouraged destruction, rather than preservation, of written records. These factors make it difficult to document Birla's early life (as it would be of any other biographical subject from that era unless the person were born to royalty). From his teens, however, it becomes possible to piece together a narrative of his life and from the 1920s onwards, as the evidence grows richer, a fuller reconstruction of his many-faceted activities becomes possible. However, certain aspects of his life elude the biographer. For instance, the impact of his two marriages and the subsequent death of both his spouses on his personality is difficult to measure. Likewise, it is difficult to reconstruct how the Birlas made their early fortunes, though from the 1920s onwards, when most of their new ventures took the form of listed companies, it becomes easier to understand the scale of their expanding businesses. While we may never know the secret of how Birla made his money, we are in a good position to understand, at least, how he spent it.

Notwithstanding these limitations, it is possible to reconstruct a good deal about Birla's life in its variety and richness. His is a remarkable story—a life of achievements so varied that they could easily qualify him to be described as one of the greatest Indians of the twentieth century.

At a simple level, this is the story of one man's life. But it also provides a window on the transformation which India witnessed during the twentieth century and in which Birla played a modest role. In some ways it is also the story of one man's vision and his struggle to see the fulfilment of this vision. In his lifetime Birla saw the small family business of trading and money-lending transformed into the second largest industrial group in the country, bidding for the number one position with the Tatas in terms of assets, turnover and profits. He saw two World Wars and a global economic depression. He saw an intense nationalist struggle waged against the Raj and he ensured that its leadership had the powerful support, at important junctures, of an important section of the

---

[1] Alan Ross, *The Emissary: G. D. Birla, Gandhi and Independence*, London, Collins Harvill, 1986.

Indian capitalist class. He witnessed the end of the domination of the Indian economy by foreign capital, as indeed the end of colonial rule in India. With the coming of independence his vision of an independent, strong, capitalist India, with private enterprise playing a pivotal role in modernizing the country, was realized. Birla could thereafter concentrate his energies on expanding his business, safeguarding the wider interests of private enterprise, and pursuing his favourite philanthropic projects.

Birla's life provides a unique vantage point for understanding several processes which have shaped contemporary India. For instance, Birla supported, for more than 25 years, 'Hindu nationalism' and 'secular' Congress-style politics at the same time and saw no contradiction in this. His career perhaps illustrates that Hindu majoritarian nationalism (designated by the abbreviated term 'Hindutva' in the present-day context) and Congress nationalism were not bipolar opposites but ideological stances within the same political spectrum, a dimension neglected by most existing accounts of Indian nationalism. Further, Birla's work as a spokesman and strategist of big business provides insights into the nexus between businessmen and politicians and unravels before us the world of corporate lobbying. It is instructive of how businessmen intervene in the political arena and the manner in which their fortunes are powerfully shaped by the changing political context. Likewise, the philanthropic side of his personality tells us about the linkages that exist between philanthropy and religion, and the political edge that often runs through gift-giving.

A Note on the G.D. Birla Papers

This book presents, for the first time, a critical assessment of Birla based upon the extensive historical evidence available in the Birla Private Papers to which the author is the first researcher to have had full and unrestricted access. The papers, are rich in the historical evidence they provide for a study of contemporary Indian history. The pre-1947 papers relate mainly to the late 1920s, 1930s and 1940s; the evidence is sketchy for the early 1920s and very few papers relate to the earlier period. The post-1947 papers contain voluminous material for the 1940's, 1950's and 1960's. They are preserved by the family in Calcutta and Delhi.

A word of explanation may be offered about the way the papers are organized and the manner in which they are cited in this work. The papers are divided into four main series: (a) Very Very Important Correspondence; (b) Important Correspondence (further sub-divided into Series I which relates mainly to the post-1947 period and Series II which relates to the pre-1947 correspondence, referred to as Series I and Series II, respectively in this manuscript); (c) Foreign Correspondence; and (d) Miscellaneous Correspondence. All correspondence is organized into files according to the names of the correspondents and these are numbered. In addition to the above four series, a number of files exist on individual subjects with distinct file numbers. One important set of such files is designated as 'Miscellaneous'.

In addition to the Birla Papers, a number of hitherto unused sources have been utilized such as the records of the Federation of Indian Chambers of Commerce and Industry and the Indian Chamber of Commerce, business journals such as *Capital* and *Commerce*, contemporary newspapers like the *Hindustan Times*, the *New Empire*, and the *Eastern Economist*, periodicals such as *Shri Marwari Agarwal, Maheshwari Bandhu, Marwari*, private papers of prominent businessmen, politicians and officials, oral interviews with members of the Birla family, and the extensive government records available in archives in Delhi, Calcutta and London.

Acknowledgements

This work originated as a Ph.D. thesis which I presented at the University of Cambridge in 1992. It has since been substantially revised and in the many years that this has taken, I have incurred many debts.

I must start with thanking my research supervisor at Cambridge, Anthony Low, for having been most encouraging and having given all the time and attention I could ask for when I was doing my thesis and in the years thereafter. I could not have completed this work without his support.

Many others have, over the years, provided help and encouragement. I must thank Chris Bayly most warmly for his consistent encouragement and generous support over the years. Judith Brown has read many chapters and I most gratefully acknowledge her encouragement. Peter Reeves has patiently read drafts of most chapters and offered valuable suggestions for which I must thank him. He has prodded me to complete this work.

I would like to thank my teachers at the Jawaharlal Nehru University, specially Bipan Chandra, for their support. Others who have been helpful with comments on parts of this work include the late Ravinder Kumar, Claude Markovits, Mushirul Hasan, Aditya Mukherjee, and Basudev Chatterji. I thank them all most warmly.

This work could not have started without the co-operation and interest of Sarala and Basant Kumar Birla. By giving me unrestricted access to the G.D. Birla Papers, they reposed their confidence in me. Above all, Sarala Birla's encouragement has been most inspiring for which I must warmly thank her. I must also warmly thank Manjushree Birla for her keen interest in this work. The late L.N. Birla kindly showed me some of the material which was in his possession for which I am most grateful. By showing me files of the *Hindustan Times*, Shobhana Bharatiya provided facilities for which I am thankful. I am also obliged to G.L. Bansal, ex-parliamentarian and long-time secretary-general of FICCI for sharing with me his considerable knowledge of the subject.

The generosity of many persons and institutions made this work possible. The award of a Commonwealth Scholarship by the Association of Commonwealth Universities enabled me to study at Cambridge. I must thank my tutor at

Pembroke College, Jay Winter, for his interest in my welfare during my years at Pembroke. The organizations that made long field trips possible are the Smuts Memorial Fund, the Ellen MacArthur Fund, the Charles Wallace India Trust, the Hammond Trust, the British Council and the Master and Fellows of Pembroke College.

The archivists and librarians of a number of institutions facilitated this research and I must warmly thank them. The staff of 'Mangalam' in Delhi, especially Ratan Lal, have been most co-operative over the years. In Calcutta, I must begin by thanking Nopaniji and Tandonji of the Maheswari Pustakalaya for their unfailing kindness and help. I am grateful to the authorities of the Bara Bazaar Kumarsabha Pustakalaya, Surajmal Jalan Pustakalaya, Marwari Relief Society, Akhil Bharatiya Marwari Sammelan, Vishudanand Saraswati Vidyalaya, and the National Library. In Delhi, I would like to thank the staff of the Marwari Library, the FICCI Library and Records Room, the Nehru Memorial Museum and Library, and the National Archives of India. In Pilani, the director and the librarian of the Birla Insititute of Technology and Science, the secretary of the Birla Education Trust and, above all, R.S. Shah deserve much thanks for their help in facilitating my research. Among the institutions that I used in England I would like to thank the authorities of the India Office Library and Records, the Centre of South Asian Studies at Cambridge, the Central Library, the Churchill College Library and Archives, and not the least, the Faculty of Oriental Studies.

I would like to thank the Jesus and Mary College, University of Delhi, especially its former principal, Sister Melba Rodriques. In Singapore, I would like to thank colleagues and friends at Nanyang Technological University, where I taught, for their support while I was revising the thesis. Two individuals offered institutional support which made my writing possible in its later stages. I am grateful to Diana Wong, formerly of the Institute of South-east Asian Studies, and Brenda Yeoh of the Centre of Advanced Studies at the National University of Singapore. I must thank George Landow, for his very encouraging comments on the first few chapters which he read.

Among friends there are many with whom I have spent enjoyable times during the course of the writing of this book. First and foremost, I must thank Tan Tai Yong and Sylvia Tan for their consistent encouragement. Since our Cambridge days, they have been unfailing in their warmth and friendship. From my time in Cambridge I thank Kamal Choudhary and Sumita Chickermane. In Delhi, I must acknowledge Salil Misra, Neerja and Hulas Singh and Visalakshi Menon for their unfailing support, generosity and for always being such good friends. In Singapore, Renu Gupta patiently went through drafts to help make the text more readable. Aradhana Talwar was most helpful with proof-reading at short notice. I would also like to thank Stephanie Rupp for her friendship, encouragement, and the good times we shared.

I thank my editors at the Oxford University Press, who have been wonderfully supportive and most tolerant of delayed submissions.

My family, especially my mother Santosh Malik, has been most supportive and understanding at all times. It is a pleasure to acknowledge all that Kamal, Anu, Ritu and Nitin have done to motivate me to complete this work. I must thank Yasmin for never failing to ask when it would be finally completed. I must also thank my father-in-law for his interest in this work. Geeta has always been most supportive. I must thank Taramani for being such a great help. My husband Gyanesh has been an invaluable source of strength and without his support this work would not have been possible. He has shared every moment of this work and his encouragement has been indispensable. Vrinda has provided much enjoyable distraction during the writing of this book. This work could not have been completed without the blessings and love of Shri Vishwa Mitter Ji Maharaj. It is difficult for me to acknowledge all that my uncle Shri Prem Ji Maharaj has done for me over the years, and it is to him that this book is dedicated.

The Birlas : A Genealogy

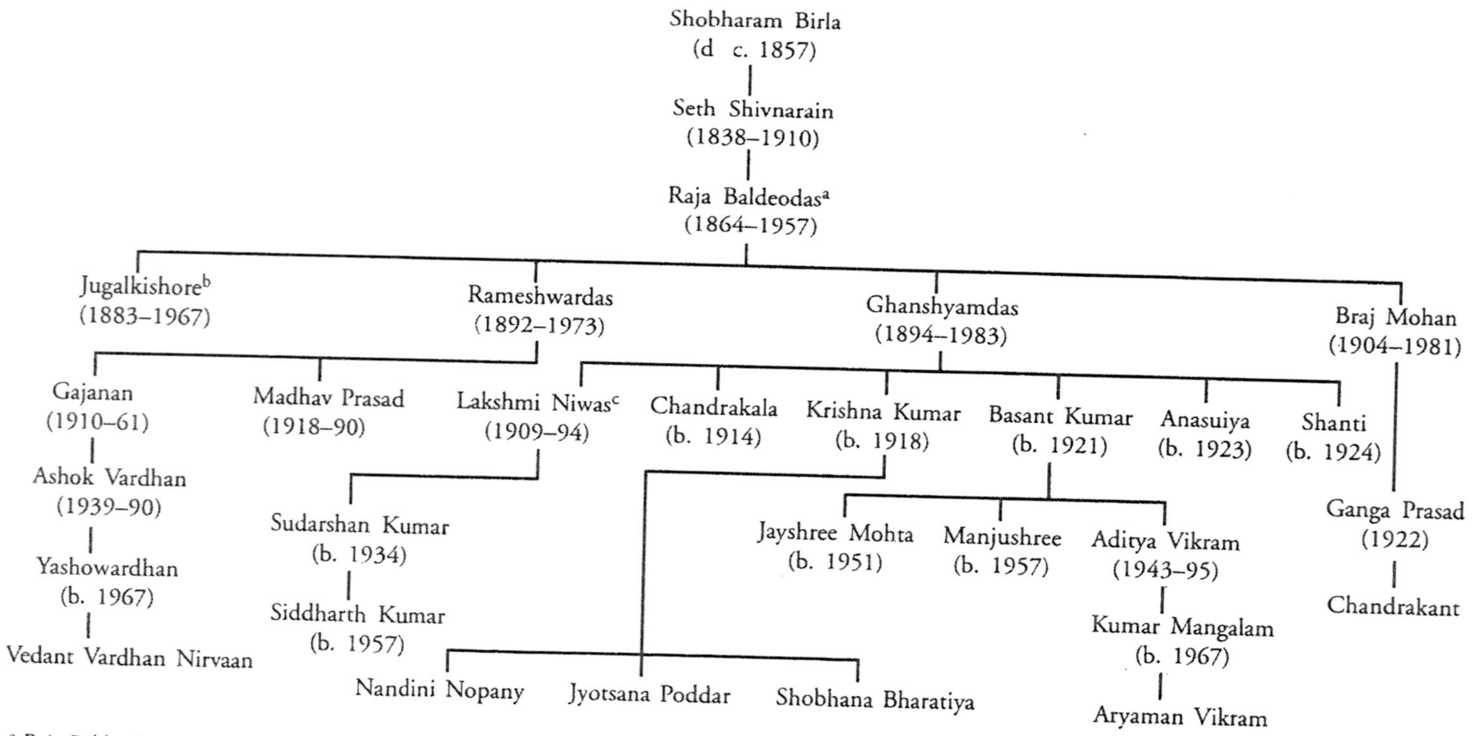

Shobharam Birla
(d c. 1857)

Seth Shivnarain
(1838–1910)

Raja Baldeodas[a]
(1864–1957)

Jugalkishore[b]
(1883–1967)

Rameshwardas
(1892–1973)

Ghanshyamdas
(1894–1983)

Braj Mohan
(1904–1981)

Gajanan
(1910–61)

Madhav Prasad
(1918–90)

Lakshmi Niwas[c]
(1909–94)

Chandrakala
(b. 1914)

Krishna Kumar
(b. 1918)

Basant Kumar
(b. 1921)

Anasuiya
(b. 1923)

Shanti
(b. 1924)

Ganga Prasad
(1922)

Chandrakant

Ashok Vardhan
(1939–90)

Sudarshan Kumar
(b. 1934)

Siddharth Kumar
(b. 1957)

Jayshree Mohta
(b. 1951)

Manjushree
(b. 1957)

Aditya Vikram
(1943–95)

Kumar Mangalam
(b. 1967)

Aryaman Vikram

Yashowardhan
(b. 1967)

Vedant Vardhan Nirvaan

Nandini Nopany   Jyotsana Poddar   Shobhana Bharatiya

[a] Raja Baldeodas also had three daughters: Bhagwanidevi Mohta, Jaidevi Kothari and Kamaladevi Mantri.

[b] No children; adopted G.D. Birla's eldest son Lakshmi Niwas.

[c] G.D. Birla's son from his wife Durgadevi. The other children were from his second marriage with Mahadevi.

1

The Birlas: From Pilani to Bara Bazaar, 1858–1910

Ghanshyamdas Birla was born on 14 April 1894 in a small windowless room in a large *haveli* in the sleepy village of Pilani which lies about 160 miles south-west of Delhi in the north Indian state of Rajasthan. He was the fourth child of his parents, Baldeodas and Yogeshwari Devi (three more were to follow), who were delighted at his birth as it took place on *Ramnavami*, the birthday of Lord Rama and one of the most auspicious days in the Hindu almanac. The newborn was called Ghanshyamdas.[1] In Hindi 'Ghanshyam' literally means dark as a cloud but it is also another name for Lord Krishna who was of dark visage. This was perhaps due to the influence of Braj language and culture (at the centre of which lies the legend of the cowherd god Krishna) in that part of Rajputana from which the Birlas originated.[2] The family belonged to the *Maheshwari* subcaste of the trading community of the Marwaris, and its members had over several generations imbibed the trading and money-lending skills traditionally associated with their caste. At the time of Ghanshyamdas' birth the Birlas were a prosperous joint family whose businesses extended to the twin metropolises of Bombay and Calcutta.

Perhaps a snapshot of the kind of world Ghanshyamdas was born into may be helpful before we discuss his lineage and family circumstances. In England, it was the fifty-seventh year of Victoria's reign as Queen, and the nineteenth of her formal accession as Empress of India. William Gladstone, the Liberal politician, had, for the last time, relinquished office as prime minister. Rudyard Kipling was writing his *Jungle Book*. Nearer home in India, Mohandas Karamchand Gandhi was still 'an Indian non-entity': having qualified as a barrister from the Inner Temple and failed to establish a legal practice at Rajkot, he had just embarked on his South African odyssey. Jamsetji Tata had successfully established the Empress and Swadeshi Cotton Mills and was keenly exploring prospects of venturing into iron and steel manufacturing. Bankim Chandra Chattopadhyaya, famous for composing the anthem *Bande Mataram*, had just died.

It is possible to reconstruct more precisely the events of 14 April 1894—the day Ghanshyamdas was born—to fill out this picture. On that morning the

Viceroy, Lord Elgin, who had arrived a few days before in Simla for the summer, presided over his Executive Council. At Simla, the 'Volunteers' and the 'Military' played a friendly cricket match in which, not unexpectedly, the Volunteers were routed. The Stanley Opera Company staged *The Colleen Bawn*, and the theatre was crowded from the footlights to the entrance. The meteorological office recorded a temperature of 70°, and a mild epidemic of measles was reported in the summer capital. In Bombay, Justice M.G. Ranade addressed the annual meeting of the Graduates' Association and urged his audience to actively take up social reform. In Aligarh, Sir Syed Ahmad Khan boarded a train to go to Lahore where the Mohammadans of the city had collected Rs 15,000 as subscription for his scheme of the Aligarh College. In London, the death was announced of Patrick Scott, veteran of the Bengal Infantry who had served in the Sikh War, and taken part in the 'Relief of Lucknow' alongside Havelock. The Queen was away in Florence with her entourage, which included her Indian *Moonshi* (secretary), where she had a quiet day. The English Mail arrived that day, and the 'Malabar' sailed from Bombay. The Calcutta and Bombay Stock Exchanges were closed and conditions were reported to be firm in the money markets. In Lahore, the police band played as usual in the evening at Lawrence Gardens, ending the performance with 'God Save the Queen!'. From all accounts it seemed to be a typical day of the Victorian era whose ideas still seemed to be in ascendancy in colonial India. It was in such a milieu that Ghanshyamdas arrived.

When his birth took place there was nothing extraordinary about the Birlas. They were a typical Marwari family from the Shekhawati region which lies at the heart of the larger Marwari cultural landscape (see map). Shekhawati today corresponds to the six subdivisions of Sikar, Fatehpur, Neem-Ka-Thana, Jhunjhunu, Nawalgarh and Khetri, which extend over Jhunjhunu and Sikar districts in Rajasthan.[3] In the colonial period Shekhawati was a part of Rajputana, a region with a distinct identity of its own, which was ruled by autocratic princely states whom the British controlled under the panoply of paramountcy.[4] From his headquarters in Ajmer a British diplomatic officer, known as the Agent to the Governor-General, controlled the whole of Rajputana through a network of Residents stationed at the courts of important princes. Shekhawati was ruled by a Rajput chieftain, who owed allegiance to Sawai Madho Singh II, the Maharaja of Jaipur, who had succeeded to the throne in 1880. The British thus had an overall presence in the region which was dominated by powerful Rajput chiefs. Across the whole of Shekhawati the Birlas had connections and ties of marriage and residence that went back several generations.

Ghanshyamdas' forebears traced their genealogy to the ninth-century trader Baidh Singh of Badhauli village in Nawalgarh. In the popular Modiya dialect of the Marwaris, the first name Baidh successively changed over the generations to 'Behada', 'Behadia', 'Bedla' and to become finally the title 'Birla'.[5] From Nawalgarh, Baidh Singh's kinsmen branched out over time to different parts of Shekhawati. By the 1850s Ghanshyamdas' family seemed to have been

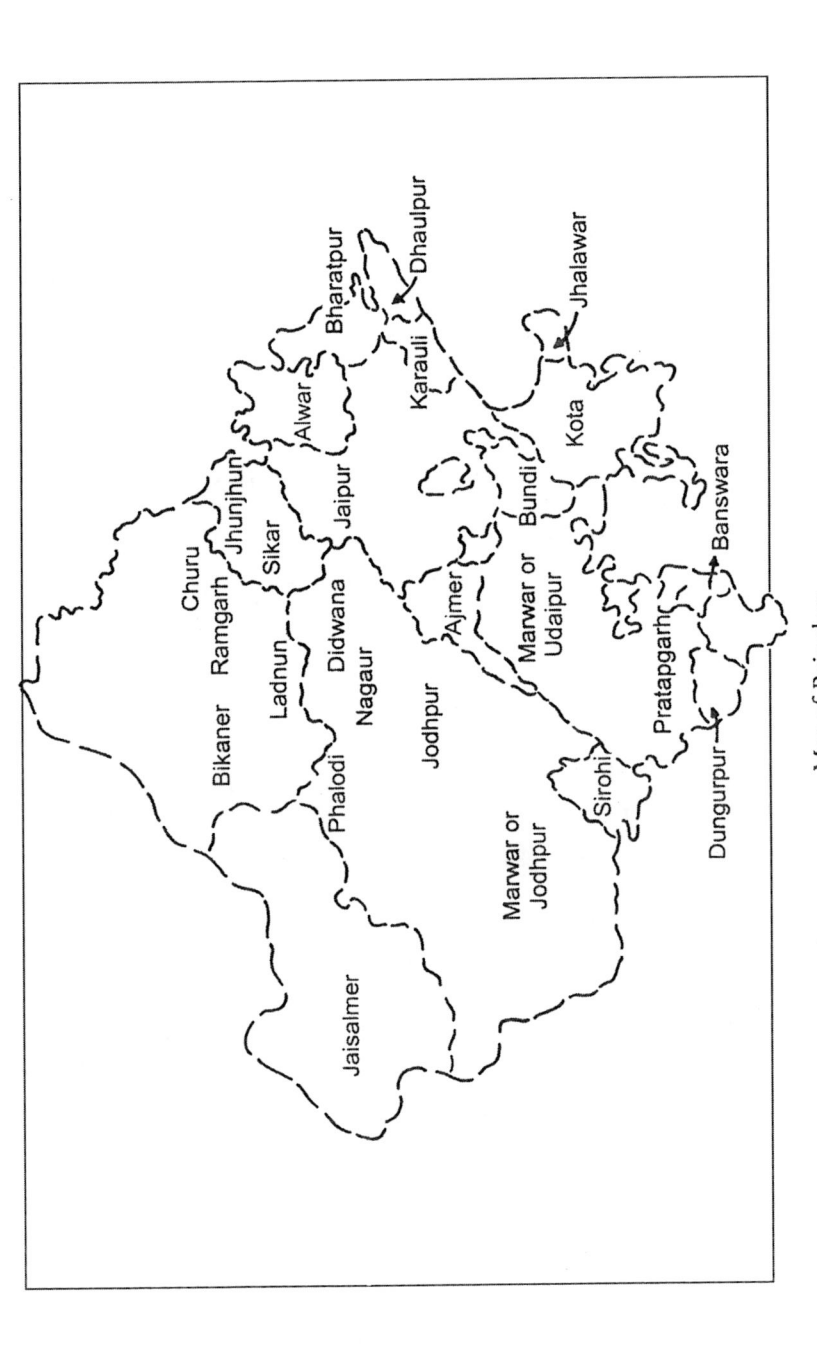

Map of Rajasthan

concentrated at Nawalgarh, and at Pilani, then a village of less than 3000 inhabitants. Although Pilani was dominated by the Agarwal subcaste, the Birlas themselves were Maheshwari.[6] As the early fortunes of the Birlas were powerfully shaped by the larger Marwari community, its vocation and its values, we need to consider what it meant to be a Marwari.

THE COMMUNITY OF MARWARIS

The term 'Marwari' is derived from Marwar, which traditionally stood for the erstwhile princely state of Jodhpur. Over time, the word gradually came to encompass people from other areas in Rajasthan, especially those from the neighbouring Jaipur and Bikaner states, since important figures in the community hailed from these areas as well. The Akhil Bharatiya Marwari Sammelan (an all-India association claiming to represent the community) nowadays officially defines the term in the present context as encompassing all those whose original homeland is Rajasthan and its adjoining areas. The Sammelan insists that the term 'Marwari' is not exclusive to traders alone but includes people from other occupations and castes also.[7] Yet while anyone from Marwar may call himself a Marwari, in colloquial use it invariably refers to traders and the word 'Marwari' has come to evoke the imagery of a wealthy merchant well ensconced in his immigrant setting while clinging to the customs, practices and manners of his kin.[8]

What are the attributes of a Marwari? How is he viewed by those among whom he functions? What is his own self-view? Bhimsen Kedia, one of the founders of the 'Akhil Bhartiya Marwari Sammelan' and a historian of the community, writes that the term epitomizes

one who is the follower of the *Sanatan Dharma* and *Ahimsa* in the Jain style, one who wears his native dress and follows the life-style, a follower of the old culture, a staunch believer in God, one who cares for the poor and homeless, one who builds *dharamshalas* wherever he goes, and one who is known among all the *jatis* for his trading abilities and his business acumen.[9]

In defining their own characteristics most Marwaris stress religiosity, piety, trading abilities, fair play, resourcefulness, strong kinship ties and an austere lifestyle. Yet, in certain localities and among some groups, a negative view vitiates this perception of the community. In these circles, the characteristics commonly attributed to them are miserliness, regressive conservatism, clannishness and superstition.[10]

The Marwaris have essentially been a diasporic community. This is particularly true of Shekhawati Marwaris who have a long tradition of migration which occurred in response to a dearth of opportunity in their native land. Factors relating to the natural terrain of Rajputana such as recurring famines propelled these migrations. So did outbreaks of plague and wars. The coming of colonial rule then quickened them. As the British established their ascendancy over north India, the traditional Marwari activities of financing the warring Rajput princely states and trading along the caravan routes, that stretched beyond Rajputana to north-west India and even Central Asia, shrank.[11] Royal courts with their conspicuous consumption of goods and services declined as centres of political power. In addition, there occurred a major shift in long-established trade routes due to the rise of new commercial centres and trading posts which the British either established or patronized.[12] All of this profoundly affected the fortunes of the mercantile and trading communities of Rajputana and soon propelled further Marwari migration. At the same time the Marwaris were also quick to spot the advantages which were to be gained from the commercial opportunities which were opening up around the mid-nineteenth century in other parts of India, especially in the twin metropolitan centres of Bombay and Calcutta.[13] Moreover, in contrast to the unsettled conditions that prevailed in their native Rajputana, the *Pax Britannica* in British India brought a new safety to life and property. This generated a sense of security that was reinforced by the introduction by the British of elaborate commercial and civil legal codes relating to exchange, credit and contract. These new conditions strengthened the propensity of the Marwaris to migrate.[14] As soon as their 'pioneers' had settled in their new environment and found the prosperity they were seeking, they acted as magnets to attract their kinsmen.[15]

One of the two new major centres of out-migration for the Marwaris was Bombay. Although they had been connected with the Marathas as bankers and military contractors, it was only between 1835 and 1850 that they arrived in Bombay in large numbers.[16] By the turn of the century their number was significant; in 1901 there were 13,000 Rajasthani immigrants there, clustered around Crawford Market and Bhuleshwar.[17] The Census reported that they constituted a little less than ten per cent of the city's mercantile population, and were mainly commission buyers and sellers of cash crops like cloth, oilseeds, grain and opium. The more enterprising among them became *banias,* chief Indian brokers to large European firms. Some of these firms were final exporters and importers of goods, while others were involved in the local speculative commodity markets, mainly of opium and spices. In addition, they operated in the buoyant stock exchange.[18] Calcutta was the other major centre to which the Marwaris headed. The first Marwari firms there date from well before 1857 but it was only during the 1870s that they arrived en masse. By the 1880s they were beginning to replace the *Khattris* and Bengalis as *bania* to British firms. Although in the ensuing decades they steadily built up a commercial position there that was second only to the British, their numbers in the city remained small, and as late as 1921 it was reckoned that there were still less than 15,000 of them.[19]

The Marwaris were by no means the only important business community in India. The Nattukotai *Chettiars* were pre-eminent in the south Indian economy.[20] The Gujarati banias controlled the economy of western India while the Sindhis (especially from the *bhaiband* segment) had trading networks that extended beyond the north-western parts of undivided India.[21] With their kinship-based networks, these communities controlled the vital flows of credit and goods. However, because these other communities originated in coastal areas, they were better placed to spread out to regions beyond the Indian subcontinent. The Chettiars thus moved into Burma, Malaya and parts of South-east Asia, the Gujaratis into much of East Africa, and the Sindhis to Afghanistan, the Middle Eastern region and even across the Central Asian trade routes. While the Marwaris shared certain basic characteristics with these communities, they remained essentially a community that concentrated its energies on the great north Indian hinterland. In due course their horizons extended from the deserts of Rajputana in the west to the tea plantations of Assam and the paddy growing areas of Burma in the east and touched the fringes of the Deccan in the south. But they did not participate in coastal trade or extend their businesses further to countries beyond India. Instead, they entrenched themselves in the economy of north India. There they acted as bankers whose principal operations lay in the inland movement of credit and produce and in meeting the needs of the import–export businesses managed and financed by the Europeans.

By virtue of the complex financial arrangements that interlocked them at several layers and generated the flow of credit, only indigenous merchants could deliver the goods at all levels of the economy.[22] The financing of the massive movement of crops and goods remained the preserve of local bankers and their agents; they also helped the production process by advancing loans to peasants and artisans. Once the produce arrived from the village to the town, it was the responsibility of the *arhatiya* to transport it to port towns and inland centres through the *hundi* network which was serviced by the *shroffs*. Traditional trading groups thus controlled the indigenous money market and had woven an intricate web of credit and exchange by which money moved across the country rapidly. The historian Rajat Ray observes that their 'critical function was to generate indigenous flows of mobile credit without which the market economy could not have functioned, and which in turn generated the opposite flows of produce, manufactured goods, bullion, currency and revenue, adjusting these two-way flows between town and country to the highly uncertain seasons and their extremely taxing credit demands'.[23]

The Marwaris thus served the new economic order under the British as sub-contractors and became an indispensible part of trade and commerce. The Calcutta Marwaris took to certain specific business activities and soon entrenched themselves in these. They became the principal distributors of Manchester piece-goods and were prominent in the supply of grain, oilseeds, raw jute and other unprocessed goods—the staple commodities of the export economy controlled by the European managing agencies.[24] Since the Marwaris had developed an extensive internal trading network by the second half of the nineteenth century, they became the natural allies of the British in the piece-goods trade. By the late 1870s their hold over jute and piece-goods trade was well established in Calcutta. Most newcomers from Rajasthan who came to Calcutta started as agents to the larger Marwari firms in the city before embarking upon their independent businesses. Some brokers became bania or guarantee brokers to importing houses and performed the tasks of bringing new orders and financing and guaranteeing bills. For about 1.5 per cent commission, the bania undertook to guarantee that the bazaar merchant would fully pay the bill of the order which the broker had bought and financed. European importing houses dealt with big bazaar merchants through the bania who bought goods on commission at the port. In metropolitan towns big merchants, in turn, passed these goods either direct to the *mufossil* shopkeeper or through the intermediacy of a wholesale dealer.[25] Through these operations, the Marwaris were able to strengthen their hold on the credit and banking structure of the indigenous economy. By the turn of the century, so well entrenched was their position that, more than half of the jute balers in Calcutta were Marwaris.[26] In addition to jute, the Marwaris also had considerable interest in the speculative markets of Calcutta. In 1860 they started futures in opium, and in 1890 in spices, hessian and later in 1905–6 in jute, and these soon became a Marwari preserve.[27] It was from this extraordinary community with its pan-Indian business networks that the Birlas originated.

The origin of the Birlas within this community was quite humble. Ghanshyamdas' forefathers operated at the village level in their traditional vocation of money-lending and retail trading. Over the years they gained valuable mercantile skills that were nurtured within the family and passed on from one generation to the next. While the Birlas showed themselves endowed with business skills they did not, however, possess the capital to set up a gaddi of their own till a few years before Ghanshyamdas' birth.[28] Shobharam Birla, Ghanshyamdas' great grandfather and the earliest of the Birla clan about whom we have some details, worked as a *munim* or chief clerk with the banking firm of Ganeriwalas, which was headquartered at Hyderabad in the Deccan. On a monthly salary of Rs 10 he worked for the firm's branch office at Nawalgarh. He was, however, only an employee of one of the larger Marwari firms of his time. Not much is known about Shobharam except that after a long stint with the Ganeriwalas he died at around the time of the Indian Revolt of 1857. Upon his death his son Shivnarain, who had set up a small retail shop in Pilani where he had moved, was offered a job as a munim by the Ganeriwalas at the firm's headquarters.[29] However, despite family pressure, Shivnarain refused this offer. Instead, he set out to seek his fortunes in the far-away metropolis of Bombay, a decision which was to be a turning-point in the family's history.

Shivnarain Birla's decision to search for greener pastures outside Rajputana was typical of Marwari men at that time. His move to Bombay came as a part of the wave of migrations from Rajputana we described earlier. In the year following the Indian Revolt of 1857, accompanied with a relative, Sukhdev Das, Shivnarain left his village of Pilani at the young age of 20. Journeys from Rajputana entailed many hardships. They were always undertaken in large *sangh* to minimize the risk of encounter with dacoits en route, and involved travel by various means such as camels, horses and boats.[30] Shivnarain headed towards Bombay and it took him an arduous journey of twenty days by camel to reach Ahmedabad, the nearest railway station, from where a train took him to Bombay.

For a young Marwari stepping out of his native Rajputana to set up business in the presidency town of Bombay, the transition was made easier by the strong kinship networks established by his fellow caste men.[31] These community networks came into play as soon as an immigrant arrived in the metropolis. Newly-arrived immigrants were housed in a *bassa* which provided them with board and lodging at a minimal rate, sometimes even free of cost. These bassas or messes were run either on a co-operative basis by the lodgers or by the larger Marwari firms as charity.[32] The bassa was more than just a means of providing subsidized lodging. It initiated the newcomers into the business and social networks of the community in the metropolis. Here newcomers forged associations and learnt the ways of city life and the bonding that took place in the early months usually lasted a lifetime. Moreover, the bassa as an institution also symbolized the care which established Marwaris showed towards the newcomers and it was not unreasonable to expect that in return, the newcomers would imbibe some of the values of the community. Most significantly, the bassa symbolized the corporate nature of the community and the strict codes of business morality which held it together. Shivnarain and Sukhdev Das lived in Pilani Mandali, a bassa set up by Marwaris from their native village. The Mandali was run on a co-operative basis and cost the residents a paltry sum of Rs 3 to 4 per month. Shivnarain found that the living conditions in it were not congenial: the rooms were cramped and sometimes shared by as many as ten people. Life in the bassa, Ghanshyamdas later wrote while reflecting on his grandfather's life, could be difficult and it appeared that the immigrant's 'life purpose seemed to be to earn large sums in the town while living under these conditions, returning to his village for much-needed rest and then returning again'.[33]

In the bassa a newcomer typically started work with a more established seth in the capacity of munim.[34] This enabled the apprentice to learn the tricks-of-the-trade while the employer was assured of accountability and, more significantly, of 'loyalty' which usually lasted a lifetime. After some years the seth could help his protégé to set up an independent business.[35] However, rivalries could sometimes erupt, with former employees setting themselves up as competitors.[36] In normal circumstances, a newcomer setting up business, irrespective of who he was, was customarily given an interest-free loan by the established members of the caste.[37] Some firms even had funds especially created for such purposes as well as to help those threatened by insolvency.[38] These practices went a long way in ensuring a smooth commercial debut for the newcomer.

It is perhaps important to recognize the strong corporate nature of the Marwari community. Financial and trade transactions interlocked the Marwaris settled in different regions of the country. Much of the transactions, involving movement of both credit and goods, used indigenous financial instruments, namely the hundi. Hundis were mercantile notes of credit used in financing trade, in movement of goods and also in transferring funds from one place to another. The hundi had no legal binding; it was not regulated by colonial laws and had no standing in a court of law. In the event of a merchant dishonouring his financial commitments or resorting to dishonest practices, there could thus be no recourse to litigation. In such circumstances interactions between fellow caste men were based on notions of trust or *sakh*. It meant much more than financial liquidity and having one's hundi accepted in bazaar transactions; sakh may be defined as 'credit worthiness' and 'business integrity'. The historian, Chris Bayly perceptively observes that sakh incorporated a moral dimension. It represented a certain moral stature which was acquired through high personal conduct. There could be several indices of this such as keeping regular account books, being frugal and displaying high personal conduct and integrity.[39] There were ways of acquiring sakh: keeping to one's financial and market obligations, extending patronage to communitarian and religious activities and showing generosity in the philanthropic work which the community undertook.

To return to Shivnarain Birla, as was typical of the Maheshwaris, he did not start his career as a munim. An attribute that set the Maheshwaris apart from other subcastes like the Agarwals and Oswals was their desire to chart independent careers rather than work as munims. They preferred mostly to speculate or to function as simple traders even though on a modest scale. They were also not known to work with English firms, at least in the early decades of their settlement in Bombay and Calcutta.[40] Shivnarain forged a partnership with Hardayal Padia, a fellow caste man from Pilani who was well established in Marwari business circles in Bombay. For the first two years Shivnarain, together with Hardayal Padia, engaged in opium *satta* (speculation). This was a vocation his son later specialized in and from which the family made much of its early fortune. He performed the more cautious, low-risk operation popularly called *average ka satta*.[41] In such transactions speculation was based on averages which were calculated in two ways. The first was based on the auction at Calcutta of opium bags meant to be exported; the auction rate was then averaged and speculation was done based on this average. The second method was by calculating the average rate of the worth of the total number of steamers carrying opium, meant for export; based on this average, speculation was carried out. In two years Shivnarain had learnt enough to have the confidence to launch an independent business. He now began to operate as an independent opium speculator from the premises of Cheniram Jasraj, a fellow Marwari.

The choice of entering opium speculation by Shivnarain was a prudent one. The opium trade was in full blast in the 1860s and 1870s after having gone through a period of lull during the years of the Opium Wars.[42] One reason for the boom was the legalization of opium sales in Hong Kong after 1845. On an average 45,000 to 48,000 chests produced in India were put on sale each year in the international market, and most of these went to China. The exports peaked in 1879–80 when 48,722 chests of Bengal opium and 46,114 Malwa opium chests were shipped.[43] Shivnarain displayed tremendous risk-taking abilities by entering opium speculation. While the huge volume of trade in opium ensured that both traders and speculators enjoyed enormous profits, it was also intensely risky in character. Opium was liable to sudden and unaccountable price fluctuations. Prices depended not only on supply factors and increasingly on competition from China-grown opium, but more importantly on the China market, news of which was not easily available. Speculating in opium meant working closely with fellow Marwaris involved in the business, as much of the success in speculation depended upon receiving accurate information about the size of the season's produce and also about the China market. Information about the size of the produce could be obtained from fellow Marwaris who were usually responsible for bringing the contracted opium into the market from the collecting centres.[44] What was especially important, however, was accurate information about the China market; every hour made a difference in price and a few hours' advantage could mean a profit of thousands of rupees. Misinformation, on the other hand, could lead to imprudent purchases and enormous losses.[45] Traders and speculators depended for news of the market upon opium-carriers which played the role of the postal service. Captains of fast moving ships named clippers, especially of the P & O Company—the largest shipping company in Eastern waters—provided valuable information which was conveyed to speculators through 'electric telegraph'.

Much of the speculation took place when chests of manufactured opium were sold by auction each month.[46] Although speculation took place at both Bombay and Calcutta, it was Calcutta that was more important especially since the abandonment of the Bombay opium auctions after 1830.[47] Speculation was a 'matter of wild excitement, bulls and bears fighting for mastery in a feverish market where the price see-sawed in the most giddy manner, soaring and then dropping, only to soar again higher than ever.' So fervent was bidding that speculators could raise prices to high levels—at one such sale at Calcutta in 1845 two speculators took the price to a phenomenal Rs 1,30,995 per chest, compared to the average price which ranged between Rs 400 and 450 per chest.[48] In these early years Shivnarain did not diversify his activities; he concentrated on speculation in opium in which he made large gains. More significantly, he had mastered the subtleties of speculation and as Shivnarain himself admitted, barely lost Rs 8000 during the firm's long years in opium speculation.[49] For the next 10 years Shivnarain perfected the art of opium speculation.

INCORPORATING THE GADDI

In 1875, Shivnarain's only son, Baldeodas, joined him at the age of 12 after his wedding to Yogeshwari Bai, daughter of Ramsukhdas Singhi, a prominent trader of Churu.[50] Together, in 1879, father and son set up a gaddi, an independent firm named 'Shivnarain Baldeodas', near Mumbadevi. Literally, the word gaddi means a seat but in the context of business it is an euphemism for a typical Marwari firm. It usually contains big *gaddas* which are covered with white shining sheets. The largest backrest is reserved for the seth, while the smaller ones are used by his munims or *gomashtas* (sub-clerks) who supervise all operations.[51] Each gomashta is responsible for a different ledger. The cashier understandably is the most important of these as he controls the *rokar-bahi* (cash book) and the *rokara* (cash box). In addition, the gaddi has a *khata-bahi*, a *hundi mukl* and a *jama-bahi*. Daily reports of cash and credit positions are compiled at the close of business. The tremendous success of the Marwaris in speculation can partly be accounted for by their ability to maximize cash flows.

The establishment of the gaddi by Shivnarain and Baldeodas after almost 25 years of endeavour signified a milestone in the Birla fortunes.[52] Evidence suggests that by the late 1870s the Birlas had reached a fair degree of affluence, as is illustrated by their activities back home in Pilani. In these years, Shivnarain made a number of visits to his native village where he had left other members of his family. During these visits he performed acts typically associated with a successful Marwari immigrant, such as opening a well for the village folk, consecrating a temple dedicated to the god Shiva and, above all, building a haveli. While the basic structure of the haveli had been constructed in 1864, major extensions were made to it over the next two decades, easily making it the most magnificent building in Pilani.[53] It consisted of eight interlocking quadrangles and its architectural style reflected both the social conservatism of the time as well as the colourful pageantry associated with the havelis of Shekhawati.[54] The outer courtyards contained rooms for Pannalal, the head munim, and the gomashtas as well as a formal gaddi where visitors were received. In the central courtyard was placed a container for a *tulsi* plant considered sacred by the Hindus. The Birla household strictly followed the segregation of women who were forbidden to use the front part of the haveli, and had to use the back exit. The women's quarter was guarded by two guards posted at its entrance. The paintings on the walls depict traditional Shekhawati motifs. 'On the ochre of its exterior walls elephants parade and horses charge... The inner and outer courtyards contain scenes of merchant activity, as well as of military action and local flora and fauna.'[55] The construction of the haveli and the performance of various religious tasks signified the coming of *Lakshmi* (the Hindu goddess of wealth) into the Birla family. Shivnarain's other acts of piety included feeding the *brahmans*, going on pilgrimage to Pushkar and organizing *kathas*.[56]

The increasing philanthropy of the Birlas within the village also reflected their affluence. The first definite evidence of this philanthropy relates to 1899 when Rajputana saw a severe drought. Shivnarain and Baldeodas, both in Pilani on a visit, opened several relief centres. A free canteen and a cheap grain store were opened in the village to feed its poor.[57] In this time of crisis Baldeodas also arranged for the village cattle to be herded together so that they could be collectively fed; preservation and feeding of cattle was considered an act of religious piety. When drought struck again in 1905 Shivnarain redeemed a pledge he had taken in 1899 to spend Rs 10,000 in constructing wells.[58] In addition, he spent Rs 22,000 in opening a dharamshala with contributions from the Thakur of Nawalgarh and help from other villagers.[59] Given that social and commercial goals interlocked, the family's growing reputation for piety must certainly have added to their reputation and commercial status within the larger Marwari community.

As father and son were beginning to enjoy their new-found affluence, an unexpected event threatened their fortunes. In August 1896 bubonic plague spread in Bombay, starting from Mandvi, on the east of the city. Despite drastic government measures to control the epidemic, such as segregation of persons who had been in contact with plague patients, removal of the afflicted to properly equipped hospitals and disinfecting of premises, it spread rapidly and by December, mortality rates in the city had reached alarming numbers. The government measures only led to panic among the city's residents and became a stimulus to large-scale evacuation.[60] Most Marwaris either moved to Calcutta or temporarily closed shop. 'Shivnarain Baldeodas', with a reported net worth of more than Rs 1,50,000, decided to move their main business to Calcutta where initially they experienced much hardship in finding their feet. However, the relocation proved to be a blessing in disguise. Calcutta was the home of the satta world as the Bombay averages (on which the Birlas hedged their bets) were calculated at Calcutta rates. Once the plague had passed, the Bombay firm was reopened as a branch office and it was decided that Shivnarain would manage it, while Baldeodas would look after the Calcutta gaddi.

THE MARWARI COSMOS OF BARA BAZAAR

By the time 'Shivnarain Baldeodas' moved to Calcutta in the 1890s, the Marwaris were well entrenched in the city. Baldeodas discovered that the Marwaris were in a relatively stronger position in the commercial milieu of Calcutta than they were in Bombay. This may have been because of the stiff competition they faced from the already established Gujarati traders in western India. In Calcutta, by contrast, the Bengali Hindus who had dominated the city's 'native' economy till the middle of the nineteenth century had nearly all lost out by the 1850s.[61] The field was thereafter left clear for the Marwaris to build their fortunes.[62] Further, Calcutta was the major market for products like opium, and in its neighbouring regions of Assam and north Bengal, the community had already begun to monopolize trade. In view of these factors it was not surprising that it was Calcutta that, over the decades, became the major centre of Marwari commerce and enterprise.

The move to Calcutta was to prove a turning point for the Birlas. Keen on an auspicious inauguration and aspiring to become a leading firm, Baldeodas inaugurated his gaddi in 1896 at Kaligodam Number 18, Mullick Street in the heart of Bara Bazaar.[63] The choice of this location was strategic: the building housed the great Marwari firm of 'Tarachand Ghanshyamdas', which had been trading in Calcutta for more than half a century.[64] Many new firms huddled into the same building which was located near the centre of the opium trade. Fledgling Marwari firms could make use of the re-discounting, insurance and other services offered by this large firm. Baldeodas managed to get a room here because of his contacts with the Ganeriwalas, with whom his grandfather had worked, and who had been associated with 'Tarachand Ghanshyamdas'. Baldeodas shared his office with three other firms of 'Devibaksh Jivanram', 'Ramnarain Bhojraj' and 'Daulatram Lakshminarain' and the meagre rent of Rs 60 was shared among the four of them. Adjacent to this room was a rest-room and a communal kitchen for the running of which a monthly contribution of Rs 10 each was made.[65] All four firms engaged in opium speculation and came to be known as 'Bare Chaurastiya' (the Gang of Four). Baldeodas also managed to get a room on the floor above his office for lodging.

Bara Bazaar (the Great Bazaar) at this period in Calcutta's history was not only the Marwari quarter of Calcutta but the centre of indigenous banking and commerce. Over the years it came to signify a Marwari cosmos. With the arrival of the Marwaris, prosperity came to the otherwise poor area of Bara Bazaar.[66] Originally, the neighbourhood had consisted only of Cross Street, but with increasing Marwari migration, it soon expanded to encompass Harrison Road, Kalakaar Street, Pagiya Patti and their adjacent areas.[67] The Marwaris began buying up property from the Bengali *zamindars* after 1870, and by 1900 they owned the bulk of the real estate in Bara Bazaar.[68] Cloth import was the most important trade in Calcutta, and most Marwaris were well entrenched in it. Bara Bazaar became the centre of this business, and over the decades trading in cloth, hessian and opium came to be concentrated here. By the late 1870s the Marwaris also controlled the crucial inland trade in jute and cotton piece-goods and by the end of the century they virtually monopolized the indigenous banking system. Bara Bazaar became the hub of these diverse businesses.

Life in Bara Bazaar proved to be hectic for Baldeodas. Trading started in the early hours with the arrival of munims and gomashtas as early as seven in the morning and continued until midnight. At about one in the afternoon the agents or *dalals* returned from the offices of the European firms to place their orders and to report bazaar conditions to their firms.[69] Gulab Saraogi, the Birla employee responsible for liaising with the European firms, would bring in their orders. Soon after the move to Calcutta, Baldeodas was joined by his eldest son Jugalkishore, who had been born in 1883. Prior to joining the business Jugalkishore had received some training in rudimentary arithmetic. The Birla firm now came to be known as 'Baldeodas Jugalkishore' and it concentrated its activities in opium speculation. From this the firm soon graduated to actual trading in opium, which had so far been an exclusive preserve of the English, and within a short time this pioneering move was emulated by other Marwaris.[70] In the years thereafter the Birlas entered the silver, grain, linseed and Manchester cloth trades. But the opium futures segment remained the mainstay of their fortune in these years.[71] The firm made rich profits in both trading as well as on the stock exchange.

Both the Bombay and the Calcutta branches experienced an impressive growth in business. Yet, when compared to other Marwaris in the same business, the Birlas seem to have operated on a modest scale at this time. The leading opium speculators in Calcutta, for instance, were Harduttrai Chamria, Sarupchand, Nirmal Lohia, Rampratap Chamria, Ramdayal Nevatia, Gajraj Singhania, Jokhiram Ruia, Nathuram Poddar and Surajmal Nagarmal. Many of them had well diversified businesses and dealt in several commodities. Harduttrai Chamria and Hukumchand were known as 'kings' of the speculative markets. Chamria, for instance, dealt in salt, gold, silver and opium and had large-scale banking and real estate operations. He organized the first futures market in Calcutta and in 1911 he was the main organizer of the syndicate which monopolized the entire opium trade and made huge profits. Likewise, Sarupchand was into opium, cotton, jute and spices. After 1909 Sarupchand is estimated to have made a windfall gain of Rs two crores in opium speculation alone.[72] Although not yet reckoned among established Marwari seths, 'Baldeo-das Jugalkishore' (Shivnarain Baldeodas) was increasingly gaining stature among the upcoming firms in Calcutta.

A CHILDHOOD IN PILANI

Away from the bustle of the business world of Calcutta, life for the women and children of the Birla clan continued at an uneventful and slow pace in native Pilani. Childhood in the village for the young Ghanshyamdas was not strikingly different from that of any other Rajasthani. Everyday life was characterized by recurrent cycles of harsh weather, water scarcity, droughts and shortages of fresh foodstuff. These early years for the young Ghanshyamdas were peaceful, disturbed occasionally only by a death or a marriage in the village or the departure of a kinsman for far-away Calcutta. In the absence of the men, Ghanshyamdas spent most of his time in the company of the womenfolk of the house, especially his grandmother, mother and elder sister.

Perhaps the only remarkable aspect of his childhood which distinguished it from that of the other children in the village was the all-pervasive religious atmosphere in the family. The Birlas imbibed strong *Vaishnavite* values. The family elders, in particular Shivnarain and Ghanshyamdas's mother, insisted on a strict regime of religious observances for the grandchildren from their early childhood. A typical day's routine started at five in the morning with prayers.[73] Shivnarain, during his periodic visits home, joined his grandson in the morning prayer. Even though neither the unlettered Shivnarain nor Ghanshyamdas, still too young, could read the prayer book, they both kept it in front of them but recited from memory. At the age of nine Ghanshyamdas was given his own prayer kit and religious books. As a young child Ghanshyamdas could recite verses from the popular Hindu texts *Vishnu Sahasranaman,* the *Ramcharita Manas* and the *Durga Saptasati.* Shivnarain also insisted that the family should strictly follow many Hindu devotional practices. In the event of an illness he called the priest to perform prayers, fed the brahmans to appease the gods, and only then followed whatever medical advice was available.[74] Fasting was observed on important occasions by the members of the family, and generous donations were made to priests who were regularly fed.[75]

This religiosity remained deeply ingrained in Ghanshyamdas and became a dominant element in his life. The lasting impression it left could be seen in his daily life, beliefs and values, and also in the causes that he later supported. Throughout his life he meticulously followed the religious routine and the disciplined regimentation imbibed in his childhood years. An important belief that went back to these early years was that the mind and the body are intrinsically linked to each other and that exercise and fitness are ways of controlling the mind and the body. Ghanshyamdas deeply imbibed this belief: he always rose three hours before dawn, exercised and read the scriptures before embarking upon any other activity. Several religious books which he read in these years also left a deep imprint. Especially dear to him were the *Bhagvad Gita,* Hinduism's main ethical text, and the *Ashram Bhajnawali,* both of which he always kept by his bedside together with a rosary.[76] While he enthusiastically read other texts such as the *Ramayana,* it was the *Gita* that he turned to and derived strength from at times of personal crisis and family problems.[77] All food in the house was cooked by brahmans to ensure ritual purity and vegetarianism was very strictly followed by the family. The religious environment in the family was nurtured by both Ghanshyamdas and his elder brother, Jugalkishore.

Among siblings Ghanshyamdas' companions were his elder sister Bhagwani Devi and brother, Rameshwardas, who was just two years older than him. His eldest brother, Jugalkishore, as we mentioned earlier, had joined Baldeodas in the business. It was Rameshwardas who became Ghanshyamdas' favourite playmate. He would piggy-back Ghanshyamdas in the lanes and alleys of Pilani. An important event which took place in these years was the marriage of his elder sister to Krishan Gopal Mohta of Rajgarh. The others in the house with whom he spent time were the three servants—Heera, Seera and Rupa. Heera, a *Jat,* was in charge of the camels and was a good marksman; Seera, called *tau* or uncle by the children, took care of the cows and was fond of telling stories and singing religious songs while Rupa was the overall 'comptroller of the household'.

Young Ghanshyamdas also spent time playing with the village lads. He was especially fond of the company of the local priest, Charandas. Swamiji, as the villagers called him, had been appointed priest by Shivnarain to a temple constructed by him. Besides being a priest, he also claimed to possess the skills of a physician and had musical talents. Ghanshyamdas learnt many devotional songs from him, much to the pride of his grandfather who asked him to perform before visitors. These musical lessons and recitations led to his becoming an accomplished vocalist in later life. However, the person who fascinated him most was the village wrestler, Qamardeen Ilahi. Ghanshyamdas admired his physical prowess and even aspired to be a wrestler himself. Another village character whose company he sought was Gigalia, who was a wrestler and marksman.

While Pilani offered many outlets for recreation, the educational facilities which were locally available were appalling. Baldeodas believed in imparting only *mahajani shiksha* to his sons, as did most other Marwaris of this time. Its curriculum typically consisted of skills like *patti pahara*, bahi-khatha, weights and measures, the Modiya and Hindi scripts, and just enough English to read telegrams. Baldeodas's self-proclaimed dictum was to 'teach only as much as helps in trading as a learned man can never be a trader'.[78] But even imparting these basic skills did not prove to be easy in Pilani. At the age of four Ghanshyamdas was put into the only school in Pilani which conducted classes up to the primary level and was housed in the open. The school functioned according to the vagaries of the weather. During winter, classes were held in an area overlooking the market square, in the hot weather under the shadow of the wall, and when the monsoons came it was holiday time.[79] Under such circumstances, not surprisingly, the school soon closed down. Shivnarain was now constrained to set up a primary school in 1900 in order to educate his grandsons. This was located in the house where the Birlas had lived before moving to their *haveli*. Rameshwardas and Ghanshyamdas joined the school and became the first in the family to receive any formal schooling. Baldeodas himself had been tutored by a relative and Jugalkishore, Ghanshyamdas' elder brother, had learnt rudimentary arithmetic from Munim Pannalal. When Rameshwardas and Ghanshyamdas were first sent to school, the blessings of *Saraswati* (the Hindu goddess of learning) and *Ganesha* (the Hindu god of auspicious beginnings) were invoked. Their education commenced under Kan Singh, who himself did not prove to be particularly learned; his proficiency in mathematics was regarded with suspicion.[80] He was then replaced by Rambilas from Bhiwani, who introduced elementary English in the school curriculum. Ghanshyamdas attended this school till the age of nine by which time he had progressed to some numeracy in mathematics and knew rudimentary English. His skills in English soon came to be tested when in 1903 he accompanied his grandfather on a long pilgrimage to the Hindu religious cities of Mathura, Brindavan and Puri: he was able to use English for sending telegrams and purchasing tickets at railway stations. Shivnarain was much impressed and he concluded that Ghanshyamdas was ready for advanced instruction which only schools in Calcutta could provide.

In Calcutta, Ghanshyamdas was admitted to the Vishudanand Saraswati Vidyalaya and placed under the charge of his elder brother Jugalkishore. The school had been set up by the Marwaris of Calcutta for the education of their children. What set the school apart from other institutions in the city was its emphasis on imparting ideals of *Sanatan Dharma* and its use of Hindi as the medium of instruction. However, Ghanshyamdas could not easily adjust to the changed circumstances of city life and his schooling took an indifferent course. He left the house every morning with his school bag and wandered the streets of Calcutta till late in the evening. Jugalkishore could not catch the recalcitrant youngster, as business gave him little time to monitor the activities of his younger brother. Playing truant, Ghanshyamdas soon knew the streets of the city as intimately as a rickshaw-puller! 'I roamed the streets whole day long. As a result I learnt nothing from the Vishudanand Vidyalaya, but from the streets of Calcutta I learnt a lot about the atmosphere', he later remembered.[81] This state of affairs did not, however, last very long as Baldeodas decided to take matters in his own hands and now took Ghanshyamdas with him to Bombay. There a tutor was appointed to help him improve his English. Again the men had little time to devote to Ghanshyamdas' education and he was soon sent back to the village. Following this he had a brief stint at the school in Pilani under a new master, Shriram Sharma, who belonged to the nearby town of Churu. Shriram taught Ghanshyamdas English, Hindi and some basic Sanskrit. From this school he passed his lower primary examination. Given his experience of schooling in Pilani, Calcutta, Bombay, and again Pilani, it is hardly surprising that Ghanshyamdas 'hated to be taught by a teacher' and that his formal education remained incomplete.

It was later upon joining business that he realized how inadequate his education had been and began reading anything he could lay his hands upon. Proficiency in English was especially essential for receiving and sending commercial information, for reading market reports and for liaising with European firms. To attain this he read newspapers with the help of a dictionary.[82] He also read the Indian classic *Arthashastra*, and some of the writings of Rousseau, Tolstoy, Plato, Aristotle, Swami Dayanand, and even Marx! In his later years he read, on an average, ten to fifteen books a year.

MARRIAGE AND APPRENTICESHIP

At the age of 12, Ghanshyamdas' apprenticeship in business began in Bombay. By this time the family firm 'Shivnarain Baldeodas' was engaged in opium speculation and increasingly in forward trading in cotton, wheat, rape-seed and silver. As the only one in the family who was proficient in English, Ghanshyamdas was given a privileged position in the firm: he was put in charge of negotiations with English brokers such as Montagu and Sharp. 'I was surrounded by illiterates and found myself the *visharad* (the wise one) among them,' he later recalled in his memoirs.[83]

In keeping with the Marwari tradition of early marriages, Shivnarain now began to search for a wife for his 12-year-old grandson.[84] He had got his own son Baldeodas married at the age of 12, his eldest grandson Jugalkishore at 11 and Rameshwardas at 10. Among immigrant Marwari families of Bombay and Calcutta marriage ceremonies continued to be performed in the village.[85] Ghanshyamdas' bride-to-be was Durgadevi, daughter of Seth Mahadev Somani of Chidawa, which lay close to Pilani in Shekhawati. The Somanis were an influential family in Chidawa where they were given the title of 'Chowdhury'. Mahadev Somani, who had migrated to Calcutta, traded in jute and hessian in which he built a reputation over the years and made a fortune when jute stocks rose during World War I.

In the tradition of his community, Shivnarain planned a grand affair and invited all the Pilani traders resident in Bombay for the marriage which took place in the village.[86] Celebrations continued over several days, beginning with a feast for the village brahmans. The groom then rode a horse to the house of the family priest to seek his blessings before leaving with the marriage party of almost 1000 persons for Chidawa where the wedding took place. There Ghanshyamdas rode an elephant in procession to the house of the bride. It is difficult to speculate what marriage must have meant for 12-year-old Ghanshyamdas. Even though he was married in 1906, Ghanshyamdas brought his new bride to their haveli in Pilani only two years later. They were given quarters on the first floor of the haveli along with the two other married brothers, Jugalikishore and Rameshwardas. The couple did not, however, spend much time together, as Ghanshyamdas' increasing business responsibilities kept him away in Bombay for the better part of the year. Marriage did, however, mean an elevated status for Ghanshyamdas; he was henceforth addressed with respect as Ghanshyam *Bhaiji* (elder brother).

A year after Durgadevi moved to Pilani their eldest son, Lakshmi Niwas was born on 11 July 1909. There was much celebration in the Birla household on the birth of a great grandson; women visitors who came to see the infant were given a scarf each. Unfortunately, soon after the birth of the son tragedy struck and Durgadevi came down with tuberculosis. Ghanshyamdas who was then in Bombay rushed back to the village and just four months after the birth, Durgadevi died. The infant was then sent to the care of his maternal grandparents in Chidawa and Ghanshyamdas returned to Bombay. From the fragmentary evidence available it is difficult to know how Ghanshyamdas responded to this bereavement.

It took his grandmother and mother three years to persuade him to remarry. In 1912 he married 13-year-old Mahadevi, the daughter of Seth Premsukhdas Karva of Sardar Shahr. The bride's grandfather was Rai Bahadur Seth Saligram. The father, Premsukhdas, himself was a wealthy trader who owned 'Rai Saligram Chunilal Bahadur' which was the principal distributor for Assam Oil Company. The firm had several branches in Assam, with its main offices in Gauhati and Dibrugarh. An active patron of the movement for the promotion of Hindi language, Premsukhdas was a key member of the Kashi Nagri Prachari Sabha, an association committed to the popularization of the Hindi.[87] His elder brother had been awarded the title MBE (Member of the British Empire) by the Viceroy. Soon after his marriage, Ghanshyamdas left for Calcutta but he kept in correspondence with Mahadevi and on visits home brought her many gifts. The couple lived in this manner separately for about three years.

In 1910 Shivnarain passed away at Pilani. He had spent the last ten years of his life in retirement. In these years he devoted himself to pilgrimage, *daan* (charity) and prayer. He also started the practice of 'sadavrata'—the daily distribution of food to the needy who came to the haveli.[88] Every afternoon he held discussions with the teacher of his grandsons, Shriram Sharma, an enthusiastic supporter of the Arya Samaj, and the learned brahmans of the village on religious texts such as the *Mahabharata, Ramayana, Ramcharita Manas* and the *Shrimadbhagvad Gita*.[89] At the time of his death the Birla businesses were based in four cities. At each of these cities ceremonies connected with his death were performed. In Pilani, sweets were distributed as Shivnarain had lived to a ripe old age and Re 1 was given to each family which attended the ceremony. In Bombay, more than 2500 people were fed while in Calcutta, 1600 brahmans were fed. At Banaras too brahmans were fed. The total expenditure incurred on these ceremonies came to Rs 55,750, a sizeable sum in those days, which indicated the growing affluence of the family.[90]

With the passing away of Shivnarain came a generational shift. Baldeodas also decided to retire to a life of prayer and spiritual pursuits, leaving the business to his sons and intervening only on an exceptional basis.[91] The story goes that Baldeodas met an astrologer in Banaras in 1910, where he had gone to perform the death rituals of his father. The astrologer predicted that Baldeodas would live only up to the age of 55. Feeling that he only had ten more years, Baldeodas decided to devote himself to prayer and retired to the sacred city of Banaras with his wife, following the ancient custom of awaiting death in the holy city. For his retirement, Baldeodas created a fund of Rs 8 lakhs and bought government securities and he intended to live off their interest. He built a house for himself at Lal Ghat which, over time, thanks to his philanthropic activities, began to be called Birla Ghat.[92] He had by now married his three daughters into influential trading families and groomed his elder three sons to take responsibility for the business. The astrologer's predictions proved wrong and Baldeodas lived to be 93 and passed away in 1956.

Baldeodas' retirement marked the coming of age of the younger generation. The three young sons—Rameshwardas in Bombay and Jugalkishore and Ghanshyamdas in Calcutta—now were the helmsmen steering the family business. How they fared in this is the story of the following chapter.

NOTES AND REFERENCES

[1] In the first two chapters of this work, Birla is referred to by his first name to distinguish him from his father and brothers who also feature prominently in the narrative; from Chapter 3 onwards the surname Birla is used to describe him.

[2] On how Braj culture has evolved around the Krishna legend, see Moti Lal Gupta, *Braj: The Centrum of Indian Culture* (Delhi, 1982).

[3] For a history of Shekhawati, see Udayvir Sharma, *Shekhawati Ka Itihas* (Lakshmangarh, 1980).

[4] See *The Imperial Gazetteer of India*, Vol. XVIII (Oxford, 1908). Also see Karine Schomer, Joan L. Erdman et al. (eds), *The Idea of Rajasthan, Explorations in Regional Identity*, Vol. I & II (Delhi, 1994).

[5] D.D. Shastri (ed.), *Ek Bindu Ek Sindhu* (Mathura, 1948), p. 114. Also see D.K. Taknet, *Industrial Entrepreneurship Among Shekhawati Marwaris* (Jaipur, 1986), p. 112.

[6] Of the many subcastes among the Marwaris, the prominent ones were Agarwals, Maheshwaris and Oswals. For profiles of prominent Maheshwaris, see S.R. Bhandari, *Maheshwari Jati Ka Itihas* (Bhanpura, 1940). Also see his *Agarwal Jati Ka Itihas* (Bhanpura, 1937) and Rishi Gemini Kaushik Barua, *Mai Apni Marwari Jati Ko Pyar Karta Hun*, especially Vols. I to III (Calcutta, 1970–2).

[7] Interview with the President of the *Akhil Bharatiya Marwari Sammelan*, Bara Bazaar, Calcutta, May 1989.

[8] Colonel Todd in his classic *Annals* mentioned as many as 128 trading castes; he, however, noted that the most important traders came from only five castes, *Annals and Antiquities of Rajasthan or the Central and Rajpoot States of India*, Vols. I & II (Calcutta, 1894). A recent study suggests that the largest numbers of successful Marwari firms belong to the Agarwals, then to the Oswals, the third in number come the Maheshwaris and finally the Khandelwals, D.K. Taknet, *Marwari Samaj* (Jaipur, 1989), p. 34. Dwijendra Tripathi and Makrand Mehta argue that the founders of four out of eight business houses in western India came from castes and communities not traditionally associated with trading, see their edited work *Business Houses in Western India: A Study in Entrepreneurial Response, 1850–1957* (London, 1989).

[9] Bhimsen Kedia, *Bharat Mein Marwari Samaj* (Calcutta [*Samvat* 2008] 1947), pp. 1–12.

[10] Here one must remember their crucial role as men who controlled rural credit and markets in a largely subsistence economy vulnerable to the vagaries of the monsoon. Understandably, most of this negative perception arises from the Marwaris' role as village money-lenders. Kedia, however, insists that rival trading groups displaced by the Marwaris are responsible for such adverse views, Kedia, *Bharat Mein Marwari Samaj*, pp. 1–12. For an interesting analysis of social perceptions of *banias*, see Richard Fox, 'Pariah Capitalism and Traditional Merchants' in Milton Singer (ed.), *Entrepreneurship and Modernization of Occupational Cultures in South Asia* (Duke, 1973). For a recent study of negative social perceptions of mercantile groups, see David Hardiman, *Feeding the Bania* (New Delhi, 1996).

[11] Lakshmi Subramanian and Rajat K. Ray, 'Merchants and Politics: From the Great Mughals to the East India Company' in Dwijendra Tripathi (ed.), *Business and Politics in India, A Historical Perspective* (Delhi, 1991).

[12] C.A. Bayly, *Rulers, Townsmen, Bazaars* (Cambridge, 1983) and his *Indian Society and the Making of the British Empire* (Cambridge, 1988), specially chapters 1 and 2.

[13] Thomas A. Timberg, 'Hiatus and incubator: Indigenous trade and traders, 1837–1857' in Asiya Siddiqi (ed.), *Trade and Finance in Colonial India, 1750–1860* (Delhi, 1995).

[14] K.L. Sharma, 'Changing aspects of merchants, markets, moneylending and migration: reflections based on field notes from a village in Rajasthan' in Philippe

Cadene and Denis Vidal (eds), *Webs of Trade: Dynamics of Business Communities in Western India.*

[15] Thomas A. Timberg, *The Marwaris: From Traders to Industrialists* (New Delhi, 1978), pp. 97–103. Also see G.D. Sharma, 'The Marwaris: Economic Foundations of an Indian Capitalist Class' in Dwijendra Tripathi (ed.), *Business Communities of India, A Historical Perspective* (New Delhi, 1984), pp. 185–207.

[16] Timberg, *The Marwaris: From Traders to Industrialists*, p. 44.

[17] Of these about 2000 came from Udaipur, 100 from Bikaner, 1000 from Jaipur and 7500 from Jodhpur.

[18] The Bombay stock exchange was founded in 1875 and reorganized in 1909.

[19] In spite of their small numbers, the Calcutta Marwaris were better positioned than their fellow caste-men in Bombay, see Timberg, *The Marwaris: From Traders to Industrialists*, p. 57. In Bombay, Marwari migrations had started after 1800 and the immigrants had gained a position in the speculative markets, especially in cotton, opium and the cloth trades. However, the vigorous competition from the Gujarati commercial groups did not allow their position to become as dominant as that of their kinsmen in Calcutta. Although large-scale migrations to Calcutta started only after 1839, the Marwaris achieved a prominent position more easily because of a lack of competition from the Khattris and the Bengalis. Another difference in their positioning in the two cities was their dominance of the commercial hinterland of Calcutta and their relative absence from the hinterland of the Bombay presidency.

[20] David West Rudner, *Caste and Capitalism in Colonial India, The Nattukottai Chettiars* (Berkeley, 1994).

[21] Claude Markovits, *The Global World of Indian Merchants, 1790–1947: Traders of Sind from Bukhara to Panama*, Cambridge, CUP, 2000.

[22] For an overview of some of the processes at work in the north Indian economy in these decades, see C.A. Bayly, 'The age of hiatus: the north Indian economy and society, 1830–50' in Asiya Siddiqi (ed.), *Trade and Finance in Colonial India, 1750–1860* (Delhi, 1995).

[23] Rajat Kanta Ray, 'The Bazaar: Changing structural characteristics of the indigenous section of the Indian economy before and after the Great Depression' in *Indian Economic & Social History Review*, Vol. 25, No. 3 (1988), p. 278.

[24] For an important study of the cotton trade in Bombay presidency in this period, see Marika Vicziany, 'Bombay merchants and structural changes in the export community 1850 to 1880' in Asiya Siddiqi (ed.), *Trade and Finance in Colonial India, 1750–1860* (Delhi, 1995).

[25] L.C. Jain's *Indigenous Banking in India* (London, 1929) explains in great detail how these networks operated.

[26] They were thus well positioned to take advantage of the opportunity of buying export-oriented jute presses that came as a result of World War I.

[27] Their interest in the stock market continued to grow before and during World War I. They acquired a position of near monopoly in speculative markets during the boom time of World War I and this, together with their advantageous positioning in sectors such as cotton import, jute and hessian enabled them to reap super profits, facilitating their debut into industry soon after. It is reckoned that the Marwaris control half of the private industrial investment in India today. Out of the 100 'top industrial giants', 28 are Marwari-owned, with 12 companies belonging to the Birla group alone. In 1986–7, out of the 11 companies with the largest turnover in the country, five belonged to Marwaris. The Monopolies

Commission reported in 1964–5 that 75 top business houses owned assets worth Rs 2605 crores. This trend of Marwari dominance has continued. In 1975 the assets of the top four Marwari houses were estimated at Rs 1395 crores and by 1986–7 these had grown to Rs 7654 crores. Out of these, the Birlas alone accounted for a staggering Rs 4772 crores. Similarly, out of 47 presidents of the prestigious Federation of Indian Chambers of Commerce and Industry (FICCI), 20 have been Marwaris.

[28] Literally, the word *gaddi* means a seat but in the context of business it refers to a firm.

[29] He worked in partnership with a fellow Marwari, see D.D. Shastri, *Ek Bindu Ek Sindhu*, p. 115. Founded in 1802, the Ganeriwalas were an Agarwal banking firm closely connected with the Nizam of Hyderabad. Along with the Pittis, they, at one time, farmed the revenue of the entire Berar province for the Nizam, Timberg, *The Marwaris*, p. 224. The offer that the Ganeriwalas made to Shivnarain involved dealings with East India Company officials and with factory-owners in the cantonments of Ajmer and Mhow.

[30] The early migrants to Calcutta hitched their rides as supercargoes from Mirzapur in UP, one of the bigger trading depots for Calcutta. The migrant would get on to river boats belonging to one of the big Marwari firms based in Mirzapur. These boats would carry goods to Calcutta and the passenger would be responsible for their safe delivery; in return he would be fed, given a small payment and taken to his destination. Nathuram Saraf of Mandawa, the first Marwari *bania* in Calcutta, came in late 1830s as a supercargo on one of Sevaram Ramrikhdas' boats from Mirzapur. Balchand Modi, *Desh ke Itihas Mein Marwari Jati Ka Sthan* (Calcutta, 1939), pp. 439–48 and Timberg, *The Marwaris*, p. 152. Journeys often took months and could sometimes even lead to fatalities, Nandkishore Jalan, *Shri Ishwardas Jalan Abhinandan Granth* (Calcutta, 1977), pp. 49–50. Popular sayings were coined in Marwar to discourage people from undertaking such journeys; one such saying was: 'Half a loaf of bread earned at home is better than a whole loaf earned in a foreign land'.

[31] A newcomer usually knew only the name of the Marwari area in the city and had no contact address upon arrival. Someone going to Calcutta, for instance, would know that his destination was Kaligodam, the Marwari settlement, and could be ignorant about all else in the city. Once he arrived in the area, he would seek others from his village and caste, see Bhawarmal Singhi (ed.), *Padam Bhushan Shri Sitaram Seksaria Abhinandan Granth* (Calcutta, 1974), p. 258.

[32] Timberg, *The Marwaris*, p. 4. Rudner also describes similar institutions in the context of the Chettiar diaspora in Southeast Asia, see his *Caste and Capitalism in Colonial India, The Nattukottai Chettiars*.

[33] G.D. Birla recalled his early days in Pilani in a brief account, *Ve Din* (n.d., n.p.), p. 6.

[34] At this stage it may be interesting to chart the career path for a typical Marwari immigrant. Most Marwari migrants to Calcutta started as agents or clerks to the larger Marwari firms and, in the fullness of time, set up their own businesses. We have the example of Ramdutt Goenka, who arrived in the early 1830s and started as clerk to Sevaram Ramrikhdas, a large firm headquartered in Mirzapur. Within a decade he had established his own gaddi and by the 1860s he was bania to several large firms. His brothers became commission agents and brokers to his old employers when he left them. He himself became an independent cloth broker to Kettlewell Bulden and then moved on to found his own firm of 'Ramdutt Ramrikhdas' in 1848. His family had connections with the Greek firm of Ralli as Sevaram Ramrikhdas, his previous employer, was the first

Ralli broker and Ramdutt's nephew, Shivbaksh, was also employed with them. When Shivbaksh resigned, he insisted on a kinsman replacing him and Ramchandra Goenka was appointed to succeed him. Over the years Ramdutt Ramrikhdas became bania to the managing agency of Ralli for the supply of jute and piece-goods. His firm was also a jute dealer and trader in its own right. Brokers often moved to the rank of bania; for instance Surajmal Jhunjhunwala became *bania* to Graham and Company in 1879 and Onkarmal Jatia to M/s Andrew Yule, see Timberg, *The Marwaris*, pp. 52 and 152–3. Similarly, Surajmal Jhunjhunwala and Nathuram Saraf encouraged Marwaris from their native villages to migrate and helped them to open shops and many of them rose to the status of dalal. They also opened a bassa for the newcomers.

[35] This tradition has been maintained by the Birlas. Many of their senior employees or associates were rewarded for their services by helping them set up independent businesses. Many of them are now industrialists in their own right. Prime examples are Tarachand Saboo and Durga Prasad Mandelia.

[36] Timberg concludes from conversations during his field-work that many firms preferred Brahman munims who were thought to be more honest and less likely to start a rival business.

[37] The amount was also laid down by custom—it could be anything from Rs 21 to 201, see Taknet, *Marwari Samaj*, pp. 145–6.

[38] For instance, Sukhanand Saraogi was known for his generosity to the newcomers and the firm of 'Joharmal Rungta' instituted a fund for granting loans to people in need of collaterals. Similarly, Khadasingh Kothari of the firm 'Maha Singh Meghraj' was reputed to have loaned thousands of rupees to fellow Marwaris.

[39] C.A. Bayly, *Rulers, Townsmen and Bazaars*, p. 180. Credit worthiness and business integrity (*sakh*) were regarded as extremely important to the Marwaris. Popular sayings like *Gayi Sakh, Rahi Rakh* (he who has lost his goodwill, his name is dust and ashes) testify to this. Individual insolvency was perceived as adversely affecting the prestige of the entire community. Marwaris, therefore, always baled out fellow men in financial trouble. Insolvency was punished with social boycott and insults. The bankrupt Marwari could not, for instance, wear his headgear (symbol of status). Also see T.A. Timberg and C.V. Aiyar, 'Informal credit markets in India' in *Economic Development and Cultural Change*, No. 33, 1984.

[40] Balchand Modi, *Desh Ke Itihas Mein Marwari Jati Ka Sthan*, pp. 628–9. Amongst the Marwaris the last to arrive in Calcutta were the Maheshwaris; they came only after the Rajputs, Agarwals and Oswals. Most Maheshwari firms in Calcutta were established only after 1880. Out of the 66 major firms in the 1890s, 44 were from the Bikaner region and nine were from Shekhawati, mostly from the Churu and Sardarshahr areas. The Maheshwaris enjoyed a reputation for proficiency in *sarrafa* (banking). They displayed a special aptitude for speculation because of their long tradition of operating in various speculative markets which had flourished in both Shekhawati and Bikaner. This may have also been because the Shekhawati Marwaris were latecomers to the cities and thus took this route, see Timberg, *The Marwaris*, pp. 165–6.

[41] See Rishi Gemini Kaushik Barua, *Raja Baldeodas Birla* (Calcutta, n.d.), p. 29.

[42] For an account of how a Bombay merchant profited from the lucrative opium trade, see Asiya Siddiqi, 'The business world of Jamsetjee Jejeebhoy' in Asiya Siddiqi (ed.), *Trade and Finance in Colonial India, 1750–1860* (Delhi, 1995).

[43] See David Edward Owen, *British Opium Policy in China and India* (Yale, 1934), p. 281 fn.

[44] Marwaris responsible for bringing opium from the countryside were often blamed for manipulating opium prices by deliberately sending innacurate information on the size of the produce for the season. W.E. Cheong, *Mandarins and Merchants. Jardine Matheson & Co., China Agency of the Early 19th Century* (Curzon Press, 1979), p. 131.

[45] David Edward Owen, *British Opium Policy in China and India*, pp. 197–8.

[46] Notifications were published annually by the government stating the number of chests that would be put up for sale. See Ellen N. La Motte, *The Opium Monopoly* (New York, 1920), p. 45.

[47] W.E. Cheong, *Mandarins and Merchants Jardine Matheson & Co., a China agency in the early nineteenth century* (Curzon Press, 1979), p. 209.

[48] Basil Lubbock, *The Opium Clippers* (Glasgow, 1933), p. 286. Also see Ellen N. La Motte, *The Opium Monopoly* (New York, 1920).

[49] Barua, *Raja Baldeodas Birla*, p. 29. It is not possible to accurately estimate the fortune he made in these years.

[50] Barua, *ibid*, p. 25. Till that time he had run a small retail shop which he then closed.

[51] A traditional Marwari gaddi is still a colourful sight. The seth transacts business wearing his traditional clothes of *pagri* (headgear), *kagri*, *angrakhan*, *dhoti* and *dupatta*. Cash boxes and red-coloured ledgers remain his main business apparatus. He usually arrives early after the morning prayers and stays till late night. During bouyant times, he and his munims do not leave the gaddi for many days at a stretch. The gaddi functions almost like a home for the Marwari. Legend has it that Marwari seths earned so much that in counting the cash after close of business, their hands pained. Instead of counting, they often weighed the bags and carried them home, Taknet, *Marwari Samaj*, pp. 52–3.

[52] Shivnarain and Baldeodas had to struggle hard to gain recognition. In spite of his setting up an independent firm, the dalals would not do business with Shivnarain until 1894 by when the Birlas were more established in banking circles. Both of them continued to live in the cramped bassa till 1891, when Baldeodas persuaded his father to buy a house in the not-so-affluent neighbourhood of Phanswari—an area looked down upon by the prosperous Gujarati traders. Barua, *Raja Baldeodas Birla*, p. 31.

[53] Both Ross and Barua date the construction of the haveli to 1864. However, since Shivnarain migrated from Pilani only in 1858, it seems improbable that within six years he could have amassed enough wealth to construct the haveli in its present magnificent form. Enquiries within the village did not produce any authentic leads. From the architecture itself, it is difficult to arrive at a conclusion. The haveli now has been converted into a museum. See Alan Ross, *The Emissary G.D. Birla, Gandhi and Independence* (London, 1986) and Barua, *Raja Baldeodas Birla*.

[54] Ilay Cooper, *Rajasthan: the guide to painted towns of Shekhawati and Churu* (Churu, 1988).

[55] Alan Ross, *The Emissary*, p. 18.

[56] For details on religious tasks performed by Shivnarain, see Barua, *Raja Baldeodas Birla*, pp. 24 and 44. Also see, G.D. Birla, *Ve Din*, p. 4.

[57] The canteen was kept open even after the drought to feed religious men and the needy. Every household contributed a handful of flour each day and collections were made at the end of each month. The nearby *mandi* (wholesale market) also had to contribute some grain; all traders bringing their camels to sell goods had to pay one paise per camel. The overall responsibility for the canteen, however, rested with the Birla family, Barua, *Raja Baldeodas Birla*, pp. 41–5.

[58] He had made a windfall profit of Rs 10,000 when the price of linseed appreciated but had deferred the realization of the sum due to a misunderstanding between his two

branches. Shivnarain vowed to donate the money for digging wells in his village, if he succeeded in realizing it, Barua, *Raja Baldeodas Birla*, p. 43. He was perhaps motivated by the popular Rajasthani superstition about digging wells, i.e. a well dug by one who had earned his money in good faith would bring out sweet water and would be auspicious for the benefactor. Another popular Rajasthani superstition prohibited one person alone to finance the digging of a well.

[59] Financing a dharamshala was considered obligatory for all Marwari families which were regarded to have come into wealth.

[60] *The Imperial Gazetteer of India*, Vol. VIII (Oxford, 1908).

[61] Bengal did not have a well-articulated commercial economy. It has been suggested that the Bengalis withdrew from trade and commerce around this time and increasingly came to be replaced by the Marwaris. N.K. Sinha sees three factors behind this—the litigious and extravagant nature of the heirs of the first generation of Bengali businessmen; the effect of various frauds perpetrated by Englishmen in the early nineteenth century which played a part in disenchanting the Bengalis from joint ventures; and finally, the existence of easy and lucrative avenues for investment in permanently-settled zamindaris and the lack of an up-country network, see N.K. Sinha, *The Economic History of Bengal*, Vol. III (Calcutta, 1970).

[62] S. Mitra and A. Prasad, 'The Marwaris of Calcutta' in S. Chowdhury (ed.), *Calcutta. The Living City*, Vol. II (Calcutta, 1990).

[63] This was to become the nerve-centre of the family's business in the years to come. During a visit in May 1989 I found the gaddi still being maintained though I could hardly see any business being transacted. Informants told me that this was because of the ritual significance of the gaddi. The annual *Lakshmi Pujan* (welcoming the goddess of wealth) is still performed by the Birla family here. This also marks the beginning of the financial year for the Marwaris.

[64] Tarachand Ghanshyamdas had been traders since the early nineteenth century; they had been in Calcutta since the 1830s and they were engaged in speculative activity in stock, opium and government paper markets in addition to discounting of hundis issued by smaller indigenous bankers and purchase and sale of gold. Timberg, 'Three types of the Marwari Firm', Indian Economic and Social History Review (*IESHR*), (January 1973), pp. 1–36. Also see his 'A North Indian Firm as seen through its Business Records, 1860–1914: Tarachand Ghanshyamdas, A Great Marwari Firm', *IESHR*, Vol. 8, No. 3 (1971).

[65] Barua, *Raja Baldeodas Birla*, pp. 57–8.

[66] A nineteenth century English observer was intrigued by the spectacle when he explored 'the inmost recesses of the Babel-like regions of the Burra Bazar... here above and below, may be seen the jewels of Golconda and Bundelkhand, the shawls of Cashmere, the broad cloths of England, silks of Moorshedabad and Benaras, muslins of Dacca, calicoes, ginghanis, chintzes, brocade of Persia, spicery and myrrh and frankincense from Ceylon, the Spice Islands and Arabia, shells from the Eastern Coast and Straits, iron ware and cutlery in abundance, as well from Europe as Monghyr, coffee, drugs, dried fruits and sweetmeats from Arabia and Turkey, cows' tails from Thibet, and ivory from Ceylon... (The variety of goods was matched by the variety of the buyers and sellers who included) Persians, Arabs, Jews, Marwarrees, Armenians, Mundrazees, Cashmeerees, Malabars, Goojratees, Goorkhas, Afghans, Seiks, Turks, Parsees, Chinese, Burmese and Bengalis,' cited in Norma Evenson, *The Indian Metropolis: A View Towards the West* (Yale, 1989), pp. 25–6. Also see 'Barabazar' in Sukanta Chowdhuri (ed.), *Calcutta The Living City*, Vol. II (Calcutta, 1980).

[67] Radhakrishna Nevatia (ed.), *Bara Bazaar Ke Karyakarta: Sansmaran Avam Abhinandan* (Calcutta, 1982).

[68] Taknet, *Marwari Samaj*, p. 53.

[69] For an interesting reconstruction of everyday life of a trader in Bara Bazaar, see Ramkrishna Nevatia, *Shri Ramdev Chokhany* (Calcutta, n.d.), p. 29.

[70] Apparently the Marwaris suffered retribution for this and some English firms even bought up the entire stock to dissuade them. However, Baldeodas and the rest of the Marwaris did not give up, Barua, *Raja Baldeodas Birla*, p. 59.

[71] See Taknet, *Marwari Samaj*, p. 57; also see Timberg, *The Marwaris*, pp. 162–3.

[72] By 1905 the Marwaris controlled more than one-fourth of the satta business of Calcutta, with a bigger share in opium and jute segments. The other big men in trading were Hanumanbaks Kanoi, 'Tea King'; Ramnarain Ruia, 'Cotton King'; and Baldeodas Dudhewala, 'Shares King', Taknet, *Marwari Samaj*, pp. 56–7.

[73] 'If there was any difference between our family and other Rajasthani families, it was the religious inclinations of our family', recalled G.D. Birla in *Ve Din*, p. 7.

[74] Barua, *Raja Baldeodas Birla*, pp. 34–44.

[75] At the wedding of a poor Brahman's daughter Shivnarain customarily gave a donation of Rs 101, *Ibid*, p. 44.

[76] Raj Kumar Gupta, *Twenty Five years with Shri G.D. Birla Glimpses of a glorious life* (New Delhi, 1982), p. 42.

[77] In his later years, as a general practice, it was only after reading three to four pages of the translation of the *Gita* by Swami Chinamayanada that Ghanshyamdas retired for the day. R.K. Gupta, *Twenty Five years with Shri G.D. Birla*, p. 53.

[78] D.D. Shastri, *Ek Bindu Ek Sindhu*, p. 116. Interestingly, in the 1930s Braj Mohan Birla advised the Ahmedabad industrialist Ambalal Sarabhai not to send his son to Oxford but to induct him into the business while he was still in his teens. See Aparna Basu, *Mridula Sarabhai, Rebel With A Cause* (Delhi, 1996).

[79] Lack of education among the Marwaris was legendary. The children of Brahmans had to be sent out of the village of Pilani to Bagad to be taught. G.D. Birla in *Ve Din* describes conditions in the school, as also in the next school he attended.

[80] For details see G.D. Birla, *Ve Din*. For details on what constituted *Mahajani shiksha*, see Bhawarmal Singhi (ed.), *Shri Sitaram Seksaria Abhinandan Granth*, pp. 251–2.

[81] G.D. Birla, *Ve Din*.

[82] Marwaris were gradually realizing the importance of English and they often appointed special tutors to teach their sons. For instance, Ishwardas Jalan had a tutor, who was paid Rs 10 a month, in addition to some cloth from the shop, Nandkishore Jalan, *Shri Ishwardas Jalan Abhinandan Granth* (Calcutta, 1977), p. 64. G.D. Birla also later noted that special tutors were appointed to teach enough English to be able to read and send commercial intelligence. See G.D. Birla, *Kuch Dekha Kuch Sunna* (New Delhi, 1962), pp. 42–54. The 1921 Census notes that most Marwari males in Calcutta were literate—on par with the elite castes of Bengal, although their level of English literacy was significantly lower. Female literacy among the Marwaris was almost nil. Among Agarwals, Oswals and Maheshwaris, the lowest level of English literacy was among the Maheshwaris, who ironically proved to be the most successful in industry.

[83] *Ibid*.

[84] Jugalkishore's marriage was an ostentatious affair with a party for 400 persons, one elephant, ten carriages, twenty horses and many camels, See Shastri, *Ek Bindu Ek Sindhu*, p. 116. During marriages in Rajasthan, camel owners traditionally accompanied marriage

parties free of cost. For the groom's party a large procession meant added safety and grandeur, while for camel drivers it meant gifts and food for themselves and the beasts. The bride's family were obliged to welcome them.

[85] Ramkrishna Nevatia, *Shri Ramdev Chokhany*, p. 38.

[86] Barua, *Raja Baldeodas Birla*, pp. 46–7.

[87] He opened a library and a school for girls in his village, Sardar Shahr and was instrumental in the opening and the running of a *goshala*. Premsukhdas was also known to have succeeded in persuading the Ruler of Bikaner to open the Jodhpur–Bikaner railway line.

[88] B.K. Birla, *A Rare Legacy. Memoirs of B.K. Birla* (Bombay, 1994), pp. 263–4.

[89] Jaju, *G.D. Birla. A Biography*, p. 24.

[90] Memorial in Birla house, Pilani cited in B.K. Birla, *A Rare Legacy. Memoirs of B.K. Birla*, pp. 264–5. Later when his wife died rituals were held at nine cities and the expenditure was approx Rs 2,00,000.

[91] His last act in trading was in 1911 when he sold Chinese silver to the Government of India. It was only in 1911 that the Bombay firm experienced a turnaround in its fortunes through a windfall gain it made when it sold Chinese silver to the Government of India. Baldeodas negotiated with the authorities to purchase silver and all transactions were carried out through the Chartered Bank. The sale was made through the intermediacy of a Parsi dalal, Meherbanji. An offer was made to the Government of India for this silver by Baldeodas on highly competitive terms. So strong was the demand that Baldeodas sold silver for eight days earning Rs 30,000 on his first deal and about Rs 8,00,000 in total. He earned more than Rs 2,00,000 on market deals alone, Barua, *Raja Baldeodas Birla*, pp. 81–2.

[92] Baldeodas' and Yogeshwari Devi's days were devoted to prayer and religious activities. After rising at four in the morning, Baldeodas took a boat to the mid-Ganges for his bath; this was followed by prayers and recitations from the scriptures in the Birla house. Each afternoon an hour was kept aside for religious discussions with the city's Hindu religious preachers and *pandits* who were invited to Birla house. He himself wrote four religious books. Other religious activites which occupied the couple during the day were feeding the birds, caring for cows and undertaking philanthropy. He took it upon himself to spend on the restoration of the *ghats* of the city.

2

In the Forefront of the Calcutta Marwaris, 1911–1919

The year 1911 is a turning-point in the story of the Birlas. In that year Baldeodas retired from active involvement in business and the responsibility for the gaddi passed over to the younger generation. Ghanshyamdas moved to Calcutta and joined Jugalkishore to assume full charge of the family business. The two brothers lived above their office on 18, Mullick Street in Bara Bazaar. As was to be expected, the coming of the younger generation at the helm of the business was marked by several new developments, three of which occurred in less than a year and are noteworthy. First, in a pioneering move the Birlas became the first Indian business house in Calcutta to begin importing Japanese cloth from the firm, Mitsui. Whether this move was prompted by a shrewd business sense which anticipated the increasing importance of Japanese trade, or due to the influence of the Swadeshi Movement, is difficult to ascertain. Initially, this line of business did not do very well but the brothers persevered and were amply rewarded as Japanese trade proved to be very lucrative in the long run. However, the considerable risk-taking which it then involved must be acknowledged.[1] Second, the Birlas joined the opium syndicate which had just been established in Calcutta by Harduttrai Chamria. This turned out to be an astute move. Among the first to join the syndicate when it was formed, the Birlas were soon reaping huge profits as the syndicate soon became a powerful cartel which began to influence the entire opium trade. Finally, as was to be expected, the two brothers reorganized the business. While they continued the old-style brokerage and trading at their traditional gaddi, Ghanshyamdas set out to launch a firm of his own. The firm 'G.M. Birla' ('Ghanshyamdas Murlidhar') was thus incorporated to provide a vehicle for the 16-year-old Ghanshyamdas to launch his business career; this was a collaboration with his brother-in-law Murlidhar and was stated under the guidance of Mahadev Somani, the father of his late wife Durgadevi.

In spite of these three significant initiatives, Ghanshyamdas understood that the family had a long way to traverse before it could consider itself established in Calcutta, in business as well as socially. The Birlas still had to carve out a place for themselves among the leading Marwaris of Calcutta both in terms of prosperity and public stature. Public stature within the community, Ghanshyamdas realized, could be acquired along two possible paths. One was through philanthropy and the other through leadership over institutions which regulated community affairs, some of which were quite unique to the Marwaris. A position of leadership over them conferred prestige and enhanced public stature. In the years to come Ghanshyamdas and Jugalkishore pursued both the paths in a determined bid for leadership. In pre-World War I Calcutta, the most significant institutions of the community were the Marwari Panchayat, the Marwari Association and the Marwari Chamber of Commerce. Let us then briefly look at each of these institutions to see how the Birlas came to position themselves vis-à-vis the institutions.

Marwari Social Organization

Set up around 1828, the Marwari Panchayat was the oldest institution of the community in Calcutta. It arbitrated in internal disputes and took up matters of common concern.[2] When Ghanshyamdas started out in Calcutta the five *panches* (headmen) who made up the *Panchayat* were Jainarain Poddar of 'Tarachand Ghanshyamdas', Lakshminarain Kanodia of 'Harnandrai Phoolchand Bhaga', Surajmal Khemka of 'Harmukhrai Ramchandra', Nankurai Surekha of 'Sekharam Ramrikhdas' and Ganeshdas Bagdia from 'Sevaram Kaluram'. They collectively represented the most powerful Marwari firms in the city at that time. Under the panoply of the Marwari Panchayat there existed smaller panchayats which represented jatis as well as specific lines of business. These panchayats settled disputes internally, discouraged members from expensive litigation in colonial law courts and attempted to keep non-Marwaris at bay so that they could not interfere in the affairs of the community. In some ways panchayats dealing with specific trades were like the early modern European guilds. The Shroffs' Panchayat, for instance, regulated all aspects connected with speculation, while the Afeem Chaurasta Ki Panchayat enjoyed complete jurisdiction over the Marwaris engaged in the opium trade.[3] These bodies had wide-ranging spheres of influence and they, interalia regulated rates of interest and commission, certified hundi transactions, dealt with cases of liquidation and insolvency and settled family disputes.[4]

While the panchayats represented a traditional form of organization, the Marwaris also set up several bodies along modern lines. The Marwari Chamber of Commerce was one such organization. Founded in 1895 it had grown out of the need to safeguard Marwari interests vis-á-vis the larger European firms in the piece-goods business. Although the community had a representative in the European-dominated Bengal Chamber of Commerce, the feeling was widespread that their voice was not adequately heard.[5] As the Marwaris were heavily involved with Manchester piece-goods—and Bara Bazaar was the centre of this trade—they felt they needed a separate body which could safeguard their interest vis-á-vis the European firms and the government.[6] In the initial years the Chamber broadly fulfilled this objective but in later years it came to be racked by dissensions between buyers and sellers of cloth. As the sellers increasingly came to dominate the Chamber, the buyers formed their own Merchants' Committee.[7]

Yet another forum in the city was the Marwari Association which had been organized in 1898 principally to represent the community in the political arena.[8] Its first annual report styled it as 'the Parliament of the Marwari jati' and declared its aims to be the enrichment of 'the political, intellectual, trade and social life' of the community as well as to 'protect the honour and birth rights of the jati.'[9] However, these claims proved to be somewhat lofty and the Association could not develop a representative, broad-based character. It came to be dominated by rich traders mostly connected with the piece-goods trade who rigidly controlled its membership.[10] These traders were inclined to be loyalists and had intimate connections with European firms and the government from which they curried favours. Several even enjoyed titles.[11] The leadership of the Association kept the younger Marwaris out of its executive committee which made it unpopular with the younger generation, which was moreover inclined towards nationalist ideas. The younger members professed to be *sudharwadis* or radicals and wanted the Association to address issues of social reform.[12] In 1903—the year of the establishment of the Birla firm 'Baldeodas Jugalkishore'—the dissenting members of the Marwari Association formed a new body, called the Vaishya Sabha.[13] The radicalism of the Vaishya Sabha was illustrated by the enthusiasm shown by its members for the Swadeshi Movement which was gaining popularity in Bengal.[14] It started a debating society called the Buddhi Vardhani Sabha which played an important role in propagating the ideal of *swadeshi* and encouraging its members to trade only in swadeshi goods.[15] The distinct identities of the Marwari Association and the Vaishya Sabha reflected the growing rift between the reforming and conservative sections of the community.[16] These institutions collectively dominated the public arena of the Calcutta Marwaris. They were, as was to be expected, controlled by the larger Marwari firms. Many of these had come to Calcutta in the 1830s and 1840s and thus enjoyed the advantages associated with pioneers. The institutions which we described earlier were primarily set up by this first wave of migrants and it was naturally they who controlled them.

In comparison, Jugalkishore and Ghanshyamdas, when they came of age and took over the reins of the gaddi, paled into insignificance as they were men of modest stature in public life as also in the world of business. Although their commercial success had been remarkable and they were gaining recognition for this, they still stood outside the institutions that controlled the corporate life of the Marwaris in the city. They were seen as latecomers, and in a world where commercial and social spheres interlocked, this was an unenviable situation.

Moreover, Jugalkishore and Ghanshyamdas had the disadvantages associated with youth and inexperience; when Baldeodas retired, Jugalkishore was 27 years old and Ghanshyamdas, merely 16.

Over the next decade, as this chapter will show, Jugalkishore and Ghanshyamdas strove to carve out a place for themselves in Bara Bazaar. They were helped in this by the transformation which the world of Marwari politics itself was undergoing. The younger generation in the community was increasingly challenging the established leadership, its policies and values. This divide was somewhat characteristic of the generational gulf that existed in Indian politics. The moderate–extremist clash within nationalist politics had not been resolved. Radical ideas were emerging but they had yet to find adherence in large numbers and the old prescriptions were yet to become discredited.[17] The ambiguities of the era are perhaps best mirrored in the career of Mohandas Karamchand Gandhi. His ideas in this decade represent a curious blend of the old and the new. For the Marwaris too, it was a time of ferment during which the Birla brothers consciously tried to identify with the aspirations of the younger generation.

DEBUT IN PUBLIC AFFAIRS

The Birla brothers' debut in the public affairs of the community illustrated which way their sympathies lay. In 1911, soon after moving to Calcutta, Ghanshyamdas, together with fellow Marwari traders Prabhudayal Himmatsinghka and Devidutt Jalan, started the Marwari Sporting Club.[18] The purpose of the Club was to encourage a culture of fitness and sports among the youth and to provide instruction in self-defence. The Club soon became a meeting-place for the younger residents of Bara Bazaar who gathered everyday for body-building, wrestling and rifle-shooting, and to learn the use of *lathi* and *lazium*. Arrangements were later made for a playground for football and cricket, a game Ghanshyamdas himself enjoyed playing in those years. It is difficult to speculate whether the Club was set up to encourage self-defence following the communal clashes which took place in 1910 in Calcutta in which Marwari loss of life and property had been substantial.[19] Although the focus of the Club remained physical fitness, its members did not restrict themselves to sports and initiated other activities such as conducting classes in Hindi. It is not surprising that initiatives that encouraged self-defence and physical fitness marked Ghanshyamdas' debut in public life. His interest in physical fitness went back to his early childhood and was part of his belief in the synthesis of mind and body which he strove to achieve in his daily life. Further, one reason for setting up a club to encourage physical exercise could have been the need to counter stereotypes of Marwaris as being weak, unfit and effeminate. In retrospect, two aspects of this debut are noteworthy: first, it was a low-key affair in a sphere of activity which the established Marwari institutions may have looked upon as insignificant; second, it was an initiative that only the younger generation in the community was likely to find attractive.

This commitment of the Birlas to institutions that promoted physical fitness came to be extended over the years. Ghanshyamdas from his early childhood had developed an admiration for and interest in wrestling and this came to be expressed in 1916 when he enthusiastically supported a new institution, the Bara Bazaar Yuwak Sangh. The Yuwak Sangh, unlike the Marwari Sporting Club, was a traditional *akhara* which laid emphasis on wrestling as a way of life. In addition to supporting professional wrestlers, it provided an arena for Marwari youth to learn wrestling and physical fitness under expert guidance. Ghanshyamdas himself frequently participated in wrestling and took an interest in the activities of the Sangh. Much of the expenditure of the *akhara* was borne by him; an annual sum of Rs 2000 was earmarked for this purpose to be used for provisions like *ghee, gur* and gram which were essential for the wrestlers' diet.[20] In addition to this recurring expenditure Ghanshyamdas gifted a house with four-room accommodation for the full-time members of the Sangh. Subsequently, the Birla brothers became the principal patrons of the Maheshwari Vyayamshala, which they set up in Calcutta in the early 1920s. This Vyayamshala also became the venue for celebrations connected with festivals such as *Ganesh Chaturthi* and *Nag Panchami* in which the larger Bara Bazaar community actively participated.[21]

The Birla brothers' patronage to akharas continued to grow beyond Calcutta and by the 1920s they were supporting similar institutions in many parts of India. Jugalkishore, in particular, took it upon himself to establish several of these akharas. So enthusiastic was his support that, not only did he patronize the akharas, but was also known to take upon himself the sponsorship of *dangals* (wrestling tournaments). This involved expenditure on the wrestlers, their food, lodging and travel and the overheads of hosting the tournament. To popularize the event, on one occasion, he paid for the tickets himself, so that the spectators could attend free of cost.[22] This patronage was paid for by the Birla firm run jointly by the brothers.

The most ambitious of such projects came in 1928 when the Birlas set up an akhara in Delhi as an adjunct to their newly-opened Birla Cloth Mills. Guru Hanuman, who later became a legendary figure in the annals of Indian wrestling was put in charge of the akhara which came to be known as the Birla Mill Vyayamshala. The relationship between Guru Hanuman and the Birlas became an intimate one, with the Birlas as the patrons becoming responsible for the image of the wrestler and Guru Hanuman, in turn, bringing them glory. Jugalkishore always took a personal interest in its growth, while the Mill in Delhi underwrote all its expenses.[23] So well recognized was Jugalkishore's patronage of wrestling that he was known as Birla Maharaj by the Hindu wrestling community.[24] The reputation of the Vyayamshala has over the years continued to grow and it has nurtured hundreds of young wrestlers, many of whom have won laurels in national and international events.[25] The akhara is reportedly the most well-endowed institution of its kind in India. For Jugalkishore and Ghanshyamdas, patronage of akharas meant much more than extending mere financial support, however substantial it might have been. Patronage meant rather an attitude of moral and ethical support—'ideological underwriting of the wrestler's way of life'[26]—which reflected a close relationship between the patron and the wrestler.[27]

To come back to the brothers' early initiatives in Calcutta, in 1911 when Jugalkishore and Ghanshyamdas had made their debut in public life, their initiative had started on the fringes of Marwari public life and had taken the form of a wrestling club. This small initiative proved to be very popular with the younger generation. The two brothers now consolidated this constituency by helping to set up in 1913 the Marwari Sahayak Samiti. The organization of the Samiti came about as a result of regular meetings of young traders at the gaddi of 'Baldeodas Jugalkishore'. These young men decided to establish facilities for medical care in Bara Bazaar and, for this purpose, they formed the Marwari Sahayak Samiti. Jugalkishore who mostly funded its activities in the early years, was elected its founder-president. The Samiti set up a hospital in Bara Bazaar which fulfilled a long-felt need for medical care. In its first year itself the hospital benefited 17,175 out-patients and 749 in-patients.[28] The Samiti soon extended its range of activities to provide flood relief in Darbhanga and Burdwan on which it spent Rs 20,000.[29] Its volunteers also established medical camps during religious fairs such as the Shitalji mela, the Gangasagar mela and the famous Kumbh mela. The Marwari Sahayak Samiti also had an agenda of social reform for the community which included eradication of child marriage, *purdah* and reduction of expenditure on death ceremonies. With such initiatives the Samiti soon became the focus of youth activities in Bara Bazaar. Its active members in these formative years were Jwala Prasad Kanodia, Prabhudayal Himmatsinghka, Hanuman Prasad Poddar, Radha Krishna Nevatia and, not the least, the Birla brothers.

Perhaps the most important initiative which the Samiti took was the Hindu Club (also called the Kaligodam Vyayaam Shala) which acted as a meeting-place for young Marwaris with an interest in physical culture. An extension of the Club was the Sahitya Sambandhini Sabha which aimed at publishing quality literature in Hindi at low rates. It used the medium of religion to propagate ideas of social reform and nationalist awareness. For instance, it brought out one of the most popular Hindi publications of its time—the *Tikawali Gita* of Baburao Vishnu Paradikar. On its cover was a picture of *Bharat Mata* (Mother India) with the *Gita* in one hand and a sword in the other! Published in 1914 by the Samiti under the presidentship of Jugalkishore, the book became so popular that two editions were sold out in quick succession. The government, fearing links with revolutionary terrorists, however, proscribed the *Gita* and the premises of the Club were searched by the police.

From these two initiatives which were especially targeted at the younger generation, Jugalkishore and Ghanshyamdas graduated to the mainstream of Marwari public arena. The founding of the Maheshwari Sabha in 1914 in which they played an active role signified this.[30] Together with Ramkrishna Mohta, a prominent Marwari businessman, the Birlas thus became its principal patrons. The Sabha formed a fund-raising committee and Jugalkishore became its moving spirit.[31] An urgent priority in these early years was the need for a building of its own for the Sabha. For this purpose a large plot of land was bought at Shobharam Baisakh Street with the help of Ramkrishna Mohta; and the Birlas contributed the substantial sum of Rs 2,80,000 for this purpose. In recognition of this generosity Jugalkishore was made a permanent trustee of the organization.[32] Later financial difficulties were experienced in the construction of the building at this site and the Birlas gave a further sum of Rs 7,70,001 to help meet the costs. They thus became the largest donors to the Sabha which was the first Marwari organization in Calcutta to be housed in a building of its own.[33] For these generous contributions, Jugalkishore came to be lauded within the community as *Daan Veer* Jugalkishore Birla.

Having established itself in a premises of its own, the Sabha started a range of activities. One activity which attracted the interest of both Jugalkishore and Ghanshyamdas was the promotion of Hindi. When the Sabha proposed to establish a library of Hindi books, which were difficult to obtain by young Marwaris in Calcutta where Bengali predominated, the Birlas showed enthusiasm in supporting this project and Jugalkishore became a member of the sub-committee established for this purpose. In a report on the activities of the Sabha it was later recalled: 'It is an absolute truth that without the support of Jugalkishore Birla ...the many proud institutions of the Maheshwari Sabha would not enjoy the status that they do.'[34] Further, educational work carried out by the Sabha was also liberally supported by the Birlas. They became the main financiers of the Maheshwari Vidyalaya which was set up in 1916 in Calcutta and in recognition of their services, Jugalkishore was made the Vidyalaya's president for 1916–17 after which Ghanshyamdas was given this responsibility which he held till 1921.[35] In 1918 alone, the Birlas' donation to the Vidyalaya amounted to Rs 51,000.[36] The Vidyalaya invited celebrities from the world of Hindi journalism and literature to be associated with it. Its principal in those years was Babu Moolchand Agarwal, editor and publisher of the well-known Hindi paper *Aaj* and a literary figure in his own right. The Vidyalaya increasingly came to play a central role in the Marwari community and regularly invited important political leaders to preside over its functions. For its first annual function, held under the presidentship of Jugalkishore, Pandit Madan Mohan Malaviya was invited. The following year, when Ghanshyamdas became the president, the guest of honour was none other than Mohandas Karamchand Gandhi.

A REVOLUTIONARY INTERLUDE

The initiatives of Jugalkishore and Ghanshyamdas and their quiet rise within the community was, however, interrupted by an episode which proved to be decisive for Ghanshyamdas personally. In 1914 he was implicated in a revolutionary terrorist case which came to be known as the Rodda conspiracy case. The Partition of Bengal in 1905 and the Swadeshi Movement which accompanied it had influenced the youth of Bengal and in its aftermath the revolutionary terrorist movement stood at its peak.[37] The younger generation of the Marwaris could not keep aloof from the revolutionary fervour which seemed all-pervasive in Calcutta. Several young Marwari men had forged links with Bengali revolutionaries and occasionally helped them financially. Among them was Hanuman Prasad Poddar, a prominent member of the Anushilan Samiti who helped the organization financially and regularly participated in its meetings.[38] Another such young Marwari was Onkarmal Saraf, known to be a close associate of Ashutosh Lahiri, a famous Bengali revolutionary of that time.[39] Prabhu Dayal Himmatsinghka, a close associate of Ghanshyamdas, had also developed revolutionary links.[40] Several impressionable young men of Bara Bazaar had thus come under the romantic spell of terrorist ideology, and one Marwari, Lala Hanumant Sahai, had even been implicated in a revolutionary conspiracy case.[41] It was rumoured that the famous Bengal revolutionary Aurobindo Ghosh used to receive regular financial contributions from sympathizers in Bara Bazaar. The forging of links with the revolutionaries must be seen in the context of the political environment in which the young Marwaris lived. It was fashionable for the young men in that era to be sympathetic with the revolutionaries. Although the fervour often lasted only so far as not to cause a major disruption in their lifestyle, it is not surprising that several young members of the Marwari Sahayak Samiti and the Hindu Club came under the spell of revolutionary propaganda. Bipin Ganguli and other extremists were known to patronize the Marwari Sahayak Samiti and it was rumoured that they sometimes even addressed its meetings. The Hindu Club, having earned the wrath of the authorities with the publication of the *Tikawali Gita*, had already been declared an illegal body, as we noted earlier.[42]

In the circumstances the involvement of seven young Marwaris including Ghanshyamdas in the Rodda conspiracy case of August 1914 proved to be a landmark for the community. The case involved the theft of a consignment of arms belonging to Rodda & Co., a prominent arms dealer of Calcutta.[43] The theft was allegedly committed by Bipin Ganguli, who enlisted the help of his Marwari sympathizers for hiding the stolen cases. Ganguli reportedly 'lodged the arms with a Marwari in the first place'. He then disposed of about 22 pistols 'when the Marwari became restive and demanded the removal of the remainder from his house. The Marwari handed him 28 of the pistols and a part of the ammunition'.[44] When news reached Bara Bazaar that the police suspected Marwari involvement, panic spread among the traders. The story goes that the crates were then moved from house to house and, at one point, they were hidden at the Birla residence in Zakaria Street.[45] Police enquiries soon confirmed the connivance of the Marwaris. Searches were conducted at several premises in Bara

Bazaar, and the Birlas' residence in Zakaria Street and their gaddi and warehouse in Harrison Road, Kaligodam, were scoured.[46] As a result of these intensive investigations, 31 pistols were recovered from a godown in Badtalla Street in the heart of Bara Bazaar. Warrants were issued in the names of Hanuman Prasad Poddar, Prabhu Dayal Himmatsinghka, Phoolchand Chowdhury, Jwalaprasad Kanodia, Kanhaiyalal Chitlangiya, Onkarmal Saraf and Ghanshyamdas Birla. Since all of them were prominent members of the Marwari Sahayak Samiti and the Hindu Club, both the organizations were asked to discontinue their activities.

While the issue of a warrant of arrest for Ghanshyamdas was shocking, his involvement in the case was not entirely surprising. He had been actively involved with the Marwari Sahayak Samiti and was its president at the time of the Rodda conspiracy case. He was also deeply involved with the activities of the Hindu Club and his social circle was made of friends who formed the core of these two organizations. Moreover, he subscribed to the radical ideas of people like Himmatsinghka, Saraf and Poddar. In any case, the police seemed to have had evidence that the cache of arms had at one time been hidden with Ghanshyamdas' connivance at one of his premises. In close circles it was believed that he had assisted the revolutionaries financially but it was difficult to confirm this.[47]

As the police began to arrest those under suspicion, Ghanshyamdas almost ended up in a prison cell. In an interview with the author, Prabhu Dayal Himmatsinghka recalled:

In 1914 I was arrested in the Rodda Arms Case and in 1916 I was externed from Bengal and interned in my house at Dhumka, Bihar, for four years. At the time I was arrested, there was also a warrant for Birla's arrest, but I managed to tip him off and he escaped to the south.

As a result of this prior information Ghanshyamdas managed to avoid arrest. His family elders, upon hearing the news of his impending arrest, made arrangements for his books and papers to be despatched to Mukundgarh in Shekhawati.[48] Ghanshyamdas escaped first to Ooty (Ootacamund) in south India, then to Nathdwara, and finally to Pushkar in Rajputana. Pushkar was not far from Pilani but Ghanshyamdas did not dare visit his village home for fear of arrest. He remained underground for almost three months and 'spent weeks sometimes dressed as a *Sadhu*' in parts of western Rajasthan.[49] Alan Ross suggests that the austerity and discipline instilled in him as a young boy stood him in good stead during these difficult times. Looking back at the episode Ghanshyamdas later recalled: 'It must be said, however, that I never had a great taste for terrorism, and after my contact with Gandhiji whatever traces remained were altogether eradicated.'[50] It was during these months of wanderings that his eldest daughter Chandrakala was born and it was several months later that Ghanshyamdas was able to see her.

Meanwhile in Calcutta, the family elders lobbied high officials and important persons close to the authorities to get the warrant rescinded. Instrumental in this was Sir Kailashchandra Bose, known 'for his contacts with high-level British officials' who were 'very fond of him'. Bose was requested by the family elders to stand guarantee for Ghanshyamdas. Further, Charles Tegart, then a senior official in the Calcutta police, was also approached for help.[51] On Bose's surety to the Lal Bazaar police that Ghanshyamdas had nothing to do with the terrorists, the warrant was finally withdrawn.[52] Ghanshyamdas then returned to Calcutta and resigned from the presidentship of the Marwari Sahayak Samiti.

BACK IN THE MAINSTREAM

The Rodda conspiracy case shook the Marwaris of Bara Bazaar. The Sedition Committee of 1918 (headed by Justice Rowlatt) was later to declare the case as an 'event of the greatest importance in the development of revolutionary crime in Bengal'. 'Few, if any, revolutionary outrages have taken place in Bengal,' it continued, 'since August 1914, in which Mauser pistols stolen from Rodda and Co. have not been used.'[53] The British later claimed that the pistols which could not be recovered in the Rodda conspiracy case were subsequently used in 54 cases of serious revolutionary crime involving dacoity or murder. In view of the great importance which the authorities attached to the case, it is not surprising that the entire Marwari leadership in Calcutta felt itself to be under a cloud of suspicion. Those were the years of World War I when the Marwaris were beginning to make enormous fortunes in business. The Marwari leadership felt that the younger, recalcitrant members were inviting the wrath of the authorities at such a time of opportunity and endangering the interests of the entire community. Elders within the Marwari Panchayat and the conservative leadership of the Marwari Association now decided to take matters in their hands and reassert control. The leadership lobbied with Sir Kailashchandra Bose and persuaded Saraknath Sadhu, the government lawyer, and Puranchand Lahiri, another prominent Calcutta lawyer, to intercede on behalf of the accused. It was due to these efforts that five of the warrants, including that of Ghanshyamdas, were withdrawn, and two others, Prabhudayal Himmatsinghka and Saraf, got off lightly by merely being externed from Bengal and only one Marwari was finally sentenced.[54]

Having succeeded in securing a remission for those involved, the older leadership now decided to turn this crisis into an opportunity to contain the younger elements and reassert its authority. Basantlal Morarka, one of the radicals who later became a prominent politician in West Bengal recalls that 'the case affected the Samaj in such a manner that the younger members trembled with fear ... they were now in no position to stand in opposition.' In Morarka's view the episode led to the taming of the younger elements.[55] The reassertion of control by the conservative leadership is best illustrated by what happened to the Marwari Sahayak Samiti with which Ghanshyamdas was closely associated. Six of the arrested men had been founder-members of the Samiti. To disassociate the Samiti from the ignominy brought upon the community, it was decided to transform its character and give it respectability. Kailashchandra Bose was now persuaded to extend his patronage to the Samiti, so that 'both the government and the public understand that this was not a political organization'. Bose, a non-Marwari, was persuaded to accept its presidentship.[56] As president, Bose's first initiative was to impress upon the general body of the Samiti that its name 'was a dangerous one, because two of Bengal's revolutionary organizations were also named samiti—the Yugantar Samiti and the Anushilan Samiti'. Unless the name was changed, he argued, the government would continue to be suspicious of the Marwari community.[57] Despite protests from the younger members, the Samiti's name was changed to Marwari Relief Society and this change in nomenclature symbolized that the conservatives' dominance over the community was now complete. The Society declared that it would only be concerned with social service, and its associated bodies such as the Hindu Club and the Sahitya Sambandhini Sabha, were disbanded.[58]

Following the Rodda case the Marwari Association clearly gained in stature and was keen to demonstrate its authority. One issue which illustrated it was that of adulteration of food. The Association received complaints that some Marwari traders were dealing in ghee adulterated with beef tallow. The leadership of the Association decided to expose these traders. It organized raids at godowns where stocks of ghee were stored, seized samples of over 70 tons and had these clinically examined. A panchayat was then called and the guilty were fined upwards of Rs 75,000 each and excommunicated from the community. Later a representation was made to the Lieutenant-Governor, Lord Ronaldshay, which resulted in legislation being enacted against adulteration of food in 1917.[59]

Ghanshyamdas, now back in Calcutta after his three-month escapade, was nominated the vice-president of the Marwari Relief Society in a thoughtful move which aimed at moulding his ideas rather than marginalizing him in the new set-up. The community elders, at the prompting of Baldeodas and Jugalkishore, hoped that working under Kailashchandra Bose as the president would bring Ghanshyamdas back into the mainstream of Marwari public life.[60] Ghanshyamdas probably felt a sense of gratitude towards those who had shielded him and were now trying to rehabilitate him in Bara Bazaar. On his part he reoriented his politics to bring it in line with the changed agenda of the Marwari Relief Society. His organizational activities thereafter were strictly non-controversial and focused on educational charities in Rajputana.[61] In this way the family elders were successful in weaning him away from the magnetic pull of radical politics which intoxicated Calcutta's youth at this time. The episode, however, left a deep impression on Ghanshyamdas. While his interest in politics had been awakened, it made him alive to the risks which direct participation in radical nationalist politics entailed. He realized that as a businessman he had his family's business interests to safeguard, and this realization influenced his subsequent involvements.

In Ghanshyamdas' own words whatever traces of revolutionary terrorism remained were 'eradicated' after his contact with Gandhi which took place in 1916 when the latter visited Calcutta. As a guest of the Marwari community Gandhi stayed at the local Vishudanand Saraswati Vidyalaya in Bara Bazaar. He was formally presented with an address by the community and he made the acquaintance of several prominent Marwari families. On his arrival Gandhi was taken in a procession through the streets of Bara Bazaar. As the procession passed the centre of the crowded business district his carriage was stopped. At this point two young men came forward, and in a dramatic gesture, unyoked the horses and insisted on hauling the cart themselves. These men were Jamnalal Bajaj, a prominent Congress leader and Ghanshyamdas Birla who had been walking alongside the cart and shouting 'Karamvir Gandhi Ki Jai'.[62] The hauling of Gandhi's cart by Jamnalal and Ghanshyamdas symbolized in a profound way the strong bonds of support and patronage which Gandhi was later to forge with the Marwaris. In the years to come it was the Marwaris who quite substantially financed the many campaigns that the Mahatma espoused in his long drawn-out struggle against the Raj.[63]

Ghanshyamdas' first encounter with Gandhi was to always remain etched in his mind. He attended all five of Gandhi's public meetings in Calcutta. Gandhi's 'manner of behaviour, his food habits, simple lifestyle, humility and less talk' impressed him greatly, although he found it difficult to wholly comprehend what Gandhi represented. Gandhi's references to Gokhale as his political mentor irked some young men who disapproved of the Maharashtrian leader's moderation 'because he spoke with common sense and not excitement—which appealed less to the youth's education and training'. Ghanshyamdas later recalled that it was the extremist leader Lokmanya Tilak who was dear to them. 'That was why we young men disapproved of Gandhiji's repeatedly calling Gokhale his political mentor.'[64] Out of curiosity, Ghanshyamdas enquired from Gandhi if he would reply to questions concerning public issues asked by an unknown, ordinary young man. Gandhi replied in the affirmative and soon enough Ghanshyamdas despatched his first letter just to verify if he would keep his word. Much to his surprise and delight, Ghanshyamdas received a prompt reply.[65]

It may, at this stage, be interesting to see what happened to Ghanshyamdas' radical associates, after the Rodda case. According to Basantlal Morarka, they had found themselves in an environment 'in which they were paralysed by the fear of government repression in the field of politics, by the obscurantism of the Brahmins in the field of religion and by the tyranny of the Panchayat in the field of social work'.[66] Although Ghanshyamdas had disavowed his revolutionary terrorism, through his public gestures, the personal links which he had forged with the radicals within the community continued. This is illustrated by his lifelong association with Hanuman Prasad Poddar and Prabhudayal Himmatsinghka. While Ghanshyamdas kept out of the political arena, his radical fervour found expression in the strong support which he extended to the agenda of social reform within the community, even at the risk of the displeasure of the community elders. One such occasion was when, in 1916, he publicly entertained Kaliprasad Khaitan upon his return from England when he had been

excommunicated by the Panchayat for overseas travel. The community threatened
to boycott the forthcoming wedding of Ghanshyamdas' younger brother Braj
Mohan as a consequence. Baldeodas, who intervened to save the situation,
consulted the Panchayat and arrived at a compromise which appeased his son,
while satisfying the conservatives. Kaliprasad Khaitan could, as a result, be
readmitted into the community by agreeing to subject himself to rituals
of purification and by undertaking a pilgrimage.[67] This illustrates that
Ghanshyamdas had not lost face with his radical associates.

Meanwhile, the radicals regrouped themselves in the Gyan Vardhini Mitra
Mandali which was started initially as a social club and disavowed any connection
with political, social or religious causes.[68] Nonetheless, it forged an important
contact with Jamnalal Bajaj who was already well established both in Marwari
and nationalist circles and, through him, with Gandhi. Bajaj was the only
prominent Marwari leader who had been sympathetic to the radicals' plight after
their involvement in the Rodda case and this had forged a bond between him
and the radicals. With his continued support, the Mandali was able to organize
the Marwari Traders' Association and merge its identity in the new organization.
The Marwari Traders' Association, under the patronage of Bajaj, now became
the vehicle of the radicals' struggle against the conservatives. It started its own
newspaper, called the *Satya Sanatan Dharma*, in opposition to the *Shri Sanatan
Dharma* brought out by the conservatives.[69]

The conservative leadership of Bara Bazaar had been effective by its tough
line in restraining the drift towards revolutionary politics among the younger
ranks of Marwaris. But it had not succeeded in assuaging the feelings of the
dissidents or bringing them wholly back into the fold. Ghanshyamdas seems to
have been more of an exception and was able to come back to the mainstream
more easily, which may have been due to the stature and influence of Baldeodas
and Jugalkishore. However, a large section of the radicals remained anchorless.
Jamnalal Bajaj was able to take advantage of this and succeeded in recruiting
many of them when he encouraged the Marwari Traders' Association in Calcutta
to merge with the Akhil Bharatiya Marwari Agarwal Mahasabha which he started
as an all-India organization of the Marwaris. Bajaj wanted to inaugurate the
Mahasabha in Calcutta, perceived to be the bastion of Marwari conservatism.
However, due to the strong opposition of the Marwari Panchayat, he was not
successful and the opening session was then held at Wardha.[70]

Bajaj was thus successful in consolidating a solid block of activists who were
to play a leading role in the passage of Marwari politics to mass nationalism.
Their increasing influence was noticed at the time of the historic Rowlatt
satyagraha, which ushered in the Gandhian era of nationalism in Indian politics.
The Agarwal Mahasabha spearheaded Marwari participation in the agitation.
On the day of the *hartal* on 6 April 1919, the call for which was given by Gandhi,
most shops in Bara Bazaar remained closed.[71] At meetings held on 6, 11, and
12 April at Nakhoda Mosque in protest over the Rowlatt Bill, a large participation

by the Marwaris was noticed.[72] When the news of Gandhi's arrest in Punjab came on 10 April, all shops were closed.[73] On the same day agitators disrupted the tram services in the north of the city. The offenders were mostly said to be 'small boys of the Marwari and Bhatia castes with a sprinkling of Muhamaddans' who were 'incited by others of more mature age who kept in the background.'[74] Among the principal speakers at a protest meeting organized at Beadon Square were two prominent traders, Ambika Prasad Bajpai and Debi Prasad Khaitan, a close personal associate of Ghanshyamdas.[75] The meeting urged the audience to observe mourning and keep their shops shut for four days.[76] The following day violence erupted in the city. At a further meeting Marwari trader Padam Raj Jain supported the suggestion that a complete hartal should be observed in memory of the dead.[77]

While the radical Marwaris enthusiastically participated in the Rowlatt satyagraha and played a leading role in making it a success in Calcutta, the Marwari Association and the Marwari Chamber of Commerce passed resolutions affirming their loyalty to the government and expressing disapproval of the violence. They also disclaimed the responsibility of the Marwari community as a whole for the disturbances, and alleged that those Marwaris who had taken part in them were 'an insignificant number of men of the lowest class'.[78] Two days later a deputation of the conservatives within the Marwari Association called upon the Governor to reaffirm their allegiance. The Governor asserted the 'responsibility of the community for the disturbances which had taken place.'[79] The delegation, on its part, continued to disassociate itself from the disturbances and assured him that 'being traders our first priority is peace in the city'.[80] It was after the Rowlatt agitation that differences between the two groups came into the open and a split became unavoidable.[81] Ghanshyamdas kept aloof from these controversies plaguing Marwari politics and concentrated on his business.

THE EMERGING PHILANTHROPISTS

A parallel focus of the Birlas' public work, as noted earlier, lay in the realm of philanthropy. The 1910s were marked by their emergence as the leading Marwari philanthropists of Calcutta. It is interesting to note the scale of their philanthropy and how much this contributed to their growing public stature.[82] The Birlas' notion of philanthropy was rooted in notions of religious piety. Central to such piety were charities done for the cause of cow protection. The Marwaris had shown a strong interest in this cause and had been the principal financiers of the strong cow-protection movements that had flourished across north India from 1880s onwards.[83] One of the earliest philanthropies which the family undertook in Calcutta involved donations amounting to Rs 1,00,000 for the establishment of *goshalas*.[84] The Birla brothers also took a keen interest in the Pinjrapole Society established in the 1880s, to provide a refuge for bereft birds whose care is considered a form of religious piety among the Marwaris.[85]

In 1904, the Birlas made a substantial donation to the Vishudanand Saraswati Vidyalaya which was the main educational institution for the community in Calcutta, and thereafter their strong support to this school continued. In 1911, the Hindu nationalist leader Pandit Madan Mohan Malaviya visited the school and made an appeal for Rs 3,00,000, so that it could be housed in a building of its own. So passionate and persuasive was Malaviya's appeal that six leading Marwaris took a pledge that they would wear their pagri only after the money had been collected. Though these six men did not include the Birla brothers, the family contributed substantially to this appeal.[86] Educational charities elsewhere also came to be supported by the Birlas. In 1912, the Birla brothers helped Jamnalal Bajaj to collect donations for a Marwari school in Bombay. In 1918, the family established the first high school in Pilani for which Baldeodas was honoured with the title of seth by Sawai Madho Singh, the Maharaja of Jaipur.

We have already noted the strong support which the Birla brothers had given to Maheshwari organizations such as the Maheshwari Vidyalaya and the Maheshwari Panchayat. Further, scholars and institutions promoting the cause of Hindi and Sanskrit were also supported liberally by the Birlas. In 1910, when Baldeodas first visited Banaras, a city with which he later had a long association, he opened a Sanskrit library there to promote classical learning. In Calcutta, Jugalkishore became the principal patron of the Maheshwari Pustakalaya, a library devoted to Hindi books. This was the second library in Calcutta devoted solely to Hindi books. He was also a patron of an association set up by the Maheshwaris to promote Hindi.[87] A Brahman Bari was opened in Bombay in 1916, and another in 1920, in Calcutta, to provide lodgings to Hindi-speaking scholars. At its opening ceremony Lord Ronaldshay, the Lieutenant Governor of Bengal, commended Baldeodas as one 'well known for his philanthropy' who supported 'impartially all projects which are designed to benefit humanity'.[88] In 1918, Baldeodas was awarded the title of 'Rai Bahadur' by the government for his generous donation to a scheme promoted by Lady Chelmsford for child welfare and for his charities to help establish facilities for the treatment of leprosy.[89] In 1919, Baldeodas helped establish the Marwari Hospital at Elmhurst Street in Calcutta with a contribution of Rs 51,001.[90] *Capital*, the European financial weekly which was usually critical of the Marwaris, commented upon Baldeodas as:

a fine type of successful Marwari merchant who realises that one of the responsibilities of wealth is to spend money for the amelioration of the place where he made it. It is consoling to find the tribe is increasing and it is not extravagant to believe that, in the course of time, the Marwaris will do for Calcutta what the Parsis have done for Bombay.

In the field of philanthropy the Birlas were clearly gaining a stature that increasingly brought them in the forefront of the Marwaris of Calcutta.[91] Meanwhile, the horizons of their charities came to be extended by the substantial profits made by them during the war years as we shall see below. At the end of the war it was reckoned that the Birlas' known charities had exceeded Rs 25 lakhs in hard cash.[92]

THE PROSPERITY OF THE WAR YEARS

Philanthropy on this scale was possible only because the Birlas had done exceedingly well in their business during the war years. As we noted earlier, in 1914, when World War I broke out, the Birlas had three firms. Two of these were branches of 'Baldeodas Jugalkishore', originally called 'Shivnarain Baldeodas' and first set up in Bombay in 1879 and then in 1896, in Calcutta. The third was the firm of 'G.M. Birla' set up by Ghanshyamdas in partnership with his brother-in-law. The Bombay firm was managed by Rameshwardas who was occasionally helped by Baldeodas, while the Calcutta business was run by Jugalkishore and Ghanshyamdas. The new firm was managed exclusively by Ghanshyamdas. While 'Baldeodas Jugalkishore' dealt in silver, opium, grain, wool, linseed and Manchester cloth, the new firm 'Ghanshyamdas Murlidhar' specialized in jute and functioned as a broker in the jute and gunny trade. At this time Marwari firms were reaping large profits from the trading and export of jute. The jute sector itself was experiencing impressive growth within the overall economy. In 1911, the year the new Birla firm was set up, Indian exports of raw jute were worth Rs 1540 lakhs and exports of jute products exceeded Rs 1700 lakhs.[93] As we earlier noted the Marwaris had been particularly well entrenched at all levels in the raw jute trade since the 1870s. In their role as arhatiyas they brought raw jute from the countryside to up-country markets where they were involved with *kuchcha* baling. Once the goods reached the jute mills they were involved in *fataka* operations on an extensive scale. Ghanshyamdas' new venture benefited from this dominance of the community in the trade as it gave him advantages in terms of prior intelligence about market and pricing trends.

The new firm meant diverse and heavy responsibilities for Ghanshyamdas. As a jute broker he had to make contact with important European managing agencies such as Bird and Heiglers, Andrew Yule, Jardine Skinner and McLeod, Begg & Dunlop. In these dealings especially helpful to him was Mahadev Somani, the father of his late wife Durgadevi. Somani had formidable contacts with the European managing agencies, who regarded him as reliable and his name featured in the lists of dalals with whom business was recommended. These links led to some of the earliest contracts which 'G.M. Birla' was able to secure. Ghanshyamdas' proficiency in English also helped him establish a rapport with the European managing agencies. Soon orders for the new firm were forthcoming and the business was off to a good start.

Interestingly, Ghanshyamdas' contacts with the European firms, particularly with the Scots who dominated the jute industry, was to leave a strong impression upon his personality. As a regular visitor to their offices Ghanshyamdas was able to closely observe the expatriate businessmen at work. As he recalled in his autobiography:

During my association with them I began to see their superiority in business methods, their organizational capacity and their many other virtues. But their racial arrogance could not be concealed. I was not allowed to use the lift to go up to their office, nor their benches while waiting to see them.

One particular incident which Ghanshyamdas could never forget was when he called upon a British businessman with whom he had taken an appointment. While the meeting was in progress Ghanshyamdas was unceremoniously asked to leave when an English broker entered the room. Ghanshyamdas vowed never to visit that firm again. 'I smarted under these insults and this created within me a political interest which from 1912 until today I have fully maintained,' he later recalled.[94] Such incidents of racial discrimination and arrogance roused in him a political consciousness. He came to deeply resent the European monopoly over the jute trade more than ever.

In 1914, World War I broke out and the ups and downs caused by the wartime economy created extraordinary opportunities for businessmen. The Birlas too stood to gain from some of these opportunities. In particular, their speculative operations in silver led to windfall gains. The increasing international price of silver and the policy of the Government of India to import large quantities made silver speculation extremely lucrative. The government needed silver for coinage as currency circulation increased during the war from 1.8 billion to 2.9 billion silver rupees. Such was the demand for silver that in a single year India managed to absorb twice the total annual world output of silver.[95] As a major speculator, 'Baldeodas Jugalkishore' made large profits. So large was the firm's turnover that the brothers could not handle them on their own and Baldeodas, who was leading a retired life in Banaras was summoned to help out.[96] Others too such as the well known trader Ramkrishna Dalmia made large fortunes during the silver boom.[97]

Meanwhile, the fortunes of the jute industry were being dramatically transformed due to the outbreak of World War I. Jute suddenly became an item of immense strategic importance for wartime supplies. The main reason for this was because trench warfare, which was the main form of combat during the war, led to a colossal demand for sandbags which were made of jute. In addition, wrappers and packing materials were required for the transport of huge quantities of war supplies.[98] As jute was principally grown in the hinterland of the Calcutta region, the metropolis became the centre of wartime production and the port from where jute products were shipped to the whole of the British empire. The Marwaris who were entrenched in the jute trade benefited greatly from this boom and the Birlas too reaped enormous profits. In their capacity as traders and exporters of jute, the Birla firms benefited from a manyfold increase in turnover and records show that they figured prominently in the accounts of clearances of jute mills.[99] At the end of the war the Birlas stood second only to the powerful European managing agency, Ralli Brothers, in the accounts of clearances of raw jute and jute fabrics.[100] Further, through their dealings in jute shares, the Birlas built up their stocks in the capital of jute mills. The Marwari Association claimed that by 1922 no less than 60 per cent of shares in jute mills were controlled by Indians. Jute shares rose in value; the ratio of net profit to paid-up capital increased from 10 in 1914 to 58 in 1915, reaching an all-time high of 149 in 1917. The industry recorded net-profit rates of over 50 per cent of paid-up capital in the war years. The Birlas were in the forefront of those Marwaris who benefited from the wartime profits.[101] A third source of profit were their speculative operations in jute stocks. The Birla firms, both in Bombay and Calcutta, reportedly made handsome profits in the stock market and in hedge transactions in raw jute and gunny. The overall scale of the growth which the entire jute sector as a whole had experienced in this period can be gauged from the fact that the Indian jute industry supplied 1378 million sand bags, 713 million yards of cloth, one million pounds of twine and a large quantity of wrappers and bags for war purposes.[102]

In view of such demand for jute, Ghanshyamdas, who had for some time been determined to move into industry, now made concrete plans. Jute was naturally the choice as it was a business which the family knew a great deal about. As noted earlier, the Birlas' involvement with jute went back to the late 1850s when Shivnarain first started out in Bombay in jute speculation. Moreover, the Birlas had for long been involved in stock exchange and hedge transactions in raw jute and gunny. By 1918 they figured among the top 15 shippers of hessian. Moreover, by the end of World War I, jute was one sector of the economy in which Marwaris dominated at its different layers from the procurement of raw materials to the intermediate stage of baling to speculation and control over jute shares.[103] Their long years of experience and their kinship-based links with other Marwaris made them insiders in the jute business. All these factors emboldened Ghanshyamdas in his plans as he felt that he could draw upon the family's experience and contacts and expect that, in difficult times, they would rally behind him.

Yet, Ghanshyamdas had to persist with his plans almost single-handedly. After the retirement of Baldeodas, Jugalkishore was the overall in-charge of the family's business and he had no enthusiasm for moving into industry. He was content with old-style trading and speculation in which the family had been extremely successful. Moreover, he was conservative and even tended to be superstitious; he believed that the elements—wood and iron—spelt ruin to the human body and dealing in these could only lead to disaster! While he made no attempt to dampen Ghanshyamdas' enthusiasm, he made it clear that personally he would keep out of his younger brother's grand schemes.[104]

The move into the industry proved to be daunting. Jute, regarded as the very life-blood of Calcutta, had been an exclusive European preserve and entering jute manufacture meant, therefore, breaking this strong monopoly. Even though the Marwaris had been involved in jute trading and baling, they had played no part in jute manufacture. So pervasive was European control over the industry that in 1911 only one jute company (Soorah Jute which owned the smallest mill) had an Indian on its board of directors. The European managing agencies thus controlled the industry tightly. In 1911 just seven managing agencies controlled 55 per cent of the jute companies, and in 1914 five of these controlled almost half of the total weaving capacity of the entire industry.[105] This dominance of the managing agencies, with their interlocking directorships, meant that they controlled all aspects of the industry. This dominance was reinforced by the Indian Jute Mills' Association (IJMA), an almost exclusively European association. Its membership extended to 44 jute mills operating 37,600 looms, making it only 800 looms short of the total industry. The IJMA enforced agreements on production limits, regulated profits, controlled prices and negotiated contracts on rail and freight rates.[106]

Costs were another consideration that Ghanshyamdas needed to take into account. Before World War I the estimated minimum investment needed to start a new jute mill exceeded Rs 20 lakhs.[107] As was to be expected, inflation pushed up these outlays once the war broke out, and it was reckoned in 1916 that a new mill was likely to cost Rs 10,000 per loom. Thus an average-sized mill of 500 looms could cost over Rs 50 lakhs.[108] When Ghanshyamdas drew up his plans he expected to commence operations with 450 looms.[109] Large capital investment was required for such a venture. However, obtaining a loan from the commercial banks which were largely controlled by the British was no easy task. Ghanshyamdas contacted the Bank of Bengal, which was heavily biased against local traders and refused to give loans to anyone except the established European firms. Its directors came from the prominent managing agencies which, in turn, controlled the jute industry. Not unexpectedly, the Bank at first refused to advance a loan to Ghanshyamdas, and it was only after 'the intervention of a British broker that they agreed to give it only at a higher rate of interest.'[110] This loan could, however, meet only a portion of the total capital requirements and the rest were raised from the profits garnered by different lines of the Birla businesses during the war years. Capital for the new Birla company was also raised by floating shares on the stock market. The total number of shares offered for subscription to the public in 1920 was 2,75,000, consisting of 2,50,000 ordinary shares of Rs 10 each and 12,500 preference shares of Rs 100 each. Initially, Rs 5 was called up on ordinary shares and preference were offered at the paid-up price per share of Rs 50, the rate of interest being $7\frac{1}{2}$ per cent.[111] Durga Prasad Mandelia, a young Marwari from Pilani, who was inducted into the new mill by Ghanshyamdas as a clerk and rose to become a close business associate and an industrialist in his own right, recalls that 'if one venture failed, a man could be ruined' and 'those were not the times for the faint-hearted'. In his view, 'an aspiring industrialist had to invest almost his entire savings in promoting his first ventures and then expand by mortgaging the assets of the first undertaking to finance the second'.

Although the initial funds for the mill were organized, over-runs cost continued to be a source of worry. After promoting the mill in 1919, Ghanshyamdas discovered that costs had escalated sharply by the time the mill came on stream. At one stage so bleak did the situation seem that Ghanshyamdas in a moment of panic contemplated selling out and even made an offer to Andrew Yule. 'When he walked into the Andrew Yule offices to conclude a deal', Radha Krishen Kanoria, one of Birla's closest associates recalls, 'a Scottish manager started criticising him for having the audacity to establish a jute mill. GDB then instantly withdrew the offer of sale and made a resolution to break the foreign monopoly of the jute industry'.[112] Ghanshyamdas gave up thoughts of selling out and decided to scale down his plans and commence operations with a smaller capacity of 392 looms. This was one way of bringing down the overall costs which nonetheless came to Rs 16,064 per loom.

Birla's determined efforts came to fruition in 1919 when the Birla Jute Manufacturing Company was registered and along with two other Marwari firms, the Halwasia Jute Mills and the Hukumchand Jute Mills Ltd—broke the European monopoly over the jute sector.[113] However, Birla Jute soon encountered opposition from the established managing agencies who resented the Marwaris' entry into industry and were 'terrified of Indian mills asserting their dominance through intense competition'.[114] Andrew Yule and Co. created various difficulties; they at first acquired a part of the land which Ghanshyamdas had wanted for his factory and the vacant land adjoining it. This forced Birla Jute to move to the south of Calcutta to Budge Budge in Shyamnagar.[115] To this were added the difficulties faced in the day-to-day functioning like transportation. The transport of raw jute was controlled by European managing agencies who had long-term deals with rail and steamship companies. The non-European new entrants alleged that higher freight rates were charged to increase costs and thereby cut their margins. Further, Ghanshyamdas was also denied membership of the IJMA for the first few years and was forced to employ English brokers to conduct transactions on behalf of his mill.[116] Despite these difficulties Birla Jute started production in 1920.

Like the other Marwari firms floated at this time, Birla Jute had on its board of directors 'gentiles from Dundee and elsewhere'. The members of the board were: G.D. Birla, C. Chowdhury, H. Gavin Wilson, G.L. Allen and Seth Badridas Goenka. At the managerial level, the necessity of employing experienced European mill managers was acutely felt.[117] Two Scotsmen were put in charge of operations and for training the mill-hands, and the Indian managers were instructed 'to learn the intricacies of the business from the Scottish managers.' As D.P. Mandelia later recalled: 'As soon as we were confident that we had learnt the basics we informed Mr Birla who promptly retired the Scotsmen.'[118]

Birla Jute got off to a good start and the new venture turned out to be highly successful. This can be seen from the fact that when trading in its shares started in January 1920, the market quotation stood at Rs $5\frac{1}{4}$ over the paid-up price of Rs 5 per share. The jute industry continued to be buoyant in the post-war years and, despite the cessation of hostilities, profitability continued to be high at first due to the massive shipments of food and agricultural products to war-ravaged Europe and later due to a significant rise in the volume of world trade.

Throughout the 1920s Indian exports of jute continued to expand.[119] So profitable did jute prove to be that it appeared doubtful if any other group of factories in the world paid such handsome profits between 1915 and 1929'.[120]

These were years of intense hard work for Ghanshyamdas and the challenge of setting up the new mill proved to be highly demanding. In the mill everything went through his personal scrutiny. No detail was too small to be ignored by him.[121] Each machine was diligently inspected by Ghanshyamdas who operated them himself to see how they worked. Managers submitted regular reports and comparative monthly statistics, graphs of production, efficiency and profit and loss, each of which he perused diligently.[122] The accounting department reported directly to him. The yearly budget was divided on a daily, weekly and monthly basis. Financial results were scrutinized closely by Ghanshyamdas. By this method, daily profit and loss could be ascertained. Drawbacks could be known immediately, so corrective action could be taken. Thus complete information of the monthly profit and loss as well as the daily profit and loss could be known on the same day. The system was based on the *parta* system of calculation, a traditional Marwari system of financial control.

Following the establishment of Birla Jute, Ghanshyamdas boldly diversified into cotton. In 1920 a cotton mill was bought in Delhi from Kanhaiyalal Bagla for the price of Rs 5,00,000. Originally owned by an Englishman, the mill was first called the Gilhari Mill and then the Hanuman Mahadev Cotton Mill. After Ghanshyamdas acquired it, it was renamed the Birla Cotton Spinning and Weaving Mill Limited.[123] In April 1920 Ghanshyamdas floated a company to formalize its take-over. Incorporated on 10 March 1920, the company's prospectus declared that the mill was to have a capacity of 13,000 spindles. Orders were placed in England for machinery and meanwhile a weaving department was started. The mill's authorized capital was Rs 15,00,000 made up of 1,50,000 shares of Rs 10 each. In 1920, 1,00,000 shares of the total value of Rs 10,00,000 were offered to the public and the share issue was fully subscribed. The directors of the company were G.D. Birla, Narsinghdas Kothari (of M/s Bagla Kothari and Co.) and Babu Ghanshyamdas Loyalka (of M/s G.D. Loyalka and Co.).[124]

Towards the end of 1919 the branches of the old family concern 'Baldeodas Jugalkishore' had been amalgamated to set up the managing agency 'Birla Brothers Ltd' with a capital of Rs 50 lakhs.[125] All the brothers were made directors but from the outset its effective management was placed in the hands of Ghanshyamdas. The other firm of 'Ghanshyamdas Murlidhar' was closed down. Jugalkishore, who had been running the Calcutta business, retired and Rameshwardas was placed in charge of the Bombay branch.[126] This change from the traditional Marwari firm of 'Baldeodas Jugalkishore' to the modern 'Birla Brothers' of 7, Royal Exchange, Calcutta, signified the transition of the family from traders to industrialists.

From ordinary beginnings in trading the Birlas achieved extraordinary success in their business activities and alongside gained a prominent position in the public affairs of the Marwaris. By 1919, it was Ghanshyamdas who firmly led the vanguard in the family's pioneering transition from old-style trading to modern industry. In the years to come he consolidated this role as the moving spirit behind the Birlas' widening horizons.

NOTES AND REFERENCES

[1] The Birlas developed close business ties with managers such as R.N.D. Senda of Mitsui, among other firms, Timberg, *The Marwaris*, pp. 62–3. Other Marwari houses which followed the Birla example and traded in cloth with Japan were those of Keshoram Poddar, Ruia and even Bachhraj & Co. (Jamnalal Bajaj's firm). In 1913 Bachhraj Jamnalal sold 40,000 bales of cloth to Japan and made an estimated profit of Rs 55,000, Taknet, *Marwari Samaj*, p. 69.

[2] One of the many disputes which the Panchayat was called upon to adjudicate was between the 'Sanatani' and 'Sudharwadi' groups, Taknet, *Marwari Samaj*, p. 54. Also see Balchand Modi, *Desh Ke Itihas Mein Marwari Jati Ka Sthan*.

[3] R. Nevatia (ed.), *Shri Ramdev Chokhany*, p. 46. The panch of the latter were Bijraj Chowdhury, Harduttrai Chamria, Vishveshwarlal Chitlangiya, Chunilal Binani and Shivnandrai Tiwari. Nandkishore Jalan, *Shri Ishwardas Jalan Abhinandan Granth*, p. 119. Not much is known about the Shroffs' Panchayat which ceased to exist by the 1920s.

[4] Even in small commercial centres, forms of such panchayats existed: for instance it is known that Marwari panchayats influenced market practices as the Sarrafa Panchayat in Agra, the Gyarah Panch in Indore and the Naupati Mahajan in Banaras. Rajat Ray mentions that the Multani Shroffs Association regulated the hundi rate, See Rajat K. Ray, 'The Bazaar: Changing Structural characteristics of the indigenous section of the Indian economy before and after the Great Depression' in *IESHR*, Vol. 25, No. 3 (1988), p. 309.

[5] Marwari importers, under forward contracts for the import of piece-goods, advanced large sums with which British manufacturers bought their raw materials in India and elsewhere. On the arrival of such goods under forward contracts, disputes often occurred between British exporters and local importers. In such circumstances Marwari traders were compelled to approach the Bengal Chamber for arbitration which often caused dissatisfaction. The Marwaris decided, as a result, to form their own independent chamber of commerce. Rajat Ray, *Urban Roots of Indian Nationalism* (New Delhi, 1979), pp. 42–4. The need for a separate body was specially felt when the dominant firms in Manchester cloth trading, the Ralli Brothers and Graham and Company made their contract rules stricter for indigenous traders. The Marwaris decided to combine to oppose this. Initially, they formed the 'Cloth Samiti of the Marwari Association' and in 1900 it was renamed the Marwari Chamber of Commerce. By this time, the larger part of the piece-goods import trade in Calcutta had passed into the hands of Bara Bazaar traders. Since the Bara Bazaar men were mainly interested in cotton textile import, this became the predominant interest of the Marwari Chamber of Commerce. See Jalan, *Shri Ishwardas Jalan Abhinandan Granth*, pp. 119–20.

[6] Marwari firms avoided the courts by either taking their differences to panchayats or by settling them by negotiation or arbitration by a prominent Marwari. It was symptomatic of the closed nature of the community that in the entire pre-Independence period, only three large firms let their affairs reach the courts: these were the disputes involving Harduttrai Chamria, Raja Shivbaksh Bagla and the Lodhas of Ajmer. According

to its first year report, the Marwari Chamber received notice of 1198 disputes and settled 1080 of these to the satisfaction of its members. It was keen to reduce instances of Marwari insolvency.

[7] Balchand Modi, *Desh Ke Itihas Mein Marwari Jati Ka Sthan*, pp. 612–14. Also see Rameshwar Prasad Patodia, *Shri Anandilal Poddar Smriti Pushpa* (Calcutta, n.d.), p. 96.

[8] The Association declared that since politics was closely connected with trade, it would interest itself in politics, Taknet, *Marwari Samaj*, p. 188. For details see Balchand Modi, *Desh Ke Itihas Mein Marwari Jati Ka Sthan*, p. 608.

[9] The Report of the Marwari Association of 1899–1903 made this clear when it stated: 'The Marwaris have now learnt to recognise the necessity and usefulness of mutual exchange of views and of concerted action in matters relating to the interests of the community. Signs of fresh activity are visible in all directions and many have already taken practical shape. New associations and sabhas have already sprung up into existence and the piece-goods branch of the Marwari Association itself has grown into a separate and very important body, now known as the Marwari Chamber of Commerce. These are no doubt hopeful indications of the approach of a prosperous future and it is a matter of great delight to remember that the first great awakening that the Marwari people received of the necessity of such united efforts was from the Marwari Association. It pleases no one more than this association to see that the colossal work which it undertook to accomplish does no longer rest on its shoulders alone but that other organised bodies have come forward cheerfully to share its responsibilities'.

[10] Jalan, *Shri Ishwardas Jalan Abhinandan Granth*, pp. 102–3.

[11] Within years of its establishment, it was denounced as having become a vehicle for self-promotion, for obtaining titles and favours, and for getting seats in the Council and the Municipality, Balchand Modi, *Desh Ke Itihas Mein Marwari Jati Ka Sthan*, pp. 610–11. Its four most powerful members were Daulatram Chokhany, Joharmal Khemka, Ramjidas Bajoria and Chimanlal Ganeriwala (timber merchant with interest in rice and money-lending, with branches in Burma). They were popularly called *chokdi* ('Gang of Four') and were staunch Sanatanis; they dominated the Association through most of the pre-war years, later forming the *chapkan party*, so called because of the frequent delegations they took to officials when they wore the formal *chapkan, chaddar* and pagris, Jalan, *Shri Ishwardas Jalan Abhinandan Granth*, pp. 102–3. The other prominent conservative members were Joharmal Khemka, Ramjidas Bajoria, Keshoram Poddar, Ramkumar Jhunjhunwala, Chimanlal Ganeriwala and Daulatram Chokhany. See also *Bhagirath Kanoria Smriti Granth* (Calcutta, n.d.).

[12] Some of the prominent younger members were Basantlal Morarka, Padhraj Jain, Bhagirath Kanodia, Prabhu Dayal Himmatsinghka, Sitaram Seksaria, Motilal Lath, Gangaprasad Bhotika, and Ramkumar Bhuwalika.

[13] The Sabha took up a range of issues such as safety arrangements, improvement of civic facilities in Bara Bazaar and railway difficulties of traders. It aimed to improve the image of the Marwari jati which it believed was increasingly becoming a target for ridicule because of its conservatism. Often members of the Association and the panch would be dalals to English firms while the new group may possibly have been independent traders. The Vaishya Sabha was formed by Ramkumar Goenka, Sadaram Kedia, Phoolchand Chowdhary, Ramgopal Khemka, Baijnath Kedia, Devivaks Saraf, etc.

[14] For details on the Swadeshi movement, see Sumit Sarkar, *Swadeshi Movement in Bengal. 1903–8* (New Delhi, 1973).

[15] Balchand Modi, *Desh Ke Itihas Mein Marwari Jati Ka Sthan*, pp. 623–4. The president of the Society, largely responsible for this, was the famous Maharashtrian editor of the Bengali *Hitvadia*—Pandit Sakharam Ganesh Deuskar, who was a follower of Tilak. Apparently the discussion initiated by him propagating the use of swadeshi was so popular that the President of the Saraswati Vidyalaya, where the meeting was being held, had to adjourn the meeting abruptly on the request of the more influential traders, who were the dalals to the European firms, see *ibid* for details, pp. 616–26.

[16] These differences continued to grow, and in 1908 the leadership of the Marwari Association was forced to convene a special session to discuss the reformist challenge posed by the Sabha, Barua, *Raja Baldeodas Birla*, pp. 63–4. The younger elements, many of whom were influenced by the Arya Samaj, challenged the leadership again in 1911 when they proposed the name of Jainarayan Poddar, chief clerk of the famous firm Tarachand Ghanshyamdas, as an office bearer of the Association. The Sanatan Dharmis countered this move by a resolution asking all members to take an oath on the *Gita* professing to be Sanatani. Although this resolution was fought by moderates like Onkarmal Saraf, Jainarain Poddar was not allowed to be nominated as he was an Arya Samaji but perhaps more importantly because he was merely a munim. The issue of oath-taking precipitated a split and the Sudharwadis, as a result, were kept out of the Association and other bodies controlled by it such as the Vishudanand Vidyalaya. See *Bhagirath Kanodia Smriti Granth*, p. 22. This struggle continued throughout the early 1920s and could not be resolved despite the intervention of prominent leaders like Jamnalal Bajaj and even Gandhi. The details of conflicts within the Association are provided by Balchand Modi, *Desh Ke Itihas Mein Marwari Jati Ka Sthan*, pp. 579–601.

[17] The ambiguities of this period are described by D.A. Low in his 'Introduction' to *Soundings in Modern South Asian History* (London, 1968).

[18] For details on the Club see R. Nevatia, *Bara Bazaar Ke Karyakarta: Sansmaran Avam Abhinandan* (Calcutta, 1982), p. 38.

[19] See Suranjan Das, *Communal riots in Bengal, 1905–1947* (Delhi, 1991) and J.H. Broomfield, *Elite Conflict in a plural society; twentieth century Bengal* (Berkeley, 1968). For the larger context see Kenneth McPherson, *The Muslim microcosm, Calcutta, 1918 to 1935* (Wiesbaden, 1974).

[20] Ram Nivas Jaju, *G.D. Birla, A Biography*, p. 67.

[21] *Maheshwari Sabha Heerak Jayanti, 1911–47* (Calcutta, n.d.), pp. 10–1.

[22] D.D. Shastri (ed.), *Ek Bindu Ek Sindhu*, p. 160.

[23] The akhara supports hundreds of wrestlers who are reportedly paid a regular monthly stipend. It involves a huge financial responsibility—in the 1970s a foreign wrestling 'rubber' mat alone cost them the sum of Rs 2,00,000. Joseph S. Alter, *The Wrestler's Body Identity and Ideology in North India* (California, 1992), pp. 88–9.

[24] D.D. Shastri, *Ek Bindu Ek Sindhu*, p. 83.

[25] Among these may be mentioned Satpal, Ashok Kumar, Suresh Kumar and Ved Prakash.

[26] Joseph S. Alter, *The Wrestler's Body Identity and Ideology in North India*, pp. 70–1

[27] For a discussion on the relationship between patron and wrestler see, Joseph S. Alter, *The Wrestler's Body Identity and Ideology in North India*, pp. 70–89.

[28] *Marwari Relief Society Karyakala Swarn Jayanti* (Calcutta, 1963), pp. 6–7.

[29] Among the founder members were J.K. Birla, Onkarmal Saraf and Harackchand Mohta. In its first few years, the total income of the organization was a mere Rs 28 per

month, with the understanding that any increase in expenditure would be funded by three of the founder members.

[30] It was founded by 12 'leading' Maheshwaris such as Shivkrishan Bhawar, Ramratandas Karnani, Hardevdas Daga, Rampratap Rathi, Govindlal Daga, Ramchandra Lakhotia, Bhishamchand Mudhra, Sitaram Sodhani, Kanhaiyalal Lokhani, Mangilal Bihani, Bithaldas Kothari and Ganpatlal Mohta.

[31] *Maheshwari Sabha Heerak Jayanti, 1914–1947*, p. 6.

[32] *Maheshwari Sabha Heerak Jayanti, 1914–1974*, p. 7 and pp. 46 and 48.

[33] *Maheshwari Sabha Heerak Jayanti, 1914–1974*, p. 48. For the contributions of Ramkrishna Mohta to the Sabha, see Vishambar Prasad Sharma Visharad, *Swaragiye Ramkrishnaji Mohta Jiwan Charitra Aur Sansmaran* (Calcutta, 1941), p. 43.

[34] Vishambar Prasad Sharma Visharad, *Swaragiye Ramkrishnaji Mohta Jiwan Charitra Aur Samsmaran*, p. 47.

[35] 'By a proposal of the Sabha's *Muladhaar* Ramkrishna Mohta the Vidyalaya was established and *Daan Vir* Jugalkishore Birla was most important in the actual establishment,' acknowledged *Maheshwari Sabha Heerak Jayanti, 1914–1974* (Calcutta, n.d.), p. 10.

[36] Among the other donors were Ramkrishna Mohta, Bangur and Kothari.

[37] The authoritative study of revolutionary terrorism is by Peter Heehs, *The Bomb in Bengal. The rise of revolutionary terrorism in India*, Delhi, 1993. Also see Sumit Sarkar, *Swadeshi Movement in Bengal, 1903–8*. Also see Rajat K. Ray, *Social Conflict and Political Unrest in Bengal, 1875–1922* (Delhi, 1984).

[38] Poddar was to become one of the most influential Marwaris in later years. Influenced by Tilak from an early age, he was a founder member of the Marwari Sahayak Samiti but had to disassociate himself from the Samiti and from its Sahitya Sambandhini Sabha when the *Tikavali Gita* published by it was banned. He was implicated in the Rodda case in 1916 for which he was interned for 21 months and later externed from Bengal. He was then invited by Jamnalal Bajaj to Bombay where he came under Gandhi's influence. Poddar decided to leave politics and dedicate himself to social work, Sangathan and to the cause of the Hindus. In 1921, along with Jamnalal Bajaj, he set up the Akhil Bharatiya Marwari Agarwal Sabha in Bombay. He was instrumental in starting the Goraksha Mahabiyan Samiti. In the late 1920s he established an ashram in Gorakhpur and started the Gita Press which brought out the monthly *Kalyan*. The Gita Press played an important role in producing and disseminating literature promoting the cause of 'Hindi, Hindu, Hindustan', see Nevatia, *Bara Bazaar Ke Karyakarta*, pp. 4–5.

[39] Studying the profiles of these men may help ascertain the extent of their involvement with the revolutionaries. Saraf, a successful Bara Bazaar trader, was a founder member of the Marwari Sahayak Samiti. He too was implicated in the Rodda Conspiracy Case in 1916. He was excommunicated by the Marwari Sanatan Dharma (Agarwal) Sabha for supporting widow remarriage. In 1926 he was founder member of the Hindu Relief Club and had set up the Sanatan Dharma Pustakalaya in his hometown of Mandava. He later set up the Calcutta Industrial Bank and helped found the Marwari Traders' Association.

[40] Himmatsinghka was to become a lifelong associate of Ghanshyamdas. He rose to establish a solicitors' firm at the Calcutta High Court. A founder member of the Marwari Sahayak Samiti, he was interned for four years in the Rodda Case. In 1912, he set up the Marwari Samaj Chattravas and the following year helped establish the Gyanvardhini Sabha. He was also a functionary of the Pinjrapole Society and was active in cow-protection movements. In the 1920s, he too was excommunicated, along with 12 others, for promoting widow remarriage. In 1927 he was elected to the Bengal Council. Between

1937 and 1948 he was elected to the Council three times. He also participated in the 1942 Quit India Movement. Interview with Shri P.D. Himmatsinghka, May 1989, Calcutta.

[41] Sahai was prosecuted in the Delhi Bomb Case in 1914 for financially helping the revolutionaries and for being a party to their plans. Taknet, *Marwari Samaj*, pp. 189–90.

[42] In 1916 Tilak was called to address the Samiti, Alan Ross, *The Emissary*, p. 26.

[43] About 202 cases of arms and ammunition were cleared by a clerk of Rodda & Co. from Customs, but only 192 cases were delivered to the company's warehouse. The missing ten cases contained 50 Mauser pistols and 46,000 rounds of ammunition. As many as 44 pistols were quickly distributed to nine revolutionary groups in Bengal and officials suspected that they were subsequently used in 54 cases of political dacoity or murder.

[44] Confession of Phanindra Chakravarty quoted from Home Department, 1917 (299–301) by Leonard A. Gordon, *Bengal: The Nationalist Movement, 1876–1940* (New York, 1974), p. 148. On the Rodda conspiracy case see also David M. Laushey, *Bengal Terrorists and the Marxist Left, Aspects of Regional Nationalism in India, 1905–1942* (Calcutta, 1975).

[45] According to Alan Ross, the crates were then thrown into the Hooglee in panic. Alan Ross, *The Emissary*, p. 27. This seems doubtful since the arms were widely used by the revolutionaries in subsequent years.

[46] Barua, *Raja Baldeodas Birla*, p. 88.

[47] This has been asserted by D.P. Mandelia, Birla's close associate of over 50 years standing, D.P. Mandelia, *G.D. Birla: A Superb Master Sculptor* (Delhi, 1983), p. 10.

[48] Barua, *Raja Baldeodas Birla*, p. 88.

[49] Alan Ross, *The Emissary*, p. 28.

[50] G.D. Birla, *In the Shadow of the Mahatma*, p. xv.

[51] This marked the beginning of a long association with Tegart, who rose to become the Commissioner of Police of Calcutta. In the years to come Tegart acquired a reputation for his successful campaign against terrorism in Bengal and was knighted, and after his retirement served on the Secretary of State's council in India Office. His private papers in the Centre of South Asian Studies at Cambridge provide details of his Indian career. Incidentally, in the 1930s he was retained by Birla to head his business operations in London, Mandelia, *G.D. Birla: A Superb Master Sculptor*, p. 10.

[52] D.P. Sharma, *Deshbhakt Udyog Pravartak Ghanshyamdas Birla*, p. 58.

[53] *Sedition Committee 1918 Report* (Calcutta, 1918). Also see J.C. Kerr, *Political Trouble in India, 1907–17* (Calcutta, 1917).

[54] For details see *Bhagirath Kanoria Smriti Granth*, p. 24.

[55] *Basantlal Morarka Smriti Granth* (Calcutta, 1957), p. 63. 'The impact of the case and the changing character of the samaj was not only in terms of the taming of the younger elements but, more importantly in the re-establishment of the control over the Samiti and society by the elders', *Bhagirath Kanoria Smriti Granth*, p. 24. The only prominent Marwari to publicly laud the young men was Jamnalal Bajaj in 1916. He applauded their bravery and even distributed sweets at a meeting to celebrate their defiance. Ram Narayan Chowdhury, *Bapu As I Saw Him* (Ahmedabad, 1958), p. 62.

[56] From its foundation till 1916, Jugalkishore Birla had been the president. *Marwari Relief Society Rajat Jayanti, 1913–1941* (Calcutta, 1941), List of office bearers, n.p.

[57] *Bhagirath Kanodia Smriti Granth*, p. 24.

[58] *Marwari Relief Society Rajat Jayanti*, p. 13.

[59] Among other causes taken up in 1917 was reducing consumption and expenditure in public feasts. Nevatia, *Shri Ramdev Chokhany*, pp. 78–80. The Association became even more powerful when under the Montague–Chelmsford scheme they were granted a seat in the Central Legislative Assembly and in the Bengal Legislative Council.

[60] G.D. Birla, *In the Shadow of the Mahatma*, p. xiv.

[61] A school was opened in Manser, and several others followed in Lakshmangarh and Behal in Hissar district and other villages of Rajasthan. *Marwari Relief Society Rajat Jayanti*, pp. 11–12. Also see D.P. Sharma, *Deshbhakt Udyog Pravartak Ghanshyamdas Birla*, p. 15.

[62] G.D. Birla, *Gandhiji Ka Pratham Darshan*, Jeevan Sahitya (Sasta Sahitya Mandal Prakashan, September 1983).

[63] For the important role of the mercantile classes in nationalist politics, see D.A. Low, 'The forgotten Bania: Merchant Communities and the Indian National Congress,' in D.A. Low (ed.), *Indian National Congress: Centenary Hindsights* (Delhi, 1998).

[64] G.D. Birla, *Gandhiji Ka Pratham Darshan*.

[65] G.D. Birla, *Gandhiji Ka Pratham Darshan*. Unfortunately, Gandhi's first letter to Birla is not available.

[66] *Basantlal Morarka Smriti Granth*, p. 64.

[67] For details see Barua, *Raja Baldeodas Birla*, p. 91.

[68] *Bhagirath Kanoria Smriti Granth*, p. 25.

[69] *Basantlal Morarka Smriti Granth*, pp. 82–3.

[70] At this session resolutions were passed calling for improvement of educational standards among the Marwaris; for social reforms such as fixing the minimum age for marriage, curtailing expenditure at wedding and death ceremonies; need for resolving differences without litigation; promotion of Hindi language and the starting of a paper in Hindi; and cow-protection. The government's policy of imperial preference was criticized and Marwaris were asked to take to Swadeshi and to encourage industry by setting up joint stock companies. For details, see Bajranglal Kanhaiyalal Jhunjhunwala, *Marwari Sudhar* (Calcutta, Samvat 1976). Interestingly, both the conservatives and the reformists were impressing upon the community to enter industry. As early as 1913, the Marwari Association urged its members to follow the examples of 'Rockfeller, Carnegie and Tata.' There seemed a large measure of consensus over vital issues like the need to acquire modern commercial intelligence and business methods; the necessity for solving all disputes internally; cow-protection; promotion of Hindi; need to build *jati shakti*; and, above all, the desirability of entering industry. Differences revolved around social issues such as widow remarriage and, more crucially, over the nature of support to be given to the nationalists, *Marwari Jati Ke Kartavya, Calcutta Marwari Association Annual Function: Babu Ranglal Poddar* (Samvat, 1969). Gandhi was invited to the Mahasabha's second session at Bombay. On his appeal for *Hindi Prachar* (spread of Hindi) in south India, the members present collected Rs 50,000. A fund of Rs 6,00,000 was also set up for the Agarwal Sahayak Kosh to help the community. See *Basantlal Morarka Smriti Granth*, p. 65.

[71] Padam Raj Jain and Ambika Prasad Bajpai were made responsible for ensuring the success of hartal by closing all shops.

[72] Reports on the meeting of 6 April commented on the audience being 'chiefly up-country Hindus, Marwaris and Muhamaddans'. On the meeting at Beadon Square on the 11th 'about 6000 people assembled mostly Marwaris, Bhatias and up-country men'.

[73] Leaflets were circulated 'urging the people to agitate for the release of Mr Gandhi and continue to urge the repeal of the Rowlatt Bill'.

[74] Report on the Rowlatt Satyagraha in the City of Calcutta. From R. Clarke, Commissioner of Police to the Chief Secretary to the Government of Bengal, in R. Kumar (ed.), *Essays on Gandhian Politics, The Rowlatt Satyagraha of 1919* (Oxford, 1971).

[75] Both were members of the Marwari Agarwal Mahasabha and both leaders of the reformists within the Marwari Association.

[76] R. Kumar (ed.), *Essays on Gandhian Politics. The Rowlatt Satyagraha of 1919*.

[77] *Ibid*, p. 342.

[78] *Ibid*.

[79] During the interview the Governor apparently 'reminded' them of their immigrant status within the city and of the precariousness of their position. R. Nevatia, *Shri Ramdev Chokhany*, p. 117.

[80] *Ibid*, p. 117. Also see *Basantlal Morarka Smriti Granth*, p. 35.

[81] By then the young men of the Mitra Mandali, who were till then in the employment of the big Marwari firms left their paid employment and were now traders in independent capacities. This resulted in their becoming more confident that they could now oppose the Sanatanis more forcefully. *Bhagirath Kanoria Smriti Granth*, p. 27

[82] Mary Elisabeth Berry observes in her 'Introduction' to 'Giving in Asia: A Symposium', that although philanthropy was motivated by a range of concerns, a universal element in gift-giving was that of securing 'reputation' or 'credit', *Journal of Asian Studies*, Vol. 46, No. 2, May 1987, pp. 305–8.

[83] For details of these movements see, Gyanendra Pandey, *The Construction of Communalism in North India* (New Delhi, 1990). Perhaps the strength of these movements can be accounted partially by the strong support they enjoyed from Hindu mercantile groups.

[84] D.D. Shastri (ed.), *Ek Bindu Ek Sindhu*, p. 116.

[85] Its founder members were Ramchandra Goenka, Surajmal Jhunjhunwala, Jugalkishore Ruia, Badridas-Mukim and Shivbaksh Bagla (major timber merchant with interests in rice and money-lending with branches in Burma).

[86] *Bhagirath Kanoria Smriti Granth*, p. 23.

[87] *Maheshwari Sabha Heerak Jayanti, 1914–1974*, pp. 6 and 9.

[88] *Capital*, 7 February 1920.

[89] *Capital*, 7 February 1920.

[90] Barua, *Raja Baldeodas Birla*, p. 167.

[91] Douglas E. Haynes argues that Surat businessmen began to engage in modern forms of philanthropy which reflected a 'negotiated' accommodation to Victorian values to secure stable ties with political overlords. In contrast, the nature of Birla's philanthropy is much more complex: their early philanthropy hardly seems to be an attempt to engage in modern forms of philanthropy to adjust to Victorian values in an attempt to appease political overlords. It was as yet rooted in traditional and religious notions of piety. However, significant changes occurred in the 1920s which bear a close similarity to the analysis presented by Haynes of the impact of Gandhian politics on the politics of gift-giving. See Douglas E. Haynes, 'From Tribute to Philanthropy. The Politics of Gift Giving in a western Indian city' in *Journal of Asian Studies*, Vol. 46, No. 2, May 1987, pp. 339–60. Also see his *Rhetoric and Ritual in colonial India, The shaping of a Public Culture in Surat city, 1850–1928* (Berkeley, 1991).

[92] *Capital*, 17 May 1920.

[93] Goutam K. Sarkar, *Jute in India, An Economic Analysis* (Calcutta, 1989), p. 7.

[94] G.D. Birla, introduction to *In the Shadow of the Mahatma, A Personal Memoir* (Bombay, 1959). Also see *Commerce*, 25 June 1983.

[95] D. Rothermund, *An Economic History of India* (London, 1988), pp. 72–3.

[96] *Barua, Raja Baldeodas Birla*, p. 83.

[97] Dalmia turned to silver speculation in a moment of desperation after he had been declared insolvent by the community. He claimed that he borrowed Rs 50 from a friend and, based on some commercial intelligence, made some speculative deals in silver. He made windfall gains which he reinvested. This continued for a week at the end of which he found himself worth more than one and a half lakh rupees. Such stories were not unusual amongst the Marwari community in those times. Seth Ramkrishna Dalmia, *Some Notes and Reminiscences* (Bombay, 1948). On Dalmia also see his *A Short Sketch of the Beginning of my Life and a Guide to Bliss* (New Delhi, 1962).

[98] Raymond K. Renford, *The Non Official British in India Till 1920* (New Delhi, 1987), p. 358.

[99] The others were Sarupchand Hukumchand, Keshoram Poddar, Bangur brothers and Baldeodas Doodhwawalla, A.K. Bagchi, *Private Investment in India, 1900–39* (Cambridge, 1972).

[100] By 1918–19, 'Marwari exporting firms accounted for 63% of the membership' of the Calcutta Baled Jute Association, which had in its 'roster names such as Birla, Sarupchand Hukumchand, Surajmal Nagarmal, Onkarmull Jatia and Randutt Ramrikhdas.' Onkar Goswami, 'Then Came the Marwaris: Some Aspects of the Changes in the Pattern of Industrial Control in Eastern India', *IESHR*, Vol. 22, No. 3 (1985), pp. 225–48.

[101] For instance, the Bangurs, ordinary share brokers, became millionaires when jute shares rose. Keshoram Poddar was known to have made Rs 2 to 4 crores after he entered hessian and jute trading and speculation, Rajat Ray, *Social Conflict and Political Unrest in Bengal, 1875–1927*, p. 228n.

[102] Goutam K. Sarkar, *Jute in India, An Economic Analysis* (Calcutta, 1989). The *Capital* observed on 12 May 1916: 'The manufacturing portion of the industry is growing and it has never taken a more extraordinary leap forward than in the past 18 months.' On the growing prosperity of the industry it commented: 'So profitable have been the contracts placed, that one Dundee firm calculates its contribution to the national funds in the last 12 months to have aggregated 1 million Sterling.'

[103] As the *Capital* remarked on 25 May 1922: 'The great prosperity of the Calcutta jute mills during the war made many mouths water in the Indian commercial community, more especially the Marwari mouths.... . Why should not Indians dominate the jute manufacturing trade as well as the cotton manufacturing trade? The Marwaris, at any rate, were determined to drive the thin end of the wedge.'

[104] Jaju, *G.D. Birla. A Biography*, p. 69.

[105] Among the large agencies were: Andrew Yule and Co., Bird and Co., F.W. Heilgers and Co., Thomas Duff and Co., Jardine Skinner and Co., Anderson, Wright and Co., and Kettlewell Bullen and Co.

[106] It also had a seat on the Bengal Legislative Council from 1909 onwards and a representative on the Calcutta Port Trust.

[107] Bagchi, *Private Investment in India*, p. 264.

[108] *Capital*, 11 August 1916. For instance, the Albion Jute Mill, set up in 1916, cost Rs 9266 per loom.

[109] *Capital*, 7 October 1920.

[110] D.P. Sharma, *Deshbhakt Udyog Pravartak Ghanshyamdas Birla*, p. 22.

[111] The other new Marwari jute company, Sarupchand Hukumchand, had a paid-up capital of Rs 80,00,000 and the paid-up price per share was Rs 10, with market quotation being Rs 11.

[112] Dilip Thakore, 'A Legend in his Lifetime', *Business World*, 30 March–12 April 1981.

[113] Although registered in 1919, they did not start operations till the end of 1922. The Halwasia mill does not appear to have been finally set up as it finds no mention after its registration in *Capital*.

[114] Onkar Goswami, 'Collaboration and Conflict: European and Indian Capitalists and the Jute Economy of Bengal 1919–39', *IESHR*, Vol. 19, No. 2, p. 143.

[115] According to J. Sarkar, 'The Beginnings in Calcutta' in *Economic Times* (26 June 1983), the dispute led to protracted legislation which ended in the Privy Council where Ghanshyamdas was vindicated.

[116] D.P. Sharma, *Deshbhakt Udyog Pravartak Ghanshyamdas Birla*, p. 26.

[117] As the *Capital* remarked: 'Like the Parsees and Bhatias of Bombay, the Marwaris of Calcutta saw the use, nay the necessity of employing in the first instance mill managers from Great Britain.' *Capital*, 25 May 1922.

[118] D.P. Mandelia 'The Superb Master Sculptor' in *The Glorious Ninety Years: G.D. Birla, 1894–1983*, p. 97.

[119] See Goutam K. Sarkar, *Jute in India An economic analysis* (Calcutta, 1989).

[120] D.H. Buchanan, *The development of capitalistic enterprise in India* (New York, 1934), p. 253

[121] B.K. Birla, *A Rare Legacy*, pp. 214–5.

[122] R.K. Gupta, *25 years with Shri G.D. Birla*, p. 48.

[123] *Ibid*, p. 25.

[124] *Capital*, 14 October 1920.

[125] *Birla Bandhuon Ki Desh Seva*, p. 43.

[126] Balchand Modi, *Desh Ke Itihas Mein Marwari Jati Ka Sthan*, p. 560. The youngest brother, Braj Mohan, did not join the business till later.

3

Widening the Horizon: In Search of a Public Career, 1920–1926

The early 1920s saw Ghanshyamdas (henceforth referred to as Birla) experience what were perhaps the happiest years of his life. After almost two generations of solitude the Birla men in Calcutta were joined by their womenfolk. The initiative for this had come from Jugalkishore and Ghanshyamdas who brought their wives and young children to the city. Initially, the family lived in Zakaria Street in a rented accommodation but thereafter moved to 6, Rainey Park, a property on the outskirts of the city which the brothers had purchased. This, however, could not fully cater to the needs of a growing family. In 1919 the Birlas made their first major purchase of real estate in a prestigious neighbourhood. A garden house extending over 19 *bighas,* which belonged to the ancestral estate of the Tagores, was bought for Rs 4 lakhs. Birla drew up ambitious plans to build a family mansion which could accommodate the growing clan under one roof. The prestigious architectural firm of M/s N. Guin was engaged which, under instructions from Birla, produced a design for a Victorian-style edifice. So came about 'Birla Park', into which the family moved in 1923. The new house had a separate wing for the family of each of the brothers, even though Rameshwardas was based in Bombay and Braj Mohan did not yet have a family, while Baldeodas lived in retirement in Banaras. Birla installed modern amenities like the telephone in the new house where the family also had the use of a two-horse carriage. For Birla's wife Mahadevi, used to the harsh conditions of life in Shekhawati, all this was quite a change. Their family now consisted of six children, five of their own—and Lakshmi Niwas, Birla's son from his first marriage, who had since been adopted by Jugalkishore and his wife (who did not have children of their own). Mahadevi and Ghanshyamdas' eldest child was Chandrakala, born in 1914 when her father was in hiding during the Rodda case. The second was Krishna Kumar, born in October 1917, followed by Basant Kumar, born in 1921 and then two daughters Anasuiya, born in 1923 and Shanti, born in 1924. The young children enjoyed living at Birla Park and especially looked forward to outings in the horse-carriage with its coachman Abdul, who took them to Eden Gardens where the band performed in the evenings.

In retrospect, while these were Birla's happiest years, they also appear to be his busiest. This was a period of consolidation for the new business accompanied by rapid diversification. Birla Jute had only recently commenced production and its operations had yet to fully stabilize. Moreover, the Birla Cotton, Spinning & Weaving Mill in Delhi had just been acquired and demanded constant attention. Further, several proposals for new ventures needed to be looked at in terms of their feasibility. Particularly exciting was an invitation from the Maharaja of Gwalior to set up industries in the princely state, which later led Birla to establish the Jiyajee Rao Cotton Mills in Gwalior. Within the family more responsibilities now rested upon Birla's shoulders as, in 1920, Jugalkishore, following his father's example, took early retirement from business to devote himself to spiritual pursuits.[1] By the early 1920s Birla had thus became the pivot around which the entire business revolved. In addition to his business commitments, there was a growing involvement with the sphere of public affairs which increasingly seemed to draw him. He was, by this time, a leading member of the Marwari Association, the Marwari Relief Society and the Maheshwari Sabha.

IN THE BENGAL COUNCIL

Birla's active involvement with the Marwari Association prompted Lord Ronaldshay, the Governor of Bengal, to nominate him in January 1921 to the Bengal Legislative Council. As Ronaldshay explained to Edwin Montagu, the Secretary of State for India:

The Marwaris are great supporters of Gandhi and are consequently inclined to support his policy of non co-operation. They are very orthodox and very emotional and easily carried away by a man like Gandhi who promises them the disappearance of Western civilization and a return to the golden days of Hindu supremacy in the land. They are very wealthy as you know and can help the non-cooperationists very considerably in the matter of finance. Among the older men there is a considerable body which views with disfavour the present day tendency of the younger members of the community to throw in their lot with the political extremists and Ghanshyamdas Birla is a capable representative of this body.[2]

Thus at the young age of 27 Birla found himself in the legislative arena as the representative of Marwari commercial interests. In making this selection the Governor passed over many Marwari stalwarts such as Sir Badridas Goenka. Instead, the authorities preferred Birla who was popular with the younger generation of the Marwaris and could be relied upon to keep it in check. The family's large donations to war funds and Birla's aloofness from politics at the time of the Rowlatt agitation must have also been factors which contributed to his nomination.

However, Birla did not prove to be a very active member of the Bengal Legislative Council. During the year that he spent there, he voted only six times. In the inaugural session he voted with the official bloc on the budget. Two months after the session had commenced, he made his one and only intervention in the Council. He raised a question concerning the insanitary conditions and the prevailing high rate of mortality in Bara Bazaar. He wanted to enquire what measures the government had taken for improving conditions there. He also raised the issue of a park that had been proposed for the area.[3] The issue of sanitary conditions was one about which the Marwari Association had been campaigning for a long time both with the Calcutta Corporation and the Calcutta Improvement Trust.[4] In the second session of the Council held during April 1921, Birla supported an official motion giving a supplementary grant to the police for increasing its strength in the 24-Parganas district. In the following session in July, he again voted with the official bloc against the proposal to publish Council proceedings only in Bengali. In the August-September meetings a bill for women's suffrage was introduced in the Council; Birla voted against the extension of suffrage rights to women. In the winter session he voted only on two occasions: the first was on a motion that survey and settlement operations be discontinued in Khulna district in view of agrarian distress there, while the second was on a demand for grants. On both these occasions Birla's vote was cast in favour of the official bloc. In this period there were several important discussions from which he absented himself such as the Bengal Tenancy Amendment Bill in July 1921 and the budget debate in February 1922.[5]

Birla's frequent absence from the Council can be explained only by his business commitments which were pressing in those years. Moreover, he still had to find his feet in the world of legislative politics with its own elaborate and unwritten code of conduct. Although he mostly voted with the official bloc, he was careful not to take an openly loyalist stand and kept out of controversial discussions. One reason for his reticence in the debates appears to have been his lack of public-speaking skills. Moreover, a debating chamber as august as the Bengal Council with its many stalwarts, must have intimidated Birla.

Birla was nominated to several house committees such as the Public Accounts Committee and the Finance Committee on Howrah Bridge.[6] In their deliberations his positions invariably reflected the interest of the Marwari community. For instance, in the Finance Committee on Howrah Bridge (January 1923), he dissented from the majority report which recommended the construction of a bridge.[7] This dissent was based on his analysis of the likely impact of such a bridge on Marwari business interests. It was feared that the proposed bridge, planned in close proximity to Bara Bazaar, would increase the tax burden on the Marwaris who would be asked to contribute to its cost. More significantly, there was apprehension that it would adversely affect real estate-values in the area.[8] Keeping these interests of his Marwari constituents, Birla opposed the bridge on the ground of its enormous costs.[9] His stand in the Council was supported by the prestigious newspaper, the *Bengalee*.[10] Birla's activities in the Legislative Council and its committees reflected his own self-view as a Marwari. His activities were largely restricted to the Bara Bazaar community, of which he saw himself as a representative.

'BARON OF THE PRESS'

Although Birla looked upon his role in the Bengal Council essentially as a representative of Marwari business, he showed great keenness in these years to widen the horizon of his public activities. This is perhaps best reflected by his acquisition of two quality English-language newspapers of Calcutta. In 1920 M/ s Birla Brothers purchased the only evening newspaper in the city, the *Empire*.[11] The paper had been associated with the European-controlled publication *Commerce* and was mainly devoted to commercial news. As its new proprietors the Birlas declared that they proposed to continue the editorial policies of the paper and the only change they made was in its mast-head. From the *Empire*, the paper became the *New Empire*.[12] This change in nomenclature symbolized continuity rather than a break and significantly the word 'Empire' was retained which was extraordinary in a context in which the Indian-controlled press was becoming increasingly radicalized.[13] Professing to be businessmen first and foremost, the new proprietors declared the newspaper's policy to be twofold: (a) 'discussion of matters relating to trade, commerce, finance and industry'; and (b) 'the protection and advancement of commercial interests'.[14] In its coverage of events, while focusing upon financial and industrial subjects, the *New Empire* also attempted to give prominence to the proceedings of the Legislative Council and to sports news in which it had carved out a niche, as was to be expected of an eveninger. By thus defining its editorial framework, the *New Empire* and its new owners carefully stayed out of dangerous political matters. For the English-language Calcutta press, the change in ownership signified a good portent. The *Capital* remarked that the *New Empire*'s take-over by the Birlas was 'a guarantee that the paper will prove an asset on the side of law and order'.[15]

In 1922 the Birlas acquired another prestigious English-language daily, *Bengalee*, which had been started by Sir Surendra Nath Banerjee, the distinguished politician of the moderate era. Birla, together with the Maharaja of Cassim Bazaar, took over the paper with the approval of Sir Surendra Nath. *Bengalee* had always been an 'independent liberal organ' and the new management intended absolutely no changes in the editorial policy and announced that the paper would continue as the sturdy spokesman of the moderate party.[16] It is interesting to ask the question what prompted Birla to enter the completely unfamiliar world of newspaper-publishing. Several explanations may be offered. Having entered industry after a protracted struggle against racial discrimination, control over a commercial newspaper from the prestigious *Commerce* marked yet another stage in the fight against European business dominance. Calcutta's commercial press had been owned by Europeans who usually looked upon Marwari businessmen with contempt. The take-over of the only evening newspaper of Calcutta challenged this European monopoly and undoubtedly enhanced Birla's profile as an upcoming representative of indigenous business. As a late entrant in industry, Birla knew that control over commercial intelligence could help position him in the forefront of Calcutta's business world. Moreover, interest in newspapers reflected his growing ambitions of a public career. By acquiring two English newspapers Birla had dared to venture outside the restricted Marwari world of Bara Bazaar.

NEGOTIATING NON-COOPERATION

One development which increasingly connected Marwari public affairs to the larger world of politics was the launching of the Non-cooperation Movement in 1920 by Mahatma Gandhi. The sphere of Marwari politics, of which Birla had been a part, was transformed forever. As a leading figure of the Marwari Association (which had only a year earlier denounced the Rowlatt satyagraha), it is interesting to look at Birla's stance towards the advent of the policy of non-cooperation. His responses may perhaps be considered at two levels: first, in terms of the editorial policies of his two newspapers, *New Empire* and *Bengalee* and second, the personal positions he took in the Bengal Legislative Council and before the Bara Bazaar community.

As the only evening newspaper of Calcutta, the *New Empire* was in the business of reporting and commenting upon political events on a daily basis. During the crucial months between the Calcutta and Nagpur sessions of the Indian National Congress in 1920, the paper frequently commented upon the debates which were raging within nationalist circles. Its editorials without fail highlighted the inadvisability of non-cooperation, especially at a time when 'far reaching constitutional changes' were placing the country 'firmly on the road of responsible self-government'. Its editorial columns went to the extent of denouncing Gandhi's scheme as unwise and impracticable and predicted that non-cooperation would create discord and strife and was doomed to failure.[17] The *New Empire* was unequivocal in its criticism:

It behoves all those who have the future welfare of the country at heart whole-heartedly to take to constructive work, without haste, without rest, and to bring health, plenty, education...and above all a feeling of relief to the Indians suffering from the demoralising effects of inferior status and aloofness from the defence and Government of their own country.[18]

Its columns pleaded the cause of the reformed councils which would 'open the road to large constructive legislation in which non-officials and officials will find themselves working together for the common good.' It would be 'so much more effective if common labour could be accomplished in a feeling of cordiality and fellow feeling', the newspaper asserted.[19]

In these crucial months the *New Empire* closely followed developments within the Congress.[20] The outcome of the Calcutta Congress was seen by it as a personal triumph for Gandhi and as proof that 'his self-denying character has stamped itself deeply upon the consciousness of the people of India.' Despite expressing strong misgivings about his programme, it confessed to 'yielding to none in our admiration for Gandhi' and observed that there 'was none who at the present moment wields the same extent of influence among the people.' It attributed Gandhi's appeal to his 'transparent honesty, his sincerity of purpose, his selflessness and his spirit of simplicity...his readiness to suffer for the cause of his country and his unflinching courage.'[21] A similar line was echoed by the *Bengalee* with regard to non-cooperation and the constitutional reforms being introduced under 'dyarchy'. It pleaded in 'earnest to give the reforms a chance and to fight tooth and nail the dangerous heresy of Gandhism.'[22] So forthright was its stand that the paper was lauded by the European-controlled loyalist *Capital* for its 'splendid fight...against Gandhism, non-cooperation and civil disobedience' and for remaining the 'sturdy spokesman of the moderate party.'[23]

While the Birla-controlled newspapers made no attempt to disguise their criticism of Gandhi's programme, in his personal capacity Birla kept a low profile during this turbulent period in Indian politics. The victory of Gandhi's formula of non-cooperation at the Nagpur Congress in December 1920 and the acquiescence in it of old stalwarts like the Punjab leader Lala Lajpat Rai deeply disappointed him. He had met Lajpat Rai in 1911 when the latter visited Calcutta.[24] Then only 17 years old, Birla had been deeply impressed by the Punjab leader's personality and ideas. 'Having never met a renowned leader,' the impressionable Birla had been 'very much awe-stricken by his presence.' At this meeting Birla had put a number of questions to Lajpat Rai which he answered patiently. Deeply impressed, Lajpat Rai had seemed to him like 'the Mount Everest whose summit it was impossible to climb'. He was now disappointed by Lajpat Rai's climb-down at the Calcutta Congress. Quite perceptibly, he noticed the sartorial transformation which accompanied Lajpat Rai's conversion.[25] Birla observed that Lajpat Rai's trade-mark 'Punjabi turban, by which he was too easily recognised by his countrymen', had now given way to the famous Gandhi cap. To him, all this was a disappointment.[26]

Although Birla believed in the reforms, he did not join some of the influential business leaders from Bombay, which included Sir Dinshaw Wacha, Sir N.C. Chandavarkar, Purshotamdas Thakurdas and Sir C.L. Setalvad, in condemning the Non-cooperation Movement as 'dangerous to the best interests of the country, calculated to paralyse the people.'[27] Neither did he support his more radical associates from Bara Bazaar who were now the Mahatma's most enthusiastic supporters in Calcutta. Rather, he kept his views to himself and made no public statements. Within the Bengal Council, as we earlier noted, he took a pro-reforms stand. In October 1921, along with 27 non-official members, he signed a cable to the Secretary of State for India asking for additional funds for Bengal to avoid excessive taxation. If their demand was refused, the legislators warned that a 'deadlock will follow, imperiling the reforms, strengthening non cooperation and greatly impairing general administrative efficiency and marring the usefulness of transferred departments.'[28]

In January 1922 Birla resigned from the Bengal Legislative Council. A convergence of factors led to this. To begin with, his business commitments in these years were so pressing that he could hardly devote time for legislative work; as we earlier noted Birla Jute had only recently started production and he was finalizing plans for establishing cotton mills in Delhi and later Gwalior. Moreover, he felt that someone else who was willing to play a more active role could better serve the interests of the Marwaris in the Bengal Council. Upon his resignation the Marwari Association nominated Debi Prasad Khaitan, Birla's trusted lieutenant and the 'shining light' of M/s Birla Brothers to the Council.[29] Although Khaitan had been an active participant in the Rowlatt satyagraha, he was, by 1922, a committed constitutionalist and continued Birla's policy of whole-heartedly supporting the reforms.[30]

In these years what is striking about Birla's political ideas was his faith in the efficacy of constitutional methods. He believed in entering the reformed councils to promote self-government—a common ground he strongly shared with the Marwari Association. But he took pains to make it clear that he was no loyalist like many other leaders of the Marwari Association, even though he had kept aloof from his erstwhile radical colleagues who were now the staunch supporters of the Non-cooperation Movement in Calcutta.

It may at this stage be helpful to take a glance at what was happening to Marwari politics at its grassroots in Calcutta. The Marwaris' overwhelming contribution to the success of the Rowlatt satyagraha in Calcutta has already been noted.[31] Following this, in 1920, Jamnalal Bajaj had established the Bara Bazaar Congress Committee, and amongst its most prominent members were Ramkrishna Mohta, Sitaram Seksaria and Basantlal Morarka. These men had been Birla's associates since the days of the Rodda case. With the victory of the Gandhian formula at the Nagpur Congress, the atmosphere in Bara Bazaar became charged with enthusiasm for Gandhi.[32] In addition to participation in meetings and hartals, most Marwari traders pledged to abstain from all forward orders at the height of the foreign-cloth-boycott campaign in 1921.[33] In such a charged atmosphere it became increasingly difficult for Birla to remain aloof and yet maintain his position at the forefront of Marwari leadership. At this time the family made two significant gestures. Birla reportedly took part in a bonfire of foreign cloth.[34] The second, more significant gesture, came at the time of collections for the Tilak Swaraj Fund which had been started by Gandhi. Marwari businessmen all over India had contributed munificently to the Fund. At a meeting in Bara Bazaar at which Gandhi was present and appealed for funds, large donations were made by the Marwaris, with Ramkrishna Mohta taking the lead with an on-the-spot donation of Rs 25,000. Many others followed and several prominent Marwari families donated up to Rs 2 to 3 lakhs each to the Fund. For instance, Anandilal Poddar donated Rs 2 lakhs, Jainarain Dani and Hiralal Kariwala were known to have donated more than one lakh each[35] and Jamnalal Bajaj himself gave one lakh. It is difficult to ascertain what prompted the Birlas to subscribe to the Fund, but a certain degree of pressure resulting from the changed mood of the community must have definitely played a role.[36] Rameshwardas, who was incharge of the Bombay branch of the Birla firm, called on the Mahatma at Mani Bhawan in Bombay and presented him with a cheque of Rs 1 lakh. Having never met him before, Gandhi did not personally know the donor, 'although he had heard about me from Malaviyaji and Jamnalalji Bajaj'.[37]

Thus Birla cautiously tried to maintain his own position in the front ranks of the Calcutta Marwaris in the turbulent years of the Non-cooperation Movement. Within the Marwari Association he could retain his standing because of the common ground he shared with its members by his faith in constitutional methods. Yet, he had not lost face with the radical elements among the Marwaris who were enthusiastic supporters of Gandhi. Quite unlike his radicalism of the pre-War years, Birla had matured politically and now took measured steps.

AN OUTCASTE

In 1921 Birla's influence in Bara Bazaar politics stood at its peak. In that year he represented the community in the Bengal Legislative Council and his lieutenant Debi Prasad Khaitan was elected president of the powerful Marwari Association. In early 1922 Birla ensured that, upon his resignation, Khaitan succeeded him as the Association's nominee in the Council. However, Birla's position thereafter became increasingly precarious as he was engulfed in several factional controversies which plagued the Association. The first of these was over the Association's memorandum before the Indian Fiscal Commission (1921–2). Birla had been nominated a member of the Commission which invited evidence from various business associations. As president of the Marwari Association, Khaitan submitted a memorandum which strongly criticized the government's fiscal and economic policies. In this memorandum and in the subsequent evidence which he presented before the Commission, Khaitan demanded protection for Indian industry and exposed the discrimination faced by indigenous business in obtaining credit from European-dominated banks and in several other areas.[38] His memorandum voiced the concerns of nascent Indian industrialists, rather than of old-style traders and middlemen who dominated the Marwari Association. Moreover, as a member of the Fiscal Commission, Birla himself did not hide the fact that he was a 'protectionist', and he boldly signed a note of dissent to the Commission's Report. These strongly nationalist positions were disliked by the loyalist traders entrenched in the Marwari Association. Many of them saw their fortunes as being dependent upon European businesses and the goodwill of the government. It may be argued that this divergence of opinion reflected a wider breach that existed between the big firms who were venturing into industry and the rest of the Marwaris who were still very largely engaged in trading and speculation.

In 1922, Khaitan, who had never been liked by the conservatives, was ousted as the president of the Association. He had been one of the principal organizers of the Rowlatt satyagraha of 1919 and he and his associates had then been denounced by the loyalist Marwari leadership as 'men of the lowest class'.[39] Nonetheless, riding on the wave of the tremendous enthusiasm generated among the Marwaris by Gandhi's call for non-cooperation, Khaitan and his associates had succeeded in wresting control over the Association. The controversy over the Fiscal Commission further embittered relations. Although both Birla and Khaitan were staunch constitutionalists, they did not share the loyalist views of the conservatives within the Marwari Association. The struggle became particularly acrimonious over the selection of the Association's nominee to the Central Legislative Assembly (CLA). The progressives, led by Khaitan, suggested that Birla be chosen as a consensus candidate. The conservatives, however, opposed this and instead proposed Vishweshwarlal Halwasia.[40] Failing to secure a unanimous nomination, the Khaitan–Birla group put up Ranglal Jajodia. A special session was convened so that voting could take place and Birla and Ramdev Chokhany were chosen its vice-presidents. The Birla–Khaitan group lost narrowly and Birla had to publicly admit defeat.[41] This turned the tide within the Association in favour of the conservatives and in 1923 they re-established control with the election of Sir Onkar Mull Jatia as president. However, the Birla–Khaitan group continued to be office bearers; Birla was elected one of the four vice-presidents and 'the inevitable' Khaitan was made honorary treasurer.[42]

This simmering discontent in Marwari politics in Calcutta inevitably led to a showdown. This final estrangement, however, occurred not over politics but over a social issue—the wedding of Birla's elder brother Rameshwardas (who was a widower) to a Kolwar Maheshwari girl. 'Kolwar' was the label given by the Maheshwaris to fellow caste members who had settled in western UP. Traditionally, the term had merely represented a regional sub-grouping without any connotation of an inferior status. However, by the 1920s the meaning of the term had changed. The non-Kolwar Maheshwaris, who called themselves 'Didu' (as they traced their ancestry to a place called Didwana), had begun to regard the Kolwars as ritually inferior and sometimes not even as fellow Maheshwaris. Conservative Maheshwaris could go to the extreme of ostracizing those who interacted with Kolwars. The issue of the status of Kolwars had been agitating the Calcutta Marwaris for some time. The Maheshwari Mahasabha had set up a committee in November 1921 to consider the matter. Of its five members, four had agreed that Kolwars were Didu Maheshwaris like the rest of the Maheshwaris. Only one member, Kanhaiyalal Rathi, had disagreed. He had pronounced that Kolwars were ritually inferior and inter-dining and marriage with them should be disallowed.[43] Taking a lead in the conflict, the Birlas arranged the marriage of

Rameshwardas, who had been widowed some time before, with a Kolwar girl. Fearing some opposition within the community, the marriage was performed in haste, even before the report of the Committee became available. The alliance had been arranged in a progressive spirit and with the complete support of the family elders.[44]

As soon as the news of the marriage became known in Bara Bazaar, the Birlas were excommunicated by the Maheshwari Panchayat. Conflict over the Kolwar issue provided an opportunity for both the conservatives and the reformists to close ranks and to consolidate their respective hold over community organizations. To the established Maheshwari bankers it provided an opportunity to dislodge the Birlas from their position of influence within caste organizations. While the conservatives, led by powerful merchants such as Rampratap Daga, Seth Govindas Kothari, Mangiram Bangur and Sukhlal Karnani, excommunicated the Birlas, the Birla allies, in turn, took control over the Maheshwari Mahasabha and the local papers, *Maheshwari* and *Marwari*.[45] In the polarization that followed, the Birla group, which included Ramkrishna Mohta, Ramgopal Mundhra, Kasturchand Kothari and Brij Vallabhdas Mundhra, was able to wrest control over the Maheshwari Sabha and the Didu Maheshwari Sangh, while the dissidents walked out and formed the Didu Maheshwari Mahapanchayat.[46] As the head of the Birla clan, Baldeodas was asked by the conservatives of the Didu Maheshwari Mahapanchayat to appear before it and present his case. Baldeodas was informally assured re-entry into the community if he gave a written apology to the Mahapanchayat. This gesture of conciliation had been offered in recognition of the respect which Baldeodas enjoyed as a community elder.[47] Completely taken aback by the turn of events, Baldeodas was tempted to apologize and conciliate the conservatives. However, Birla took a bold stand and dissuaded him. Within the Akhil Bharatiya Maheshwari Sabha, he resolutely declared that the distinction within the community was false and needed to be done away with.[48] Meanwhile, the Mahapanchayat organized a campaign to enforce the excommunication and volunteers were sent to different parts of the country to propagate the news.[49] The excommunication naturally affected the Birlas' standing within the community. Although they controlled two of the Maheshwari organizations, they were pitted against community elders and powerful Marwari families.

MALAVIYA'S DISCIPLE

The excommunication proved to be a time of anxiety and stress for the Birla family. In this hour of crisis Birla turned for help and guidance to two individuals—the prominent nationalist leader, Madan Mohan Malaviya and Gandhi. For Gandhi he was still a mere acquaintance, but with Malaviya his family had by these years developed close links. Malaviya enjoyed the status of a learned guru for the community, and Birla sought his advice and solace. He knew that Malaviya had excellent credentials for intervening in this dispute as he enjoyed a pre-eminent position among the Calcutta Marwaris. His close links with them went back many decades to the time when he had solicited their support for the propagation of Sanskrit and Hindi as well as cow-protection which had a particular religious appeal for the Marwaris and was considered a special form of piety by them. The Marwaris had been one of the most enthusiastic supporters of the cow-protection movements and for several similar causes which contributed to Hindu resurgence at the turn of the century, which Malaviya championed. The links between Malaviya's politics in Allahabad and local commercial interests have been highlighted by Chris Bayly.[50] By the 1910s Malaviya had drawn up an ambitious scheme for his Banaras Hindu University (BHU) which over the years became the rallying symbol for Hindu nationalists. Malaviya's project of the Hindu University, given its magnificent scale, was aimed at building up an all-India movement for the resurgence of Hindu nationalism. The support of local commercial groups which had so far been available to Malaviya was clearly not sufficient to support this scheme which needed an all-India campaign to seek patronage and to collect the funds required to establish the University. For a project of such a grand scale there were only two groups which Malaviya could tap—the Hindu princely states and the mercantile groups, mainly the Marwaris.

Malaviya thus fostered links with powerful Marwari families who could be potential donors to the BHU. In 1911, during a visit to Calcutta, he was honoured by the Marwaris of Bara Bazaar. In January 1912 he again visited the city to appeal for donations for the Hindu University and reportedly received hundreds of currency notes on the spot.[51] Among the Marwaris he began to enjoy a 'reputation for piety, a knowledge of the Sanskrit classics, acquaintance with English history and literature,...researches in current finance and economics'. The community increasingly looked upon him as a great social reformer and modernizer. His work as a member of the CLA where he showed much interest in commercial and industrial questions, had also made him particularly popular among mercantile groups. His strong advocacy of their interests before the Industrial Commission of 1916–18 had reinforced his credentials as a champion of indigenous business and industry.[52]

In view of his superb credentials among the Marwaris who revered him as a guru, it was natural for Birla to seek Malaviya's guidance in the crisis caused by the family's excommunication. He sent two telegrams to Malaviya requesting him to personally come to Calcutta. As Malaviya could not undertake the journey because of ill health, Jugalkishore was sent to Banaras to consult him. Malaviya advised a conciliatory attitude towards the Marwari Panchayat. He wanted the Panchayat to be informed that the family had settled the alliance in the knowledge that four out of five Committee members had pronounced that Kolwars enjoyed the same status as Didu Maheshwaris and intermixing with them was permissible. In case the Panchayat decided to appoint another committee, Malaviya advised the Birlas to abide by its decision. As a gesture of conciliation, he wanted Birla to personally inform the Panchayat that, 'from your side it is not the intention to go against the *biradari*'. He counselled that the crisis be handled by the family with a measure of humility.[53]

The family had been completely shaken by the social ostracism which it faced. So strong was the boycott that day-to-day relations within the community were strained. The Birlas became the target of ridicule from the conservative elements and even cartoons depicting members of the family appeared in propaganda materials.[54] Entertaining, receiving visitors, inter-dining and participating in social events were all affected. An index of how entrenched was the conservative opposition is illustrated by the example of Rukmani Devi, wife of Birla's younger brother Braj Mohan. She could not visit her parents, the Tapariahs, who were on the side of the conservatives, for 12 years.[55] No clear evidence is available about how the excommunication affected the Birlas' business activities. Probably the business too was adversely affected, as their social standing in Bara Bazaar must have been lowered and, as we earlier noted, among the Marwaris credit is principally dependent upon sakh. However, it is probable that they could take the risk, as their major interests by this time lay in industry.

In the face of this stiff opposition the family elders, Baldeodas and Jugalkishore, began to waver. They were inclined to take the view that an apology be made to the Panchayat. Rameshwardas and Birla, however, were not in favour of bending at this stage. They requested Malaviya to persuade Baldeodas and Jugalkishore to remain steadfast. Malaviya reasoned with Baldeodas not to be excessively worried or agitated.[56] He reassured them that the alliance was, after all, within the *Vaishya* caste and not with a lower caste. Moreover, previous alliances with Kolwars had been approved by the Panchayat.

Following Malaviya's advice the family stood united. In a few years the conservative opposition died down. Although Birla and his supporters succeeded in retaining control over the Maheshwari Mahasabha and continued to enjoy support among the moderate and younger elements within the community, the entrenched conservatives made it impossible for Birla to have any future leadership role in the community. Within Marwari politics the episode meant that he had reached the end of the road, although he retained strong community links with the Calcutta Marwaris once the controversy had settled. The Kolwar incident proved to be a time of introspection for Birla, who increasingly felt that the Marwari public arena was too restricted for his ambitions and too narrow for his vision. The conclusion he drew from this was that he must broaden his horizons and seek wider linkages.

At another level the Kolwar issue drew him closer to Malaviya and the two discovered a number of common interests. Malaviya involved him in several of his projects which were aimed at a resurgence of Hindu nationalism. In the main Malaviya enlisted Birla's support for his scheme of the Hindu University at Banaras. Central to this notion of Hindu nationalism lay a strong belief in a resurgent and progressive Hinduism. In this construction of Hinduism the restoration of the pristine glory of the Hindu religion, as enshrined in the classical vedas and *shastras*, was emphasized. Yet, this view of Hindu resurgence laid equal importance on modern learning. It was significantly different from the Hindu reformist movements that had flourished in the nineteenth century in that it did not have a revivalist philosophy. While being uniquely modern in its ideas, it did not start altogether a new set of doctrine as the Arya Samaj had done so successfully in the Punjab. Instead, it aimed to address the Hindu masses who subscribed to the mainstream of Sanatan Dharma. Its discourse employed the language of classical Sanskrit learning to call for the resurgence of the Hindu 'community' and 'society' with a view to modernizing it for the twentieth century. In this discourse spiritual progress (dharma) went side by side with the attainment of material prosperity (*artha*) for which scientific knowledge and industrial progress were essential. Malaviya's 1905 prospectus for the BHU summed it up when it proclaimed on its cover page: 'That is religion which ensures temporal prosperity and eternal bliss'.[57]

In the political arena this discourse meant the building up of the unity of the Hindu community, the formation of a strong political party to represent the interests of this community, and the conception of a political system in which the interests of different religious communities were negotiated through politics. It was this construction of a homogenized pan-Indian Hinduism that drew Birla so strongly towards Malaviya.[58] It was not Birla alone, but his father Baldeodas and brother Jugalkishore who were also attracted to Malaviya and towards them he was particularly affectionate. 'The Revered Malaviyaji loved Jugalkishoreji throughout his life like his own son,' wrote Padam Kant, Malaviya's son.[59] Further, he notes that it was his father who was responsible for Jugalkishore's conversion from his staunch leanings towards Arya Samaj to Sanatan Dharma. He writes that 'whatever work Malaviyaji did for Hindu religion, Hindu pilgrims and the reform and upliftment of the Hindu community, in all such activities the Birlas' full support, either secret or explicit, was always forthcoming'.[60]

The Birlas supported Malaviya's Hindu University in a variety of ways. 'Whenever Malaviyaji faced any financial crisis, the Birlas always kind-heartedly supported him. The reality was that if the Birlas were to be eliminated from among the benefactors of Malaviyaji, the success of his projects would have been in doubt', recalls Kanhaiyalal Mishra.[61] Both Jugalkishore and Birla gave Rs 75,000 to Malaviya to train Hindu preachers for propaganda. Jugalkishore established a fund in the Hindu University to propagate the *Gita*. Its purpose was to support discourses of the *Gita* all over India. A separate department for Indian Religion and Philosophy was founded in the Central Hindu College by the Birlas. They also endowed a Sanskrit Mahavidyalaya in the University. A hostel for 400 inmates, the Birla Chhatravaas, was founded by them. In 1926 they helped establish the Rajputana Hostel and a wing of the Women's Hostel. The Music Faculty was started with funds provided by them to promote classical Indian music. In the early years of the University, 100 scholarships of Rs 15 per month were instituted by Jugalkishore to help needy students. In addition, a number of other activities within the University were supported by the Birlas. They contributed to the setting up of the university press and a research laboratory for *Ayurvedic* medicine. In addition, a gymnasium and a teachers' training college were also endowed by them. In recognition of these charities Birla was made a member of the Court of the University in 1925 and later Baldeodas was awarded an honorary degree of D. Litt.

Outside the University, the family supported a number of activities under Malaviya's inspiration. The Birlas gave money to the Kashi Pracharini Sabha for the propagation of Hindi. Padam Kant writes that Jugalkishore spent lakhs of rupees under Malaviya's inspiration to restore temples and dharamshalas or to build new ones at major Hindu pilgrim centres. The most important of these involved the restoration of the Shri Krishna Janmabhumi in Mathura. 'When Malaviyaji resolved to undertake this work, Jugalkishoreji became his right hand'.[62] Within Banaras the Birlas established the Birla Ayurvedic Hospital and a maternity home and a dental hospital. An institution was set up by Jugalkishore for sadhus and *sanyasins* and an old women's home for Marwari women who wished to spend their last years in Banaras. The Birlas also spent money on the restoration of temples and cremation sites in the city. Among the temples which they generously supported were the famous Durgaji temple, the Balaji temple at Pandeghat and the Gauri Shankar Mahadev temple at Lalghat.[63] A number of cremation sites were also restored by them: among these were the famous Manikarnika Ghat, Tulsi Ghat, Lal Ghat and Bundi Ghat. They also constructed dharamshalas and shelters for those visiting the city to cremate their dead.

Perhaps the emotional relationship between Malaviya and the Birla family can best be illustrated by an incident which occurred when Malaviya lay on his deathbed. His son, Padam Kant, recalls that for more than two days Malaviya struggled between life and death and everyone present realized that he was worried about something. 'On the third day suddenly Jugalkishoreji came. As soon as father saw him, he regained consciousness. Jugalkishoreji immediately knew the desire of his heart and said: "Maharaj, I promise that the Vishwanath Temple will be constructed according to your desire. You must depart peacefully".' His son recalls that Malaviya died soon after with an immense sense of satisfaction.[64] The Birlas then constructed a magnificent temple at Banaras which is regarded as one of the finest examples of Indian temple architecture, with its tower 19 feet taller than the Qutab Minar in Delhi.

The Birlas were thus Malaviya's major benefactors from the 1920s. A commemorative volume published by BHU in 1936 acknowledged them as the largest donors to the University. It was reckoned that by 1935 itself they had donated Rs 8,36,700 to the University—more than the contributions of the Maharajas of Udaipur, Bikaner, Alwar and Mysore put together.[65] According to Raja Baldeodas' biographer, the total charities of the Birlas to BHU were in excess of Rs 30 lakhs.[66]

Outside Banaras, in other spheres too, the Malaviya–Birla connection was strengthened by several new projects. Birla came to be deeply involved with the other much-prized project of Malaviya—the *Hindustan Times*. This newspaper had been started in September 1924 by the Akalis, allegedly with funds provided by Ghadar party activists based in San Francisco.[67] K.M. Pannikkar was appointed its editor. From the beginning the paper failed to achieve financial stability, and by early 1925 it badly needed injections of cash just to survive. Malaviya was very keen to acquire a prestigious all-India paper, especially since Delhi as the capital city had no other English daily. In March 1925 he decided to acquire a controlling interest in the *Hindustan Times* and requested Birla for a loan. The money was supposed to be returned once a company had been floated. While Birla doubted the wisdom of Malaviya taking over the paper, he felt he could not disobey him: 'Your word is law to me,' he wrote, 'I do not know whether I have got great sympathy for issuing a newspaper from Delhi. However, since you order me to pay I will do so... I only feel glad when I get an opportunity to serve you people occasionally.'[68] Despite regular help from Birla, the finances of the paper could not stabilize. In August 1925 Malaviya was again knocking on Birla's door for a further contribution of Rs 15,000: 'You have been so kind to me,' he wrote, 'and our relations are such that I feel sincerely sorry and pained to ask you for *further* help to enable me to discharge the responsibility which I unwisely took upon myself in connection with the Hindustan Times.'[69] Malaviya wanted the contribution as a loan but added that, 'should it unfortunately so happen that the loan cannot be repaid, you will kindly regard it as one of the many contributions you have made to the public cause.'[70] The amount, together with another Rs 5000, was paid by Birla, and Malaviya blessed the donor: 'May God grant you and yours the purest wisdom and bhakti.'[71]

In spite of these injections of cash, the *Hindustan Times* still did not become financially viable for several months. In January 1926 Malaviya needed a further contingency loan, as he had been let down by those who had promised to help.[72] To Birla, the enterprise appeared to be yet another example of Malaviya's lack of financial judgement. He admonished Malaviya for his unrealistic optimism and advised him to discontinue the paper, which was proving to be a source of regular trouble. Birla could foresee that the newspaper would continue to be a losing concern, and he wanted Malaviya 'to stop it and free yourself from unnecessary anxiety.'[73] Malaviya, however, persisted in his efforts, and in September 1926 was able to register it as a joint stock company and constitute a board of directors. He persuaded Birla to become a director: 'It is a very important journalistic venture,' he wrote. 'We are going to publish Lahore and Lucknow editions and I expect it will become a very important and self-supporting paper in course of time.'[74] Among those who joined the board were Lajpat Rai, N.C. Kelkar, M.R. Jayakar, K. Ramayyangar, Lala Baijnath Sayan, Lala Shri Ram and Malaviya himself. Birla's entry into the board was reluctant and, not unexpectedly, by 1927 the financial responsibility for the *Hindustan Times* had fallen largely upon his shoulders.

LAJPAT RAI'S BENEFACTOR

In the 1920s, while Birla provided financial support to Malaviya, politically he was in sympathy with Lala Lajpat Rai. Although the two had met nine years earlier, they had remained mere acquaintances until late 1923. On his release from jail at that time, Lajpat Rai's overriding concern was the organization and consolidation of the Hindus of north India. This led him to establish contact with the Birla brothers.[75] He had heard of the Birlas' reputation for supporting causes relating to the Hindus and of their large-scale philanthropy. Within three months of his release from prison in 1923, Lajpat Rai wrote to them expressing a wish to meet them to discuss 'the problem of Hindu unity' and 'how to save our depressed classes'. Any delay in solving these, he wrote, would be suicidal. Impressing upon them the urgency of the situation, Lajpat Rai felt that the 'present is the time of quick decision and prompt action if we want the Hindu community to be saved from ambitious and enterprising enemies.' The task, as he saw it, was twofold: first, 'to strengthen the Hindus of the Punjab' who were to provide the 'advance guard' in the resurgence of Hindu nationalism at a pan-Indian level; and second 'to take in all the depressed classes.'[76] Lajpat Rai believed that the depressed classes must be integrated with the larger Hindu community. He proposed to start work among the depressed classes in provinces where they were concentrated, such as the Central Provinces, Madras, Bihar and Orissa, and he proposed to train volunteers for this purpose.[77] However, Lajpat Rai made it clear that he was 'ready to undertake this work if sufficient funds' were placed at his disposal. For further discussions, he proposed a trip to Calcutta in early 1924 'principally to meet you brothers.'[78]

As we have seen earlier Birla had felt attracted to the Punjab leader from the days of the Non-cooperation Movement. He later recalled that Lajpat Rai was 'built entirely on a different pattern and was moulded in a different philosophy from that of Gandhiji.' Lajpat Rai was 'impatient with the slowness of our progress', and his desire for 'a life full of strength and speed' attracted young Birla. Birla felt that Gandhi's programme of satyagraha with all its philosophy appeared before Lajpat Rai's politics 'so docile, meek and boring'. Lajpat Rai's politics, on the other hand, appealed to Birla, who 'placed him on a higher pedestal than Gandhi'.[79] Lajpat Rai's initiative in 1923 soon led to a strong relationship. Within three months of his visit to Calcutta in 1923, Rai planned a trip to Europe. He wanted to visit England to act as the Congress' informal emissary at a time when the Labour Party had come to power there; he also wanted to seek medical treatment in London. All arrangements for the journey, such as purchase of steamer tickets for him and a companion were made by the Birlas.[80]

Lajpat Rai's efforts for the removal of untouchability appealed to Birla as deserving of support. Birla, who later became the president of the Harijan Sevak Sangh, acknowledged that it was Lajpat Rai who was the 'first to attract me towards the work of the removal of untouchability.' In addition, several other projects of

Lajpat Rai impressed the Birla brothers, such as the Boy Scouts scheme and the publication of Rai's political writings. Soon Lajpat Rai was receiving a monthly stipend of Rs 3000 from them for his Servants of the People Society.[81] In 1925 Birla provided Lajpat Rai with a car and a driver for his personal use in Lahore.[82]

The support by the Birlas to Lajpat Rai took several other forms. Jugalkishore promised him Rs 5000 for work among the Akalis.[83] Rai regularly discussed plans of work among the depressed classes with Birla.[84] He also tried to involve him in the activities of the Tilak School of Politics and, on its first anniversary, invited him to preside over its celebrations.[85] Lajpat Rai's books, *Young India* and *England's Debt to India*, had been banned during World War I. However, in 1926 the proscription order was cancelled; Lajpat Rai wanted *Young India* to be reprinted and *England's Debt to India* brought up-to-date. For this he asked Birla to write a chapter on 'the Currency Policy of the Government and its Effect,' and he wanted him to update the chapter on the cotton industry. Lajpat Rai was also engaged in writing a book which was to be a reply to Katherine Mayo's *Mother India*. He wanted all three books 'to be placed in the hands of every member of the British Parliament, every member of the American Congress and all members of the German and French Parliaments.'[86] The question was of finding money for it.[87] Birla, ever ready to help, agreed to meet the costs.[88] The *Hindustan Times* promoted the books in its editorials. 'Among the front rank leaders in India today we cannot think of anyone who has a better title to write of India's struggle than Lala Lajpat Rai,' it wrote. Its editorials declared that *Young India* surpassed other writings of the time; 'Neither in the autobiography of Sir Surendranath Banerjee nor in Mrs Annie Besant's "India's Fight for Freedom" can one obtain such a realistic and intimate picture of the eventful days of 1907 and 1908 as in this book of Lala Lajpat Rai.'[89] Birla also partly paid for the cost of the book written in reply to Katherine Mayo's.[90]

By the mid-1920s the Birla brothers had become the chief benefactors of Lajpat Rai. Birla made provision for money he gave Lajpat Rai in his annual budget, and set aside large sums to promote his political activities. In 1926 the Bombay office of Birla Brothers gave Rai Rs 2000 to 3000 for his trip to Europe to attend the International Labour Conference.[91] Indeed, his firm maintained a regular account where all transactions concerning Lajpat Rai were recorded. In 1927, for instance, Birla asked Lajpat Rai 'how much money you wish me to set apart for these heads or any other item you wish me to include in my next year's budget'.[92] Another project of Lajpat Rai which Birla financed was the establishment of a gymnasium in Lahore.[93] Lajpat Rai greatly appreciated the interest which the Birla brothers took in his projects. In recognition, he wanted to place a photograph of Jugalkishore and Birla himself in the illustrated edition of *Young India*. Birla felt that only Jugalkishore's photograph should be published, since it was he who had done 'whatever has been done for the untouchables'. Moreover, he felt that Lajpat Rai had been such a kind guide in politics and hence must not give so much prominence to him.[94]

Another area of Birla's support to Lajpat Rai was his help to Arya Samaj institutions. In February 1927 Birla performed the opening ceremony of the Dayanand Anglo Vedic (DAV) High School in Delhi. Speaking on this occasion, Birla commended the Arya Samaj for its splendid work in the field of education. He said the D.A.V. institutions were the 'messengers of the old *rishis*' of India and that their 'very foundation was built on self-sacrifice'. He paid a 'glowing tribute to the works of Mahatma Hans Raj and late Swami Shradhanand Saraswati' and lauded them as the pillars of the samaj.[95]

IN THE HINDU WING OF NATIONALISM

The support to Malaviya and Lajpat Rai soon led Birla into active politics after all. By 1925 he found himself becoming involved again in mainstream politics. Despite his earlier withdrawal from the Bengal Legislative Council, he was again playing a key role in the formation of the Independent Congress Party in 1926 and found himself contesting an election on its behalf to the CLA. What was the nature of Birla's involvement in politics? To be able to answer this question we must understand the wider context of nationalist politics in the 1920s.

After Gandhi's suspension of the Non-cooperation Movement in 1922, acute differences arose among various political groups over the future course of the nationalist movement. Broadly, political opinion was polarized into two opposite camps—the 'Pro-changers' led by Motilal Nehru and C.R. Das and the 'No-changers' led by Rajendra Prasad, Vallabhbhai Patel, Rajagopalachari and Jamnalal Bajaj. The Pro-changers were the advocates of council- entry and wanted a change in the course of the Congress programme. Both Malaviya and Lajpat Rai were broadly in sympathy with this programme. In 1923, Motilal Nehru and C.R. Das succeeded in bringing together diverse elements on the question of council-entry under the name of the Swarajya Party. The Swarajists described themselves 'as a party within the Congress, and as such an integral part of the Congress'.[96] In 1923 the Swarajya Party won an impressive victory in elections to the CLA and to the provincial councils.[97] Although Malaviya had contested the 1923 Assembly elections as an Independent, he cooperated with the Swarajists in the CLA to form the Nationalist Party within the Assembly as a united front against the official bloc. Lajpat Rai, just out of prison, also supported the Swarajya Party candidates in the Punjab and campaigned actively for them.[98] Both Malaviya and Lajpat Rai subsequently joined the party after the latter was elected to the CLA in December 1925.

Although both Lajpat Rai and Malaviya fully supported the programme of council entry and had little faith in Gandhi's Non-cooperation Movement, they found that they were still not in a position to wholeheartedly support the Swarajists. One reason was the old tension between Malaviya and Motilal Nehru, who had sharp and well-known differences, centred mainly on the communal question.[99] Both Malaviya and Lajpat Rai were convinced that the Swarajists were willing to go too far in conciliating the Muslims, even at the cost of sacrificing the political interests of the Hindus. Both shared a common vision of organizing and consolidating Hindu political interests. Such a vision, however, was anathema to Motilal Nehru and his secular colleagues.[100] Further, Malaviya and Lajpat Rai were sympathetic to what came to be known as 'responsive co-operation': their support for Tambe and Jayakar in the Central Provinces clearly breached relations with Motilal Nehru and these dissensions rocked the Swarajya Party.[101] In August 1926 Lajpat Rai resigned from the Swarajya Party, and on 7 August 1926, together with Malaviya, formed the Independent Congress Party (ICP). They were joined by M.R. Jayakar, B.S. Moonje, N.C. Kelkar and others. Chris Bayly has characterized the ICP as a 'loose gathering of those contacts which had been pioneered in the Hindu University movement or even earlier in the Madhya Hindu Samaj of the 1880s'.[102]

Birla was delighted by the coming together of Malaviya and Lajpat Rai to form the new party. Since 1925 he had been trying to convince Lajpat Rai to consider 'the matter of organising a new party in co-operation with Panditji'.[103] He had wondered why 'in spite of India being so fortunate to possess leaders like Gandhiji, yourself, Malaviyaji, Motilal, Jayakar and so many others, we cannot unite and lay down some common, sensible and practical programme'. He was excited by the news of the formation of the party: 'I have got a great desire to come and see you', he wrote, but he was prevented from doing so by ill-health. He hoped that the ICP would succeed in achieving what others had failed to achieve.

From benefactor and financier of Lajpat Rai, Birla soon became a political colleague in the cause of Hindu nationalism. Lajpat Rai, in particular, consulted him on all important decisions. For instance, before accepting the president-ship of the ICP, he wired Birla: 'Friends insist my accepting the Presidentship of the Independent Congress Party. What do you advise? Will you support me?'[104] Birla played an indispensable role in bringing together Malaviya and Lajpat Rai and helped them resolve their differences. Though both of them were committed to the movement for a 'resurgent Hindu nationalism', many of their ideas and personality traits sharply differed. For instance, Lajpat Rai believed that Malaviya had involved himself so much with the BHU that he neglected questions of practical politics. Birla often acted as a mediator between the two leaders and his role in the formation of the ICP had been absolutely crucial. He soon became a key member of the inner group of the ICP, and played a vital part in planning its 1926 election campaign. He was a member of the select group which drafted the manifesto of the Party and laid down the programme it would follow in the CLA and in the provincial councils.[105] The ICP manifesto announced that the Party would work within the legislature to bring full responsible government and declared itself in favour of council-entry.[106]

The main contest in the elections which took place all over India in 1926 was between the Swarajists and the ICP. Birla became closely involved in the formulation of his party's electoral strategy. For instance, Lajpat Rai inquired of him if he could procure the services of B.C. Pal, the famous Bengali leader of the Moderate era, to campaign in the Punjab, 'provided the cost is not exorbitant'.[107] Worried by moves by Motilal Nehru to put up strong candidates against Lajpat Rai, Birla assured him that in such an eventuality, 'I will ask Panditji to put one against Mr. Nehru'.[108] When the Swarajists put Raizada Hansraj and Dewan Chamanlal against Lajpat Rai in both his constituencies in the Punjab, Malaviya was pressured by ICP members in the United Provinces (UP) to contest against Motilal, a move which Lajpat Rai vetoed.[109]

Birla himself was drafted by Lajpat Rai to contest for the CLA on behalf of the ICP. Lajpat Rai had been prospecting a constituency for Birla ever since the second half of 1925. At first he had his name registered as a voter in Punjab. Birla was, however, interested only when a seat was guaranteed and did not want to go in for competition in any election.[110] The electoral situation in Punjab was not easy for Lajpat Rai and he felt that he could not hold out any strong hopes about his chances in this province. But he assured Birla of support in Delhi or anywhere else.[111] However, plans for Birla's election to the CLA had to be kept in abeyance till the 1926 elections were actually announced.

Birla was then nominated by the ICP to stand from the 'non-Mohamaddan rural constituency of Banaras–Gorakhpur' in UP. Birla had no links with UP politics and hardly knew any local politicians of the region which he was meant to represent. The only reason for his contesting from the Banaras–Gorakhpur constituency was Malaviya' s great influence in the area. The seat was chosen for him by Malaviya himself. Birla could also derive some credit from the fact that his father had made Banaras his home and the family had donated large sums in charity to the city. Here he was pitted against Sri Prakasa, son of the seasoned Congress politician Bhagwandas and a personal friend of Jawaharlal Nehru. Birla had been keen to avoid a contest and tried to work out a compromise between himself and Sri Prakasa. It was suggested that if Birla contested from Faizabad, leaving the Banaras–Gorakhpur seat to Sri Prakasa, electoral adjustments could be made in such a way that both did not have to face a direct contest.[112] These efforts at conciliation, however, failed because Malaviya and Motilal Nehru could not finally agree, and Birla found himself locked in a tough fight.

Birla's election campaign was high-pitched. He was able to get Lajpat Rai, Malaviya and Swami Shradhanand to canvass personally for him. Shradhanand toured many areas on Birla's behalf. He declared Birla to be 'one of those few persons who were ever eager to do as much as they could for every good cause and in the interest of Hindus particularly and his countrymen generally'.[113] Malaviya personally visited many places and advised Birla to visit every district himself.[114] Lajpat Rai at first sent a message to be used in the campaign. In this he congratulated Birla on contesting the Banaras–Gorakhpur seat, since 'there are few men' who have 'greater and more substantial claims on the confidence of the Hindu community'. He complimented him for 'the services he had rendered to the Hindus' and for his 'purse... {which has} always been open for every good cause' and for 'every useful movement, aiming at the uplift of Indians in general and Hindus in particular.' He lauded Birla for having placed large sums of money at the disposal of many Indian leaders, and commended his services on the tariff committee. He felt 'confident that your practical knowledge of commerce and finance will enable you to take an intelligent lead in the discussion of all questions bearing on public finance and the development of industries that come before the Assembly'.[115] Later he personally visited the constituency and spent three days canvassing in Banaras and Gorakhpur districts.

In his campaign speeches Birla reiterated support for Hindu *sangathan* and declared it to be the most important work before the country which would be incomplete without the uplift of the depressed classes.[116] In spite of this strong support and hectic campaigning, the contest proved to be much tougher than Birla had imagined. He later confessed to Lajpat Rai that 'had I known that there would be such a keen contest I would never have plunged into this troublesome water'.[117]

Polling took place on 26 November 1926. Out of the total electorate of 12,608, over 74.72 per cent voted. Birla secured 7236 votes (76.81 per cent), as compared to 2185 votes (23.19 per cent) which were cast for Sri Prakasa.[118] Elsewhere too the Swarajya Party suffered badly in the elections. It lost ground everywhere except in Madras. In Bihar and Orissa it could barely maintain its position. In Bengal and the Central Provinces, even though it emerged as the single largest party, it still was powerless to create a constitutional deadlock. The electoral success of the ICP put the Swarajists in disarray. During the campaign communal passions had been roused, creating an unhealthy atmosphere and leaving Motilal Nehru and many others in the Congress bitter.[119]

Birla had contributed substantially to this success of the party both in terms of strategy and finances.[120] After this extraordinary electoral success Malaviya and Lajpat Rai were well positioned to demonstrate their new strength at the forthcoming session of the Congress at Gauhati. Malaviya urged Birla to play an active role at this session:

You have thoroughly identified yourself with the party and the work we wish to do for the country and the part I wish you to play in it demands that you should go to the Congress and speak at it. The Congress is yet a power, and I wish it to become a greater power, as it used to be by adopting a sound policy. We should not ignore it. We should be represented at it in our best strength. Please therefore make up your mind to attend it and ask other capable friends to join us in doing so.[121]

Birla was then made responsible for persuading 'as many men of intellect, position and wealth' as possible to go with the ICP delegation to the Congress.[122] He, however, could not attend due to ill-health. He felt that as Bengal and Assam would be very strongly represented, it would be difficult for the Congress to come to some unanimity about the present split.[123]

The Malaviya–Lajpat Rai combination now stood at the apex of its influence in nationalist politics. This influence came from its rousing electoral success in which Birla had played an instrumental role. Malaviya and Lajpat Rai, having been vindicated at the polls, now demanded that their programme of council-entry be accepted by the Congress as its official creed. Indeed, many within the organization looked upon their stance as a bid to capture the Congress. Motilal Nehru complained to Jawaharlal Nehru that, 'The Malaviya–Lala gang aided by Birla's money are making frantic efforts to capture the Congress. They will probably succeed as no counter effort is possible from our side.'[124] Many looked upon the ICP's tactic as 'a veiled attempt to pursue the policies of the Hindu Mahasabha in the name of the Congress.'[125]

Following his election as a member of the CLA and his increasing organizational responsibilities in the ICP, Birla was inevitably drawn into the wider factional politics of the Congress. He came under intense pressure from his mentors to play a more active political role. Malaviya wanted him to develop skills as a legislator and foresaw a prominent role for him in that capacity. Lajpat Rai's expectations from him were even greater. He believed that 'there are not many men among the Hindus on whom we could desire the mantle of leadership to fall.' What was needed was 'a reliable Hindu leader who would inspire love and confidence among his colleagues and co-workers to lead the Hindus of North India.'[126] Lajpat Rai believed that Birla had the potential to be such an all-India leader and he wanted to groom him for this role. He was convinced that Birla had 'the make of a great leader and all the qualities of a really generous one'. While he recognized that Birla's business interests were important as they 'supply the sinews of war', Lajpat Rai, nonetheless argued that, having 'entered politics you cannot neglect political issues.' Impressing upon him the importance of his future role as a politician, Lajpat Rai wrote to Birla: 'I have my eyes on you and Jayakar for the future leadership of the Hindus in politics'.[127]

Birla now stood at the crossroads of his public career. Would he pursue the high road of political leadership of pan-Indian 'Hindu nationalism' which his mentors were urging him to take or would he rather follow his own counsel?

NOTES AND REFERENCES

[1] Balchand Modi, *Desh Ke Itihas Main Marwari Jati Ka Sthan*, pp. 557–60.

[2] Ronaldshay to Montagu, 6 January 1921, Zetland Papers, India Office Library and Records/Mss.Eur.D. 609/4.

[3] The official reply stated that the Calcutta Corporation and the Calcutta Improvement Trust were the authorities responsible for this. The report of the committee appointed by the Calcutta Improvement Trust had recommended a park to be opened at the intersection of Badtalla Street and Jai Mohan Mullick Street. Birla was informed that the Calcutta Improvement Trust was still considering this report.

[4] See 'Minutes of Marwari Association Meetings, 1922–23' in R.K. Nevatia (ed.), *Shri Ramdev Chokhany.*

[5] *Bengal Legislative Council Proceedings*, 1921, Vol. I.

[6] *Capital*, 21 April 1921.

[7] While 11 of the 19 members agreed to the proposal of such a bridge, the rest dissented. *Capital* in its 2 August 1923 issue commented that 'they would not object to an even more magnificent and enduring structure, if the interests they represented were not asked to contribute to the costs.'

[8] 'Bara Bazaar may have secular objection to anything which involves the remotest risk of depreciating the value of land and houses in that neighbourhood', commented *Capital,* 14 April 1927.

[9] The *Capital,* usually uncharitable to the Marwaris, commented: 'The Marwaris are not sweet on bridges that encroach on their property, and are not above calling in a foreign power to resurrect some old-forgotten and lapsed treaty to delay if not defeat the encroachment. The legend of Bally is as instructive and amusing as the "Hunting of the Shark." ' *Capital,* 14 April 1927.

[10] The *Bengalee* added a religious argument to the opposition. It enquired if the Governor was 'sure that there will be no satyagraha of the non-violent type if a bridge be erected on which non-Hindus may sit, stand or walk with shoes on, while Sadhus, reverential women and men gather below for a bath in the Ganga?,' cited in *Capital,* 14 April 1927.

[11] A joint stock company with a capital of Rs 5,00,000 was floated for the purpose of the take-over of the paper, *Capital,* 31 July 1920.

[12] The *Commerce* sold out the evening paper because of problems of logistics and financial viability. The paper was auctioned by the official liquidator on 15 July 1920 when the Birlas bought it.

[13] On these issues, see Milton Israel, *Communication and power: propaganda and the press in the Indian nationalist struggle, 1920–1947* (Cambridge, 1994).

[14] *Empire,* 19 July 1920.

[15] *Commerce,* 22 July 1920.

[16] Unfortunately, I have not been able to locate old issues of the *Bengalee* in archives in Delhi and London.

[17] The *New Empire* commented that 'many more persons anxious to take their places' would move into the services and the posts would be filled with 'men who would in many cases be less experienced, less independent and less patriotic and less able.' This would make the 'work of officialdom easier and much less onerous' and the government would continue its business 'without the advice and controlling influence of those who besides being gifted with the power of clear and accurate thinking, think, feel and act for the people undeterred by any sacrifices they themselves may be called upon to make.' It thus argued that the real object of the movement would be defeated, *New Empire,* 6 September 1920.

[18] *Ibid.*

[19] *New Empire,* 10 September 1920.

[20] *New Empire,* 4 September 1920.

[21] *New Empire,* 6 September 1920.

[22] While praising the policy followed by the new proprietors, the *Capital* optimistically observed: 'The prestige which Sir Surendranath Banerjee gave the paper during his long and arduous struggle for home rule will gain a new lustre if the present direction guide their steps by the beacon light of his fine speech in the Bengal Council,' *Capital,* 26 January 1922.

[23] *Capital,* 3 February 1922.

[24] As Birla later recalled their first meeting: 'An old friend of mine who was an Arya Samajist, but not interested in politics, took me to Justice Chowdhury's house to see him.' Birla's Note, 'Lala Lajpat Rai', Birla Papers, Series Miscellaneous, File No. 123.

[25] For a fascinating description of a similar sartorial transformation of Motilal and Jawaharlal Nehru, see Emma Tarlo, *Clothing matters: dress and identity in India* (Chicago, 1996).

[26] Birla's Note, 'Lala Lajpat Rai', Birla Papers, Series Miscellaneous, File No. 123.

[27] The Bombay businessmen declared: 'The non-co-operation movement is dangerous to the best interests of the country, calculated to paralyse the people and lead not only to political dissensions but also social and domestic anarchy and add to the existing forces which retard amity and union among the different castes and creeds of India and as the movement will result in violence and consequently set back the steady and stable progress of the country, this meeting resolves that the following steps be taken to educate public opinion against the movement and point out to the masses in particular the dangers to which they are inevitably exposed by the movement.' The statement recommended strong measures by the government against the Movement. Also see Dwijendra Tripathi, 'The Congress and the Industrial Question 1919–35 in B.N. Pande (ed.), *A Centenary History of the Indian National Congress (1885–1985)*, Vol. II (New Delhi, 1983), pp. 493–524.

[28] The legislators demanded: 'Bengal Council being in recess, we members present in Calcutta desire to express our deep sense of the inadequacy of the relief granted to Bengal by the Government of India in the present financial crisis and pray that you will intervene for the allocation to Bengal of either one-third of the income and super tax, or three-fourths of the jute export duty. We consider this the irreducible minimum, otherwise taxation being inevitable for ordinary expenditure. Such taxation will assuredly be rejected by the Council and a deadlock will follow, imperilling the reforms, strengthening non-co-operation and gravely impairing administrative efficiency and marring the usefulness of transferred departments. We assure you that for future improvements in sanitation, education and other nation-building activities, we are prepared to tax ourselves but not for normal expenditure.' *Capital*, 6 October 1921.

[29] Debi Prasad Khaitan was an old associate of Birla. Born in 1888 Khaitan was the first Marwari attorney and started practice in the Calcutta High Court in 1911. He was invited to join Birla Bros Ltd., and in 1911 was made the firm's General Manager. He was in the Bengal Legislative Assembly in 1922–6; nominated member of the Board of Industries, 1928; attended the International Labour Conference as the employers' representative in 1928; was President of the Indian Chamber of Commerce, 1930; elected to the Calcutta Corporation in 1939; member of Jute Association, 1933; President, FICCI, 1936; member, International Chamber of Commerce, 1934–6; Commissioner, Calcutta Port Trust, 1937; in charge of the UP and Bihar Commission on setting up sugar mills (later called the Khaitan Commission), 1937; represented Indian industry at the Indo-Japanese Trade agreement and the Indo-Lancashire Agreement. For details of his career, see D.P. Sharma, *Desh Bhakt Udyog Pravartak Ghanshyamdas Birla*, pp. 212–4 and *Indian Year Book and Who's Who 1941–42* (Bombay, 1942).

[30] In his maiden speech, Khaitan took a strong pro-government stance. He opposed proposals to refuse financial measures to compel the government to release C.R. Das and other imprisoned non-cooperators. During the council debate on the Bengal Amusements Tax Bill, the opposition advocated the defeat of the measure as a way of protesting against the government's repressive policy. This was in sharp contrast to Khaitan's staunch stance

of economic nationalism which he had exhibited at the Indian Fiscal Commission. Also see *Capital*, 26 January 1922.

[31] It was the Bara Bazaar contingent which had influenced voting in Gandhi's favour at the Calcutta Congress. As Basantlal Morarka later wrote: 'The Bara Bazaar *dal* were the supporters of Mahatmaji. The Bengal camp was divided into two groups. One day at the session an argument broke out between the two Bengal groups and they disagreed with each other acrimoniously. On hearing of this Mahatmaji came to the Bengal camp and urged the supporters that the leader of Bengal was Deshbandhu Das. He told his supporters to explain their views to Das but not fight with him.' *Basantlal Morarka Smriti Granth*, p. 35. According to the *Bengalee*, the Bengal vote at the Calcutta Congress was 'determined by the votes of the Marwari and Hindu communities, who are here on purposes of business'. Judith Brown, *Gandhi's Rise to Power Indian Politics, 1915–1922* (Cambridge, 1972), pp. 267–8.

[32] The atmosphere in Bara Bazaar can be gauged by the recollections of the hartal on the visit of the Prince of Wales in 1921 which 'was far more successful than any other hartal till today. All trade in Calcutta came to a complete stand-still; even the local store that sold pan was closed, passengers at Howrah were stranded and the whole city was engulfed in darkness ... Even the electricity supply at night was stopped. That fateful day in 1921 was a complete black-out for the city.' *Basantlal Morarka Smriti Granth*, p. 36.

[33] The *Capital* alleged that they did so because they had surplus stocks in a depressed market and they made a virtue of necessity since it was in their interest to gain time to work off old stocks. *Capital*, 10 August 1922.

[34] D.P. Sharma asserts that Birla participated in a bonfire of foreign cloth. However, there does not appear to be any other evidence to confirm this.

[35] As Sitaram Seksaria recalled 'When Gandhiji appealed on behalf of the Congress for the Tilak Swaraj Fund, not only the wealthy members of the Marwari Samaj, but the middle level and ordinary people donated money. Calcutta's Anandilal Poddar, Jainarainji Dani, Hiralal Kariwala and Birla brothers gave many lakhs. None of them gave less than rupees one lakh.' Bhawarmal Singhi (ed.), *Padam Bhushan Shri Sitaram Seksaria Abhinandan Granth*, p. 281.

[36] The role of Jamnalal Bajaj may have been crucial in the donation. Bajaj, being the Treasurer of the Congress and also one of those responsible for the collections, must have persuaded the Birlas to contribute. For Bajaj's involvement with the Tilak Swaraj Fund, see B.R. Nanda, *In Gandhi's Footsteps: The Life and Times of Jamnalal Bajaj* (New Delhi, 1990), pp. 62–5.

[37] R.D. Birla's interview to *Current*, Bombay, May 1964.

[38] Evidence of D.P. Khaitan in *Report of the Indian Fiscal Commission, 1921–22, and Minute of Dissent, 1922* Cmd 1764, Vol. II (Calcutta, 1923), particularly see the Minutes of the Evidence Recorded.

[39] R. Kumar (ed.), *Essays on Gandhian Politics, The Rowlatt Satyagraha of 1919* (Oxford, 1971), p. 342.

[40] According to Chokhany, Birla himself proposed his own name. However, it is difficult to find any evidence to confirm this view which may be biased. R. Nevatia, *Shri Ramdev Chokhany*, pp. 135–6.

[41] *Ibid*, p. 35.

[42] The other office bearers were Onkar Mull Jatia as president and Badridas Goenka, Ramdev Chokhany and Ram Chandra Poddar as vice-presidents. 'There has been a rich infusion of young blood in the Committee of the Marwari Association. Sir Onkar Mull

Jatia is the new President and Mr Ramdev Chokhany Vice-President. The son of Hari Ram Goenka is a member of the Committee. And there is the inevitable Mr D.P. Khaitan as Honorary Secretary. Such a phalanx of talent and determination should be able to make the Government sit up and take notice. How much longer is the Alsatia of Burra Bazaar to be allowed to disgrace the Queen of the Eastern seas.' *Capital*, 29 March 1923.

[43] The Maheshwari Mahasabha had been founded in 1914, and Jugalkishore Birla and Mohta were its chief patrons.

[44] According to Baldeodas' biographer, the alliance of Rameshwardas was an attempt to take a reformist stand. Barua, *Raja Baldeodas Birla*, p. 92.

[45] The conflict engulfed the entire community, not only in Bara Bazaar, but all over north India. 'No one could be left unaffected. Members of the community were forced to align with one section or the other.'

[46] A publication of the Didu Maheshwari Mahapanchayat, the *Maheshwari Bandhu* gives the list of anti-Birla leaders. Its 48th number, published on 21 February 1926 contains evidence by religious scholars against the reformists claims about the Kolwars. It also contains cartoons which ridicule the reformers and the Birlas in particular. Some of these cartoons are included by Timberg in *The Marwaris*.

[47] According to *Maheshwari Bandhu*, Rameshwardas replied to this invitation by replying: 'We have purposely had an alliance with the Kolwars. The *Samaj* may do what it pleases. I am not concerned about the *Samaj*,' Rampratap Daga 'Vartman Andolan Par Spasht Vichar' in *Maheshwari Bandhu*, 21 February 1926.

[48] D.P. Sharma, *Desh Bhakt Udyog Pravartak Ghanshyamdas Birla*, p. 98.

[49] The Didu Maheshwari Mahapanchayat condemned the 'English pandits' who had taken over the Maheshwari Mahasabha. They proclaimed their own purpose to be 'the purification of the jati, dharma and protecting the community's honour and pride.' The propagation by the Mahapanchayat may have exaggerated the popularity of the excommunication. For the Mahapanchayat's view, see 'Bharatvarshiya Shri Didu Maheshwari Mahapanchayat' in *Maheshwari Bandhu*, 21 February 1926.

[50] C.A. Bayly, *Local Roots of Indian Politics Allahabad 1880–1920* (Oxford, 1975).

[51] M. Vishveswaraya, 'Pandit Madan Mohan Malaviya: Some Personal Reminiscences' in *Malaviya Commemoration Volume–BHU–1932* (Allahabad, 1932), pp. 989–90.

[52] In his minute to the Commission Malaviya had argued 'how Indian industries have suffered in the past by discouragement and ... how vital it is to foster industries on modern lines for the economic upliftment of the country,' *ibid*. Malaviya's minute was lauded 'as the true Indian view of the industrial needs of the country'. Also see Madan Mohan Malaviya 'Note on the report of the Indian Industrial Commission' in *Speeches and Writings of Pandit Madan Mohan Malaviya* (n.p., n.d.), pp. 269–493.

[53] Malaviya to Birla, 12 Samvat 1981, Birla Papers, Series Very Very Important Correspondence, File No. 12.

[54] The cartoons were first published in the *Maheshwari Bandhu* of 21 February 1926.

[55] R.N. Jaju, *G.D. Birla. A Biography*, p. 82.

[56] 'She is the daughter of a vaishya, not of a shudra ...There are many people in the jati who are with you in this and those who are opposed to you may be so out of jealousy ...You and Kakaji [Baldeodas] should be relaxed about all this', Malaviya to Jugalkishore Birla, 3 July 1924, Birla Papers, Series Very Very Important Correspondence, File No. 12.

[57] The classic statement of this discourse is to be found in Malaviya's 'Prospectus of a Proposed Hindu University for the Promotion of Scientific, Technical and Artistic Education Combined With Religious Instruction and Classical Culture', which was

issued in 1905 from Allahabad and has been reproduced in S.L. Dar and S. Somaskandan, *History of the Banaras Hindu University* (Banaras, 1966).

[58] For recent studies of similar constructions of Hinduism as a homogenized entity, see Vasudha Dalmia and Heinrich von Stietencron (eds) *Representing Hinduism, The Construction of Religious Traditions and National Identity* (New Delhi, 1995), David Ludden (ed.) *Making India Hindu* (Delhi, 1996), and Christophe Jaffrelot, *The Hindu Nationalist Movement and Indian Politics, 1925 to the 1990s* (Delhi, 1996).

[59] Pandit Padam Kant Malaviya, 'Mahamana Malaviya aur Jugalkishore Birla' in D.D. Shastri, *Ek Bindu Ek Sindhu*, p. 68.

[60] *Ibid*, p. 70.

[61] Kanhaiyalal Mishra, 'Varanasi Ko Birlaji Ki Den' in D.D. Shastri, *Ek Bindu Ek Sindhu*, p. 169.

[62] Padam Kant Malaviya, 'Mahamana Malaviya aur Jugalkishore Birla' in *ibid*, p. 70.

[63] For the importance of these sites in the overall landscape of Banaras, see Diana L. Eck, *Banaras, The City of Light* (Princeton, 1984).

[64] *Ibid*, p. 70.

[65] Sundaram and Dar (eds), *Benaras Hindu University 1905–35*, p. 360.

[66] Barua, *Raja Baldeodas Birla*, pp. 113–5.

[67] Durga Das, who was for long editor, recalls in his memoirs *India From Curzon to Nehru and After* (London, 1969), p. 109.

[68] Birla to Malaviya, 21 March 1925, Birla Papers, Series Very Very Important Correspondence, File No. 12.

[69] Malaviya to Birla, 2 August 1925, Birla Papers, Series Very Very Important Correspondence, File No. 12 (emphasis original).

[70] Malaviya to Birla, 2 August 1925, Birla Papers, Series Very Very Important Correspondence, File No. 12.

[71] Malaviya to Birla, 8 August 1925, Birla Papers, Series Very Very Important Correspondence, File No. 12.

[72] 'As you have already spent so much in your attempt to serve the country through the press, I hope you will not mind giving Rs 5000 more for the same cause.' Malaviya to Birla, 8 January 1926, Birla Papers, Series Very Very Important Correspondence, File No. 12.

[73] Birla to Malaviya, 12 January 1926, Birla Papers, Series Very Very Important Correspondence, File No. 12.

[74] Malaviya to Birla, 24 September 1926, Birla Papers, Series Very Very Important Correspondence, File No. 12.

[75] For a study of Lajpat Rai's politics in this phase, see J.S. Dhanki, *Lala Lajpat Rai and Indian Nationalism* (Jalandhar, 1990). The suspension of the Non-cooperation Movement by Gandhi in March 1922 had completely disheartened Lajpat Rai. He 'castigated the Mahatma's blundering tactics, particularly his reliance on the Muslims and his decision at Bardoli, just when his followers hopes were at the highest', cited in Judith Brown, *Gandhi's Rise to Power*, pp. 342–3. He also began to criticize the Congress doctrine of a united Indian nation and contended that the Hindus were a nation in their own right as distinct from the Muslims and other communities. He even went to the extent of saying: 'If the Hindu community does not want to commit Hara Kiri, they must move every nerve to be communally efficient and united', cited in Satya M. Rai, *Legislative Politics and Freedom Struggle in Punjab 1897–1947* (New Delhi, 1984), pp. 123 and 177.

[76] Although an all-India politician, Lajpat Rai's political base was in the Punjab. He was a key figure in the revival of the Punjab Hindu Sabha which provided the 'rallying point for a multitude of Hindu revivalist groups; the Shuddhi Sabha, the Arya Samaj and the orthodox Sanathan Dharma Sabha.' Mushirul Hasan, 'Communalism in the Provinces: A Case Study of Bengal and the Punjab' in Mushirul Hasan (ed.), *Communal and Pan Islamic Trends in Colonial India* (New Delhi, 1985), p. 273.

[77] Initially, the training of 100 volunteers was proposed, each of whom was to be paid Rs 25 to Rs 50 for three to six months and then sent to the field. Volunteers were eventually to be recruited from among the depressed classes themselves. Lajpat Rai was critical of others working with similar aims, who 'take too many schemes in hand, make all schemes very big and take too much time to come to decisions.' In this category, he placed Malaviya whom he criticized for his 'dilatoriness' and for 'devoting all the monies and all the time' for the Banaras Hindu University, while ignoring 'important' practical problems.

[78] Lajpat Rai to Birla, 30 December 1923, Birla Papers, Series Important Files II, File No. L–7.

[79] In many ways Birla's analysis of Lajpat Rai's political differences with Gandhi in the early 1920s echoed his own political ideas. Over the debates on Gandhi's programme for non-cooperation, Lajpat Rai had till the Nagpur Congress in December 1920 supported C.R. Das. It was later said that 'Lajpat Rai was forced into this position by the Punjabi delegates who urged him to support Gandhi or imperil his position of provincial leadership.' See Judith Brown, *Gandhi's Rise to Power*, p. 295.

[80] Since steamer tickets had to be purchased in Bombay Lajpat Rai sent a wire to Birla Bros, Bombay to 'pay the passage money (return) for the two passages.' For Lajpat Rai, the alliance with the Birlas was an extension of his well-formed political constituency of commercial groups of traders, money-lenders and urban educated groups in the Punjab. The middle classes which formed the back bone of the Arya Samaj in the Punjab had belonged predominantly to the commercial castes of Khattris, Aroras and Banias. A revealing index of this is the composition of the Managing Committee of the DAV College, the premier institution of the Arya Samaj. Of the 25 members, 18 had the prefix of 'Lala' showing their Khattri origins. S. Bhatia, *Social Change and Politics in Punjab, 1898–1910* (New Delhi, 1987). Also see Kenneth Jones, *Arya Dharma: Hindu Consciousness in 19th Century Punjab* (California, 1976) and Nina Puri, *Political Elite and Society in the Punjab* (Delhi, 1985).

[81] Lajpat Rai to Birla, 14 March 1924, Birla Papers, Series II, File No. L–7.

[82] Lajpat Rai to Birla, 5 September 1926, Birla Papers, Series II, File No. L–7.

[83] It is difficult to ascertain the nature of Lajpat Rai's involvement with the Akali movement. Lajpat Rai visited the Nanakana Sahib Gurudwara in 1921 to express sympathy with the Akalis. In 1924 he again supported the cause of the Akalis over the Jaito incident in Nabha state, Mohinder Singh, 'The Congress and Nationalist Sikh Politics', in B.N. Pandey (ed.), *A Centenary History of the Indian National Congress*, pp. 353–407.

[84] Lajpat Rai to Birla, 14 March 1924, Birla Papers, Series II, File No. L–7.

[85] Lajpat Rai to Birla n.d., Birla Papers, Series II, File No. L–7. The School, founded by Lajpat Rai in 1920 after his return from America, was modelled on the New York Rand School of Sociology by which Rai was very impressed.

[86] Lajpat Rai to Birla, 29 November 1927, Birla Papers, Series II, File No. L–7.

[87] Lajpat Rai to Birla, 6 October 1927, Birla Papers, Series II, File No. L–7.

[88] Lajpat Rai to Birla, 13 October 1927, 15 October 1927, 22 November 1927 and 6 October 1927, in Birla Papers, Series II, File No. L–7.

[89] *Hindustan Times*, editorial 4 January 1928.

[90] Besides helping with the costs of the book, Birla took a keen interest in its production. He found the cover of *Unhappy India* 'very hideous'. Charlie Andrews also agreed that the cover needed to be changed. The original cover depicted photographs of lynching of Negroes in America. Birla wrote to Rai: 'You are quite correct in condemning the hideous crime of lynching Negroes which had been perpetrated by the so-called Whitemen in America. But I think it will do no good if such photographs are given prominence.' Birla believed that 'being a very weak nation we cannot afford to retaliate; our weapon should be only persuasion.' Birla to Lajpat Rai, 5 May 1928, Birla Papers, Series II, File No. L–7. His intervention had the desired effect and the cover was withdrawn.

[91] Lajpat Rai to Birla, 14 April 1926, Birla Papers, Series II, File No. L–7.

[92] Birla to Lajpat Rai, 10 October 1927, Birla Papers, Series II, File No. L–7.

[93] A donation was required by Lajpat Rai for 're-establishing' himself with the 'Hindu community of Lahore' by redeeming a promise he had made during the 1926 elections. He had promised to raise Rs 10,000 for promoting the cause of physical training among the Hindus. Lajpat Rai to Birla, 28 July 1928, Birla Papers, Series II, File No. L–7. Later he felt 'upset by people charging me with failure to keep a promise made in election days.' Birla to Lajpat Rai, 21 July 1928, Birla Papers, Series II, File No. L–7. At first, Birla felt that the two 'might probably have a discussion before we actually paid,' but later he paid up: 'I will abide by your instruction in any case,' he wrote. Birla to Lajpat Rai, 16 July 1928, Birla Papers, Series II, File No. L–7.

[94] Birla to Lajpat Rai, n.d., Publicly acknowledging their generosity he complimented the Birlas during a CLA debate in 1928 in the following terms: 'I know of one Hindu individual who has been spending in the last five or six years from Rs 15,000 to 25,000 a month on the education of the depressed classes and that is the elder brother (Shri Jugalkishore) of my friend Mr G.D. Birla.' *Central Legislative Assembly Debates*, Vol. I, No. 15, p. 693, 23 February 1928, cited in *Shradhanjali Swaragiya Jugalkishore Birla* (n.d., n.p.).

[95] *Hindustan Times*, 1 March 1927.

[96] B.R. Nanda, *The Nehrus* (London, 1962), p. 207.

[97] In the CLA, the Swarajists were elected from 45 of the total 104 elected seats in a house of 145. In the provinces their success varied. In UP they won every seat wherever they opposed a Liberal candidate; in Bombay out of 43 non-Muslim seats they won 23; in the Central provinces out of 114 seats open to general and special constituencies they won 45 seats. In Madras they won only a few seats and in Punjab, Bihar and Orissa they fared very poorly. S.R. Bakshi, *Swaraj Party and the Indian National Congress* (New Delhi, 1985), p. 72.

[98] Satya M. Rai, *Legislative Politics and Freedom Struggle in Punjab*, p. 130.

[99] For a general background, see Richard Gordon, 'The Hindu Mahasabha and the Indian National Congress, 1915 to 1926' in *Modern Asian Studies*, Vol. 9, No. 2 (1975), pp. 145–203.

[100] See B.R. Nanda, *The Nehrus*.

[101] B.R. Nanda, 'The Swarajist Interlude' B.N. Pandey (ed.), *A Centenary History of the Indian National Congress*, Vol. II, pp. 112–61.

[102] C.A. Bayly, *Local Roots of Indian Politics*, p. 215.

[103] Birla to Lajpat Rai, 27 October 1925, Birla Papers, Series II, File No. L–7.

[104] Lajpat Rai to Birla, 14 September 1926, Birla Papers, Series II, File No. L–7.

[105] Malaviya wired to Birla that: 'Meeting of select members of our party here on 18th and 19th to discuss and lay down programme and policy for the Assembly and for provincial Councils. Hope you'll attend.' Malaviya to Birla, 11 December 1926, Birla Papers, Series Very Very Important Correspondence, File No. 12.

[106] S.L. Gupta, *Pandit Madan Mohan Malaviya A Socio-Political Study* (Allahabad, 1978), p. 218.

[107] Lajpat Rai to Birla, 5 September 1926, Birla Papers, Series II, File No. L–7.

[108] Birla to Lajpat Rai, 8 October 1926, Birla Papers, Series II, File No. L–7.

[109] He wrote to Malaviya: 'I read a statement in the press to the effect that the members of the Independent Congress Party in UP are pressing you to contest the same seat as Pandit Motilal is expected to stand for in the coming elections to the Legislative Assembly .... I would beg you not to follow the advice of your friends in this matter, as in my judgement the country needs both of you in the Legislative Assembly. As for myself I think I can take care of myself. I do not believe in the doctrine of retaliation.' Lajpat Rai to Malaviya, 14 October 1926, cited in J.S. Dhanki, *Lala Lajpat Rai and Indian Nationalism*, p. 312.

[110] As he wrote to Lajpat Rai in August 1926: 'Unless a seat is guaranteed to me from any province I won't stand' and asked him not to 'trouble yourself over the matter if you think you cannot do much.' Birla to Lajpat Rai, 27 August 1926, Birla Papers, Series II, File No. L–7.

[111] Lajpat Rai to Birla, 24 October 1925, Birla Papers, Series II, File No. L–7.

[112] Sri Prakasa to Birla, 21 August 1926, in G.D. Birla, *Bapu A Unique Association* (Bombay, 1977), Vol. I, pp. 53–4.

[113] According to J.T.F. Jordens, Shradhanand was initially reluctant to campaign for Birla as he had been out of politics for some years and because his own son, Indra, was supporting the Congress. But Birla's personality appealed to the Swami and he agreed to campaign for him as a person rather than for his party. Jordens points out that there were two considerations which impelled Shradhanand to support an ICP candidate. 'His gesture was one way of publicly reiterating his disapproval of the Mahasabha entering the arena of politics, and of reaffirming his conviction that the Congress policy of reconciliation with the Muslims spelled disaster for the Hindu cause.' J.T.F. Jordens, *Swami Shradhanand His Life and Causes* (Delhi, 1981), pp. 165–6.

[114] Malaviya to Birla, 17 September 1926, Birla Papers, Series Very Very Important Correspondence, File No. 12.

[115] Lajpat Rai to Birla, 16 September 1926, Birla Papers, Series II, File No. L–7.

[116] Jordens, *Swami Shradhanand*, p. 165. For Birla's views on *Hindu sangathan*, also see G.D. Birla, 'Quo Vadis?' in L.N. Birla (ed.), *Birla Park Annual 1928* (Calcutta, 1928).

[117] Birla to Lajpat Rai, 8 October 1926, Birla Papers, Series II, File No. L–7. Writing about this Birla later recalled: 'When I was made a candidate I did not know that I was jumping into a fight. This I realised afterwards. I even thought of withdrawing but being caught in this it was very difficult to withdraw.' See Birla Papers, Series Miscellaneous, File No. 123.

[118] P.D. Reeves, B.D. Graham, J.M. Goodman (eds), *A Handbook of Elections in Uttar Pradesh, 1920–51* (New Delhi, 1975), p. 34

[119] Durga Das, the journalist, recalls in his memoirs: 'When I met Motilal after the elections he confessed that his nominees had been worsted because the question of cow

slaughter had been dragged into the campaign by rival parties and he himself had been denounced as a beef-eater.' *Ibid*, p. 123. Also see Motilal Nehru to Jawaharlal Nehru, 2 December 1926, in *A Bunch of Old Letters: written mostly to Jawaharlal Nehru and some written by him* (Bombay, 1958), pp. 51–2. Motilal complained to Jawaharlal: 'Publicly I was denounced as an anti-Hindu and pro-Mohammadan but privately almost every individual voter was told that I was a beef eater in league with the Muslims to legalise cow slaughter in public places at all times.'

[120] Although it is difficult to ascertain his exact contributions, there is evidence that his contribution was considerable. For instance, in September 1926 he provided Malaviya with Rs 10,000 which he needed urgently and in December when Malaviya needed another Rs 5000 to meet his overdraft from the bank and Rs 7000 to 'pay certain dues' for the daily *Abhyudaya* for the next two or three months, Birla provided these. In December 1926, Malaviya wanted a further Rs 12,000 for the ICP: 'You have helped the party so generously and spent so much on your own election, that I feel it wrong to ask you for any further contribution just now,' he wrote, yet made his request even so. Malaviya to Birla, 17 December 1926, Birla Papers, Series Very Very Important Correspondence, File No. 12.

[121] Malaviya to Birla, 17 December 1926, Birla Papers, Series Very Very Important Correspondence, File No. 12.

[122] Malaviya to Birla, 17 December 1926, Birla Papers, Series Very Very Important Correspondence, File No. 12.

[123] Birla to Malaviya, 19 December 1926, Birla Papers, Series Very Very Important Correspondence, File No. 12.

[124] Jawaharlal Nehru, *A Bunch of Old Letters*, p. 52.

[125] Durga Das, *India from Curzon to Nehru and After*, p. 123.

[126] Lajpat Rai to Birla, n.d., Birla Papers, Series II, File No. L–7.

[127] Lajpat Rai to Birla, 26 August 1927, Birla Papers, Series II, File No. L–7.

4

'In the Shadow of the Mahatma'

Although throughout the 1920s Birla politically remained very much under the spell of Malaviya and Lajpat Rai, his relationship with Gandhi was evolving alongside. This was happening in a context which was marked, on the one hand, by political fluidity, and on the other, by undercurrents which were to sway the course of events later in the 1930s. While Gandhi's Non-cooperation campaign had established his supremacy over the Congress, it was clear that the phase of agitational politics was over. Nationalist politicians like Lajpat Rai, Malaviya, Motilal Nehru and others were exploring ways of working within the constitutional framework, while trying not to dilute their commitment to Swaraj. Further, there was a growing polarization after the mid-1920s over the communal question. The platform of Hindu–Muslim unity built in the heyday of the Khilafat agitation had collapsed. Both Hindu and Muslim politicians were returning to their respective constituencies, and increasingly adopting sectarian postures. In this fluid context Birla found himself caught in the political undercurrents and came to be associated with several of the important initiatives of this period. Yet, it was his deepening relationship with Gandhi which was perhaps of the greatest consequence, and we must, therefore, turn our attention to this relationship.

Birla had, as we have noted in Chapter 2, first met Gandhi in 1916 when the latter visited Calcutta as the guest of the Marwari community. Birla had, like many others from his community and background, been fascinated by the Mahatma's religious character and traits.[1] However, it was not until the 1920s that he came to know the Mahatma personally. It was only in 1924 that they actually began to correspond with each other. There is no clear evidence about how this came about but we do know that it was sometime in 1921 after the Birlas had contributed Rs 1,00,000 to the Tilak Swaraj Fund. Later in 1924, in response to a request from Bajaj, Birla offered his services to Gandhi. In a letter to Bajaj, he wrote:

I am enmeshed in business. My revered father and elder brother do not like my abandoning business. I do everything to please them. This is also my dharma....However, if any financial help or personal service is required by Mahatmaji I shall be happy to render it. My situation is peculiar; I want one thing and do another.[2]

This was the period when the Birla family was faced with a crisis due to its excommunication by the Calcutta Marwaris as we have seen in Chapter 3. This perhaps led Birla to approach Gandhi. In the fight with the conservatives, Birla tried to win over as many sympathizers as possible. Birla knew quite well that Gandhi enjoyed immense popularity with the younger generation of the Marwaris in Calcutta. Enlisting the moral support of Gandhi in such a situation could help the family immensely. At the height of the trouble over his excommunication, Birla approached Gandhi for moral support and guidance. In the first available letter to Birla dated 7 February 1924, Gandhi seems ambivalent about the help he could offer: 'When both parties are in the wrong, it is difficult to decide which one deserves greater blame. I have, therefore, worked out a simple plan—to do good even to the evil-doer.' He advised the family to adopt an attitude of forbearance. In case his brother and father decided to apologize to the community, he advised Birla to hold firm and not bend to pressure. He wrote reassuringly:

I am sure an attitude of forbearance on your part will prove fruitful ultimately. We all have within us the forces of light and darkness working side by side. Therefore, some mental agony is inevitable. But this need not frighten us. Sustained resistance will defeat the forces of darkness in the end but we must remain confident in our heart of hearts that it is our sacred duty to strengthen the forces of light.[3]

Such lofty advice could not have been of much practical help to the distraught Birla, but nonetheless he felt reassured and wrote back to Gandhi. 'Your letters always contribute to my mental peace.' Thus began a regular correspondence between the two men. Just two months after the first letter, Gandhi acknowledged another letter from Birla: 'Bhai Ghanshyamdas, your letters are pouring in.' He found it difficult to reply to all of them for want of time.[4] In 1924 itself Gandhi wrote 11 letters to Birla The subjects of these letters were wide-ranging. They also reveal that often the two men did not agree on a number of issues.

In a long letter to Gandhi, for example, Birla argued that if people followed the Mahatma's advice on non-violence, they would become incapable of protecting themselves. 'We also see,' he explained, 'that those who were converted to Islam by resort to force 200 years ago had been full of hatred for their tormentors then, but they are now as good Muslims as those hailing from Arabia and Iran. This only goes to prove that it is possible to proselytize forcibly.' Birla confessed that he often doubted his own belief in the concept of non-violence. He also acknowledged that he often found it difficult to understand the complexities of Gandhi's teachings and doubts continued to plague him. 'I have no doubt, whatever, in my mind that non-violence is something worth attaining. But, supposing somebody kills another for the good of society, will that be an act of violence? We are told through dramatized allegory that an act done without passion falls in the category of inaction.'[5]

At the level of practical politics too, there were marked differences. For instance, Birla raised with Gandhi the question of absolving the Swarajya Party of the charge of acquiring office. The Swarajya Party had been formed by C.R. Das and Motilal Nehru to advocate council-entry, in opposition to Gandhi's own scheme of boycott of legislatures. He told Gandhi that he thought Sarojini Naidu was not a suitable candidate for the Congress presidentship. Gandhi assured him that he would do full justice to his complaints about the Swarajya Party if he was furnished with proof. On the second charge, he stood his ground and argued that Sarojini Naidu was a very capable leader. Along with these discussions were others on non-violence, *shuddhi* and the Swarajya Party and often the two disagreed. As they grew closer, Gandhi also offered his characteristic dietary recommendations. He asked Birla, for instance, to 'take milk for at least 15 days if you like. Take fruit, but no bread. Make it your habit to take buttermilk'.[6]

Despite their differences, a measure of affection and intimacy seems to have developed quite early between the two. The attraction and awe with which Birla held the Mahatma made him increasingly believe that 'he must somehow be right in a sense that I could not grasp'.[7] Barely six months after their first letters had been exchanged, Birla signed his letter 'Yours affectionately'. Gandhi also reciprocated fully. He wrote: 'God has given me mentors, and I regard you as one of them. Among them are some of my own children, some sisters and some others like yourself and Jamnalalji who are grown-ups'.[8] The measure of intimacy that developed in such a short time is somewhat surprising.

Throughout 1925 Gandhi wrote on average one letter every fortnight to Birla. In late 1925 Gandhi requested Birla to send a donation of Rs 50,000 to the Aligarh Muslim University.[9] This put Birla in a difficult position. If he donated money to a Muslim cause he would face opposition from two sources— from Malaviya who was involved in fund-raising for the BHU and from his own family elders who would object to such a large donation to a Muslim institution. It was easier for Birla to explain the situation to Malaviya. To him, he confided that the only reason he was giving in to Gandhi's demand was because of the difficulty of refusing when 'one of the world's greatest men comes begging to the door'. Birla found it more difficult to face the opposition from his family. So he obtained a promise from Gandhi that his name as a donor would be kept anonymous, so that they should not hear of it.[10] The Hindu–Muslim issue was one on which Birla disagreed with Gandhi and it cropped up repeatedly in their later discussions. Birla empathized with the views of Malaviya and Swami Shraddhanand, the Arya Samaj leader, and wanted Gandhi to work closely with them in finding a solution to the communal problem.[11]

Thereafter, throughout 1926, Gandhi wrote to Birla on an average of one letter every fortnight in which they discussed various matters. In June 1926, when Birla asked for advice on his desire to contest for the Central Legislative Assembly, Gandhi frankly responded: 'What can I say about the question of

Council-entry? I have fundamental differences with Pujya Malaviyaji on this count. The only thing I can usefully say in regard to this matter is that if you believe that some public good is achievable through council entry, you should go there as a matter of course'.[12] However, Gandhi did not impose his own views on Birla but rather assured him that he would not stand in his way. He wrote:

If you are harbouring the notion that you have given me a pledge not to enter the Council, you must get rid of it. No such ban was ever decided upon. You should consider yourself free of any such inhibition and decide upon entering the Council purely from the operational, i.e. moral point of view.[13]

At the same time Gandhi gently tried to influence Birla by advising him that the matter could be left till the elections and even suggested that he could get out of it on the grounds of ill health which could come as a 'blessing in disguise.' To Gandhi, Birla's electoral success was merely another political battle. Though he refused to comment on it, he advised Birla to be watchful of the proceedings in the Assembly and not submit to any pressures.[14] Birla followed Gandhi's advice when, in 1926, he was offered a knighthood by the Government of India. He refused to accept it, which immensely pleased Gandhi: 'You have declined to accept a title. This I liked very much indeed. This refusal to accept a title does not mean that we treat the Government as our enemy, nor that titles are bad in themselves, though I for one consider them bad in our present condition.'[15] Yet the occasions when he followed the advice of the Mahatma on political matters were rare in the 1920s, and it was only later that he became much closer to Gandhi on public issues. Their relationship was much more of a guru and a disciple as far as spiritual and personal matters were concerned. In politics they continued to differ. In these years while making his political views known, Gandhi allowed Birla to choose his own path and made no demands on Birla's allegiance. Though Birla repeatedly went back to Gandhi for advice, he took his own decisions and followed his own independent counsel.[16] Yet, Birla respected him immensely and his faith in him was growing. Reflecting on his early relationship with the Mahatma, he later wrote:

There was not much in common between us so far as our mode of life went. Gandhiji was a saintly person who had renounced all the comforts and luxuries of life...His outlook on economics, however, was different. He believed in small-scale industries—*charkha*, *ghani* and all that. I, on the other hand, led a fairly comfortable life and believed in the industrialization of the country through large-scale industries. How then did we come to have such a close association? Why did I continue to inspire his trust and affection? I should attribute this mainly to his greatness and generosity. I have not come across many men possessing the charm, the affection and the devotion to their friends that Gandhiji had. A saint is not very difficult for the world to produce and political leaders are put forth in plenty, but real men are not to be found in abundance on this earth. Gandhiji was a man among men—a rare specimen not produced by the world even once in a century. And yet people have known so little of him as a man. The result was that, although I did not agree with him on many problems, I never refused to obey his wishes.

For his part, he not only tolerated my independence of thought, but loved me all the more for it, as a father would his child.

A TRAGEDY

Just when his political career seemed to be on the upswing and he was growing closer to several important figures in Indian politics, Birla faced one of his greatest personal challenges. Soon after the birth of their youngest daughter, Shantidevi, in 1924, Mahadevi developed tuberculosis. She had to spend part of the year in a cool climate and Birla moved her and the children to Solan, a hill station where he rented two houses. He spent as much time as he could with her and the family. Malaviya found a 'guardian tutor' to care for the children that would give Mahadevi some rest. The deterioration in her condition was rather rapid and she was moved to Delhi to be under constant medical attention. In these trying times, Birla turned for emotional support to Gandhi who did not hesitate to offer advice even on intimate matters. Gandhi made dietary suggestions and, more significantly, advised Birla to develop himself spiritually to face the daunting challenge. Repeatedly chanting God's name, the Mahatma told him, would give him the 'strength to be free from passions'. To help him take his mind off his problems, Gandhi personally chose a charkha for him to ply.[17]

Gandhi took time to visit the ailing Mahadevi. On one of his journeys, he stopped at Delhi and drove with Birla to Okhla, 15 miles away where Mahadevi had been taken. This visit meant a great deal to both Mahadevi and Birla, given the spiritual aura with which they saw Gandhi and the deepening religious character of their relationship with him. 'Now that you have come, I am satisfied. ...I was very keen to have your *darshan*. Now that my last wish has been fulfilled, I shall die in peace', Mahadevi is reported to have said to the Mahatma.[18] Gandhi prayed for her and blessed her. It was clear that Mahadevi's end was near and Gandhi wanted Birla to take a vow in front of her that he would not marry again.[19] Whether Birla followed Gandhi's advice is not known. Birla turned to all he could as it became clear that Mahadevi's condition was not improving. He leaned towards Malaviya for emotional strength. He desired Malaviya's darshan in the hope that his 'blessings might still make her recover'. He craved for Malaviya's company which gave him 'great peace of mind'.[20] Unfortunately, Mahadevi did not survive for long after this and passed away in February 1926.

At the age of only 33, Birla became a widower for the second time. Deeply saddened, he put up a brave front. Those around him admired him and thought he bore the calamity with fortitude. However, he was a changed person who refused to enter into any deep emotional attachments after this experience. Years later he confided to a friend that 'from the day Mahadeviji died he never gave another woman a thought. Desire ended with the loss of her'.[21] In the months following her death, he came under considerable pressure from his mother to marry again, in view of his relatively young age and the responsibility of bringing up six young children. So strong was the family pressure on him that his mother sought Malaviya's intervention to persuade him to agree. Malaviya also advised him to obey his mother but Birla remained firm.

Unsure of his ability to play the new role of both parents that was now required of him, Birla made arrangements for the care of the children. The children were still very young—Lakshmi Niwas was the only one who was capable of taking care of himself. He had already been adopted by Jugalkishore who did not have a child of his own. Krishna Kumar and Basant Kumar were just eight and five years old. His daughter, Chandrakala was merely ten years old and Anasuiya just three. The youngest, Shantidevi, was an infant of two.[22] The girls were sent to Bombay under the care of Rameshwardas. Krishna Kumar and Basant Kumar were put under the charge of Braj Mohan in Calcutta. Mahadevi's demise meant an end to the complete family life that Birla had enjoyed after his wife had moved to Calcutta. He was separated from the children. He found that immersing himself in business and public activities was the easiest way to forget the sorrow and loneliness that now surrounded him.[23]

SOJOURN TO THE WEST

Once the family arrangements had been settled, Birla decided to take up an invitation by the Government of India, following a nomination of the FICCI, to attend the Tenth International Labour Conference held at Geneva in May 1927. It had been barely a year since his bereavement and Gandhi saw no advantage in Birla's decision to attend and asked him to stay in India and 'hold your soul in patience'. If the purpose was to gain experience of travelling in Europe, he advised him to go independently but warned: 'My inner voice tells me the present is not the moment for it.' However, once again he left the decision open by adding: 'Do what your inner voice wants you to do'.[24] When he learnt that Birla had taken the decision to go to Europe, Gandhi thoughtfully sent him a list of guidelines to follow while travelling abroad, on behaviour, eating habits and on general instructions for the trip.

Birla saw his nomination to the Geneva Conference as a major step forward by Indian business. So far the government had always made such nominations from European Chambers of Commerce. This practice of excluding Indian capital from such meetings had been strongly criticized by Indian commercial bodies and it was only after repeated protests that an Indian had been chosen to represent Indian employers.[25] Birla's nomination thus marked the end of the European monopoly. Besides Birla, the delegation consisted of V.V. Giri (the labour representative), J. Sethi (adviser to the labour representative) and Sir Atul Chatterjee, the head of the delegation.[26]

Birla's decision to travel abroad and to cross the 'black waters' was seized upon by a section of Calcutta's Marwaris to revive old conservative sentiments against the family. Some Marwaris even approached Raja Baldeodas in Banaras to dissuade Birla from risking the loss of caste. But for Birla the break with the conservative caste groups was complete, and he merely brushed aside their objections.[27] While Birla was reluctant to listen to orthodox members of his own community, he submitted to an 11-point code of conduct which Gandhi laid out for him as 'rules necessary for maintaining good health in foreign countries.' In this code of conduct, Gandhi advised him not to eat unfamiliar food; not to eat more than three times a day or after eight in the evening; to walk six miles daily; to refrain from eating chocolates; to avoid 'mental debauch' that came from being in a foreign country, and to read the Hindu holy texts of the *Gita* and the *Ramayana*.[28] In addition, Gandhi suggested that Birla should meet the Secretary of State for India and, if possible, the British Prime Minister. However, he did not think it advisable for Birla to seek an audience with the King, unless the Secretary of State or the Prime Minister suggested it.[29] Gandhi also felt that it was important for Birla to acquaint himself with the living conditions of the lower classes in England. This could be done, he suggested, by visiting jails and by walking through poor localities. 'Station yourself near the bars in poor as also prosperous localities on Saturday nights for making comparative study', advised Gandhi to the first-time visitor.

Birla set sail on S.S. Rawalpindi in May 1927 with Lajpat Rai, who was going for medical treatment, as his companion.[30] The steamer took them from Bombay to Aden and then to Marseilles where Birla and Lajpat Rai took the train to Geneva. The sea journey gave Birla his first real exposure to European society. His reaction to Europeans, with whom he had only had business dealings so far, was one of shock. The sight of short-haired European women drinking and smoking in public and dancing till the early hours of the morning disturbed him. To Birla, these appeared as symptoms of a hedonistic and self-indulgent society which was heading towards ruin. It made him wonder how, in spite of such decadence, the English ruled over such a large Empire and why India, for all its glorious past and ancient culture, was still subservient to Britain. Much of Birla's thought during the voyage turned on seeking an answer to this question. The answer, he felt, lay in the fact that patriotism was supreme for the English. Indians, by contrast, disguised cowardliness as forgiveness and were 'alien to the concept of a nation, self-rule, public duty and public welfare'. 'Even now', he lamented, 'our people lack any ardent desire for freedom and independence as a nation'.[31] The voyage gave him a respite from his busy schedule and provided an opportunity to contemplate the political situation in India, the nature of British rule, the sacrifices made by political leaders like Gandhi, Lajpat Rai and Malaviya, and the expectations of the Indian masses. He enjoyed long discussions with Lajpat Rai, and his respect for his simplicity and humility grew.[32] During the three and a half months that they spent together, they used to discuss a lot of India's problems and the intimacy between the two grew considerably.

Marseilles, the first port of call, did not impress Birla. He was, however, enthralled by the cathedral of Notre Dame in Paris and it made him wonder why there could not be an equally magnificent temple in London for the Hindu community.[33] The train journey from Marseilles to Geneva brought to him thoughts of home. The view of lush green fields, rich orchards and abundant water turned his thoughts to the plight of the poor Indian farmer, specially in his native Rajasthan. From Geneva he took a long flight to London, his first experience of air travel. He repeatedly chanted God's name and was relieved to feel only a slight dizziness compared to many on board who felt sick. London, a city which later became his favourite summer time retreat, seemed almost like a huge tree nest. Its crowded streets, fast pace of life, smoke and fog did not endear it to him.[34] He was struck by the difference between the governmental system of Britain to the one obtaining in India. He attributed it to the presence of foreign rule in India and the total lack of accountability of the Raj to Indian people.

Meanwhile in Geneva, the Labour Conference, attended by the representatives of 42 countries, commenced its business on 25 May 1927. Sir Atul Chatterjee, the Indian High Commissioner in London, was elected its chairman. Among the key issues on its agenda were sickness insurance, freedom of association for trade unions and the need to evolve machinery to fix minimum wages in unorganized sectors. In his address Birla concentrated on problems facing Indian industry and raised a number of crucial issues. For instance, the Conference had recommended the creation of offices of national correspondents and it was proposed that the International Labour Organization's (ILO) national correspondent in India should be based in Delhi. Birla opposed this, and suggested that the correspondent, if he was to be in touch with labour, must be based in an industrial centre, like Bombay or Calcutta. He believed that the ILO representative should not confine his activities to merely dealings with the government, but should maintain close contact with both labour and capital.[35] He further demanded that the ILO representative should be an Indian. He also proposed that all literature issued by the ILO in India should be in a vernacular language, preferably Hindi.[36] This was a staunchly nationalist stance to take. Birla was, in effect, arguing that European delegates who had been nominated to the Conference so far represented their own narrow interests, rather than that of the entire Indian business community. 'We are all alive to the necessity of representing ourselves through people of our own nationality, and I hope that more will be done in this direction in the future', he declared.[37]

It is significant that during the Conference, Birla and Giri, although representing the divergent interests of capital and labour, worked together. Each emphasized the importance of appointing Indians to represent both capital and labour at the ILO. Both highlighted the difference in the economic conditions between India and the West, and called upon the Conference to address itself specifically to conditions obtaining in developing countries.[38]

After the Conference, Birla left Geneva to join Lajpat Rai in London. There he met a number of 'businessmen, social workers and influential politicians.' He also had a number of business engagements. Unfortunately, no detailed records of these meetings are available. Among the important persons he met were Lord Birkenhead, the Secretary of State for India, and Lord Lytton, a former Governor of Bengal. He also had the privilege of being received by the King. In these meetings he discussed the political situation in India, if he found an opportunity to do so. This visit convinced Birla of the importance of lobbying for India among not only political circles but influential business circles.

In their weeks together in London, Lajpat Rai observed Birla closely and felt towards him almost like 'a father who wants his son to be greater, bigger and better than himself.' He was convinced that Birla had 'the make of a great leader and all the qualities of a really generous one,' provided he changed his manners. He told Birla that he needed to do away with the 'impression of...curtness and abruptness which might induce some people (who do not know you well) to run away with the idea that you are a conceited man.' He wanted him to imbibe the manners of Gandhi who was very particular in his behaviour towards friends and co-workers. Although Birla was very generous, he often left an impression of being an autocrat.[39] Lajpat Rai gently pointed out to Birla that in public life what was needed 'was a different kind of equipment both mental and that of manners from the one which went to make you a successful businessman.'[40]

Their time together convinced Lajpat Rai that Birla should be groomed for the political leadership of the Hindu community. Lajpat Rai believed that 'there are not many men among the Hindus on whom we could desire the mantle of leadership to fall.' What was needed, he said, was 'a reliable Hindu leader who would inspire love and confidence among his colleagues and co-workers to lead the Hindus of North India' and Birla fitted the bill.[41] His keenness to groom Birla for a political role led Lajpat Rai to convince him that, instead of being in Europe, he should be in India where the CLA was in session. Although Birla's business interests were important, because they 'supply the sinews of war', nonetheless, Lajpat Rai argued, having 'entered politics you cannot neglect political issues.' The CLA session would be important for India in general and Indian trade and industries in particular and his 'influence among Indian businessmen' would be crucial at such a stage.

Lajpat Rai wanted Birla to take a more active political role. He considered it to be 'absolutely necessary for you to become an All-India man.' Impressing upon him the importance of his future role as a politician, Lajpat Rai wrote: 'I have my eyes on you and Jayakar for the future leadership of the Hindus in politics and I wish you to address some public meetings in all provinces.'[42] On his part Birla reassured him that the ICP was in very good position, as it had the greatest advantage of having the best of all the sensible men. Following Lajpat Rai's advice, Birla returned to India in time for the CLA session.

Birla's five-month stay in Europe left a strong impression on him. But it did not significantly influence either his lifestyle or his values.[43] He followed his strict vegetarian habits and remained a teetotaller. In fact, he strictly adhered to the 11-point regime prescribed by Gandhi. Thereafter, he became a regular visitor to England as he discovered the importance of keeping in contact with British politicians. As we shall see later, establishing this contact with British policy-makers later became an integral part of his public activities. He also became a seasoned traveller, and discovered his love for air travel, which over the years, became the only luxury that he allowed himself in an otherwise austere lifestyle.[44]

INNER PARTY CONFLICTS

On his return from Europe, Birla found to his dismay that the position of his party, the ICP, was in a disarray. The euphoria that had followed its electoral success in 1926 had subsided. The party had joined with other groups like the 'responsive co-operators' and the Hindu Mahasabha to form a loose parliamentary bloc known as the Nationalist Party. This had about 20 legislators, with Lajpat Rai as the president of the bloc and Malaviya its vice-president. However, the Nationalist Party was plagued by lack of unity and discipline. Its members found it difficult to work together, since each functioned as a leader in his own right. The only common bond holding it together was the belief in 'responsive co-operation' and a faith in the need for a common Hindu platform. They were, however, riven by personal jealousies as Birla found out. Both Lajpat Rai and Malaviya had strong disagreements about strategy, future policy and discipline within the party, and these were made worse by their interpersonal conflict. Malaviya often found it difficult to function strictly within the confines of the ICP and wanted greater freedom. Matters came to a head soon after Birla returned from Europe when Malaviya had an interview with the Viceroy on the Reserve Bank Bill without informing his colleagues and without even the approval of the party executive. When he was questioned by other party members, Malaviya asked Birla to intervene. He told Birla that, having never been controlled by a party in the past, he did not wish to be restricted by one now. He explained to Birla that he had no time to attend party meetings, nor did he want to abide by its decisions. He further told Birla that if the ICP wanted to use him, it ought to consult him and try to mould his position. Malaviya admitted that his position might be unreasonable, but he was prepared to resign from the party unless it was accepted.[45]

Birla fully understood the critical importance of Malaviya to the party which had sprung from and been nurtured by the religious movement he had pioneered. He was also aware of the immense political support that Malaviya was capable of mobilizing in northern India. Birla thus believed that Malaviya was central to the party's fortunes and his wishes must, therefore, be fulfilled. He accordingly intervened on behalf of Malaviya and tried to persuade both Lajpat Rai and others asking them to agree to Malaviya's demands. Birla reasoned with Lajpat Rai and others that, 'if we want to utilise the great personality we ought to make ourselves suit his convenience.' Lajpat Rai was pained by Malaviya's position. He retorted that Malaviya's apolitical attitude was creating problems within the party and making it difficult for it to function as a collective body.[46] As a way out of the difficult situation, Lajpat Rai was prepared to surrender the party's leadership to Malaviya. He proposed that 'the party should elect Malaviyaji as its leader. Then perhaps it may be possible for him to persuade the party to follow him in every respect'. It was not just differences between Lajpat Rai and Malaviya but the differences among the others too, that were plaguing the party. Lajpat Rai complained to Birla about how intraparty differences frequently led to open breaches of discipline and how things had come to such a pass that both he and Malaviya were threatening to resign. Birla urged Lajpat Rai to take a more conciliatory view and arranged a meeting between him and Malaviya to sort out their differences. He drew Lajpat Rai's attention to the brighter side of the picture: 'Please do not worry about our party...The greatest advantage to our party is that it has the best of all the sensible men and, therefore, I do not anticipate much difficulty.'[47]

However, the announcement in late 1927 of the appointment of the all-British Simon Commission brought matters to a head. Nationalist opinion across India was outraged at being excluded from this body charged with the task of producing the draft of a future constitution of India. It stirred all shades of political opinion and reinvigorated Indian politics. The ICP was now faced with an internal crisis. It needed to urgently resolve its differences and put up a show of solidarity to meet this new challenge. However, Malaviya and Lajpat Rai once again differed about the strategy their party should follow. Malaviya wanted a total boycott of the Commission, together with a campaign for non-payment of taxes, boycott of British goods and withdrawal from legislatures, accompanied by a constructive programme focusing on educational reform and physical training.[48] Lajpat Rai felt that Malaviya's programme was extreme and impracticable. He told Birla: 'I regret I don't agree with Pandit Malaviya's scheme. To talk of non-payment of taxes in the present atmosphere is nothing more than a bluff. Nor am I in favour of abstaining from the assembly...Let us be practicable and not indulge in bluffs. We should not do anything which is not in our power to make effective.'[49] It was Malaviya's schemes which personally appealed to Birla. He too advocated a complete boycott and agreed that a walk-out from the legislature was necessary. As he told Gandhi: 'Hartals should be observed at every place on the arrival of the Commission and subsequently every town at the time the Commission goes to visit should observe hartal with a huge mass meeting.'[50]

But the overriding concern of Birla was the need for party unity. He wanted his party colleagues to forget old differences and work together to make the boycott a huge success. He urged Malaviya and Lajpat Rai to make the most of the opportunity afforded by the Commission and unite with other political leaders to forge a broad nationalist front. The need of the hour, Birla pleaded, was an effective boycott of the Commission.[51] To Birla it was an opportune moment for Gandhi, Malaviya and Lajpat Rai to come together and evolve a common programme. In an almost desperate tone, he told Lajpat Rai: 'I wish you to think out very carefully and lay down a constructive programme before the people. Gandhiji has got his own programme; he wants to stick to Khadi, removal of untouchability, and Hindu–Muslim unity. You, besides Gandhiji's programme, want to train the young men of India physically. Malaviyaji wants to educate them politically, economically and socially. Now why can't you three unite? I think if you did that you can give a clear lead to the country'.[52] 'It would be a thousand pities', he later wrote, 'if owing to dissentions among the big leaders, India could not pursue a common programme.'[53]

To his frustration however, Birla found that there seemed to be almost irreconcilable differences plaguing the ICP. In a most forthright manner, he told Malaviya: 'What a shame that a party consisting of hardly twenty members should have four different sets of views...Under these circumstances, is it desirable that the Nationalist party should at all exist any longer?'[54] The inability of the top leadership to work together made Birla impatient. He conveyed some of his frustration to Lajpat Rai when he wrote: 'I am really impatient, but unless you big guns move, nothing is possible in this country.'[55] He believed that much of the inertia in the country was due to the political leadership which was 'confused and puzzled' and unable to show a clear direction. Amidst such disunity within his own party, Birla now looked towards Gandhi to whom he wrote:

How I wish the old non cooperation spirit ruled again; but I feel rather nervous as I fear that this momentary effervescence may subside if not properly led. I do not find any single person who can command confidence of all the people. Don't you think that the time for which you have so far waited has come.[56]

The ICP was finally able to put together a common programme after hectic efforts by Birla. Although the party decided not to boycott the legislature, it resolved to participate in all other anti-Commission activities.

The countrywide hartals, black flags demonstrations and mass meetings in early February 1928 against the Commission excited Birla. Commenting on a disturbance at Madras where the police opened fire on crowds in which two persons were killed, he wrote: 'It was a pity that there was a disturbance at Madras. But such things are inevitable. They should not deter the leaders of the boycott from preaching hartal on such occasions in future. What other alternative have we got to give an effective demonstration of our resentment.' It was his conviction that 'any agitation against the Government, since it is always based on justice, can do us no harm.'

During the anti-Simon protests, he generously supported Malaviya and the ICP with funds and placed additional resources at the party's disposal to meet the situation. Money earmarked for activities such as the scout movement was channelled into political propaganda against the Simon Commission.[57] Large sums for propaganda were provided at Malaviya's request. For instance, early in 1928 Birla sent Rs 15,000 in addition to his regular contribution to Malaviya. The scale of Birla's financial support can be seen from the fact that, after six months of regular withdrawals by both Lajpat Rai and Malaviya from the political fund created for the party by Birla, the ICP was still left with over Rs 50,000 in July 1928 for the remaining months of the year.[58]

FORGING NEW POLITICAL LINKS

Alongside the trying task of keeping the ICP together during these difficult months, Birla found himself playing an important role in the deliberations which led to the Nehru Report in 1928 which was an attempt by Indian political parties to produce by consensus a draft constitution for India. His support for the Nehru Report marked a turning point in his political career and was significant for a number of reasons. Birla's experiences of the making of the Nehru Report led him to form strong political convictions as a constitutionalist, a position from which he never swerved. At the same time, his involvement with the Nehru Report led to his abiding conviction in wider nationalist unity to which he was willing to subordinate his personal, staunchly Hindu, sympathies. So far his political career had been nurtured first within the narrow Marwari caste politics, and then within the Hindu nationalist wing of Malaviya and Lajpat Rai. By adopting a strong position on the Nehru Report, Birla showed that he could not be confined by the narrow Hindu sectarianism of his political mentors and had the ability to work independently with secular politicians for constitutional progress.

Birla became involved at an early stage with the making of the Nehru Report. When the Madras Congress of 1927 resolved to sponsor an All-Parties Conference to frame a constitution for India, Birla was elated at this prospect of nationalist solidarity. He persuaded Malaviya and other colleagues of the ICP to join enthusiastically with other leaders in this common enterprise.[59] The All-Parties Conference met in February and May 1928 and Birla took an active interest in its proceedings. He kept close contact with Motilal Nehru, who was given the responsibility of drafting a constitution. He had first made the acquaintance of Motilal Nehru during his election campaign in 1926 when he had opposed Sri Prakasa, the Swarajist candidate who was a personal favourite of Motilal. Although their acquaintance had started with both of them belonging to opposite camps, Birla increasingly impressed Motilal as they came to know each other closely during CLA sessions in Delhi and Simla. His pragmatism and frankness were much to Motilal's liking, in spite of the fact that Birla was perceived as a camp follower of Malaviya, Motilal's traditional rival in UP politics.

It was this perception which led Motilal Nehru to seek Birla's active help in framing his report. Motilal extended a personal invitation to Birla to the May

1928 meeting of his committee. 'I am sure,' he wrote to Birla, 'your presence will be very helpful.'[60] Although Birla did not personally attend the Conference, he played a part in ensuring that both Malaviya and Lajpat Rai fully co-operated with the Nehru Committee. He was infuriated with the Hindu Mahasabha for taking an extreme position on the communal issue which was the main obstacle in evolving a common constitution. 'I am afraid', he wrote to Motilal, 'the...Hindu Mahasabha on the one hand and the reactionary type of Muslims on the other are doing great disservice to the country at present.'[61] In spite of his known Hindu sympathies, Birla was wary of extreme communal positions, especially when they undermined nationalist solidarity and threatened constitutional progress. As he wrote to Motilal:

I am sorry that both the reactionary Hindus and the reactionary Mohamedans are trying their best to put obstacles in the way. But, I think we should go ahead with our plans undaunted. Eventually we are bound to succeed and I hope that both the communities will realise that the best interest of the country lies in mutual cooperation and not in quarrels.[62]

These words of encouragement comforted Motilal. But so strong were the differences on the minority question that they threatened the Committee with a breakdown. The extremist opinions of both the Hindu Mahasabha and a section of Muslims made it difficult to arrive at a consensus. Motilal lamented that few communal leaders were really interested in resolving their differences and forging a united front. 'The truth is,' he confided to Birla, 'that while Swaraj is on everybody's lips there are few who really and earnestly desire it.'[63] During the tedious proceedings, Motilal constantly sought Birla's presence. He saw Birla as being in a unique position to mould the views in the Hindu camp, especially because of his influence over Malaviya to help ensure that 'an ignominious surrender to the reactionary forces now at work is to be avoided.'[64] Motilal pleaded with Birla to come for the final session of the Conference at Lucknow where the Nehru Report was to be formally accepted by all the parties concerned. 'I shall be in sore need of the help of friends like you,' he wrote, 'and i do hope you will come in time.'[65]

On the formal acceptance of the Nehru Report, Birla was well pleased with his ICP colleagues, especially Malaviya.[66] He now decided to offer his whole-hearted support to Motilal in organizing propaganda to popularize the Report. A Central Publicity Bureau with provincial bodies was set up and Birla provided the main financial support to ensure that the Nehru Report did not languish in political obscurity. Though the Nehru Committee had hoped to elicit Rs 25,000 for propaganda work, the actual funds it possessed were only Rs 2000, contributed equally by Birla and Purshotamdas Thakurdas, the Bombay-based businessman and close personal friend of Birla.[67] Funds were badly needed for provincial propaganda committees, to organize tours of committee members and for printing and distribution. Motilal turned to Birla for help with an estimated expenditure of Rs 30,000 to 40,000.[68] Birla responded and promptly sent Rs 15,000. Placing the funds entirely at Motilal's disposal for allocation to provincial committees, he made it clear that he did not want to deal with other leaders involved in publicity and would rather deal with Motilal only.[69] His financial support for the Report's propaganda continued till he heard that sufficient publicity had been undertaken and funds were needed no more.[70]

The making of the Nehru Report saw Birla functioning in a completely new political context. The possibilities which seemed to open up in 1927–8 for constitutional advance enthused Birla. They enabled him to resolve an internal conflict between his faith in the sectarian Hindu ICP, in which his political career had been reared, on the one hand, and on the other hand, his growing belief in the efficacy of constitutionalism, in favour of the latter. He showed flexibility on the communal issue and was impatient with the extreme positions of Hindu nationalist politicians, which he increasingly described in these years as reactionary. More significantly, he showed an ability to overcome the sectarianism of party politics and to work with all-India politicians like Motilal Nehru, as he was convinced that this would best promote the nationalist interest. But, above all, he now developed a deep and growing frustration with the restrictive nature of Hindu nationalist politics, of the puritan Arya Samaj and Hindu Mahasabha type, and its more political variant in the ICP.[71]

DISILLUSION WITH POLITICS

Birla's growing disillusion with the ICP was hastened by the unexpected death of Lajpat Rai in November 1928. It was widely believed that Lajpat Rai had died a martyr's death two weeks after receiving lathi blows while leading an anti-Simon demonstration.[71] Birla was stunned to hear of his death. In a press statement, he paid glowing tributes to his early mentor:

The country loses in him a man of transcendental patriotism who made untold sacrifices in its cause. It was my proud privilege in recent years to count myself as one of his followers in the Assembly and outside, but politics was not the only tie that bound him to me. I mourn today the loss of one who was to me more an affectionate elder than a political guide and mine is a personal loss whose extent I can ill calculate.[72]

In spite of their growing differences, Birla and Lajpat Rai had come closer in their personal relations in the last phase of Rai's life. In these years Lajpat Rai had become prone to bouts of depression and often confided in Birla whom he had begun to call his 'father confessor'.[73] Lajpat Rai wrote to Birla in July 1928: 'I thought I was committing a sin in passing this lava of pessimism into the ears of a journeyman full of hopes, aspirations and ambitions. Yet I don't know why I am choosing you of all the persons on earth to be my confidante...I am sick of life—both mentally and physically...I have no zest left in me, no go, no desire.'[74] Lajpat Rai showed signs of withdrawal from public activities and wanted to curtail his needs and expenses. He felt guilty that he had raised his standard of living at the expense of friends like Birla, and resolved 'to reduce my wants and my cost of living. The first thing to do away with is the motor car. The car which I possess is yours and I wish to return it to you.'[75]

With Lajpat Rai dead, Birla plunged into raising funds to commemorate him. Along with Malaviya and prominent Congress leader M.A. Ansari, he launched an appeal for the Lajpat Rai Memorial Fund in January 1929.[76] The appeal was supported by Gandhi and Birla himself became the treasurer. In less than a year, over Rs 2,00,000 were collected.[77] His efforts ensured that some of the institutions founded by Lajpat Rai were put on a sound financial basis, which he regarded as a lasting tribute to the departed leader. Lajpat Rai's death marked a crucial landmark in Birla's political career, hastening his break with the ICP, as his differences with Malaviya continued to grow. Their differences on the question of religious freedom and the communal problem had been of long-standing. They came to a head in 1927 when Birla differed sharply with Malaviya over the latter's position on issues such as religious freedom and cow-slaughter. Birla found Malaviya unreasonable and wanted him to distance the ICP from the 'fanatics' of the Hindu Mahasabha. He was of the opinion that the Hindus must recognize the freedom of religion of the Muslims and try to win their goodwill by making concessions on issues such as music-before-mosque and cow-slaughter. Before Lajpat Rai's death he had frankly told him that 'I think you big leaders ought to persuade Hindus to come to reasonable mind. We cannot help our cause if we put up a most unreasonable opposition to the reasonable demands of the Muslims.'[78] Birla's notes of a discussion he had with Malaviya in October 1927 also confirm the strong disagreement between the two over religious freedom.

Such differences increasingly came to the fore in the later 1920s. Birla wanted Hindu politicians to take a pragmatic view and conciliate the Muslims, so that further constitutional progress could be made.[79] More than these differences, what most disillusioned Birla as far as Malaviya was concerned was his actual experience of the functioning of the ICP. He recognized that the ICP, in spite of its extraordinary electoral success and the fact that it boasted leaders with the stature of Lajpat Rai and Malaviya, could never really be anything more than a rump. The intraparty tensions which plagued the ICP and the personal jealousies among its leaders left Birla disillusioned, not only with the party's functioning, but also with his own career as a politician. He was spending too much time resolving inter-personal problems and pushing the leadership to work together. This was a role he clearly did not enjoy. He felt the ICP was a rudderless ship, lurching from crisis to crisis. He also increasingly believed that the politics of both Lajpat Rai and Malaviya were too sectarian to be part of a broader nationalist front. His experience of the making of the Nehru Report convinced him that sectarian communal politics were fundamentally injurious to constitutional progress. In a letter written to Lajpat Rai just before he died, Birla confessed how he had been disappointed by the big leaders. 'I do not at all feel encouraged,' he wrote, 'to take interest in present day politics'.[80]

His drift away from Malaviya and the politics of Hindu nationalism had started even when Lajpat Rai was alive. After Lajpat Rai's death, his differences with Malaviya widened, and after 1928 there is no evidence of any regular correspondence between them. The final break with Malaviya, however, came in 1932 at the Round Table Conference when Malaviya's position on the minorities question differed fundamentally from Gandhi's. Malaviya's extreme position on communal issues such as the opening of temples to the lower castes and the Communal Award further reinforced the breach. In a letter written to Malaviya in 1934 Birla blamed Malaviya for the gulf that existed between them:

I sincerely feel that you took up a very wrong attitude in London, and thereby caused great harm not only to the Hindu–Muslim cause but also to the political cause of India. Had you not taken up this stiff attitude that you took in London, we could have settled the things with the Muslims on better terms than you were prepared to give them in Allahabad. Besides, Mahatmaji would have been saved the great humiliation that was caused to him on account of the failure of the Gandhi committee. It is very unfortunate that on such critical occasions, you take up rather uncompromising attitude. Even now, I feel that you are going to deal a staggering blow to the cause of solidarity... And, I frankly confess that I feel a sort of *dharm sankat* [moral dilemma] in the letter. You know my views fully well. I never concealed them from you. In fact, I went to the extent of even expressing things in a language which with my respect for you should not have been done...In the Assembly, the Communal Award is going to be a regular item on the agenda. There we will want men who can take up the correct attitude towards matters, financial, fiscal and political. And the Hindu Mahasabha crowd whom you are going to include in your party is, I am sure, not out to help ... All the same, you know my regards or rather deep reverence for you. Our relations are no longer those between a political leader and an admirer. I prize myself as one of your pet children...I am, at present, torn between my duty towards you and towards my conscience... I do not know of a man who can take offence at anything that you say. And besides, you know my relations with you. I am one of those who aspire to have your *Ashirwaad* [blessings] in every walk of my life.[81]

Such sentiments reveal how far the two men had drifted apart. After 1932 Birla severed all political links with Malaviya, and the two hardly ever discussed political issues. Nevertheless, a close personal bond remained between the Birla family and Malaviya. Birla's elder brother, Jugalkishore, continued to provide a monthly allowance of Rs 3000 to Malaviya, an arrangement which went back to the early 1920s. Jugalkishore and Baldeodas continued to support Malaviya's religious, educational and social activities relating to the BHU and the Hindu Mahasabha. In fact, the larger part of the Birlas' charities to the BHU were made in the early 1930s, and Birla himself continued to take a personal interest in the University's financial affairs.

NOTES AND REFERENCES

[1] As D.A. Low observes: 'Gandhi himself was a Bania; Indian nationalism's principal figure was one of their own. He was in addition a deeply religious figure. Given the

importance of their religious commitments in the culture and values of these merchant communities, adherence to him accordingly involved not only a political but a religious involvement. This proved to be especially important for the powerful, wealthy and now very extensive Marwari community, which was especially influential in Calcutta. Two of its principal leaders, Birla and Bajaj, soon established highly personal associations with him of a quasi-filial and religious character.' See D.A. Low, 'The forgotten Bania: merchant communities and the Indian National Congress' in his *Eclipse of Empire* (Cambridge, 1991), pp. 101–19.

[2] B.R. Nanda, *In Gandhi's Footsteps*, pp. 326–7.

[3] Gandhi to Birla, 13 May 1924, Birla, *Bapu*, Vol. I, pp. 5–6.

[4] Gandhi to Birla, 21 April 1924, *ibid*, pp. 4–5. Unfortunately, most of Birla's early letters to Gandhi have not been preserved and are not available.

[5] Also see Gandhi to Birla, 23 May 1924, *ibid*, pp. 6–7.

[6] Gandhi to Birla, n.d., *ibid*, p. 15.

[7] Birla, *In the Shadow of the Mahatma*, pp. XV–XVI and 2.

[8] Gandhi to Birla, 20 July 1924, *ibid*, pp. 10–11.

[9] Gandhi confessed that the tensions between the two communities worried him: 'I have been going deep into the Hindu–Muslim question and have been placing increasing reliance on my own conclusions even though the path is strewn with difficulties.' Gandhi to Birla, 22 Jan 1925, Birla, *Bapu*, Vol. I, pp. 19–20.

[10] Gandhi to Birla, 8 March 1925, *ibid*, p. 23.

[11] Gandhi to Birla, 28 July 1925, *ibid.* Also see Gandhi to Birla, 7 August 1925, Birla, *Bapu*, Vol. I, pp. 32–3.

[12] Gandhi to Birla, 8 June 1926, Birla, *Bapu*, Vol. I, pp. 47–8.

[13] Gandhi to Birla, 8 June 1926, *ibid.*

[14] Gandhi to Birla, n.d., *ibid*, p. 60.

[15] Gandhi to Birla, 4 April 1926, Birla, *Bapu*, Vol. I, pp. 43–4.

[16] *Ibid*, p. XV.

[17] Gandhi to Birla, February 1925, 1 February 1925, 30 April 1925, See Birla, *Bapu*, Vol. I, pp. 21–2, also see pp. 20 and 28.

[18] Basant Kumar Birla, *A Rare Legacy. Memoirs of B.K. Birla* (Bombay, 1994), pp. 8–9.

[19] Gandhi to Birla, 30 April 1925, *Ibid*, p. 28. Jaju, *G.D. Birla A Biography*, p. 89.

[20] Birla to Malaviya, 12 October 1925 and 4 September 1925, Birla Papers, Series Very Very Important Correspondence, File No. 12.

[21] Alan Ross, *The Emissary*, p. 45.

[22] Jaju, *G.D. Birla A Biography*, pp. 87–90.

[23] *Ibid*, pp. 90–1.

[24] Gandhi to Birla, October n.d., *ibid*, p. 56.

[25] FICCI, *Silver Jubilee Souvenir 1927–51* (New Delhi, 1952). Also see S.N. Dhyani, *International Labour Organisation and India, In pursuit of Social Justice* (New Delhi, 1977).

[26] V.V. Giri, *My life and times*, Vol. 1 (Madras, 1976). Other members were Sir Louis J. Kershaw and government advisers J.C. Waton and S. Lall. R.P. Paranjpe was later nominated as a substitute for Atul Chatterjee, as the latter was elected President of the Conference. The *Commerce* wrote on 2 July 1927: 'The 10th session of the congregation was unique in two respects. For the first time in its history it was presided over by an Indian—Sir Atul Chatterjee ... Again it was the first time that Indian employers were

represented by an Indian—Mr G.D. Birla—and the entire delegation was, as it should be, predominantly Indian.' The usually pro-European *Capital* observed that in Geneva Birla's 'natural charm of manner will gain him many friends at the conference, but his jejune views on the great labour problem will not cut much ice in this solemn and serious audience.' *Capital*, 21 April 1927. Birla was felicitated upon his nomination by several Indian commercial organizations. Among these were the Indian Chamber of Commerce, the Indian Mining Federation, the Indian Produce Association of Calcutta, the Cotton Brokers Association, the Grain and Seed Brokers Association and the Marwari Association of Bombay, *Hindustan Times*, 16 April 1927. At these functions Birla urged the Indian business community to come together and 'present a united front on occasions which called for united action.' He declared that 'we must learn the value of unity and solidarity' the lack of which 'was the root cause of the country's maladies.' He was enthusiastic about participating in the forthcoming conference, and declared that his aim was to convey that under foreign rule the interests of Indian labour and capital were identical.

[27] Excommunicated in 1924, the Birlas had only recently been accepted back into the community. Among conservative Marwaris, crossing the 'black water' was regarded as inevitably leading to loss of caste. Foreign travel and the excommunication of those who had crossed the seas had caused a split among the Agarwals in Calcutta before World War I. According to Timberg, 'The Maheshwaris did not apparently have a clear line drawn on the issue, though it was one of the numerous points of division between the reform and conservative parties.' Timberg, *The Marwaris*, pp. 73–4. In Chapter 2 we have seen how Baldeodas had intervened in the case of Kaliprasad Khaitan. In 1927 Baldeodas expressed his inability to influence the decision of his son and told the conservatives that he could not interfere with the independent decisions of his son. Barua, *Raja Baldeodas Birla*, p. 97.

[28] Gandhi to Birla, 16 March 1927, Birla, *Bapu*, Vol. I, pp. 65–7.

[29] Gandhi to Birla, 26 May 1927 cited in Birla, *In the Shadow of the Mahatma*, pp. 33–4.

[30] Among others travelling on the steamer were other nominees to the Conference Giri and Sethi, two members of the Agricultural Commission—Sir Gangaram and B.S. Kamat, and the former resident of Jaipur, Colonel Ben, and the Maharaja of Dungarpur. See *Hindustan Times*, 7, 8 and 10 May 1927.

[31] Birla maintained an irregular journal of his impressions during these days. See his 'Desh-Videsh Mein' in Birla, *Bikhre Vicharon Ki Bharoti* (New Delhi, 1978), pp. 239–54. This frame of mind led him into an argument with a British MP about the opposition of Indian business to the Rupee–Sterling ratio, and the role of the British in Hindu–Muslim troubles. Birla strongly differed with the MP and their argument turned acrimonious. See his 'Steamer Mein' in 'Desh-Videsh Mein' in Birla, *Bikhre Vicharon Ki Bharoti*, pp. 239–42.

[32] In his journal he wrote about one of his many discussions with Lajpat Rai: 'We began to discuss the state of our country and reached the conclusion that we were lacking in self sacrifice. Lalaji in a loving gesture raised his hand and said that "in our country there are only two truly great men, Gandhiji and Malaviyaji" ... Lalaji's humility and simplicity won my heart. I said, "Lalaji, after that you are the next." Birla, 'Marseilles Se Geneva', in 'Desh-Videsh Mein' in *Bikhre Vicharon Ki Bharoti*, pp. 247–50.

[33] After visiting the cathedral Birla wrote: 'I see no difference between our temples and this. For me, Jesus in Mary's lap was like Krishna in Yashoda's lap ... With my devotion I derived peace from seeing Jesus in Krishna's incarnation ... I began to wonder why could

there not be one of our temples 50 feet high, as the Notre Dame ... and I realised that a good temple could not be built without 10 lakhs. Understanding the reality I sighed. But then told myself—'Is there God in a temple? God is within you!' *ibid*, p. 247. Interestingly, Birla succeeded in helping realize this vision within a few months. In early 1928 he contributed substantially to a scheme to build a Hindu temple in London and to provide a residence for orthodox Hindu merchants and commercial travellers visiting Britain. The *Hindustan Times* reported that G.D. Birla and Ramgopal Mohta made 'substantial donations.' The Management committee had H.S. Polak, N.S. Sen and M. Bathiya representing Birla. The paper reported: 'A house is now being decorated and furnished in orthodox Indian style and is expected to be ready in April. No definite arrangement hitherto to erect a temple has been made and the necessary sanction of the London City Council has not yet been asked,' *Hindustan Times*, 2 February 1928.

[34] Birla observed: 'Our lagging behind in the race in the world becomes clear on coming here. Planes overhead, cars and trams on the road, the underground rail down beneath—the two to three alternate ways to commute from one place in the city to another; big gardens in the middle of the city, the magnificent buildings, the clean streets; the wealth, intelligence and strength of character—all this can be seen in London, yet London did not appeal to me.' See his 'Bhishan Kai London' in 'Desh-Videsh Mein' in his *Bikhre Vicharon Ki Bharoti*, pp. 250–2.

[35] As Birla argued at the Conference: 'While the appointment of such a correspondent is a move in the right direction, I do not think Delhi is the proper place for his permanent seat. As Delhi is the capital of India, the National correspondent will undoubtedly be able to keep himself in touch with the Government of India, but Delhi is not an industrial centre. The largest industrial centres in India are Calcutta and Bombay, and therefore, if the National Correspondent is to keep in touch with Indian labour, it is only proper that his office should be either in Bombay or in Calcutta.' G.D. Birla's speech at the sixth sitting of the plenary session on 2 June 1927. See *International Labour Conference, Tenth Session, Geneva*, Vol. I, 1927, see the record of proceedings.

[36] The proposal that all literature be issued in Hindi was accepted by the Secretary-General.

[37] After the plenary meeting, the business of the Conference was delegated to three main committees and one Indian delegate was elected to each of these. Birla was drafted on to the Committee on Sickness Insurance, while Giri was nominated to the Committee on Minimum Wages. These were the Committee on Article 408, the Committee on Sickness Insurance and the Committee on Freedom of Insurance and Minimum Wages. Due to the absence of advisers accompanying the Indian delegates and because many of the committee meetings overlapped, the Indian delegates could not be represented on many of the committees. The non-appointment of advisers with the Indian delegates was later raised by Birla in the CLA: 'The delegate who is sent from here is put to great inconvenience for want of suitable advisers to assist him. I had that experience because I was given no advisers when I was sent as the Employers delegate to Geneva with the result that out of at least nine committee meetings I could attend only one committee meeting. One has to work from seven in the morning till seven in the evening, and it is very difficult for one man to attend all the committee meetings and keep himself in touch with the deliberations of all of them ... While the delegate for labour got one adviser and the Government also sent their delegates in full strength, the employers delegate was not provided with even one adviser ... I hope, therefore, that this time, when the Government nominate delegates to the International labour conference, they will bear

this point in mind and see that the full quota is sent to represent India.' 13 March 1928, *Legislative Assembly Debates*, Vol. 4 (Simla, 1928). Birla's suggestion was implemented and the following year advisers were nominated for the employers delegate. In the 1928 session Narottam Morarjee was nominated and his two advisers were R.K. Shanmugham Chetty and D.P. Khaitan, *Commerce*, 14 April 1928.

[38] Birla argued that conditions in India had to be kept in view while drafting legislation; Giri also emphasized the same. At the Conference Giri declared: 'Ungrateful though it may sound to many, I have to draw the attention of this Conference to the fact that ... the International Labour Conference has not devoted that time, energy and attention which it was to be hoped to the investigation and amelioration of conditions ... in countries like India, where the Government is foreign and where the interests of rulers and ruled are at variance and where the workers are not well organised.' *International Labour Conference, Tenth Session, Geneva*, 1927. See the record of the proceedings, pp. 96–7.

[39] Lajpat Rai to Birla, n.d., Birla Papers, Series II, File No. L–7.

[40] Also see Lajpat Rai to Birla, n.d., Birla Papers, Series II, File No. L–7.

[41] Lajpat Rai to Birla, n.d., Birla Papers, Series II, File No. L–7.

[42] Lajpat Rai to Birla, 26 August 1927, Birla Papers, Series II, File No. L–7.

[43] This was in contrast with others like Motilal Nehru who were deeply influenced by the first contact with the West. As B.R. Nanda writes: 'This trip to Europe accelerated Motilal's westernisation. Thorough-going changes ensued, from knives and forks at the dining table to European governesses for the children. To the new influence may be attributed the adoption of "Nehru" as a surname.' B.R. Nanda, *The Nehrus*, p. 40.

[44] 'Perhaps the only indulgence that Birla allows himself is his passion for travel. He is always on the move, travelling within the country in his 25-year-old convertible Dakota DC-3 which has an office and 13 seats, and frequently journeying abroad.' Dilip Thakore, 'A Legend in his Lifetime' in *Business India*, 30 March–12 April 1981. Within a decade and a half of his first journey to Europe, Birla started his own airways.

[45] Birla's, 'Notes on Talk with Malaviyaji', 17 October 1927, Birla Papers, Series Very Very Important Correspondence, File No. 10.

[46] 'I am writing this letter in confidence to you, but it appears to me that it would be extremely difficult for any group of men to work with Panditji. I wish Panditji were to devote himself exclusively to the University affairs which are in a hopeless condition. Even in social matters, he takes up a stand which makes our position ridiculous. It seems to me that we shall have to do something drastic to get out of this ridiculous position ... I have the greatest possible respect and love for Pandit Malaviyaji. I will rather retire from public life than come into clash with him. I am even prepared to resign my seat in the Assembly, but I cannot go on under the present circumstances. My health is being undermined by these worries. I want to have a heart to heart talk with you if you could kindly manage to come to Delhi for one day. I beg of you to come there, for which I shall be very grateful. The fact is that I am very much upset and I want somebody to whom I can open my heart frankly and unreservedly.' Lajpat Rai to Birla, 27 October 1927, Birla Papers, Series II, File No. L–7.

[47] Birla to Lajpat Rai, 30 September 1927, Birla Papers, Series II, File No. L–7.

[48] S.L. Gupta, *Pandit Madan Mohan Malaviya A Socio-Political Study*, pp. 220–2.

[49] Lajpat Rai to Birla, 2 December 1927, Birla Papers, Series II, File No. L–7.

[50] Birla to Lajpat Rai, n.d., Birla Papers, Series II, File No. L–7 and Birla to Gandhi, 8 December 1927, Birla, *Bapu*, Vol. I, p. 75.

[51] Birla to Malaviya, 5 January 1928, Birla Papers, Series Very Very Important Correspondence, File No. 6.

[52] Birla to Lajpat Rai, 2 May 1928, Birla Papers, Series II, File No. L–7.

[53] Birla to Lajpat Rai, 2 December 1927, Birla Papers, Series II, File No. L–7.

[54] Birla to Malaviya, 26 January 1928, Birla Papers, Series Very Very Important Correspondence, File No. 6.

[55] Birla to Lajpat Rai, 2 December 1927, Birla Papers, Series II, File No. L–7.

[56] Birla to Gandhi, 8 December 1927, Birla, *Bapu*, Vol. I, p. 75.

[57] Birla to Malaviya, 25 July 1928, Birla Papers, Series Very Very Important Correspondence, File No. 6.

[58] Birla to Malaviya, 26 January 1928, Birla Papers, Series Very Very Important Correspondence, File No. 6.

[59] Birla to Malaviya, 5 January 1928, Birla Papers, Series Very Very Important Correspondence, File No. 6.

[60] Motilal Nehru to Birla, 8 May 1928 cited in *Nehru Family and Ghanshyamdas Birla* (New Delhi, 1986), pp. 3–4.

[61] Birla to Motilal Nehru, 18 May 1928, *ibid*, p. 7.

[62] Birla to Motilal Nehru, 24 May 1928, *ibid*, pp. 7–8.

[63] Motilal Nehru to Birla, 1 June 1928, *ibid*, p. 8.

[64] Motilal Nehru to Birla, 28 June 1928, *ibid*, pp. 9–10. It is well known that it was due to Malaviya's efforts that the Hindu Mahasabha initially accepted the Nehru Report. S.L. Gupta, *Pandit Madan Mohan Malaviya A Socio-Political Study*, p. 224.

[65] Motilal Nehru to Birla, 19 August 1928 cited in *Nehru Family and Ghanshyamdas Birla*, pp. 11–12. Birla was again unable to attend the conference.

[66] Malaviya to Birla, 19 August 1928, Birla Papers, Series Very Very Important Correspondence, File No. 6.

[67] Motilal Nehru to Birla, 29 September 1928, cited in *Nehru Family and Ghanshyamdas Birla*, pp. 13–14.

[68] Motilal Nehru to Birla, 6 October 1928, *ibid*, p. 15.

[69] Birla to Motilal Nehru, 6 October 1928, *ibid*, pp. 15–16.

[70] Lajpat Rai to Birla, 8 November 1928, Birla Papers, Series II, File No. L–7.

[71] Dhanki, *Lala Lajpat Rai and Indian Nationalism*, pp. 331–41.

[72] The *Hindustan Times* wrote: 'He lived the life of a hero, he died the death of a martyr! A prudent and foreseeing statesman, a man of indomitable courage, a fearless and devoted patriot, a true friend of the poor and the depressed, Lala Lajpat Rai wielded a pen of steel and was gifted with a tongue of fire.'

[73] Lajpat Rai to Birla, 31 July 1928, Birla Papers, Series II, File No. L–7.

[74] Lajpat Rai to G.D. Birla, 12 July 1928 Also see Dhanki, *Lala Lajpat Rai and Indian Nationalism*, p. 341.

[75] Lajpat Rai to Birla, 24 July 1928, Birla Papers, Series II, File No. L–7.

[76] An appeal was launched for Rs 5,00,000. The money was to be distributed to different organizations started by Lajpat Rai. Rs 4,25,000 was to be given to the Servants of Peoples Society, Rs 25,000 for the completion of the Lajpat Rai Hall which was half finished, and Rs 50,000 for the work done by the Society for the uplift of depressed classes. *Hindustan Times* 14 January 1929 and 21 March 1929.

[77] The Hindustan Times played a major role in fund raising. For instance, it wrote on November 1929: 'The 17th of November is a sacred day in the Indian calendar ... On the 17th India will celebrate the death anniversary of Lala Lajpat Rai. There is,

however, no true Indian who can contemplate the coming of this important day without a guilty conscience. In commemoration of his great and varied services to the nation, the nation undertook to collect 5 lakhs of rupees ... Barely 2 lakhs of that sum have been collected. It is the duty of every Indian if he owes any debt of gratitude to the late Lajpat Rai and his services, and if he has any regard for redeeming a national pledge, to strain every nerve to complete the quota of 5 Lakhs before the 17th.' *Hindustan Times*, 13 November 1929.

[78] Birla to Lajpat Rai, 10 October 1927, Birla Papers, Series II, File No. L–7.

[79] To Lajpat Rai, Birla wrote: 'My personal opinion is—whether other fanatic Hindus agree or not—that we must recognize freedom of religion for the slaughter of cows on the one hand and playing of music or slaughter of pigs on the other. If we want to save cows we must depend on the goodwill of the other religionists.' He later wrote: 'I cannot help feeling that we have been most unreasonable in asking for freedom of music while disallowing them freedom in observing their own religious ceremonies.' Birla to Lajpat Rai, 30 September 1927, Birla Papers, Series II, File No. L–7. To Gandhi he wrote: 'I personally think that Hindu–Muslim unity should be based on religious freedom and toleration. This may mean full freedom to Mohammedans to perform Kurbani anywhere within the four wall of the house, of course with due regard to the sense of decency and to the Hindus full freedom to play music before mosques at any time.' Birla to Gandhi, 8 December 1927, Birla, *Bapu*, Vol. I, pp. 74–5.

[80] Birla to Lajpat Rai, 13 November 1928, Birla Papers, Series II, File No. L–7.

[81] Birla to Malaviya, 15 August 1934, Birla Papers, Series Very Very Important Correspondence, File No. 6.

5

The Spokesman of Indian Big Business

As we have seen, Birla's stint in the Central Legislative Assembly (CLA) and his active role within the Independent Congress Party (ICP) had given him a ringside view of Indian political life at its apex. His close relationship with Gandhi acquainted him with top Congress leaders, and within the august chamber of the CLA he came to rub shoulders with the tallest political figures of his time. Yet, he discovered that his temperament and his business commitments were not compatible with the life of a typical politician. He did not see himself joining their ranks, nor did he entertain any grandiose notions of himself as a future political leader. For him this was an important lesson in self-clarification. Yet, these experiences in the political arena did not de-politicize Birla, nor did they diminish his belief in the efficacy of politics. His interest in public affairs continued, although he repositioned himself, away from the political centre-stage, to carve for himself a role as a spokesman of Indian business.

The years 1926 to 1936 saw Birla consolidate his new role as an influential spokesman of Indian big business. He also came to advise the Gandhian wing of the Congress on economic matters, and began to play the role of an emissary between the Mahatma and the British in the late 1930s.

Protagonist of Business Solidarity

The mid-1920s saw Birla emerge in political and business circles as a protagonist of solidarity within Indian big business. From 1925 he devoted considerable energy in attempting to create commercial bodies which brought together Indian business for the first time on an all-India scale. His efforts led directly to the formation, in 1927, of the influential Federation of Indian Chambers of Commerce and Industry (FICCI) which increasingly became the vehicle of the struggle by Indian big business against domination by European capital. His personal experiences first as a broker and then as an upcoming mill-owner in Calcutta's jute industry had instilled in him a missionary zeal to promote the solidarity of indigenous business. His resentment at the racial discrimination he faced from Europeans who dominated the jute trade was deepened when in 1919 he faced the daunting task of launching his jute mill. He found Andrew Yule and Co., the powerful European managing agency, creating many hurdles to stall his plans. Further, his attempts to obtain credit from the presidency banks were thwarted due to the influence of powerful European firms. The last straw was the pervasive influence of the European-controlled Indian Jute Manufacturers' Association (IJMA) which practically controlled all aspects of the industry. The Association enjoyed extraordinary influence with government agencies like the railways, municipalities and the local administration. Although Birla remained undaunted by these obstacles and successfully broke the European monopoly in jute by setting up the first Indian mill, the experience imprinted upon his mind a great sense of injustice. He was later to recall: 'I smarted under these insults, and this created within me a political interest which, from 1912 until today, I have fully maintained.'[1] Such experiences convinced him that economics could not be divorced from politics, and led him to seek the guidance and company of many nationalist leaders.

As Birla expanded his business interests in the 1920s, he increasingly came to realize the formidable influence which the European chambers and commercial bodies enjoyed. He knew that this influence was, to a large extent, due to the strength of their organization. 'The number of the European merchants in this country is much smaller than ours,' he told fellow businessmen, 'but their combination, their unity has secured an influence for them which Indian merchants ought to aspire for.'[2] He well understood that Indian businessmen could advance their interests only if they created an organization which could speak with one voice against the European managing agencies. 'I remember a friend of mine', he observed in a speech before the Indian Industrial and Commercial Congress in 1926, 'who was...the President of the Bengal Chamber of Commerce, remarking a few years back that it was not the Government of India but the Bengal Chamber of Commerce which ruled the country. I have to confess unfortunately that I do not find much untruth in his remarks.'[3] He set about convincing his fellow businessmen of the need for the solidarity of Indian business.

Birla came to articulate with great foresight the needs of Indian business in the changed context of the post-World War I era. The War had loosened the hold of European business over the Indian economy. Indian entrepreneurs had entered European preserves, engineering and other areas catering to the military needs of the state. There had also been a phenomenal growth in the cotton textile industry, which demonstrated that Indian capital was no longer restricted to the older type of mercantile activity but could now compete with European capital. On the political front, the introduction of the Government of India Act of 1919 had opened new arenas for a fight against European capital, since it gave commercial and industrial interests special representation in the expanded legislative councils. Further, the post-War period witnessed a deep polarization of opinion over economic and fiscal policies between Indian and European business. This polarization was epitomized in their attitude to several questions like the protection of Indian industry and the rupee–sterling ratio.

One important public forum where this polarization was apparent was the Indian Fiscal Commission which had been appointed to examine the long-standing demands of Indian businessmen on the issue of protection and to consider the 'question of the desirability of adopting the principle of imperial preference,' that is, preference to British industry. Birla was nominated a member of this Commission to represent Indian business. The Commission disagreed on several fundamental issues and its Indian members, which included Ibrahim Rahimtoola, T.V. Seshagiri Ayyar, Jamnadas Dwarkadas and Narottam Morarjee, signed a note of dissent in which they demanded a policy of unqualified protection.[4] But they were outnumbered and the Commission's report was adopted solely on the recommendation of its European members.[5] It reinforced his view that Indian capital would have to fight for itself as a unified force. He recalled:

Five of us including the President wrote a minute of dissent, differing in their conclusions from the majority consisting of six, mainly because the main recommendation of the latter had been qualified by the condition that protection should be applied with 'discrimination along the lines of the report'...Indians recognised long ago the urgent necessity of giving Protection to their industries, and in the absence of any popular control over the fiscal policy they had to content themselves with propaganda in favour of swadeshi and for the boycott of foreign goods.[6]

To Birla the increasing gulf between British and Indian business was further demonstrated by the government's adamant position on the rupee–sterling ratio question.[7] Indian business, almost unanimously wanted a revision of the exchange rate to favour exports. Birla felt strongly that Indian business needed to fight together on this. In a speech, he declared:

You can see very well how today in spite of four successive good crops that India has had her purchasing power crippled and is at a very low ebb and what misfortune it is that, to add to our misery the Government wants to appreciate the rupee by $12\frac{1}{2}$ ...Gentlemen, I am not a pessimist. I do not wish to alarm you, but I want to put only bare facts before you. Because of the manipulation of exchange, we did not reap the full advantage of the world rise in prices during the war. During the depression we suffered most of all countries...It is better that we took time by the forelock and set about devising ways and means to fight the menace which like the Democles' sword is hanging over your head.[8]

As far as he could see, there was only one solution and it lay in Indian business coming together to form an all-India organization so that their voice could be effectively heard.[9] He now took every opportunity to convince fellow businessmen to pool their resources and present a united front. He called upon them to 'learn... the value of unity and solidarity, the lack of which at present is the root cause of the malady'.[10] He declared that 'our unity in thoughts, words and deeds...will prove to the country as well as the Government that the Indian mercantile community couldn't be so easily ignored'.[11] In his view the need for unity within Indian business was absolutely critical.[12]

The 1920s further aggravated the fears of Indian business and its sense of vulnerability. To begin with, the European chambers of commerce, in an unprecedented show of strength, came together in 1920 to form the Associated Chambers of Commerce of India and Ceylon (ASSOCHAM).[13] The historian Rajat Kanta Ray has suggested that the immediate impetus for the formation of an all-India body by Indian big business came from a 1923 resolution of ASSOCHAM against protection to the steel industry.[14] Alarmed by the activities of ASSOCHAM, Birla tried to convince fellow business colleagues of the need to form an Indian counterpart to ASSOCHAM.[15] For instance, in a letter to Purshotamdas Thakurdas he wrote in 1923:

I have been watching very closely the activities of the Associated Chambers for the past few years, and I feel their strong organisation will be very detrimental to Indian interests if steps are not taken to organise a similar institution of the Indians....If you take the lead, I am sure you will have the whole hearted support from Calcutta, and it would be a great glory to see merchants from all parts of India standing on one platform and putting their well considered and combined views before the Government with a force which will carry greater weight than those of the combined European institutions.[16]

However, Thakurdas and others whom he approached were not enthusiastic about the proposal. After the recent Non-cooperation Movement, many believed that Indian business should remain aloof from politics and utilize the forum provided in the Legislative Assembly.[17] Notwithstanding this lack of interest, Birla persevered in trying to unite Indian big business under an all-India umbrella organization.

This anxiety to start a new forum was, in part, due to Birla's difficulties with his own Marwari Association. As we have seen, Birla had been isolated by 1923 in the internal politics of the Marwari Association and was publicly forced to admit defeat. Moreover, he believed that the Marwari Association was too restricted in its nature and too steeped in tradition to function along the lines of a modern chamber of commerce. Matters within the Association were further complicated by the growing tensions between traders entrenched in the piece-goods market and those that had made the break into industry. These factors contributed to Birla's resolve to form an alternate body. In 1925 after sustained efforts the Indian Chamber of Commerce (ICC) was founded in Calcutta. The two most important persons behind the new body were Birla and his close lieutenant, D.P. Khaitan.

The ICC claimed to represent all interests and all communities.[18] Birla's sense of achievement knew no bounds. The Chamber soon overshadowed older commercial organizations in Bengal such as the Bengali-dominated Bengal National Chamber of Commerce in Calcutta. The ICC had Indian shippers, importers and other mercantile interests within it and on its board were influential and upcoming firms.[19] It set up tribunals to arbitrate in disputes relating to particular trades such as jute, piece-goods, iron and steel, coal and minerals. 'We have got among us industrialists', Birla boasted to the Government of India's Finance Member, Sir Basil Blackett, 'exporters and colliery owners. Similarly we have got among us Hindus, Mohamedans and Parsees. We claim, therefore, to be the premier mercantile body as far as Indian interests are concerned'.[20] So influential did the ICC become that within two years of its foundation, Birla could proudly claim:

The Chamber here is getting very powerful day by day...We are organising Indian trade in Calcutta in every direction, and all the newly-formed associations are getting themselves affiliated to the Indian Chamber of Commerce. A scheme is on foot at present to build an exchange for the Indian trade and commerce in Calcutta. We want to locate all our mercantile bodies in one building of our own. ...The Europeans are getting very jealous of all this. Privately, they are non co-operating with the Marwaris even in business. Of course, we do not mind this.[21]

The growth in membership was rapid and the ICC could within a decade claim corporate affiliation of 18 of the foremost trade associations.[22] Although the ICC could not call itself truly representative of Indian businessmen on an all-India scale, it succeeded in entrenching itself in eastern India where European chambers had been most dominant. Birla recognized its regional limitation and continued to work for the establishment of a truly all-India association.

Meanwhile, other businessmen had also been making efforts to bring Indian big business together into an all-India body, although nothing concrete had emerged by the mid-1920s.[23] In 1927 a conference of different commercial organizations was called and it led to the formation of the Indian Industrial and Commercial Congress (IICC). Its president, prominent Punjab industrialist, Lala Harkrishan Lal, moved a resolution to establish an Indian Associated Chamber of Commerce.[24] Then at a special session of the IICC a resolution was passed proposing the formation of the Federation of Indian Chambers of Commerce and Industry.[25] A formal constitution of the new body was proposed by Bombay businessman Sir Purshotamdas Thakurdas and seconded by B.K. Sarkar.[26] The Federation declared that its primary objective was 'to promote Indian business in matters of inland and foreign trade, transport, industry and manufacture, finance and all other economic subjects'. A feature which distinguished the Federation from previous Indian commercial associations was that it was to be based in the capital Delhi 'to get a proper foothold before the executive at Delhi, so that the claims of Indian commerce and industry would not be at a disadvantage in comparison with those of European interests'.[27]

In its first year about 24 business associations and chambers of commerce joined the Federation.[28] Within five years, however, nearly 45 commercial bodies had become affiliated to FICCI. These included the entire Indian-controlled insurance, shipping, tea, jute, bullion and banking sectors of the economy.[29] Unlike older commercial organizations, FICCI was not confined to any particular region but commanded the affiliation of commercial bodies from all over India, including Burma. It was at the forefront of this formidable network of business organizations that Birla now stood in his capacity as one of the pioneers of FICCI.

IN THE LEGISLATIVE ARENA

When, in 1927, Birla entered the CLA, he found himself in a completely new and unfamiliar environment. He was thrust into the company of some of the most prominent public figures of the country.[30] Among the prominent members on the official benches were Basil Blackett (Finance Member, succeeded in 1929 by George Schuster), Alexander Muddiman (Home Member) and B.N. Mitra (Member for Industries and Labour). The Assembly was presided over by Vithalbhai Patel. The largest single opposition party in the CLA was the Swarajya Party led by Motilal Nehru; they numbered about 40 out of a total of 104 elected members. Then, there was the 20-strong group of Nationalists led by Malaviya and Lajpat Rai. Other political groups were those which functioned around Jinnah's Independent Party and the Central Muslim Party under the leadership of Zulfiqar Ali Khan. Representatives of commerce had a strong presence and included Sir Purshotamdas Thakurdas (Indian Merchants' Chamber, Bombay)[31]; Sir Victor Sassoon (Bombay Millowners' Association— succeeded by Homi Mody in 1928)[32]; Vidya Sagar Pandya (Madras Chamber); Cowasjee Jehangir (Bombay Millowners' Association) and Sir Walter Stuart James (ASSOCHAM).[33] In addition there were several members who had considerable interests in commerce, even though they had been elected on party tickets. Prominent among them were Fazal Ibrahim Rahimtoola,[34] R.K. Shanmugham Chetty,[35] S.N. Haji,[36] and Birla himself.

Once the CLA session started Birla found himself grappling with a variety of new issues. He kept pace with the proceedings but felt most comfortable when economic issues were raised. On political issues he seldom raised any points and just voted following the writ of Lajpat Rai and Malaviya. He increasingly saw his role as an expert in economic affairs. He forged a strong working relationship with Thakurdas and together they took the lead in economic discussions and actively participated in budget debates and important legislation. During the three years he spent in the CLA, he developed a close relationship between big business and the nationalist leadership.

Birla emerged as one of the most important critics of the government's fiscal policies. For instance, in 1927, during the budget session, he argued that the government's budget surplus was illusory and was possible only because of a manipulation of the exchange rate and increased taxation. Budget discussions became a battleground between Birla and his colleagues and officials of the government in their fight over the ratio question. For example, Birla demonstrated how the government, in balancing the 1929 budget, was merely juggling with figures.[37] Birla's forthright criticism of the government's financial policies led him to raise many issues. In particular, he often spoke on the question of protection to Indian industry. 'Let me make it clear', he declared, 'that protection is nothing like a religious creed; it is a philosophy of bread and butter. If we are to impose a tax on our own consumer, if we are to put a burden on the Indian taxpayer, we can do so with justification only in the interest of the truly Indian industries and not in the interest of those industries in which Indians have no interest.'[38]

Birla came to be increasingly recognized for his expertise on the budget and his incisive analysis of fiscal questions as an expert in political circles. In 1929 he was appointed to the Royal Commission on Labour in India as the employers' delegate. The *Capital* remarked that Birla's appointment 'will tear him away now and again from the Legislative Assembly and his absence will be keenly felt by his non-official friends, as it will mean the loss of a prominent member who could offer tough opposition to the Treasury benches by his trenchant and expert criticism of the Government's currency and financial policy.'[39] Similarly, the *Hindustan Times* described him and Thakurdas as 'among the best financial brains on the opposition benches' and 'the most invincible critics of the Budget.'[40] They showed such expertise and skill in critiquing the budget that year after year it became 'a torn and tattered remnant' of the government's proposals.

In those years the CLA was an important policy-making arena. As a legislator Birla came to be involved with the debates and drafting of the Steel Protection Bill of 1927, the Currency Bill of 1927, the Coastal Reservation Bill of 1928 which became a *cause celebre* for Indian shipping and the Cotton Textile (Protection) Bill of March 1930 upon which hinged the fortunes of the large cotton textile industry. The CLA provided an arena for Birla and other business representatives to present their claims for protection, debate the currency question and argue for the 'Indianization of industry'. So effective was their campaign in shaping the industrial and fiscal policies of the Government of India that ASSOCHAM launched a counter campaign to lobby support in the British Parliament against the alleged tendency of the CLA to enact discriminatory legislation.

As a result of his hectic legislative work Birla now spent more time in Simla and Delhi than at home in Calcutta. Initially, during visits to Delhi he stayed with Thakurdas, but in 1928 he built a large house in the new capital's Albuquerque Road. Birla House in Delhi was situated in close proximity to the residences of many of the members of the Viceroy's Council and senior officials. Jugalkishore also moved in and both brothers lived together in Delhi.

With his strong political credentials within the ICP and the pre-eminent position he held in Gandhi's eyes, Birla was able to slowly ensure that Indian politicians within the Assembly took an interest in economic issues. In this he was helped by Thakurdas who too had close ties with politicians. In particular they were able to rally the support of the Swarajya Party led by Motilal Nehru.[41] Together they were very successful in forging a close working relationship with the nationalist leadership within the CLA. They were able to lobby and mobilize wide-ranging support from politicians on a number of economic questions.

The manner in which this close relationship worked is best seen when we consider some of the most important bills. The first such legislation related to the protection of the steel industry. The steel industry in India had been synonymous with the Bombay-based business house of the Tatas and had enjoyed protection since World War I.[42] In 1927 the Government of India introduced a bill to extend this protection for a further period of seven years. However, it also introduced the principle of imperial preference which proposed significantly lower duty for British steel in contrast to imports from other countries. Birla and his business colleagues raised a storm in the Assembly and opposition to imperial preference soon became their battle cry. Birla personally led the campaign, arguing that imperial preference must be opposed tooth and nail. He declared that import duties should be based on the quality of goods, rather than on the country of origin.[43] Birla and Thakurdas successfully rallied the support of nationalist politicians for their position. Although Birla and Thakurdas failed to change the course of the legislation, they succeeded in mobilizing almost the entire political leadership within the CLA. Lajpat Rai was the first to raise his voice against the measure which, he declared, would establish a precedent and would lead to the extension of imperial preference to other industries.[44] Similarly, Motilal Nehru roundly condemned the bill and so vehement was his opposition that it led to uncharitable speculation in the press regarding his close links with the Tatas and about their generous funding of the Swarajists' recent election campaign.[45] The debate on the bill demonstrated the success of Birla and Thakurdas in enlisting the support of a wide range of political leaders on an issue which was basically the concern of a single industrialist. Birla personally had no interest in steel, nor did he have any close business ties with the Tatas. As a matter of fact, he differed with Sir Dorabji Tata on the political strategy of big business,[46] and the Tatas had refused to join FICCI.[47] Notwithstanding these differences, Birla whole-heartedly took up the issue and made it an occasion for a show of solidarity by big business.

The close relationship which Birla worked hard to forge between big business and the nationalist leadership was further cemented by their experience of the Currency Bill of 1927. The bill was introduced to give statutory recognition to the Rupee–Sterling ratio which had been fixed at 1s. 6d. in 1923.[48] The conflict between the government and Indian business over the currency question had been long-standing.[49] Indian opinion had consistently argued for a lower ratio. Business leaders used a variety of methods to disseminate propaganda against the government on the ratio question.[50] Big business succeeded in convincing the nationalist leadership that the currency question was not merely a capitalist agitation, but affected the common people. Birla wrote to Gandhi claiming that a lower currency ratio would help 'agriculture...village craftsmen, such as chamars, potters, herdsmen and other producers while it will go against bankers, security holders, money-lenders.'[51] He also carried out intensive lobbying among legislators and members of the Congress Working Committee.[52]

So effective was this lobbying that Thakurdas was invited to attend a special meeting of the Congress Working Committee to decide the party's position, and he successfully persuaded the Working Committee to issue a whip to its legislative members.[53] By the time the Currency Bill was tabled in the Assembly, Birla and Thakurdas had prepared a solid ground to oppose the bill. In a spirited speech Birla reiterated that the ratio question affected not only the Indian commercial community, but the agricultural classes.[54] Political leaders from diverse shades of the spectrum such as Malaviya, Srinivasa Iyengar, Jinnah and Jamnadas Mehta condemned the bill. All the non-official members of the CLA closed ranks and voted in a single bloc, and the government only managed to pass the bill with a very narrow majority.[55]

Another example of a purely business demand being taken up by the entire political leadership in the Assembly was provided by the Inland Coastal Reservation Bill of 1928. This bill was piloted by S.N. Haji, a Bombay-based shipper, who had sought election to the Assembly with the single object of obtaining concessions for Indian coastal shipping.[56] Reservation of coastal shipping largely concerned the fortunes of a single Indian company—the Scindia Steam Navigation Company, in which businessmen Narottam Morarjee and Walchand Hirachand had interests. Notwithstanding the fact that only a single company was likely to benefit from the bill, Birla was once again successful in mobilizing the entire nationalist leadership within the CLA. The bill directly hit the interests of the powerful shipping group headed by the influential British shipping tycoon, Lord Inchcape, and was strongly opposed, not only by the European chambers but also by official members. The European chambers declared that the bill was based on racial discrimination and appealed directly to the British Parliament to intervene.[57]

Birla strongly refuted the European viewpoint. He disputed the argument that freight rates would increase if control over shipping passed to indian hands. He declared that India's aspirations for a mercantile fleet of her own were legitimate, and the time had come for public opinion to rally around this demand.[58] On the political plane, the triumph for big business came when Gandhi was persuaded to take up Scindia's cause in an article in his journal *Young India* entitled 'Indian shipping'.[59] The demand for the support of Indian shipping was even adopted by the Indian National Congress in its resolutions. Within the Assembly, political leaders stood out amongst those who supported the bill. It was apparent to observers that 'the Coastal shipping bill is essentially a triumph of propaganda, persistent, well organised and well directed.'[60] Much of the strength of the campaign for the Coastal Reservation Bill was due to the energy and skill of the lobbyist Birla.[61]

A close relationship between big business and the nationalist leadership could only be based on reciprocity. We have seen the manner in which the political leadership, on its part, supported the demands of big business within and outside the Assembly. Big business, for its part, broadly followed the overall leadership of the Congress on political matters. Several outstanding examples of this two-way relationship may be provided. Perhaps the most significant was the example of the Public Safety Bill of 1928. The bill was introduced by the government to acquire the power to deport undesirable and subversive foreign activists, especially Philip Spratt and Ben Bradley, of the Communist Party of Great Britain who were active in organizing trade unions in India. The government tried to create the panic of 'a red scare' and much propaganda was carried out alleging infiltration into Indian trade unions by Russian agents. The Public Safety Bill was opposed by the entire nationalist leadership as an attack on civil liberties.[62] Birla and others followed the lead of the Congress leadership in opposing the bill. Birla declared that, while he was not at all in favour of communism, he was not prepared to support a measure which curtailed civil liberties. 'I and other Indian capitalists very strongly disapprove', he declared, 'of any principle which vests the Government with a power, enabling them to deport or intern or imprison people without a trial.'[63] Repressive laws enforced in an arbitrary manner, he warned, would not check communism as the government was attempting to do. To the charge that Indian capitalists generally supported the official measure, he produced telegrams from 29 chambers of commerce affiliated to FICCI which whole-heartedly endorsed Birla's opposition to the bill. Such a show of solidarity enabled the Congress to prevent the bill from being enacted.

A similar instance of big business following the path of the nationalist leadership was provided by the Trades Disputes Bill of 1929. The bill was designed to curtail strikes and to impose a system of tribunals on the trade union movement. The Congress declared its opposition to the bill which was then referred to a select committee of which Birla was a member. He strongly protested against the introduction of the bill, and when it was presented in the Assembly, joined hands with Malaviya, Motilal Nehru and Jayakar in opposing it. These two examples illustrate how close the alliance between big business and the political leadership had grown in the Assembly.

The only occasion when the government succeeded in causing fissures in the alliance was over the Cotton Protection Bill of 1930. The bill proposed a 20 per cent duty on the import of cotton piece-goods from all countries except England, and 15 per cent on goods from England. The bill had a mixed reception among business leaders. Bombay industrialists, who had suffered from depressed conditions for some time, badly needed whatever protection the bill afforded them. The rest of Indian big business, led by Birla, felt that accepting the paltry concessions given by the bill meant compromising on the principle of imperial preference. He took the position that big business should not break rank on the issue with the nationalist leadership which did not want any concessions to be made to Lancashire. Birla argued that the Bombay businessmen should take a long-term view and not alienate the nationalist leadership. The bill had been introduced at the time when Gandhi had just launched the Civil Disobedience campaign. All Congress members of the Assembly had already resigned their positions in response to Gandhi's call. When the bill was tabled, only a section of the nationalist opposition was present to oppose it. Among those who vehemently did so were Malaviya, Kunzru, Jayakar and Vithalbhai Patel.[64] In the debate on the bill, Birla actively championed the cause of the Bombay textile industry.[65] In the most outspoken speech he made during his tenure in the Assembly, he declared:

I say that if any self-respect is left in the millowners, they should declare a lock-out and say to Government they do not want to go the dogs. They may ask Government to go to the dogs, but they should refuse to consider this most humiliating proposal. I am afraid they have not got that courage, but surely it is the duty of this House to say that we are not going to stand this humiliating proposal and we are not going to accept it.

Malaviya proposed an amendment which imposed a uniform duty of $3\frac{1}{2}$ annas per pound on all imports irrespective of their country of origin. This was supported by Birla.[66] Birla's foremost concern during this debate was to keep the Bombay mill-owners close to the political leadership. As he reasoned:

I have spoken to my friends, the millowners, of the disadvantageous situation in which they are putting themselves and I will tell them that, by accepting this proposal, they are doing the greatest disservice to themselves. First of all, they are alienating the sympathy of the people...It is impossible for any Government, until we get responsible Government to fight against the Lancashire interests and, Sir, what they are doing at present is inviting death for themselves. As I said, they have lost their nerves, and it is the duty of this House, however impatient the Bombay mill-owners may be... in their impatience they may not do something which is against their own interests and against the interests of this country.[67]

In spite of Birla's best efforts, Bombay businessmen, led by Thakurdas, did not vote along with Birla's group and Malaviya's amendment was defeated by 60 votes to 44. The ICP members, led by Malaviya, resigned from the Assembly to protest over their defeat over the Cotton Protection Bill.[68] The attitude of the Bombay industry deeply disappointed Birla. He had worked hard to make the business leadership realize that only by working in close co-operation with the political leadership could their interests be furthered, and on this occasion they badly let him down.[69]

During his years in the Assembly, Birla learnt the critical importance of big business working closely with the nationalist leadership. In early 1929 he even explored with Motilal Nehru and Malaviya the possibility of FICCI and the Congress forming an alliance to contest the forthcoming Assembly elections. 'I think that times are so critical,' he told Thakurdas 'that unless we realised the situation and fought the elections with right seriousness in order to get the best men in the Assembly all our time in the Assembly is bound to be wasted.'[70] It was agreed among Birla, Malaviya and Motilal Nehru that a common election fund should be started. Birla proposed that a committee of Motilal, Malaviya, Thakurdas and himself should be formed to allocate funds to candidates all over India. He was confident that he and Thakurdas could get 40 donors to contribute Rs 10,000 each to launch the fund by providing the initial outlay of Rs four lakhs.[71] The first instalment of the election fund was placed at the disposal of Motilal Nehru and Malaviya.[72]

A further example of the maturity of the relationship which Birla and Thakurdas forged between big business and the nationalist leadership was provided by their attempts in 1929 to prevent some industrialists from forming a separate 'capitalist party' to fight the threat of communism. In 1929, prominent Bombay industrialists, Ibrahim Rahimtoola, Cowasji Jehangir and Dorabji Tata made a move to organize a party of capitalists, both Indian and European. They had felt alarmed at the growing influence of the left-wing within the trade union movement, as had been witnessed in recent prolonged strikes in Bombay's textile mills and in the Tatas' steel plant at Jamshedpur. These businessmen felt that mill-owners should unite and co-operate with the government in fighting communist infiltration in the trade unions. The move alarmed Birla and Thakurdas who warned Dorabji Tata that a purely capitalist party would lose the sympathy of all nationalist groups within the Assembly. Birla thought that the move was ill-advised and harmful. He personally found 'it difficult to understand the stupid mentality of the Mill-Owners who in their interests are losing the sympathy of all right thinking men.'[73] Writing to Thakurdas, he fully set out his objections to such a multi-racial capitalist party:

So far as the new organisation is concerned, by no stretch of imagination, it can even touch the fringe of communism. Because if we analysed the membership of the new association, we find that none of the members of the new association carries any weight either with the masses or with the middle classes...Most of the capitalists ignore the fact that to some extent they themselves are responsible for breeding communism, and I have not the least doubt in my mind that a purely capitalist organisation is the last body to put up an effective fight against communism. What we capitalists can do towards driving this evil out of India is to remove the root causes as far as we are concerned and also co-operate with those who through constitutional means want to change the government for a national one. The salvation of the capitalist does not lie in joining hands with the reactionary element...The politicians feel that our capitalists are out for exploitation hand in hand with the foreign capitalists, and this new association can only confirm this suspicion.[74]

Birla was confident that the scheme drawn up by the Bombay capitalists would soon 'come to grief'. Thakurdas fully shared this viewpoint. Both men now ensured that the moves for organizing the separate capitalist party were stalled. They thus ensured that the close relationship which they had worked so hard to forge between business and the nationalist leadership was not undermined by any change in tactics.

In retrospect, the extraordinary success of Birla and Thakurdas in the Assembly could be seen in the extent to which they were able to make the nationalist leadership aware of economic issues and the strong support which they were able to obtain from the Congress. This is illustrated by the 11-point demand which Gandhi put forth before the Raj in January 1930 as his charter of demands before embarking on his Civil Disobedience campaign. The long-standing demands of Birla and his business friends were incorporated by Gandhi—such as reduction of the rupee–sterling ratio, protective tariff on foreign cloth and the passage of the Coastal Reservation Bill. In addition, business could identify with a number of other demands in Gandhi's 11-point manifesto. These related to a reduction of military expenditure by 50 per cent, the abolition of salt tax and a reduction of salaries of higher officials by one-half.[75] The Mahatma acknowledged that these 11-points constituted the 'essence of Swaraj' for him and by identifying these he had given 'a body in part to the elusive word, Independence.'[76] That out of Gandhi's 11-points, three were the specific demands of Indian business was a testimony to the success of Birla and Thakurdas.

DAYS OF CIVIL DISOBEDIENCE

Soon thereafter Gandhi launched the Civil Disobedience Movement. The strategy which Birla had pursued for advancing the interest of business had to be refashioned. Himself an avowed constitutionalist and staunch believer in the efficacy of negotiations, Birla could not agree with the methods which the Mahatma propounded of not co-operating with the Raj. Before Gandhi embarked upon the campaign Birla had tried to convince him of the need to explore the possibility of a compromise with the government. Birla tried to persuade Gandhi to consider attending the first Round Table Conference which had been called by the British to arrive at a negotiated settlement of the Indian problem. He also met the Viceroy, Lord Irwin, to discuss possibilities of a conciliation with the Congress.

Birla reported his meeting to Gandhi to persuade him to give up his plans for a campaign. He claimed that a 'new spirit' prevailed among British policy-makers and both the new Secretary of State, Wedgwood Benn, and the Viceroy sincerely wanted to help resolve the political impasse. Birla pleaded with Gandhi to make the most of what was likely to be offered and be a realist in believing that 'we are not going to get full Dominion status now. But even then we could do many things with what we would get, securing the rest in 5–10 years.'[77] Unsuccessful in convincing Gandhi by his letters, Birla visited Wardha to see him. For all his efforts, he was, however, unable to persuade Gandhi to look at things in the perspective in which he did. Gandhi, instead, made it clear to him that 'his distrust of the British was acute and he urged that members should have nothing more to do with the legislature.'[78]

A month after Birla visited Wardha, the Congress passed the resolution for complete independence or *Purna Swaraj*. It called upon legislators to resign and asked Congressmen to prepare for Civil Disobedience. In response, the Swarajists resigned from the legislatures. However, Birla doubted the wisdom of this move, as he believed that the Assembly 'was providing a useful experience for Indians of the working of parliamentary institutions'. He personally did not resign in response to Gandhi's appeal, as he was bound by the discipline of his own party, the ICP. In March 1930 when Gandhi, with his band of followers, had embarked on his celebrated march from Sabarmati to Dandi, ICP legislators resigned from the Assembly. However, the issue upon which they resigned was the Cotton Protection Bill.[79]

In the following months Birla actively supported the Congress as president of FICCI. He launched a vigorous attack on the government's economic policies and denounced excessive government expenditure, demanded a large-scale retrenchment of officials, a reduction in the budget of the army, policies promoting agriculture, and 'unqualified protection' to industry to replace discriminating free trade.[80] Linking his ideas with the Gandhian cause, he declared in his annual presidential address to FICCI before an audience which included the Viceroy and the Finance Member:

It is impossible in the present circumstances and in the present political condition of our country to convert the Government to our views; but I think the only solution of our present difficulties lies in strengthening the hands of those who are fighting for the freedom of our country. I have repeated it from other platforms and I want to repeat it here again, that Swaraj is not a question of sentiment; it is a question of bread. The prosperity of the country depends entirely on the amount of political freedom which we get and I think that not only in the interests of the country but in the interests of the capitalists, the employers and the industrialists we should try to fight and strengthen the hands of those who are fighting for Swaraj.[81]

Gandhi's movement proved to be successful beyond all expectations. He was able to construct around the symbols of swadeshi and salt a powerful campaign which challenged colonial authority. Its most visible forms were the picketing of cloth shops which traded in foreign cloth and the ritualized production of salt in public places. The movement soon spread across much of India eliciting strong support in urban centres and pockets of resistance in rural areas. The entire leadership of the Congress including Gandhi was arrested, as the British realized that they were faced with a large scale and determined campaign to challenge their authority. As news of the popular enthusiasm poured in, Birla was excited by the demonstration of public spirit.[82] Birla's enthusiasm ran counter to the conservative position taken by his family elders. His father, Baldeodas, was opposed to his family taking part in anti-British activities. Through the course of the movement, he refused to sever social links with high British officials. In November 1930, for example, Sir Hugh Stephenson, Governor of Bihar, performed the opening ceremony of the Birla Women's Hospital in Ranchi. The hospital was funded by Raja Baldeodas.[83] Notwithstanding such opposition, Birla's faith in Gandhi prevailed over the lingering doubts that he had had about the course of the campaign. 'Your faith gives you an overpowering feeling of elation', he wrote to Gandhi. 'A businessman like me', he continued, 'careful about counting his pennies, could be deeply upset by fear of a failure. Anyway, your Herculean labour is bound to yield fruit. That much faith I do have.' He undertook a tour of important industrial centres and in his press interviews tried to dispel the view that the Congress' Civil Disobedience was behind the prevailing economic distress, which he blamed squarely on the ruinous financial policy of the government.[84]

Birla was especially supportive of one of the important components of the Congress' programme, which was the boycott of foreign cloth. Given how this could immensely benefit the indigenous mill industry Birla canvassed support for the boycott of British goods among piece-goods importers of Calcutta and called upon them, most of whom were Marwaris, to 'wash their hands clean of foreign piece-goods business and devote themselves to the swadeshi cloth business'. He tried to arrange for foreign cloth dealers in Calcutta to establish contact with the Bombay and Ahmedabad cotton mills.[85] He wrote to industrialists in Ahmedabad such as Ambalal Sarabhai that the decision of the Marwaris to stop the import of piece-goods could perform miracles in promoting the cause of swadeshi. He asked Sarabhai to coordinate with the Bombay and Ahmedabad mills to ensure a regular supply of swadeshi cloth to the Calcutta Marwaris.[86] He also publicly associated himself with Gandhi's scheme for the promotion of *khadi*. Just before his arrest on 4 May 1930, Gandhi held a series of talks with Birla and Sarabhai about what mill-owners could do to promote khadi.[87] In these talks Birla promised to open a khadi store near his village in Rajasthan.[88] He, however, differed from Gandhi on the issue of mill-made coarse cloth. He tried to convince him that Indian textile mills could play an important role in popularizing khadi, since mill-made coarse cloth was both affordable and durable.[89] He maintained his belief that the common man benefited greatly from mill-made cloth which had the potential of totally replacing foreign cloth.[90] In contrast to Birla's view, Gandhi believed that mill-owners would not give up their profits and that the boycott of foreign cloth could only be successful through the use of hand-made khadi.[91] Notwithstanding these differences with Gandhi on mill-made cloth, Birla opened a number of stores selling khadi.[92]

As the Civil Disobedience campaign gathered momentum, Birla intensified his efforts to enlist the support of the chambers of commerce and organizations of big business for the Congress cause. Under his guidance, the Calcutta-based Indian Chamber of Commerce, proved to be one of the most enthusiastic supporters of Civil Disobedience among commercial bodies.[93] Yet, the strong support which Indian capitalists showed to the Congress campaign must be seen in the wider context of the increasing radicalization of business in the late 1920s.[94] This was the direct result of a number of factors such as the government's adamant position on the rupee–sterling ratio which 'had passed far beyond the Bombay agitators and went right through the country with the strength of a religious demand'.[95] Further, the imposition of differential duties and the government's unsympathetic response to the growing demand for the protection of Indian industry, together with the effects of the world depression pushed big business to extend its support to Gandhi's movement.[96] The extent of support given by some business organizations to the Congress cause can be seen in their responses to the highly symbolic issue of salt. The Indian Chamber of Commerce was the first to take this up when it recommended that the position of the salt industry should be given protection.[97] Then, in its annual meeting, FICCI also urged the immediate reference of the salt industry to the government's Tariff Board, and later brought out a Monograph on Common Salt. The monograph was recommended by Jawaharlal Nehru to the Congress committees all over India for propaganda.[98]

Among business organizations perhaps the most important was the support of FICCI whose executive decided in May 1930 to adopt a resolution on the political situation. Drafted by Ambalal Sarabhai and moved by Birla, it declared that, without Gandhi, no solution to the political situation could be found.[99] In the months that followed, FICCI took up a number of issues such as the violent encounters between the police and the satyagrahis which marked the campaign. Alongside, the organization directed its affiliated bodies and members 'to patronise only Indian goods to the maximum extent possible and to reduce consumption as far as possible of such goods as are either not made or insufficiently made in the country.' Prominent members of the organization including Birla put forth measures which could be adopted by the Federation and its members to promote swadeshi.[100] It also formed a Swadeshi Prachar Association for the boycott of foreign cloth and the promotion of swadeshi.[101] There is considerable evidence to suggest that there was much business support for the Civil Disobedience Movement in its initial phase. Purshotamdas Thakurdas conveyed some of the sense of sympathy which many business leaders felt for Gandhi's campaign when he wrote to Lord Irwin in May 1930:

Esteemed friends of mine all over the country whose views I value, have repeatedly brought to my notice lately that the estrangement between the commercial community and the Government is on the increase. What with the boycott movement, picketing of shops, and the lathi charges and other rough handling by the Police of the crowd, things are looking definitely ugly. I submit that it is not necessary nor advisable at this stage to say that all this is the doing of Gandhi and his friends. It is true that they started the civil disobedience movement. But Government must not overlook the fact that owing to the extremely depressed economic condition of the agriculturists and the masses in the districts, Mr Gandhi is now proved to have started at a psychological moment.

Emphasizing the strength of the movement, he told Irwin that 'every Indian is, as it were, captured by the bonafides of Mr Gandhi's movement', and asked Irwin to come forward with a reconciling step. He wanted Irwin 'to make a statement that, in the next constitution, Indians will be masters in their own house, barring of course the questions of military defence and foreign and political relations which require further consideration. The "economic exploitation" of the country, as it is called, will have to be stopped by entrusting full control over finance, currency, fiscal policy and railways to popular ministers responsible to the legislature.'[102]

However, studies of the participation of business in Gandhi's movement by the historians Sumit Sarkar and Claude Markovits have argued that by the autumn of 1930 the enthusiasm of business for Civil Disobedience began to decline because of difficult business conditions. Business groups now wanted to conciliate. In September 1930 Birla wanted FICCI to remove its self-imposed ban on attending the forthcoming Round Table Conference in London in the absence of Gandhi. He now wanted to keep the door to negotiations open. He wrote to Lala Shri Ram, the FICCI president, that the ban was unjust and wrong and ought to be lifted. Ironically, he himself had moved the resolution proposing the self-imposed ban in May 1930. He explained that he had done so because of his personal political commitment, but he now felt that some good might come out of the forthcoming Round Table Conference.[103] There were also other members of the FICCI executive who shared Birla's view, and FICCI informed its member bodies that the earlier resolution on the boycott of the Round Table Conference should be considered as recommendatory, not mandatory.[104]

Birla's two most important concerns in these months were to keep the commercial support of FICCI solidly behind the Congress and to persuade Gandhi to conciliate with the British. While ensuring that big business strongly supported the Congress, Birla fully realized the limitations of the support which big business in general and he personally could extend to the Congress cause. From his early experience of the Rodda conspiracy case, he had learnt the lesson that a direct confrontation with the government would jeopardize his career and his commitment to strengthening the interests of Indian big business in their struggle against foreign capital. However, to him, the centrality of upholding the position of Gandhi was paramount and his views are best summed up in a letter he wrote to Thakurdas in January 1931:

Regarding the present agitation and the results of the Round Table Conference, I agree that we should try our best to get the country out of the present political turmoil. But I do not see my way so far. There could be no doubt that what we are being offered at present is entirely due to Gandhiji... This leads one to the conclusion that if we are to achieve what we desire the present movement should not be allowed to be shaken. We should, therefore, have two objects in view: One is that we should jump in at the most opportune time for a reconciliation and the other is that we should not do anything which might weaken the hands of those through whose efforts we have arrived at this stage.[105]

Birla was looking for signals for conciliation from the government, so that the Congress leadership could be persuaded to settle for peace without losing face. Thakurdas too had been driven by similar motives when he wrote to Irwin earlier in June 1930:

You can, I am sure, realise that Mr Gandhi cannot now abandon the movement without some agreement regarding the future constitution. If such an agreement is arrived at, I

An early photograph of Birla

As a young boy, in traditional Marwari attire

Mahadevi

The Birla brothers: Jugalkishore, Rameshwardas, Ghanshyamdas (in spectacles), and Braj Mohan

feel that Mr Gandhi can be persuaded to take the first step of calling off his movement...We wish to press our view on Mr Gandhi with all emphasis and do not apprehend failure. It is for Your Excellency to strengthen our hands to enable us to press our plan on Mr Gandhi.[106]

The most opportune time, according to Birla, came in January 1931. Gandhi was unconditionally released from jail and the ban on the Congress organization withdrawn. Not having met the Mahatma for several months, Birla rushed to Allahabad to see him. There are no records available of what transpired but it appears that Birla pressed for conciliation. From Allahabad where the Congress high command was in session, Birla maintained close contact with Thakurdas who was in Delhi and regularly reported developments to him. Thakurdas trusted Birla to explain the views of the commercial community to the Congress leaders and 'to impress Gandhi with the view that the country could not go on as at present for any length of time without catastrophic consequences'.[107]

After his early talks with Gandhi, Birla informed Thakurdas that there were good prospects for peace, although he felt some issues which Gandhi might raise could present difficulties.[108] The Viceroy, Lord Irwin, realized the importance of Birla's efforts. He reported to the Secretary of State, Benn, that both Birla and Thakurdas were 'working very hard...to get Gandhi to be reasonable'. While, in Allahabad, Birla was trying to get Gandhi to bid for peace, in Delhi, Thakurdas was discussing with Irwin the possibilities of resolving issues such as salt and the picketing of liquor and foreign cloth shops.[109] Lord Irwin was delighted to find that Birla and Thakurdas were working in earnest to persuade Gandhi. 'Though I should have supposed that the outlook of Birla must be poles apart from that of Gandhi', he wrote to the Secretary of State, 'it is I think significant that he and Purshotamd as should be busying themselves to the extent they are in the cause of peace.'[110]

As things eventuated, Gandhi signed a pact with the Viceroy in March 1931 and the first phase of civil disobedience was suspended. It marked, said Thakurdas, a return to political sanity.[111] FICCI hailed the Gandhi–Irwin Pact as 'a distinct landmark in our history, a signal stage in the building up of our national constitution and a pact that every member of the commercial community in India will be grateful for.' Similar sentiments were echoed by Indian chambers of commerce all over the country.[112]

IN LONDON WITH GANDHI

One of the provisions of the Gandhi–Irwin Pact had been the decision by the Congress to attend the second Round Table Conference—something which was welcomed by Birla and many within the business world. As the premier organization representing Indian business, FICCI endorsed the Congress decision and elected three representatives to attend the Conference—Birla, Thakurdas and Jamal Mohammed, the FICCI president for 1931. Both Birla and Thakurdas had emerged as the foremost spokesmen of Indian big business since the mid-1920s and were regarded as best suited to represent its interests. Although FICCI decided against giving a specific mandate to its representatives, Birla and Thakurdas informed fellow colleagues that they would follow Mahatma Gandhi's lead at the forthcoming Conference. Within FICCI there was some support for the idea that its representatives should do this.[113]

The formal announcement by the government of the invitees to the Conference in August 1931, however, came as a rude shock to Birla. The government excluded the names of both Birla and Mohammed, although that of Thakurdas was included. Instead, they chose Maneckji Dadabhoy and Padamji Ginwala, both Bombay-based pro-government men, to represent Indian business. This seriously challenged the position of FICCI and it carried out a long correspondence on the issue with the government, threatening even to boycott the Conference. In a representation to the newly arrived Viceroy, Lord Willingdon, the FICCI leadership warned that 'if any agreement is arrived at the Round Table Conference in the absence of the representatives of the Federation such agreement will not be binding on the Indian mercantile community'.[114] Birla's omission was regarded by the FICCI executive as a deliberate attempt by the government to undermine his stature. Birla himself attributed the government's hostile attitude towards him to his close association with Gandhi which, he believed, made him suspect in the eyes of the Raj.[115] The issue of FICCI's representation was taken up by Gandhi. He personally took charge of all its correspondence with the government and joined issue with the Viceroy. Gandhi demanded that the government should honour the promise made by Lord Irwin that FICCI would be granted adequate representation at the Round Table Conference. Even more significantly he declared that:

My usefulness would be largely curtailed if the interests represented by these three gentlemen...are not to be represented at the Round Table Conference. The Federation is to a certain extent working in conjunction with the Congress...If there were any negotiations...in connection with Indian commerce I should be perfectly helpless without the assistance and cooperation of these gentlemen and the purpose for which I am being sent to London is in danger of being defeated.[116]

Willingdon was, however, not well disposed to the FICCI cause. When Gandhi did not get a favourable response from him he was willing to go further—even take up the issue with the British Prime Minister.[117] The continued campaign by FICCI and Gandhi's persistent efforts forced the government to yield, and both Birla and Mohammed were finally invited in September 1931 as delegates to the Round Table Conference. Thakurdas was appointed to the Federal Structure Committee and Birla to the Minorities Committee, while Mohammed was only allowed to attend the plenary session. Birla was also permitted to attend the sessions of the Federal Structure Committee, but only in the absence of Thakurdas, and on the condition that he would only observe and not participate in the proceedings. Birla turned down this reluctant concession which was offered so grudgingly to him.

Birla accompanied Gandhi on the voyage to London. They set sail from Bombay on S.S. Rajputana on 29 August 1931 along with a number of other delegates including Malaviya.[118] On the ship and later in London, Birla was privileged to be Gandhi's constant companion during their European sojourn.[119] Gandhi stayed at Kingsley Hall in the East End of London and, despite Birla's persuasion, refused to move to Arya Bhavan in Hampstead where Birla stayed. He kept in close contact with Birla and conferred with him on a daily basis about his engagements.[120] Although they stayed at separate places, the overall responsibility for looking after Gandhi's needs rested with Birla. He provided transportation and was in charge of the well-being of Gandhi and members of his entourage.

RUPEE AND THE GOLD STANDARD

A few days after they arrived in London, the Indian delegates were faced with a most unexpected development. On 21 September 1931, the sterling quite unexpectedly went off the gold standard. This had major repercussions for the Indian rupee which was linked to sterling by the Currency Act of 1927. So long as sterling was convertible to gold, the position of the rupee was also secure and it too was virtually convertible to gold. But with sterling no longer linked to gold, the Government of India had to re-assess the basis and the rate of the Indian rupee.[121] With sterling off the gold standard, there were three main policy alternatives for the Government of India for Indian currency: (a) to continue to link the rupee to sterling at the existing ratio or at a lower one; (b) to abandon the link and allow the rupee to find its own level; or (c) to link the rupee to gold at a convenient parity.[122] The first alternative was preferred by the India Office while Indian commercial opinion felt inclined to the second. The government argued in favour of maintaining the sterling value of the rupee, on the grounds that otherwise the rupee would seek conversion into foreign currencies in large quantities thereby causing a fall in its exchange value. In contrast, Indian commercial opinion had for a long time wanted a free rupee and the substance of its demands from the early twentieth century had centred on the need to lower the currency ratio. The de-linking of the rupee from sterling, it was argued by Indian experts, would ensure that the rupee would find its own independent level.[123] To Indian commercial opinion, the divorce of sterling from gold in 1931 was seen as an opportunity to secure the de-linking of the Indian rupee on a permanent basis.

However, the currency question was a subject which few among the Indian delegates to the Round Table Conference understood. Gandhi faced a difficult situation, as he was confronted with an issue of great importance on which he had to respond immediately and in which he had little expertise. In such a situation, Birla proved to be the man on the spot. Being the only Indian business representative in London at the time (Thakurdas was still in India), he became the sole spokesman for Indian commercial interests in London. FICCI and other commercial bodies wired to Gandhi to take up the issue of the future of the rupee and to consult Birla on what should be done.[124] Birla first briefed the entire Indian delegation. He explained the technicalities of the fiscal situation to Gandhi, who was well aware of his own ignorance on the subject of finance.[125] In mid-1932 he confessed to Birla: 'I have been reading books on economy. I can understand better than before. But as yet the picture of the whole subject does not come before me.'[126] Gandhi and other delegates looked to Birla for expertise on this question. He even promised Birla that he would not make any statement on financial questions without first consulting him.[127] It was most fortuitous that Birla was in London. He was readily accepted by the Indian delegates as the spokesman of Indian popular opinion on the rupee–sterling issue in the many meetings which followed with the India Office.

Conscious of the critical role he had been called upon to play, Birla gave extensive interviews to the press criticizing the government's decision of continuing to link the rupee to sterling at the rate of 1s.6d. He was interviewed by *Reuters* and given much coverage by the *Manchester Guardian*. He claimed that the Secretary of State in London and the Finance Member of the Government of India had spoken with two different voices, highlighting the conflict of opinion within the Raj on the wisdom of the decision. He charged that the Government of India had been balancing its budget by resorting to excessive borrowing and taxation in order only to maintain the rupee–sterling ratio.[128] In response to Birla's effective campaign, the India Office was forced to organize a number of meetings with Indian delegates to elicit their views.

A meeting was arranged with the Secretary of State at which Henry Strakosch, Member of the India Council, put forth the official viewpoint.[129] Although Gandhi and other Indian delegates were invited to this meeting, Birla was excluded.[130] Gandhi did not respond.[131] Discussions were then resumed on 8 October 1931, and this time both Birla and Thakurdas were invited.[132] Birla forcefully presented the Indian case while Strakosch argued the official line. Strakosch argued that, if the rupee was left to find its own course, there would be a wholesale flight from the rupee, with the result that the exchange rate would decline in its silver value. This would, in turn, lead to a constant disturbance in budgetary arrangements, the setting off of a vicious spiral of inflation, and the inevitable ascent of prices. Thus the best course available, he concluded, was the continuation of the rupee's link to sterling.[133] Birla put forth the view that just as the rupee could not be based on gold because of a lack of gold reserves, it could not be linked to sterling as there were not enough sterling balances either. If the rupee continued to be linked to sterling, then the government would be forced to either sell silver or borrow sterling to fulfil its obligations. Moreover, he argued, being a debtor country, it was important for India to increase productivity and export surplus, for which a devaluation of currency and the raising of internal price levels were essential.[134]

The issue seemed almost intractable and many informal discussions followed, with Birla and Thakurdas playing a leading part. They argued that both from the point of view of the agriculturist as well as industry, what was needed was to give an impetus to India's exports so that she could discharge her liabilities. To be able to do so, she needed an independent financial policy.[135] Needless to say, Gandhi strongly supported the case which was put forward by Birla and Thakurdas.

In concrete terms these meetings did not lead to any results as there was no change in government policy on the rupee–sterling question. Birla and Thakurdas, however, knew what their real achievement was. Reporting to the FICCI general body on their return from London, they declared: 'The net gain from the discussion was that Gandhiji and many of our politicians who had attended the meetings were convinced that in asking for the rupee to be left alone the Indian commercial community were asking for something which was in the best interests of the masses and Gandhiji told the Secretary of State after the third meeting that the verdict must go against him in the matter.'[136] During the currency crisis Birla had convinced Gandhi of his financial expertise and that when he spoke on fiscal policy, he did so in the best interest of the country.

THE AGENDA OF BIG BUSINESS

The currency crisis was, however, an unscheduled item on the agenda. Birla and Thakurdas were principally in London to present their case for Indian control over federal finance in the new constitutional arrangements which were being worked out at the Round Table Conference. More specifically, the concerns of the business representatives were commercial discrimination (that is, discrimination in favour of Indian-controlled industry) and financial safeguards (that is, transfer of finance to popular control under the new constitution). The question of commercial discrimination was taken up in the Federal Structure Committee and in several informal meetings. Discrimination in favour of indigenous industry had long been one of the main demands of Indian business associations. As we have seen, a major concern for both Birla and Thakurdas during their time in the Assembly had been to gain protection for Indian industry.[137] FICCI strongly believed that 'the future legislature of the country should have unfettered powers, if necessary, in the interests of the country to discriminate against non-nationals'.[138]

Things became somewhat complicated because during his visit to Manchester and in his talks with Sir Edward Benthall, the influential spokesman of ASSOCHAM, Gandhi promised that there would be no commercial discrimination along racial lines. To Gandhi it was part of his philosophy that the British were India's best friends and should not be discriminated against. But for FICCI representatives, it was not quite as simple as that. They were not pleased with Gandhi's informal promise. However, they felt that by insisting on their demand for commercial discrimination in the face of Gandhi's promise to European business, 'we would go against both Gandhiji and the Congress who want no racial discrimination'. More significantly, in return for the unqualified support that Gandhi gave them on two of the three main items on their agenda (that is, on the rupee–sterling question and financial safeguards), Birla and Thakurdas were now forced to stand by Gandhi.

A number of meetings were arranged between representatives of Indian and British business. At the first meeting which took place, Gandhi, Birla, Benthall and Herbert Carr (European businessman from Calcutta and president of the European Association) were present. At this meeting, Birla conceded Gandhi's principle that there should be no racial discrimination, but he demanded 'adequate provision for the protection of such concerns as might require protection in the national interest against stronger concerns, in all probability British.' Thakurdas made the same point in meetings of the Federal Structure Committee.[139] At the meeting, Indian and European business representatives could not come to any agreement.[140] Ultimately, the Federal Structure Committee Report recommended a clause prohibiting both legislative and administrative discrimination. FICCI representatives had strongly objected to the inclusion of such a clause. Thakurdas protested that if such measures were to be incorporated in the new Act, they would not pave the way for a workable constitution.

Another major demand on the agenda of Birla and Thakurdas related to the complete transfer of control over federal finance in the new constitution. Thakurdas declared in the Federal Structure Committee, 'nothing but a minister completely responsible to the legislature will satisfy us and... no safeguards devised by this Conference in the shape of control from outside India will be acceptable.'[141] For the administration of currency, Birla and Thakurdas recommended the establishment of a Reserve Bank to be created by the Indian legislature and to be independent of both Whitehall and the Bank of England. The recommendations of the Federal Structure Committee regarding financial safeguards dissatisfied Birla and Thakurdas. They were particularly unhappy with the recommendations which vested the Viceroy with control over all currency matters, the Reserve Bank, railways, budgetary control over debt service, sinking fund charges, military charges, and salaries and pensions. They argued that such extensive powers gave the Viceroy effective control over 88.5 per cent of the budget. Birla strongly criticized this continuing hold over finance and declared that little actual control in the area of finance was being given up by the British. He further argued that, although a Reserve Bank was proposed, the power of amending the Indian Currency Act and stabilizing the rupee was still being reserved.[142] In a strong presentation of the case for Indian control over finance, Birla said: 'I maintain Sir that as long as 80 percent of our revenue is mortgaged there is no way of avoiding these safeguards. Therefore the financial control could never be effective whether it is today or 20 years hence or even 100 years hence so long as this position is maintained.' To him the new financial system that was proposed was 'something like having possession of the treasury vaults without its contents.'[143]

Gandhi strongly endorsed the views of FICCI when he declared:

Three experts from the Federation of Commerce and Industry have in their own manner each...told you out of their expert experiences how utterly impossible it is for any body of responsible ministers to tackle the problem of administration when 80 per cent of India's resources are mortgaged irretrievably. Better than I could have shown to you they have shown out of the aptitude of their knowledge what these safeguards mean for India. They mean the complete cramping of India.[144]

In their meetings with the City of London bankers and financiers Birla and Thakurdas reiterated the position that the 'Governor-General should not occupy a better position than that of a debenture holder in respect of reserved items...and that he should step in only in case of default'.

Whilst Birla and Thakurdas were preoccupied with economic and financial issues the Round Table Conference was floundering on the communal issue. Representatives of different communities and political groups spoke in different voices. The claim put forth by Gandhi that the Indian National Congress represented all communities in India was refuted by representatives of the minorities, princes from the Indian states as well as leaders of the depressed classes. This jeopardized all discussions and it was soon clear that the formal consultations within the Conference had lost all meaning and real negotiations were being carried out informally. Gandhi was disappointed at the disunity showed by the Indian delegates and by the attempts to pull down the stature of the Congress. Birla, however, continued to impress upon Gandhi not to lose faith but to continue to persist in seeking a solution.[145] Till as late as mid-November 1931 Birla continued his efforts to convince Gandhi that a settlement was still possible and that the English were sincere in their efforts for a solution.[146] Notwithstanding this optimism, it was clear that no progress was being made in the deliberations of the Conference. The Conference ran into trouble when Sir Samuel Hoare, the Secretary of State for India, floated the idea of provincial autonomy being granted as a first step, with control over the centre to be transferred later. The Muslims and other minority leaders favoured the idea, but the Congress rejected it outright. Gandhi, along with Sapru, Moonje, Malaviya, V.S.S. Sastri, Pheroze Sethna and the business representatives Cowasji Jehangir, Thakurdas and Birla, signed a letter to the British Prime Minister rejecting the scheme. The letter pleaded that the communal deadlock should not be allowed to 'block the way to a full and comprehensive scheme of responsible government, which alone could provide an adequate settlement of the pressing problems.'[147] Birla personally found the failure of the Conference very painful and lamented:

We have proved how useless we people are. There is absolutely no unity at all. Each one is concerned with increasing his own prestige...Gandhiji is the captain and the fact that he should be helped is of no consideration to anyone...Vallabhbhai, Jawaharlal etc have not even looked towards the Viceroy's house, and all the responsibility has been left on Gandhiji. Here the situation is such that Gandhiji meets the Prime Minister, then the Aga Khan, the leader of the Muslims, then Ambedkar, the Untouchables leader, then leaders like Ujjal Singh and then Sapru, the Liberal leader. In all these meetings each one gives his own point of view. Our disunity has been displayed as never before.[148]

While realizing that disunity among the delegates was the root cause of the failure of the Conference, Birla warned the British of the dangers involved in taking undue advantage of this disunity and to allow Gandhi to go back empty-handed:

The Conference may be wound up and Mahatma Gandhi may be sent back, but may I ask, what next? Have you got any programme?...We were sermonised on the efficacy of persuasion and reason. It was said that the policy of Congress was a policy of negation, a policy of destruction, a sterile policy. What have you proved? We have been discussing, reasoning and trying to persuade you for the last nine weeks. What is the result? We are nowhere. Has it not been proved by your actions that the policy of persuasion and of reason has failed?...You are challenging the Congress to start the civil disobedience movement again....I warn you again that you will be making the greatest mistake of your life if you do not take the opportunity of coming to a friendly settlement...I know the youth of my country. It is quite possible that a few years hence you will not have to deal with men like Mr Gandhi who has proved in many respects a greater Conservative than many of you, you may not have to deal with Princes, you may not have to deal with capitalists like myself, you may have to deal with new men, new conditions, new ideas and new ambitions. Beware of that.[149]

As the Conference drew to a close towards the end of 1931, Birla and Thakurdas took stock of the position. They realized that not much progress had been made in securing major concessions on the agenda which they had pursued at the Conference. The rupee–sterling ratio question stood as it did before; the resolution on commercial safeguards adopted by the Conference prevented the new government from passing any discriminatory legislation against British business; and numerous financial safeguards ensured that the budget in the new constitution largely remained under the control of the viceroy. All this seemed a bitter disappointment to them. They felt the Conference had left important economic questions either 'untouched or undecided and attention was deliberately diverted to peripheral details to the neglect of the centre.'

It was with such feelings that Birla returned to India. Upon arrival he and Thakurdas were subjected to intense criticism from some of the member-bodies of FICCI who blamed them for returning empty-handed from the Conference. More significantly, they were condemned for their stand on commercial discrimination. It was alleged that they had subordinated a long-standing policy of FICCI to their allegiance to Gandhi[150]—for having 'tied up our conscience to the apron strings of the Congress'.[151] Birla and Thakurdas faced this widespread criticism by arguing that as FICCI delegates they had to be a part of the broader nationalist mainstream. They asked FICCI members: 'Do those who insist on racial discrimination as such seriously believe that they have any chance of success in a fight in which the weight of the Congress is against them?'[152]

SHIFTS IN STRATEGY

The collapse of the Conference from the point of view of business and the criticism that Birla faced on return from London taught him the important lesson that it was wise not to identify too openly with the Congress leadership. This shift in its position was noticeable in the resolution passed by FICCI which explored the possibility of working with non-Congress politicians who were inclined to cooperate in the new constitutional arrangements:

In the near future there is no possibility of an agreement being arrived at between a radical India and a reactionary Parliament, but we feel that it would be possible at some time in the near future for the Conservative Party to try and come to an understanding at least with the progressive Indian opinion, which though not identified with the Congress may yet be a force in Indian politics. In our opinion, such an agreement may not be acceptable to Gandhiji, but may not meet with his active opposition. Such a progressive party at present is non-existent. We feel, however, that the Federation, though not a political party, may with its progressive views yet aspire to do substantial service to the country's cause by doing what it can to rightly explain Gandhiji and bridge the gulf between him and the Government.[153]

Meanwhile, Gandhi renewed the Civil Disobedience campaign in early 1932. In retaliation, the British banned the Congress organization and the entire political leadership at the national, provincial and local levels was arrested using draconian powers. A political deadlock ensued. The FICCI leadership viewed these developments with alarm. While not keen to be seen breaking rank with the Congress, they realized the need for continuing to negotiate with the government. Their strategy now was to distance itself from the Congress leadership. The initial steps in this direction had been taken by Birla in London itself towards the end of the Conference. In late January 1932 when Gandhi was in jail, Birla had met the Secretary of State, Sir Samuel Hoare and urged him to set up a special committee consisting solely of business representatives, both from India and Lancashire, to negotiate the issue of financial safeguards. Discussing financial questions with politicians who did not understand the subject, Birla argued, was merely a waste of time. He felt that the time had come to have across-the-board discussions among Indian and British commercial interests, with the politicians kept out.[154] Birla conveyed similar views in meetings with Sir George Schuster, the new Finance Member and impressed upon him that 'experienced businessmen of both sides should sit at a table and come to an agreed solution'.[155]

Whereas Birla and Thakurdas were extremely keen to continue negotiations, FICCI was divided over further participation in talks with the government. Its member-bodies overwhelmingly wanted non-participation, but the executive committee, under the sway of Birla and Thakurdas, was prepared to stake its position over the issue and declared that if its resolution in favour of continued negotiations was not passed, the executive would resign *en masse*.[156] In the end, the FICCI general body endorsed the executive's decision and it was widely seen as a personal triumph for Birla. Birla informed Hoare of this mandate and renewed his offer of co-operation. 'If at any time you think we could serve the cause of peace and progress in India we would be delighted to offer our help,' he wrote. He further assured Hoare that Thakurdas would be delighted to attend the forthcoming Imperial Economic Conference at Ottawa, a further sign of the keenness to seek peace with the government.[157] He assured Hoare that in the dealings between Indian business and the government, 'past history' could be left behind. 'So far as we are concerned', he continued, 'you will find us always ready to work for the economic interest leaving aside sentiments and politics.'[158]

In spite of the initial signs of encouragement, Birla heard no more. He was astute enough to realize that Hoare must have been criticized in official circles for carrying on a 'private correspondence' with him. He was correct in his assumption. Hoare had wanted to include Birla and Thakurdas in the Indian delegation to Ottawa, but Willingdon would not have it. Willingdon distrusted Birla whom he described rather contemptuously as 'that basically non-cooperating fellow, motivated by selfish interests'.[159] His hostility went back to the time when he had tried to stall Birla's nomination to the Round Table Conference. He perhaps rightly regarded Birla as a camp follower of Gandhi and was determined to keep him out of the Imperial Conference at Ottawa. Birla himself later confessed that Willingdon considered him as an untouchable.[160] As a result, FICCI was not consulted by the government over the representation to the Ottawa Conference but merely asked if it was interested in deputing observers. This was seen as an insult by the FICCI executive which immediately turned down the offer and registered its strong protest to the Secretary of State. It declared, that 'until India got effective control over her fiscal policy, no commitment would be binding on her which would restrict her freedom to develop her indigenous industries in future.'[161] The Ottawa agreement to create an imperial trading bloc was vehemently denounced by FICCI.[162] The FICCI declared that the delegation to Ottawa did not represent the business side of India. Thakurdas, Birla and M.A. Master were deputed by the FICCI executive to campaign against the arbitrary and unjust attitude of the Government of India on this issue.[163] Other prominent commercial bodies and the nationalist leadership also joined FICCI in condemning the agreement reached at Ottawa.[164] Birla played a leading role in orchestrating the public campaign against the agreement. In an article in the *Leader* he declared that the Ottawa Pact was harmful to India's interests as it underrated the value of preferences granted to Indian goods and overrated those granted to British goods.[165]

In spite of the strong opposition of FICCI to the Ottawa Pact and its anger at being ignored by the government, Thakurdas attended the third Round Table Conference in his individual capacity which FICCI and most commercial associations decided to boycott. Thakurdas was censured for his decision to attend the Round Table Conference by the Indian Merchants' Chamber and had to resign from its executive. Birla maintained an uneasy silence on Thakurdas' position. According to Claude Markovits, the continued closeness between the two during these months 'suggests a sort of "division of labour" between them and underlines the flexibility of the approach taken by that section of the big business leadership due to the fact that the final shape of the new Constitution was not yet known'.[166] Federal finance was, however, once again the most important issue for Indian business at the third Round Table Conference but once again no practical gains could be made from its point of view.[167] In March 1933 the 'Proposals for Indian Constitutional Reforms' were published in the form of a White Paper.[168] To Birla the White Paper appeared to be an improvement over previous schemes.

CONFRONTING LANCASHIRE

While Indian business was responding to the White Paper, Lancashire lobbyists were nervous about the reform proposals, especially because of the worsening trade situation due to the flooding of Japanese goods into the Indian market after the devaluation of the yen. The Manchester Chamber of Commerce (MCC) wanted statutory preferences to be incorporated in the reform proposals, but had been informed by Hoare that he could not tamper with the principle of fiscal autonomy and tariffs could not be lowered, and that the only solution lay in direct negotiations for a trade treaty with India. This led Manchester to negotiate directly with Indian business and to the signing of a pact in October 1933 between Homi Mody of the Bombay Millowners' Association and Clare-Lees who headed the Lancashire textile delegation. Under the Mody–Lees Pact, the Bombay mill-owners accepted preferences as fair and desirable and obtained from Lancashire a commitment for the increased import of Indian raw cotton in exchange for a lower rate of tariff on British textiles.[169]

The Pact was condemned by almost all chambers of commerce in India, including the Bombay-based Indian Merchants' Chamber which forced Mody to resign from its executive. FICCI took the lead in condemning the Pact, and so widespread was the criticism that Mody backtracked and told Clare-Lees that the Indian commercial community should have been consulted more widely. Congress bulletins in Bombay called Mody 'the hireling of the mill-owners' and 'lackey of Lancashire who feels more for Britain than for Bombay'.[170] The almost unanimous condemnation by the Indian business community of the Ottawa Pact and then of the Mody–Lees Pact, and the leading role played in this by Birla, convinced the India Office that FICCI could not be ignored, if a share of the Indian market was to be secured for Lancashire. Even British businessmen realized this, and in late 1934 the Lancashire lobbies contacted Birla to explore the possibilities of negotiation. Birla, on his part, understood that the moment was right to enter into talks. Lancashire was at its most vulnerable, with the reforms not promising them any significant concessions. Further, Lancashire had learnt from the bitter experience of the Mody–Lees Pact that little could be achieved in India without the cooperation of men like Birla and Thakurdas. Behind Birla's responsiveness to Lancashire lay a deep understanding of the power structure in Whitehall. He knew full well the important role that Lancashire played as a pressure group on the India Office and realized that it would be most prudent to deal directly with Lancashire. He was realistic in conceding that Lancashire had to be accommodated in the Indian market. The challenge for him lay in ensuring that such an accommodation should take place on the terms of Indian business, rather than those advanced by Lancashire. Birla reasoned that if Lancashire could be convinced that it could get a share of the Indian market, Lancashire could be trusted to put pressure on the India Office to negotiate with Gandhi. This, in turn, would lead to a change in the India Office's attitude towards Gandhi and would facilitate an acceptance of the reforms scheme. Moreover, the interests of Indian business, Birla believed, would not be harmed, as Indian mills no longer felt threatened by competition from Lancashire and could easily compete as equals.[171]

Birla was in close contact with Lancashire lobbyists like Sir Reginald Clarke and William McColin Kirkpatrick, a member of Parliament (MP) from Lancashire. Both had been old acquaintances of Birla from their Calcutta days.[172] Clarke and Kirkpatrick, after consulting Birla, held talks with Hoare, and R.A. Butler, the Under Secretary of State for India, was then deputed to hold talks with the Lancashire MPs.[173] Both Clarke and Kirkpatrick realized the powerful influence which Birla enjoyed in Indian commercial circles, especially in Calcutta. Clarke now took the opportunity to write to Birla: 'What is required is for someone of your standing to let the Lancashire industrialists know what the Indian mercantile community is prepared to support to secure a basis of agreement and to create machinery for cooperation.'[174]

Birla replied by setting the record straight and said that Lancashire had been terribly wrong in dealing with men like Mody and ignoring the 'real representatives' of the Indian mercantile community.[175] He further pointed out that Lancashire would still be mistaken if it persisted in seeking a settlement with the government to the exclusion of FICCI. Even if Lancashire were successful in striking a deal with the government, he explained, it would not be enforceable and would 'result in greater hostility and intensification of Swadeshi spirit.' Moreover, Indian mills could easily make things difficult for Lancashire by intensifying competition. The only solution, Birla impressed upon Clarke, lay in dealing with those who would count in the new dispensation:

In their own interest they should have a pact with and assurance from those who will count in future...I think it would be very wise on the part of Lancashire to take the Indian politician with them on political grounds and I am ready to help them. If, on the other hand, Lancashire relied too much on the Government they may get a pact but not the market.

Birla encouraged Lancashire to meet right-wing Congressmen to obtain their support. The man to meet, he told Clarke, was Bhulabhai Desai, the 'Bombay man'. He promised that, if Indian business and Lancashire could settle amicably, he would ensure that the Congress would no longer give a call for the boycott of foreign goods.[176] Birla tried hard to get Lancashire to recognize the influence of FICCI and to consult the 'real representatives' of Indian business in all future negotiations. However, only a section among Lancashire business valued his advice. In 1935, disregarding Birla's opinion, Lancashire persisted in signing a trade agreement with the Government of India without consulting Indian business. Birla's position was vindicated when the agreement failed to be endorsed in the CLA where the official motion was defeated. Bhulabhai Desai, the leader of the Congress party in the Assembly, declared that the vote was a protest against those ignoring the interests of both the consumer and Indian mercantile community.[177]

Birla's fight to secure recognition for FICCI as the sole representative of Indian commercial interests was finally successful in April 1935 when he, along with Thakurdas, Kasturbhai Lalbhai and Walchand Hirachand, was invited by the government to act as unofficial advisers to negotiate the Indo-British Trade Agreement.[178] This recognition came belatedly as both the Government of India and the India Office were forced to recognize the stature of Birla and FICCI. Lancashire played a major role in bringing about this change of perception. At last, by the stiff opposition put forward to the Ottawa Pact and by the successful undermining of the Mody–Lees Pact, Birla and his associates had been able to demonstrate both to Lancashire and to the government that they were the men with whom business had to be done.

The negotiations for the Indo-British Trade Agreement started in 1936. By this time the political situation had changed significantly for Birla. Willingdon, who treated him as an 'untouchable,' had left India. Provincial autonomy was high on the political agenda, and Birla was excited at the prospect of seeing Congress ministries assume power in the provinces. His mission now was to get the Congress right-wing to accept office under the Government of India Act of 1935 and to see how Indian control over federal finance could be expedited by the early inauguration of Federation, a story we continue in the following chapter.

Notes and References

[1] Birla, *In the Shadow of the Mahatma*, Introduction, p. XV.

[2] Speech by Birla at the 4th session of the Indian Industrial and Commercial Congress, 31 December 1926, cited in *Indian Annual Register (IAR)*, 1926, July–December, pp. 423–5.

[3] *Ibid.*

[4] On the other hand members such as the representatives of European capital such as *Holberton* and *Montagu*, E. Webb from the Bengal Chamber of Commerce favoured a policy of protection with discrimination. See *Report of the Indian Fiscal Commission 1921–22, and Minute of Dissent, 1922*, Cmd 1764. Also see speech by Sir Campbell

Rhodes of Bengal Chamber of Commerce at Assocham's Fourth Annual Meeting, 8 January 1923, *Indian Annual Register*, 1923, Vol. I, pp. 713–28.

[5] As a staunch believer in protectionism, Birla's experience of the Fiscal Commission of 1921–2 was a bitter one, as he felt that Indian views were disregarded, in spite of 'the almost complete unanimity with which Indian witnesses opposed the principle of Imperial preference.' *Report of the Indian Fiscal Commission 1921–22*, chapter XIII, p. 139.

[6] Presidential address to FICCI, 14 February 1930 cited in G.D. Birla, *Path to Prosperity* (Allahabad, 1950), pp. 141–2. Birla saw the advantage that the political affinity of European businessmen with the administrators gave them and he understood the intimate connection between European capital and administration. Citing the example of the British ICS (Indian Civil Service) officers he wrote that they were influenced by 'the die-hard views freely expressed among the businessmen, with whom they closely associated socially. Indeed it could be remarked that, whereas some of the businessmen of humble origins were anxious that their sons should enter the Indian Civil Service or the Indian army because they regarded this as a rise in the social ladder that they wished to climb, officials on the contrary, besought their business friends to take their sons into firms in order that they should have more prosperous financial careers than fell to the average official.' G.D. Birla, 'India's War Prosperity' in *ibid*, p. 183 cited in Rajat Kanta Ray, *Industrialisation in India, 1914–47 Growth and Conflict in the Private Corporate Sector* (Delhi, 1979), p. 298.

[7] In the years of the World War I the rising price of silver threw the old ratio out of gear, and by the time the War had ended the value of the rupee, in a silver coin, had risen to 2s. The Babington Smith Committee on the suggestion of Keynes recommended to fixing the value of the rupee at 2s. 0d. in 1919, even though the actual rate was 1s. 8d. at that time. The worldwide fall in the prices of silver and other commodities put pressure on the high exchange rate of the rupee. In 1921–2 there was a sharp decline of the exchange rate and a deflationary policy had to be followed to support the exchange rate. The contraction of currency resulted in exchange reaching the level of 1s. 4d. by 1923. In 1925 the Hilton Young Commission, despite the dissent of Purshotamdas Thakurdas, recommended fixing the rupee at 1s. 6d. Indian commercial opinion wanted it to be fixed at the pre-War level of 1s. 4d. Indian business argued for a devaluation of the rupee. The new rate was advantageous to the British exporters to India and would hurt the Indian exporters. For a detailed study of the question see D. Rothermund, *An Economic History of India*, especially chapter 7. For Keynes' arguments, see Anand Chandavarkar, *Keynes and India. A Study in Economics and Biography* (London, 1989), chapter 4. Also see, D.K. Malhotra, *History and Problems of Indian Currency 1835–1939* (Lahore, 1939).

[8] Birla's speech at the fourth session of the Indian Industrial and Commercial Congress cited in *IAR*, July–December 1926, pp. 423–5.

[9] Although Indian merchants had organized in chambers of commerce and trade organizations these had remained very restricted in nature. The earliest chamber was the Coconada Chamber of Commerce formed in 1868. The Coconada chamber restricted membership to merchants or firms carrying on business in Coconada or other places within the districts of Kistna, Godavari, Vizakapatnam and Ganjam. The Bengal National Chamber of Commerce established in 1887 restricted itself with its objective to 'aid and stimulate the development of commercial, agricultural and industrial enterprises in Bengal and Assam and to protect the commercial interests of all persons trading therein'; the Marwari Association established in 1896 was primarily concerned with the interests

of the Marwari community; the Indian Merchants Chamber established in 1907, although it did not state so was largely concerned with the interests of the Bombay region. Other chambers such as the Maharashtra Chamber of Commerce also clearly restricted themselves to regions or to specific trades.

[10] *Hindustan Times,* 7 May 1927.

[11] Birla's speech at the Fourth Session of the Indian Industrial and Commercial Congress cited in *IAR,* July–December 1926, pp. 423–5.

[12] He cited the successful example of concerted action by indigenous business which had led to the abolition of excise duty in the cotton textile industry.

[13] In the changed circumstances of the post-War years, the European chambers of commerce felt the need for increased consolidation into an all-India body. The consolidation of the Cochin, Karachi, Coconada, Upper India, Punjab, Tuticorin, Chittagong, Calcutta, Bombay and Madras Chambers in the ASSOCHAM in 1920 can be directly attributed to the increasing scope of legislation, the breakthrough by Indian business into hitherto European-dominated industries and the 'sharper spirit of trade rivalry' between Indian and European interests. A study of the Bengal Chamber of Commerce states that although 'occasional informal consultations between the Chambers in the three presidency capitals had for long been the practice, the integration of economic policy into an all-Indian pattern, an enlarging corpus of legislation, the rapid growth of Indian business and a sharper spirit of trade rivalry, as well as the mobilization of important Indian industrial financial support for political purposes and the hiving off of indigenous concerns into national and communal organisations, all pointed to the desirability of more regular and formal processes of consultation between the older chambers of commerce, which became less representative of Indian interests from the end of the Ist World War.' G.W. Tyson, *The Bengal Chamber of Commerce and Industry 1853–1953. A Centenary Survey* (Calcutta, 1953), pp. 122–3 For a history of the European Bombay Chamber of Commerce see Rusi J. Daruwala, *The Bombay Chamber Story* (Bombay, 1986).

[14] According to Ray, 'the ASSOCHAM resolution produced an immediate impact on Indian business organisation in its political aspects. The resolution galvanised Indian businessmen into a new effort to build up an all-India organisation of their own.' Rajat Ray, *Industrialisation in India*, p. 304. For the story of the resolution and the dissent on it by the Bombay Chamber of Commerce see R.J.F. Sullivan, *One Hundred Years of Bombay. History of the Bombay Chamber of Commerce 1836–1936* (Bombay), p. 161.

[15] Thakurdas (1879–1961) was the most important Bombay businessman in the inter-War years. He was a founder member of the Indian Merchants' Chamber, member, Indian Retrenchment Committee, member, Royal Commission on Indian Currency and Finance (1926), delegate to the Round Table Conferences 1930–3 and one of the most prominent members of the FICCI. Closely associated with the Tatas, he had a range of business interests.

[16] Birla to Thakurdas, 7 December 1923, Purshotamdas Thakurdas Papers, (henceforth, PT Papers), File 42, Part IV.

[17] Thakurdas to Birla, 11 December 1923 and Thakurdas to Birla, 7 January 1927, PT Papers, File 42, Part IV.

[18] Indian Chamber of Commerce Calcutta, *Diamond Jubilee 1925–1985 Commemorative Volume.*

[19] For instance, there were the Scindia Steam Navigation Co., Soorajmull Nagarmull, A.C. Bannerjee and Co., and Anandji Haridas and Co.

[20] *Ibid.* The Chamber had two types of membership, local and mofussil. Merchants, bankers, ship-owners, representatives of commercial, transport or insurance companies, brokers and persons engaged in trade who were Indians were eligible for membership.

[21] Birla to Purshotamdas Thakurdas, 2 May 1928, PT Papers, File 42, Part III.

[22] The most prominent among these were the Indian Sugar Mills' Association, Indian Chemical Manufacturers' Association, Indian Paper Mills' Association, Indian Insurance Companies' Association, Indian Jute Balers' Association, East India Jute Association, Indian Colliery Owners' Association, Indian Tea Merchants' Association, Shareholders' Association, and the Indian Coal Merchants' Association.

[23] In 1913 an attempt was made by Sir Fazulbhoy Currimbhoy Ibrahim, a leading mill-owner of Bombay. Ibrahim planned for an Indian Commercial Congress but his proposal was delayed due to the outbreak of the War and the first Indian Commercial Congress could only be held in 1915. The Congress resolved to establish an Associated Indian Chamber of Commerce and elected a provincial committee to carry on the work of getting the Association registering and enrolling members. Nothing, however, came out of these attempts. In 1920 the Indian Industrial Congress , which had been started in 1905 under the presidentship of R.C. Dutt, and the Indian Commercial Congress were amalgamated to form the Indian Industrial and Commercial Congress (IICC). Federation of Indian Chambers of Commerce and Industry, *Silver Jubilee Souvenir 1927–1952* (New Delhi, 1952), pp. 1–15.

[24] The next session of the IICC was held in Calcutta on 31 December and 1–2 January 1927 under the presidentship of Sir Dinshaw Petit. Birla was the president of the reception committee and made a memorable appeal to Indian businessmen at the session. Birla's speech at the fourth Industrial and Commercial Congress, 31 December 1926, cited in *IAR*, July–December 1926, pp. 423–5. A committee was appointed consisting of one representative of each association and chamber affiliated to the IICC with Harkrishan Lal as president and J.K. Mehta as secretary to draft a constitution to be placed before a special session.

[25] Malaviya himself supported the resolution: 'You can influence the course of events, commercial, industrial and agricultural and even political, in a larger way and to a greater extent by making this federation a living institution than probably any people at present imagine.' Two years later the term industry was added, making it FICCI.

[26] A provisional committee consisting of Dinshaw Petit, Thakurdas, Birla, Jamal Mohammad, Lala Harkishen Lal, Adamji Haji Dawood, Jamshed N.R. Mehta, Vikramjit Singh, Shri Ram, W.C. Bannerjee, B.F. Madon and Kasturbhai Lalbhai was appointed to undertake the preparatory work. D.P. Khaitan and A.C. Banerjee were elected joint treasurers.

[27] Purshotamdas Thakurdas, 'My Associations with the Federation' in *ibid*, p. 184.

[28] *Ibid.*

[29] Speech of Birla at the Second Round Table Conference cited in FICCI, *Report of the Representatives of the Federation on the Round Table Conference, 1932* (Bombay, 1932).

[30] One of Birla's contemporary in the CLA was H.P. Mody. In his memoirs he recounted the atmosphere that prevailed in the House: 'In the first year, I felt rather subdued in the presence of such outstanding figures in the national movement as Pandit Motilal Nehru, Pandit M.M. Malaviya and Mr M.A. Jinnah. Mr V. Patel was in the chair at the time and ruled with a rod of iron, and even as a new Member I had to wait before I could catch his eyes. The Assembly was impressive in other ways too—members of Govt, officials and leaders of the various parties wore morning dress in the House. What a far

cry from the bush-coats and flopping jackets which are so much in fashion nowadays.'
See Mody's, 'As I look back' in H.P. Mody, *Reflections. Wise and Otherwise* (Bombay,
1961), p. 104.

[31] Thakurdas was nominated to the Council of State in 1923 by Lord Reading and
in 1924 was nominated to the CLA.

[32] Sassoon was a leading mill-owner in Bombay. He headed the E.D. Sassoon United
Mills, the Alexandra, Edward Sassoon and Myer Sassoon Mills and other dye works. He
had been nominated for a term earlier in 1921 by Lord Reading. For details of his career
see Stanley Jackson, *The Sassoons. Portrait of a Dynasty* (London, 1989). He was succeeded
by Mody who was a prominent Bombay industrialist and was a partner in the textile firm
of C.N. Wadia. He had been member of the Bombay Municipal Corporation since 1913;
in 1927 was elected chairman of the Bombay Millowners' Association; in 1928, president
of the Indian Merchants' Chamber and in 1930 was a delegate to the first Round Table
Conference.

[33] Elected only in 1930, the year Birla and Thakurdas resigned, Jehangir was a major
financier in Bombay and controlled two cotton mills. He had earlier been a nominated
member of the Bombay Legislative Council in the 1920s and was the president of the
Bombay Municipal Corporation in 1919–20. Later he was also a delegate to the Round
Table Conferences.

[34] A Bombay-based merchant, Rahimtoola had been a member of the Bombay
Municipal Corporation during 1919–1930, and had been nominated to a number of
official committees. He was elected from the Muhammadan Rural constituency of
Bombay Central division.

[35] Chetty, a businessman and vakil was elected on a Congress ticket from the non-
Muhammadan Rural constituency of Salem and Coimbatore cum North Arcot. He was
the Congress chief whip in the legislative assembly from 1926 to 29. He was also a
prominent member of FICCI.

[36] Haji was the manager of the Rangoon office of Scindia Steamship Company and
was known to be close to Walchand Hirachand on whose persuasion he had stood for
the CLA. Haji represented the Bombay central division non- Muhammadan constituency.
In 1926 he had attended the Maritime session of the International Labour Conference
as a representative of the Indian Industrial and Commercial Association.

[37] Birla declared that he was only administering a warning to the Finance Member
that popular opinion would not agree to additional taxation and the only remedy lay in
curtailing recurring and non-recurring expenditure. He opposed sterling borrowings, the
high bank rate and currency contraction by the government to maintain the ratio and
argued for protection of industry. See Birla's speech in the CLA, 4 March 1929, cited
in Birla, *Path to Prosperity*, pp. 326–7.

[38] Birla was attacked by W.S. Lamb who alleged that Birla was supporting the increase
in excise duty on kerosene because he was interested in oil imports. Birla defended his
position: 'It is quite correct that I have a small interest in the import of kerosene oil, but
in this House, Sir, I represent only one interest, ... Sir, it is a mere coincidence that I
happen to have a special interest in all the five things which it is proposed to tax in the
present finance bill. Sir, I am a small importer of sugar, and as such I do not like the import
duty; and yet, in the national interest, I have supported it. Then, Sir, I carry large stocks
of silver, and therefore, the silver duty has benefited me considerably, and yet I have
opposed the silver duty. Then again, Sir, the income tax touches my pocket directly, but
I have not said a word against it. And Sir, the proposal for Imperial Preference is calculated

to benefit my own mills—situated as they are in up-country—more than the Bombay mills, and yet, in the national interest, I have opposed it. Therefore, Sir, if I have supported the present proposal I have done so because I felt that the national interest demanded that the excise duty and the import duty should be equalised', *Legislative Assembly Debates*, 20 March 1930, Vol. 1, No. 38 (Delhi, 1930), pp. 2074–5. Thakurdas also came to his defence and informed the Assembly that after the Birla firm started importing oil, telegrams had been sent by mischief-makers to the principals of oil companies in America alleging that Birla was selling oil under the brand 'Gandhi oil' and was encouraging political agitation in the country, *Legislative Assembly Debates*, 21 March 1930, Vol. 1, No. 39 (Delhi, 1930), pp. 2126–37.

[39] *Capital*, 2 April 1929.

[40] *Hindustan Times*, 6 March 1929.

[41] The links between the Swarajists and Bombay industrialists are well known. From the early 1920s Motilal Nehru's party had enjoyed the support of businessmen such as Sir J.B. Petit, and from 1925 onwards the Swarajists were patronized by Bombay and Ahmedabad millowners. Motilal was known to be personally close to the Tatas with whom he regularly stayed during his trips to Bombay. Thakurdas too was close to Motilal. Their close links are illustrated by the fact that in 1925 they discussed the possibility of buying a paper for Swarajist propaganda, and that in 1927 Thakurdas was nominated by Nehru, then heading the All-Parties Committee, as the chairman of a sub-committee to enquire into the financial aspects of the separation of Sindh. Motilal also had close links with other industrialists such as Kasturbhai Lalbhai who attended most of the private meetings of the Swarajists and was regarded by Motilal as a better Swarajist than many party members. For a study of Kasturbhai, see Dwijendra Tripathi, *The Dynamics of a Tradition: Kasturbhai Lalbhai and his Enterpreneurship* (Delhi, 1981).

[42] For a general background of the steel industry, see D.M. Wagle, 'Imperial Preference and the Indian Steel Industry 1924–39', *Economic History Review*, Vol. XXXIV, No. 1, 1981, pp. 120–31.

[43] He argued that the Indian producer would have to pay a higher duty to protect the British manufacturer; that under the differential duty introduced in the scheme the UK manufacturers would be tempted to lower quality and that there was the danger of the fall in prices of the UK products in which case the duty on the UK products would have to be increased and that the differentiation between standard and non-standard steel which the Bill used did not exist at all except in structural sections. Birla speech in CLA, 14 February 1927, cited in *Path to Prosperity*, pp. 146–53.

[44] *Hindustan Times*, 20 February 1927.

[45] For Motilal's speech see Manoranjan Jha, *Role of Central Legislature in the Freedom Struggle*, New Delhi, 1972, pp. 117–8.

[46] Their differences went back to 1921 when Sir Dorabji was a leading member of the Bombay capitalists who publicly denounced Gandhi's Non-cooperation Movement, while Birla advocated moderation. Later, in 1929 Dorabji supported moves by Rahimtoola to start a 'capitalist party' of both Indian and European members in the CLA to fight the 'red scare' and to break the strike waves. This was contrary to Birla's views as we shall see later.

[47] The Tatas joined FICCI only in 1937 and then withdrew with the start of the World War II. For a study of J.R.D. Tata's career and politics see R.M. Lala, *Beyond the Last Blue Mountain. A Life of J.R.D. Tata* (Bombay, 1992).

[48] The bill was introduced to amend the Indian Coinage Act of 1906 and the Indian Paper Currency act of 1923 and to fix the rupee at 1s. 6d.

49 For a background of the ratio controversy see Aditya Mukherjee, 'The Rupee Question, 1926–8: Rupee–Sterling Ratio and the Gold Standard' in *Studies in History*, Vol. 5, No. 1 new series (1989).

50 For instance, they had come together in a Currency League which generously funded the Bombay-based newspaper *Free Press of India* which transmitted over 86,755 words of currency propaganda between October 1926 and February 1927, A.D.D. Gordon, *Businessmen and Politics. Rising Nationalism and a Modernising Economy in Bombay 1918–1933* (New Delhi, 1978), p. 184.

51 Birla to Gandhi, Undated Note 1926 in PT Papers, File 111, cited in Gordon, *Businessmen and Politics*, p. 186.

52 B.F. Madon, a prominent member of the Indian Merchants' Chamber and a currency propagandist, was drafted by FICCI to come to Delhi and speak to legislators about it. Many legislators were unaware of the implications of the ratio question, and Madon reportedly spent four hours with one Congress politician alone. A special memorandum was drafted by Birla along with Thakurdas, Madon and Jamnadas Mehta to clarify the issues involved for the benefit of the legislators. Frank Moraes, Sir Purshotamdas Thakurdas (Bombay, 1957), pp. 102–3.

53 *Hindustan Times*, 8 February 1927; the paper commented: 'It is true that the Congress Working Committee is not a committee of economic experts, but a body consisting of able politicians. There is some sense in the argument of those who urge that an economic question of the nature of the currency question should not be made a party question. If the Assembly were a body on which there was any likelihood of Government members voting not en bloc but according to their discretion, it would have been proper for the parties of the opposition to adopt a similar attitude. But when Government benches are determined to vote en bloc for a ratio which is decidedly against the economic interests of the country, the nonofficial benches must perforce act together to save the country from ruin.' *Hindustan Times*, 9 February 1927.

54 'I wish to say to the members of this House that their duty is very clear. It is quite possible that the Govt may be able to carry this measure through, with the support of nominated members, mysterious brokers, reputed contractors and pampered professors, but I may say that even if we are defeated, our defeat will be glorious and if the Govt are victorious, their victory will be the victory of wrong over right. I again beg to appeal to this House to vote solidly against the 1s. 6d. ratio with one will and one voice.' Appealing to the European bloc he said: 'I wish to tell my European friends in this House, that although they were not all of them born and bred in this country, they have eaten the salt of India and I hope they will not be untrue to the salt.' Birla's speech in the CLA, cited in Birla, *Path to Prosperity*, p. 231.

55 Birla was very upset with the voting results which he attributed to the government's ploy of 'snatching votes' that the Bill passed. In a speech to the fourth Maharashtra Commercial Congress he said: 'I need not dilate on the opposition which the measure met at the hands of the popular parties in the Assembly and the defeat of the opposition with the help of snatching votes. It proved to be at any rate the proverbial "last straw on the camel's back." *Hindustan Times*, 6 December 1929.

56 The bill was first drafted at the instigation of Walchand Hirachand who got it drafted by a lawyer and retired high court judge of Madras and then tried to have it brought before the CLA by K.C. Neogy. However the necessary number of votes for taking it into consideration were not forthcoming and thus it could not be taken up. Moreover, there were doubts whether such legislation could be taken up by the Assembly.

Walchand conferred with legal experts to get an opinion on this and only then was the bill introduced by S.N. Haji. G.D. Khanolkar, *Walchand Hirachand* (Bombay, 1969), pp. 204–6.

[57] They objected to the Bill on the ground that it was economically unsound, Indian capital would not be forthcoming adequately to replace foreign lines, and reservation would lead to higher freight rates which would adversely affect the consumer. *Capital*, echoing the sentiments of the European chambers, observed: 'As long as the pioneer and non paying stage of development lasts, or if the venture is a complete failure, nothing much is said. But when the risks have been run, when large sums have been spent in establishing trade channels, when, in a word, the enterprise has become profitable, the cry is raised that the pioneer must withdraw and give place to those who have stood aside while the trail was blazed for them ... How often do Indian politicians, industrialists and workers in many other spheres endeavour to supplant British efforts when they would be so much more usefully occupied in striving to supplement it! And what a tremendous benefit it would confer on India to take the latter word as the watchword instead of the former! Whether it is banking, insurance, jute manufacture, river steamships, or any other sphere of effort or enterprise, public or private, Indian effort seems to concentrate on dispossessing the men in possession instead of cultivating new ground'. *Capital*, 24 May 1928.

[58] Birla accused ASSOCHAM of resorting to 'dirty tactics' and condemned its attitude as a 'desperate attempt of the British commercial interest in India to maintain their unnatural position at the sacrifice of the most vital interests of the country.' FICCI published a reply to the European Chambers written by Birla, who was its president, which set out the case for Indian shipping and refuted the allegations of ASSOCHAM. Federation of Indian Chambers of Commerce and Industry, *A Statement on behalf of the Federation of Indian Chambers of Commerce and Industry in reply to the circular letter dated the 27th July 1929 issued by the Associated Chambers of Commerce of India and Ceylon to influence opinion in England against India's right to adapt her economic policy to her own needs* (henceforth FICCI reply to ASSOCHAM), (Calcutta, 1929).

[59] Gandhi wrote that he would welcome all action that would protect them against foreign aggression especially when the latter is grossly unfair. *Young India*, 2 August 1928, cited in Khanolkar, *Walchand Hirachand*, pp. 222–3, fn 13.

[60] *Capital*, 22 August 1929.

[61] Big business' demand for the reservation of coastal shipping remained unfulfilled inspite of its continued efforts throughout the late 1920s and the 1930s.

[62] Motilal Nehru led the opposition by denouncing the Bill as a 'direct attack on Indian Nationalism, on the Indian National Congress and as the Slavery of India Bill Number One. Bipan Chandra, *India's Struggle for Independence* (New Delhi, 1988), p. 244.

[63] Birla's speech in the Central Legislative Assembly on 5 February 1929, *Legislative Assembly Debates 4*, Vol. 1 (Delhi, 1929), pp. 485–90.

[64] The *Capital* observed: 'Pandit Malaviya and President Patel indulged in a good deal of hysterical nonsense implying that India had been coerced and tricked by a Machiavellian administration into making heavy and pecuniary sacrifices in the interests of Lancashire mills.' *Capital*, 3 April 1930.

[65] In his speech he said: 'I think Bombay is in a frightful condition, and it is the duty of this House to treat her case sympathetically, and not to criticise her at a time when she requires a sympathetic word and sympathetic treatment more than she required at any other time. I also wish to say that whatever be the criticisms against Bombay, that is the only place where you get a little glimpse of Indian management and Indian enterprise. You kill Bombay

and you kill the entire Indian trade ... It is true that Bombay has become impatient, as one of my friends remarked. She has lost her nerves. It is therefore all the more necessary that we should not allow her to commit suicide by taking a cup of poison when she requires a cup of milk, that is judicious nourishment and wise counsel.' Birla's speech in the CLA, 25 March 1930, cited in Birla, *Path to Prosperity*, pp. 173–6. Also see *Legislative Assembly Debates*, Vol. 1, No. 42 (Delhi, 1930), pp. 2417–27.

66 Birla declared that, while he sympathized with the case of the Bombay industry for protection, the proposals in the Bill did not give adequate protection. He claimed with the Bill the price of imported English goods would be regulated on the basis of prices of non-British goods which would have to be sold at a higher price on account of the 5 per cent extra duty. He thus argued that if 5 per cent extra raises the price of all imports from UK, it would mean that the Indian consumer would be paying Rs 2 crores annually for the benefit of Lancashire. The *Capital* commented: 'Some of the opposition speeches in the Legislative Assembly (including Birla's and Malaviya) in order to create prejudice against the Cotton Tariff Bill, asserted that its adoption would amount to "making Lancashire a gift of Rs $2\frac{1}{4}$ crores yearly, at the cost of India". This, of course, is a gross miscalculation ... In the Assembly, however, except on the official benches, the consumers have few champions and are envisaged only as sheep to be fleeced. The leaders who should be protecting the interests of the consumers are blinded by political prejudice, and would not miss an opportunity to inflict an injury on Lancashire even at the price of inflicting an even greater injury on a considerable section of their own countrymen.' *Capital*, 3 April 1930.

67 Birla's speech in CLA, cited in Birla, *Path to Prosperity*, pp. 174–93. Also see *Legislative Assembly Debates*, Vol. 1, No. 42 (Delhi, 1930), pp. 2417–27.

68 M. Jha, *Role of Central Legislature in the Freedom Struggle*, pp. 166–7.

69 In a speech to the Maharashtra Commercial Congress he warned the Bombay Millowners' Association not to think of supporting imperial preference as they would be 'alienating the sympathy of the whole country'. He warned that Bombay business would be isolated and that 'he could foresee that not only all the sections of the popular block in the Assembly, but the whole Indian mercantile community, irrespective of province and caste and creed would oppose any such plea for Imperial Preference by the back door.' Birla's speech as President of the Fourth session of the Maharashtra Commercial Congress in December 1929. *Hindustan Times*, 6 December 1929.

70 Birla to Thakurdas, 26 April 1929, PT Papers, File 42.

71 Birla to Thakurdas, 26 April 1929, PT Papers, File 42.

72 With the change in the party's plans, Motilal offered to return the balance in the election fund to Birla in March 1930. Birla asked him to utilize it 'for any good purpose which is not against my creed or purpose.' Motilal Nehru to Birla, 28 February 1930 and Birla to Motilal Nehru, 3 March 1930, in *Nehru Family and Ghanshyamdas Birla*, pp. 16 and 18.

73 Birla to Thakurdas, 19 June 1929, in PT Papers, File 42.

74 Birla to Thakurdas, 30 July 1929, PT Papers, File 42.

75 'Young India', 30 January 1930. *The Collected Works of Mahatma Gandhi*, Vol. XLII, October 1929–February 1930 (Ahmedabad, 1970), pp. 432–5. For an overall picture see Judith Brown, *Gandhi and Civil Disobedience: the Mahatma in Indian politics 1928–1934* (Cambridge, 1974).

76 'Young India', 20 March 1930, in *Collected Works of Mahatma Gandhi*, Vol. XLIII, March–June 1930 (Ahmedabad, 1971), pp. 40–5. Also see D.G. Tendulkar, *Mahatma*, Vol. II (New Delhi, 1969), p. 15.

[77] Birla's views resonated in Thakurdas' letter to Gandhi in late January 1930 when he too tried to dissuade the Mahatma from launching his satyagraha: 'I do not believe that India will benefit now or within a few decades by revolution as by the process of evolution ... if the constitution is not sufficiently changed after the Conference in London as to make us masters in our own house, I can understand your impatience, but to resort to civil disobedience does strike me as being a hasty step.' For Gandhi's reply to Thakurdas, 9 February 1930, see *Collected Works of Mahatma Gandhi*, Vol. XLII, October 1929–February 1930, p. 465.

[78] Birla, *In the Shadow of the Mahatma*, p. 44.

[79] Birla's radical support came despite opposition from family elders; his father was known to be opposed to the Movement. Confidential note by A.H. Ghuznavi, MLA, 15 September 1930, Home Poll. F N 190/1930 cited in Sumit Sarkar, 'The Logic of Gandhian Nationalism: Civil Disobedience and the Gandhi–Irwin Pact (1930–31)', in *Indian Historical Review*, Vol. III, No. 1, July 1976, p. 121.

[80] He said: 'Indians recognised long ago the urgent necessity of giving protection to their industries, and in the absence of any popular control over the fiscal policy, they had to content themselves with propaganda in favour of Swadeshi and for the boycott of foreign goods. It may be easy to misrepresent the motive of the capitalist when he advocates protection and to depict him as the arch-enemy of the consumer. But what about the Indian National Congress which is certainly not a capitalist organisation?...What does the popular propaganda for a boycott of foreign goods mean if not protection to the indigenous industry.' Birla's presidential address at the third annual meeting of FICCI, 14 February 1930, cited in Birla, *Path to Prosperity*, pp. 141–2.

[81] He further continued: 'I am not so much concerned with what the Government is going to do, as with what we are going to do. I think our duty to the country is clear, and we businessmen must give a clear lead to the country as to what is demanded in the best economic interests of the country.' Birla's speech at the FICCI session, 16 February 1930, *Proceedings of the Annual Meeting FICCI February 1930–35*, Vol. III (Delhi, 1935), pp. 263–5. The nationalist press lauded Birla's speech in glowing terms. The *Hindu* wrote: 'It is a thought provoking utterance. The essence of his conclusion is a gravely disturbing proposition that India is sinking deeper and deeper into the condition of financial embarrassment verging on insolvency.' The *Indian Daily Mail* commented: 'The Viceroy and the members of the Executive Council who listened to it have seldom had the plain and untarnished truth about the fiscal policy so forcibly dinned into their ears.' See *Hindustan Times*, 19 February 1930.

[82] See his letter to Gandhi, 28 April 1930, in Birla, *Bapu*, Vol. I, pp. 140–2.

[83] At the ceremony, the Governor paid glowing tributes to the family's philanthropy. See *Hindustan Times*, 1 November 1930.

[84] He asserted that 'to maintain that the present economic depression is due mainly to the political distress is to make a statement entirely lacking in truth ... It would be sheer absurdity to maintain that due to the movement of the boycott of the foreign cloth, Indian mills are adversely affected. The matter of the fact is that, but for the boycott movement most of the Bombay mills would have shut their doors long ago.' *Hindustan Times*, 17 August 1930.

[85] There was a substantial drop in cloth imports during 1930: net import of cloth into India was 1897 million yards in 1929–30. In 1930 it fell to 873 million yards and in 1931–2 to 760 million yards. Sir Sorabji Sakalatwala of the House of Tatas commented on this sharp decline: 'It can be fairly stated that 80 per cent of the reduction in imports

between July and December (1930) can be attributed to the boycott; in other words the boycott was responsible for reduction of 460 million yards in piece-goods imports, and nearly 6 million lbs. in yarn imports. There may be some recovery in imports before the end of the financial year, but a total reduction of at least 800 to 1000 million yards in piece-goods imports may be expected during the year which comes to a close on 31st March 1931.' S.D. Mehta cited in Arun Joshi, *Lala Shri Ram* (New Delhi, 1975), p. 225.

[86] Birla to A. Sarabhai, 30 April 1930, PT Papers, File 100.

[87] 'Interview with J.B. Kripalani', 4 May 1930, *Collected Works of Mahatma Gandhi*, Vol. XLIII, pp. 384–6.

[88] Birla to Gandhi, 11 October 1927, in Birla, *Towards Swadeshi* (Bombay, 1980), p. 3. Birla took to wearing khadi in 1927.

[89] Birla to Gandhi, 11 April 1928, Birla, *Towards Swadeshi*, pp. 4–7.

[90] Also see Birla to Gandhi, 28 April 1930, *ibid*, pp. 11–12.

[91] Rameshwardas Birla also sent Gandhi a scheme for popularizing khadi with the co-operation of Indian mills. Gandhi to R.D. Birla, 28 April 1930, *ibid*, p. 10.

[92] Birla to Gandhi, 8 April 1930, *ibid*, pp. 11–12.

[93] In February 1930 its president Gangjee warned the Government that, if 'in addition to the tenseness of the atmosphere in the political situation, the unrest in the economic sphere and the question of the gnawing poverty and the unemployment of the people is not solved, I am afraid the result would be calamitous and I warn the government to consider this very carefully.' *Hindustan Times*, 9 February 1930. In March 1930 Birla's old associate, D.P. Khaitan, a leading member of the Chamber, declared: 'At long last there is dawning upon our minds the realisation of the stubborn fact that unless India attains self government it is difficult for her to improve her economic position.' D.P. Khaitan's speech at the special meeting of the Indian Chamber of Commerce, Calcutta, 5 March 1930, Annual Report for 1930, p 189. Cited by S. Sarkar, 'The Logic of Gandhian Nationalism: Civil Disobedience and the Gandhi–Irwin Pact (1930–31)' in *Indian Historical Review*, Vol. III, No. I, July 1976, p. 122.

[94] Endorsing many of Birla's views at the FICCI session, Mody declared: 'As you know, the outlook of our President Mr Birla on economic affairs is national as it properly should be; our great grievance is that our government's outlook on economic matters is anything but national with the result that today the industrial and commercial community of India are among the strongest critics of the present government.' H.P. Mody's 'Vote of thanks to the President' Minutes of third annual meeting held on 14 to 16 February 1930 at Delhi in FICCI, *Proceedings of Annual Meetings 1930–35*.

[95] Sir Malcolm Hailey, cited in Sir George Schuster, *Private Work and Public Causes* (Cowbridge, 1979), p. 109.

[96] Perhaps a typical business viewpoint was represented in the speech of M.L. Dahanukar, the vice-president of the Maharashtra Chamber of Commerce, when he explained why civil disobedience was deriving such an enthusiastic response from business organizations. Dahanukar explained: 'Businessmen as a rule love peace, but when even they seem to welcome such stormy days, it is up to those who hold power to pause and think.' He further declared: 'If the business community have expressed their sympathy with the present political movement and in places they have actually supported the same, it is due to their realisation this time (a realisation which was absent on the previous occasion, 1919–21) that they undoubtedly stand to gain in the end like the other classes in the country, when the nation as a whole benefits in consequence of the Congress achieving the goal after the necessary struggle.' *Hindustan Times*, 13 August 1930.

[97] The Chamber criticized the government resolution which turned down the recommendation of the Taxation Enquiry Committee Report for referring the case of the Salt industry to the Tariff Board for enquiry of the grant of protection to it. The Committee in its recommendation indicated 'how all the arguments adduced by the government were hollow and prejudiced.' *Capital*, 14 March 1929.

[98] Circular to PCCs, 22 February 1930, S. Gopal (ed.), *Selected Works of Jawaharlal Nehru*, Vol. IV (New Delhi, 1973), pp. 271–3, cited in Sarkar 'The Logic of Gandhian Nationalism: Civil Disobedience and the Gandhi–Irwin Pact (1930–31)' in *Indian Historical Review*, Vol. III, No. 1, July 1976, p. 122.

[99] FICCI's resolution stated: 'In the opinion of the Committee of the Federation, no conference (of the nature of the Round Table Conference) convened for the purpose of discussing the problem of constitutional advance can come to a solution of the present political difficulty which will be acceptable to the country, unless such a conference is attended by Mahatma Gandhi, as a free man, or at least has his approval. For this reason the Committee feel it necessary to recommend to the various member-bodies of the Federation not to nominate representatives of Indian commercial interests to the Round Table Conference unless Mahatma Gandhi is a party to the said Conference. The Committee desires to suggest to the member-bodies to inform their individual members of the undesirability of attending such a Conference if any individual members of the member-bodies be invited in their individual private capacity to such a conference.' FICCI, *Proceedings of Annual Meetings 1930–35*. Thakurdas later told Irwin that he was one of those anxious to attend the Conference but had been forced to boycott it because of the pressure by his Chamber. Irwin to Wedgwood Benn, 10 October 1930, Halifax Papers, Mss.Eur.C.152 (microfilm), Roll 16.

[100] Minutes of third annual meeting held on 14 to 16 February 1930 at Delhi in FICCI, *Proceedings of Annual Meeting 1930*.

[101] This Association prepared lists of cotton mills which were under Indian control and did not use foreign yarn, the type of goods manufactured by them and the names of their selling agents all over India. These lists were then widely advertised in the national press on behalf of FICCI to promote the cause of swadeshi. Many mill-owners, moreover, signed a declaration that they would not use imported yarn. The Ahmedabad mill-owners even went to the extent of agreeing not to import machinery from Britain unless it was absolutely unavoidable. Arun Joshi, *Lala Shri Ram*, pp. 224–5.

[102] Thakurdas to Irwin, 12 May 1930, Halifax Papers, Mss.Eur.C.152 (microfilm), Roll 15.

[103] As he explained, 'it is a fact that there are people in the country equally patriotic and honest if not more than some of us who believe that some good might be done to the country by their attending the Round Table Conference.' Birla to Lala Shri Ram, cited in Venkatsubbiah, *Enterprise and Economic Change. 50 Years of FICCI*, pp. 14–5.

[104] Birla received strong support from Shanmugham Chetty who also argued that Indian commerce must not go unrepresented at the Round Table Conference. He wrote to Shri Ram that 'as businessmen we have to take a more practical view of affairs and taking such a view I feel that whether the Round Table Conference gives to India what she demands or not its potentialities are considerable for harming Indian commercial interests in case such interests are not taken care of at the conference,' *ibid.*

[105] Birla to Thakurdas, 16 January 1931, PT Papers, File 42.

[106] Thakurdas to Irwin, 10 June 1930, Halifax Papers (microfilm), Roll 15. While Thakurdas was impatient for an immediate settlement, Birla was biding his time. He

wrote to Thakurdas that Gandhi could not be blamed: 'I do not think I can altogether blame Gandhiji. At first sight people may think Gandhiji to be very unreasonable, but stripped of all verbiage, his demand amounts to nothing else but Dominion Status. The Government by giving assurances to him could have easily won him over.' Birla to Thakurdas, PT Papers, File 104/1930 cited by Sumit Sarkar, 'The Logic of Gandhian Nationalism: Civil Disobedience and the Gandhi–Irwin Pact (1930–1)' in the *Indian Historical Review*, Vol. 3, No. 1, p. 137n.

[107] As Joseph Bhore, Commerce Member of the Viceroy's Council, confided to George Cunningham, the Viceroy's private secretary, 31 January 1931, Halifax Papers, Mss.Eur.C.152 (microfilm), Roll 16.

[108] Gandhi wanted to know from Thakurdas what the Bombay business community would regard as minimum proposals for peace..

[109] That Thakurdas had some influence on the thinking of Irwin can be seen by two of the specific suggestions he made. He suggested that, while not repealing the salt acts or allowing people to defy them, permission could be granted to those who dwelt by the sea-shore to manufacture salt for themselves provided they did not engage in its sale. He argued that such a concession would amount to little in practical terms, but was important since it would have a great sentimental value for Gandhi. Thakurdas took a similar line in regard to the picketing of liquor shops and suggested that the government should not place obstacles in the way of volunteers who exhorted people not to sell or consume liquor. Both these issues were resolved in the Gandhi–Irwin Pact along the lines suggested by Thakurdas.

[110] 'I find some ground for chastened hope in what I guess is a growing desire for peace among the commercial community.' Irwin to Wedgwood Benn, 2 February 1931, Halifax Papers, Mss.Eur.C.152 (microfilm), Roll 16.

[111] Markovits, *Indian Business and Nationalist Politics 1931–1939 , The Indigenous Capitalist Class and the Rise of the Congress Party* (Cambridge, 1985), p. 78.

[112] The following month Gandhi was invited by FICCI to perform the opening ceremony at its annual session. In May 1931, FICCI undertook to compile a Directory of swadeshi manufacturers on Gandhi's suggestion, FICCI, *Report of Proceedings of the Executive Committee for 1931*. The Indian Merchants' Chamber and the Bombay Swadeshi League were also involved with this work.

[113] Ambalal Sarabhai, the Ahmedabad based mill-owner, for instance, believed that 'whatever be the numerical strength of any interest represented at the Round Table Conference the interest that will carry most weight will be that of the Congress whose representative will be Gandhiji.' Sarabhai to Lala Shri Ram, 15 June 1931, cited in Venkatasubbiah, *Enterprise and Economic Change*, p. 16.

[114] Minutes of fourth annual meeting 7–9 April 1931 in FICCI, *Proceedings of Annual Meetings 1931*. Supporting FICCI, the *Hindustan Times* wrote: 'The Federation has in its possession documentary evidence to prove that Lord Irwin agreed to nominate three of its elected representatives to the resumed Round Table Conference ... Lord Willingdon's government, however, without giving any reason, went back on the pledge of Lord Irwin, and nominated only Sir Purshotamdas Thakurdas. To add insult to injury, the European commercial community's delegation was increased from three to five, and two reactionary Indian merchants, Sir Maneckji Dadabhoy and Sir Padamji Ginwala who represent nobody but themselves, were nominated to deceive the outside public that they were the spokesmen of the Indian mercantile community. Whatever may have been the reasons that inspired the Government's decision, the fact remains that the Indian mercantile

community is not represented at the Round Table Conference.' *Hindustan Times*, 3 September 1931.

[115] By the autumn of 1931 the spirit of cooperation that characterized the Gandhi–Irwin pact had been replaced by a widening gulf between the Congress and the Raj. For this story see, D.A. Low, *Britain and Indian Nationalism: the Imprint of Ambiguity 1929–1942* (Cambridge, 1997), chapter 4.

[116] Gandhi to Viceroy, 29 August 1931, *Collected Works of Mahatma Gandhi* Vol. XLVII (Ahmedabad, 1971), pp. 382–3.

[117] Birla's diary entry dated 17 September 1931, in 'Diary Ke Panne' in Birla, *Bikhre Vicharon Ki Bharoti*, p. 304.

[118] The journey proved to be eventful for Birla. Quite in contrast to his first voyage in 1927, the whole character of travelling seemed to have changed in the presence of Gandhi. In contrast to the formal dress and stiff behaviour that he experienced in his first journey, the voyage in 1931 was marked by informality, with most delegates wearing Indian style dhoti-kurta and Birla regretted having dressed in Western style clothes. Birla maintained a regular diary during the trip. He observed how Malaviya and Gandhi made unusual companions. Malaviya carried his own holy Ganges water, separate utensils and provisions for his own food. Gandhi was surrounded for much of the time by admiring and curious crowds. He often proved to be very difficult to his companions. For example, he insisted on sitting on the most uncomfortable part of the ship and refused to move despite the entreaties of Birla and others. See Birla's 'Diary ke Panne' in *Bikhre Vicharon Ki Bharoti*, pp. 283–95.

[119] They had frequent discussions about the Conference in particular and the political situation in general. From the start Gandhi was not very hopeful of the outcome of the Conference, but Birla tried to convince him that the British were well intentioned in inviting him and that much could be achieved at the Conference. After one such discussion, his diary entry records Birla telling Gandhi: 'Why is the government calling you? The government knows very well what your demands are. The Karachi resolution also is in front of them. Even then they are calling you. This means that your demands are going to be fulfilled.' *Ibid*, pp. 289–90.

[120] Arya Bhavan was constructed by Birla, after his 1927 trip to London, for the benefit of visiting Hindu merchants. Gandhi insisted on staying in Kingsley Hall on the ground that he preferred to live among the poor. Birla tried hard to persuade Gandhi to move to Arya Bhavan. 'To-day after dinner' he wrote in his diary, 'we went to Kingsley Hall ... I asked him [Gandhiji] whether he would move residence ...Yesterday Devdas told me on the phone that Bapu has been slightly convinced about moving residence and it is possible that he may move to Arya Bhavan ... All arguments were put to him ... but all this had no impact on Mahatmaji.' *Ibid*, pp. 297–8.

[121] So sudden was the decision of Whitehall that even Sir George Schuster, Finance Member of the Viceroy's Council, was taken by surprise when he received a wire from the India Office on the morning of 21 September 1931. Schuster recalls in his memoirs that the following few days 'proved an unforgettable experience. In our discussions on the Viceroy's Council I myself, greatly influenced by the strong opinion of the head of my Currency Department, felt bound to urge that the change in the position of sterling created entirely new conditions which gave us a legitimate opportunity to escape from what had proved to be a most damaging commitment to the 1/6d. ratio ... The result of our deliberations was that the Viceroy and all members of the Council supported my view and the Viceroy informed the Secretary of State that they would all resign with me

if my advice was not accepted.' Schuster, of course, finally did not resign and agreed to go along the decision of the India Office. Sir George Schuster, *Private Work and Public Causes*, pp. 112–15. Two contradictory official statements were made—one by the Finance Member and the other by the Secretary of State. The Finance Member declared that currency offices were being closed and the statutory obligation of the government to sell sterling or gold against rupees was temporarily suspended, thereby implying that the rupee would be allowed to take its own course and would not be linked to gold or sterling any longer. The India Office contradicted this. At the Federal Structure Committee, Samuel Hoare declared that it had been decided 'to maintain the present standard on sterling basis.' Behind the contradictory statements lay a difference in opinion between the Government of India and Whitehall. The Government of India had for some time been trying to impress Whitehall that its currency policy was very damaging from the political point of view in India. When the currency crisis erupted they were now tempted to de-link the rupee from sterling. London differed sharply over the issue, and the Government of India was finally forced to retreat. On the general background see D.E. Moggridge, *British Monetary Policy 1924–31* (Cambridge, 1972).

[122] The third alternative was not seriously considered by either the Government of India or by Indian opinion because there were not enough gold reserves and wide fluctuations in gold prices could lead to a sharp fall in the external value of the rupee.

[123] On the issues involved in the debate see B.R. Shenoy, 'The Rupee–Sterling Ratio and the Exports of Gold' in Radhakamal Mukherjee and H.L. Dey (ed.), *Economic Problems of Modern India* (London, 1941), pp. 267–8. Also see D.K. Malhotra, *History and Problems of Indian Currency 1835–1939* (Lahore, 1939).

[124] FICCI asked Gandhi to 'protest against attempt to link rupee to sterling. It is unwarranted, unjustified, most injurious to Indian economic interests.' *Hindustan Times*, 27 September 1931. Also see FICCI, *Report of Proceedings of Executive Committee for 1931*. Gandhi sent these telegrams to the Secretary of State and to Henry Strakosch. See Gandhi to Sir Samuel Hoare, 28 September 1931 and Gandhi to Sir Henry Strakosch, 28 September 1931 in *Collected Works of Mahatma Gandhi* XLVIII, September 1931–January 1932 (Ahmedabad, 1971), pp. 81–2. He also sent copies to Sapru and suggested to him to discuss the question 'with Mr Birla or Prof Shah or both and form an opinion and perhaps support my letter to the S of S.' Gandhi to Sapru, 28 September 1931 in *ibid*, p. 82.

[125] Birla had been periodically sending Gandhi literature on the currency issue and other economic questions. Over these years he sent many books on the currency question, including his own writings. Gandhi could not understand the intricacies of many of the questions. He wrote to Birla in February 1932: 'The more I familiarise myself with the science of currency, the more convinced I am that what is adumbrated in these books is not the way to solve the problem of the people's poverty. The only way is to devise some method whereby income and expenditure function in close cooperation. That is possible only through a resurrection of cottage industry.' Gandhi to Birla, 5 July 1932, *Bapu*, Vol. I, pp. 197–8.

[126] Gandhi to Birla, 28 June 1932, *Collected Works of Mahatma Gandhi*, Vol. L (June–August 1932), (Ahmedabad, 1972), p. 108.

[127] Gandhi addressed the House of Commons on 23 September and his statement on financial issues was disliked by Birla. Birla's diary entry for the following day reads: 'At night we again talked about this issue. I asked him why he gave statements on such matters without any consultation. We had a big argument. Mahatmaji claimed that his

words did not mean as I had interpreted them. He said, "I have learnt all the good things one can from law. I have not said even one thing on which I can be caught." Finally, we agreed that in the future he would not say anything on such matters without my advice.' Birla's diary entry, 24 September 1931, Birla, 'Diary Ke Panne' in *Bikhre Vicharon Ki Bharoti*, p. 305.

[128] FICCI *Report of the Representatives of the Federation on the Round Table Conference, 1932* (New Delhi, 1932), p. 3. In an interview to *Reuters* he claimed that the government had let an opportunity to undo the wrong in its currency policy pass and had added 'insult to injury'. He asserted that 'India will continue to suffer' under the exchange policy 'and the suffering will be simply because the Government is alien and irresponsible.' *Hindustan Times*, 24 September 1931. In a letter to the *Manchester Guardian* he appealed to the British public to take notice of the injustice of the situation, especially at a time when a Round Table Conference was being held to make India an equal partner in the British Commonwealth. Letter to the editor, the *Manchester Guardian*, 29 September 1931, cited in FICCI, *Report of the Representatives of the Federation on the Round Table Conference, 1932*, Appendix A, pp. A–1 to A–4.

[129] Strakosch was closely associated with South African industrial development, especially the gold mining industry and he was the author of the South African Currency and Banking Act of 1920. He was member of the Council of India from 1930 till 1937, delegate to the Imperial Economic Conference at Ottawa in 1932, member of the Royal Commission on Indian Currency and Finance 1925–6 and delegate of India at the Monetary and Economic Conference of 1933.

[130] Reporting about Birla's omission the *Hindustan Times* observed: 'Sir Samuel Hoare could not ... be unaware of the presence of Mr Birla in London. Besides Mr Birla is known to be one of the few outstanding Indians whose opinions on financial matters are accepted as authoritative in India ... The neglect on the part of the Secretary of State was obviously deliberate. The Secretary of State feared that Mr Birla might ask awkward questions, and might make the task of the so-called financial experts a bit difficult.' *Hindustan Times*, 28 September 1931.

[131] FICCI, *Report of the Representatives of the Federation on the Round Table Conference, 1932*, p. 4.

[132] Among the others invited were Gandhi, Jinnah, Sir Maneckji, Sir Pheroze Sethna, K.T. Shah (Bombay economist), Joshi (Bombay economist) and Rangaswami Ayyangar (editor of the Madras-based *Hindu*).

[133] Much of the discussion revolved around Birla's recently published pamphlet 'The Present Depression and Monetary Reform.' Strakosch said that he agreed with the first part of the pamphlet in which Birla had argued for a stable price level. Birla said that they were his private views and the delegates were now 'not there to plead for stabilizing the price level but for leaving exchange alone.'

[134] FICCI, *Report of the Representatives of the Federation on the Round Table Conference,1932*, p. 5. Also see Birla, 'Diary Ke Panne', *Bikhre Vicharon Ki Bharoti*, p. 315.

[135] FICCI, *Report of the Representatives of the Federation on the Round Table Conference, 1932*, pp. 5–8.

[136] *Ibid*, p. 8.

[137] Birla had fought for protection for Indian industry ever since his membership of the Indian Fiscal Commission in 1922 when he, along with others, had signed a note of dissent. For a background to the use of the term 'discriminating protection', see D.

Rothermund, *India in the Great Depression 1929–36* (New Delhi, 1992), especially pp. 168–70.

[138] FICCI, *Report of the Representatives of the Federation on the Round Table Conference*, 1932, p. 9.

[139] 'We are all unanimous', he stated, 'that we want to exercise ... no discrimination against a person or a company because it is a European or non-Indian company; but surely that does not mean that we shall agree to shut out for ever the power of discrimination both against a non-national and against a national on other grounds more reasonable and more justifiable.' FICCI, *Report of the Representatives of the Federation on the Round Table Conference*, 1932, p. 11. Afterwards businessmen from both sides traded allegations casting aspersions on the motives of the other. Benthall claimed that in private conversations with British business, Birla was prepared to guarantee non-discrimination against British business interests and that Birla had declared that 'for the last ten years of his life, he had been taking up an attitude of opposition, which was more often than not of a bitter nature because it was the only way he could put pressure to bear on the objects he had in mind, but that, henceforth, he desired to work in collaboration and to drop all his hostility.' Benthall Papers, Box XI, File I, Cambridge Centre of South Asian Studies. The FICCI representatives, on their part, alleged that Benthall gave an untrue account of the informal meetings and presented a 'distorted version' of events, see FICCI, *Report of the Representatives of the Federation on the Round Table Conference*, 1932.

[140] The discussion moved to a number of other issues such as subsidies to concerns. While European businessmen felt that concerns that were subsidized on economic and not racial grounds could be acceptable, but such cases would be few, and that subsidies would arise in regard to trade and not concerns; this could not be accepted by the Indian delegates.

[141] FICCI, *Report of the Representatives of the Federation on the Round Table Conference*, 1932, p. 15.

[142] 'Out of a budget of 90 crores, 72 crores or even more is to be reserved for the Crown. Out of the total functions of the Finance Department, currency and exchange is to be controlled by the Governor-General ... May I ask, Sir, what is left after that? ', demanded Birla at the plenary session, see *ibid*.

[143] 'I do not think any self-respecting Finance Member could carry on with all these rigid safeguards and will care to accept office with a stipulation that 72 crores each year, without questioning the justification, shall be handed over to the Governor.'

[144] FICCI, *Report of the Representatives of the Federation on the Round Table Conference*, 1932, p. 19.

[145] His diary entry for 5 November 1931 reads: 'Baldwin has told Mahatmaji clearly that you will not get what you want. I told Mahatmaji that if we got even 8 annas it would be because of you, so you must not leave just like that.' Mahatmaji replied "I know, I will not run away." His strategy is not to accept if too little is gained.' Birla, 'Diary Ke Panne', in *Bikhre Vicharon Ke Bharoti*, pp. 327–9.

[146] Birla continued to interpret various gestures optimistically to Gandhi. See for instance his 'Diary Ke Panne', in *Bikhre Vicharon Ki Bharoti*, p. 337.

[147] Letter to the Prime Minister, 6 November 1931, *Collected Works of Mahatma Gandhi*, Vol. XLVIII, pp. 271–2.

[148] Birla, 'Diary Ke Panne,' in *Bikhre Vicharon Ki Bharoti*, pp. 332–3.

[149] Speech of G.D. Birla at the plenary session on 30 November 1931, cited in FICCI, *Report of the Representatives of the Federation on the Round Table Conference, 1932*,

Appendix RC (2). The audience was very impressed with Birla's lucid presentation of his case. After hearing him, Campbell Rhodes complimented him and said: 'Mr Birla, if you are ever out of a job, go to Henry Strakosch for a recommendation. You will get a good one.' Diary entry for 4 December 1931, Birla, 'Diary Ke Panne', in *Bikhre Vicharon Ki Bharoti*, p. 344.

[150] Defending their stand on the issue of commercial discrimination, the returned delegates said 'Our own attitude was as firm as reasonable. We did not press for racial discrimination but at the same time we made it amply clear that we would not agree to anything which curtailed or restricted India's right to pursue the economic policy which she considered to be in the best interests of the country irrespective of the fact whether those adversely affected by it were nationals or non- nationals.' FICCI, *Report of the Representatives of the Federation on the Round Table Conference*, 1932, p. 10.

[151] Letter to the Federation, 9 August 1932, cited in Venkatasubbiah, *Enterprise and Economic Change*, p. 17.

[152] FICCI, *Report of the Representatives of the Federation on the Round Table Conference*, 1932, p. 12.

[153] FICCI, *Report of the Representatives of the Federation on the Round Table Conference*, 1932.

[154] Samuel Hoare to Birla, 27 January 1932, in Birla, *Bapu*, Vol. I, pp. 171–2. Also see FICCI, *Report of the Representatives of the Federation on the Round Table Conference 1932*, p. 19. Also Birla to Hoare, 14 March 1932 in Birla, *Bapu*, Vol. I, pp. 178–80. Birla emphasized the point which Thakurdas had made at the RTC deliberations that what mattered most to Indian commercial opinion was whether the financial safeguards came to 5 per cent or 95 per cent. After talks with Hoare, Birla wired to Thakurdas that the authorities had 'promised consideration' but that unless 'full, free discussion with British authorities on reduction mortgage, adjustment of past liability, with popular composition' was assured, the talks would not be worthwhile.

[155] Birla to Samuel Hoare, 14 March 1932, in Birla, *Bapu*, pp. 178–80.

[156] Birla to Samuel Hoare, 14 March 1932, in Birla, *Bapu*, pp. 178–82.

[157] The FICCI executive also showed an interest in the Conference when in March 1932 it asked George Rainy, the Commerce Member about the Conference's agenda and details of the nominations of the Indian delegation. FICCI, *Report of Proceedings of Executive Committee for 1932*, Vol. I (New Delhi, 1933).

[158] Birla to Samuel Hoare, 28 March 1932, in Birla, *Bapu*, Vol. I, pp. 182–3.

[159] See Markovits, *Indian Business and Nationalist Politics*, p. 85 and Willingdon to Hoare, 21 March 1932 in B. Chatterjee, 'Business and Politics in the 1930s, Lancashire and the Making of the Indo-British Trade Agreement, 1939', *Modern Asian Studies (MAS)*, Vol. 15, No. 3, 1981, p. 547.

[160] Birla to Mahadev Desai, 21 December 1934, in Birla, *Bapu*, Vol. I, pp. 459–60.

[161] FICCI, *Report of Proceedings of Executive Committee for 1931*.

[162] By the agreement the Government of India agreed to preferences for 160 manufactured British goods including motor vehicles, chemicals, drugs, building and engineering materials, hardware, tyres and items of food and clothing in return for a guarantee for preference in the British market for Indian raw materials including tea, cotton, jute and tobacco. On the Ottawa Conference see Ian M. Drummond, *British Economic Policy and the Empire 1919–1939* (London, 1972) especially Part I, chapters 3 and 4. Also see its review by Max Beloff, 'The Political Blind Spot of Economists' in *Government and Opposition*, Vol. 10, No. I, Winter 1975, pp. 107–12. Also see W.K.

Hancock, *Survey of British Commonwealth Affairs, Problems of Economic Policy 1918–1939*, Vol. II, Part I, especially chapter 3, section III.

163 In a statement made on behalf of FICCI they declared that they 'could not help feeling that the British government were anxious to seek protection for their industries in the preserved markets of the Empire behind preferential tariffs as their industries could not face the severe competition from their rivals, the United States of America and Japan in the Far Eastern markets ... the Government of India had no industrial policy of their own which would foster indigenous industries and encourage utilization of agricultural produce .... In conclusion, the Committee of the Federation had no hesitation in stating that the Agreement as read and understood in the light of the Delegation Report was undoubtedly detrimental and disadvantageous to the national interests of commerce and industry of the country.' FICCI, *Report of Proceedings of Executive Committee for 1932*.

164 Only some Bombay-based industrialists supported the Pact; the more loyalist businessmen such as Mody were effectively silenced by the government.

165 Markovits, *Indian Business and Nationalist Politics*, p. 87. Later in 1936 FICCI brought out a report on the working of the Ottawa Scheme of Preferences and recommended 'the termination of the present trade agreement between the UK and India as it has resulted in no material benefit to India's agricultural produce and has unnecessarily called for retaliation—however subconscious from her other foreign customers'. The report concluded: 'a) That India's export trade in agricultural produce with the United Kingdom did not show any substantial advance owing to the fact that the British dominions securing similar preference gained a better and stronger footing in the United Kingdom market over India's produce and b) That the intense economic nationalism initiated by the United Kingdom in creating an economic bloc within the Empire has restricted the growth of internationalism of trade instead of encouraging it and forced a number of manufacturing non-Empire countries to resort to import licenses, quota restrictions and exchange control to arrest the passivity of trade, which measures, in case of India, affected her export trade to these non-Empire countries.' FICCI, *Note on the Ottawa Scheme of Preferences* (Cawnpore, 1936), p. 73. For a detailed study of the pact and a position contrary to that of FICCI see B.N. Adarkar, 'The Ottawa Pact' in Radhakamal Mukherjee (ed.), *Economic Problems of Modern India*, Vol. II (London, 1939), pp. 378–95.

166 Markovits, *Indian Business and Nationalist Politics*, p. 90.

167 In the new arrangements being finalized it was proposed that it would continue to remain a reserved subject. Most powers were to be vested with the Viceroy who would have an ICS person in charge of reserved finance; the Viceroy could veto the budget; all sterling and foreign loans were to be managed by him and the rupee ratio and the currency question were to be under a Crown-appointed Reserve Bank.

168 It envisaged an all-India federation in which the Viceroy would have direct control over the army, foreign affairs and the power to veto finance, for essential details see Carl Bridge, *Holding India to the Empire* (London, 1986).

169 Mody was trying to obtain Lancashire's support to back Indian interests to 'pressurize Whitehall into agreeing to the Indian demand for protection against the Japanese inroads' into the Indian market. Under the Pact the Indian side agreed: a) to offer to Lancashire a 5 per cent decrease in the Indian import duty for two years, from 25 to 20 per cent; b) not to make fresh proposals with regard to the duties applicable to the UK imports of cotton piece-goods, when the revenue position of India made it possible for the Government of India to remove the surcharge on all imports imposed in October 1931; c) so far as imports of cotton yarns from the UK were concerned, the

duty might be 5 per cent *ad valorem* with specific duty of $1\frac{1}{4}$ anna a lb; and d) that duties on artificial silk piece-goods in the case of UK might be 30 per cent ad valorem or $1\frac{1}{4}$ per square yard for 100 per cent artificial silk fabrics, and 30 per cent or 2 annas a square yard for mixture fabrics of cotton and artificials. In regard to the Empire and other overseas markets for piece-goods and yarns, any advantages which might be arranged for Britain were to be extended to India and India could participate in any quota which might be allocated to UK in respect of overseas markets. The MCC agreed to arrange contracts between Indian manufacturers and British business in these markets. D.R. Mankekar, *Homi Mody, A Many Splendoured Life* (Bombay, 1968), pp. 67 and 71–2.

[170] The Pact ran into deep trouble in Britain too. Churchill, out of tune with the party leadership over the Indian question, charged Hoare of putting pressure on Manchester Chamber of Commerce to alter its evidence before the Joint Select Committee and alleged that a breach of parliamentary privilege had been committed, see Carl Bridge, *Holding India to the Empire*, chapter 5. Mody later recalled that: 'Never was a move so grossly misunderstood and so bitterly criticised. For weeks on end, a violent campaign went on in the press and all manner of people and associations denounced the pact. It is interesting to recall that, amongst the bodies which passed condemnatory resolutions, was one which had been prompted for the promotion of the interests of Hindu widows!' H.P. Mody, 'As I Look Back', Talk from the Bombay station of All India Radio, 15 July 1956, in Mody, *Reflections Wise and Otherwise*, pp. 105–6.

[171] He initially felt that Indian mills may experience some difficulty after the removal of the 25 per cent tariff against Lancashire, but they could easily adjust and compete by increasing their efficiency. Moreover, Indian business was aware that 'products in which Britain would now cherish preferences did not by and large compete with Indian goods', B. Chatterji, 'Business and Politics in the 1930s, Lancashire and the Making of the Indo-British Trade Agreement, 1939', in *Modern Asian Studies*, Vol. 15, No. 3, 1981, p. 561. As he explained to Mahadev Desai: 'I personally feel that a trade pact without sacrificing the Indian interests and yet benefiting Lancashire interests is possible but the greatest quid-pro-quo could only be Lancashire's political support. Mody–Lees pact for them is of no value. On the other hand, Gandhi–Lees pact could be of great value. Should not Bapu give his thoughts to the position to find out whether it is not possible to utilise their anxiety to our mutual advantage?' See Birla to Mahadev Desai, 10 November 1934 in Birla, *Bapu*, Vol. I, pp. 428–30.

[172] Sir Reginald Clarke had been a retired Indian Police official in Calcutta and had held several important positions like the Deputy Commissioner of Calcutta Police in the 1920s. Kirkpatrick too was a former '*box-wallah*' from Calcutta and had been a partner in Bird and Co., the managing agency. He held directorships of several jute mills and mining companies till 1923. In 1931 he was elected Conservative MP from Preston and held the seat till 1937.

[173] Sir Reginald Clarke to Birla, 8 December 1935, Birla Papers, File No. 5.

[174] Reginald Clarke to Birla, 28 December 1934, Birla Papers, File No. 5.

[175] 'Mr Mody has no stake in the Indian cotton industry and consequently in the pact that he made, he had to sacrifice nothing. People make unkind remarks about him and no one takes him seriously' Birla to Reginald Clarke, 14 January 1935, Birla Papers, File No. 5.

[176] He wrote to Clarke: 'When I take up a thing, I see that it is of lasting value ... If therefore I help in making a pact with Lancashire it becomes my duty to see that

Lancashire really retains a footing in the Indian market. I should then see that boycott becomes an impossible thing. But I do not know whether anyone wants it ... The future alone will show who is the real friend.'

[177] The Viceroy told Birla that the pact was made by Hoare to win 60 votes of Lancashire in the House of Commons and it did not really give away anything. Birla asserted that it was the 'wrongful manner' in which the pact had been concluded that mattered most. He pointed out that while in Britain, Runciman consulted Lancashire interests at every step, in India, Bhore even refused to meet the FICCI deputation, despite the fact that the Mody–Lees pact was disapproved. Birla, 'Interview With the Viceroy', 1 February 1935, Birla, *Bapu*, Vol. II, pp. 15–18.

[178] Birla to Clarke, 1 April 1935, Birla Papers, File No. 5. Birla assured Clarke that FICCI representatives would 'be delighted to come, if invited, but would also be prepared to discuss matters in a friendly way. But as I have suggested ... it would be very premature to invite anyone officially and therefore the best thing would be to talk without commitments and without representing anyone and only in an unofficial way.'

6

In the Mainstream of Nationalist Politics

In April 1934, Birla turned 40—a mid-point in his life. Let us pause to take stock of his circumstances at that point in time. For someone his age, he had evolved an impressive public persona. His association with Gandhi had made him a familiar figure in top nationalist circles. His proximity to Gandhi had brought him into close contact with several important leaders like Vallabhbhai Patel, C. Rajagopalachari and Rajendra Prasad, and he was widely accepted as an insider in the Gandhian camp. In 1932 he had been made the founding-president of the All-India Harijan Sevak Sangh and this had intensified his involvement with Gandhi's favourite constructive programme. He was recognized as a press baron of some standing. His *Hindustan Times* was still the only major English daily newspaper published from the capital and had a growing circulation. He and the family enjoyed a growing reputation for philanthropy all over the country. In Rajasthan, he was well known for his educational philanthropy having set up a large number of primary schools in the 1920s under the aegis of the Birla Education Trust. Within business circles, he was regarded as the moving spirit behind FICCI and, not the least, as the spokesman of an influential section of big business. He and his brothers ran a diversified all-India business which was expanding into challenging areas such as sugar, paper and insurance in the early 1930s. Within political circles in India and London he was perceived as somebody with influence on Gandhi. With such credentials, Birla had clearly arrived within Indian public life.

How did Birla harness these credentials? We have noted that his short career as a politician had disillusioned him. However, he had found his feet in the important role he carved out for himself as a spokesman of Indian big business, as an expert on economic matters for the Congress high command and as an emissary between the Mahatma and the British. How these new roles, which he had taken upon himself in the early 1930s, came to be consolidated and the manner in which he took an interest from outside the political arena is a story we take up here. Of his new roles, what took much of Birla's attention in the 1930s was his interest in mainstream Congress politics.

It may be remembered at the outset that Birla was not formally a Congressman; nor did he regard himself as a politician any longer. He liked to describe himself as a 'Gandhi man' and carefully distinguished between the politics of the Gandhian right-wing and that of the Congress as a whole. As we have seen, Congress right-wing leaders looked upon him as an expert on economic and fiscal questions. They increasingly regarded him as a colleague in the wider nationalist struggle and several of them became his intimate friends. With many he came to share close personal ties.

Foremost among them was Jamnalal Bajaj, fellow Marwari businessman, treasurer of the Congress for over two decades and a political leader in his own right.[1] Birla's association with Bajaj went back to 1912 and they shared close ties of kinship and community.[2] As we have noted, Bajaj had been responsible for bringing the Birlas to Gandhi's notice. They also shared common interests in the Gandhian establishment and its constructive programme. Both took a keen interest in cow-protection, promotion of Hindi, Harijan welfare and temple-entry for the untouchables. Both were regarded as his close lieutenants by Gandhi. Since the late 1920s, Bajaj had taken a keen interest in the family's philanthropy and in the work of the Birla Education Trust which Birla had set up in 1929 to spearhead educational development in Rajasthan. Birla, in turn, regularly advised Bajaj on business matters.[3] Their intimacy is revealed by the fact that during Bajaj's frequent jail sentences, it was Birla who was often called upon to advise the Bajaj family on business matters.[4]

Yet another close associate was C. Rajagopalachari, or 'Rajaji' as he was widely known. Birla came in contact with Rajaji through his association with Gandhi, and by 1930 was close enough to be asked for help to find employment for Rajaji's eldest son-in-law Varadarajan.[5] Their intimacy grew through the 1930s, especially after 1935 when Devdas Gandhi, Rajaji's second son-in-law and Gandhi's son, joined the *Hindustan Times* as its editor, a position he held till his death in 1957. Rajaji was also co-opted by Birla to be a trustee of his Krishnarpan Trust which did charitable work of a diverse nature.[6]

Among other prominent nationalist leaders Birla was particularly close to Rajendra Prasad, the Congress stalwart from Bihar. In an article, he recalled that Rajendra Prasad gave the first impression of 'a simple man perhaps a fourth rate Mukhtaar in some backward District Court'. But, he continued: 'Rajendra Babus are not born in every society or in every age. All his qualities are packed so tightly and concealed with such naturalness under his simple pose that his appearance has become completely deceptive. All his big qualities are buried so deep that in order to know Rajendra Babu one has to dig deep with him to discover and be profited'.[7] Birla had high regard for his 'deep wisdom, erudition and intelligence'.[8] This relationship also matured through the 1930s. An instance of their close relationship was seen in 1936 when the Prasad family's finances were adversely affected after the sudden death of Rajendra Prasad's elder brother, Mahendra Prasad.[9] The family was deeply in debt and some assets had to be disposed of in order to clear it. It was to Bajaj and Birla that Rajendra Prasad turned at this time for help. A loan of Rs 45,000 was arranged to be provided by Birla. Rajendra Prasad was, however, hesitant to accept a personal loan from Birla as he was concerned about possible criticisms by his political colleagues. It was, therefore, arranged that the money provided by Birla would be transacted to Rajendra Prasad as a loan from Bajaj who was his colleague in the Congress Working Committee.[10] Later, in 1942, Birla helped the Prasad family sort out its financial matters in connection with its investment in the Chapra Electric Supply Company.[11] From the 1930s, Rajendra Prasad was a frequent guest at Birla House and took a keen interest in the Birla educational establishments at Pilani.[12]

The 1930s saw the cementing of relations by Birla with major Congress leaders. Another leader who became a close personal friend was K.M. Munshi, the prominent Bombay-based politician and lawyer. Although Birla had made acquaintance with Munshi in the 1920s, it was his strong support for the Bharatiya Vidya Bhavan that brought him in close contact with Munshi. The Bhavan had been set up in 1938 by Munshi and his wife Lilawati who was a reputed social worker. Among its many projects which Birla supported was the Bharatiya Itihas Samiti (Committee on Indian History) which was established to prepare the series 'History and Culture of the Indian People'. It planned to bring out an eleven-volume history of India under the supervision of the well-known historian R.C. Majumdar. When Munshi sought Birla's help in 1943, a donation of Rs 1,50,000 was agreed for the project.[13] For the publication of these volumes, a committee composed of Munshi as chairman and Birla as vice-chairman was set up.[14] The close friendship which Munshi and Birla enjoyed extended to other spheres also. For instance, Munshi sometimes advised Birla on legal matters, especially in relation to his educational institutions.[15]

Of all the Congress leaders he knew, it was, however, with Vallabhbhai Patel that Birla came to share a special relationship. Birla claimed that he fell under the spell of the Sardar in the early 1920s.[16] Although we do not know the details of their early association, by 1930 Patel had come to know Birla intimately. Birla became a familiar figure in the Patel household, someone who could always be relied upon.[17] As Birla later recalled:

I would get a telegram, sometimes just two words 'Come immediately' and when I arrived he would tell me what I had to do. Inevitably the question of collection would come up. Once I told Patel what Gandhi had said to me, 'I do not like the Sardar collecting money from businessmen.' His reply was characteristic: 'This is not his concern. Gandhi is a Mahatma. I am not. I have to do the job.'[18]

This association continued to grow during the 1930s.

The Birla homes came to be frequently used by nationalist leaders during their travels. Gandhi had begun to regularly stay at Birla House in New Delhi, and as a result, a number of Congressmen frequented it too which brought them in proximity with Birla.[19] Over the years, 'Birla Houses' came into being not only in the cities of New Delhi, Bombay and Calcutta, but at Ranchi in Bihar, the hill resort of Mussorie in UP, and in Simla, the summer capital of the Raj.[20] Gandhi stayed at Birla House in New Delhi during several crucial points of his political career. For instance, he was at Birla House just before he met Lord Linlithgow in October 1939 to carry out vital negotiations on the future policy towards the War. During the Cripps Mission crucial negotiations were carried out there too. In August 1942 Gandhi was arrested from Birla House in Bombay after he gave the call for 'Quit India'.[21] At the time of the Simla Conference in 1946, most members of the Congress Working Committee stayed at Birla House. Over the years, Birla House in Delhi acquired a role similar to the one that Anand Bhavan (the home of the Nehrus in Allahabad) had earlier played in nationalist politics. This led Gilbert Laithwaite, the influential private secretary to the Viceroy, to remark: 'The real capital of India is not just New Delhi but Birla House, where Mahatma Gandhi and other Congress leaders stay and where the Congress Working Committee meets and major political decisions are taken.'[22]

THE CHALLENGE OF THE CONGRESS LEFT-WING

Given his close involvement with Gandhi and the Congress leadership, it is hardly surprising that Birla came to be well aware of the internal dynamics of the top echelons of the party. A major political concern for Birla in the early 1930s was the rise of the left-wing within the Congress. As is well known, the Congress party was riven by divisions which were both factional and ideological. Of all these the most worrisome to him was the increasing influence of the leftists within the party. Nehru was emerging as the Left ideologue and a number of younger Congressmen felt attracted to his ideas. Much before other public figures noticed the development of socialist trends within the Congress, Birla was trying to evolve strategies to meet the challenge. As we have seen, although he had supported the Civil Disobedience Movement, his faith lay in constitutional methods. He had for some time believed that the Raj's failure to make terms with Gandhi would strengthen the hands of the radicals within the Congress and would make a negotiated settlement of the Indian political problem impossible to attain.

Birla wanted the British to realize that in a context of growing left-wing tendencies in India, Gandhi was the best defence against extremist politics. His great fear was that the failure of the government to arrive at a settlement with Gandhi would strengthen the radical element within the Congress. Soon after the second Civil Disobedience Movement had been suppressed by the extensive use of extraordinary powers embodied in the civil–martial-law package, Birla reiterated this belief. 'I wish I could convert the authorities,' he told Samuel Hoare, the Conservative leader, 'to the view that Gandhiji and men of his type are not only friends of India but also friends of Great Britain and that Gandhiji is the greatest force on the side of law and order.' It was, he said, Gandhi who 'alone is responsible for keeping the left wing in India in check,' and he urged the British to renew the dialogue with the Mahatma.[23] Birla believed that British intransigence would ultimately undermine Gandhi's leadership and strengthen the radicals.[24]

In his view, the best strategy to counter the rising challenge of the Left within the Congress was to promote constitutionalism. An opportunity for this was at hand with the White Paper which had been put forth by the government in March 1933 consisting of reform proposals of a federation between British and Princely India and a grant of autonomy to the provinces of British India. An acceptance of the white paper would put the Congress firmly on the constitutional path. Though Birla was not uncritical of the proposals, he was anxious that the Congress should work the reforms for what they were worth. The acceptance of the constitutional method, his *Hindustan Times* propounded, would 'have a pacifying effect on the left-wing of the Congress'.[25]

Birla was growing restive with the increasingly vociferous propaganda by the leftists and those he called the 'fire-eaters' within the Congress and the threat they posed to dominate its leadership through the figure of Nehru. He noticed how effectively the left-wing within the Congress had intensified its activities in the early 1930s. Matters came to a head when in October 1933 Nehru published a set of his writings provocatively titled 'Whither India' in which he openly attacked 'capitalists and vested interests'.[26] He defined the political goals as independence and socialism and proposed the destruction of all class privileges and vested interests.[27] Then, in what seemed an even more threatening move to Birla, a few months later, in May 1934 leftist elements organized themselves into the Congress Socialist Party (CSP).[28] Although Nehru was not formally associated with the new party, it was apparent to all that he was the inspiration behind it. The CSP appeared, to Birla, to consist of avowed communists who seemed to place all loyalties secondary to their leftist commitments. Birla was filled with apprehension at the growing influence of the leftists and their vigorous propaganda against 'vested interests' alarmed him. The CSP seemed intent on launching a well-orchestrated attempt at 'spreading hatred' against business and depicting the businessman 'as a blood sucker who has joined the vested interests of the Britishers for the exploitation of the masses'.[29] The prospect of the Congress moving towards the Left deeply perturbed Birla.

Birla took every opportunity to speak with his friends within the Congress leadership to evolve a strategy to deal with the leftist challenge. The fact that many within the Congress viewed the rise of the leftists with suspicion relieved him. It was with some satisfaction that he heard of the Congress Working Committee of June 1934 denouncing class war as contrary to the Gandhian creed of non-violence. This gave Birla an insight into how the leftist challenge could be dealt with and helped him evolve the essentials of a strategy which he thereafter consistently advocated.[30]

The first element of this strategy was that public figures should pressure the Congress to become 'constitutional-minded'. The acceptance of constitutional methods by the Congress would keep the leftists at bay and strengthen the right-wing. The other crucial element was the *desiradatum* that the left-wing should not be directly attacked but rather the hands of the right-wing be strengthened. 'Vallabhbhai, Rajaji and Rajendra Babu are all fighting communism and socialism', he perceptively said to his old friend, Purshotamdas Thakurdas. 'It is, therefore, necessary that we who represent healthy capitalism should help Gandhi as far as possible and work with a common objective,' he added.[31] In his scheme it was important to garner support for the Congress Right and he wanted his business colleagues to keep behind the party and to challenge the leftist view that business was not a reliable partner in the struggle against British imperialism. He was anxious that leftist rhetoric should not drive away business leaders from supporting the Congress as this would weaken the hands of those who were fighting the leftists internally within the party. Birla made strenuous efforts in these years to ensure that big business did not break ranks in its overall support for the Congress.

This was no easy task. Nehru's scathing attacks on capitalism were not restricted to 'Whither India' but also surfaced in public speeches. What made the task of maintaining business solidarity even more daunting was the prospect of the Congress rejecting the proposals of the Government of India Act of 1935 which had been based on the White Paper of 1933. The Act provided for a two-stage devolution of power. In the first stage, power was to be transferred to the provinces and in the second, to the centre under the scheme of federation if the princely states agreed to join in. However, initial reactions by Congress were critical, suggesting that the party might reject the opportunity of gaining office in the provinces. This made several Bombay businessmen anxious to start a 'Reforms Party' of their own. Homi Mody in Bombay gave a call to businessmen to create a separate party and sever their links with the Congress because of its flirtations with extreme socialist elements.[32] Though Birla too was worried by these signs, this was not his way of dealing with the emerging crisis. Mody's call was a complete contrast to the strategy which Birla had worked out. Mody came under attack for undermining the Congress and the Birla-owned *Hindustan Times* editorially described him as a 'rat' and his party as a 'party of reaction'[33]. Ultimately, nothing came of Mody's call for a separate party.[34]

Birla also knew that it was not only business that needed to support his strategy of keeping the left-wing at bay within the Congress, but that he also needed the co-operation of influential British politicians. He, therefore, applied himself to the task of persuading those British politicians whom he knew of the need to conciliate the right-wing so that it would accept the reforms. He wrote to Sir John Anderson, the Governor of Bengal, whom he knew well because of his business interests in the province. Birla emphasized the need of a rapprochement with the Congress right-wing. In the absence of an understanding between the Congress right-wing and the government, he feared that 'the right wing may retire and leave the field to the left-wing'. He tried to convince him to strengthen

Gandhi's hands as otherwise the Mahatma's influence would erode, leading to a drift which would strengthen the 'hands of firebrands'.[35]

In the summer of 1935, Birla embarked on a goodwill mission to England to win support for his ideas. He obtained letters of introduction to several politicians from Gandhi and Sir John Anderson. He spent three and a half months in England and met as many influential politicians as he possibly could. Among them were Lord Zetland, the new Secretary of State for India,[36] Ramsay MacDonald, the former Prime Minister, the Earl of Halifax, the former Viceroy, Lord Salisbury,[37] Sir Henry Page-Croft and Lord Derby,[38] the last three being die-hard conservative politicians, and Stanley Baldwin, the then Prime Minister. He had an especially fruitful meeting with Linlithgow, the Viceroy designate, [39] and seems to have immediately struck a rapport with him. In addition, he met the Archbishop of Canterbury, several India Office officials like Sir Findlater Stewart[40] and R.A. Butler,[41] some Labour leaders,[42] Winston Churchill,[43] men from the City, and representatives of the press.[44] In these meetings, Birla drove home a single point: that by not resolving the constitutional issue, the Government of India was indirectly strengthening the leftist forces within the Congress.[45] He emphasized that the British should establish personal contact with the Mahatma and the Gandhian wing of the Congress and remove the fear and distrust that permeated the Raj's relationship with the party.[46]

Through his meetings with British politicians in those months Birla pleaded the cause of the Congress Right. His consistent message was that the Congress was experiencing an intense ideological struggle; that the left-wing was gaining strength; that the right-wing was under attack for having 'achieved nothing'; that the Government of India by ignoring the moderate Congressmen was indirectly helping leftist forces; that the struggle had reached a critical phase; that if the Congress rejected the reforms it was because of its distrust of the government; and that all this would jeopardize the success of the new constitution which the British were incorporating.[47] He promised several influential politicians such as Zetland, Halifax, Hoare and Lothian, that he would use his personal influence with Gandhi to ensure that the Congress would not close the door on the reforms until Linlithgow, the Viceroy-designate, had taken charge. Although no concrete results emerged from his goodwill mission, Birla returned to India with the conviction that the British were sincere in their intentions to institute the new reforms fully. He believed that it would be a great folly for the Congress to reject the new constitution.

On his return to India in September 1935, Birla proceeded straight to Wardha to give Gandhi a first-hand report of his visit. Here he appraised Gandhi and other leaders such as Patel and Rajagopalachari who were present at the Mahatma's ashram. Birla provided them with a detailed account of his talks. He entreated Gandhi to promise that the Congress would take no decision about the new constitution until the new Viceroy had taken charge. Even though Gandhi found it difficult to accept the cheerful view of Birla and was sceptical of whether the positive spirit he talked of really existed among official circles in India, he promised that no new commitments about the reforms would be made at the forthcoming Congress session at Lucknow.[48] From his close observation of Congress politics, Birla could see that the struggle between the forces advocating office acceptance and the leftists opposed to office would be played out quite quickly. As he expected, the clash occurred at the Congress session in Lucknow where Nehru was elected president of the party.

The Lucknow session marked the apogee of Nehru's socialism and saw a number of radical resolutions proposed. Yet, in a very real sense it proved to be a triumph for Birla.[49] The leftist resolution against office acceptance was defeated, and Nehru's attempt to secure the direct affiliation of trade unions and Kisan Sabhas (farmers' unions) to the Congress was stalled.[50] Most significantly, the Congress decided to fight the forthcoming elections. Further, ten out of the fourteen members of the new Working Committee publicly disapproved of Nehru's socialism.[51] The outcome was much in keeping with what Birla expected after his discussion with Mahatma, Patel and Rajagopalachari. Birla was delighted as he boasted to Thakurdas:

Mahatmaji kept his promise and without his uttering a word, he saw *that no new commitments were made.* Jawaharlalji's speech in a way was thrown into the waste paper basket because all the resolutions that were passed were against the spirit of his speech...It must be said, however, to the credit of Jawaharlalji that he fully realized his position and did not abuse his powers. The Working Committee which he has constituted contains an overwhelming majority of 'Mahatmaji's group'.[52]

Birla was finally satisfied that things were moving in the right direction. He was optimistic that as long as the new Viceroy, Lord Linlithgow, handled the situation properly, there was every likelihood of Congressmen coming into office.[53] The Lucknow session made Birla completely confident that ultimately the Vallabhbhai group would prevail and, 'with a little friendly handling, he (Nehru) could be made into a real friend.'[54]

However, Birla's perceptive analysis of Nehru's character was not shared by an important section of capitalists—especially those from Bombay. Unlike Birla who was attuned to the inner workings of the Congress's decision-making, these men continued to be alarmed by Nehru's socialist pronouncements.[55] Even though the Lucknow Congress had rejected most of Nehru's proposals, a month later 21 important Bombay businessmen signed a manifesto denouncing his views. They declared that: 'We have no hesitation in declaring that we are unequivocally opposed to ideas of this kind being propagated, as in the present condition of widespread economic misery in the country, they were likely to find ready though unthinking reception'. 'We are convinced,' they continued that, 'there is a grave risk of the masses of the country being misled by such doctrines into believing that all that is required for the improvement of their well-being is a total destruction of the existing social and economic structure.'[56]

The Bombay Manifesto disturbed Birla. In private he too shared the sentiments of the Bombay businessmen, but a public attack on the Congress president by an important section of big business was repugnant to his thinking. It marked a sharp departure from the careful strategy that he had assiduously worked out. In particular, he was painfully surprised to see the name of his esteemed friend Purshotamdas Thakurdas in the crowd of signatories. Birla sharply chided him:

Of course, on principle we are all opposed to socialism or communism, but in my opinion the way in which the manifesto was worded did not do full justice to Jawaharlal...You are such a cautious man that you never take a step without careful consideration. Therefore I was rather surprised that you should put your name to a document the contents of which, to my mind, were liable to be seriously misinterpreted...The manifesto has given impetus to the forces working against capitalism.[57]

He also reprimanded Walchand Hirachand, another seasoned business leader, for having 'rendered no service to your caste men'. 'It is curious,' he told Hirachand, 'how we businessmen are so short-sighted. It looks very crude for a man of property to say that he is opposed to expropriation in the wider interest of the country.'[58] Birla's strong reprimand to Thakurdas and Walchand led to a change in the attitude of some Bombay businessmen. With the result that when Nehru visited Bombay a few weeks later, he received a warm welcome from many in the business world and several chambers of commerce presented him with purses and addresses.[59] Birla also used his influence to see that the mistake made by the Bombay capitalists was not repeated by business organizations elsewhere. On his part, he continued to share his views of the ambivalent character of Nehru's socialist pronouncements with his friends. As he put it:

Socialism is only another name for the impatience of Jawaharlal. He has however realized that he is in a very small majority in the Congress, but in spite of all this, there has been no split and I don't think there will be any split. Both the sides are wise enough to know that split would not pay any of them. So the net result has been that Jawaharlal has recently calmed down and he is no more talking of socialism and all that.[60]

Though Birla knew that Nehru's socialism had been contained, a decisive victory over the left-wing could only be achieved after the Congress had decided to accept office. He tirelessly continued his efforts towards that end. He repeatedly wrote letters to the British politicians he had met while in London, like Halifax and Lothian, to impress upon them that the reforms must be worked in the most liberal manner.[61] When the Congress made it a pre-condition that the Governor's 'special powers' would not be used before it accepted office, Birla tried to break the deadlock by going to see the Viceroy. He told Linlithgow that all Gandhi wanted was a 'gentleman's agreement' and urged him to hold direct talks with Gandhi to settle the issue rather than leave it to provincial leaders. He told Linlithgow that there existed no real division within the Congress over office acceptance, and that ultimately Nehru would simply follow Gandhi. He continued to impress upon Congress leaders the need to exercise moderation.[62] In these months, Birla often visited Gandhi in Gujarat and spoke with him at length to expedite the process of office acceptance.

While the Congress debated the issue and protracted negotiations followed, Birla left for England in early 1937 in his capacity as unofficial adviser to the Indo-British Trade Negotiations. He sailed regretting that the deadlock between the Congress and the government had resulted from '75 per cent misunderstanding and 25 per cent mutual fear' and hoped that a way out would be found.

A Sentinel of Provincial Autonomy

Only in July 1937 could the stalemate finally be resolved and the Congress agreed to form ministries in the provinces. Well aware of how hard Birla had worked for this, Gandhi had him informed by telephone as soon as the decision was taken. Birla was simply overwhelmed with joy to hear the news and felt very cheerful and happy.[63] He saw the decision as a vindication of the Congress right-wing and he wired his friends in the 'high command' congratulating them on their triumph.[64] Birla's enthusiasm sprang from the vital importance he attached to office acceptance by the Congress in his overall political vision. He believed that the successful working of provincial autonomy would pave the way for a devolution of power at the centre.[65] It would 'lead the Congress towards a permanent policy of constitutionalism' which 'may be the speedier method of achieving our goal'.[66]

Although between July and September 1937 Birla was in London, he received regular news about the functioning of the new ministries from Mahadev Desai, Gandhi's secretary, Rajagopalachari, now the Madras Premier and several other Congressmen.[67] They sent him important pronouncements of Gandhi, speeches of ministers and news-reports about the early measures of the ministries. On his part, Birla passed these on to British politicians whom he regarded as influential— Halifax, Lothian, Zetland, Butler and Churchill among others—as proof of the success of the constitutional arrangements. He emphasized the positive spirit with which the ministers looked upon office.[68] He even used personal letters written to him by Gandhi to drive home his point.[69] Rajagopalachari, he told Halifax, was working like a Trojan and ministers elsewhere were much engrossed in constructive work.[70] He stressed that a good beginning had been made and that 'both the Governors and the Ministers are pulling on extremely well'.[71] He tried to impress upon British politicians that the Congress had finally given up the path of confrontation and was now keen to make a success of constitutional work.[72] But the British 'must be helpful and not obstructive', and it was important for the Governors and the services 'to play the game'.[73] Only then, he said, 'will constitutionalism prevail, otherwise the Congress would be compelled again to resort to direct action.'[74] During his three months stay in London, Birla tirelessly reiterated this message to British politicians.[75] His consistent refrain to the many politicians he met—Sir George Schuster, Lord Zetland, R.A. Butler,

Lord Derby and Oliver Stanley among others—was that the experiment of Provincial Autonomy must be worked as successfully as possible by both the Congress and the Raj.

By now Birla enjoyed easy access to important figures in the British political establishment. Many British politicians looked upon him as a personal emissary of Gandhi. Moreover, they regarded him as a conciliator who could be relied upon to work sincerely for the success of the new constitution. This perception of Birla in British political circles went back to the moderating influence he was believed to have exercised upon Gandhi in 1930–1 at the time of the Gandhi–Irwin Pact. A more recent feather in his cap had been his success in keeping the promise he had made in July–August 1935 that the Congress would not reject the new constitution until the arrival of Linlithgow in India. Birla, therefore, enjoyed an impeccable reputation in London and many British politicians regarded him as an insider in the Gandhian establishment and were more than willing to lend him a serious ear.[76]

On his return to India in October 1937, Birla was pleased to see for himself the change that had occurred in the political atmosphere and that the overall policy of the Congress ministries in the provinces was being steered by the party's high command, made up of Rajendra Prasad, Rajagopalachari, Sardar Patel and other leaders he trusted. His optimism about the success of the ministries is reflected in an article he wrote in the Quaker weekly, the *Friend*:

I can say from personal knowledge that never in the history of British rule in India has there been a more congenial atmosphere for a mutual understanding between Great Britain and India. Bureaucracy, such a 'repugnant enemy' of Nationalist India, is now its faithful servant. Popular ministers are protecting and supporting them against misdirected attacks. And the Service too, is giving its most loyal co-operation to its former enemy; the policy of personal contact established by that most noble Viceroy, Lord Irwin (now Lord Halifax) and broken by Lord Willingdon, creating so much bitterness in India against England and Englishmen, has again been established by Lord Linlithgow.[77]

Through the following months while the Congress held office, Birla discussed a number of issues with the leaders. His overriding concern was to ensure the smooth functioning of the ministries. One way was to establish what he called the personal touch between the Viceroy and Gandhi at the centre and the Governors and Congress premiers in the provinces. This could help resolve areas of tension and would settle many thorny problems.[78]

To Congressmen who had taken up office, he continually stressed that the reforms needed to be worked in a spirit of co-operation. It was of great importance that the new ministries should create a good impression of governments that were functioning successfully.[79] It was important too to set healthy precedents and to give up the mentality of agitation. He strongly disagreed with the rhetoric of some Congressmen that the ministries did not possess real power. 'It does not enhance our prestige to say that we are merely puppets of the Governors and as we have no power, we cannot do much,' he observed. Nothing could be more damaging in his view than establishing the 'convention of puppetism'.[80] He wanted the ministries to devote themselves to constructive work and to give priority to the real issues which in his view were economic. He urged them to address the economic problems of the masses, as their record would ultimately be judged by their ability to provide relief to the people. He frankly declared:

It is quite likely that after the first flush of enthusiasm is over and the excitement...has subsided, there will set in a phase of reaction. The masses will ask themselves: 'Have we been able to get more nourishment than before?... Are we any the better in respect of our standard of living?' A man needs 3000 calories of balanced diet..., 40 yards of cloth, a decent hut to live in...The masses will ask, 'Are we getting all this?' And the answer will definitely be 'NO'. Because for such vast constructive work, experience, efficiency, proper planning and administrative capacity will be needed, which few among the Congress men yet have.[81]

Birla saw the solution in economic planning to increase income levels by encouraging production. Issues of reform in the agrarian sector, especially zamindari abolition did not interest him. Birla had no patience with raising slogans of zamindari abolition, especially in UP and Bihar. Though he was willing to accept that the zamindari system needed great reform as a lot of tyranny was sheltered behind it, he believed that it was premature to raise the demand for its abolition.[82] In his view zamindari was merely a symptom rather than the cause of rural misery. 'There are provinces', he observed, 'where there is no zamindari and yet the masses are as poor as in the zamindari provinces.'[83] In his view zamindari abolition could not be allowed to become the catch-word for economic reform.[84] He wanted economic reforms to focus on increasing production and addressing the problem of unemployment.

Another challenge for the Congress ministries, in Birla's view, concerned their ability to maintain law and order. The popular demonstrations, marches and celebratory processions that characterized the early months of Congress rule appeared to him as signs of indiscipline. He wanted Congress ministers to take firm control of the law-and-order machinery. He believed that, as the party in power, the Congress needed to move away from its old agitational style of politics. As reports of demonstrations poured in from several Congress provinces, he observed that, 'it looks as if everybody wants to have his own way under the Congress regime...I will not be surprised if some day I heard of marches led to the house of the minister with flags and slogans'. Such signs of indiscipline among the people must, he believed, be actively discouraged as it was important to learn the lesson 'that even under swaraj they have to be law abiding, reasonable and disciplined.'[85] Throughout the Congress' tenure in office, Birla continued to stress the need to maintain discipline within party ranks. He was of the opinion that the Congress ministries' performance should be exemplary and was anxious that ministers should acquit themselves well in the field of law and order, and discipline fellow party-men in order to avoid any situation in which the Governors could intervene by using their special powers.

An issue that exercised Birla considerably in these early months related to the Congress' attitude towards working-class disputes. Under the Congress ministries, trade unionists' expectations of increased wages and improved conditions of work led to labour unrest in several provinces.[86] The Congress' response to this was to appoint enquiry committees to investigate labour grievances. Two of its important committees in Bihar and UP were headed by Rajendra Prasad. Birla took a keen interest in their proceedings, especially in the UP labour enquiry because of a prolonged industrial strike in Kanpur.[87] He was disturbed by the tendency of the trade unions to resort to strikes. While he believed that trade unions should not do this, he also stressed that employers should accept the arbitration of the Congress. He accordingly persuaded the Kanpur employers to make concessions to labour and to abide by the Congress' arbitration. He was, however, critical of the UP Labour Enquiry Committee's report, as it misrepresented many basic facts about the employers.[88] Moreover, the inept handling of the Kanpur situation by the Pant ministry made matters worse for him. He believed that Rajendra Prasad as chairman of the enquiry committee had made a grave error in not distinguishing between 'our men' (such as Padampat Singhania, the pro-Congress mill-owner and leading member of FICCI) and 'other employers' (such as the loyalist Sir J.P. Srivastava).[89]

A striking feature of Birla's position on labour–capital relations during the Congress' tenure in office was his complete non-interference in strike situations. This is all the more significant because Birla was by this time one of the largest Indian employers. Moreover, his interest in labour problems went back at least a decade to his work in the International Labour Conference of 1927, followed by his membership of the Royal Commission of Labour in 1929. In spite of these formidable credentials, Birla was careful not to be seen playing the role of the employers' representative or influencing the Congress leadership to look upon working class unrest from a capitalist point of view. In this he showed his deliberative caution in not responding aggressively to leftist attacks.

Throughout these years, Birla continued to play the role of unofficial economic adviser to the Congress high command. He was personally called upon to advise the Congress leadership on a number of economic issues. In June 1938, for instance, when the Congress Working Committee tried to formulate its position on the question of the rupee–sterling ratio, the leadership turned to Birla. 'This is a technical question involving highly technical financial knowledge and in such matters we have always looked to you for advice,' Patel wrote to him.[90] Birla had only recently drafted a representation which the Indian Chamber of Commerce had addressed to the Government of India on the issue and thus he responded promptly. He sent the draft to Patel along with very detailed suggestions which then provided the basis of the official Congress response on the subject.[91] While Birla was always at hand to offer advice, FICCI also increasingly emerged as the economic think-tank which the Congress leadership consulted on a regular basis. Durga Das, the journalist, recalled that FICCI was widely perceived by this time as the economic wing of the Congress.[92] FICCI greatly expanded its activities to take advantage of the enlarged role that it was now called upon to perform. It enlarged its secretariat,[93] its staff increased manifold and its headquarters in New Delhi was reorganized.[94] In late 1936, Birla, along with other businessmen such as Seth Padampat Singhania and Lala Shri Ram, established the 'Lala Diwan Chand Political Information Bureau' to encourage research and analysis that would enable legislators to formulate economic policy.[95]

As the months in office passed there was often trouble which the Congress ministries encountered in their dealings with the Raj. On several occasions, Birla's trouble-shooting skills were sought by prominent Congress leaders. A most striking example of this was in February 1938 when two of the ministries formed by the Congress in the north Indian states of UP and Bihar threatened to resign. Birla's qualification for intervention was the good relations he had with officials of the Raj, especially with the Viceroy. Due to disagreements between the Congress ministries and the Governors of the states a crisis loomed which potentially endangered the working of provincial autonomy all over India. As negotiations moved towards a deadlock, G.B. Pant, Congress leader and Chief Minister of UP, approached Birla. On Pant's request Birla met Viceroy Linlithgow who took 'copious notes' of all that he said.[96] Notwithstanding Birla's efforts the talks at the level of the state between the Chief Minister and the Governor broke down completely, and the Congress ministries resigned in UP and Bihar. It was again left to Birla to defuse the crisis and he put forth several possible solutions.[97] However, the crisis continued and once again Birla's help was sought—this time by Gandhi who wired him at Pilani to return to Delhi immediately.[98] Birla rushed and re-established contact with Pant in Lucknow and Linlithgow in Delhi. After protracted talks the ministerial crisis was resolved and the Congress ministries came back into office at the end of February 1938. In the resolution of the crisis, Birla had played a crucial role. It had proved his point about the efficacy of the personal touch. 'I realised the weakness of the position that I, a non-Congressman without any authority from anyone, should be an instrument in doing some good work', he later said.[99]

By 1938 Birla's concern with the successful working of provincial autonomy was overshadowed by the increasing challenge posed by radical leftists especially by the Congress leader Subhash Chandra Bose to the Gandhian right-wing. Birla personally had no links with Bose, although, being based in Calcutta, he had closely observed his style of politics. Not unexpectedly, Birla was critical of Bose's general attitude towards the Gandhian wing of the Congress, and much more after his election to the Congress presidentship in 1937.[100] At his presidential speech at the Haripura Congress session, Bose had urged the agitational path and wanted the Congress to take an uncompromising attitude towards the Raj. This went against the creed which Birla propounded and had tried so hard to achieve in the last few years. Moreover, Bose's speech came just at a time when Birla was very anxiously trying to resolve the UP ministerial crisis and was urging both the

Congress and the Raj to be conciliatory. He intensely disliked Bose's speech and saw it as yet another threat to Gandhi and the right-wing within the Congress. The ideological debates that followed the Haripura session and the factional differences that openly surfaced within the Congress deeply disturbed him.

It was obvious to Birla that although Nehru had 'sobered down', the leftist threat remained.[101] Birla felt that right-wing Congress leaders should fight back and consolidate their position over the organization. For several months he had closely observed how the Congress high command, and especially Patel, had become the victim of a continuously hostile campaign.[102] Patel had, on certain occasions, taken stands which were opposed by many within the Congress and had, in Birla's view, been unjustly seen as having his way. There were lessons to be learnt, Birla told his friends in the Congress high command, especially Patel, who, he said, needed to make a concerted effort to improve his public image. In a tone of warning, he told Patel:

A strong impression is gaining ground that you are leading the Working Committee by the nose. It has been reported that Subhas Babu too feels that the Working Committee takes decisions at your orders. There is a lot of jealousy with the result that our best ministers are the most criticized ones of the day. People call you and Rajaji 'Dictators'. I would not mind if all this was confined to a few malcontents but unfortunately this feeling is now spreading also among friends.'[103]

All that was required was a little more propaganda which could be done by undertaking more tours, not just in Gujarat, but all over India, to establish contact with local Congressmen. He cautioned Patel not to neglect the important aspect of his public image.[104]

Throughout 1938–9 Birla kept a close watch on the activities of the leftists.[105] As the rift in the Congress Working Committee widened and the right-wing leadership was faced with an open revolt by Bose, he was convinced that the time had come for the right-wing to assert its control. The increasingly defiant stance of Bose after the Congress session at Tripuri and his formation of the Forward Bloc led Birla to impress upon Patel that there was now no alternative except to take disciplinary action. He was clear that Bose's revolt could not go unpunished and strict action must be taken. The best course, he advised Patel, was to convene a special session of the Congress rather than let the AICC (All India Congress Committee) take disciplinary action. 'If you take disciplinary action without going to the country', he cautioned Patel, 'it will help Subhash to become a martyr and perhaps it may eventually weaken your hands.'[106] In August 1939 Bose was disqualified from the president-ship of the Bengal Congress and debarred from the membership of any elective Congress committee for three years. This came as a relief to Birla.

In overall terms, Birla played an extremely important role in these years. His efforts were directed at creating a political climate conducive to the successful inauguration of provincial autonomy which he hoped would soon lead to the introduction of Dominion Status by the British. Birla was helped in these efforts because he had been able to consolidate relations with many in the British political establishment and was, by the mid-1930s, widely acknowledged as the personal emissary of Gandhi. Working the new constitution, in his view, would give the British and the Congress leadership the confidence to negotiate the devolution of responsibility at the centre. These hopes were, however, belied in late 1939, as we shall see later.

NOTES AND REFERENCES

[1] For a biographical study of Jamnalal Bajaj, see B.R. Nanda, *In Gandhi's Footsteps: The Life and Times of Jamnalal Bajaj* (Delhi, 1990). Also see, Kamalnayan Bajaj, *Kakaji, Bapu, Vinoba* (Delhi, n.d.), Kedar Nath (ed.), *Shreysadhak Jamnalal Bajaj* (Delhi, 1968), T.V. Parvate, *Jamnalal Bajaj* (Ahmedabad, 1962) and Kaka Kalelkar (ed.), *To A Gandhian Capitalist* (Bombay, 1951).

[2] On their first meeting, see Birla's recollections in *Shri Jamanalalji* (n.d., n.p.). Also see Haribhau Upadhyaya, *Shreyarthi Jamnanalalji* (New Delhi, 1951), pp. 30–1.

[3] Bajaj was the first Chairman of the Trust. On his involvement with the Trust see, Sukhdeo Pandey, *Mere Pilani Ke Sansmaran* (Pilani, Samvat 2029), pp. 157–9. Also see, *The Birla Education Trust Golden Jubilee Volume* (Pilani, 1951), p. 191; *The Birla Education Trust and Its Institutions* (Pilani, 1944); *The Changing Face of Pilani. Diamond Jubilee of the Birla Education Trust, 1900–1961* (Pilani, 1961); and V.P. Verma (ed.), *Diamond Jubilee Souvenir 1901–1961, Birla Education Trust* (Pilani, 1961).

[4] For instance in 1931 when Bajaj was incarcerated in Dhulia jail for participation in the Civil Disobedience Movement, the Bajaj-controlled Hindustan Sugar Mill ran into trouble with the UP Government which refused to grant it a licence for sulphur essential for the production of raw sugar (and also used in the manufacture of explosives). At this time Bajaj elicited the help of Birla. Ramkrishna Bajaj (ed.), *Patra Vyavahaar*, Vol. VII, *Correspondence With Social Reformers and Businessmen*, pp. 61–3. For details of the growth of the company, see *Hindustan Sugar Mills Golden Jubilee 1932–1982*, pamphlet (Bombay, 1982).

[5] Bajaj to Rajagopalachari, 9 March 1930, Ramkrishna Bajaj (ed.), *Patra Vyavahaar*, Vol. VII, pp. 125–6.

[6] Rajagopalachari to Birla, 16 October 1942, Birla Papers, Series II, File No. R–5.

[7] G.D. Birla, 'Rajendra Babu' in Birla Papers, Series Miscellaneous, File No. 121.

[8] Their association was strengthened by the friendship that existed between Prasad and Durga Prasad Khaitan, Birla's close lieutenant, from the time the two studied together in Presidency College, Calcutta, in the early 1900s. Kali Kinkar Datta, *Rajendra Prasad* (New Delhi, 1970).

[9] Mahendra Prasad used to support the family ever since Rajendra Prasad joined the nationalist movement and gave up his own legal practice. Along with a zamindari in Zaradei village in Chapra district, Mahendra Prasad was manager of the Chapra branch of the Bank of Bihar and had also started a rice mill and invested in an electric company, the Chapra Electric Supply Company. These ventures had not been successful and on Mahendra Prasad's sudden death it was left to Prasad to sort out the family's finances. The burden was so heavy that Prasad had asked Gandhi to be relieved from the Congress presidentship for 1936. See K.L. Panjabi, *Rajendra Prasad* (London, 1960), p. 86.

[10] Bajaj to Birla, 5 July 1936, and Birla to Bajaj, 9 July 1936, in Ramkrishna Bajaj (ed.), *Patra Vyavahaar*, Vol. VII, pp. 98–100. Also see B.R. Nanda, *In Gandhi's Footsteps*, pp. 252–3.

[11] Prasad to Birla, 25 July 1942, Birla Papers, Series II, File No. C–3.

[12] He visited Pilani often for health reasons since the dry weather suited him as he suffered from asthma. For details on Prasad's close association with the Birla Education Trust and the keen interest he took in its work, see Sukhdeo Pandey, *Mere Pilani Ke Sansmaran*, pp. 138–43.

[13] Munshi later noted: 'In the course of my studies I had long felt the inadequacy of our so-called Indian histories. For many years, therefore, I was planning an elaborate history of India in order not only that India's past might be described by her own sons, but also that the world might catch a glimpse of her soul as Indians see it. The Bharatiya Vidya Bhavan, ... took over the scheme. It was, however, realized only in 1944, when my generous friend Shri G.D. Birla ... lent me his co-operation.' cited in R.C. Majumdar, 'Reminiscences' in *Modern India Heritage and Achievement, Shri Ghanshyamdas Birla Eightieth Birthday Commemoration Volume* (Pilani, 1977), pp. 113–5.

[14] The other members were Sir S. Radhakrishnan, Sir Tek Chand, Sir T.R. Venkatramana Shastri, N.C. Mehta, Acharya Jinavijayaji Muni and Paras Nath Sinha, Munshi to the Trustees, Krishnarpan Trust, 13 April 1944, Birla Papers, Series II, File No. M–34.

[15] In June 1944, for example, Munshi advised Birla on the legal aspects of the take-over of the Nasik Military School from Moonje and he helped him revise the school's constitution. Munshi to Birla, 15 June 1944 and 21 December 1945, Birla Papers, Series II, File No. M–34.

[16] G.D. Birla, 'Introduction', *In the Shadow of the Mahatma*, p. XIX.

[17] Maniben Vallabhbhai Patel, 'Shri Ghanshyamdas Birla' in *Words to Remember*, np. On Patel's association with the Birla Education Trust, Pilani see Sukhdeo Pandey, *Mere Pilani Ke Sansmaran*, pp. 171–4.

[18] Birla cited in D.V. Tahmankar, *Sardar Patel* (London, 1970), pp. 17–18.

[19] Mira Behn, a part of Gandhi's *entourage*, recalls that Birla House was regarded by her as 'our Delhi home'. Mira Behn, *The Spirit's Pilgrimage* (London, 1960), p. 235. The Birlas maintained at Pilani several guest houses, all of different types and suited to either more Western or to more traditional needs.

[20] The houses were all named 'Birla House' except the one at Simla which was called 'Snow View.'

[21] D.P. Sharma, *Deshbhakt Udyog Pravartak Ghanshyamdas Birla*, pp. 84–5.

[22] Cited in D.P. Sharma, *Deshbhakt Udyog Pravartak Ghanshyamdas Birla*, pp. 82–3.

[23] Birla to Samuel Hoare, 14 March 1932, Birla, *In the Shadow of the Mahatma*, pp. 54–7.

[24] 'The loss of his influence' Birla told Reginald Clarke, 'among the youngsters and the fire-eaters is going to have a very serious consequence on the methods of future political struggles, as it is the youngsters who would count in future ... But now the young men are having a reaction. They are definitely leaning towards the Western ideas such as Communism, Bolshevism and all that it implies...The dream therefore of some of us is now receding in a far distant ground. But is there any remedy?' Birla to Reginald Clarke, n.d., Birla Papers, Foreign Correspondence, File No. C–3.

[25] *Hindustan Times*, 10 March 1933.

[26] The *Hindustan Times* editorial commented on Nehru's radical speeches when it wrote 'We all agree, that the ideal system of Government should provide for the

recognition of the masses, but the Indian problem consists, in the first place, of minimising the hurt of foreign rule and then probably of socialising in the best sense of that much-abused word, the amenities of life. In this respect, Mahatma Gandhi has greater faith in the patriotism of the "vested interests" at least to the extent of the fact that they gradually realise the effects of subjection which are more corrosive and wasteful than the loss of privilege under self-government. Pandit Jawaharlal is restless about defining the "self" in the term before getting hold of the "government" itself.' *Hindustan Times*, 17 September 1933.

[27] Michael Brecher, *Nehru, A Political Biography* (Delhi, 1998), p. 194.

[28] The *Hindustan Times* characterized the new party as 'inconsistent to the creed of the Congress' and added 'as regards the Congress Socialists, we would sound a note of warning. They may hold their beliefs sincerely but let them not be under the impression that those who do not agree with them are less sincere in their beliefs. Mahatmaji's straight talk to them at Benaras where he is reported to have told them that they should either abide by the Congress decision or take charge of the Congress Executive is due to resentment at the constant sniping at the Working Committee indulged in by certain socialist leaders who believe that they only have the welfare of the masses at heart and not the present leaders of the Congress.' *Hindustan Times*, 29 July 1934.

[29] Birla to Reginald Clarke, n.d., Birla Papers, Foreign Correspondence, File No. C–3.

[30] This section, as will be apparent, draws considerably upon the analysis presented by Bipan Chandra in his 'Jawaharlal Nehru and the Indian Capitalist Class 1936'. Bipan Chandra has rightly analysed Birla's role in 1936; our evidence, however, suggests that the essentials of Birla's strategy towards the left had been worked out as early as 1931. See Bipan Chandra, 'Jawaharlal Nehru and the Indian Capitalist Class, 1936' in his *Imperialism and Nationalism in India* (Delhi, 1979), pp. 171–203.

[31] Birla to Thakurdas, 3 August 1934, PT Papers, File 42, Part IV.

[32] Mody called on Bombay to take the lead and to 'put herself at the head of a movement which would give her an opportunity to proving once again her capacity for constructive statesmanship.' Mody's speech cited in his *Reflections Wise and Otherwise*, pp. 11–4

[33] D.R. Mankekar, *Homi Mody*, p. 117.

[34] Within three months Mody gave up his plan. The *Hindustan Times* commented that: 'Liberal circles in Bombay did not view with any enthusiasm the formation of a new party, the only reason for its existence would be antagonism towards the Congress, and the Liberal party was not willing to merge its identity in a nondescript rabble, every one of whom would have a grievance of his own against the Congress. The Liberals, having given him a cold shoulder Sir Mody has now beaten a strategic retreat and is attempting to rope in the Europeans to form an anti-Congress combination with the object of preventing the Congress from capturing the citadels of honour under the new reforms.' *Hindustan Times*, 2 November 1935. On the change in Mody's views about the 'Reforms party' see Mankekar, *Homi Mody*, p. 117.

[35] Birla, 'Interview with the Governor of Bengal', 1 May 1935, Birla, *Bapu*, Vol. II, pp. 44–7. He emphasized that the 'right wing Congressmen are thus fighting against two forces—the Government and the Socialists. The latter are making a direct attack by discrediting the leaders for having "achieved nothing." The Government is helping indirectly the Socialists by ignoring the right wing; between the two the right wing is being crushed.' Birla to J. Anderson, 5 July 1935, *ibid*, p. 190.

[36] Zetland was an old acquaintance of Birla from his days as Governor of Bengal. After meeting him Birla wrote: 'I went to see him in London and found him a good listener. One of his rare interruptions was to ask if Mr Gandhi was a practical man. I said, Hoare, Halifax, Findlater Stewart and Smuts could give Mr Gandhi a certificate on that point ... I said, "You should not doubt his practicality. He is not after quantity but quality; it is the spirit that he wants." ... He wished he could make friends in India realise how they had to fight here and against these heavy odds to get the Bill passed. I said I could get them to realise this only if the right atmosphere were created. The policy of "see me not" had spoilt the atmosphere ... He would do his best to help and would talk to me again'. Birla, *In the Shadow of the Mahatma*, pp. 172–3.

[37] After meeting Salisbury, Birla wrote in his notes: 'Old deaf man. Not much grit or wit, but feels his responsibility.' Further he noted that 'he is a nice man, but I don't think he could be of much use.' Birla, *ibid*, pp. 188–9.

[38] Birla found Derby 'the most charming personality' he had met in England. He reported to Gandhi that 'He stands on no ceremony. When I wanted to see him he came at once to my hotel rather than see me at his own place. He will arrange any interviews for me that I want. He has told me to ring him up whenever I need his help and he will either come to me or send for me. He talked to me with great paternal affection and I liked the man very much.' Birla to Gandhi, 29 June 1935, Birla, *ibid*, pp. 173–81.

[39] On Linlithgow, he noted: 'Tall, well-built, not brilliant but capable and sound; no imagination, matter-of-fact, at the same time straightforward, frank and well-intentioned.' Birla, *ibid*, pp. 186–7.

[40] After meeting him, Birla reported to Gandhi that 'the most helpful of them is Sir Findlater Stewart and I think he counts a lot. He is very friendly towards you and never tired of singing your praises, and when I gave him your letter he read it with great affection and emotion. He has promised and is giving every help.' Birla to Gandhi, 29 June 1935, Birla, *ibid*, pp. 173–81.

[41] Birla was very impressed by Butler whom he found 'a very capable and intelligent man, with a wide outlook. He has no tinge of racial bias or superiority'. Birla, *In the Shadow of the Mahatma*, pp. 169–70. Also Birla to Gandhi, 29 June 1935, in *ibid*, pp. 173–81.

[42] He met Major Attlee, Rhys Davies, Morgan Jones and other labour leaders together and found 'almost all of them unintelligent and dull ... all agreed that the atmosphere required improving but they were helpless. They had no power and no influence and, they might also have added, no intelligence! They suffer from an inferiority complex.' Birla, *ibid*, pp. 184–6.

[43] Birla met with Churchill at his country home and had a long discussion about India; 'It was never boring', he later noted continuing, 'at times he showed great enthusiasm. But he is badly informed about India. He has peculiar notions. Villages, he thinks, are entirely cut off in India from towns. I corrected this. No townsman is a pure townsman in India; everyone maintains touch with the village ... He thought motor-cars had not reached the villages. I corrected him again ... He thought that educated men, graduates and politicians were all in the towns. I again corrected him.' Birla, *ibid*, pp. 189–92.

[44] Among them were Bone and Crozier of the *Manchester Guardian*, Geoffrey Dawson, editor of *The Times*, Sir Walter Layton and Kingsley Martin of *The New Statesman*.

[45] He pressured British politicians for three conciliatory measures—the release of non-violent political prisoners still in jail, the return of lands confiscated during the Civil Disobedience Movement and conciliatory measures to solve the terrorist movement.

[46] As Birla reported to Anderson: 'I thus tried to impress upon them my conclusion that the atmosphere and not the bill was the more important ... Mutual co-operation in this atmosphere became impossible and along with it any good constructive work. Congressmen, due to the present atmosphere, were getting more irresponsible, and there was the danger that the Right Wing being wiped out of the picture by the Left Wing, which has already gained ground, and in order to vie with the Left Wing, the Right Wing may adopt wrecking tactics.' Birla to John Anderson, 5 July 1935, Birla, *Bapu*, Vol. II, pp. 83–7, also Birla to Gandhi, 29 July 1935, *ibid*, pp. 67–75, and Birla to Dawson, 11 July 1935, *ibid*, pp. 100–1.

[47] For instance in a note to Halifax, he presented his analysis and explained the power balance between the left and the right-wing. He told him that: 'When the Congress Working Committee met at Jubbalpore recently this section (the Congress Socialist Party) openly revolted against the parliamentarians when the work of the Assembly was under review. More radical resolutions were presented and a nominal victory secured; the situation was saved only by the tact and wisdom of the right wing—particularly of Mr Rajagopalachari. The right-wing Congressmen are thus fighting against two forces—the Government and the Socialists. The latter are making a direct attack by discrediting the leaders for having "achieved nothing". The Government is helping the Socialists indirectly by ignoring the right-wing; between the two the right-wing is being crushed. The result may be either the retirement of the right wingers, leaving the field free to the Socialists, or the adoption of some extreme programme in respect of reforms in order to carry public opinion. *This is the effect of the present atmosphere on the right wing of the Congress.*' Birla, 'Some Notes About The Political Situation In India', Note given to Halifax in Birla, *In the Shadow of the Mahatma*, pp. 192–5 (emphasis original).

[48] Interview with Viceroy, 5 August 1936, Birla, *Bapu*, Vol. II, pp. 261–5. Also see Birla to Linlithgow, 23 September 1935, *ibid*, p. 146, and Lothian to Birla, 11 October 1935, *ibid*, p. 152.

[49] Before the session the *Hindustan Times* editorial declared: 'The socialist ideology, with its materialist conception of human relationships and insistence of class war, is alien to the traditions and temperament of the East so as to make the Indian peasants enthuse over their wholly artificial and mostly intellectual idea of how society is to be reconstituted is scarcely a feasible proposition. Especially, at the present time, when the Parliamentary programme of the Congress has come in handy at a psychological moment to save the country from the despondency of defeat and failure, any reference to the "revolutionary" spirit is peculiarly inappropriate and can be made only by people entirely out of touch with the actualities of the political situation, as it is today.' *Hindustan Times*, 24 March 1936.

[50] See D.A. Low, 'Congress and "Mass Contacts" 1936–37: Ideology, Interests and Conflict over the Basis of Party Representation' in his *Rearguard Action: Britain and India: Selected Essays*, New Delhi, 1996.

[51] Bipan Chandra observes that 'the Lucknow Congress was both the high water mark and the swan song of Nehru's radicalism,' see his 'Jawaharlal Nehru and the Indian Capitalist Class in 1936', p. 196.

[52] He described Nehru to be 'like a typical English democrat who takes defeat in a sporting spirit. He seems to be out for giving expression to his ideology but he realizes that action is impossible and so does not press for it.' Birla to Thakurdas, 20 April 1936, PT Papers, File 144/ 1936–43.

[53] *Ibid*.

[54] Birla to Carl Heath, 25 February 1936, Birla Papers, File No. 29.

[55] The first signs of the businessmen's unease were reflected at the first quarterly meeting of the Indian Merchants' Chamber when A.D. Shroff, the Vice-President, criticized Nehru's pronouncements and urged the commercial and industrial community to make it 'clear to the Congress that they could not accept such utterances' Reporting Shroff's speech, the *Hindustan Times* wrote that 'an announcement of this character coming from a person of the position of the Congress President, in his [Shroff's] opinion, was most likely to injure the best interests of the country, if it resulted in checking industrial enterprise and encouraged the flight of capital from India.' *Hindustan Times*, 29 April 1936. The chamber declared that they needed to have a 'frank talk' with Nehru to tell him what 'merchants with a stake in the country think about his theories and philosophy.' *Hindustan Times*, 30 April 1936.

[56] The signatories included Purshotamdas Thakurdas, A.D. Shroff, Chunilal Mehta, A.R. Dalal, V.N. Chandavarkar, Homi Mody, Cowasji Jehangir, Chimanlal Setalvad and others. The *Hindustan Times* asked Nehru to see the Manifesto as a warning of 'the complications which persistence in socialist propaganda is likely to lead to,' and to keep two considerations before him in the future. These were firstly that 'India is already a land broken up into diverse creeds and sections which are so full of self-consciousness that nationalists are finding it hard to make a nation of these heterogeneous elements.' It asked further: 'Should Pandit Jawaharlal introduce another division into this land of warring sects by propagating the doctrine of class war which forms such a prominent feature of socialism as elaborated by Karl Marx? Secondly, the biggest task before the country today is the attainment of freedom...At such a time, is it wise to drive into the opposite camp vast sections of the people like the small businessmen, the petty landlords and the *bourgeiose* whose sympathies are sure to be alienated, if the Congress instead of being a purely national body becomes the organ of socialist propaganda? If Pandit Jawaharlal gives due weight to these two considerations, there is only one course open to him. And we are sure he has the courage to take it.' *Hindustan Times*, 22 May 1936.

[57] Birla to Thakurdas, 1 June 1936, PT Papers, File 177/ 1936–43 and Birla Papers, Series II, File No. T–5.

[58] Birla to Walchand Hirachand, 26 May 1936, PT Papers, File 177/ 1936–43, cited by Bipan Chandra, 'Jawaharlal Nehru and the Indian Capitalist Class, 1936', pp. 192–3. In an editorial called 'Failure of Socialism', the *Hindustan Times* argued that Nehru's belief that capitalism would collapse on its own inequalities was 'an essential weakness of his faith' and asserted that 'socialism is too artificial a conception to fit into the complex realities of modern life ... In India, especially, where most activities are conducted with the religious background behind, the anti-religious conception of life which goes with socialism everywhere is not likely to make the least appeal.' *Hindustan Times*, 17 May 1936.

[59] For details of Nehru's reception in Bombay by commercial organizations, see Bipan Chandra, 'Jawaharlal Nehru and the Indian Capitalist Class, 1936', p. 195.

[60] Birla to Reginald Clarke, 27 July 1936, Birla Papers, Series Foreign Correspondence, File No. C–3.

[61] For instance, see Birla to Lothian, 7 August 1936, Birla, *Bapu*, Vol. II, pp. 269–72. Also Birla to Halifax, 12 March 1937, *ibid*, pp. 330–2, Birla to Lothian, 31 March 1937, *ibid*, pp. 336–8.

[62] 'For God's sake, don't take any extreme step', he wrote to Rajagopalachari, 'you have put yourself in the right by taking a moderate attitude, and if you continue this situation,

I have no doubt that in the course of time your opponents must realize the reasonableness of your position. So I hope you will continue the counsel of moderation.' Birla to Rajagopalachari, 20 April 1937, Birla Papers, Series Very Very Important Correspondence, File 8. Birla also told Mahadev Desai: 'The authorities in Delhi are most unhappy ... If the present position is maintained, I think a solution must come out and with great honour. I hope the Working Committee will not nullify the atmosphere created by Bapu's moderation. He has put the whole of India in the right and his opponents in the wrong. His last wire to the *Times* was splendid. He has made clear that he does not stand on false prestige.' Birla to Mahadev Desai, 16 April 1937, Birla, *Bapu,* Vol. II, pp. 342–3.

[63] Birla to Halifax, 15 August 1937, Birla Papers, File No. 33. 'I have no doubt in my mind that Bapu has taken the right decision and no one but Bapu alone could have done this,' he wrote to Mahadev Desai. Birla to Mahadev Desai, n.d., Birla, *In the Shadow of the Mahatma,* p. 218.

[64] Birla's view was confirmed by Mahadev Desai who sent him the details of the Working Committee's meeting. The decision was 'another personal triumph for Bapu' he wrote, adding 'Jawahar and his friends of course behaved splendidly but without Bapu it would have been difficult.' Mahadev Desai to Birla, 9 July 1937, Birla, *Bapu,* Vol. III, pp. 6–8. Also Mahadev to Birla, 16 July 1937, *ibid,* pp. 9–10. He wrote to Rajaji, 'Your trial has now begun and you have to demonstrate what you can do under Congress administration.' Birla to Rajagopalachari, 7 July 1937, in Birla Papers, Series Very Very Important Correspondence, File No. 8.

[65] 'After working the constitution for two or three years successfully, we should send a small delegation of our public men to England who would talk informally with the Cabinet ministers here and would tell them how they had done their best to advance through constitutional lines but then had come to a dead stop because no further progress was possible without a new Act. They should try to persuade the Government here to give them something of their own liking and they should tell them clearly that India need not be satisfied with her present position. And unless there was a permanent agreement there was likelihood of direct action.' Birla to Mahadev Desai, 30 July 1937, Birla, *Bapu,* Vol. III, pp. 34–7.

[66] Birla to Halifax, 15 August 1937, Birla Papers, File No. 33.

[67] He had written to Rajagopalachari: 'Please keep me well informed so far as it helps my work here. You must be very busy now with the administration but please don't forget that two years hence you will have again to negotiate and we should prepare ground from now onward for the same.' Birla to Rajagopalachari, 27 July 1937, Birla Papers, Series Very Very Important Correspondence, File No. 8.

[68] See for example Birla to Mahadev Desai, 27 July 1937, in Birla, *Bapu,* Vol. III, pp. 29–32.

[69] Birla to Mahadev Desai, 27 and 30 July 1937, *ibid,* pp. 29–31 and pp. 34–7.

[70] Birla to Halifax, 15 August 1937, also Birla to Halifax, 11 August 1937, Birla Papers, File No. 33.

[71] Birla to Halifax, 15 August 1937, Birla Papers, File No. 33.

[72] For instance, while giving Zetland an article written by Gandhi in the *Harijan,* Birla specifically pointed out two sentences—'one in which Bapu had recognized the attempt by Great Britain to replace the rule of the sword by the rule of the majority' and the second in which he had stated that 'office acceptance was an attempt to avoid bloody revolution on the one hand and civil disobedience on the other hand.' See Birla's report to Mahadev Desai. Birla to Mahadev Desai, 27 July 1937, Birla, *Bapu,* Vol. III, pp. 29–32.

[73] Birla to Mahadev Desai, 8 July 1937, Birla, *Bapu*, Vol III, pp. 3–6.

[74] Birla to Mahadev Desai, 8 July 1937, Birla, *Bapu*, Vol. III, pp. 3–6. If the Governors and the services cooperated, he assured Halifax, there was 'no doubt that Gandhiji will strive every nerve to see that no cause arises for a break.' Birla to Halifax, 15 August 1937, Birla Papers, File No. 33.

[75] See for instance, the report of his meeting with Findlater Stewart and Halifax sent to Mahadev Desai, 8 July 1937, Birla, *Bapu*, Vol. III, pp. 3–6. He was invited to Chartwell by Winston Churchill, the conservative leader, whom he assured that, although the Congress stood for independence, it was not against Englishmen. Birla to Mahadev Desai, 22 July 1937, *ibid*, pp. 21–2. He also met Roger Lumley, the Governor-designate of Bombay, with whom he discussed ways and means of facilitating social contact between Congressmen and governors in the provinces. Birla to Desai, 20 July 1937, *ibid*, pp. 19–20.

[76] Zetland, for instance, regarded him as 'much more anxious for peace and much more alive to the reasonableness of the Government's case' than most leaders. Secretary of State to Viceroy, 28 June 1937, L/PO/6/96 (1) in P.N. Chopra (ed.), *Towards Freedom 1937–47*, Vol. I, *Experiment with Provincial autonomy 1 January–31 December 1937* (henceforth *TOFE*), (New Delhi, 1985), Doc. No. 338, pp. 694–5.

[77] G.D. Birla, 'Congress and Progress in India', 22 April 1938, in the *Friend*, The Quaker Weekly Journal, Vol. 96, No. 1 (London, 1938).

[78] Birla to Rajagopalachari, 7 July 1937, Birla Papers, Series Very Very Important Correspondence, File No. 8.

[79] 'Don't you think that, as a newly formed Government with no experience behind us, we have to judge all our actions according to the impressions they create on the general public?' he asked Patel. Birla to Patel, 13 July 1938, Birla Papers, Series Very Very Important Correspondence, File No. 4.

[80] Birla to Mahadev Desai, 26 January 1938, Birla, *Bapu*, Vol. III, pp. 146–7. Also see Birla to Mahadev Desai, 26 January 1938, *ibid*, pp. 146–7.

[81] Birla 'Congress and Progress in India', in the *Friend*. Similarly, he told Mahadev Desai, 'All this enthusiasm about the release of prisoners will begin to fade after some time. People will demand more bread and the bread is not going to come out of the confiscation of zemindaris. Our ministers will therefore have to decide from this very moment as to what they are going to do for ameliorating the condition of the people. If they think that the amelioration depends on the confiscation of the properties, then I think they are deceiving themselves.' Birla to Mahadev Desai, 4 December 1937, Birla, *Bapu*, Vol. III, pp. 104–7.

[82] Birla, 'Congress and Progress in India', in the *Friend*.

[83] Birla, 'Congress and Progress in India', in the *Friend*.

[84] 'Unless the Congress tells the peasants clearly that their position could be improved ultimately through their own hard work and not by any stroke of wand, I don't think this discontent will subside' he told Mahadev Desai. Birla to Mahadev Desai, 4 December 1937, Birla, *Bapu*, Vol. III, pp. 104–7.

[85] Birla to Mahadev Desai, 16 August 1937, Birla, *Bapu*, Vol. III, pp. 54–7. An instance of such 'indiscipline' was the march by peasants in Bihar to the Assembly in September 1937. This was very much disliked by Birla. What was equally distressing was the reaction of the Bihar Premier who, Birla reported to Mahadev, 'told them all sorts of sweet things without telling them that they were wrong in occupying the Assembly seats and refusing to vacate them.'

[86] For details of the increase in industrial disputes during this period, see Markovits, *Indian Business and Nationalist Politics*, pp. 155–7.

[87] The Kanpur strike had started before the Congress ministry came into office; when the Pant ministry came in they asked the mill-owners to recognize the workers' Mazdoor Sabha which they agreed to. The Kanpur Labour Enquiry Committee submitted their report in April 1938 and recommended a 21 per cent increase in wages; this was rejected by the Employers' Association and in the meantime the mill-owners withdrew their recognition of the Mazdoor Sabha. This led to another two-month strike.

[88] It was not the necessity of increasing wages, Birla told Patel, that the employers were objecting to but rather that the report was 'full of inaccuracies.' The most basic facts in it such as the price of commodities were incorrect and this led to incorrect conclusions. Moreover, he stressed that the UP Government passed a resolution on the strike without consulting the mill-owners and this had made it more difficult for the employers to accept arbitration by the Congress since they had lost all faith in the Congress government. Birla to Patel, 9 May 1938, and Birla to Patel, 20 June 1938, Birla Papers, Series Very Very Important Correspondence, File No. 4.

[89] Birla to Patel, 25 May 1938 and Patel to Birla, 11 June 1938, Birla Papers, Series Very Very Important Correspondence, File No. 4.

[90] Patel to Birla, 29 June 1938, Birla Papers, Series Very Very Important Correspondence, File No. 4, also see Birla to Mahadev Desai, 24 July 1938, Birla, *Bapu*, Vol. III, p. 176.

[91] Birla advised the 'High Command' not to be 'very aggressive at this stage, but if further sign of weakness in the exchange is discerned, the Congress and the public will have to be more assertive.' Birla to Patel, 2 July 1938, Birla Papers, Series Very Very Important Correspondence, File No. 4. He advised no hasty step, but rather that the Congress 'should watch the conditions before it embarks on a definite policy.' He thought it was expedient to 'pass a resolution for a lower ratio in the interest of the country' but told Mahadev Desai not to 'start any aggressive agitation at this stage' since in the prevalent political situation, there was not much that could be done. 'Besides, until Federation comes in,' he said 'I don't see what definitely could the Congress do except agitating.' Birla to Mahadev Desai, 24 July 1938, Birla, *Bapu*, Vol. III, p. 176. In keeping with Birla's expert advise, the Working Committee passed a resolution in favour of a lower ratio at the end of 1938.

[92] Durga Das observes that 'In fact, the comments of the Federation on the Central Budget were awaited by the Congress and other legislators to decide what line to take in the general discussion on it.' Durga Das, *Curzon to Nehru*, pp. 316–7.

[93] With the changed political situation, the FICCI Committee felt that 'it is necessary for the Federation to express its considered opinion on the several measures of far reaching importance coming before the Assembly and affecting trade and commerce of the country. In consequence of this change ... the work of the Federation office has increased materially during the course of the year'. FICCI, *Proceedings of the Annual Meeting 1938–9* (New Delhi, 1939).

[94] It was decided that the 'Federation Office should be adequately equipped with additional staff for the purpose of making a proper study of the numerous problems which called for the Federation's attention from time to time.'

[95] Lala Diwan Chand Trust to the Federation, 16 May 1936, and Federation to the Lala Diwan Chand Trust, 3 August 1936, in FICCI, *Correspondence and Relevant documents relating to Important questions dealt with by the Federation during the year 1936–7* (New Delhi, 1937).

[96] Birla to Gandhi, 20 February 1938, Birla, *Bapu*, Vol. III, pp. 149–52.

[97] Laithwaite assured Birla that the Viceroy would make a statement within two or three days in which he would take a stand on the principle of individual review of prisoners cases; he would state that he had 'no desire to torpedo the Congress governments'; would admit that 'law and order was the province of the ministers and he had not the slightest desire to interfere' and 'would make some sort of appeal' and then the final step of the ministers and the Governors meeting could be taken and the releases could begin. Birla to Mahadev Desai, 20 February 1938, Birla, *Bapu*, Vol. III, pp. 149–52.

[98] Birla to Gandhi, 25 February 1938, *ibid*, p. 152.

[99] Birla to Zetland, 2 June 1938, Birla Papers, File No. 33.

[100] Birla's differences with Bose can be seen from his attitude towards the National Planning Committee. Towards the end of 1938 a conference of provincial ministers of industry met, presided over by Bose. The conference aimed at formulating a comprehensive scheme of planning for the following 10 to 15 years. Birla was one of the special invitees to the conference along with other business leaders such as Lala Shri Ram and Lala Shankar Lal. From this conference emerged the National Planning Committee under the chairmanship of Nehru. A number of business leaders were nominated to the Committee such as Thakurdas, A.D. Shroff, Ambalal Sarabhai and later Walchand Hirachand. Birla too was invited to join the committee as chairman of the Sub-committee on Trade. However, he excused himself and explained to Rajendra Prasad: 'From the very beginning I have kept myself out of touch with this Planning Committee and have also felt in my heart of hearts that a lot of work being done at present is a waste of time. If I am given any constructive work, I am always at the disposal of the Congress, but to me it looks as if it is more of an academical committee and thus I may perhaps find myself a square in a round hole.' Birla to Rajendra Prasad, 29 June 1939 and 30 June 1939, Valmiki Choudhary (ed.), *Dr Rajendra Prasad. Correspondence and Select Documents*, Vol. III: January to July 1939 (New Delhi, 1984), pp. 242–3 and p. 139. For details on the work done by the National Planning Committee see R. Chattopadhyaya, 'Attitude of Indian Business Towards Economic Planning, 1930–56', Indian Institute of Management, Ahmedabad, Seminar Series in Business History (IV), Business and Politics in India: A Historical Perspective (Ahmedabad, 1989), (mimeograph).

[101] Birla to Arthur Moore, 6 March 1938, Birla Papers, File No. 32.

[102] K.F. Nariman, a prominent Bombay Congress leader, had alleged that Patel had misused his official position in the 'High Command' to impose a person of his own choice, B.G. Kher, during the election for the Bombay premiership in July 1937. Nariman insisted upon an enquiry into Patel's role. Although the enquiry cleared Patel, his image suffered within Congress circles.

[103] Birla to Patel, 13 July 1938, Birla Papers, Series Very Very Important Correspondence, File No. 4.

[104] Birla to Patel, 30 July 1938, Series Very Very Important Correspondence, File No. 4. Patel was completely unperturbed by the criticisms levelled against him: 'The Bengal Press has never spared me and I do not attach any importance to that kind of propaganda. The Working Committee was unanimous in the decision about the C P crisis ... We cannot help people forming their own opinions, nor can we surrender our judgement or abdicate our functions for fear of being styled "Dictators", "Fascists", "Hitlers" or the like ... Much of the propaganda is engineered by the Maharashtra group who controls the press as they have mastered the art of carrying on unscrupulous agitation against their opponents.' Patel to Birla, 1 August 1938, *ibid*.

[105] For instance, Pyarelal, Gandhi's secretary, informed him about Bose's meeting with Gandhi in February 1939. 'Subhas was here, closeted with Bapu for three hours. The report that has appeared in the Press is substantially correct. As I wrote to you before, Bapu's outspoken advice fell absolutely flat upon him. He is out for personal adventure. I wonder where the crew on whose shoulders he has mounted to his Presidential chair will lead him. It is a dangerous crew. But Bapu hopes that if he can rightly put into operation the whole technique of non-violence, it will be well with the Congress and the country.' Pyarelal to Birla, 22 February 1939, Birla, *Bapu*, Vol. III, pp. 252–3.

[106] Patel disagreed with Birla's suggestion of going to the Congress as a whole and replied: 'I do not think there is any cause for going to Congress as a whole. In such matters proper course is for the Working Committee to deal with the situation and whatever Bengal may do and feel we cannot afford to ignore this defiance. It would mean certainly the end of Congress.' Birla to Patel, 15 July 1939, and Patel to Birla, 18 July 1939, Birla Papers, Series Very Very Important Correspondence, File No. 4.

7

A Crucial Decade for the Family

Birla could play his new public role only because of the strong support network which he enjoyed from within the larger family, especially from his brothers Rameshwardas and Braj Mohan. Birla's most active years in public life were also the most momentous for the family. The children were at a crucial age—all in their early teens when they needed attention. However, between 1930 and 1943 all of Birla's children were married and the boys were inducted into different branches of the family business. After 1926, following Mahadevi's demise, the children were placed under the charge of different branches of the family in Bombay and Calcutta. Birla tried hard to keep track of how they were doing. However, as his public life increasingly grew more hectic and his business commitments multiplied, he was required to spend long periods travelling within the country and to the UK. In view of these circumstances Birla increasingly realized that he could not provide the care which his young children needed and had to depend upon the help of his brothers and their wives.

Responsibility for the children came to be shared by Rameshwardas and Braj Mohan. Rameshwardas lived at Birla House on Mount Pleasant Road in Bombay while Braj Mohan was based at Birla Park, the family's Calcutta home. Birla, as we have noted earlier, had moved to Delhi in 1929 along with Jugalkishore. There were five running establishments which the family maintained by the late 1920s—in Banaras, Delhi, Bombay, Calcutta and Pilani to which periodic visits were made. Yet, the geographical distance was not allowed to upset the family's cohesion and solidarity. Over the years, the brothers had assumed well demarcated roles within the family. After Baldeodas' retirement, Jugalkishore donned the mantle of the patriarch and his views were considered binding on all. While keeping a sharp eye on what he saw as important family and religious matters, Jugalkishore, however, remained uninvolved with the daily concerns of care-taking and upbringing. Birla could take an interest in the children only when critical decisions were to be made. Rameshwardas and Braj Mohan looked after day-to-day socialization, education and apprenticeship. Birla could leave all these matters to them because of the manner in which the family functioned.

FAMILY AS A SOCIAL GROUP

The family functioned as a social group and sustained the children through their growing-up years. Close contact was maintained among the different households. All important decisions were taken by the elders, and the younger generation— which consisted of Birla's own six children, six of Rameshwardas' and two of Braj Mohan'—moved easily between Calcutta and Bombay. Relations among the cousins were intimate. Because of a fortuitous set of circumstances, all the children of the Birla brothers had, by the late 1920s, come to live together. When Rameshwardas' first wife expired in 1923 he sent his sons to be cared for by Braj Mohan and his wife in Calcutta, while his daughters remained with him. Although he later remarried, this arrangement continued. Then, when Mahadevi expired in 1926, Birla too made similar arrangements for the care of his children. The sons were put under the charge of Braj Mohan and his daughters under Rameshwardas. Thus, all six sons of the three Birla brothers came to live together in Calcutta. Their education and upbringing became the responsibility of Braj Mohan and his wife. The seven daughters of Rameshwardas and Birla came under the care of Rameshwardas and his second wife in Bombay. The family met once a year during the holidays which were spent either in Calcutta or Bombay, or in one of the family houses in the hills.

Whilst their relation with their uncles was an intimate one, the relation of the children with Birla was somewhat aloof and formal. Meeting him sometimes after long intervals the children grew to be intimidated by their father. Most often these meetings were short—while he was on a business visit to Bombay or Calcutta and he barely had time to spend with them. Overall the atmosphere was of deep respect mingled with fear for elders. The youngsters felt deserted and yearned to be with him. Even when he was at home, their formal relation made it difficult for them to express their emotions frankly. So much did they fear him that they almost never had the courage to question his long absences.[1] It was only many years later, when their father was well into his eighties, that the children dared to confess what they had dearly missed him. As Shanti, his daughter, told Birla: 'I wish you could always have loved us as much as you do now. When we went to Delhi or you came to Bombay, we only knew of your arrival and departure; you could seldom spare us any time.'[2]

However, it seemed to Birla that arrangements for their care could not be better under the circumstances. Keeping them close to him and Jugalkishore in Delhi in the absence of a matriarchal figure made little sense.[3] He felt inadequate to care for the young children on his own. Moreover, the Delhi home was more like an official residence while Bombay and Calcutta remained family homes where they lived amidst the extended family and community networks.

However, in the early 1930s, the experiment of keeping the children with him in Delhi was made. Both Krishna Kumar and Basant Kumar along with Gangaprasad (Braj Mohan's son) and Madhav Prasad (Rameshwardas' elder son) were called to stay in Delhi. Lakshmi Niwas, already in his twenties, was based in Delhi and was involved in the family business. The younger two—Krishna Kumar and Basant Kumar were admitted into the prestigious Modern School. However, the arrangements did not work. The boys were both forcibly admitted to the school hostel, Krishna Kumar came down with pneumonia and the children missed the warmth of the Calcutta family home. What made matters worse was Birla's hectic schedule. Finally, the boys, to the relief of all, were sent back to Calcutta.[4] Circumstances thus conspired so that in their crucial growing-up years the children could not enjoy a satisfying relationship with their father. He grew to know his sons only after they joined the family business, and while grooming them, developed an appreciation of their abilities, strengths and weaknesses. His relation towards his daughters remained formal. This had much to do with the way the girl-child was perceived by the elders. In an orthodox family such as theirs the status of a girl was markedly different from that of a boy. Though as children they all enjoyed an equally affectionate relationship with their elders and shared in the family's prosperity, the girls were brought up on the premise that the family's responsibility did not extend beyond giving them primary education and finding suitable grooms for them. Like other Marwari families, it was taken for granted that the girls would not play any role in business nor inherit immovable properties.[5] The family's responsibility was to nurture them in an affectionate environment, impart to them 'some education' and find a 'good husband'.

Through these early years, the values which the family elders hoped to instil in the daughters were of service, restraint and renunciation. The position of a daughter is perhaps best captured by a conversation which Shanti, Birla's youngest daughter had with her father. He told her: 'The first lesson in the *Gita* is to do your duty at all costs. Spinning, reading, domestic chores—all these are your work and duty... The greatest duty is to serve your household and make it a happy home.'[6] The girls thus came to appreciate that their primary loyalty lay with their husband's family. They were to become their 'husband's associate and protector of his righteousness.'[7] Daughters who resisted early marriage or expressed ambitions for higher education were counselled. When Shanti expressed a desire to complete her High School examination before her marriage Birla told her that mere degrees would not take her far. 'Real examinations are held in everyday life and success or failure are assessed there', he said.

Sons were, however, given a different treatment. The expectation from them was that they would train to take up the responsibility of the family business and demonstrate qualities of leadership. They were expected to complete their school education although higher education was not encouraged. Hands-on training in business was considered more valuable than a formal college degree. Among Birla's sons and nephews only Ganga Prasad, Braj Mohan's son, became a graduate. Although Birla's younger sons Krishna Kumar and Basant Kumar too spent some time in college they soon left to join business.

DEFINING THE FAMILY 'TRADITION'

A great deal of emphasis was placed in inculcating a sense of tradition among the children. This was typical of a Marwari business family. The joint-family structure and its hierarchies were paramount. The children were taught to respect the framework of the joint family and not allowed to differentiate among the elders. They thus called Jugalkishore *Bade Baboji* or elder father even though he had no children of his own. Rameshwardas was addressed as *Baboji* or father, Birla as *Kakoji* which meant elder uncle, and Braj Mohan was called *Chachoji* or uncle. Likewise, their wives were also addressed similarly by the new generation. Jugalkishore's and Rameshwardas' wives were called *Badi-Ma* or elder mother in keeping with their exalted status and Braj Mohan's wife was addressed as *Kakiji* or aunt by all the children of the family.

A strict regime of traditional Hindu rituals was inculcated in the daily lives of the youngsters. Jugalkishore ensured that the family strictly followed religious practices prescribed by the Sanatan Dharma tradition of Hinduism. Astrologers were consulted before all important occasions. Jugalkishore kept the horoscopes of the entire family in his charge and regularly organized prayers and religious ceremonies, to 'ward off suspected obstacles and neutralise evil influences.'[8] From a young age, the children were exposed to important holy texts and made to 'memorise good quatrains from the *Ramayana* and also verses from the *Gita*.'[9] Jugalkishore instructed the younger generation to 'carry on with *bhajans, kirtans* and *havans*' and to strictly observe the chanting of prayers.[10]

Another essential element of the family tradition was the shunning of individuality. The importance of the family as a social unit rather than the individual was emphasized to the Birla children. Individualistic behaviour was discouraged and they were expected to respect decisions made by elders. In social life a strict 'code of restraint' was practised at home. This meant an austere lifestyle which emphasized control over individual expenditure. 'Never utilise wealth only for fun and frolic', Birla told Basant Kumar. He compared expenditure of wealth on 'worldly pleasures' to the demon-like conduct of Ravana in the epic *Ramayana*.[11] A frugal lifestyle was emphasized to the children who were instructed to 'spend the bare minimum on yourself'. Birla regarded over-spending as 'committing sin' which would 'destroy our business'.[12] This code translated into a control over consumption. To 'waste money on worldly pleasures' was derided. The youngsters were discouraged from taking to enjoyments such as the theatre. On learning that his elder daughter, Chandrakala, had developed some interest in theatre, Birla immediately took her to task. He derided her interest in theatre, declaring that it was purely for entertainment, not for instruction. 'Girls should pay more attention to holy thoughts and sinless conduct.'[13] All pleasures should be shunned, he told her. During vacations, which were sometimes spent in hill stations, the children were discouraged from mixing with 'Anglicized ladies and gentlemen'.[14]

In keeping with Sanatani practices, the entire family followed a strict vegetarian diet and even the consumption of onions and garlic was disallowed.[15] 'Those who eat food only for taste die prematurely,' Birla warned Basant Kumar and asked him to 'take food as you would take medicines'. Sweets, cakes, pastries were regarded as European and were also taboo to the children for fear of encouraging spendthrift tendencies.[16] Consumption of *paan*, betel-nuts and tobacco was discouraged and children who dared indulge, were reprimanded. Consumption of alcohol was regarded no less than a sin.

Signs of opposition or revolt against the austere lifestyle invited censure and punishment. The case of Gajanan, Rameshwardas' son provided a living example of how unbecoming conduct was dealt with. When Gajanan showed a 'fondness for high living, for gourmet style food, ... for song and dance, and for smoking' he was severely taken to task.[17] Birla was given the responsibility of disciplining the youngster. Birla advised his 25-year-old nephew to give up his bad habits and to follow the family's traditions. When his discussions and warnings to Gajanan failed to have the desired effect, severe measures were taken. He was ostracized by the family elders. An unrelenting Gajanan, however, found it difficult to follow the beaten path. He had, in 1929, been married against his wishes. Although he had two children, his marriage was not successful. He was unable to mend his ways. Then the family discovered that he had developed another relationship and wanted to separate from his wife. This proved to be the last straw for the family elders. Birla and Rameshwardas worked out a legal settlement in 1935 which severed Gajanan's ties with the family. Under its terms he was disinherited and given an allowance of Rs 1000 every month. His wife and her two children were taken under the family's charge while he was forced out of Birla Park, his home. The family elders continued to give the respect and privileges due to his wife as a daughter-in-law.

This served as an example to all the youngsters. They understood that no deviations from the family tradition would be tolerated and acquiesced in all important individual decisions made by the family patriarchs, including marriage alliances. Such alliances were seen to be critical in continuing the family's traditions. Considerations of compatibility in terms of status within the community were paramount. Marriages were seen to be important for building networks and enhancing the family honour and prestige within the larger Maheshwari community. Brides were chosen from families which were seen to have superior status within the community. It was hoped that alliances would bring contacts and valuable advice on business matters. The *kutumb*—or in-laws—were invaluable for forging community links. Thus Birla's eldest son, Lakshmi Niwas, was married in 1927 to the daughter of Shyamsundarlal Loiwal, who held the important position of Diwan in the princely state of Kishangarh in Rajputana.[18] So well connected was the family that the Maharaja of Kishangarh himself attended the wedding. It was perceived by the elders to have 'elevated the prestige of the Birla family in the Maheshwari community' after the setback to its reputation over the unfortunate Kolwar controversy. The other boys were also married into prominent families—Krishna Kumar married into the prominent Taparia family.[19] Perhaps the most prestigious was the match for Basant Kumar in 1942 with Sarala, the daughter of Brijlal Biyani, who had been president of the All India Maheshwari Mahasabha and a prominent leader from the Central Provinces known among political circles as Berar Kesari.

Marriages of the daughters was less complex. While considerations of ritual status were important, the prominence of the family was not an important consideration. Since he was based in Calcutta where community networks existed, it often became the responsibility of Braj Mohan to find marriage alliances. Chandrakala was married in August 1931 to Bansi Dhar who came from the Daga family which had businesses in Jalpaiguri. The family had a flourishing business in tea, textiles and insurance. Chandrakala was then only 14 years old. After the marriage ceremonies which took place at Birla Park in Calcutta, Birla gave her the following advice for her married life:

You must remember, you now have to cement relations in your new home. You must do your duty unflinchingly. Do not lose patience. I gave you some education and found you a good husband... What else can I do for you now? May God give you moral strength... Never neglect your duty. Service, restraint and renunciation... You must love your life-partner, which you must already do, I am sure... Remain happy and do not neglect your daily prayers.[20]

In 1941 the family was able to find suitable matches for the younger daughters, Anusuiya and Shanti. Anusuiya was married to Narendra Singh Taparia, a scion of a Calcutta Maheshwari family. Shanti was married to Krishnagopal Maheshwari.[21] The following year when the marriage of Basant Kumar and Sarala was celebrated Birla had the satisfaction of seeing all his children settled. He developed a close relationship with his daughters-in-law. With Sarala he developed a special bond as Gandhi, who knew the Biyani family well, had played a role in encouraging the match. Although he had warned Sarala that 'the Birla family is used to traditional methods. There won't be much freedom for you', he had been delighted at this alliance and the engagement had taken place in his ashram at Wardha.[22] This made the youngest daughter-in-law special in Birla's eyes. In later years he looked upon her as the lady of the house.

BUSINESS GROOMING

An essential element of the family tradition was the initiation and apprenticeship of sons into family business and their grooming for future leadership. Sons were initiated into the business once they finished schooling. Birla and Braj Mohan took active interest in their apprenticeship.

The new apprentice typically underwent initial training for approximately a year. In this period he was put under the charge of a trusted senior manager who regularly reported progress to Braj Mohan and Birla. Having lived with Braj

Mohan through their childhood years, the boys found it easier to work with him and felt intimidated if they had to deal with Birla at the work-place. Thus Lakshmi Niwas started his apprenticeship in the jute trade with Braj Mohan. Krishna Kumar was initiated into the sugar mills in the late 1930s. Basant Kumar initially began with stock operations and then joined the Kesoram Cotton Mill. Birla's nephews Ganga Prasad and Madho Prasad started out with shipping and jute respectively.[23] Senior managers played a critical role during the apprenticeship years. Basant Kumar, for example, was placed under the charge of Sitaram Khemka, a trusted kinsman and employee. An essential component of the training was in learning financial and accounting matters. 'Keeping accounts, maintaining cash books, ledgers, vouchers, bills and outstanding accounts, reconciling bank records' were part of this preliminary training which also included preparation of 'daily reports, parta, monthly and annual income and expenditure accounts, sales procedures'. Such training continued for as long as it took them to single-handedly prepare the 'entire cash book, balance the receipts and payments, meticulously account for every paisa'. This could sometimes even take up to a year. Thereafter they were attached to other departments such as sales and manufacturing.

Perhaps more significant than learning these skills was the inculcation of the family's code of business in the young initiates. This was not difficult to imbibe as it was merely an extension of the code of restraint which they had been taught at home. They were taught that the dignity and status of the family within the community and in the industrial world were the most important. They were repeatedly reminded that the family name must not be dishonoured. 'It didn't matter', Birla told the younger generation as they took their first steps in the world of business, 'if we should expand slowly, but we should proceed with abundant caution'. The reputation of the family was most important since the 'community had reposed full faith on us. Even if a single enterprise failed, the blame would fall ... on the entire Birla family'.[24]

There were certain fundamental rules which were always to be followed. Foremost was the need to keep a tight control on the finances by monitoring daily financial performance achieved through the parta system which was followed in all Birla enterprises. This entailed the calculation of cost, output and profit on a daily basis. Their training emphasized an almost obsessive concern with financial performance and control which characterized the Birla business philosophy. 'Major effort' was to go 'into financial and commercial matters.' Each parta statement was looked at on a daily basis and sometimes up to ten to twelve days of each month were spent in examining the accounts of the previous month. Birla himself insisted that daily parta statements from each of the mills under his charge be sent to him each day wherever he might be.

Other principles which were passed on to the next generation related to the extended family. Complete loyalty was expected from senior employees. They were considered to be a part of the extended joint-family staff. Senior employees inevitably came from the Marwari community preferably from the Maheshwari subcaste. Many of them also had a Pilani connection and had spent long years with the business. They were often indebted for help rendered in personal affairs. A prime example was Durga Prasad Mandelia—called *Chachoji* by the younger generation. He had started his career with Birla at the age of 14 and had risen to become a key business associate. The new generation was similarly encouraged to select a team of their own and were encouraged to recruit sons of senior employees. This ensured stability and loyalty which was sometimes rewarded by giving away of agency and distribution rights. Thus from within the community satellite groups were created which strengthened the business network, provided managerial talent and enhanced trust.

Once their apprenticeship was completed and real business responsibilities started the younger generation were given charge of the units where they had been trained. By 1940 Birla's three sons and nephews had completed their initial training and taken over individual charge of different factories. Thus Lakshmi Niwas was looking after the New Asiatic Insurance Company and had opened a starch unit in Rangoon. Madhav Prasad had taken charge of the Birla Jute Mill. Basant Kumar had been elevated to become the chairman of the Kesoram Cotton. Krishna Kumar had a number of sugar mills under his control. Ganga Prasad too had begun to take responsibility. It was only Gajanan who had been left out of these business endeavours.[25]

While the new generation had taken charge of different units, Birla and Braj Mohan continued to keep a watchful eye on their progress. They had to be consulted before any major investment decisions were made. As Basant Kumar recalls his early days in the family business: 'I did have to approach Kakoji for permission whenever I wanted to raise fresh capital. Without his advice and clearance, I did not raise even Rs 50 lakhs from the market.'[26] Diversification plans were discussed carefully with the elders and had to be approved by them. Certain areas of business were considered taboo such as the hotel business because it involved 'drinking and dancing' which was not in keeping with the austere tradition of the family.

As they expanded their horizons, the younger generation knew that the family tradition had to be adhered to. For example, in 1938, Basant Kumar started a new company, Kumar Chemical and Pharmaceutical Works Ltd., for the manufacture of pharmaceuticals. He made a substantial investment of over rupees two and a half lakhs and hired a foreign expert from Hungary to help set up the new enterprise. When his plans were well advanced, Jugalkishore was horrified to learn that the manufacturing process would involve the use of animal glands to produce hormone-based medicines.[27] Uncle and nephew argued over the issue for over two months. However, Jugalkishore remained adamant and Basant Kumar ultimately had to give in and abandon the project.[28]

By the early 1940s the Birla brothers had the satisfaction of seeing the next generation take up business responsibilities. Except for Gajanan, all other sons had successfully completed their apprenticeship, and moved easily into the roles earmarked for them in the business empire. This was welltimed as the business was poised for unprecedented growth thanks to the economic opportunities thrown up by the outbreak of World War II in 1939.

Notes and References

[1] Basant Kumar Birla, *A Rare Legacy*, p. 20.

[2] R.N. Jaju, *G.D. Birla: A Biography*, p. 172.

[3] Jugalkishore's wife had expired in 1927.

[4] *Ibid*, pp. 18–19.

[5] For a valuable study of how family businesses function see Sudipt Dutta, *Family Business in India* (New Delhi, 1997).

[6] *Ibid*, p. 151.

[7] Birla to Chandrakala, in Jaju, *G.D. Birla: A Biography*, pp. 99–100.

[8] Basant Kumar Birla, *A Rare Legacy*, p. 283.

[9] Birla to Shanti, in R.N. Jaju, *G.D. Birla: A Biography*, p. 131.

[10] See Basant Kumar Birla, *A Rare Legacy*, p. 281.

[11] Basant Kumar Birla, *A Rare Legacy*, pp. 350–1.

[12] Basant Kumar Birla, *A Rare Legacy*, pp. 350–1.

[13] R.N. Jaju, *G.D. Birla: A Biography*, p. 110

[14] Basant Kumar Birla, *A Rare Legacy*, p. 23.

[15] Basant Kumar Birla, *A Rare Legacy*, p. 280.

[16] Basant Kumar Birla, *A Rare Legacy*, pp. 350–1.

[17] Basant Kumar Birla, *A Rare Legacy*, pp. 310–13.

[18] Loliwal had been an important figure in the Maheshwari community. He was instrumental in the establishment of the Maheshwari Mahasabha in 1890 and had inaugurated the first session of the Maheshwari Mahasabha which had been attended by Maheshwaris from all over the country.

[19] Gajanan married the daughter of Jamnadas Malpani of Jabalpur, in 1929. The Malpanis were 'considered then to be one of the finest in the Marwari community' and Madhav Prasad's bride was from the Mohta family, a prominent Maheshwari family from Sirsa.

[20] R.N. Jaju, *G.D. Birla: A Biography*, pp. 99–100.

[21] R.N. Jaju, *G.D. Birla: A Biography*, p. 131.

[22] Basant Kumar Birla, *A Rare Legacy*, p. 36.

[23] Basant Kumar Birla, *A Rare Legacy*, pp. 25–6.

[24] Basant Kumar Birla, *A Rare Legacy*, p. 80.

[25] Basant Kumar Birla, *A Rare Legacy*, pp. 310–13.

[26] Basant Kumar Birla, *A Rare Legacy*, p. 80.

[27] Basant Kumar Birla, *A Rare Legacy*, pp. 31–2

[28] Basant Kumar's first independent venture was thus stopped in its tracks by Jugalkishore. The Hungarian consultant was stupefied by what appeared clearly to be a completely irrational decision, involving large financial losses.

8

The War Years

As the clouds of a European war loomed on the political horizon, Birla grew increasingly restive about the future of the Congress ministries. His sympathies however lay with the British in their times of difficulties. As soon as hostilities broke out, he wired Churchill with whom he had discussed the threat of war on his last visit to England, to congratulate him on joining the government. He assured him that the 'sympathies of most of us who belong to the Gandhi school of thought are whole-heartedly with Great Britain'. 'If our prayers can have any influence on the ultimate results of the war, the victory will undoubtedly be yours', he continued.[1] While he believed that India should support the Allies, he felt that a war should not be imposed upon her. India must co-operate voluntarily in return for a promise that after the war she would be granted full Westminster-style Dominion Status. In the interim he envisaged an expansion of the Viceroy's Executive Council and the inauguration of Federation.

POLITICAL DISAPPOINTMENT AND DEADLOCK

The Viceroy's unilateral declaration that India was party to the war without consulting Indian opinion led to resignation of the Congress ministries in October 1939. The deadlock arose as the British involved India in the war, imposing heavy demands upon men and material for a cause in which India had little stake. This arbitrary decision outraged Indian political opinion and the Congress leadership took the view that India could not participate in the war without the consent of its political leadership and without the explicit promise of independence. That ended the experiment of co-operating with the British in governing India, which Birla had believed could ultimately lead to the complete devolution of power into Indian hands. A deeply disappointed Birla found it hard to accept the fact that after the extraordinary success of the Congress ministries, political events could take such an adverse turn. It appeared to him no less than a tragedy that a unique experiment showing 'greater inclination on both sides for mutual understanding and friendship' had terminated so abruptly. Birla approached his British friends at the highest levels of the political establishment not to alienate the Gandhi school of thought which was eager to help. He emphasized that Gandhi alone could keep peace in India for the duration of the war. 'India is extremely peaceful not by accident but by *design*,' he told Laithwaite. 'Gandhiji wants to convert peaceful India into a *friendly India*, full of goodwill towards England,' he added.[2] Hoping to play a role in bringing the Gandhian leadership close to the Raj, he made many overtures to the Viceroy. He wanted to meet with him to explain the Gandhian point of view. 'At the slightest encouragement from you,' he told Laithwaite, 'I should like to run down to Delhi.'

Notwithstanding Birla's overtures, there was no response from official quarters and there was little Birla could do. The British were in no mood to give in to the Congress' demand for a role in central government which might have endangered India's ability to satisfy wartime imperial needs. By March 1940 it was clear that negotiations between the government and the Congress had reached a deadlock and the party resolved to unhesitatingly start Civil Disobedience and empowered Gandhi to initiate it. Upset by this decision, Birla censured Gandhi that 'we are going the wrong way,' and urged him to reconsider the decision.[3] 'Avenues of honourable settlement', he pleaded with the Mahatma, still existed and must be explored. It was a particularly trying phase because Birla felt torn between his loyalty to Gandhi and his own belief in the constitutional path:

When I consult my heart I feel that eventually Bapu must win...God must guide him. But this is talking with faith. When I consult my head and do a bit of 'rational thinking', I come to no other conclusion than that we have not played our cards well.[4]

Between March and October 1940 he swamped Gandhi with long notes about his thoughts and doubts about the course the Congress was embarking upon. Instead of abandoning the framework of the 1935 Act the Congress, he maintained, should work for reconciliation with the British.[5] He urged the Mahatma to try, for once, to be pragmatic, to make accommodations and not take the whole country 'wandering in the wilderness'.[6] He pressed him to take larger issues into consideration and to settle for Dominion Status, in view of his health and old age. 'Become more practical and try to face realities and settle as practical men instead of taking a rigid position,' he told the Mahatma. It was only reasonable, he stressed, to 'adjust our demands in relation to our strength and circumstances.'[7] Though his views fell on deaf ears, Birla persisted throughout the summer of 1940 in putting forth his views for Gandhi's consideration.

In the meantime, the political situation was changing rapidly. Though the Viceroy promised the Congress a voice in his Executive Council, the offer was rejected by Gandhi who now decided to launch the Individual Civil Disobedience Movement in October 1940. This was again a decision that Birla vehemently opposed. Two months after it commenced, he made another attempt to convince Gandhi of its futility. In a meeting at the Mahatma's ashram, he showed his scepticism at the progress of the campaign and frankly asked him to accept the Viceroy's offer of the expansion of his Council. Thereafter, he was forthright in letting Gandhi know that his Individual Satyagraha campaign was losing its character. He was well aware that important Congress leaders such as Rajagopalachari, S. Satyamurti from Madras and Bhulabhai Desai from Bombay were growing increasingly restless and that there existed a gulf between them and Gandhi.[8] Birla made no headway with Gandhi and was forced to find consolation in his loyalty to the Mahatma. 'Since Bapu is in charge of leadership, only good can come out of it,' he concluded.[9]

Ironically, at just the time when Birla w.. pleading with Gandhi to give up his satyagraha and explore avenues of negotiation with the government, his credentials as a conciliator were being doubted by the Viceroy and his advisers. Linlithgow had come to believe that Birla was secretly financing Gandhi's Civil Disobedience campaign and, at the same time, maintaining the appearance of a peace-maker between the government and Gandhi. To Linlithgow such a position was quite untenable and he now decided that he could no longer receive Birla as long as Gandhi persisted in his campaign. Birla first heard that he had fallen out of favour with the Viceroy, from S.C. Mitra. Much surprised, he immediately sought an interview with the Viceroy but was received instead by Laithwaite's private secretary, who confirmed the news. Birla was furiously angry. He felt completely let down having spent so much effort in the last few years building up a close rapport with the Viceroy and having worked so hard to be recognized as a conciliator. He confided to Mahadev Desai:

The Viceroy should have known by this time, that no man among Indians has worked harder to help him or stood more loyally by him than myself...If the Viceroy feels that on the one hand I come to him as a friend and on the other I am secretly acting against him, then I have no desire to waste his time any more.[10]

He felt angered that 'the Viceroy has wronged me by suspecting my honesty' and saw behind it the 'wooden minds these men have got!'[11] Though he wanted to clear the air, there was no way to do so as the Viceroy would have nothing to do with him. Feeling let down and humiliated, Birla believed the rift between the Congress and the Raj was growing wider and felt his own row with Linlithgow was a tragic manifestation of this gulf. This episode ended Birla's role of playing negotiator between the Gandhian leadership and the British. For many years he had worked hard to establish the personal touch in an attempt to bring about a reconciliation between a section of the Congress leadership and the British. For his part, it had been a role he relished.

TESTS OF ALLEGIANCE

In the months that followed, there was a marked change in Birla's attitude towards the evolving political situation. He had been extremely keen throughout 1940 that the Congress should co-operate in the war effort in return for

Dominion Status at the end of the war, and in the interim, a voice in the central government. In late 1940, he had opposed Gandhi's decision to embark upon Individual satyagarha, and later criticized it when it was already in full swing. However, gradually, a significant shift took place in his views. Birla no longer saw any sagacity in conciliation with the British. There were many factors that led to this change of heart. The breaking of his relations with Linlithgow in late 1940 indicated to him that official attitudes had now hardened. Further, the complete lack of response of the government to Gandhi's satyagraha led him to doubt the government's sincerity to secure Indian co-operation for the war effort. Moreover, the rapidly changing fortunes of the British in the war also altered Birla's views. Following Hitler's invasion of Russia and the Japanese successes in South-east Asia in 1941, Birla believed that the war was coming nearer to India. The sinking fortunes of the Allies, together with the economic dislocation caused by the war effort in India, worried him. In such a situation it appeared to him that Gandhi had adopted the right course by his symbolic protest through Individual Civil Disobedience, without actually impeding the war effort or seriously threatening the Raj. He felt that the moderation shown by Gandhi and the Congress had, however, not been reciprocated by the British.

What made matters worse and alienated him further was his experience of the Raj's handling of economic affairs during these years. Like many businessmen he had seen in the war an opportunity for the expansion of industry and a time when the government would co-opt Indian industry in planning for it. This did not happen. All these experiences brought a radical change in Birla's perception. As he confessed to Gandhi:

When I exercise my faith and my powers of reasoning I feel that the path chosen by you was the only one and the best that could have been taken during the early stages of the struggle. I was sceptical as to the value of the path you had taken ... Now I feel convinced that there was no alternative to the course we have adopted. This because the British have betrayed no anxiety to give us anything substantial ... now we have amply demonstrated that although our soldiers are taking part in the fighting, India as a nation has rebelled against participation in this massive act of violence. This conflict will end in universal destruction; there will be no victor at the end of it and even he who wins is sure to invite self destruction. If in this situation we remain uninvolved in this conflict we would thereby be rendering service to humanity.[12]

There was now no further scope for negotiations. 'Destinies are being shaped just now', Birla observed, 'by hidden hands and all calculations are mere waste of time'.[13] He now found himself agreeing with Gandhi's attitude towards the war. Although he had always been a protagonist of co-operation with the Raj and, since the introduction of the Government of India Act of 1935 had worked particularly hard to achieve this, he was now prepared to follow Gandhi and confront the Raj in whatever way the Mahatma chose.

When Sir Stafford Cripps, leader of the British House of Commons, arrived in India in early 1942 with an offer of an independent India as a Dominion under the British after the war, Birla was not one of those upon whom he could count for support for his mission.[14] Though not directly involved with the talks that took place in March–April 1942, his home in Delhi became the unofficial headquarters of the Congress leadership.[15] Of the three Congress negotiators, Nehru, Patel and Azad, two stayed at Birla House.[16] Gandhi, who was present only during the early weeks of the talks, was also a guest of Birla. Thus, Birla was in the thick of the protracted negotiations. However, the talks did not go far and were dismissed by Gandhi as a 'post dated cheque on a failing bank.' Birla too fully subscribed to this view and told Mahadev Desai that the concessions offered by Cripps came a bit too late.[17] His *Hindustan Times* also echoed a similar view and commented that the Cripps Mission came thirty months too late,[18] and FICCI too endorsed Birla's position.[19]

As Gandhi prepared himself for a renewed campaign against the Raj, Birla kept in close touch with how his ideas were evolving and with the developments in the Congress camp. Gandhi's activities were regularly reported to him by the meticulous correspondence he kept with Mahadev Desai. At the end of April 1942 he spent four days at Wardha with Gandhi. At the end of June 1942 Gandhi sent a hand-delivered letter to Birla in which he shared his inner turmoil and revealed his plans for the coming campaign:

What I am occupied with at the present moment derives its inspiration from my inner urging which hourly grows in intensive [sic!]. The regime is bent on mischief. Whatever is being said in order to oppose me, angers me besides adding to my distress, though both these are unjustified. All these are fleeting impulses which leave after a while and I am at peace with myself once again.

My mind is made up; my plans for the coming struggle are nearing completion. I am only waiting for the Working Committee meeting. I have made my preparations.[20]

Mahadev Desai confirmed to Birla that Gandhi was preparing for the final struggle and was 'determined to throw his last throw this time'. Gandhi was determined that 'he must stake everything—his most precious possession—his life.' 'There is no arguing with him,' Desai informed him.[21] Like many insiders Birla knew that a storm was brewing and that the coming struggle would be very different from previous Congress campaigns. Concerned about what might eventuate, he tried to gauge the official reactions to a possibly violent movement. On 2 July 1942 he met G.N. Molesworth, the Deputy Chief of Staff of the Indian Army whom he had never met before. He invited Molesworth to tea at his Delhi home. What then transpired is best described in Molesworth's own words:

Mr Birla was a very wealthy Indian industrialist who was known to be a close adviser of Mr Gandhi and to supply many of the financial 'sinews of war' to the Congress party. I had to obtain the Viceroy's permission before accepting and was told to 'keep my eyes skinned'. (I might have added 'and fingers crossed'.) I duly went to his large and imposing mansion on Kingsway. It had a great central hall out of which a wide oak staircase rose and was furnished in English style with several antique pieces. Tea was served on a silver tea service with china and other accessories which would have put many a 'stately home' to shame.

Mr Birla was...clad in white Congress 'uniform' of home-spun cloth, very courteous, speaking perfect English. He was a most interesting and well-informed person. When tea was over I had to listen to a long dissertation on political ideologies and aspirations and the increasing dangers of the time. It was clear to me that I was intended (although this was never mentioned) to convey a warning to the Viceroy. Finally, he asked me the same question which had been put to me by Louis Fischer. What would happen to the Congress leaders if there should be political disturbances in the future? I gave the same answer as before. He pressed me further, but I would not go beyond saying that the question was hypothetical. It was obvious that he was hinting that a storm was brewing, as we suspected, and his talk to me confirmed our impressions. The only question was: When will the storm break? Our talk was very friendly and we parted with expressions of cordiality on both sides.[22]

Less than a fortnight after this meeting, the Congress Working Committee met in Bombay on 14 July 1942 and passed the resolution demanding that the British quit India. Swallowing his pride, four days later, Birla requested a meeting with the Viceroy. His last correspondence with him had been more than a year and a half back: 'You shut the doors against me', he wrote to Laithwaite. Birla lamented the lack of contact between the Congress leadership and the British, and urged that contact be maintained. The fear he had was that 'there is a friendliness behind this fight which should not be allowed to die out'.[23] His request for an interview with Linlithgow was turned down.[24] Undeterred Birla persisted. He got together with fellow businessmen such as Thakurdas and J.R.D. Tata to approach the Viceroy. In a letter candidly putting forth their views on the political situation, they wrote:

We are all businessmen and, therefore, need hardly point out that our interest lies in peace, harmony, goodwill and order throughout the country. We are also nationalists but we may add that our nationalism is not of a narrow type ... Analysing the Congress resolution, we read in it nothing more than a demand for political freedom such as would enthuse the people to fight the aggression and die while fighting ... We submit that the need of the hour is not strong action, but a proper and sympathetic understanding and tactful handling of a grave situation. We feel that during the midst of war political freedom to India could be granted. In time of peace the question of political independence could have waited but a time of peril for the United Nations in all war theatres is, we submit, the psychological moment for making the country free in order to enable it to visualize the peril to its own freedom and to play a full part in retaining it.[25]

On 8 August 1942 the All India Congress Committee met at Bombay and formerly adopted the Quit India resolution, and Gandhi give his famous call to 'Do or Die'. Birla had, by then, arrived in Bombay to be with the Mahatma at this historic moment. This was the first time that he openly stood by the Mahatma at the time of the launch of a political agitation. At dawn the following morning, the police came to Birla House to arrest Gandhi. As they waited to take him, Birla insisted that prayers be held and Rameshwardas' wife, Shardadevi, applied *tilak* on Gandhi's forehead. Birla also entreated Gandhi to promise not to embark upon a fast in haste while he was in jail and thus endanger his well-being.

The popular response to the Quit India Movement and the large-scale repression that followed are well known.[26] Over 91,000 people were arrested, and several hundred police stations destroyed in attacks on government institutions. Civilian or military authorities resorted to firing on 534 occasions and the British had to deploy $57\frac{1}{2}$ battalions to restore their control and stamp out the challenge posed by the Movement.[27] Birla now worked hard to mobilize the support of big business for the Congress cause. He found fertile ground. The experience of the war years had radicalized big business and it was openly critical of the government's war-related economic policies. Growing apprehensions about the fortunes of the British position after the rapid fall of Singapore, Malaya and Burma had further fuelled discontent. Then, in July 1942, had come the bitter blow when Sir Edward Benthall was appointed Member of War Transport in the Viceroy's Executive Council.[28] Benthall, a Bird and Co. businessman from Calcutta, epitomized to Indian capitalists the aggressiveness of European commerce. His elevation to such an important position struck at the very roots of Indian industry's aspirations of the previous two decades. One of its fundamental demands had been that British commerce should not enjoy a privileged position. This is what Birla and Thakurdas had fought fervently for since their years in the Central Legislative Assembly in the late 1920s. By inducting Benthall into its highest decision-making body, the government confirmed the privileged position of European business. Moreover, the portfolio of shipping, for long a matter of contention between Indian and British commerce, now came under Benthall.[29] Indian big business reacted to the appointment with dismay. FICCI conveyed its serious objections and strong resentment to the Viceroy.[30] The bitter disappointment of big business to Benthall's appointment in July 1942 helped to condition its response to the Quit India Movement.

In the months that followed, Birla worked together with the FICCI president, G.L. Mehta and other business leaders and frequently drafted the resolutions brought out by FICCI.[31] Together, they ensured that FICCI was unequivocal in its support for Gandhi and his movement. Immediately after his arrest and that of other Congress leaders, FICCI sent a telegram to the Viceroy deploring the government's repression and the arrests.[32] It demanded 'that any further deterioration in the situation should be immediately prevented by Government's recognition of India's legitimate demand for a national government at the centre in order to enable India to play her part in the war as an independent and self-respecting member of the United Nations.'[33] G.L. Mehta gave press interviews declaring that the interests of the commercial community were identical with those of the nationalist movement. He asserted that 'whatever ideological sympathies existed among the people at the start of the war had gradually changed into apathy and eventually into ill-concealed hostility, owing to the unimaginative policy of the Government'.[34] Birla, for his part, requisitioned an immediate meeting of FICCI which could not, however, be held in view of the breakdown in communications. However, on 26 August 1942, a conference of business leaders boldly condemned the repression of the government:

The commercial community is strongly of opinion that it is only by the establishment of a representative national government, with full and unreserved powers, that the country's resources can be fully mobilised towards winning the war and that they can trust that the British Government will even now take immediate steps to accede to this legitimate demand to prevent the situation from deteriorating further.[35]

Another conference of Indian commercial and industrial bodies met in Calcutta, presided over by Badridas Goenka, a prominent Calcutta businessman, and it adopted a similar resolution.[36] In the months that followed FICCI played a prominent role in condemning the government. It demanded immediate reconciliation on the part of the government and declared that it 'will only be possible if effective power is transferred forthwith from Britain to India...A National Government is, moreover, essential not only for war effort but also for safeguarding India's economic and financial interests.'[37] It was vehement in its response to Churchill's allegation that Indian commercial interests were behind the subversive Congress movement. Mehta declared at a press conference:

Indian commercial organisations do not feel apologetic about the fact that they are an integral part of the national movement and that they are fully in accord with the essentials of the Congress demand for freedom and transfer of power ... They believe that without the achievement of self-government, economic advancement of the people is not possible and therefore urge an immediate and satisfactory solution between the government and the people.

Indian commercial interests, irrespective of political affiliations, demand the establishment of a representative National Government at the centre, not only in order to mobilise the economic front which is vital in this war but also to ensure India's status and safeguard her economic interests in post war period.[38]

It publicly proclaimed its nationalist commitment when G.L. Mehta declared at its session that:

The Indian commercial community has come to realise after long and painful experience that without the achievement of full self-government economic advancement of the people is not possible and they will not be severed from their primary obligation as patriotic Indians to assist their countrymen in all their legitimate efforts to achieve political and economic emancipation.[39]

FICCI's commitment and Birla's new radical stand were put to test when Gandhi embarked on a 21-day fast in February 1943 against government aggression. Although Birla fully understood Gandhi's reasons for fasting, he was naturally alarmed at the prospect in view of Gandhi's failing health and advanced years. The fast immediately became a highly emotive issue for Birla. He took the initiative in canvassing public support for an appeal to the authorities to release Gandhi. Birla well understood that there was little that he could do himself and that the best strategy in the circumstances would be to involve the Liberals since they were the only credible political leaders out of jail at this time. With K.M. Munshi, he 'decided to summon a conference as representative as possible in the hope of moving the Government'. Together, they wired C. Rajagopalachari and the Liberal leader Sir Tej Bahadur Sapru to obtain their support for the conference.[40]

Out of this initiative emerged the Leaders' Conference which met at the FICCI premises in New Delhi on 19–20 February 1943 under the chairmanship of Sapru. Birla ensured that a number of influential businessmen lent support to the main resolution of the Conference, and these included G.L. Mehta, Purshotamdas Thakurdas, Kasturbhai Lalbhai, J.R.D. Tata and Sir Ardeshir Dalal, along with prominent politicians such as M.R. Jayakar, S.P. Mukherji, C. Rajagopalachari, K.M. Munshi, Bhulabhai Desai and H.N. Kunzru. The conference demanded Gandhi's immediate and unconditional release.[41] A second session took place in Bombay on 9–10 March 1943. Birla also made a personal appeal to Linlithgow to release Gandhi in a final gesture of conciliation to mark the end of his viceroyalty in India.[42] He wanted to meet Linlithgow personally and present the case for Gandhi's release. Yet again his request for a meeting was turned down.[43] However, the government remained unmoved.

Nevertheless, Birla and his business friends left no stone unturned to pressurize the government relentlessly. They now changed their strategy to mobilize Indian support within the highest councils of the Government of India itself. This entailed putting pressure on the Indian members of the Viceroy's Executive Council. Birla enjoyed excellent personal relations with Nalini Ranjan Sarkar, a Calcutta businessman who was the Member for Education, Health and Agriculture. He influenced Sarkar (with whom he was on first-name terms) to take the issue up in the Council. Similarly, Homi Mody, the Supply Member and prominently associated with the Tatas, was also persuaded by Thakurdas and Birla to work for conciliation.[44] So effective was this strategy that the Viceroy's Executive Council was rocked with dissensions. Both Sarkar and Mody tried to influence the Council to order the release of Gandhi. Several other Indian members like Jogendra Singh, M.S. Aney, Sultan Ahmed and Feroz Khan Noon also vigorously supported them. As Gandhi's condition deteriorated, Sarkar and Mody came under irresistible pressure from their fellow businessmen to resign their positions.[45] On the seventh day of Gandhi's fast Sarkar, Mody and Aney, who was the Member for Overseas Indians, resigned. Their resignations seriously undermined the prestige of the Government of India at a crucial juncture, as it was deserted by its most prominent Indian ministers.[46] Linlithgow was outraged. He could see behind the resignations the most determined efforts of Birla and Thakurdas.[47] As is well known, Gandhi later fulfilled his fast. It, however, provided the occasion for big business to demonstrate its solidarity in the nationalist cause.[48] It proved to be a moment of reckoning for Sarkar and Mody. Birla was delighted that they stood their ground.

Such forthright support by Birla and big business for the Quit India Movement made it highly suspect in the eyes of the government. In November 1942, Linlithgow asked the Central Intelligence Bureau to probe the role of big business in supporting the movement. He especially suspected Birla as being the main financier of the Congress.[49] Linlithgow hoped that the evidence collected by the Central Intelligence Bureau would lead to a stage 'when we could strike against Birla Brothers and other leading financiers'.[50] Instructions were also sent out to provincial governors to direct provincial Intelligence Departments to investigate the source of Congress funds and report their findings to the Director of the Central Intelligence Bureau. The enquiries, however, presented a mixed picture. While some provinces confirmed that business and commercial interests were the main supporters of the Congress, several other criminal investigation departments (CIDs) reported that 'ad hoc' collections made by Congressmen from the common people were equally important. These findings did not satisfy Linlithgow and he wanted the matter to be pursued further.[51] Although he obtained some evidence about Congress' funds, especially concerning the prominent part played by M/s Bachhraj and Co., the family firm of Jamnalal Bajaj, he could not get to the root of the matter.[52]

For obvious reasons, it was difficult to find evidence of funding that big business was providing for the Quit India Movement as well as to Congress activists who had gone underground. Businessmen knew the threat they faced and surreptitious methods were used. The Birlas, for instance, channelled funds through Suresh Desai, then secretary of the Indian Chamber of Commerce and later a Member of Parliament. Braj Mohan had agreed to provide whatever funds were required on the condition that their source would not be revealed. The money was then personally handed over by Desai to Jayaprakash Narayan, who was a prominent leader of the underground movement.[53] Others who provided substantial sums were Walchand Hirachand,[54] and G.L. Mehta. Smaller business houses such as those headed by Rameshwar Lal Nopani (prominent Marwari businessman of Calcutta), B.K. Rohtagi (proprietor of India Fans) and M.G. Bhagat (proprietor of Jay Engineering) joined hands to provide Rs 10,000 to Rs 12,000 per month to the underground movement led by Jayaprakash Narayan and Ram Manohar Lohia. This willingness to support the Congress underground movement, even if it was led by socialists like Jayaprakash Narayan, was an index of the strong commitment that big business now unequivocally showed to the nationalist cause.

THE WAR EFFORT

A parallel, though a more gradual, process of Birlas' and big business' disappointment with the government, was discernible in their experience of the war effort. Businessmen had regarded World War II as a time when 'India's industrial expectations coincided with Britain's economic needs,' and looked upon it as a great opportunity for expansion. They had expected to play the role of economic partners of the government in planning the war economy.[55] They envisaged, not just an increase in business profits, but also the rapid development of basic industries. Such a perception was reflected at the 1940 session of FICCI which declared its support for the war effort.[56] To the business leadership, participation in the war effort meant:

not a mere transference of the war effort of the United Nations to Indian shores but a reorganisation of Indian industry with a view to get the maximum output on the background of the full utilisation of Indian resources...What would suit the war ought to suit the peace as well and nothing less than an effort to set India on her feet as a powerful self-sufficient industrial unit would be regarded as satisfactory.[57]

The war gave an impetus to economic activity and created opportunities for import substitution.[58] The emergence of India as a supply base gave a 'strong and direct stimulus' to industrial activity. The sectors of the economy which profited the most were iron and steel, monopolized by the Tata Iron and Steel Company, which was the largest producer of steel in the empire,[59] jute, which experienced a short-lived boom,[60] cotton, which supplied *khaki* uniforms and canvas,[61] sugar, which experienced a dramatic growth after the fall of Java and the Philippines and now became the chief supplier for the Empire,[62] coal which was essential for wartime transportation,[63] paper, which benefited from import substitution, cement, which made huge profits as the government undertook construction of aerodromes and other buildings, and finally leather, which produced boots, harness and saddlery.

In overall terms, Indian industry made immense profits from the wartime expansion of the economy.[64] The Birlas personally made huge profits in many areas. They owned five large sugar mills; Bharat Sugar Mills Ltd. (established in 1931) in Saran, Bihar, Upper Ganges Sugar Mill Ltd. (established in 1932) in Bijnore, UP, New India Sugar Mills Ltd. (established in 1933) in Darbhanga, Bihar, Awadh Sugar Mills Ltd. (established in 1932) in Sitapur, UP and New Swadeshi Sugar Mills Ltd. (established in 1931) in Champaran, Bihar. They also made large profits from their paper mills—Sirpur Paper Mills Ltd. (established in 1938) in Hyderabad and Orient Paper Mills Ltd. (established in 1936) in Brajnagar, Orissa. For example, as a result of wartime gains, Orient Paper Mills was able to increase its capacity more than threefold.[65]

With such high levels of profitability, the British expected Indian big business to whole-heartedly support the war effort. This expectation was, however, not borne out by actual experience. The relationship of big business and the government, on the contrary, came to be vitiated by a number of developments. The first blow to big business came in January 1940 when the Government of India introduced the Excess Profits Tax (EPT). By this measure it intended to cream off 50 per cent of all profits above an income of Rs 36,000. Business circles reacted with alarm. Birla strongly criticized it as a measure that frustrated economic expansion and dealt a serious blow to Indian industry. He accused the government of hypocrisy in attempting to assume the 'role of a saviour of the consumer' while, by implication, tarnishing the image of industry as a profiteer. He criticized the measure as a tax not on income but on consumption. The government, he alleged, intended to get 'the consumer heavily taxed, escaped all the unpleasantness arising therefrom and put the industry in the role of a profiteer!'[66] To show opposition to the new tax, public meetings were organized by FICCI in Calcutta, Bombay, Madras and several other cities. At a public meeting held on 9 February 1940 in Bombay under the auspices of the Indian Merchants' Chamber, as many as 51 chambers of commerce and industry joined hands to denounce the new tax.[67] They condemned it as a tax on capital and not on income, and blamed it for checking the flow of new capital that was badly needed to finance wartime industry.[68] FICCI took the lead in organizing this protest and sought to take a deputation to the Viceroy but its request was turned down. It was also not permitted to present its evidence before a select committee of the Central Legislative Assembly appointed to enquire into the tax.[69] Despite FICCI's strong protest, the government remained unmoved. Not only was the EPT introduced, but it was later made even more punitive.[70] This conflict over EPT set the tone of the relationship between business and the government during the war years.

A number of other factors further alienated business. A bureaucratic approach to the war economy and the inefficiency and red-tapism that characterized it appalled businessmen.[71] In particular, it annoyed those businessmen keen to cooperate in the war effort and who hoped that they would be co-opted into government committees involved with planning.[72] They believed that a rapid increase in production needed technical expertise which bureaucrats could hardly be expected to possess.[73] Their exclusion from wartime economic planning alienated them. To an extent, their grievances were rectified late in 1940 when Linlithgow appointed Homi Mody, as the Supply Member of his Executive Council. Later, in June 1941, Nalini Ranjan Sarkar, Bengal businessman and politician, was inducted as Member for Education, Health and Lands. Yet, the overall perception remained that they did not signify a real desire for a partnership between business and the government in organizing the wartime economy.

This perception was confirmed by the attitude shown when the Roger Mission arrived in India in late 1940 to advise the government on ways and means of expanding war production. Indian businessmen were not invited to join its deliberations and Roger's recommendation to incorporate businessmen on official bodies was not heeded.[74] This experience was repeated at the Eastern Group Supply Conference of October 1941.[75] Although several FICCI representatives and European chambers of commerce were invited,[76] Indian businessmen found themselves excluded from all decision-making at the conference.[77] An insight into the alienation of big business is provided by its response to the mission of Louis Johnson, the personal emissary of President Roosevelt who came to India in April 1942.[78] In Johnson's entourage was included Henry Grady as head of the American Technical Mission. Birla met Johnson on his own initiative and put before him the point of view of Indian big business. He also organized meetings between Johnson and other business leaders such as Kasturbhai Lalbhai, Walchand Hirachand, and J.R.D. Tata. The FICCI president, G.L. Mehta, arranged a reception at which Johnson was told that Indian industrialists could increase production by 250 per cent, only if they were assured that the war that was being waged was in reality a 'people's war'.[79]

By 1942 Birla's disillusion was complete.[80] Underlying this lay a fundamental difference in perception about the nature of economic development during the war. He expected that the British would help develop basic industry in India, whereas the government was solely interested in producing goods for the war. Perhaps the most striking example of this difference was provided by the government's response to the plans put forth by Birla and Walchand Hirachand to set up automobile plants. Their proposals were rejected on the ground that automobiles did not fall within the war-effort category.[81] This came as a bitter disappointment to them, a deliberate attempt by the government to curtail the potential of Indian industry.[82] Although their proposals were rejected, the Ministry of Supply in London commissioned M/s General Motors to set up a motor-car factory in India to commence production with imported parts. This added to the resentment of Indian business and they vehemently condemned the government.[83] FICCI declared that the automobile industry 'suffered postponement merely to satisfy the pressure of alien influence'[84] and even persuaded Nehru to write an article in January 1942 against the discrimination faced by Indian industry.[85] Similarly, the ship-building industry faced discouragement and this caused still more resentment.[86]

A further cause of discord arose over the government's 'scorched-earth' policy. After the Japanese advances in late 1941, the Allies became nervous about land attacks on India and the Government of India now proposed to introduce this policy. Under this all land resources were to be destroyed in a policy of denial to the enemy. In a speech before FICCI, Birla denounced the government's proposal.[87] Other business leaders also opposed this proposal. FICCI declared that India's economic capacity would be severely impaired by even its partial implementation. G.L. Mehta asserted that FICCI could not accept a policy formulated by an army command which was not in Indian hands. Business leaders appealed to the Congress leadership to take up this cause, and persuaded Gandhi to write an article in the *Harijan* opposing the policy.[88] Fortunately, the scorched-earth policy was not implemented and plants and equipment were not destroyed. But Indian business learnt the lesson that their hard work of many years could easily be destroyed if it suited military objectives.

Still another cause for resentment arose over the plight of the refugees from Burma. As is well known, commercial life in Burma had been dominated by Indian businessmen, especially Marwaris and Chettiars. When they were forced to evacuate Burma after it fell to the Japanese, there was much resentment over government apathy. FICCI alleged that the evacuation policy of the government was racist, as preferential treatment had been given to British refugees. As thousands of Indian traders arrived in Assam and Bengal after losing their all, FICCI formed an Indian Evacuees' Relief Committee with Birla as its chairman.[89] Birla was extremely active in directing the vigorous activities of the Committee.[90] He co-ordinated efforts being undertaken in this direction by the Bengal and Assam Congress provincial committees.[91]

INITIATING A PUBLIC DEBATE

The plight of the Burma refugees and the widespread dislocation that was being increasingly witnessed in the country because of the war effort made Birla even more vociferous in his criticism of the government. He believed that the government was running the war economy without consulting Indian opinion and insisted that this had to be challenged. He feared that structural changes were being made in the economy without the consent of Indian opinion. He was convinced that a public debate on economic policies during the war years was needed. To initiate this debate he started a journal devoted solely to the economy. The new weekly was called the *Eastern Economist* (modelled on the *Economist* of London) and its first issue appeared on 21 May 1943. P.S. Lokanathan, an England-trained economist and the author of several influential works on the Indian economy, was persuaded to edit the journal. The *Eastern Economist* was to be a pioneering effort in the history of Indian economic journalism. Although commercial journals like the *Commerce* and the *Capital* had existed for over half a century, they were devoted almost entirely to commercial and market news. The *Eastern Economist* blazed a new trail by focusing on questions of economic policy. The new weekly had no space for commercial news. Its focus was on presenting views on vital economic questions. The lead article of the second issue, for instance, was on the new fiscal ordinances of the government. The issue also contained a special article on price controls in the Punjab and another detailed discussion of the role of regional planning in industry. Its editorial column was aptly called Delhi Diary. Several pages were devoted to regional economic news and there was a section devoted to book reviews on current topics. There were also special pages devoted to trade, agriculture and industry.[92] Birla took a great personal interest in the planning of each issue.[93] He wanted the *Eastern Economist* to be the forum of Indian opinion on vital economic questions of the time. This expectation was more than realized, as the *Eastern Economist* continued to publish high-quality articles on economy and planning from the 1940s onwards.

Notwithstanding these commendable efforts in initiating a public debate, economic policies continued to be formulated and enforced without reference to Indian opinion. By 1943 business was unanimous in its view that the government's economic policies were leading to large-scale dislocation and suffering. This was reflected, to give one example, in the extremely high rate of inflation and the acute shortage of essential commodities.[94] The government's response to this economic crisis was to impose one control after another.[95] While Birla recognized that a degree of control was necessary to deal with the extraordinary situation that prevailed, he, like other businessmen, had an aversion to government controls as they severely restricted their freedom in production, distribution and pricing of goods. The failure of government controls in the distribution of essential commodities like wheat and sugar convinced him that the government possessed neither the machinery nor the experience required to enforce its policies. Further, the government could hardly be expected to ensure effective distribution of essential commodities in situations of scarcity. This led him to advise important official functionaries such as N.R. Sarkar that the government's involvement merely led to the 'creation of black market, corruption and all the consequential evil.' In his view what was needed was self-regulation by industry rather than coercion by the state.[96] He believed that each sector of industry should organize its expansion and distribution and control its prices. This would provide the 'incentive to do the right thing' and not lead to the 'unproductive centralization' that characterized the bureaucracy of the Raj.[97] He took the initiative in bringing together representatives of the cotton industry to formulate a scheme for the self-regulation of the industry.[98]

In March 1943 he presented this scheme to the government. Although it was at first turned down, the government later changed its mind when it realized the colossal failure of its controls in the face of the unfolding tragedy of the Bengal famine. A meeting of representatives of the textile industry was now convened by Akbar Hydari, Secretary of Industries and Civil Supplies, to work out a plan for the self-regulation of the textile industry.[99] This proved to be a great success, and within one year four price reductions of almost 40 per cent were made.[100] However, the co-operation over the textile industry was untypical if one takes an overall view of the relations between big business and the government. Big business remained trenchant in its criticism of the government's wartime economic policies. As the government failed to deliver and prices rose to unprecedented levels, Birla found himself increasingly drawn by the human misery that was now manifest in the streets of Calcutta.[101] He looked upon the Bengal famine as a man-made catastrophe which could have been avoided if the government had pursued a different set of economic policies. He laid the blame for the enormous human tragedy that occurred in eastern India at the door of the government. The 'methods of our war finance' and the scale of expenditure incurred by the government on the war had, he declared, brought the economy to breaking point. The famine could, he believed, easily have been avoided if the principle of increased production had been the sheet-anchor of war finance.[102] At the same time he accused the British of depleting the country's scanty resources of consumer goods for the war effort. 'We have time and again repeated', he declared, 'that only after a minimum of basic needs is guaranteed to the Indian masses, should resources be drawn for war purposes.' He attacked the government for failing to heed the warning of big business to increase production to avoid civil scarcities. 'That cry went unheeded', he wrote, 'and so today the human tragedy is writ large on the face of this country which has done nothing to deserve this fate except perhaps its toleration of inefficient governments.'[103]

Unable to influence the government by his policy prescriptions, Birla turned his attention to the immediate challenge of alleviating the human misery caused by the famine. By setting up cheap grain and cloth stores in scarcity-ridden Orissa in late 1942, he successfully demonstrated to the government that it was possible to keep down prices and prevent hoarding.[104] In Calcutta the Birla family became the single most important private benefactor of the relief effort.[105] By the end of 1943 M/s Birla Brothers were responsible for six cheap canteens in Calcutta which served over 12,000 people daily.[106] In addition, three cheap foodgrain centres were opened which provided relief to over 500 people. The Birlas also drew up schemes for the distribution of cheap cloth and cloth worth Rs 30,000 was distributed to destitutes.[107] Further, cheap rice stores were opened to 'help middle-class families who cannot buy at market prices or take advantage of controlled supplies'. These stores were intended to serve 20,000 persons.[108] Arrangements were also made to send 280 children to Pilani for free education under the Birla Education Trust. In addition to their own charities, the Birlas supported other relief agencies.[109] Such was the scale of these charities that Linlithgow became anxious that they would overshadow the relief efforts of the government itself and could be portrayed as an abdication by the government of its efforts.[110]

The experience of the war years emboldened Birla to challenge the credentials of the government to regulate the Indian economy. During the war years FICCI, with Birla at the forefront, emerged as the nationalist watch-dog on economic matters.[111] It provided a consistent and fearless critique of the Raj's wartime economic policies.[112] FICCI's official historian writes that during its wartime deliberations Birla was known to be a hardliner in its critique of the government.[113] This confidence expressed itself when Birla and FICCI approached the question of the post-war reconstruction of the economy.[114] Birla now raised the pertinent question of:

Who is going to plan for India?...A promise has been made that after the termination of the war India will get its own government. Will it be right for this Government to make any commitments for something which is to be executed by another Government?[115]

By 1943 Birla was supremely confident that the days of the Raj were numbered.

In retrospect, the late 1930s proved to be critical years in Birla's public career. By late 1942 he, along with other important business leaders, was convinced that they would soon be called upon to play a crucial role in the post-war Indian economy. To prepare for this role, they consulted with each other and on 11 December 1942, Birla, Thakurdas, J.R.D. Tata, Kasturbhai Lalbhai, A.D. Shroff and Lala Shri Ram held their first meeting at the Bombay office of Tata to discuss what later came to be widely known as 'the Bombay Plan'.[116] Although this plan went through various stages and was announced only in January 1944, even at their first meeting the business leaders envisaged the fundamental premise upon which the plan was based—that India would be completely independent in economic matters after the war. However, one major impediment stood in the way of the economic future they envisaged for an independent India—the worsening communal situation—and it was to this that Birla now directed his attention.

Notes and References

[1] Continuing he wrote: 'There are leftists in India who believe in the slogan of England will prevail in the end. But I hope Gandhiji's voice will prevail in the end. And I hope from your end we would get such response as will go to strengthen the hands of those who are called the rightists. I am not suggesting this in a bargaining spirit. I am only describing our own difficulty when I say that with the question of responsibility at the Centre still unresolved and the responsibility of defence being entirely out of our sphere, we are facing an uphill task in pressing the view that England is fighting a battle for the defence of democratic principles.' Birla to Churchill, 7 September 1939, Birla Papers, File No. 22.

[2] Birla to Laithwaite, 8 February 1940, Birla Papers, File No. 22.

[3] Birla to Mahadev Desai, 14 March 1940, Birla, *Bapu*, Vol. IV, pp. 32–3.

[4] Birla to Mahadev Desai, 15 March 1940, Birla, *Bapu*, Vol. IV, pp. 33–4.

[5] According to Birla, this had the added advantage of being capable of solving the communal question since, as he told Gandhi, 'we will have to fill only such gaps as to convert the present constitution into one of full responsible government.'

[6] Birla, 'Notes for Discussion with Gandhiji', n.d., Birla Papers, Series Miscellaneous, File No. 130. 'I repeat again..Why not make Great Britain go to the maximum limit and take charge of government and then travel the rest of the journey in cooperation and wrest full freedom through the path of cooperation?' Also see Birla's 'Questions for discussion with Bapu', 22 March 1940, Birla Papers, Series Miscellaneous, File No. 130.

[7] *Ibid.*

[8] Birla to Mahadev Desai, 24 January 1941, Birla, *Bapu*, Vol. IV, pp. 199–201.

[9] Birla's 'Questions for Discussion with Bapu', 22 March 1940, Birla Papers, Series Miscellaneous, File No. 130.

[10] Birla to Mahadev Desai, 29 December 1940, Birla, *In the Shadow of the Mahatma*, pp. 306–8.

[11] For details see Birla's account in 'A Personal Explanation' in his *In the Shadow of the Mahatma*, pp. 305–8.

[12] Birla to Gandhi, 4 November 1941, Birla, *Bapu*, Vol. IV, pp. 263–6.

[13] Birla to Mahadev Desai, 3 November 1941, Birla, *Bapu*, Vol. IV, p. 262.

[14] The mission envisaged an independent India after the war which would be united to Britain by allegiance to the Crown, with the provision that any province was free to

opt out. In the interim, political leaders would be invited to participate in the war effort in an expanded Executive Council.

[15] Cripps even so held some meetings with Congress leaders at Birla House such as with G.B. Pant and B.G. Kher. Bhupen Qanungo, 'The Quit India Movement, 1942' in B.N. Pandey (ed.), *A Centenary History of the Indian National Congress*, Vol. III.

[16] See Azad's letter to Cripps dated 10 April and 11 April, both sent from Birla House, New Delhi, M. Subramanayam, *Why Cripps Failed*, The Hindustan Times Press (New Delhi, 1943), pp. 72–5 and 77–9.

[17] Birla to Mahadev Desai, 23 May 1942, Birla, *Bapu*, Vol. IV, p. 302.

[18] M. Subramaniam, *Why Cripps Failed?* p. 7.

[19] Cripps' refusal to meet the representatives of Indian business and his statement that British commerce would 'in certain events have a particular position' were particularly resented by business leaders. G.L. Mehta, the FICCI president, condemned the proposals of Cripps. 'The fact ... that Indian commercial interests do not demand any recognition as a special entity during the constitutional negotiations does not mean that they are at all satisfied by the existing structure and working of the central government especially in the economic sphere or that they are any less keen for the establishment of an autonomous government at the centre. Political autonomy would, in fact, be of little value and significance unless it was such as to ensure economic independence and enable full economic development of the country. That would not be possible unless the central government is responsible to the people whose representatives should be able to control the fiscal, currency, credit and transport policy of the country.' He further stated that: 'Indian constitutional interests have a stake in the country and they are vitally concerned in any constitutional development. I strongly feel that no constitution which does not guarantee complete fiscal autonomy and recognise the right to shape India's economic policy in accordance with Indian interests can prove acceptable to the Indian commercial community.' G.L. Mehta's interview to the press, 1 April 1942, in FICCI, Vol. II, *Correspondence and Relevant Documents relating to Important Questions dealt with by the Federation during the year 1942–3* (New Delhi, 1943).

[20] Gandhi to Birla, 24 June 1942, Birla, *Bapu*, Vol. IV, p. 306.

[21] Mahadev Desai to Birla, 16 July 1942, Birla, *Bapu*, Vol. IV, pp. 318–20.

[22] Molesworth was then asked the same question by Miraben who met him at Birla House in New Delhi later in the month. G.N. Molesworth, *Curfew on Olympus* (London, 1965), pp. 228–32.

[23] Birla was writing to the Viceroy after a gap of almost a year and a half. He told Laithwaite that 'You shut the doors against me. But may I earnestly submit that you pick up someone else who can be trusted.' Birla to Laithwaite, 18 July 1942, Birla Papers, File No. 23.

[24] Linlithgow to Amery, 22 July 1942, N. Mansergh (ed.), *Constitutional Relations between Great Britain and India: The Transfer of Power, 1942–47* (henceforth *TOP*), Vol. II, Doc. No. 307. Birla did see Laithwaite on 22 July, though we have no record of the meeting.

[25] Letter to the secretary of the Viceroy, 4 August 1942, from Birla, J.R.D. Tata, Thakurdas and others in Birla Papers, Series II, File No. G–II.

[26] Birla to Mahadev Desai, 20 February 1938, Birla, *Bapu*, Vol. III, pp. 149–52. On the Quit India Movement see Francis Hutchins, *Spontaneous Revolution: the Quit India Movement* (Delhi, 1971); A.C. Bhuyen, *The Quit India Movement: the Second World War*

and Indian Nationalism (New Delhi, 1975) and P.N. Chopra (ed.), *Historic Judgement on Quit India movement: Justice Wickenden's Report* (Delhi, 1989).

[27] G. Kudaisya, 'Foreshadowing "Quit India": The Congress in Uttar Pradesh 1939–1941' in Neera Chandoke (ed.), *Mapping Histories. Essays presented to Ravinder Kumar* (Tulika, 2000), pp. 225–54.

[28] The government decided to divide the Commerce Department into two portfolios, one of War Transport and the other of Posts and Air to meet the war needs. The portfolio of War Transport included Roads and Water Transport, Major Ports, Petrol Rationing and Shipping.

[29] The details of Birla and Thakurdas championing the cause of Scindia shipping have been discussed earlier.

[30] Communication dated 17 July 1942 from FICCI to the secretary to the Viceroy. 'The appointment of a representative of the non-official British community as a member of the Council is open to serious objection as it is tantamount to a recognition of the British community in India as a minority entitled to a separate seat on the Central Executive of the country ... The present scheme of expansion does not involve any advance on the previous scheme of last year but, on the contrary, is extremely disappointing in that ... it does not involve any transfer of the reality of power from Britain to India. It constitutes, in fact, a negation of the demand for autonomous and representative Government at the centre which alone can rally national opinion and enable India to have an equal and self-respecting status among the United Nations'. Press communique, 9 July 1942. Statement on the Expansion of the Executive Council, Vol. II, *Correspondence and Relevant Documents Relating to Important Questions Dealt With During the Year 1942–3 by the Federation* (New Delhi, 1943).

[31] It was not easy for Birla and other leaders to get FICCI to speak so openly in nationalist terms. There were many within the Federation who preferred a more passive approach and felt that FICCI should not openly associate itself with the cause of the Congress. However, the more nationalist business leaders persuaded the Federation to take an open stand. Looking back on such problems in 1942, G.L. Mehta later wrote: 'Frankly, the sympathies of many Indian businessmen were at variance with their interests. They wanted to support the Congress but did not want to take risks ... It was no easy task even to express sympathy with the national movement, let alone support it without jeopardizing the position of the Federation which, while broadly at one with national aspiration, naturally comprised various shades of political opinion ... Throughout the critical year, it was my endeavour to find the largest measure of agreement between the different elements in the Federation, not excluding even Muslim businessmen. To find this common denominator was difficult but not impossible.' G.L. Mehta, 'An Unforgettable Year' in FICCI, *Silver Jubilee Souvenir 1927–51.*

[32] A number of mills went on token strikes to protest the arrests, such as the Birla Mill in Delhi, the Delhi Cloth Mill of Lala Shri Ram and the Tatas' factory at Jamshedpur. However, the only mill where the strike was prolonged and took place with the consent of the proprietor appears to have been the strike in Kasturbhai Lalbhai's mills in Ahmedabad. Lalbhai, along with Khandubhai Desai, and the labour leaders in Ahmedabad, decided that the mills would be closed down and the workers were sent home to avoid confrontation with the authorities. One hundred thousand workers thus remained on strike and the mills were closed for a period of three months, see D. Tripathi, *Dynamics of a Tradition, Kasturbhai Lalbhai and his Enterpreneurship*, p. 118.

[33] Telegram from G.L. Mehta, president, FICCI, to the private secretary to the Viceroy, n.d., FICCI, *Correspondence and Relevant Documents relating to Important Questions dealt with during the year 1942–3 by the Federation.*

[34] G.L. Mehta, press interview, n.d., Birla Papers, Series II, File No. G–11.

[35] Among the chambers which sent representatives to the conference were the Bengal National Chamber of Commerce, Moslem Chamber of Commerce, Indian Chamber of Commerce, Marwari Chamber of Commerce, Marwari Association, Bengal Millowners' Association, Indian Chemical Manufacturers' Association, Indian Mining Federation, Indian Sugar Mills' Association, Bengal Banks Association, Indian Insurance Companies Association and the Indian Paper Mills Association. A total of 29 business chambers attended the meeting and signed the resolution. *Statesman*, 27 August 1942, news clipping in Birla Papers, Series II, File No. G–11.

[36] 'We are all businessmen and need therefore hardly point out that our interest lies in peace, harmony, goodwill and order throughout the country. We believe also in the vital necessity of establishing a National Government, deriving its strength and power from the people and which would constitute a solid foundation for the Defence of India ... We submit that the only method of improving the existing situation is to change the atmosphere in the country. The people should be made to feel that it is their own government, their own country for which they have to fight and sacrifice and die and that their prestige, honour, independence and very life are at stake.; this would be possible by an immediate recognition of the national demand for the transfer of real power from British to Indian hands ... Our primary concern is the advancement of the economic interests of the country and not politics. But we are nationalists believing in the need of economic and political freedom of India and are naturally moved and affected by the recent events ... We represent commercial and industrial interests, but in the last resort, these interests themselves depend on the welfare and advancement of the mass of people. We have nothing to gain and everything to lose by unrest, disturbance and dislocation. We therefore say it with all the greater emphasis and with the full realization of our responsibilities that the Government should immediately open negotiations with the principal political parties so as to end the present impasse and to enable the realization of Indian aspirations for a free India as a self-respecting and self-reliant member of the United Nations.' Resolution Adopted by the Joint Conference of Indian Industrial and Commercial Concerns, held in Calcutta on 27 August 1942, Birla Papers, Series II, File No. G–11.

[37] FICCI press communique, 13 September 1942, FICCI, *Correspondence and Relevant Documents relating to Important Questions dealt with by the Federation during the year 1942–43.*

[38] Report of a press conference addressed by G.L. Mehta, president of FICCI in FICCI, *Correspondence and Relevant Documents relating to Important Questions dealt with by the Federation during the year 1942–43.* Later in the year FICCI reacted sharply to Churchill's famous statement that he had not become the Prime Minister to oversee the liquidation of His Majesty's Empire; according to FICCI, this characterized his policies as aiming to perpetuate the 'domination and exploitation' of the country. FICCI Statement, 19 November 1942, in *ibid.*

[39] Speech of G.L. Mehta, 27 March 1943, in FICCI, *Proceedings of the 16th Annual Meeting, Delhi, 27–28 March 1943* (Delhi, 1943).

[40] For details see Birla, *In the Shadow of the Mahatma*, pp. 263–4.

[41] The resolution stated: 'This conference representing different creeds, communities and interests in India, gives expression to the universal desire of the people of this country that, in the interests of the future of India and international goodwill, Mahatma Gandhi should be released immediately and unconditionally. This Conference views with the gravest concern the serious situation that will arise if the Government fail to take timely action and prevent a catastrophe. This Conference therefore urges the Government to release Mahatma Gandhi forthwith.' Sapru to Laithwaite, 20 February 1943, *TOP*, Vol. III, Doc. No. 506; also see Sapru and others to Churchill, 21 February 1943, Telegram, *TOP*, Vol. III, Doc. No. 512.

[42] Birla to Laithwaite, 22 February 1943, Birla Papers, File No. 23.

[43] Linlithgow to Amery, 22 February 1943, *TOP*, Vol. III, Doc. No. 515.

[44] Both N.R. Sarkar and Mody had been closely associated with the Federation; Sarkar was associated with it from 1929 when he represented FICCI on the Central Banking Enquiry Committee. From 1930–2 he was on the Executive Committee of FICCI and in 1932 was vice-president and then in 1933 was elected its president. So close was Sarkar's association that he later recalled that the presidentship of the Federation was an 'honour which I still prize the most—more probably than that of being a member of the Government.' Even when he was on the Viceroy's Executive Council, Sarkar often attended FICCI meetings as, he confessed, 'old ties die hard.' See N.R. Sarkar, 'My Days in the Federation' in FICCI, *Silver Jubilee Souvenir 1927–1950*, pp. 193–8. Mody, although not an office bearer had been associated with the Federation from the 1920s. Mody had been closer to the Bombay Millowners' Association of which he had been president in 1928.

[45] FICCI had first called upon the Indian members to show their disapproval of the government's policies as early as September 1942. After the repression unleashed by the government as a response to the Quit India Movement, FICCI had asked the Indians in the Council to convey the 'intense feeling of public resentment at the policy pursued by the Government and to persist in their demand that, unless a truly representative National Government is installed at the Centre in the country and real power is immediately transferred ... to Indian hands, there can be no fully effective mobilisation of all forces for the defence of India or an adequate solution to the existing turmoil', press communique, 13 September 1942, FICCI, *Correspondence and Relevant Documents relating to Important Questions dealt with by the Federation during the year 1942–43*. Although it did not openly address the businessmen in the Council, the FICCI appeal pointed to them. At this time the businessmen did not respond to FICCI but over the ensuing months they appear to have been under considerable pressure. With the Federation taking such a frankly nationalist stand during this Movement, it was extremely difficult for the businessmen to remain uninvolved, especially in view of their intimate involvement with FICCI from the 1920s.

[46] In their joint resignation letter they made it clear that 'The majority decision not to release Mr Gandhi unconditionally, even when danger to his life accrued from the fast he had undertaken, is one which we cannot possibly support, and as the matter at issue raises a very important question of policy, we have no option but to tender our resignations.' Mankekar, *Homi Mody*, pp. 187–8.

[47] Linlithgow to Amery, 11 February 1943, *TOP*, Vol. III, Doc. No. 453.

[48] FICCI proudly commended itself on the resignation of the two businessmen when they met in early March 1943. The President proclaimed that the fact that the business community had felt as keenly and strongly on Gandhi's fast as other nationalists was clear

from the resignation of the two businessmen from their posts which 'they had accepted and in which they had worked even at the risk of unpopularity and misunderstanding.' 'Never, indeed,' the FICCI President continued, 'have we had a bitter lesson to learn than from these events—the lesson that our salvation ultimately lies in our own hands.' See G.L. Mehta's Speech, FICCI, *Proceedings of the Annual Session, Delhi, 27–28 March 1943.*

[49] Linlithgow felt that business was fearful of the ability of the British to protect India and in the face of the Japanese aggression were afraid that their plant and machinery would be destroyed and that this made them make terms with the Japanese. He went so far as to suspect that 'a clique of financiers in India who, taking a leaf out of Japan's book, and even possibly with Japanese assistance, are endeavouring to use the Congress organization and the political ferment which it has brought about to establish for themselves a position of financial domination in India comparable to that obtained by the "Big Four" in Japan ... It is generally assumed that the Hindus are naturally sympathetic towards the Buddhist culture of Japan and would welcome its support against the Muslims if the Japanese come to India. There may be some such feeling but it may well have been fostered by the Birla Brothers with a view to their ulterior objects.' Linlithgow to all provincial governors, 2 November 1942, *TOP*, Vol. III, Doc. No. 132.

[50] Linlithgow to all provincial governors, 2 November 1942, *TOP*, Vol. III, Doc. No. 132.

[51] He asked his governors to 'discover all there is to be known about the identity, aims, policy, contracts, ramifications and methods of business groups'. Linlithgow to all provincial governors, 16 March 1943, *TOP*, Vol. III, Doc. No. 595.

[52] The Intelligence Bureau had gathered information of the assets of the Gandhi Seva Sangh and the part played by Bajaj's family in the investing of the funds.

[53] P. Chentsal Rao, *B.M. Birla: His Deeds and Dreams* (Foreword by L.K. Jha, New Delhi, 1983), pp. 15–6.

[54] Khanolkar, *Walchand Hirachand*, p. 593, also see p. 427.

[55] Venkatsubbiah, *Enterprise and Economic Change*, pp. 43–4.

[56] It called upon the government to protect 'industries which are found vital in themselves or as auxiliary to other industries during the war', to 'undertake immediately *ad hoc* enquiries for granting protection to minor industries', to 'preserve India's exports and find new ones in place of those lost in the enemy territory', to 'secure a fair share of the additional demand created by the war' for Indian industry and pursue a policy regarding purchase of wartime supplies keeping in view the 'necessity of informing the people that the wartime supplies were purchased with dire regard to the interests of Indian industries.' C.S. Ratnasambapathi Mudaliar's speech at the annual meeting of FICCI, 1940.

[57] *Indian Express* (Madras), 5 June 1942, in Birla Papers, Series II, File No. G–11. Business leaders regarded the dividing line between war and peace industries to be thin.

[58] The total purchases made by the Chief Controller of Purchase (Munitions) in India were worth Rs 13 crores in 1940, Rs 38 crores in 1941 and Rs 52 crores in 1942. The value of orders handled by the Supply Department was Rs 85 crores in the first sixteen months of the war, Rs 118 crores in 1941, Rs 223 crores in 1942 and Rs 142 crores in the first five months of 1943. L.C. Jain, *Indian Economy During the War* (Lahore, 1944), p. 30.

[59] In 1941–2 the output of finished steel was estimated to be at least 50 per cent more than in 1939. By 1943 the pre-War output had doubled. An idea of the profits made by the industry can be gained from the company profits. In 1941, profits of four

companies amounted to Rs 5.7 crores as compared to Rs 4.3 crores in 1939 that is, an increase of 33 per cent. L.C. Jain, *ibid*, pp. 33–4.

[60] The average dividend in jute mills rose from 6 per cent in 1938 to 10 per cent in 1939 to 19 per cent in 1940. However, the jute boom was short-lived due to the loss of markets, transport difficulties and coal shortage. Birla's interest in jute lay in his Birla Jute Manufacturing Company Limited which had been established in 1919.

[61] Cotton mill profits in 1941 were about $5\frac{1}{2}$ times higher than 1938 and twice as high as 1937, L.C. Jain, *ibid*, pp. 35–6. Birla owned one cotton mill—the Keshoram Cotton Mill Limited (established 1919).

[62] An idea of the profits made is clear from the capital index of shares which rose from 100 in August 1939 to 366 in May 1944. L.C. Jain, *Indian Economy During the War*, pp. 38–42. Also see, *Birla Bandhuon Ki Desh Seva*, n.p.

[63] Coal industry had a record output of 29 million tons in 1940 which was maintained in 1941–2. Birla entered coal production after the World War II broke out, see Chentsal Rao, *B.M. Birla, His Deeds and Dreams*, p. 24.

[64] An index of the overall wartime industrial prosperity can be seen from the fact that within the first six months of the operation of the control of capital issue scheme in 1943, nearly 500 applications for either starting or expanding industries, involving an aggregate capital of Rs 15 crores were approved. L.C. Jain, *Indian Economy During the War*, pp. 29–31.

[65] Chentsal Rao, *B.M. Birla, His Deeds and Dreams*, pp. 24–5. Also see, *Birla Bandhuon Ki Desh Seva*.

[66] Birla, 'Budget and its Effects on Prices' in *Eastern Economist*, 31 March 1944. For Birla's view of the programme the Finance Member should follow see Birla, 'War Finance under National Government' in *Eastern Economist*, 14 April 1944.

[67] FICCI, *Correspondence and Relevant Documents relating to Important Questions dealt with by the Federation during the year 1940–41* (New Delhi, 1941).

[68] The high level of income tax and EPT, they argued, would leave no margin to allow industry to build up reserves, which were needed especially because of the heavy wasting of assets during the war and the high layout and replacement costs which would have to be met as soon as the war ended.

[69] Prominent business leaders moved to Delhi to lobby members of the select committee such as M.A. Jinnah, with whom the FICCI had two meetings, M.S. Aney, leader of the Congress Nationalist Party, A.C. Datta, deputy president of the Assembly, Sir Abdul Halim Guznavi, Sir Abdoola Haroom, Sardar Sant Singh and Mody. FICCI, *Correspondence and Relevant Documents relating to Important Questions dealt with by the Federation during the year 1940–41* (New Delhi, 1941). Both the European chambers and FICCI joined together in these protests. It became an 'occasion when the Federation was willing to merge its class interests with the otherwise non-national interests which it often equated with anti-national interests.' Venkatsubbiah, *Enterprise and Economic Change*, p. 44.

[70] For the government, the EPT was too important a source of revenue to be given up. It was expected to yield Rs 40 crores (33.8 crores from corporations and 6.2 from other incomes) which would cover more than half of the deficit of the state budget of 1940–1. In 1941, EPT was raised to 66.66 per cent and from May 1943 its collection was made even more stringent. From May 1943 all assessors of EPT were required to make a compulsory deposit with the government of an amount equivalent to 13.5 per cent of their excess profits. In April 1944 this was raised further.

[71] Even *Capital*, the loyalist mouth-piece of British commerce, complained about the 'all-pervading tendency, for convenience, is called Red Tape.' Controllers, responsible for making important decisions were 'glorified office boys' unable to give correct information, 'concerns which have lost their finance are given quotas', the Indian Stores Department was 'full of formalities' and the Supply Board was inefficient and took a long time to make payments. It further noted that 'the Government suffers from a deep-seated constitutional inability to trust anybody. Everyone—suppliers, industrialists and its own officers is a potential criminal. Traders are given the discredit for being pretty slick and its own officers are assumed to be fools. The result is that every action is so trammeled that any action is difficult.' *Capital*, 17 October 1940.

[72] In a representation to the Government of India the Bengal National Chamber of Commerce asked for representation for Indian industry on the Supply Department which they claimed was exclusively manned by Europeans and was thus out of touch with Indian public opinion and the mercantile community. To the *Capital* this demand seemed to be the clearest sign that 'Indian business is keen to play a part in India's war effort—which its hitherto close association with the Congress might have led one to doubt.' *Capital*, 24 October 1940. Also see *Capital*, 6 March 1941.

[73] The civil servant, declared the *Eastern Economist*, is 'a child in economic administration' and 'the problems of modern economic government are so complex and call for so much technical knowledge that it becomes doubtful whether non-technical civil servants with general education and common sense only can deal with them efficiently.' *Eastern Economist*, 3 December 1943.

[74] J. Voight, *India In the Second World War* (New Delhi, 1987), pp. 72–3.

[75] The Conference was convened by the Viceroy to 'co-ordinate arrangements for production and supply of munitions and stores in various countries in South and East Africa, Asia and the South Pacific area.'

[76] Welcoming the move the *Capital* wrote that 'after a long and stubborn resistance the walls of the bureaucracy have fallen, ... it is typical of the way the real problems of war have so far been evaded by the vested interests of the Civil Service that several long weeks have been spent in establishing a principle that had its roots in obvious and elementary common-sense.' *Capital*, 17 October 1940.

[77] Not only were they 'not entrusted with any responsible work, either on the committee or sub-committees,' but 'even before the plenary session of the conference was held to consider the reports of the various sub-committees and formulate their conclusions the advisers' presence was dispensed with by a letter of thanks, which clearly conveyed the impression that their presence was no longer necessary.' See the letter from the Indian Merchants' Chamber to secretary, Commerce Department, 28 November 1940, cited in Venkatsubbiah, *Industry and Enterprise*, p. 46. It was therefore not surprising that businessmen disagreed with the work of the Conference. The Eastern Supply Conference concluded that new heavy industries should not be encouraged since the war effort needed to concentrate on maximum output in the shortest possible time. In contrast, FICCI declared that 'basic industries' which 'would be capable of expansion in times of emergency' should be developed by the government.

[78] On the overall context of Johnson's mission see B.K. Srivastava and Venkatramani, *The Quit India Movement: The American Response* (New Delhi, 1979).

[79] Khanolkar, *Walchand Hirachand*, pp. 472–8.

[80] Birla candidly expressed this disappointment when he warned FICCI's general body that 'unfortunately in India we have had so many missions and missionaries in the past

that we seem to dread any onslaught of a new mission or a new commission. We have to take everything with a bit of suspicion.' FICCI, *Proceedings of the 15th Annual Session, 7–8 March 1942* (New Delhi, 1942).

[81] Birla, however, persisted in his plans but he was forced to wait till late 1942 and could finally set up his factory not in British India but in the princely state of Baroda with large subscriptions and promise of subsidies for supporting the industry by V.T. Krishnamachari, the Dewan of Baroda. The project started only in 1944. Chentsal Rao, *B.M. Birla, His Deeds and Dreams*, pp. 25–6. Walchand Hirachand's plans went back to 1939 when he was assured by the Congress government of Bombay that they would guarantee the payment of interest for part of the capital needed on the condition that the central government promised it protective tariff. When the war broke out Walchand proposed to the government that he would undertake production of 5000 motor cars a year for the Defence Force in return for support for setting up the plant. See J. Voight, *India in the Second World War*, pp. 74–5. For the full story see Khanolkar, *Walchand Hirachand*, pp. 431–56. Both Birla and Walchand Hirachand had to wait till 1944 before they were given permission by the central government to raise capital for their automobile ventures. L.C. Jain, *Indian Economy during the War*, p. 52.

[82] 'You cannot have a hard and fast line,' declared G.L. Mehta, the FICCI president, 'between industrial development during the present (war) period and in the post-war period because, after all, you will have to provide for the safeguarding of such industries, as have grown up now, from depression as well as competition in the post-war period' cited in Venkatsubbiah, *Enterprise and Economic Change*, p. 45.

[83] G.L. Mehta's speech, FICCI, *Proceedings of the 15th Annual Session 7–8 March 1942*.

[84] *Indian Express* (Madras), 5 June 1942, news clipping in Birla Papers, Series II, File No. G–11.

[85] In January 1942, Nehru criticized the government in an article entitled 'Apathy to Indian Motor Industry'. Khanolkar, *Walchand Hirachand*, p. 465.

[86] Again Walchand's project did not receive any support from the government and ultimately the plant was set up in Vizakapatnam in May 1941. FICCI made its position clear when it declared that 'India desired, for example, not only to repair ships but to build them, and a long-range policy was necessary ... in view of the ... need of economic self-reliance.' FICCI press communique in Birla Papers, Series II, File No. G–11. Also see Khanolkar, *Walchand Hirachand*, pp. 393–7.

[87] He declared that 'we cannot be sure what the position of the enemy in respect of India will be, but supposing in a time of panic we just destroy all the good work that we have done in half a century and if after a few months or few weeks we find ourselves able to push back the enemy into the sea, we would realise that just in a mood of panic we destroyed all the good work that we had done in a generation.' Birla's speech at FICCI, see FICCI, *Proceedings of the 15th Annual Session 7–8 March 1942*.

[88] *Ibid*, p. 108.

[89] The Committee also took up the cause of refugees from Singapore, Malaya, and other Far Eastern countries. It worked in co-operation with local chambers of commerce such as the Burma Indian Chamber of Commerce, Nattukottai Chettairs Association and the Burma Indian Association.

[90] Among the causes they took up were claims by Indian merchants in respect of damage done to goods; claims for supplies made to the civil department for which merchants had not received payment or had received only part payment upto the time

of the Japanese occupation; claims made to the military department which were not paid for especially in respect of motor vehicles, stocks-in-trade etc requisitioned by the government under the 'Defence Rules' and claims of compensation to owners of immovable property, stocks-in-trade left behind or which were demolished under the Denial policy. The Committee also took up the rehabilitation of refugees with the Government of India, especially their employment and granting of relief. Letter from Federation to M.S. Aney, 1 June 1942, in FICCI, *Correspondence and Relevant Documents relating to Important Questions dealt with by the Federation during the year 1942–3.*

[91] J.B. Kripalani to D.G. Mulherkar, secretary, FICCI, 27 July 1942, and general secretary, AICC, to all Provincial Congress Committees, 27 July 1942, in FICCI, *Correspondence and Relevant Documents relating to Important Questions dealt with by the Federation during the year 1942–3.*

[92] See the *Eastern Economist*, 28 May 1943.

[93] His extensive correspondence with P.S. Lokanathan is available in Birla Papers, Series II, File No. L–3.

[94] Birla boldly put forth his views on the economic situation in March 1943, in a pamphlet entitled *Inflation or Scarcity?* To him, the root of the problem was not the rise in prices, but more the scarcity of essential commodities, made worse by the war eating up a large proportion of goods which should have been available to the civilian population. He asserted that deflationary policies would not help the situation but the remedy lay in increasing production. Birla established a 'direct connection' between the government purchases for the war and the rise in prices and he showed that no amount of currency deflation or control of prices or enforced saving would solve the problem of rising prices. Birla made a fervent plea for increasing production to deal with the rising prices rather then a policy of deflation. G.D. Birla, *Inflation or Scarcity?* (n.p., 1943). Birla's pamphlet was published at a time when there was an enormous debate on inflation and its causes. C.N. Vakil had only recently published *The Falling Rupee* which showed the seriousness of the inflationary situation and a month later 20 economists issued a manifest affirming the causal relationship between expansion of currency and rise in prices and declared that India was passing through a 'deficit-induced flat money inflation.' Birla criticized them for being 'inspired more by text-books than by the verdict of those who with their experience of actual production knew what could be achieved and what would be the result of this neglect.' See G.D. Birla, 'War Finance under a National Government.' In October 1943 V.K.R.V. Rao published his *War and the Indian Economy*. Rao argued that part of the wartime rise in prices was due to the shortage of consumer goods and would have taken place even in the absence of currency expansion. But further he said that 'this scarcity-induced rise in general prices could only take place as a result of increased spending power released through dis-hoarding, dis-saving and deficit-budgeting.' Rao had conceded to Birla's point that scarcity played a role in bringing the rise in prices but had said that it was principally money-induced. Birla's view, which was close to that of Sir Jeremy Raisman, the Finance Member, was supported by the Indian Chamber of Commerce (ICC) whose president, M.L. Shah, criticized the Bombay economists for their 'academic proposals to combat an inflationary spiral which hardly exists with methods borrowed from other countries which are not in consonance with our conditions and might react prejudicially on our national economy.' The ICC blamed the increase in prices on the decrease of consumer goods and on defective distribution. Commenting on the speech given by Shah the *Capital* wrote that 'no one will be more surprised than Sir Jeremy Raisman himself at receiving from so unexpected a quarter so complete an

absolution from the sin of inflation, as he himself hoped in his budget speech only for a partial remission for having steered clear of pure credit inflation, if not of inflationary conditions.' The FICCI, however, took a different stand on the debate; in its session of 1943 it recognized the extent of inflation and later suggested remedies to it. For the debate see Birla's, 'Budget and its Effects on prices' in the *Eastern Economist*, 31 March 1944. V.K.R.V. Rao, *War and the Indian Economy* (Delhi, 1943). Also see G.P. Gupta, *The Reserve Bank of India and Monetary Management* (Bombay, 1962), pp. 288–9, *Capital*, 21 October 1943. Birla to Mahadev Desai, 20 February 1938, Birla, *Bapu*, Vol. III, pp. 149–52. *Capital*, 22 April 1943. Birla continued to hold this view all along. See Birla's lecture at Joint Meeting with the Overseas League, 3 August 1949, *The Asiatic Review*, Vol. XLV, No. 164 (London, October 1949).

[95] At first trade controls were introduced which included export and import control-prohibited export of specific commodities to enemy countries and to restricting their flow to neutral and friendly countries and the control of foreign exchange to conserve dollar resources. However, what were more significant from the point of view of big business were the commodity controls. Commodity controls covered wheat, food grains, textiles and sugar among other commodities. By these regulations the government placed restrictions on production and prices. Production levels, technical specifications of the goods, price levels and movement and distribution of goods were regulated.

[96] Birla to Sarkar, 31 January 1943, Birla Papers, Series II, File No. S–4.

[97] G.D. Birla, 'War Finance Under National Government.' The *Eastern Economist* declared that what was needed was to evolve 'a technique of state control, which, while giving scope for individual enterprise and initiative will also curb anti-social tendencies.' See *Eastern Economist*, 3 December 1943.

[98] On Birla's initiative, prominent businessmen such as Purushottamdas Thakurdas, Lala Shri Ram, Haridas Madhavdas, Padampat Singhania and Kasturbhai Lalbhai met at Birla House in March 1943 and put forth a scheme of self-regulatory control by the industry. They proposed that measures would be adopted by industry itself to bring down the prices of cloth and yarn and cotton. Mills would agree to sell their produce within two months of production and wholesalers would sell off their goods within thirty days of actual receipt. The government, on its part, would legislate against storage of cloth and would impose restrictions on industry not to manufacture cloth beyond certain peak levels. By these measures, they felt, the prices would automatically come down. The mill-owners asked to be given statutory power to make it possible for industry to control standard production and in return they were willing to ensure that they would provide cloth at reasonable prices. Report of meeting held at Birla House, New Delhi, in Birla Papers, Series II, File No. K–4.

[99] The new scheme was 'substantially the same' as that put forth by the industrialists in March. *Capital*, 17 June 1943. The mill-owners were promised a strong voice on the Control Advisory Board Committee and the industry was promised enough autonomy to increase production and settle many questions such as working hours. Major questions such as limitation of varieties and qualities of production, profit margins and prices would be decided by the Control Advisory Board. *Capital*, 17 June 1943. The involvement by the government of the cotton industry was hailed both by government officials and industrialists. M.S. Hydari, called the involvement of the industrialists the 'triumph of mutual understanding and common sense over suspicion and lack of information' and prominent mill-owners such as Sir V.N. Chandavarkar welcomed the agreement. This 'co-operative method of control' declared the *Eastern Economist* avoids 'ignorant bureaucratic

interference with the technical matters of industry' and alongside harnesses the 'talents of the trade to social good.' *Eastern Economist*, 23 June 1944.

[100] *Eastern Economist*, 23 June 1944.

[101] For a detailed account of the Bengal famine, see Paul Greenough, *Prosperity and Misery in Modern Bengal* (New York, 1982).

[102] G.D. Birla, 'War Finance under National Government' in *Eastern Economist*, 14 April 1944.

[103] Typescript of article in Birla Papers, also published in *Eastern Economist*, 5 November 1943. He called for a 'quick and revolutionary rise in production' to fight the famine. From his intimate knowledge of Indian labour, he perceptively suggested that it was important to address problems of morale and the 'wear and tear of labour on account of ill-nourishment and diseases which should receive as much attention at least as the wear and tear of machinery which is being excessively worked up.'

[104] Amery enquired from Linlithgow whether there was a lesson to be learnt by the government from the success of Birla's efforts in keeping down prices. Amery to Linlithgow, 16 December 1942, *TOP*, Vol. III, Doc. No. 280.

[105] A large number of institutional charities came forward for relief work. The Birlas' relief effort constituted the largest that was undertaken by an individual or a single family. The prominent relief organizations which were set up largely on the initiative of the Marwaris were the Bengal Relief Committee (president, Badridas Goenka) with which the Hindu Mahasabha leader Shyama Prasad Mookerjee was associated, the Marwari Relief Society (president, Mangturam Jaipuria), Arya Samaj Relief Society (president, Seth Dhipchandjee Poddar), Stock Exchange Relief Committee (president, Gobindlal Bangur), Howrah Relief Society (president, Chiranjilal Bajoria), and the private relief work of Birla Brothers and Messrs Soorajmull Nagarmull. For details on the charities carried out by these organizations see *Relief Organisations Fight Bengal Famine* published by the Relief Co-ordination Committee (Calcutta, 1943). Also see *Bhagirath Kanodia Smriti Granth*, pp. 42–50.

[106] These were located at Rashbehari Avenue, Kalighat Park, Old Ballygunge Road, Ritchi Road, Ashoka Road and Dholapara Akra Road. *Relief Organisations Fight Bengal Famine*.

[107] *Ibid.*

[108] *Eastern Economist*, 23 July 1943.

[109] The *Hindustan Times* launched a public appeal which, in its first instalment, contributed 11,696 maunds of rice and Rs 25,000 to the Bengal Relief Committee. *Bhagirath Kanodia Smriti Granth* (n.d., n.p.), p. 45.

[110] He wrote to Sir John Herbert that 'I am disturbed also to hear reports (which I recognize may be incorrect) that Birla and the Marwaris have apparently been allowed by your Government to take over a substantial responsibility for opening communal kitchens in Calcutta, selling rice at concession rates, I have had no report from you on this subject, and no comment on the serious reflection on your Government which the existence of this state of things if correct would represent, for you will realise the extent to which it would admit of being regarded as an abdication by Government of its functions.' Linlithgow to J. Herbert, 8 August 1943, *TOP*, Vol. IV, Doc. No. 75.

[111] Venkatsubbiah writes that FICCI deliberately 'watched out for any turn or new move of official policy that was potentially prejudicial to the post-war industrialisation of India.' Venkatsubbiah, *Enterprise and Economic Change*, p. 45

[112] The varied character of the issues it took up, for instance, in its 1943 session gives an idea of this role. It took up, *inter alia*, India's sterling credits, the question of representation at international conferences, sale of Indian silver in England, allocation of defence expenditure, utilization and safeguarding of Indian sterling balances and post-war reconstruction.

[113] Venkatsubbiah, *Enterprise and Economic Change.*

[114] This is apparent from their discussions on the sterling credits accumulated during the war. This question was vigorously pursued by FICCI which insisted that the government should take no important decisions in regard to financial settlement and adjustment of India's credit until the Congress leadership was out of jail, the political situation had settled and the Central Legislature was 'effectively functioning.' It asked the government for 'adequate safeguards' to maintain the 'value and free convertibility' of India's sterling assets and to control whole or at least part of the sterling into gold or dollars to ensure this. FICCI also vehemently criticized the government's plans for setting up a 'Reconstruction Fund' which would finance India's post-war reconstruction. It claimed that the fund would 'merely subsidize British exports and assist the rehabilitation of British industry in the post war period.' They clearly told the government that it should 'not make any commitments about India's sterling resources which would freeze our sterling balances only for purchases exclusively from the UK.' FICCI press communique, 3 March 1943 in FICCI, *Correspondence and Relevant Documents relating to Important Questions dealt with by the Federation during the year 1942–3*. Also see *Capital*, 28 January 1943.

[115] Birla to D.G. Mulherkar, 11 December 1943, cited in Venkatsubbiah, *Enterprise and Economic Change*, p. 49.

[116] At this meeting, they decided the general attitude on planning which was broadly that it would embrace the whole of India, would be on a federal basis with residual powers in the provinces and would be completely free in economic matters.

9

The Political Economy of India's Partition

Among the prominent public figures of pre-independence India, what set Birla apart was his extraordinary ability to take a pragmatic approach to day-to-day politics without losing sight of an overall vision. This is most strikingly demonstrated in his analysis of the communal problem and his prescriptions for resolving it. Birla was no communalist. Neither was he intolerant of the minority communities, their distinct identities and their political aspirations. On the contrary, he was sympathetic to what he regarded as their legitimate rights relating to language, culture and religion. He was cast in the mould of a liberal who above all believed in settling disputes through negotiation and dialogue rather than taking to the streets. Yet, a study of Birla's public position from the late 1930s onwards reveals that he became convinced of the inevitability of India's partition along religious lines. He looked upon the prospect of partition not in purely negative terms but as the path towards peaceful coexistence. He was led to this conviction by his characteristic pragmatism and political foresight. He became an early votary of the idea of partition. He was soon, however, heartened to find that a large number of public figures, especially within the business world, shared similar views. Their pragmatism and their long-term strategy of rapid industrialization led by a strong state enforcing homogeneous economic policies left them with no alternative but to look increasingly upon partition as a lasting solution to the country's communal troubles.

Birla's ideas on partition had evolved over the years. It must be emphasized that the partition that Birla wanted was quite different from that which eventuated in August 1947. He was horrified by the violence that accompanied the partition and he had never envisaged the exchange of populations which took place. The fundamental premise of his scheme was that India and Pakistan would co-operate in economic affairs and in defence matters. Unfortunately this did not happen.

EARLY IDEAS OF PARTITION

Birla prided himself on being a practical man and not a visionary. Indeed, in the 1930s he described himself as a hard-headed businessman with a practical view of politics.[1] It is remarkable that his early views on the communal problem contained the germs of the idea of the partition and the creation of two separate states. The first exposition of this idea can be found in his thinking as early as October 1927, when he was involved with the Independent Congress Party—two decades before partition actually eventuated and much before Mohammad Ali Jinnah or the Muslim League formulated the idea of Pakistan *vide* the demand in the Lahore Resolution of March 1940. It was during a discussion with his political mentor, Malaviya, that Birla first expressed this idea in the following terms:

Communal representation in Legislature should go, with reservation of seats for each community, and if possible redistribution of Provinces should be made. I do not know whether splitting the Punjab and Bengal would be liked by the people but I would personally welcome it. The West Punjab and the Frontier and Sind might be composed into one province thus giving a decided majority to Mohammadans in East Bengal and the West Punjab and the seats should be reserved on the basis of population. Mixed volunteers and Scouts Corps should be constituted in every town consisting of a population of 20,000 or more and it should be the duty of the Hindu volunteers to see that in Hindu quarters no Mohammadan was assaulted and vice versa. Similarly arbitration boards should be formed in each town. Besides provincial and district arbitration boards should also be formed to decide communal disputes.[2]

What Birla clearly wanted was a re-drawing of political boundaries to create a distinct agglomeration of Muslim-majority states.[3] In such ideas lay the nucleus of his thinking on the communal question. One can see that although Birla at this time was not an advocate of the division of the country into two nation-states, he definitely believed in the need to re-draw the political map of the country to create formations based on the principle of communal interests. In many ways much of Jinnah's demand for Pakistan (even as late as in the 1940s) approximated to such ideas, as has been shown by the historian Ayesha Jalal.[4] Over the years such nebulous ideas took a more concrete form in Birla's mind,[5] and he began to articulate them with greater clarity and confidence. For instance, in a letter to Gandhi (addressed to Mahadev Desai), he wrote:

I wonder why it should not be possible to have two Federations, one of Muslims and another of Hindus. The Muslim Federation may be composed of all the provinces or portions of provinces which contain more than two thirds of Muslim populations and the Indian states like Kashmir which is composed of Musalmans. Another Federation may be of Hindus and such states as are composed of Hindus. In this case at least we will have been spared a civil war because I fear if anything is going to check our progress, it is the Hindu–Muslim question—not the Englishman, but our own internal quarrels.[6]

Such ideas crystallized in the 1930s. As we have seen Birla's chief concern in the 1930s was that constitutional progress must not be hindered and that the new reforms embodied in the Government of India Act of 1935 should be successfully introduced. However, the events of the late 1930s disappointed Birla. He saw communal dissensions leading to a widening rift between the

Congress and the League on the question of the formation of coalition ministries
after the introduction of the 1935 Act. Once negotiations over coalition ministries
failed the League retaliated by mounting a propaganda campaign against the
Congress' alleged misrule. By the late 1930s, Birla was impatient for a solution
to the communal deadlock which threatened the successful working of provincial
autonomy.[7] The prospect of the wrecking of the Federation on the shores of the
communal issue horrified him. This provided the context in which his ideas on
the communal issue crystallized. In a letter to C. Rajagopalachari, he wrote:

You remember I had a discussion with you very seriously about the question of division
of India into two units, namely Hindu India and Muslim India. I now find that the
Muslim League also is wanting the same thing. The only difference, of course, is that they
will have the Punjab and Bengal included in Muslim India without the accession of Hindu
districts. Similarly, they want Kashmir and Hyderabad both to be included in Muslim
India which, of course, is wrong and their claim could not be sustained. On the other
hand I think it should be possible on equitable basis to divide India into two units. All
the Indian states having Hindu majority of population should be included in Hindu India
and a state like Kashmir which has got a majority of Muslim population will have to go
to Muslim India. The provinces should be reconstituted with a view to allow the Hindu
districts into Hindu India and similarly Muslim districts into Muslim India.

I had spoken to Bapu also in Delhi about this idea and he was not shocked. But he
said the Sikhs would never agree to it. We dropped the discussion because Bapu said that
the question at present did not arise. But I find happily that this has arisen and I think
if we want to have a peaceful India, we must encourage this division and after that we
will have no reservation of seats, no minority problem and no communal problem.

I suggest that we allow Muslims to carry on propaganda in favour of this division
without approving or disapproving of their demand. And when they make full commitment
then alone we may accept the principle.[8]

Behind his advocacy of the idea of partition lay a complex analysis of the
communal situation. He regarded the communal discord as a stumbling block
in constitutional progress and strongly disliked the fact that it was becoming an
insuperable obstacle in political advance.

Birla analysed the communal situation in the context of the wider political
developments of the 1920s and 1930s. He viewed the problem against the
background and the history of pacts made by leaders of different communities.
He was convinced of the futility of such agreements as these made an alliance
with the minority community something to be achieved by the 'highest bidder'.
He was acutely aware of the futile nature of negotiations and agreements as
shown by the successive failures of a number of initiatives such as the Lucknow
Pact of 1916, the Nehru Report of 1928, the disastrous bickering at the Round
Table Conferences of 1930–1 and the Communal Award of 1932. He had also
been a witness to the bitter communal dissentions that led to the failure of the
second Round Table Conference in London.[9] These experiences convinced Birla
that, 'as soon as a certain position had been gained, there started a fresh agitation
for another. While one section accepted the settlement made, another began

denouncing it, and the section that indulged in denunciation came to be recognized as the leader of the community.'[10] Birla was becoming increasingly convinced that there could be no finality to such negotiations and agreements. He blamed the 'impossible demands' of the Muslim League for this. He was sympathetic to the League's demands for safeguards on cultural and religious grounds. But what was being asked for by the League was to be treated on an equal basis with vetoing power in the central and provincial legislatures. This seemed to him most unreasonable, almost a situation where '25% of the population should determine the course of political change'.[11]

After 1937 the issue of the formation of coalition ministries caused him much concern. Having closely analysed the demand for separation, he traced its roots to the United Provinces (UP) and Bombay, not to the Muslim-majority provinces. The Congress, he later admitted, made a grave mistake in not admitting Muslim League members to its provincial ministries. This convinced Muslim League leaders like Jinnah that the Congress could not be relied upon to accept equitable power-sharing arrangements and the Muslims as a minority must unite. Birla felt that 'when important Muslims were ignored' by the 'Congress their vanity was hit'.[12] The League's separatist politics initially appeared to him 'only as a bluff', but soon he realized that important issues were at stake. His own position was that coalition ministries merely accentuated communal bitterness, instead of reducing tension and restoring confidence among the Muslims. He maintained that coalition ministries were untenable in 'Congress provinces since in all such provinces, except Assam and the North-West Frontier Province (NWFP), the Muslim minority constituted less than 15% of the population'. They were, in his view, 'a sure means to perpetuate the communal colour of the governments.'[13]

He also believed that coalition ministries in the Muslim-majority provinces of Punjab and Bengal would not lead to a lasting solution as they would 'always pull their weight community-wise and in opposite directions and will practically perpetuate the communal colour of the Cabinets and ministers.'[14] In other provinces, where the Muslims did not constitute a majority (besides Bengal, Punjab, Assam, NWFP and Sind), he went on to argue that, 'if power is given to them, it would mean that 10 per cent of the population...would have the power of wrecking any measure they like.'[15] By late 1939 his dejection with the communal discord had reached such a point that he even doubted whether the 'Muslims also wanted freedom'.[16] He suspected that 'the game' of the Muslim League under Jinnah's leadership was to 'destroy democracy' and jeopardize both provincial autonomy and federation.[17] Birla was convinced that the intransigence of the League was encouraged by the support it covertly enjoyed from the British.[18] There could be no rapprochement as long as the Muslim League was encouraged by the government to serve as a check on constitutional progress. He, therefore, believed, that no lasting settlement was possible between the two communities.[19]

Birla accordingly wanted the Congress leadership to confront the problem with a fresh approach and with a sense of urgency. This was especially so since he saw signs of the Congress losing its grip and the Muslim League making headway in mobilization not only in British India but in the princely states too. Already many Muslim states which had so far remained aloof from the League were now suspicious of Congress intentions.[20] Birla feared that these states were being driven into the League's camp by the unpragmatic policies of the Congress. A 'States Muslim League' had already been launched and he feared that prominent Muslim states like Hyderabad might join it.[21] In his view it was high time for the Congress leadership to sense the dangers that lay ahead and to seek an urgent solution to the communal impasse.

TIME FOR CONCILIATION

The experience of provincial autonomy and the communal bitterness it engendered convinced Birla that the time had come for the Congress and the League to settle their differences. He further believed that if the communal problem could not be resolved through negotiations, a parting of ways would be inevitable. After 1939 he tried hard to impress upon the Congress to open negotiations with the Muslim League to bring about a conciliation between the two. He took the initiative to formulate a set of proposals for this purpose. In his initiative, a crucial role was assigned to the government which alone could bring the minority community to the negotiating table by declaring that Dominion Status would be introduced, irrespective of the position of the Muslim League. He believed that while legitimate minority demands relating to language and culture should be conceded and several other concessions made to the League, its demand for the power of veto should on no account be conceded.[22] In his scheme, negotiations should take place 'not with A or B but with duly elected and accredited representatives of Muslims.'[23] Thus talks could be held only with those with proven credentials to represent the minority community. One way of ensuring this was by holding a premiers' conference, Birla suggested to Gandhi in March 1940.[24] This would have the advantage of not compelling the Congress to recognize the League as the sole representative of the Muslims. An alternative course, in his view, was to hold a representatives' assembly made up of an electoral college of the provincial assemblies.[25] A third choice might be by way of arbitration by an impartial authority.[26] Birla communicated these proposals to Gandhi and other important Congress leaders and in March 1940 stressed the importance of working within the framework of the Government of India Act of 1935, especially since the Muslims were 'satisfied with $\frac{1}{3}$ of representation' provided by the terms of the Act. By moving out of the orbit of the Act, the Muslims would feel encouraged to ask for more which, according to Birla, would be disastrous.[27] He argued with Gandhi against abandoning the 1935 Act and adopting the demand of a constituent assembly, as desired by Nehru and a section of Congressmen.[28] He urged upon Gandhi that the British were sincere in their promise of granting India Dominion status after the war.

There was an essential pragmatism in Birla's approach of taking advantage of whatever was offered by the British.[29] In his view renewed efforts were needed at conciliation between the Congress and the League. Behind Birla's restlessness to negotiate lay an impatience with the slow pace of constitutional progress. The way of securing a responsible government at the centre, he told Gandhi, lay not in insisting on complete independence or '16 annas of the rupee', but in settling for Dominion status by 'adjusting our demands in relation to our strength.'[30] In late 1940, Birla persuaded Purshotamdas Thakurdas, his Bombay-based associate, to meet Jinnah to discuss his demand of Pakistan and to find out what exactly it was that he wanted.[31] In January 1941 he attempted to arrange talks between Maulana Azad, the Congress president, and Sir Nazimuddin, the Bengal Premier, whom he described as 'a very reasonable man'.[32] At the same time he continued to explore other avenues of negotiation. The idea of the premiers' conference, suggested by him in early 1940, was overruled by Gandhi. His proposal for a representative assembly also did not find favour among Congressmen. During 1940–1 he strongly lobbied them to accept the Viceroy's offer of Congress participation in his Executive Council.[33] He hoped that the experience of the Congress and the Muslim League in working together at the centre would 'build a bridge between the Hindus and the Muslims.'

However, all these proposals languished for lack of support. In the meanwhile, C. Rajagopalachari put forth his scheme to resolve the communal deadlock. This scheme, which came to be widely known as the 'Rajaji Formula', appealed to Birla.[34] The Rajaji Formula proposed an understanding between the Congress and the League on the basis of the Congress' acceptance of the League's Lahore Resolution and its underlying principle of self-determination, including the separation of Muslim-majority provinces, if necessary. If accepted by both the parties, the formula was to pave the way for the Congress' participation in a popular government at the centre. Birla and Rajagopalachari had shared similar views about the communal problem since the late 1930s.[35] In the early 1940s too they frequently held discussions and Birla often found himself in agreement with Rajagopalachari on the communal question.[36] Birla threw his weight behind this formula, as it met his long standing desire for an immediate transfer of power at the centre, irrespective of the communal deadlock. In February 1942 he implored Gandhi to consider seriously the merits of the Rajaji Formula and to encourage Rajaji 'to have a dialogue with Jinnah'.[37] On his part, he maintained close contact with Rajagopalachari and frequently communicated to him the reactions of important politicians to his proposals.[38] Eventually, in November 1942, Rajagopalachari and Jinnah came together to discuss the scheme. Birla took a keen interest in their deliberations. In his view Rajagopalachari was on the right track. Yet he was no longer hopeful about the success of the talks because he realized that 'after all Rajaji can't deliver the goods.' He knew that Rajagopalachari was in a hopeless minority within the top echelons of the Congress and that his 'formula' did not command much support among

Congressmen. Although he sympathized with Rajagopalachari's views and was even willing to finance a mission to England by him to lobby British politicians, he knew that the official mind of the Congress high command[39] was against it and this made him cautious in continuing his support.[40]

Instead, Birla now explored other avenues for renewing the dialogue with the Muslim League. In June 1942 he himself took the initiative to meet Liaquat Ali Khan, a prominent leader of the party. After their lengthy discussions Birla gathered the impression that a negotiated settlement with the League was possible after all. Negotiations in this direction need not necessarily be held with Jinnah but could take place with other important Muslim leaders like Liaquat Ali. He realized, however, that the precondition for this would be the Congress' acceptance of the principle of separation. In his view it all boiled down to one question: 'Are we prepared to accept the principle of separation?' If the Congress leadership showed its willingness to accept this, there could be plenty of room for discussion.[41] When Gandhi was briefed about these talks, he was concerned that Birla might have committed himself in some way which could be a most dangerous thing.[42] Birla, however, followed up his talks with Liaquat Ali by meeting Jinnah, the *Quaid-e-Azam*, himself. Fazal Rahimtoola, the Bombay-based industrialist and Birla's old colleague from his days in the Central Legislative Assembly in the late 1920s, arranged the meeting, which took place in September 1942. They had a 'good talk,' and Birla returned with the strong impression that Jinnah could not clearly define the Pakistan he wanted. He was convinced that until Jinnah defined his Pakistan, it was inadvisable to get involved in talks with him, as that could only lead to further trouble. After this point he decided not to press for a dialogue.[43] He responded with caution to other initiatives which were put forth, such as by Sikander Hyat Khan, the Unionist Premier of the Punjab in late 1942. He, moreover, also resisted the temptation to expound his views publicly.

A milestone in the attempts at reconciliation were the Gandhi–Jinnah talks of 1944. Birla carefully followed the progress of these talks. From the accounts he received he concluded that Gandhi was now willing to accept the substance of the Rajaji Formula, and that 'Jinnah did not object to Gandhi's proposal on the constitution of a central machinery,' but he wanted the central authority to 'be based on negotiations between the two states'. In overall terms, he gathered that 'Gandhiji was prepared for separation based on such districts predominantly Muslim but he would like this to be done after a plebiscite and he demanded a treaty which would create a central machinery...The greatest objection of Jinnah was to a plebiscite and boundaries.'[44] Birla's views were echoed by his weekly newspaper, the *Eastern Economist*, when it observed that the talks showed Gandhi as a great leader and statesman who had gone to the utmost length to accommodate Jinnah without conceding to the two-nation theory. It lauded Gandhi's efforts as seeking 'a solution for family members who wished to effect a separation' and strongly blamed Jinnah for the failure of the talks.[45]

THE GATHERING MOMENTUM OF PARTITION

The experience of all these negotiations with League leaders eventually convinced Birla that it was no longer possible to conciliate the League. An important change came about in his perception of the communal situation in 1945–6. By then the issue was no longer whether the Muslim League would be given Pakistan. The question now was what would be the terms under which Pakistan would be conceded. The various schemes being proposed for the division of the country consumed his attention. In the context of eastern India he regarded the Muslim League's demand as quite unacceptable. In Assam, for instance, where the Muslims constituted only 30 per cent of the population and in the western districts of Bengal which were predominantly Hindu, he wondered whether the Hindus would be 'coerced to join the Pakistan which the League demands'.[46] In the context of the Punjab, where the southern and eastern parts were largely inhabited by Hindus, similar anxieties plagued him. He was now concerned to ensure that the League 'should not be encouraged to demand more than their due'.[47] At the same time the idea that partition was inevitable was by now firmly implanted in his mind.

The victory of the Labour party in Britain in July 1945 made Birla optimistic that the process leading to a transfer of power would at last be speeded up. The ensuing constitutional negotiations, however, filled him with apprehension. What made him especially apprehensive was the tiresome negotiations at a conference called at Simla by the Viceroy to select leaders to form an Executive Council which would include equal proportions of caste Hindus and Muslims. The Simla Conference confirmed his fears that there were real difficulties to be surmounted and he dreaded that a breakdown between the two communities was at hand. As all negotiations broke down, Birla blamed the intransigence of Jinnah who claimed the sole right to nominate all Muslim members to the Viceroy's Executive Council.[48] Birla lamented that 'one man turned the whole table because he was given the vetoing power'. The collapse of the Conference further confirmed for him that the path of a negotiated settlement to the communal problem had now reached a dead-end. The time had come for the Congress to fight the forthcoming elections to display its strength and prevent the Muslim League from claiming more than its share. It was crucial in his view that the Congress should join the new interim government at the centre and he urged upon Patel that 'we must take charge of the machinery even though we may not be fully satisfied...I have no doubt that you are aware about the danger of the existing situation. In fact without governmental machinery we are feeling helpless'.[49]

Birla was no longer alone in advocating partition of the country to seek a lasting solution to the communal deadlock. Other business leaders strongly supported the idea too. For instance, Ramkrishna Dalmia, prominent Marwari businessman, openly claimed to be the first among business leaders to publicly endorse the scheme of partition.[50] Another important businessman who held similar views was Sir Homi Mody, as we shall see later in this chapter. There is considerable evidence to suggest that by the mid-1940s the groundswell of opinion within big business was receptive to the idea of partition.

It is important to understand why partition made good economic sense to Birla. He had three principal considerations. First, his support for partition came from his hard-core pragmatism. In practical terms simple considerations of public order dictated that a workable solution should be found to communal tensions which had begun to affect the economic fabric of the country. Rioting and communal disorders in the late 1930s and 1940s had threatened the collapse of all economic activity. Birla articulated this anxiety when he wrote to Rajagopalachari:

It is hardly necessary for me to draw your attention to the economic consequences of the disturbed conditions. If I do so it is only to emphasize the danger and I hope that our Government may be able to take timely steps to prevent the catastrophe which is hanging on our head... In provinces like Bengal, Bihar, UP, production is seriously affected. Today you can't even build a house...serious labour shortages, coal shortages, no bricks, Muslim *mistries* don't come in Hindu areas and Hindu labour don't enter Muslim areas.[51]

Protracted communal tensions, he feared, would paralyse economic activity. Moreover, communal arson created fears of attacks on property to which businessmen in general and industrialists in particular were vulnerable. Birla was astute enough to realize that negotiations and pacts between leaders of the two communities scarcely ever worked and resulted only in a fragile peace. What increasingly made good economic sense was to seek a long-term solution; partition appeared as the only way forward.

Second, an important consideration was the great economic opportunity which Birla saw in the post-war situation. As we have seen, he looked upon post-war reconstruction as an opportunity for the large-scale development of Indian industry. Throughout the 1940s, the necessity of improving the pace of economic growth had been his battle-cry. He had, as we know, repeatedly pleaded in his public utterances that the economic situation needed immediate attention and that political issues must be subordinated to a programme of economic recovery. He warned that 'time is the essence of the whole question and we are woefully losing it.'[52] At such a time what was needed was rapid constitutional progress to ensure Indian control over the centre. This made him impatient for constitutional advance. The communal deadlock was seen as a stumbling block towards this. Birla had warned as early as 1938 that, 'if anything is going to check our progress, it is the Hindu–Muslim question—not the Englishman, but our own internal quarrels.'[53]

THE CASE FOR A STRONG CENTRE

Above all, the reason for Birla's and big business' vigorous support for the idea of partition sprang from their long-term political strategy. Big business preferred a division of the country to the Muslim League's scheme of a loose confederation with a weak centre which only controlled defence.[54] Birla's particular genius lay in ensuring that his business colleagues realized that all schemes for a united India would inevitably be predicated on a weak centre, surrounded by strong provinces. He successfully convinced business leaders that if partition were to be averted the Muslim League would accept nothing other than a weak centre with the real power concentrated in the provinces. As his *Eastern Economist* explained:

From the economic point of view the country needs a strong central Government. Politically while the Congress and Hindu opinion may be in favour of a strong centre, Muslim opinion can only be assuaged by a Federation which will limit the powers and aims of the Centre to very narrow and limited aims and grant all essential powers including residuary authority to the provinces. What is, therefore, politically practicable may not be economically satisfying or adequate.[55]

All plans for a united India necessarily implied that political power would be concentrated in strong provincial governments to give the Muslim-majority provinces the autonomy the League demanded.[56] For big business the essentials of rapid industrialization entailed economic planning, and fundamental to this was a strong central government which could enforce economic homogeneity within the country. It envisaged a future in which the government at the centre would undertake the planned development of the economic infrastructure.[57] The importance that business men placed on the role of state planning is clear from its several policy pronouncements. Business leaders were quick to recognize that the state would play a crucial role in the economic sphere in independent India, and they advocated a large role for the state in the industrial sector in particular. This was because Birla and his colleagues knew that large-scale state enterprises would be needed for developing the basic industrial infrastructure of the country. They realized too that private enterprise would be unable to make investments in developing this infrastructure, where returns were only possible after a long gestation period. The capital, technology and managerial resources needed for large projects to develop basic industries could only be mobilized by the state.[58]

On this there existed a remarkable degree of consensus among Birla and other business leaders like Purshotamdas Thakurdas, J.R.D. Tata and Walchand Hirachand. It would not be incorrect to say that planning for big business in these years was merely a euphemism for state enterprise. As a matter of fact, there had long existed a close relationship between the Congress and FICCI on the need for economic planning, as was demonstrated by the work of the National Planning Committee of the Congress.[59] The clearest statement on the role of planning and state enterprise in independent India was made in the Bombay Plan itself for which Birla and his associates were responsible.[60] The most fundamental assumption underlying the Plan, which was announced in January 1944, was that a national government would be formed after the war.[61] Such a government would be constituted on a federal basis and its jurisdiction over economic matters would extend over the entire country. The Plan's objective was to achieve a doubling of the country's per capita income within a period of fifteen years. It proposed an ambitious scheme not only for increasing production but also for improving the general standard of living of the common man.[62] The Plan represented a comprehensive economic blueprint by big business for independent India. It envisaged a massive investment of the scale of Rs 10,000 crores over 15 years in sectors such as industry, agriculture, communication, health, education and other social activities.[63] It proposed a phased approach to industrialization. In the first phase key industries such as power, mining and metallurgy, engineering, chemicals, armaments, transport and cement were to get priority as it was upon them that the economic superstructure of the country would be built.[64]

In overall terms what was most striking about the Bombay Plan was the central role it envisaged for the state. It contemplated three kinds of state intervention in economic activity—government control, government ownership and government management. The state was to exercise control over distribution of industries; to minimize regional disparities; develop public utilities and basic industries; and undertake non-remunerative enterprise.[65] At the FICCI annual session of 1944, Birla proudly called the Bombay Plan the 'non-official plan for the economic development of India,'[66] and as things eventuated the Plan became the basis of independent India's first Five-Year National Plan. The Bombay Plan did not even mention the partition of the country. It would have been out of character for him and business to have indulged openly in such political controversy. But the Plan laid down the essentials of what they wished independent India was to be in economic terms. And it clearly implied that a divided India was preferable to big business, rather than a united India with a feeble centre and weakened by divisive elements.[67]

ESTABLISHING THE ECONOMIC FEASIBILITY OF PARTITION

Given such an approach to partition, Birla and other business leaders took steps to analyse seriously what various schemes of partition would entail in economic terms.[68] Though he gave a good deal of thought to the economic implications of Pakistan, the first economic feasibility study of the Pakistan scheme was made public in 1945 by John Mathai and Homi Mody, both signatories to the Bombay Plan and closely associated with the Tata Group.[69] In their study Mody and Mathai analysed in detail the economic consequences of the Pakistan demand. They assumed that Pakistan would consist of two economic zones, as demanded by the Muslim League. They visualized two possible scenarios. In the first scenario partition would be carried out according to the then existing provincial boundaries, that is, the Muslim-majority provinces would form the new state. In the second scenario boundaries would be re-drawn according to the contiguous Muslim-majority districts of Punjab and Bengal. Mody and Mathai concluded that Pakistan would be a viable economic unit if partition was to occur provincewise. However, if the boundaries were to be drawn on the basis of Muslim-majority districts, the position of Pakistan would not be a happy one. They concluded that, in both the scenarios, there would be a need for the two independent states of India and Pakistan to co-operate in the spheres of economy and defence. They emphasized that a large free-trade zone would be essential for the future development of the two economies. They put forward the concept of the 'optimum economic unit' under which the two states would have minimum custom barriers and large-scale trade and exchange. They also envisaged a common policy on defence.

Mody and Mathai thus came to two major conclusions. If the objective was to maintain existing standards of living and budgetary requirements on a pre-war basis (excluding the provision for defence), partition was feasible on economic grounds. But if the goal was to raise the general standard of living, then there existed the need for effective co-operation between the two states in areas of defence and economy. Without such co-operation, they pronounced partition to be a recipe for economic disaster for the two newly independent countries.[70] Interestingly, what concerned Mody and Mathai was not political separation but the underlying economic content of the partition scheme. They agreed that, while there could be political separation, what was needed was economic co-operation between the two states. So long as political separation did not prohibit a free exchange of raw materials and finished products, they regarded partition as quite feasible. Their study emphasized the pre-eminent economic position of Calcutta in the future division of the country.[71] It concluded that, without Calcutta, the eastern zone of Pakistan would be no more than a rural slum. In view of the fact that the political situation was extremely uncertain in 1945 when the study was conducted, all Mody and Mathai could do was to visualize different scenarios. However, what they succeeded in doing was to establish in the minds of big business leadership the pre-eminent position of Calcutta, and the vital importance of retaining it within India.

EXPERIENCES OF THE INTERIM MINISTRY AND THEREAFTER

While the business leadership comprehended the implications of Mody and Mathai's feasibility study, Birla continued his efforts to impress upon the political leadership to address the real issues which, for him, were economic. During these years, it was in Vallabhbhai Patel that Birla placed his hopes, carefully distinguishing his politics from the rest of the Congress. Their association had grown especially close since Birla had played a key role in the collection of funds for the Congress in the 1946 elections. It was to Patel that Birla now looked for guidance to steer the Congress policies on the communal issue. It is well known that Patel played a crucial role not only in organizing the 1946 election campaign but also in the Congress' decision to form the interim government and later in directing its course. Birla had all along pleaded with the Congress high command to take on the reins of the government, irrespective of the League's position. When the crucial decision to form the interim government was taken by the Congress, Birla felt that it was a splendid thing to happen. 'The credit for all this goes to Sardarji', he observed. 'It is curious' he continued, 'how at the age of 70, he is showing quite new lights. Even he did not come to such prominence 10 years ago. That was our misfortune. If he gives another ten years and keeps control, I think we may yet settle down peacefully.'[72] Birla wasted no time in drawing up a set of proposals of what the new government should do in the economic sphere.[73] At the same time he continued to press the Congress leadership to take a realistic view of the communal situation which by late 1946 was now clearly getting out of hand. He argued that communal polarization had reached such a stage that '80 per cent of the Muslims are behind the League' while the Congress had '90 per cent of the Hindus and 10 per cent of the Muslims at the most' behind it. He strongly pressed on Gandhi and other Congressmen the urgent need to concede the principle of separation. However, he was concerned that the Hindu-majority areas in Bengal and Punjab should be protected from the Muslim League's extravagant demands. 'After all Jinnah is right in demanding a separation,' Birla observed. 'Of course, his Pakistan and my Pakistan would be quite different. Why can't we demand a separation from the Muslims? *But why can't we* demand a separation of the Hindu areas from the Punjab and Bengal and then have a new Hindustan. But of course, there is no chance of it since neither the Congress nor H.M.G. [Her Majesty's Government] like it.'[74]

The arrival of a Cabinet Mission to look into the nature of the state that would succeed the Raj and an interim government in the meantime, did not particularly enthuse Birla who took a gloomy view of all attempts at a reconciliation with the Muslim League. The Mission in his view was faced with 'a ticklish job made more ticklish by the past which always created fears and distrust'.[75] He wished that the major parties involved in the deliberations with the Mission would make it clear to the Muslim League leaders 'that the intransigent must miss the bus.' He asked the Mission to keep in view the failure of the many pacts in the past and he asked them to work for a final solution, once for all.[76] He cautioned the members of the Mission that Jinnah's demand for a parity in the interim government would be unacceptable both to the Congress and the Hindus. He argued that the Muslim League already had one-fourth of the total seats in provincial legislatures with which it should be more than satisfied.[77]

The Cabinet Mission proposed the setting up of an interim government in which both the Muslim League and the Congress would participate. It was a last attempt by the British to transfer power to a united India. However, to accommodate both the Muslim League and the Congress it granted strong autonomy to the provinces so that the Muslim-majority areas could enjoy autonomy. The proposals of the Mission were completely unsatisfactory from the point of view of Birla's and other business leaders' economic plans. The Mission essentially envisaged a weak centre with minimum powers. As the *Eastern Economist* declared, a weak centre, as proposed by the Mission, would be incapable of performing even the minimum functions of a modern state, and more significantly would lack economic foundations. Autonomy for the provinces 'will effectively kill the economic unity of India, render planning almost impossible, bring about veritable inter-unit economic confusion and blast all hopes for any reasonable increase in living standards for the common man'.[78] A 'circumscribed' centre, as proposed by the League and embodied in the Cabinet Mission's plan, was regarded by Birla and his business colleagues as a matter for disquiet. They were acutely aware that a weak centre meant 'a complete redrawing of all the economic plans which have been in preparation these few years and involve a serious reduction in the resources available to each group.' Further, it meant that 'no all-India planning would be possible, and the constitution would be a reversion of decentralization even in the determination of economic policies.'[79] Fortunately for big business, the mission was unsuccessful. However, Birla recognized the underlying sincerity of the British to immediately transfer power to Indian hands, and that although the mission had failed, it had 'taught the rank and file to unreservedly recognize the bonafides of the Labour Government and this changed the whole atmosphere.' Its 'greatest achievement was the establishment of an atmosphere of trust and friendliness,' he acknowledged to Sir Stafford Cripps, member of the three-man Commission.[80]

Meanwhile there had been a rapid deterioration of the communal situation and, in August 1946, occurred the 'Great Calcutta Killings' in which the entire metropolis was paralysed by bitter violence that continued for days. It is estimated that 4000 persons died and that there were over 10,000 casualties.[81] The scale of communal violence shook big business in eastern India to its very foundations and outraged Birla.[82] He implored the Bengal Governor, Sir Fredrick Burrows, to take all necessary measures to restore normalcy: 'the military must enter streets and by-lanes and help recover lost property, shops must be opened, especially food stalls, and people should be persuaded to go to work and resume their normal activities'.[83] In his view the Calcutta killings destroyed whatever little possibility that existed of a compromise with the League. It marked a point of no return in the relationship between the two communities. He could see that communal politics had begun to affect the harmonious relationship that had existed in the everyday life of the two communities. Bitterness and acrimony characterized day-to-day activities of the common man. In such an environment he feared a total collapse of all economic activity in the cities. Birla could see that industrial production was threatened by strikes and communal disturbances. And this could be terrible when 'neither the worker nor the agriculturist is interested in working hard and producing more. And whatever he was producing half-heartedly is now (being) affected by communal disturbances,' he observed to Sir Stafford Cripps.[84] He was specially perturbed about the worsening situation in Bengal which faced the twin dangers of industrial strikes and communal rioting. The incident convinced him that Bengal was no longer a safe place for either business or industry as with '48 per cent destructive minded Hindus and 52 per cent fanatic Muslims (it) is not going to be a helpful place for any large scale industry.'[85]

Birla had been keen to move out of Calcutta and had, with great foresight, planned in the late 1930s and early 1940s the diversifications of his operations and their move either to Gwalior or to the Bombay region. His major industrial assets in Bengal other than the headquarters of Birla Brothers were only one jute mill and the Textile Machinery Company (Texmaco).[86] He had begun to feel that, in any case, the Bengali Hindu was definitely unfriendly towards Marwari business and, since Marwaris were men of property, they were much more vulnerable to communal arson, especially when their own Hindu brethren were not particularly co-operative.[87] To a business associate, Birla was later to claim, with some degree of relief that, all he had in Calcutta were 2000 clerks![88]

Soon thereafter, the Muslim League agreed to join the interim government at the centre in October 1946—an act which Birla portrayed as having been committed 'in a sullen mood'. In a letter to Cripps, he visualized two possible scenarios. In the first scenario, the League would create problems from within. In the second, he speculated that the day-to-day experience of administration may lead to a better appreciation of facts and understanding.[89] As the League joined the interim government, riots broke out in many areas of east Bengal. On hearing rumours about the danger of violence escalating, Birla personally appealed to Huseyn Suhrawardy, the Bengal Premier, and the Governor to act together and prevent further disturbances.[90] When Gandhi rushed to Noakhali, one of the main scenes of communal riots, in October 1946, Birla was concerned to place at the disposal of the Mahatma all the resources he could to ensure the success of his peace-keeping mission. When Birla learnt that money and essential commodities were urgently needed to provide relief to the victims of communal violence, he enlisted the cooperation of fellow mill-owners by writing to them about the plight of weavers 'who are practically ruined,' as their looms had been destroyed during communal arson. He told them that Gandhi needed yarn, and he proposed a gift of 200 bales of yarn for the weavers from the mill-owners, costing about Rs 80,000.[91] Through this communal rioting Birla hoped that the Congress leadership would finally concede to Jinnah's demand for separation. 'Perhaps this mutual killing which has already caused a loss of a few thousand lives, may make us realize the futility of this task', he wrote to Cripps.[92] It was time for the Bengal Congress to act on the side of peace and order. He wanted Congressmen to take the initiative to form a National Guard of volunteers to protect life and property, at least in the Hindu-majority areas.[93]

However, a communal discord threatened the interests of big business in a quite unexpected way. On the entry of the Muslim League in the interim government, the crucial portfolio of finance was given to Liaquat Ali Khan. As

The young jute broker

With Patel and Maniben

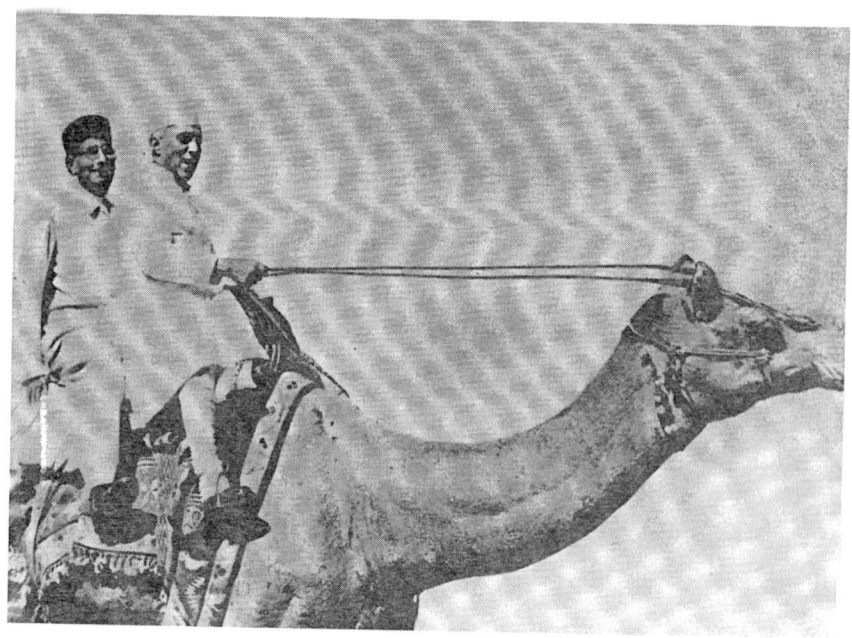

On Nehru's visit to Pilani

With Gandhi. Birla Temple, Delhi, opens to untouchables

On a pilgrimage with Basant Kumar and Sarala

G.D. Birla

Finance Minister, Liaquat Ali formulated the budget proposals which were presented before the Central Legislative Assembly in March 1947. The budget proposed a business tax on profits and a graduated tax on capital gains.[94] Birla felt that a concerted attempt by the League was underway to throttle the development of industry. He accused Liaquat Ali of framing the budget in such a way that it would 'kill the substantially Hindu industry'.[95] He led the strong protest which big business lodged against the budget. So vehement was business reaction that all stock exchanges closed down in protest. Important business leaders like Thakurdas and Tata rushed to Delhi to lend their support to Birla in his efforts to scotch the budget proposals. So effective was this campaign that Liaquat Ali was forced to drop many of his tax proposals, and Birla was widely credited for this.[96]

Although Birla and big business leaders were successful in spiking the guns of Liaquat Ali, their overall experience of the interim ministry was disappointing. They considered the economic performance of the ministry to be dismal. The *Eastern Economist* accused the Muslim League of setting itself up as an independent policy-making body in the economic sphere with its control over the crucial portfolios of finance and commerce. Dissensions within the ministry led to the economic confusion that characterized government policies. Birla was deeply disappointed that ministers, including Congressmen, were ignoring the economy. In his view the ministry had 'no peace, no leisure, no time for attending to all these matters'. The Congress ministers were equally to blame as they had no time to deal with economic issues. The communal issue, he complained, was leading to an 'obsession with Jinnah and the Muslim League' and the Congress Ministries 'looked down with contempt' on issues that dealt with matters such as the economy.[97]

More than the attitudes and policies of the interim ministry, the economy now reeled under the strain of civil strife and communal disorders. Civil strife held the economy at ransom, lamented the *Eastern Economist*. Business in Calcutta came to a complete standstill during much of 1946 and trading conditions in Bombay too were disturbed by communal unrest. The provincial governments remained completely preoccupied with maintaining law and order to be able to pay any attention to the economy. All these strains and pressures further propelled big business to seek an immediate and lasting settlement to the communal deadlock. Birla was personally dissatisfied with the way the Congress was handling the situation. The strike waves showed that the Communists were building independent political bases. Calls for hartal in Calcutta could be successful even without the co-operation of the Congress. He was disappointed with the slowness of the Congress in coming to decisions about the future. He was now exasperated by the slow pace of solving the communal problem as well as the way in which it was beginning to affect the economy. 'I am not quite sure whether we are at all interested in independence or merely in quarrelling, gaining our points and keeping the people excited', he observed to a close friend.[98]

Birla now took upon himself the task of analysing the economic implications of partition. In April 1947, the *Eastern Economist* published a series of studies focused on the economics of partition. These considered the implications of partition in terms of the division of natural resources, budget allocations, the distribution of industry and the agrarian situation. They declared in particular that the partition of Bengal was an administrative necessity in view of the unwieldy size of the province and its complex polity which had been made worse by mutual antagonisms. It concluded that the Indian Bengal would be at an advantage in economic strength.[99] In Punjab the picture was, however, different. The *Eastern Economist* concluded that 'Muslim Punjab' would get more fertile land, as compared to eastern Punjab[100] but in industrial assets the advantage rested with 'Hindu India'.[101] From its study of the total revenues, defence budgets, industrial capacity and agricultural production, the *Eastern Economist* concluded that there would be a major gap in the economic resources between India and Pakistan. It predicted that Pakistan would become a viable economic unit only after about a decade, and till then 'co-operation with the Indian Union on mutually advantageous terms is inescapable'.[102] Two months later, in June 1947, a study by Birla, called *Basic Facts Relating to Hindustan and Pakistan*, further explored the problem.[103] Birla first set out his ideas in a paper meant for private circulation and after obtaining feedback from influential quarters, published his findings in the *Eastern Economist*.[104] He prefaced his study with the bold statement that 'Hindu India' would be stronger than Pakistan but he acknowledged that Pakistan could also be strong and prosperous. He advocated economic co-ordination between the two states for a higher rate of economic growth and concluded that 'it would be in the interest of both the parts to put up co-ordinated efforts in order that the whole of India may be able to achieve high economic prosperity, strength and dignity'. What distinguished Birla's pamphlet from Mody and Mathai's earlier study was that Calcutta was not recognized even as a possible issue of contention; it was assumed that the city would be part of Indian Bengal. Birla took the position that, even without Calcutta, Pakistan was economically feasible.[105]

Between 1945 and 1948 Birla played a critical role in formulating ideas about partition and clarifying them within the higher echelons of the Congress. Both the historians Sumit Sarkar and Markovits have suggested that business pressures played a not insignificant role behind the decision of the Congress leadership to accept partition.[106] There is considerable evidence to suggest that Birla played a crucial role in this decision-making process. In these years, it was Patel rather than Gandhi who was steering the Congress and it is hardly surprising that, despite Birla's close attachment to Bapu, he increasingly looked to the Sardar for action. In a general sense, Birla also played an important role in advising the Congress leadership on economic issues. Indeed, during these years the Congress high command increasingly relied upon Birla for direction in the economic sphere.[107] His centrality is illustrated by the crucial role he was to play in the division of assets and liabilities between India and Pakistan after independence.[108]

LIVING THROUGH THE HOLOCAUST

The country was partitioned amidst turmoil and violence in which an estimated half to one million were killed in communal riots and more than 18 million were uprooted.[109] Amidst the turmoil in which the country was partitioned and the tremendous dislocation that followed, Birla took upon himself the task of convincing the newly-constituted Government of India to give foremost importance to the economy. He looked upon the holocaust in the Punjab as a very bad economic experience.[110] He also wanted the government to draw up contingency plans to deal with the alarming food situation that prevailed to prevent a collapse of the public distribution system similar to that which had occurred in Bengal a few years before. The influx of refugees and the scale of the catastrophe made him feel 'as if the whole world had gone to the wrong track'.[111] Feeling very much depressed, he lamented that 'unless we can cope with the situation India is doomed'.[112] He threw himself into the work of the rehabilitation of refugees. He believed that it was necessary to provide immediate employment to people who had been uprooted. Lack of gainful employment created 'bitterness and excited the people to retaliate'. He placed his considerable resources at the disposal of the newly-created Ministry of Relief and Rehabilitation and other agencies involved in relief work.[113] His employees worked for the government in honorary capacities and his companies provided motor vehicles first for evacuating the refugees from West Punjab and then for dispersing them internally.[114] His airlines, Bharat Airways, undertook sorties to evacuate fleeing refugees from Pakistan and his mills provided essential commodities such as flour and cloth to refugees living in temporary camps.[115] He diverted money from his other charities to concentrate on relief work. 'Every bit of energy and every available amount of money just now is going towards the refugee problem. It all looks quiet on the surface but you have no idea what amount of tension there is and what is in store for us,' he told K.N. Katju, the UP Congressman.[116] Among the many relief organizations that benefited from Birla's advice and financial support was the United Council for Relief and Welfare. He was invited to join the Council by Lady Edwina Mountbatten, its chairperson.[117] The Council was headquartered at the Government House in Delhi and coordinated the work of a large number of relief agencies. Birla worked closely on the Council's executive committee and became a key member of its finance sub-committee.[118]

Birla's financial and technical expertise was also sought by the Ministry of Relief and Rehabilitation. He advised the ministry to draw up long-term plans for economic rehabilitation. He suggested that an economic census should be taken to ascertain the areas in which industry could face scarcities of labour due to migration. 'We are feeling great scarcity of skilled workers', he observed to the Secretary, Ministry of Relief and Rehabilitation, and suggested that incoming refugees could be absorbed in industrial units all over India. To generate employment for unskilled workers, public works such as hydro-electric schemes could be undertaken. Birla advised that 'capital expenditure plans should be examined and should be taken up without delay.'[119] He brought an entirely new approach to solving the refugee problem. He recognized that relief was the need of the hour but emphasized that basically what was needed in the long-run was economic rehabilitation of the refugees. Towards this goal, he worked hard, never losing his characteristic optimism. 'Let us work with faith and leave the rest in the hands of God,' he wrote.[120]

On the business front, the Birlas seemed better prepared to handle trouble than most businessmen.[121] Foreseeing the upheaval, they had planned ways in advance of protecting businesses located in riot-prone areas. For instance, the plant and machinery of their Textile Machinery Company in Calcutta had already been removed to Gwalior by April 1947.[122] There were, however, two areas where they were particularly vulnerable—one related to the operations of their United Commercial Bank in the Muslim-majority provinces of Punjab and Sindh, and the other was a large cotton mill, the Sutlej Cotton Mill, at Okara near Lahore. Preparing months in advance of the partition, the bank's branches in Punjab and Sindh removed 80 per cent of their liquid assets to safer areas. The bank was thus able to save a large part of its movable assets. It also made changes in credit policies to deal with the new situation. All fresh lending was stopped till there was a scheme for riot and civil commotion insurance. In cases where advances of money had already been made, the bank now insisted upon riot and civil commotion risks being covered.[123] A policy decision was also taken that no trading in the bank's shares could take place 'till market conditions were more favourable'.[124] While the liquid assets of the bank could thus be saved, many of its premises suffered during the riots. Its godowns were looted and in many places its staff fled. The Custodian of Evacuee Property could provide little relief to help the bank. Birla took up the issue of his bank and of other Indian banks with the highest authorities in Pakistan. He complained against the complicity of local and district officials in lootings and disturbances, and wanted the issue to be taken up at the highest level so that the Indian banks could be compensated for their losses.[125]

The only Birla concern that ran into major trouble during the partition riots was the Sutlej Cotton Mill at Okara near Lahore. The mill had a net worth of Rs 3 crores in 1947 out of which Rs 2 crores were in stocks and Rs one crore was the investment in plant and equipment. It employed about 4000 workers. Trouble started in Okara in August 1947, after a large influx of Muslim refugees from Amritsar. Riots broke out and many Hindu families of Okara fled. Alarmed at the events, Birla requested the Governor of East Punjab to deploy the military to guard the property of the fleeing families and to make arrangements for their evacuation, in addition to the posting of a military picket to guard his mill. He also demanded the deployment of the Punjab Boundary Force for this purpose.[126] However, the mill was looted and taken over by representatives of a 'Sheikh' from

Lyallpur. These men seized the mill quarters, while the factory itself was taken over by the Pakistan Government which handed it over to one Gholan Farid Latif, originally an entrepreneur from East Punjab. Birla raised the matter with the highest authorities and approached Nehru and Patel to take it up with the Pakistan Prime Minister, Liaquat Ali Khan. He wanted military protection, so that the mill could be restarted.[127] The Indian Ambassador to Pakistan, Sri Prakasa also took pains over the security of the mill and personally called upon the Finance Minister to discuss the problem. Sri Prakasa gave the Pakistan Commerce Minister, Chundrigar, an assurance on behalf of Birla that the mill would now employ 'Muslim labour to the fullest extent.'[128] Although the mill started once again, the situation remained tense. The mill staff continued to get threatening letters, and Birla had to ask Liaquat Ali to put in a word with the local officials. The experience of his mill with the Pakistani authorities underscored the sense of frustration that Birla felt over the crucial issue of economic co-operation between the two newly independent countries. 'There is so much work for both the countries', he told Liaquat Ali, 'that it would be foolish to continue to fight and not settle down to the real task.'[129]

THE ECONOMIC BALANCE SHEET OF PARTITION

As it happened, the manner in which partition took place and Pakistan came into being took Birla unawares. His best hope had been that the two countries would cooperate in economic and defence matters, somewhat in the same manner as the present day European Economic Community.[130] But such hopes floundered in the face of the bitterness and the violence that accompanied the partition. Nonetheless, the prior considerations which he and his business colleagues gave to the idea of partition left its indelible imprint on the consequences of partition. This can be seen from the fact that the overall cost of partition to Indian big business was relatively small. With Calcutta remaining in India, there was little that business lost. In overall economic terms, Indian big business enjoyed a distinct advantage. This is clear from a number of indices. Over 90.4 per cent of the total industry of undivided India remained within India. In 1945 there existed a total of 14,677 industrial establishments in India, out of which 13,263 or 90.4 per cent remained in India while Pakistan got 1414 or 9.6 per cent. Of the total industrial employment of 3,141,774, the share of India was 2,935,729 or 93.5 per cent while that of Pakistan stood at 206,045 or 6.5 per cent.[131] Of the total joint-stock companies before partition, as many as 22,674 companies with a combined paid-up capital of Rs 56,953 lakhs remained within India, while 2867 companies with a total paid-up capital of Rs 1596 lakhs went to Pakistan. In terms of basic infrastructure too India again had the edge. For instance, in electricity generation India got 94.7 per cent of the total installed plant capacity in kilowatts, while 5.3 per cent was Pakistan's share (of this 4.8 per cent to West Pakistan and 0.5 per cent to East Pakistan).[132] In the area of transportation, out of the total railways route mileage of 41,141 in undivided India, over 34,157 miles stayed within India and 6981 miles went to Pakistan. In terms of engines and wagons, 7248 locomotives stayed in India and Pakistan received 1339. Likewise, India got 20,166 coach vehicles and 2,10,799 goods vehicles, while Pakistan's share was 4281 and 40,221 respectively.[133]

This pattern was repeated in specific sectors of industry. In textiles out of the total business establishments, 1656 remained within India and 46 went to Pakistan. In the case of engineering establishments, 1734 remained within India while Pakistan got 278. Of the total chemicals establishments, 1009 remained in India and 56 went to Pakistan. Out of the total of 108 jute mills in undivided India, none went to Pakistan; of the 394 cotton mills, 380 remained in India with less than 5 per cent going to Pakistan; of the 280 mills producing silk, 274 stayed in India; Pakistan got only 10 of the 166 sugar mills; out of 25 cement factories, 19 remained in India; of the 175 glass factories, most remained in India; all the 49 paper mills of undivided India remained in India, as did all the 18 iron and steel mills; 38 match factories remained in India, while eight went to Pakistan; of the heavy chemical factories, 38 stayed in India and two went to Pakistan; 28 paint factories remained in India, while Pakistan got four; 93 rubber factories remained in India while the share of Pakistan was 21; 30 heavy engineering factories remained in India while Pakistan got four. In certain areas, the contrasts were particularly striking such as in the case of the automobile industry in which India had an installed capacity of 36,854 automobiles per year, while Pakistan had no capacity at all.[134]

However, there were temporary difficulties. The jute industry in Calcutta saw its supply of raw material threatened, as 70 per cent of raw jute production was based in East Pakistan. But Indian industrialists were reassured that supply was likely to continue, and India would continue to be the main buyer of East Pakistan's raw jute. Moreover, jute cultivation could be developed in Indian Bengal. In any case, by the 1940s, jute was more or less a sunset industry. In overall terms, Birla felt confident that the country had the basic resources needed to put India firmly on the path of rapid capitalist development and he looked to the future with much optimism.

Notes and References

[1] Birla to Reginald Clark, 14 January 1935, Birla Papers, File No. 5.

[2] 'Notes of Conversation With Malaviyaji on 17 October 1927, Banaras' by Birla, Birla Papers, Series Very Very Important Correspondence, File No. 10.

[3] His early views on the communal problem bear close similarity to those of the Punjab Unionist leader, Fazl-i-Husain. In the 1930s, Fazl-i-Husain also wanted a re-adjustment of boundaries and a 'Muslim India' existing as a separate entity within India. For details see Aziz Husain, *Fazl-i-Husain: A Political Biography* (Bombay, 1946), pp. 248–9.

[4] Ayesha Jalal, *The Sole Spokesman Jinnah, the Muslim League and the Demand for Pakistan* (Cambridge, 1985). For a background to the communal problem see Uma

Kaura, *Muslims and Indian Nationalism, The Emergence of the Demand for India's Partition 1928–40* (New Delhi, 1977), Prabha Dixit, *Communalism: A Struggle for Power* (New Delhi, 1974). Also see K.K. Aziz, *The Making of Pakistan: A Study in Nationalism* (London, 1967) and Hector Bolitho, *Jinnah: Creator of Pakistan* (London, 1954).

[5] Birla to C. Rajagopalachari, 24 January 1936, Birla Papers, Series II, File No. H–10.

[6] Birla to Mahadev Desai, 11 January 1938, in G.D. Birla, *Bapu: A Unique Association*, Vol. III, pp. 142–4

[7] He was convinced that it was time that 'the whole process of the achievement of the goal should be expedited even though we have to adopt some short cuts and make accommodations.' Birla in his private notes entitled 'Questions for Bapu', n.d., Birla Papers, Series Miscellaneous, File No. 130.

[8] Birla to C. Rajagopalachari, 12 October 1938, Birla Papers, Series II, File No. R–8.

[9] We have seen his involvement with the Nehru Report and his participation at the Round Table Conference.

[10] 'The Present Impasse', note given by Birla to the Viceroy's Secretary, n.d., Birla Papers, Series Miscellaneous, File No. 130. Birla's private notes cited in this section, many of which are not dated, appear to have been written by him in the late 1930s.

[11] Interview with Viceroy on 11 November 1939, Birla Papers, File No. 38. Birla wrote in his notes: 'I told him very frankly that India was the only Hindu country in the world and when Englishmen talked about its ancient civilization and traditions, they mean the Hindu civilization and nothing else ... I was not prepared to accept the position that 25% of the population should check our advance. We were quite prepared to satisfy them on reasonable grounds. But we can not give the position of majority that they were demanding.' Similarly, in 1938, he wrote to Arthur Moore: 'But what Hindus are not prepared to do is to admit the claim of Muslims to be treated as if they were a majority community. The fact that they are a minority must be realized. In democracy it is the majority which is generally bound to dominate ... What they want is a dominating position.' Birla to Arthur Moore, 13 December 1938, Birla Papers, Series Foreign Correspondence.

[12] G.D. Birla, 'My Analysis of the Situation', n.d., Birla Papers, Series Miscellaneous, File No. 127.

[13] G.D. Birla, 'The Present Impasse', Birla Papers, Series Miscellaneous, File No. 130.

[14] *Ibid.*

[15] *Ibid.*

[16] G.D. Birla, 'Notes After Meeting Mahatma Gandhi', n.d., Birla Papers, Series Miscellaneous, File No. 127. Also see Birla, 'My Analysis of the Situation', n.d., Birla Papers, Series Miscellaneous, File No. 127. Discussing the situation with Cripps in December 1939 Birla told him that the Congress may have made a mistake in excluding non-Congress Muslims from the provincial cabinets in 1937, and this led the Muslims to demand the power to veto legislation. He said that now he saw only one solution—the separation of the Hindu and Muslim nations 'with the cessation of districts and appropriate population movements, followed perhaps by a loose federation holding the minimum powers necessary.' R.J. Moore, *Churchill, Cripps and India, 1939–1945* (New York, 1979), pp. 11–12.

[17] G.D. Birla, 'The Present Impasse', Birla Papers, Series Miscellaneous, File No. 130.

[18] This support encouraged the Muslim leaders that 'they can either secure a position of virtual majority or they can check the constitutional advance', 'The Present Impasse', Birla Papers, Series Miscellaneous, File No. 130.

[19] Birla to Sir George Schuster, 4 March 1940, Birla Papers, File No. 38.

[20] For an analysis of the Congress' involvement in Rajkot, see J.R. Wood, 'Indian Nationalism in the Princely Context: The Rajkot Satyagraha of 1938–39' in R. Jeffery (ed.), *People, Princes and Paramount Power: Society and Politics in the Indian Princely States* (Delhi, 1977).

[21] *Ibid.* During a talk with T.T. Krishnamachari he discussed how some states were helping the League and pointed out that the parliamentary secretary to Sikander Hyat Khan was also the secretary of the Chamber of Princes; see Birla's notes of his talk in Birla Papers, Series Miscellaneous, File No. 127.

[22] G.D. Birla, 'The Present Impasse', Birla Papers, Series Miscellaneous, File No. 127. Also Birla to Schuster, 4 March 1940, Birla Papers, File No. 38.

[23] Birla to Halifax, 2 May 1940, Birla Papers, File No. 38.

[24] Birla, 'Talk With Mahatmaji on 26 March 1940', Birla Papers, Series Miscellaneous, File No. 130

[25] Birla to Hicks, 1 May 1940, Birla Papers, File No. 38.

[26] The nature or composition of this authority was not explained by him; see 'The Present Impasse', Birla Papers, Series Miscellaneous, File No. 127.

[27] Notes by Birla, n.d., Birla Papers, Series Miscellaneous, File No. 127.

[28] G.D. Birla, 'Talks With Mahatma, 26 March 1940', Birla Papers, Series Miscellaneous, File No. 130.

[29] 'Notes on Meeting With Mahatma Gandhi', n.d., Birla Papers, Series Miscellaneous, File No. 130.

[30] Birla's 'Notes on Talks With Gandhiji', 26 March 1940, Birla Papers, Series Miscellaneous, File No. 130.

[31] Birla to Thakurdas, 18 December 1940, Birla Papers, Series II, File No. T–5. Thakurdas appears to have been in contact with Liaquat Ali Khan, the prominent League leader

[32] Birla to Mahadev Desai, 24 June 1941, *Bapu*, Vol. IV, p. 199.

[33] Birla, Notes on Meeting With Gandhi, 25 December 1940, *Bapu*, Vol. IV, pp. 185–7.

[34] Rajagopalachari pressed for an understanding between the Congress and the League to open the way for Congress participation in the Indian government and defence. The League's claim for separation of certain areas and the Muslim's right of self-determination was to be conceded. Rajagopalachari declared that he was against 'compelling people of a territorial unit to remain in the Indian Union against their declared and established will.' Rajmohan Gandhi, *The Rajaji Story* (Bombay, 1984), p. 85.

[35] The two men had shared a close relationship. Birla had supported him during 1937–9 at a time when most of his colleagues in the Congress displayed 'most unappreciative and graceless conduct' concerning his tenure as the Premier of Madras. For instance, see Birla to Rajagopalachari, 25 November 1937, Birla Papers, Series Very Very Important Correspondence, File No. 11.

[36] Birla to Thakurdas, 8 November 1941, Birla Papers, Series 2, File No. T–5.

[37] Birla to Gandhi, 28 February 1942, *Bapu*, Vol. IV, pp. 283–4.

[38] For instance, he gathered from indirect sources that 'Jinnah was slightly critical ... but was not entirely hostile' to the formula. The Liberals in England, he cheerfully told Rajapolachari, were also in favour of his scheme, and he commended it to prominent Congressmen such as K.M. Munshi. Birla to K.M. Munshi, 6 March 1942, Birla Papers, Series 2, File No. M–13.

[39] Birla to Thakurdas, 10 November 1942, Birla Papers, Series II, File No. T–5. In November 1942 Birla wrote to Lord Wedgewood: 'Rajagopalachari is now working very hard to bring about a solution of the present deadlock. I am helping him. He wants to go to England, but do you think it would do any good? If the Prime Minister would seriously put his mind to this job with sympathy and determination, I think the problem could be solved. I have advised him not to go unless he got some encouragement from those who are in power.' Birla to Lord Wedgewood, 14 November 1942, Birla Papers, Series Foreign Correspondence, File No. W–22.

[40] Later the *Eastern Economist* sympathized with Rajagopalachari who it said was the Congress politician who had tried very hard to understand Jinnah even at the risk of making the 'greatest sacrifice of his life—the abandonment of the well-earned role of a Congress spokesman.' Jinnah, it continued, had emerged from these negotiations as one not interested in negotiations and had made it clear that he 'wanted his proposition of Pakistan to be accepted absolutely, leaving him to define it in future according to his convenience and the contingencies of his own party politics.' *Eastern Economist*, 14 April 1944.

[41] In their talks Liaquat Ali had claimed that even Congress Muslims wanted separation which prompted Birla to write to Mahadev Desai. 'Besides, we should not forget,' he told Desai, 'that the Muslims—every one of them—now want it.' Birla to Mahadev Desai, 14 July 1942, *Bapu*, Vol. IV, pp. 315–7.

[42] Gandhi to Birla, 16 July 1942, *ibid*, pp. 318–20.

[43] Birla to Padampat Singhania, 25 September 1942, Birla Papers, Series II, File No. S–20 A. No details seem to exist about the exact nature of these talks. Jinnah later claimed before Nehru that Birla was in favour of Pakistan, see Birla to Nehru, 3 June 1947, Birla Papers, Series II, File No. N–4.

[44] Birla's Notes, n.d., Birla Papers, Series Miscellaneous, File No. 124.

[45] *Eastern Economist*, 29 September 1944.

[46] Note by Birla, n.d., but probably written before the Cabinet Mission, Birla Papers, Series Miscellaneous, File No. 124.

[47] Birla to Badridas Goenka, 10 January 1946, Birla Papers, Series II, File No. G–1.

[48] The Simla Conference proposed the setting up of an entirely Indian Executive Council except for the Viceroy and the Commander-in-Chief. It broke down in view of Jinnah's demand that the League must have the right to choose all the Muslim members and that within the Council all decisions opposed by the Muslim members would need a two-third majority. For details see Anita Inder Singh, *The Origins of Partition*, pp. 118–24.

[49] Birla to Patel, 14 September 1945, Birla Papers, Series II, File No. P–7. In 1945–6 Birla was instrumental in the collection of funds for Patel for a variety of reasons—for the Jawahar Purse Fund, the 1946 elections and for the Congress Central Parliamentary Board. These collections were made at the behest of Patel himself—the main fund-raiser of the Congress. In the 1946 elections Birla was responsible for the 'Calcutta quota' while his brother Rameshwardas was one of Patel's key men in Bombay. Birla used his strong Marwari network and enlisted the help of the Ruias, Poddars, Jalans, Seksarias, Somanis and the important Berar leader Brijlal Biyani. He also advised Patel that the best method for conducting the fund collection drive was by centralizing collections at the national level rather than letting the provincial leaders get involved. Birla to Patel, 17 October 1945, Birla Papers, Series II, File No. P–7.

[50] Ramkrishna Dalmia, *Some Notes and Reminiscences*, p. 33.

[51] Birla to Rajagopalachari, 12 November 1946, Birla Papers, Series II, File No. R–5.

[52] For instance, see Birla's speech to the fourth annual meeting of the Birla-controlled United Commercial Bank Ltd., 18 April 1947, in the *Eastern Economist*, 25 April 1947.

[53] Birla to Mahadev Desai, 11 January 1938, in G.D. Birla, *Bapu: A Unique Association*, Vol. III, pp. 142–4.

[54] This idea was first suggested by Claude Markovits in a preliminary form in his 'Businessmen and the Partition of India' (mimeographed), paper presented at IIM–Ahmedabad, March 1989.

[55] *Eastern Economist.*

[56] The suspicions of big business were confirmed by the policies of the Muslim League. For instance, at the end of 1943 the premiers of the five Muslim League provinces met at Delhi and Lahore to discuss the economic problems of their provinces. The majority opinion was that they should 'evolve a common economic policy' for their provinces. Such policies struck at the very root of the principle of centralized state planning that was espoused by big business. On the Conference see, *Eastern Economist*, 17 December 1943.

[57] Birla spoke of the role of the centre as early as 1934 when he said that 'we cannot improve our lot until we decide to take mass action, well thought out, well planned, as part of a scheme of co-ordination launched with the necessary authority to make it a success. Government intervention thus becomes necessary.' G.D. Birla, 'A Plea for Planning' in his *A Path to Prosperity* (1950).

[58] *Eastern Economist* published a series of seven articles in mid-1943, just a few months before the Bombay Plan was published, to highlight the fundamental importance of planning. They stressed that planning by the state was absolutely essential since 'private capitalism has failed to meet the needs of the community and in spite of all administrative inefficiency, planned economy will make possible a much greater rate of economic progress, because it could provide for a far more rapid rate of capital formation than could be possible under private capitalism.' They further emphasized that the 'entire state machinery will remain fully amenable to democratic controls' and 'private enterprise will function under defined limits subject to overall co-ordination' by the centre. See 'The State and the Private Sector', 13 August 1943, *Eastern Economist*. For the articles on planning see the issues from 2 July to 13 August 1943.

[59] The researches of Aditya Mukherjee and Raghabendra Chattopadhyaya demonstrate this quite clearly. See Aditya Mukherjee, 'Indian Capitalist Class and the Public Sector', *Economic and Political Weekly*, Vol. II, No. 3 (17 January 1976), pp. 67–73, and 'Indian Capitalist Class and Congress on Planning and Public Sector, 1930–47' in K.N. Panikkar (ed.), *National and Left Movements in India* (New Delhi, 1980), pp 45–79. R. Chattopadhyaya, 'Attitude of Indian Business Towards Economic Planning, 1930–1956' (mimeographed), paper presented at the IIM-Ahmedabad seminar on 'Business and Politics in India: A Historical Perspective', 29–31 March 1989.

[60] J.R.D. Tata recollects that it was Birla's initiative in December 1942 that brought together the authors of the Bombay Plan. R.M. Lala, *Beyond the Blue Skies: A Life of J.R.D. Tata* (New Delhi, 1992). Tata was approached by Birla and Thakurdas and the businessmen first met at Bombay House, the headquarters of Tata Sons. Among those present were Lala Shri Ram, A.D. Shroff, Kasturbhai Lalbhai, Ardeshir Dalal and John Mathai, in addition to Birla, Thakurdas and Tata. An 'Informal Committee' was set up to formulate the draft of the plan and the Tatas provided the secretarial support and the help of their statistical department. Many of the background papers were prepared by John Mathai, then in the employment of Tata Sons. Among those who helped Mathai was P.S. Lokanathan, a Birla employee and the editor of *Eastern Economist*. R. Chattopadhyaya,

'Attitude of Big Business Towards Economic Planning, 1930–1956' (mimeographed), paper presented at the seminar on 'Business and Politics in India: A Historical Perspective' at the IIM Ahmedabad, March 1989.

[61] G.D. Birla, Purshotamdas Thakurdas, J.R.D. Tata *et al. A Plan for Economic Development of India*, Parts I and II (Bombay, 1944 and 1945). Also see *Eastern Economist*, 28 January 1944.

[62] The comprehensive nature of the Plan was explained by Birla in a speech delivered at the 1944 annual session of FICCI in which he declared that the target of the Plan was 'that the people in this country should be ensured a minimum in respect of food, clothing, shelter, education, health and other social matters. That they should get about 2888 calories of balanced food per capita, 30 yards of cloth per man and decent accommodation of 100 square feet per head, guarantee of good health by proper provision of medical facilities in the shape of hospitals, dispensaries ... water and sanitary arrangements, adequate education and reasonable leisure. We estimate that if the present income that is about Rs 65 per capita is raised to about Rs 130 it should be sufficient to cover all these needs.' G.D. Birla, 'The Plan Explained', *Eastern Economist*, 10 March 1944.

[63] To augment agricultural production it suggested increasing the size of agricultural holdings and readjustment of the areas under cultivation of different crops. It even suggested the introduction of co-operative farming even if it involved a degree of compulsion.

[64] Alongside consumer goods industries were also to be developed. Small-scale and cottage industries were to be promoted so that both 'heavy and light industries move forward in a balanced way.'

[65] For instance, the state was to control key industries and public utilities and exercise overall control over economic processes. The authors of the Plan were, however, careful to point out that even in key industries private capital was to be allowed to invest if it was forthcoming, and in such areas they did not want state ownership. See R. Chattopadhyaya, 'Attitude of Big Business Towards Economic Planning.' For a study of the Bombay Plan and other non-official plans such as the 'People's Plan' promoted by M.N. Roy and the 'Gandhian Plan' of S.N. Agarwal, see A.H. Hanson, *The Process of Planning: A Study of India's Five Year Plans 1950–1964* (London, 1966), pp. 41–4. To popularize the Bombay Plan, Minoo Masani published a shorter version entitled *Picture of A Plan* (Bombay, 1945). On the Bombay Plan, also see P.A. Wadia and K.T. Merchant, *The Bombay Plan: A Criticism* (Bombay, 1945). Also see Dwijendra Tripathi, 'Congress and the Indian Industrialists (1885–1947)', (mimeographed), paper presented at IIM–Ahmedabad seminar, 1989.

[66] 'Businessmen in Conference', *Eastern Economist*, 10 March 1944.

[67] When the Bombay Plan was discussed in the Central Legislative Assembly many Muslim League members objected to the Plan's basic assumption with regard to the powers of the centre. Ziauddin Khan moved a resolution against it on the ground that it proposed a national government whose jurisdiction in economic matters extended to the whole of India. Muhammad Nauman declared that 'we representing the Muslims are opposed to the very principle of it as it envisages a central and unitary government.' Shaikh Fazl-i-Haq Piracha also said that the establishment of a single national government would not be acceptable and that after the war the Muslim-majority provinces would insist on autonomy in the economic field. Manoranjan Jha, *Role of Central Legislature in the Freedom Struggle*, pp. 278–9.

[68] Among the earliest studies of the economic consequences of the division of India was one carried out in mid-1943 by Charles H. Behre, of Columbia University. Behre demonstrated that most of the coal, iron, ferro-alloys and other industrial raw materials would come under India while Pakistan would take the oil reserves. Pakistan, he said, would desperately need India's resources in a 'closed-trade' system to survive. He concluded that without this Bengal 'would industrially speaking, die.' The *Eastern Economist*, 24 September 1943. Among contemporary observers R. Coupland was one of the first to direct his attention to this problem. See his 'Note on the Financial prospects of Pakistan' (Appendix IV) in R. Coupland, *The Future of India: Report on the Constitutional Problem in India*, Part III (Oxford, 1943).

[69] H.M. Mody and J. Mathai, *A Memorandum on the Economic and Financial Aspects of Pakistan*, (Bombay, 1945). Mody and Mathai had originally submitted their findings to the Sapru Committee on Constitutional Reforms in 1944 (Later in September 1945 they published their findings independently). The Economic subcommittee of the Sapru Committee consisted of Mody, Mathai and N.R. Sarkar. While the main Committee headed by Sapru reported against the partition of India, Mody and Mathai disagreed with this recommendation and signed a note of dissent. They stated that 'if a scheme which pre-supposed the political unity of India was not acceptable to the Muslim community, and if the results of the forthcoming elections were to vindicate generally the Muslim League position, separation as a means of ending the political deadlock should not be ruled out.' They clearly declared that the priorities of the time were such that the communal deadlock should be settled immediately. 'As things stand at present,' they wrote in their note of dissent, 'the settlement of our political problems admits of no delay. Issues of greater consequences and urgency which may affect the future of India permanently are facing us, and it is of the highest importance that the present political deadlock should not be allowed to continue and that the direction of political affairs should, without further delay, be placed in the hands of Indian leaders who have the confidence of the country.' They suggested partition on the basis of districtwise division of Muslim areas to form contiguous blocs in Muslim-majority provinces. They also advocated cooperation on economy and defence between the two new states. For this they proposed the setting up of an Inter-Governmental Council. *Constitutional Proposals of the Sapru Committee* (Bombay, 1946), pp. 343–5. In another note which Mody made alone he frankly declared that 'I am not in favour of ignoring the Pakistan demand. If our approach to the political problem of India is to be realistic, we cannot afford to forget the events of the last two or three years.' See Mankekar, *Homi Mody*, p. 201. N.R. Sarkar, the third member of the Economic subcommittee of the Sapru Committee disagreed with Mody and Mathai's recommendations. Sarkar declared that division, both provincewise and especially districtwise as proposed by Mody and Mathai would be highly prejudicial to Pakistan. He argued that Pakistan would have only 5 per cent of the mineral wealth of undivided India and even in oil, in which it was supposed to be in an advantageous position it would not have sufficient supplies. The division of India, he claimed, would be disadvantageous because of the economic interdependence of the countries which were 'almost inextricably bound up and interdependent.' Districtwise division would not make Pakistan economically feasible and Sarkar concluded that Pakistan was not a practical proposition either economically or financially. For Sarkar's view see *Sapru Committee in Constitutional Reforms*, Appendix III. Also see K.N. Chaudhuri, 'Economic Problems of Indian Independence' in C.H. Philips and M.D. Wainright (ed.), *The Partition of India. Policies and Perspectives, 1935–1947* (London, 1970).

70 They conducted their feasibility study of Pakistan by considering (a) its budgetary position, i.e. public revenue and expenditure; (b) the standard of living of its people, i.e. economic conditions; and finally (c) its defence requirements. Each of these indices was studied to consider the scenario of a province-wise division as well as one based on a division according to contiguous districts. The study clearly stated that both the eastern and the western zones of Pakistan could maintain their provincial administrations and their pre-war standards of living but their revenue would not be sufficient for their defence needs. Neither would their resources allow any large-scale industrial development in the future. These impediments could, however, be removed by co-operation with India in defence and economic matters. Mody and Mathai concluded that first, in terms of provincial and central expenditure (excluding defence), the two zones of Pakistan would be viable whether formed district-wise or province-wise. Second, in terms of food production, industrial employment and trade, the standard of living of Pakistan would compare favourably with India, if formed province-wise. However, if formed district-wise, Pakistan would be equally well placed in food production but not so in other respects. Third, the future economic development of Pakistan (formed on either basis) would depend upon the free movement of trade and economic co-operation with India.

71 Coupland also believed that 'while North-East India including Calcutta would constitute an effective partnership with Pakistan with a balanced economy, North-East India without Calcutta would be an almost wholly agrarian appendage, served by the one minor port of Chittagong.' R. Coupland, *Report on the Constitutional Problem in India*, Part III, pp. 95–6.

72 Birla to S.N. Sinha, 12 August 1946, Birla Papers, Series Miscellaneous, File No. 119–A. The *Eastern Economist* lauded the interim ministry headed by Nehru as 'homogeneous and judged by any standards, contained some of the best men of India, who could, in ability and integrity do good to administration in any country.' *Eastern Economist*, 3 January 1947.

73 In a detailed note Birla identified some of the most pressing economic problems that faced the country and suggested the measures the ministers should take. The most pressing problem in his view was of food production. He wanted the government to set a target to increase food production by 30 per cent within five years. He wanted other consumer goods such as cloth and essential items to also be treated on a priority basis. The remedy lay, according to Birla, in increased production. Birla stressed that if the National Government was 'full of determination, it had competence and efficiency and had the capacity and the will to mobilize co-operation from every quarter and thus with its popularity and earnestness ensured the stability and continuity of its administration and above all, it had external and internal peace, then it could within 15 years build up a new India, healthy, educated, clean, beautiful and prosperous.' See Birla's note to the Interim Government cited in the 'Economic Problems before the Interim Government' in *Eastern Economist*, 6 September 1946.

74 Birla to Devdas Gandhi, 31 July 1946, Birla Papers, Series Miscellaneous, File No. 119–A (emphasis original).

75 Birla to Cripps, 27 June 1946, Birla Papers, Series Foreign Correspondence, File No. C–3. For details on the Cabinet Mission see R.K. Perti, 'Cabinet Mission' in B.N. Pandey (ed.), *A Centenary History of t he Indian National Congress (1885–1985)*, Vol. III (New Delhi, 1985), pp. 640–82.

76 Note by Birla, undated but seems clearly addressed to the Cabinet Mission, Birla Papers, Series Miscellaneous, File No. 130. In this note, Birla advocates the intervertion

of the United Nations to solve the communal tangle, in case Britain was unsuccessful in solving it.

[77] Birla to Cripps, 6 June 1946, Birla Papers, Series Foreign Correspondence, File No. C–3. The *Eastern Economist* unequivocally condemned Jinnah for his intransigence during the negotiations with the Cabinet Mission. 'Mr Jinnah imagines he is in 1707 calling out Aurangzeb from his grave, erasing with a wave of his hand the whole disgraceful period of history since the Great Collapse and resuming the grand career of the Mughal Empire at the point where the hand of destiny stopped him from his appointed mission of hunting down the Hindus into the Indian Ocean' it wrote and asked the Congress leadership to 'call the bluff.' *Eastern Economist*, 3 May 1946.

[78] *Eastern Economist*, 31 May 1946.

[79] *Eastern Economist*, 17 May 1946. The *Eastern Economist* analysed for its readers the implications of the Cabinet Mission's plan. The centre would have to depend upon the provinces for essentials such as financial aid, customs revenue etc and it would be very difficult for such a state to survive for very long since the units could prove very difficult. Studying the Federal and Concurrent Legislative lists of the Government of India Act of 1935, on which the journal assumed much of the division of power between the centre and the units would be based, it declared that the vesting to the provincial units of currency, coinage, legal tender, public debt, census, import and export, customs, tariff, insurance, excise duty, income, factories, labour disputes etc would mean that India would no longer be one economic unit. This would be extremely harmful for the economy. For instance, it argued that the omission of currency from the jurisdiction of the Union Centre would lead to the lack of a common structure of prices and it would thus not be possible to avert steep rise and fall in prices. Moreover, the existence of diverse monetary blocs would lead to the creation of 'so many economic sovereign bodies negotiations among which for common monetary ideals will be lifted right out of the economic plane.' Moreover, each province would legislate over banking, insurance and company laws which would restrict the free movement of capital and other productive resources from one unit to another which was so vital for economic development. Customs and tariffs under the units would, declared the journal, 'distort the :ry pace and direction' of economic development. The economic fragmentation that would come to be in case the Mission's proposals were accepted, declared the *Eastern Economist*, would deal a 'fatal blow at the economic cohesion and strength of the country' and would 'deliberately take the county in reverse, retrograde direction of disintegration'. See 'The Cabinet Proposals II: The Economic Aspect', *Eastern Economist*, 31 May 1946; also see 'India 1946. Political survey 7' in *Eastern Economist*, 3 January 1947.

[80] Birla to Cripps, 12 December 1946, Birla Papers, Series Foreign Correspondence, File No. C–3.

[81] Suranjan Das, *Communal Riots in Bengal, 1905–1947* (Delhi, 1991), p. 171. Also see Begum Shaista Suhrawardy Ikramullah, *Huseyn Shaheed Suhrawardy, A Biography* (Karachi, 1991), pp. 54–7.

[82] The *Eastern Economist* demanded from the Central Government the immediate dismissal of the Suhrawardy ministry and the imposition of Governor's rule in Bengal. In its view, Suhrawardy and his ministers should not only be dismissed from their positions but 'should be charged and tried for incitement to murder and violence'. It also asked the Congress to concede Jinnah's demand to nominate all Muslims in the interim cabinet as, it explained, 'once the principle of taking into the Government minority groups on *communal* bais is accepted, there is no point in sticking to the right to choose

any person without regard to the feelings of the minority community.' *Eastern Economist*, 23 August 1946.

[83] Birla to Governor of Bengal, 18 August 1946, Birla Papers, Series II, File No. B–11. The *Eastern Economist* blamed the ministry for much of the ills of the 'problem province' and especially for the complete breakdown of law and order, see *Eastern Economist*, 18 October 1946.

[84] Birla to Cripps, 2 November 1946, Birla Papers, Series Foreign Correspondence, File No. C–3.

[85] Birla to L.P. Misra, 26 May 1946, Birla Papers, Series Foreign Correspondence, File No. C–3.

[86] Birla to L.P. Misra, 26 May 1946, Birla Papers, Series Foreign Correspondence, File No. C–3

[87] Birla to Chatterjee, 2 March 1947, Birla Papers, Series II, File No. C–1.

[88] Birla to L.P. Misra, 26 May 1946, Birla Papers, Series Foreign Correspondence, File No. C–3

[89] Birla to Cripps, 21 October 1946, Birla Papers, Series Foreign Correspondence, File No. C–3.

[90] Birla to Burrows, 15 November 1946 and Birla to Suhrawardy, 15 November 1946, Birla Papers, Series II, File No. B–10. For an account of communal tensions see Suranjan Das, *Communal Riots in Bengal, 1905–1947*, pp. 192–206. Also see Begum Shaista Suhrawardy Ikramullah, *Huseyn Shaheed Suhrawardy, A Biography*.

[91] Birla to Krishnaraj M.D. Thackersay, November 1946 , Birla Papers, Series II, File No. K–14.

[92] Birla to Cripps, 9 November 1946, Birla Papers, Series Foreign Correspondence, File No. C–3.

[93] Birla to Patel, 12 November 1946, Birla Papers, Series II, File No. P–7. Hindu self-defence had been one of Birla's main concerns all through the 1940s. He had always stressed the need to build up Hindu strength, so that they could protect themselves fully in 'any emergency' and fight to defend their rights. He wanted the Hindus to 'build up their strength and develop self-confidence in their capacity to defend their interest.' Birla to C. Parmeshwaran, 10 October 1946, Birla Papers, Series II, File No. P–6. He wanted the Hindus to 'rely on themselves' and was confident that 'the Hindus are capable of defending themselves even though the whole Muslim community may stand up against them.' Birla to C. Parmeshwaran, 5 October 1946, *ibid*. Birla's support to the idea of Hindu self-defence was manifested in the consistent help he gave to a Hindu para-military school—the Bhonsale Military School. This school had been established in 1937 for the purpose of giving Hindu boys physical and military training and its chief patron was the Maharaja of Gwalior. The school, headed by B.S. Moonje, the Hindu Mahasabha leader, provided training to students in guerrilla tactics and other advanced military skills. The school benefitted from the Birla family's regular support throughout the 1940s. Jugalkishore Birla provided a monthly subscription to the school. In 1947 Moonje paid tribute to Jugalkishore Birla in the following terms: 'He is the one person of the one family called the Birla family who are unique in their reputation of earning money in mints and distributing equally in mints in the public cause, though Seth Jugalkishoreji Birla's charities are almost entirely concerned with the cause of the Hindus.' Moonje to Birla, 28 February 1947, File No. M–21, Series II. In 1944 the Birla Education Trust had considered taking over the school. In mid-1944 Birla and Moonje held negotiations to explore possibilities of a take-over. The evidence suggests that these negotiations did not

lead to a change in management. See Moonje to Maharaja Scindia of Gwalior, 13 June 1944, *ibid*; also Birla to Moonje, 21 July 1944, *ibid*. Also see the 'Proposed Changes in the Memorandum of Association and Fundamental Rules of the Central Hindu Military Education Society' n.d. Birla Papers, Series Important Correspondence, File No. 13–M. Although the Birla Education Trust eventually did not take over the school, the Birlas continued their support to the school. For instance, in September 1946 Birla donated Rs 10,000 to Moonje for the school. Birla to Moonje, 16 September 1946, *ibid*. Birla also pleaded with the Congress members of the Interim Ministry to help the school with a government grant to enable it to tide over financial difficulties. 'Don't worry. Your school will not be closed,' he assured Moonje. Moonje to Birla, 16 December 1945, *ibid*. Also Moonje to Birla, 22 December 1946, Birla Papers, Series II, File No. M–21. He also followed the school's application to the Central Government for arms licences for service rifles for target practice. Moonje was apprehensive that Muslim ministers like Liaquat Ali and Azad may be hostile to his request. 'But', he wrote to Birla, 'I have full faith in your ability and skill of moulding the minds of Congressmen and particularly of Maulana Azad.' Moonje to Birla, 6 January 1947, *ibid*. In January 1947 he again took up the issue of arms licences with Patel—the Home Minister. Birla to Moonje, 8 January 1947, *ibid*. In April 1947 he assured Moonje that the Home Minister 'was considering your request very sympathetically'. Birla to Moonje, 15 April 1947, *ibid*. He pursued the case relentlessly until Moonje got the licences later in the year.

[94] The budget proposed new taxes on business activities and the appointment of a commission to enquire into allegations regarding evasion of taxes and to devise means of recovering them. The most important tax proposed in the budget was a special income tax of 25 per cent on business profits exceeding Rs 1,00,000 per annum. In addition, there was a capital gains tax which taxed profits made from capital transfers of more than Rs 5000 a year and increased corporation tax from one-sixth of the rupee to one-eighth. Export duty on tea was to be raised and the structure of supertaxes was also changed to increase liability on the higher bracket slabs.

[95] The *Eastern Economist* condemned the budget as an attack on the 'saving-investing classes' and for its failure to recognize the role they played in a free enterprise economy. It condemned Laiquat Ali for introducing a budget which was trying to bring 'social justice' at a time of political instability when the common man did not know to which government he would owe allegiance the following year. It accused him of populism, of not verifying facts technically, and characterized his attempt as trying to 'dramatise his own action and ideology' for 'an itch of immortality'. See 'Second Thoughts on the Budget' in the *Eastern Economist*, 14 March 1947. Even the report of the central board of directors of the Reserve Bank of India criticized the budget for 'defeating its own purpose and hindering the formation of capital for productive purposes.' *Capital*, 7 August 1947.

[96] This is confirmed in Wavell's journal entry of 17 and 18 March 1947. See P. Moon (ed.), *Wavell The Viceroy's Journal* (London, 1973), pp. 429–30. For details of business reactions to the interim government's budget see R. Chattopadhyaya, 'Liaquat Ali's Budget of 1947–48, The Tryst With Destiny' in *Social Scientist* (181–2), Vol. 16, No. 6–7 (1988). Also see Claude Markovits, 'Congress Policy Towards Business in the Pre-Independence Era' in R. Sisson and S. Wolpert (ed.), *Congress and Indian Nationalism: The Pre-Independence Phase* (California, 1988).

[97] Birla to Devdas Gandhi, 31 July 1946, Birla Papers, Series Miscellaneous, File No. 119–A.

[98] Birla to Devdas Gandhi, 31 July 1946, Birla Papers, Series Miscellaneous, File No. 119–A.

[99] It declared that 'better administration will be secured immediately by partition and greater balance as between agriculture and industry will be forced on the separate provinces'. 'Bengal Divided' in the *Eastern Economist*, 25 April 1947 and 27 June 1947.

[100] Out of a net sown area of 2.109 million acres in NWFP, 1.025 acres roughly were irrigated; of the total sown area of 5.14 million acres in Sind, 4.446 were irrigated; and in Muslim Punjab the irrigated area was approximately less than 12 million acres.

[101] Based on an analysis of the 1942 industrial statistics, The *Eastern Economist* projected the following picture. It forecast that India would have 857 cotton spinning and weaving mills compared to 15 in Pakistan; 11 jute mills with none in Pakistan; all the 13 sugar mills, 36 iron and steel mills, all the 19 paper mills, 57 cement factories in India with 8 going to Pakistan and 112 glass factories in India with 5 in Pakistan.

[102] *Eastern Economist*, 25 April 1947 and 27 June 1947.

[103] G.D. Birla, Basic facts Relating to India and Pakistan, *Eastern Economist*, Pamphlet No. 5 (New Delhi, 1947).

[104] Birla's pamphlet is difficult to understand as it mainly consists of statistical data on India and Pakistan on population, area, agricultural resources, potential water power, industrial distribution, mineral resources, communications, literacy, taxation. It also contains specific data for the two provinces of Bengal and Punjab. The statistics, based largely on government publications, showed that 'Hindu India' would have 'larger population, larger area and larger resources and will in many respects be stronger than the smaller India.' The data demonstrated that except in raw jute and water power resources, India would have a distinct advantage as compared to Pakistan.

[105] The *Capital* commented that it was 'at a loss to understand whether Mr Birla is seeking to reassure Hindustan or warn Pakistan. Perhaps it is a bit of both, and Mr Birla, like most businessmen, is anxious to maintain the economic unity of the country no matter what the political divisions may be.' *Capital*, 11 June 1947.

[106] Sumit Sarkar, 'Popular Movements and National Leadership, 1945–47' *Economic and Political Weekly*, Vol. 17, Nos. 14–16 (annual number, 1982), pp. 667–89. Claude Markovits, 'Businessmen and the Partition of India', paper presented at the IIMA Seminar Series in Business History (IV), 'Business and Politics in India: A Historical Perspective', 29–31 March 1989.

[107] Hasan Ispahani, the Calcutta businessman and financier of Jinnah who in 1947 became Pakistan's first ambassador to the USA, writes that Birla 'was considered by the Congress High Command to be a great financial brain and an economic expert. His views on such matters had almost the sanctity of law in the eyes of the Congress leaders.' M.A.H. Ispahani, 'Factors Leading to the Partition of British India' in C.H. Philips and M.D. Wainright (ed.), *The Partition of India Policies and Perspectives, 1935–1947*, pp. 331–59. For the point of view of a Muslim businessman see M.A.H. Ispahani, *Quaid-e-Azam Jinnah As I Knew Him* (Karachi, 1966).

[108] Birla's crucial role in informally advising the Indian government on the division of assets and liabilities between the two states is made clear from his correspondence of July–August 1947 with H.M. Patel, who was then India's representative on the Steering Committee of the Partition Council that was set up to work out the division. This correspondence is available in Birla Papers, Series II, File No. P–9 and P–10. The Pakistani representative was Chaudhari Muhammad Ali whose account of the proceedings of the Partition Council is available in his *The Emergence of Pakistan* (London, 1967),

especially chapter 9. For details see Ayesha Jalal, *The State of Martial Rule: the origins of Pakistan's political economy of defence* (Cambridge, 1990).

[109] See Tai Yong Tan and Gyanesh Kudaisya, *The Aftermath of Partition in South Asia* (London, Routledge, 2000).

[110] As Birla wrote to G. Stein on 2 September 1947: 'Perhaps people will realize very soon that the whole economy will collapse if this continues for long. In India the standard being very low people do not feel the pinch too much, as long as food and cloth is available, but even those things are now getting scarce.' Birla Papers, Series Foreign Correspondence, File No. 43–S.

[111] Birla to J.K. Anderson, 5 October 1947, Birla Papers, Series Foreign Correspondence, File No. 24–A1.

[112] Birla to K.N. Katju, 29 September 1947, Birla Papers, Series II, File No. K–2.

[113] S.K. Kripalani, Secretary, Ministry of Relief and Rehabilitation, to Birla, 11 and 16 October 1947, Birla Papers, Series II, File No. K–16.

[114] G.B. Pant to Birla, 19 September 1947, Birla Papers, Series II, File No. P–3; also S.K. Kripalani to Birla, 4 October 1947, Birla Papers, Series II, File No. K–16.

[115] K.B. Lall to Birla, 18 September 1947, Birla Papers, Series II, File No. L–12.

[116] Birla to K.N. Katju, 29 September 1947, Birla Papers, Series II, File No. K–2.

[117] Birla to Lady Mountbatten, 18 September 1947 and her reply of 19 September 1947, Birla Papers, Series II, M–26.

[118] In this capacity he worked with Lala Shri Ram, Rajkumari Amrit Kaur, the Health Minister, K.C. Neogy, Minister for Refugees, Hannah Sen, the president of the All India Women's Conference, Sucheta Kriplani, prominent Congresswoman, and a number of important social workers. 'Minutes of Meetings of the Executive Committee of the United Council of Relief and Welfare', September 1947 to March 1948, in Birla Papers, Series II, M–26.

[119] Birla to S.K. Kripalani, 8 November 1947, Birla Papers, Series II, File No. K–16.

[120] Birla to Sri Prakasa, 5 October 1947, Birla Papers, Series II, File No. S–24.

[121] That big business was nervous about the division and had begun preparing in advance for it was clear from the flight of capital that was witnessed in the months preceding the partition. Flights of capital were reported especially from Punjab. By May 1947 at least three premier banks and insurance companies were planning to move their headquarters out of Lahore. In all the flight was estimated to be to the tune of about Rs 250 crores by May. A bank with a working capital of Rs 50 crore was also reportedly moving out. Although we do not have the names of the banks and other companies that were moving out, there is evidence that a number of concerns pulled out. *Eastern Economist*, 16 May 1947.

[122] Birla to J.K. Anderson, 24 April 1947, Birla Papers, Series Foreign Correspondence, File No. 24 A–1.

[123] R.S. Saraiya to Birla, 10 April 1947, Birla Papers, Series II, File No. S–2.

[124] *Ibid.*

[125] Birla to R.K. Shanmukham Chetty, 24 December 1947, Birla Papers, Series II, File No. S–12.

[126] Wire from Birla to Chandulal Trivedi, 22 August 1947; also wire dated 23 August 1947, Birla Papers, Series I, File No. T–15.

[127] Birla to Sri Prakasa, 21 September 1937, Birla Papers, Series II, File No. S–24.

[128] Sri Prakasa to Chundrigar, 4 October 1947 and Sri Prakasa to Birla, 18 September 1947, Birla Papers, Series II, File No. S–24. Mill officials went in deputation to the

Pakistan Prime Minister, the Premier of West Punjab and the local Nawab to resolve the matter.

[129] Birla to Liaquat Ali, 27 November 1947, Birla Papers, Series Important Correspondence, File No. P–2.

[130] Calls for cooperation continued to be raised by business leaders and policy-makers even till August 1947. In June 1947, M.P. Birla advocated co-operation in the jute industry in his presidential speech at the Indian Jute Mills' Association. For details see *Capital*, 11 June 1947. Big business continuously stressed the need for economic co-operation. For instance, Driver, the President of the Indian Chamber of Commerce called the coming Independence in the July 1947 meeting a 'Swaraj scattered, insecure and split into twins and more' and called for co-operation, *Capital*, 24 July 1947. The Report of the Central Board of Directors of the Reserve Bank of India (RBI) also advised economic co-operation. Sir Chintamani Deshmukh, the Chairman of the RBI pressed for the retention of economic unity between the two independent states. He stated that 'despite political division, efforts must not be spared to continue to the fullest extent possible by mutual agreement, the economic unity of India. India and Pakistan, political limbs of what will always remain a geographical and economic unit can hardly afford to forget what the world is discovering after painful experience, that prosperity, like peace, is indivisible.' *Capital*, 7 August 1947. Similar sentiments were expressed by the *Capital* which wrote 'Economically division will create two weaker parts where one much stronger one existed before. Both, therefore, may expect to be faced with financial problems. Trade balances will be upset, and give rise to further difficulties. Customs barriers, currency convertibility and other headaches will arise to try the abilities of administrators of both sides. None of these problems are insoluble, perhaps, but before they can be solved much harm will be done to the existing system which might easily be avoided. This is a problem which actually demands high priority from the Government of both Dominions for as long as uncertainty with regard to the future persists the economic deterioration will continue.' *Capital*, 7 August 1947.

[131] C.N. Vakil, *Economic Consequences of Divided India, A Study of the Economy of India and Pakistan* (Bombay, 1950), p. 247.

[132] The break-up of various types of power generation was as follows: in steam capacity 95.3 per cent to India and 4.7 per cent to Pakistan; in oil 75.8 per cent to India and 24.2 per cent to Pakistan; and in hydroelectricity capacity, 98.1 per cent to India and 1.9 per cent to Pakistan, *ibid,* p. 225.

[133] *Ibid*, pp. 309–40 and pp. 402–5.

[134] There existed a wide disparity between the economic resources of West Pakistan and East Pakistan (later Bangladesh). For further details see N. Ahmed, *An Economic Geography of East Pakistan* (London, 1956) and A. Tayyeb, *Pakistan: A Political Geography* (London, 1966). Much more research needs to be done on the disparities and regional imbalances that existed in post-Independence India, Pakistan and Bangladesh. D.A. Low has highlighted the contrasts that exist in the political systems of the three states in his introduction to *The Political Inheritance of Pakistan* (London, 1991).

10

Hosting the Mahatma

On 15 August 1947, the *Hindustan Times*, the largest circulated newspaper from the capital, carried on its front page accounts of the stirring midnight ceremonies where Jawaharlal Nehru made his famous 'Tryst with Destiny' speech heralding the birth of India as an independent nation. A smaller item gave details of how Gandhi had ushered in independence quietly in a Muslim neighbourhood in Calcutta. The same page carried a signed article by Birla. Entitled, 'The Tasks Ahead', it contained his Independence Day message. His pragmatic tone stands in sharp contrast to Nehru's exuberance. The establishment of the nation-state, Birla wrote, could only be a means to an end. Swaraj by itself meant nothing. It could lead to *Ram Rajya* (nation of peace) or degenerate into *Ravana Rajya* (nation of chaos). A new experiment in nation-building had begun and its success critically depended upon a pragmatic approach by the political leadership to the challenges the new state faced: of ensuring peace, providing education and health-care and bringing about economic transformation in a backward, poverty-stricken land.[1]

Birla and many others missed Gandhi's presence in the capital on Independence Day. However, in just over three weeks, circumstances forced the Mahatma to come to Delhi for what turned out to be his longest stay in the city. In early September en route to riot-stricken Punjab, Gandhi stopped at Delhi. He was met at Shahdara station on the outskirts of the city by Sardar Patel and Rajkumari Amrit Kaur, a prominent member of the Congress, who had alarming news. They told him that there had been an outbreak of large-scale communal violence in Delhi, that the old walled areas had been the scene of murders, and that fires were raging through parts of the city. The Harijan quarters, where he normally stayed, were overflowing with Hindu and Sikh refugees from West Punjab. As the Home Minister, Patel was anxious about Gandhi's safety and he insisted on his staying at Birla House, his other 'Delhi home'.

GANDHI AT BIRLA HOUSE

The Birla family was well prepared to receive the guest and his large *entourage*. Elaborate arrangements had been made for their stay. Members of the family had moved their rooms to the second floor of the house, so the entire first floor could be used by the guests. Rooms were kept ready for Brij Krishna, Gandhi's associate, Gandhi's two secretaries, Pyarelal and Shivbalak Bisen, his personal physician, Sushila Nayar, and his two nieces, Abha and Manu. Another close associate, Miraben, was already staying on the first floor. She had been staying at Birla House since August when she had come to Delhi for a heart examination.[2] Some additional rooms were prepared for any unexpected guests whom Gandhi might invite to stay with him.

A small area had been set aside to serve as a reception room for the many visitors the Mahatma was expected to receive. Gandhi's large room—in which he stayed every time he was at Birla House—had been fitted out according to his tastes. From this room of approximately 25 by 16 feet all furniture had been removed and, instead, mattresses and woven mats placed on the floor. In one corner a cooking stove had been placed and in another two electric heaters kept for use on colder days. The room opened onto a terrace. Here a cot had been placed so that Gandhi could sleep outside if he so chose. Wicker chairs were placed next to it for his guests. To go out to the gardens, Gandhi merely had to step out of the room into a porch which was surrounded by rose beds and then walk under a row of red sandstone.[3]

All housekeeping arrangements were thus well in place. Curfew in parts of the city and communal incidents in the wholesale *subzi mandi* (vegetable market) meant a shortage of vegetables and fruit, and alternative sources were explored. One of Birla's white Packard cars was kept ready for the Mahatma's use. Members of the domestic staff had been allotted specific duties to serve the Mahatma in the days ahead. The lawns had been primed for Gandhi's evening prayers. A small pavilion of grey sandstone had been erected in the garden on which about 20 people could sit. On it had been placed a raised wooden platform, covered with pillows and cushions for Gandhi and his companions. Loud-speakers had been installed, amplifying systems put in place, electricity provided for, seating plans for the public worked out and arrangements made with All India Radio for Gandhi's prayer speeches to be broadcast nationwide.

Gandhi's arrival on 9 September 1947 completely transformed the atmosphere in the Birla home. The large gates of the otherwise exclusive residence were thrown wide open to the public and anyone who desired to see Gandhi could walk in. Streams of visitors poured into the house: the unknown came for a darshan of the Mahatma; refugees, to tell him of their plight; Muslims from the walled city who feared for their lives, to ask for help; deputations of trade unionists and women's organizations, to give petitions; the local and foreign press, to obtain interviews; members of the Cabinet, to seek advice and confer on important matters of state. Frequent visitors included Lord Mountbatten, Patel, Nehru and Azad who came for counsel and to discuss pressing political issues with the Mahatma.

A typical day started early at Birla House. Gandhi woke at 3.30 am every morning. Prayers were held at 3.45 am on the verandah just outside his room which were attended by members of the household. This was followed by a massage, reading of the newspapers, and then breakfast which Gandhi either had in his room or in the garden just outside. Visitors were allowed to come to Birla House from 5.30 am, when Gandhi began his meetings over breakfast, and these continued as he walked in the gardens till 8 am.[4] That Gandhi appreciated the efforts the family had made to make him comfortable was obvious as he perceived their single-minded devotion.[5] He felt that wherever he stayed in the capital, he remained a guest of Birla—whether at the Harijan quarters or at their home.

Given Birla's own strict morning religious routine which involved a reading of several Hindu scriptures, it is not surprising that he often missed the morning prayer meeting. He made it a point, however, to seek his darshan before Gandhi left on his visits to different parts of the city. As he left in Birla's white car, members of the family worried for his safety and silently prayed that he would return alive.[6] Delhi had been the scene of large-scale rioting in the previous weeks. The city had been flooded by refugees—Hindus and Sikhs from areas which had become Pakistan—and Indian Muslims who had lost their homes during the riots. The refugees had occupied the city's schools, colleges, military barracks, dharamshalas, temples, railway platforms and even its pavements. During his visits Gandhi spent time talking with the refugees, urging them to be calm, to shed their anger and repose their trust in God. Upon his return home, he took his afternoon nap after which he was ready to meet those who wanted to see him. The meetings were either held in his room or just outside in the open. On an average, Gandhi received up to 40 visitors a day.

In the evenings 'an almost Biblical atmosphere' overtook Birla House as Gandhi held his prayer meetings in the gardens. The audience at these meetings could vary between less than a hundred (on days of curfew and on Mondays which Gandhi observed as a day of silence) to six hundred on other days, depending on the mood in the city. Once the audience had been seated on the grounds, Gurbachan Singh, one of the attendants, would clear a passage for the Mahatma. Gandhi would then walk down the garden path, accompanied by his two nieces, to take his place on a mattress under the ornamental arch work. Recitations from the *Koran*, the *Gita*, the *Bible*, the *Guru Granth Sahib* and the *Ramdhun*, a chant in praise of the Hindu god Rama, which gave Gandhi much solace in these difficult days, filled the air. After the prayers were over Gandhi would speak to the audience for about fifteen minutes and his words were broadcast to the nation.

On most evenings Birla sat unnoticed amongst the large audience. Concerned about the security of his guest in the hate-filled atmosphere that prevailed in the city, he hid a pistol in his belt and suspiciously observed the people who approached Gandhi.[7] In his speeches, Gandhi took up a number of issues such as removal of food controls, the workings of the government, tensions in Kashmir and the challenge of refugee rehabilitation. However, he spoke most about the communal situation and the need to restore peace and amity. As is well-documented, these were months of extreme personal anguish for Gandhi. Much of what he had worked for in his long political career seemed to be falling apart: he had consistently opposed the partition of the country, and the scale of the disturbances that accompanied it completely bewildered him. The violence he witnessed made him feel 'nothing but agony in his heart'.[8] His thoughts were haunted by the plight of the refugees. At night as he heard the gentle drops of rain on the roof of his large room, he was saddened to think of the plight of the thousands who slept in open camps throughout the city without a roof over them. As he drove through the curfew-ridden streets, Delhi appeared as the 'city of the dead'. Day after day he visited the refugee camps and met people who lived in fear, anger and suffering. Camps had been set up all over the city—at Humayun's Tomb, Idgah, Old Fort, Daryaganj, Jamia Millia, Diwan Hall in Chandni Chowk and Kingsway, among other places. The famous Lakshmi Narayan Temple in New Delhi (popularly referred to as the Birla Mandir) had also been converted into a refugee camp. He spoke to thousands during the day and pleaded with them to stop the madness.

He asked the Muslims to stick to their homes even if they 'might be molested by their Hindu neighbours... unto death.'[9] He could not accept the argument that the Muslims should leave India for Pakistan. He pleaded with the minorities to forget and forgive. He even told the Hindu refugees that one day they should return to their homes in Pakistan. He asked them not to eye the evacuee property vacated by the Muslims but to be content with the land on which they were with its 'canopy of sky above their heads'.[10] It was the responsibility of the majority, he entreated, to repent and to make amends. Gandhi often met cynical crowds who looked at him with anger in their eyes and to whom his advice seemed incredible, given their own experiences of uprooting and violence. On a visit to the Muslim refugee camp at the Old Fort the angry crowd had to be coerced to sit down and listen to him.[11] When he met Hindu refugees from Bannu in the NWFP, he was told by one of them that he had done enough harm and was asked to 'stop and disappear from the scene'.[12] On one occasion Gandhi met with 500 members of the Rashtriya Swayamsevak Sangh (RSS), at the Harijan Colony, many of whom were fiercely opposed to him for being 'the protector of the Muslims'. He appealed to them to be tolerant; if the Hindus felt that there was no place for anyone except the majority in India, 'they would kill Hinduism'.[13] Their leader, M.S. Golwalkar, had been to see Gandhi at Birla House and had assured him that their hands were clean.

In these weeks Gandhi went to as many camps as he could. Yet, through this period, the violence continued. As many as 137 mosques had been damaged in the capital, some had been converted into Hindu temples and idols placed in them. It pained him when one day a Muslim came to see him at Birla House and tearfully placed before him a torn copy of the holy *Koran* and went away without speaking a word. He had no desire to see what looked like the 'ruin of India through fratricide' and the removal of all Muslims from India by force. His incessant prayer in these months was 'that God would remove him before such calamity descended upon their fair land'.[14] The misery and tragedy of the times distressed him and filled his heart with anguish.

Given such an atmosphere it was with a sense of foreboding that Gandhi celebrated his seventy-eighth birthday at Birla House. On that day a stream of distinguished visitors came to see him—members of the Cabinet, representatives of foreign embassies and Lady Mountbatten, among others. Flowers poured in, monetary donations came from all over, and there was a flood of telegrams and letters from different parts of the country. Gandhi had often said that he aspired to live to be 125 years old but now he had no desire to live on in such an atmosphere of darkness and hatred. He felt unable to 'appropriate' the greetings: 'Would it not be more appropriate to say condolences?' he asked.[15] Gandhi felt his was a lone voice, with none willing to follow him. Given the dismal situation, Gandhi saw no cause for the celebration of festivities, and a few weeks later he declared that there was no reason to celebrate Deepawali, the Hindu festival of light, till all the Muslims who had left for Pakistan out of fear were brought back to India.[16] In deference to Gandhi's sentiments, Birla House stood in complete darkness on the night of Deepawali.[17]

Ironically, it was at Birla's home that Gandhi undertook his last great mission: that of ensuring a secure place for the Muslims in independent India, and a righteous settlement over partition with Pakistan.[18] His host had, as we have seen, long believed in the futility of negotiations over the communal problem and disagreed vehemently with Gandhi's ideas in these months. To Birla the communal problem was an intractable one which could be solved only with the division of the country. He had made no secret of his views on the communal problem, and Gandhi knew them all along. In characteristically frank talks with Gandhi during these weeks, he confessed that he held views opposed to what Gandhi had been preaching. He told Gandhi that he had lost all faith in the Muslims after observing Pakistan's policy towards its Hindu population.

In the months which Gandhi spent with him, their differences over the communal situation accentuated. On 12 January 1948 Gandhi declared that he proposed to go on a fast unto death unless the atmosphere of communal hatred was removed from the capital. 'My greatest fast', as he called it, was undertaken in the hope of 'bringing peace to the hearts of people of all religions in India'. The fast was, however, more than an attempt to bring about an atmosphere of communal amity; Gandhi was also fasting against the omissions of the new government. The Indian government, at the insistence of Sardar Patel, had decided to withhold the payment of Rs 5500 lakhs to Pakistan, which was its unpaid share of cash balances under the financial settlement made after partition. Patel argued that the payment should at least be postponed, if not withheld, given the fact that fighting had broken out between the two dominions in October 1947 over Kashmir. To Gandhi the refusal of payment was an immoral and indefensible act. At noon on 13 January 1948 he began his fast. Given his proximity to Patel, it is not surprising that Birla objected to the payment of money to Pakistan. He fully agreed with the argument that the transfer of money should be postponed, as it would only be used by Pakistan to purchase arms against India. In a long talk with Gandhi, Birla placed all his arguments before him to convince him of the disadvantage of the transfer of money.[19]

Gandhi's decision to go on an indefinite fast alarmed Birla. No one among his close associates had been able to read his mind or was in a position to exert any influence over him to make him change his decision. Birla was sad and disappointed at this turn of events. The whole situation upset him and he found himself in a terrible dilemma. He was opposed to the cause Gandhi was championing through his fast, and quite frankly told him so. Yet the fast was taking place at his home and he was completely helpless—all his attempts at convincing Gandhi had failed. As the host he felt responsible for the Mahatma's well-being and feared for the fragile state of his health. Gandhi's rationale of subjugating the flesh and purifying himself in order to acquire the strength to deal with the events appeared nothing less than faulty to Birla. The inner cleansing which Gandhi was trying to achieve, he argued, was possible only when he preserved his physical state, and for that reason it was necessary for him to stop fasting. Many were upset at Gandhi's decision. Sardar Patel found it difficult to take what was happening and even left the city for Bombay to stay at Birla's Malabar Hill home. Birla was also tempted to follow him but was torn by a moral dilemma between his responsibilities as the host and his friendship with the Sardar. He posed his dilemma to the Mahatma who persuaded him to follow Patel to Bombay. His 'presence near Sardar', Gandhi insisted, 'would be more useful than in Delhi'. Before leaving for Bombay, Birla made one last attempt to persuade Gandhi to stop fasting. Drawing upon Hindu mythology, he narrated the story of Nachiketa and Yama. 'Even Yama was perturbed when Nachiketa fasted at his door. How can I help feeling anxious and remorseful when a Mahatma fasts in my house', he asked.[20] 'Yama, even though he was god, feared that he were inviting divine wrath by allowing Nachiketa, a Brahman, to fast at his door'. Birla argued that he, a mere mortal, would invite '*paap* (sin) on my head'. Gandhi light-heartedly retorted that, unlike Nachiketa, he was not a Brahman; Birla told him he was more than that—he was a 'Maha Brahman.'[21] Birla also invoked the story of Savitri who secured a boon for a son from Yamaraj who had come to take her husband's life and asked Gandhi for a similar boon— that he should give up his fast. For all the efforts of Birla at persuasion Gandhi remained adamant and started his fast.

As Gandhi's fast entered its second day an atmosphere of gloom descended upon Birla House. Gandhi was too weak to walk to the garden and a radio microphone had to be hooked to his bed, so that he could send his prayer message to the nation. People anxious for a darshan began to line up in pairs and walked through the garden to see Gandhi who lay on a cot in the porch just outside his room. Thousands swarmed Birla's home—which was opened to the public through day and night—on foot, on cycles, in trucks and in Rolls Royces. There are no estimates of the numbers that converged every day at Birla House, but it ran into thousands. On the fifth day, from one meeting alone—held at Urdu Park near the old city—five thousand cyclists and five thousand on foot came to Gandhi's bedside. Processions marched to Birla House—railway workers' unions, posts and telegraph workers, government press workers and women's groups. 'It was a thrilling sight', recalled Margaret Bourke-White, *Life* correspondent, who was a frequent visitor during those months, with 'procession after procession with their many coloured banners pouring through the Birla gates, overflowing the lawn, the flower beds, the broad marble terraces.'[22]

The atmosphere outside the gates was equally highly charged. Convoys of trucks lined the streets of Albuquerque Road, some with banners declaring 'Mahatmaji's life is more precious than ours'.[23] Chants of 'Hindu-Muslim *bhai bhai*', 'Mahatma Gandhi *ki jai*' and prayers for his health filled the skies. Some times there were hostile cries of 'Mahatma Gandhi *murdabad*', 'We want blood for blood', 'If he wants to die, let him die' and 'Stab! Kill.' Many dramatic scenes were witnessed at the gates. One night Nehru, on hearing the hostile slogans, jumped out of his car and confronted the group by declaring that they would have to kill him before they repeated such a slogan. On another night, seeing the adoring crowds, Nehru climbed the top of the cement pillar by the gate to address them. Quite predictably, the Cabinet relented and agreed to make the payment to Pakistan. The citizens of Delhi too responded to the Mahatma's appeal. On the sixth day of the fast a large number of politicians and leaders drawn from different communities came up with a joint plan for the restoration of peace in the city. Gandhi now agreed to break his fast with a glass of orange juice amidst much relief and celebration. The hundred odd people who had crowded the room were each handed oranges and bananas as a gesture of celebration by members of the Birla family.

An Assassination at Birla House

The sense of relief that followed the end of the fast was short-lived. Just two days later, the serenity of Birla House was disturbed by a bomb blast which took place just a few feet away from Gandhi at his evening prayer meeting. Although no one was hurt, a large portion of the garden wall had been blown into pieces. Security arrangements were immediately strengthened. There was now to be a guard consisting of one sub-inspector, one assistant inspector, six constables, three plain clothes policemen, one non-commissioned officer and 20 other policemen on duty. Yet, these precautionary measures failed, as just a few days later on Friday, 30 January 1948, at 5.07 pm, as Gandhi walked down the garden path of Birla House to his evening prayer, he was assassinated by Nathuram Godse. Godse and his co-conspirators knew the gardens well. Some of them had been there ten days earlier—on the morning of 20 January.[24] They had entered

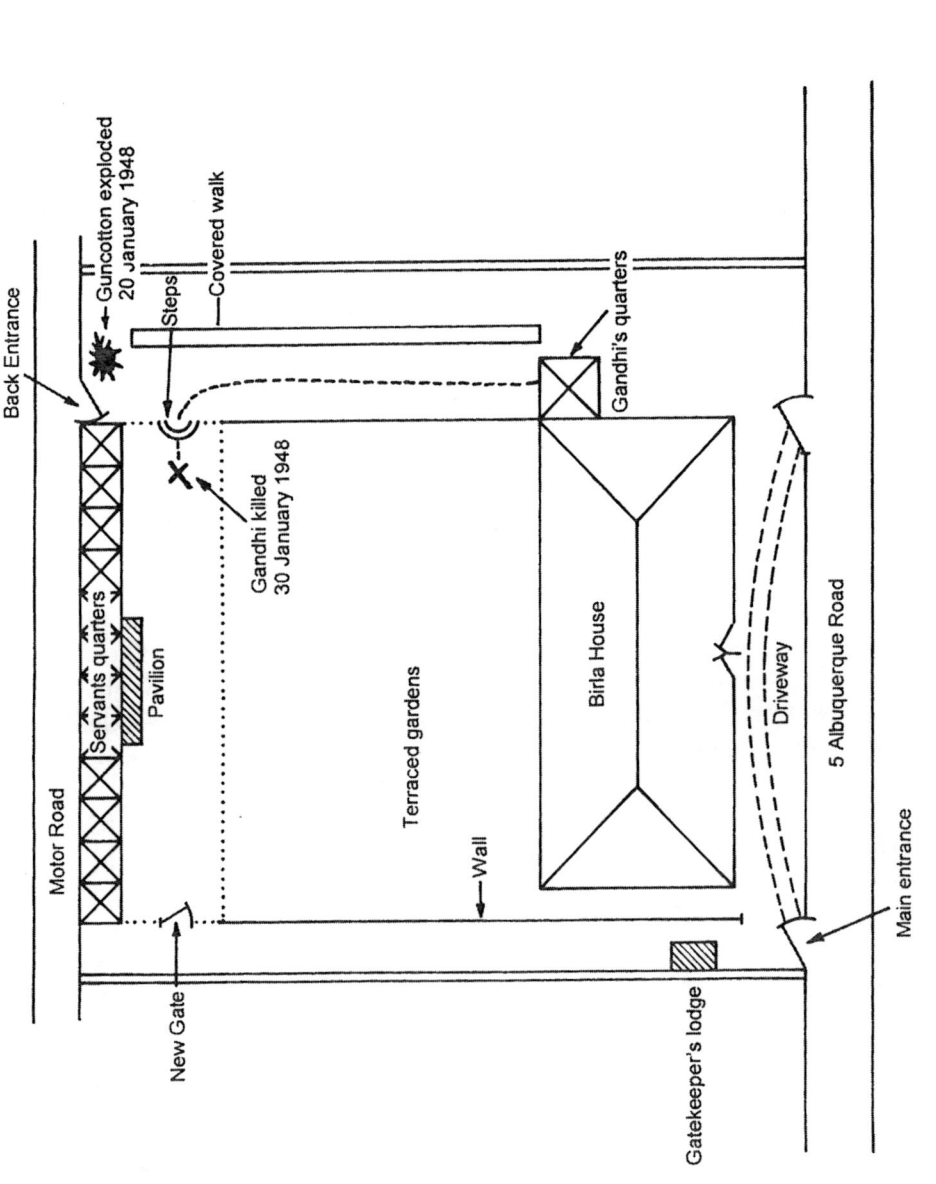

Map of Birla House, Delhi

the Birla estate through a small gate at the back which led to the prayer area by passing the servants quarters. They had even taken photographs of the area. (see map of Birla House)

As the news of the assassination spread that evening, the entire city seemed to converge on Birla's home. Important people filled the rooms while the rest occupied the gardens and terraces. The crowd which stood outside Birla House was driven by anxiety to know what had transpired and who was the culprit. As they milled outside, Nehru climbed on top of the cement pillar by the gate to announce: 'Mahatmaji is gone'. Birla was not home that evening. He had left early that day for Pilani to accompany a minister on a visit to the educational complex being developed there. He had not met Gandhi that morning because he had left in the early hours before the Mahatma awoke. The tragic news was broken to him on the phone 45 minutes after the assassination, but it was too late in the evening for him to be able to return to Delhi. After a restless night during which he dreamt of Gandhi, Birla flew to Delhi early next morning in his private aircraft. He also asked Durgaprasad Mandelia, who was in Gwalior, to reach Delhi. By the time he returned thousands had converged at Birla House to pay their last homage to the Mahatma. A lamp had been placed to mark the spot where Gandhi had fallen to the assassin's bullet. Hectic arrangements were being made for the funeral service scheduled at 11 am. A long queue of mourners was filing past the window of the room where Gandhi's body lay. Birla had to enter the room through a side entrance to pay his last respects. He could hear the chanting of the *Gita* and saw Gandhi lying, with his chest uncovered. The bullet marks were distinctly visible. However, the expression on the face held his attention—Birla could see nothing but compassion and forgiveness, a sight he could never forget.

Over one and a half million people are estimated to have walked with the Mahatma's funeral cortege for the six-mile journey from Birla House to the Yamuna river. Thousands had lined the route singing his favourite hymns and shouting his name. Gandhi's body was mounted on a gun carriage and around it sat prominent leaders—Nehru, Patel, Baldev Singh, Kripalani, Rajendra Prasad and Devdas Gandhi. Sadly, there was no place on the cortege for Birla. He walked behind the carriage for a while but was pushed aside by the milling crowds. He returned to his empty house to hear a live commentary on the event being broadcast by the All India Radio.

Not unexpectedly, Gandhi's assassination led almost immediately to allegations of lapses in security. The onus was placed on Patel, who was not only Deputy Prime Minister, but also Home Minister and thus directly responsible for the security arrangements. Socialist leaders like Jayaprakash Narayan and Ram Manohar Lohia immediately charged the government with negligence. In early February 1948 the matter was raised in the Central Assembly.[25] As these charges were levelled, Birla rushed to the defence of Patel. He declared that as Gandhi's host, he had been critical of the increased security arrangements as he never believed that anyone would dare attack the Mahatma. In a radio broadcast, he confessed that he had personally opposed the increased security arrangements as it was his conviction that 'security measures would not avail much ... if God ordained otherwise'.[26] The enhanced security cover was not liked by Gandhi either who resisted searches of persons being carried out at his prayer congregation, as he believed that his life was in the hands of God. As a disciple of Gandhi, he said he fully accepted such reasoning. Just a week before the assassination, on 21 January 1947, he had discussed the new arrangements with Gandhi who told him that he was giving in only to assuage the sentiments of Patel and Nehru. Banning the police would only add to the heavy burden which they were already carrying, he had said. Birla even discussed the arrangements with Patel who, on his objections, had sharply reprimanded him: 'this is not your department, we can't take such a risk'.[27]

As Patel replied to the charges of official negligence levelled in the Central Assembly, Birla's *Eastern Economist* raised questions about this line of thinking, which meant 'quarrelling over the hypothetical question whether anything which the government could have done would have saved Gandhiji.' It commented:

How many people have not been under the impression that his was a charmed life, to protect which no ordinary human precautions were necessary? And even if anyone could bring himself to believe that Gandhiji needed protection—one had to cross the further hurdle of persuading him that searching of his audience was necessary. Gandhiji was intensely loyal to his colleagues. But even Sardar Patel could not cross this hurdle. The Government had to choose between respecting his wishes and surrounding him with restrictions in a manner which undoubtedly would have felt as a restraint upon his liberty. And Government would have been less than human if on being faced with this choice, it failed to choose the former alternative.

Following Gandhi's assassination, the government launched a massive campaign against extreme communal organizations. In early February 1948 it banned the extreme paramilitary Hindu organization, the RSS, and arrested 25,000 members and sympathizers of the Hindu Mahasabha. There were two different interpretations of Gandhi's assasination. Nehru looked upon the murder as part of a larger conspiracy by the extreme Hindu right-wing and believed that the RSS and the Hindu Mahasabha held some responsibility. Patel, on the other hand, took the view that the assassination was not the result of a wide conspiracy but was restricted to a handful of men. Echoes of these differences could be seen within Birla's own family. There was much discussion about the role of the Mahasabha which Jugalkishore had patronized so generously over the years. In the sweeping arrests which had followed, many activists and leaders of the Mahasabha and its affiliate bodies had also been put behind bars. These included Hanuman Prasad Poddar, the founder of *Kalyan*, a weekly magazine devoted to the propagation of Hindu dharma, as well as Jai Dayal Goenka, the magazine's acting editor. Both were Marwaris and had been close to the Birla family; Poddar had even been a co-accused with Birla in the Rodda Conspiracy Case of 1914. Birla came under pressure from Jugalkishore to intercede in the cases against the two. Birla personally had no sympathy towards them, especially Poddar. He was critical of the role of the Hindu Mahasabha, especially the opposition it had consistently posed to the Congress throughout the late 1940s. He had 'no doubt ... that these people have spread poison against the Congress and Gandhiji and the sentences in the "Kalyan" are liable to interpretation of incitement to murder'. He had seen recent issues of the magazine and believed that such writings had been motivated by the desire to 'discredit the Congress and Gandhiji.' Poddar and Goenka as well as the Mahasabha leadership appeared to him 'stupid people and so [they] don't realize that under no circumstances they could take the place of the Congress leaders who have made so many sacrifices and fought for the freedom'. Birla censured Sir Badridas Goenka, fellow Marwari businessman, when he pleaded the case on behalf of Poddar and Goenka: 'I don't know why you believe that they have been propagating Sanatan Dharma. They have been propagating some sort of *Shaitan* Dharma', he retorted. Despite intense pressure from his elder brother, Birla refused to intervene.[28]

A MEMORIAL FOR THE MAHATMA

Given his close personal association with Gandhi, Birla felt a sense of responsibility for his immediate family and inner circle of associates. He was particularly anxious about Gandhi's two grand-nieces, Manu and Abha. Soon after the funeral, Birla called upon Devdas and Kanu Gandhi to discuss the two girls' future plans: he learnt that Manu wanted to go back to her father while Abha was still contemplating her future. He then turned his attention to Gandhi's associates. Pyarelal and Sushila Nayar received particular attention from him. He assured them of any support that they may need and even gave Sushila Nayar a blank cheque.[29] Further, in July 1948, a joint account was opened in their name, with an initial sum of Rs 5000 credited by Birla to meet their personal expenses.[30]

Meanwhile, Birla whole-heartedly joined the efforts, both official and non-official, which were being made to perpetuate Gandhi's legacy. He wanted to ensure that Gandhi's life, especially its last phase, was recorded for posterity. Pyarelal, given his unique position, showed an interest in undertaking a biographical project which documented various phases of Gandhi's life. Soon after Gandhi's death it was Pyarelal's foremost concern to ensure that documents, letters, notes and other materials related to the Mahatma's life which he was aware of, be secured at one place and preserved for posterity. He was also interested in recording the testimony of eminent public figures associated with Gandhi. Clearly, such pioneering work, given its ambitious nature needed institutional support. While official efforts which were later channelled into the Navajivan Trust, the *Collected Works of Mahatma Gandhi* project and the Gandhi

Memorial Fund, took time to fructify, Pyarelal was impatient to embark upon his project. Birla saw the merit in supporting Pyarelal's biographical venture and extended his enthusiastic support to it. He ensured that Pyarelal had at his disposal the resources he needed for this work. He assured him that he could ask for his help just like a member of the family.[31] A vehicle was placed at Pyarelal's disposal, the services were offered of Birla's own staff for secretarial and translation work and provision made for his personal expenses. This support continued through the 1950s and enabled Pyarelal to carry out substantial research and writing.[32] Birla maintained a close interest in the progress of the writing and commented upon drafts of *Mahatma Gandhi, The Last Phase*.[33] Pyarelal valued this support: 'I do not know of anyone on whom I can count more than upon you, not only for material help but also practical advice', he told his benefactor.[34] Birla's support extended into the early 1960s, and helped Pyarelal make substantial progress in his project.[35]

Meanwhile, the official efforts to perpetuate Gandhi's memory gathered momentum and Birla inevitably came to be closely involved. In mid-1948 Patel and Nehru convened a meeting of leading industrialists to canvass support for the Gandhi Memorial Fund. This fund-raising initiative was strategically launched from Birla Niwas in Mussoorie where Patel had been convalescing after a heart attack.[36] Important business figures and captains of industry from all over India, representing different business segments, were invited by Birla and personally called upon by Nehru and Patel to contribute to the national memorial for Gandhi. At that meeting, it was decided to raise a sum of Rs 5 crores from the business community. To meet this ambitious target, an Industrial Committee was set up and Kasturbhai Lalbhai and Birla named as its chairman and vice-chairman respectively.[37] Birla urged his business colleagues to show their generosity in perpetuating the legacy of the Father of the Nation: 'This collection is going to be a test case as far as the dignity and prestige of the industry are concerned and we should all try and help,' he urged them.[38] Both Lalbhai and Birla set to work immediately and evolved a detailed strategy. An office was set up at the FICCI headquarters in Delhi and Murlidhar Dalmia, a key Birla employee, was put in charge. Target amounts to be collected from different industries were set. To arrive at these, Lalbhai and Birla analysed profitability figures of different sectors. They then worked out industry-wise quotas.[39] Thus quotas were fixed at Rs 250 lakhs from the cotton textile industry; Rs 50 lakhs from jute; Rs 25 lakhs from coal; Rs 25 lakhs from the tea gardens of Bengal and Assam and Rs 7 lakhs from the south Indian tea estates; Rs 50 lakhs from sugar; 8 lakhs from paper; 25 lakhs from steel; 10 lakhs from cement and 10 lakhs from the woollen industry.[40] The remaining industries were to pay at the rate of 5 per cent of their gross profits based on 1945–6 or 1947–8, whichever was higher.[41] Birla and Lalbhai aimed at an overall target of Rs 638 lakhs, far in excess of the Rs 5 crores figure agreed upon at Mussoorie.

Their next step was to co-opt important industrialists from different sectors—'leaders' as Birla called them—and entrust them with the responsibility for collections. Kasturbhai Lalbhai took responsibility for the cotton industry; J.R.D. Tata was allocated steel; D. Narang made responsible for sugar; M.P. Birla was allocated jute; A.L. Cameron was made responsible for coal mines; Tulsidas Kilachand given charge of banking and A.D. Shroff, of the insurance sector.[42] Birla maintained overall charge, and quite characteristically, put strenuous efforts into the fund-raising drive. No detail was too small for his personal attention. For instance, he insisted on signing each letter, sometimes three to four hundred in one day.[43] He refused to consider using a rubber-stamp on the ground that a stamped letter would have no value or effect.[44] All follow-up action was taken by him personally. All reminders were drafted by him and every letter of thanks carried his signature.[45] So obsessive was his involvement with this work that he kept a notepad close to his bed in these months to jot down names of potential donors that might strike him at night. The names were then passed on in the morning to Murlidhar Dalmia.[46] Once the collections started, Birla regularly reviewed progress. Reports were tabulated periodically which highlighted the status of contributions from each major industrial unit in the country which had been contacted. 'Defaulters' were identified and a strategy worked out of how they could be best persuaded to contribute. Many of the 'leaders' who had been given responsibility for the collections reported problems in meeting their targets.[47] Defaulters were handled in several ways. Often Birla made personal appeals; the Birla brothers used their personal contact to elicit collections and, as a last resort, the threat of Patel's intervention was invoked.[48]

Given the economic conditions then prevalent, getting large donations from big business did not prove to be an easy task. Businessmen resented official policies on controls and food-grains. Moreover, many were uncertain about the future of private enterprise. Some found it ironical that they were now being approached for donations, while the government showed callous disregard for their views. Purshotamdas Thakurdas, Birla's old friend and himself a staunch supporter of Gandhi, candidly expressed some of his reservations:

I do not like to take it lying down as I feel that with the death of Mahatmaji, all the high precepts which he taught and which he got the Government of India to put into force regarding the control policy, have disappeared, and it is such a mockery to my mind that whilst people have thrown to the winds his sound advice regarding decontrol, they are toppling one over the other to collect large sums of money from the same capitalists including black-marketeers who pay them handsomely only because they expect more favours to come their way hereafter.[49]

Notwithstanding such feelings, the majority of businessmen contributed generously to the collection.[50] By early 1950 the targets set by Lalbhai and Birla at their Mussoorie meeting with Nehru and Patel had been exceeded.[51] On 4 April 1950 Birla wound up collections and he sent the last cheque for the Gandhi Memorial Fund to Patel.[52] The total collection stood at Rs 5 crore, 27 lakhs.[53]

'A Unique Association'

The national memorial to Gandhi became possible primarily because of the energy and commitment shown by Birla in collecting a substantial corpus of money from the corporate sector. Contributions from other quarters were less than enthusiastic and lagged far behind expectations, notwithstanding repeated appeals made by the national leaders. Thus Birla had the personal satisfaction of ensuring that the financial foundations of the Gandhi Memorial Fund were put on a strong footing. Not unexpectedly, he was invited by the Prime Minister to become a trustee of the Fund.

With the foundations of the national memorial to Gandhi secured, Birla could look back upon his relationship with the Mahatma with a sense of pride. While the national and international media in which he had received frequent publicity, especially during the 1940s, liked to describe him as the Mahatma's 'millionaire host', the label grossly oversimplified his relationship with Gandhi which was deep and complex. Their association went back 32 years and Birla looked upon it in spiritual terms. It was not Gandhi's politics that had drawn him, but his inner religious quest. The strong adherence to Hindu values to which both subscribed from childhood was a common element in their character. Both came from Vaishnavite family backgrounds and had been nurtured in deeply religious environments. This was reflected in the daily religious regimen which they both unfailingly followed throughout their lives. Both had irrevocable faith in *Rama-nama*, the prayerful recitation of the name of Rama, from which they derived much sustenance.[54]

Above all, what attracted Birla most towards Gandhi was his own belief in the ideal of the *Karmayogi*—one devoted to duty without ego, pride, attachment or expectation of reward.[55] Only two persons, Gandhi and Baldeodas, in his eyes, fulfilled the true ideal of the Karmayogi, which he himself aspired to achieve. Yet although he deeply venerated the Mahatma in a spiritual sense, he differed with him on many other issues. Their relationship was never one of unquestioning obedience. Birla often countered many of Gandhi's political ideas and the Mahatma, on his part, demanded no blind allegiance and respected his independent thinking. Given such strong spiritual bonding, the disagreements over political questions seemed inconsequential and the closeness of their relations remained unchanged even in Gandhi's twilight years. In retrospect, Birla acknowledged Gandhi as the greatest personal influence on his life besides his own father. Birla thus had the satisfaction of having unhesitatingly supported the causes that had been dear to Gandhi. As he reflected in an interview to the British Broadcasting Corporation:

In some [causes], you see, I believed; in some I did not believe. I told him: 'Don't go into the merits. I've got my own views. But I want to help you because I believe in good actions and good actions could be done only by good people.' Therefore I never hesitated to help him and I'd made a promise to him that whatever he wanted, as far as finance was concerned, if it was within my reach I would never say no. And thank God that I never had the opportunity to say no. He many times tried to give me accounts you see, even smallest details. But I was not interested.[56]

It had been, in his words, 'a unique association' which he cherished throughout his life.

NOTES AND REFERENCES

[1] G.D. Birla, 'The Tasks Ahead', in *Hindustan Times*, New Delhi, 15 August 1947.

[2] She had since come down with malignant malaria and was being cared for by members of the Birla family. Miraben, *The Spirit's Pilgrimage* (New York, 1960), pp. 284–5.

[3] Louis Fischer, *The Life of Mahatma Gandhi* (London, 1951), p. 513.

[4] Louis Fischer, *The Life of Mahatma Gandhi*, p. 452.

[5] M.K. Gandhi, *Delhi Diary, Prayer Speeches from 10–9–47 to 30–1–48* (Ahmedabad, 1948), p. 3.

[6] Miraben, *The Spirit's Pilgrimage*, pp. 287–8.

[7] Birla, *In the Shadow of the Mahatma*, p. xviii.

[8] M.K. Gandhi, *Delhi Diary*, p. 57.

[9] *Ibid*, p. 28.

[10] *Ibid*, p. 34.

[11] *Ibid*, pp. 10–12.

[12] Rajmohan Gandhi, *The good boatman: a portrait of Gandhi*, p. 433.

[13] D.G. Tendulkar, *Mahatma: life of Mohandas Karamchand Gandhi* (Bombay, 1954), p. 144

[14] See for example M.K. Gandhi, *Delhi Diary*, p. 39.

[15] *Ibid*, pp. 56–7.

[16] *Ibid*, p. 166.

[17] In the same month, an unexpected visitor arrived at Birla House—Richard Symonds, a British missionary, whom Gandhi had met in Bengal. Symonds had come down with the dreaded typhoid and Gandhi invited him to Birla House to recover.

[18] His continued residence at Birla House, he believed, suited these needs. The Muslims would feel safer visiting him there and it was easier for members of the Cabinet to meet him as most lived in the neighbouring areas.

[19] Birla to Pyarelal, 23 January 1955, in Birla Papers, Series I, File No. P–1, Pyarelalji.

[20] Birla, *In the Shadow of the Mahatma*, p. 325.

[21] Birla to Pyarelal, 23 January 1955, in Birla Papers, Series I, File No. P–1, Pyarelalji.

[22] Bourke White, *Halfway to Freedom, A Report on the New India* (New York, 1949), p. 54.

[23] *Ibid*, p. 53.

[24] For details on the planning of the assassination, see Manohar Mulgaonkar, *The Men who killed Gandhi* (Delhi, 1978).

[25] On 5 February 1948 Patel offered his explanation to the Assembly in which he stated that increased security had been provided following the 20 January 1947 abortive bomb attack on the prayer meeting at Birla House.

[26] Birla, *In the Shadow of the Mahatma*, p. 325.

[27] Watson, *Talking of Gandhiji: four programmes for radio, first broadcast for the British Broadcasting Corporation* (London, 1957), p. 121.

[28] Not only had the two men been closely involved with the magazine, but Poddar had been an organizer and fund collector of a working session of the Hindu Mahasabha at Gorakhpur which had an estimated audience of 6000–7000 and which had taken up so-called Muslim atrocities during the partition.

[29] She, however, does not appear to have encashed it. Sushila Nayar to Birla, 5 April 1957 in Birla Papers, Series I, File No. N–16, Dr Sushila Nayar.

[30] Pyarelal to Birla, 28 January 1951 and Birla to Pyarelal, 2 February 1951, in Birla Papers, Series I, File No. P–1, Pyarelalji.

[31] Pyarelal to Birla, 9 July 1962, in Birla Papers, Series I, File No. P–1, Pyarelalji. He also supported Agatha Harrison when she wanted the Arya Bhavan to be used for Indian students in England.

[32] A provision was made to meet his expenses in writing the biography in the Navajivan Press budget, but Birla insisted that he would pay for all his personal expenses. Pyarelal to Birla, 1 February 1951, in Birla Papers, Series I, File No. P–1, Pyarelalji. In 1954 he sent him small sums for the repair of his jeep and also for renovation work on the residence. Birla to Pyarelal, 22 October 1954, in Birla Papers, Series I, File No. P–1, Pyarelalji.

[33] Birla to Pyarelal, 1 February 1955, Pyarelal to Birla, 18 November 1955, Pyarelal to Birla, 1 November 1956, in Birla Papers, Series I, File No. P–1, Pyarelalji. Birla's support for his writing was unequivocal in most instances. In only one instance did Birla not support Pyarelal when he needed many hours of Gandhi's recorded voice which was with the All India Radio. The radio had agreed to give it to him as a special case, the manufacturer had presented him with a tape recorder and the Ministry of Commerce and Industry issued a special licence to enable him to obtain 150 spools of recording tape which would be needed. Given the large expenditure tax of the government, Birla felt they should ask the Gandhi Memorial Fund for help. The costs came to about Rs 2500 and were finally not borne by Birla. Pyarelal to Birla, 24 June 1957, in Birla Papers, Series I, File No. P–1, Pyarelalji. Birla to Pyarelal, 11 July 1957, in Birla Papers, Series I, File No. P–1, Pyarelalji.

[34] Pyarelal to Birla, 9 July 1962, in Birla Papers, Series I, File No. P–1, Pyarelalji.

[35] He needed office accommodation close to his apartment in Connaught Circus in New Delhi and once again approached Birla for help in this regard. The buildings requisitioned for the war were being de-requisitioned and vacant possession restored to the owners. Pyarelal thus needed to find new accommodation. Pyarelal to Birla, 27 July 1962, in Birla Papers, Series I, File No. P–1, Pyarelalji.

[36] So overwhelming was the response from the business community that the participants far exceeded the original guest list. Birla had to move into a tent which was pitched in the House's compound to accommodate house guests. See the reminiscences of Birla's secretary, R.K. Gupta, *25 years with Sri G.D. Birla*.

[37] Birla to Datar Singh, 27 November 1948, in Birla Papers, Series I, File No. D–1, Datar Singh, Sir.

[38] Birla to K.D. Jalan, 6 Aug 1948, in Birla Papers, Series I, File No. J–8, Jalan.

[39] The decision was taken to collect 5 per cent of the total income calculated on the basis of profits for 1945–6. 'Minutes of meeting of the Industrial Committee of the Gandhi Memorial Fund held on the 14th and 15th June 1948 at the office of Birla Brothers Ltd., Bombay', in Birla Papers, Series Miscellaneous, File No. 1, Gandhi Smarak Nidhi.

[40] 'Minutes of meeting of Industrial Committee of the Gandhi Memorial Fund held on Thursday, the 8th July 1948 at New Delhi', in Birla Papers, Series Miscellaneous, File No. 1, Gandhi Smarak Nidhi.

[41] 'Minutes of meeting of Industrial Committee of the Gandhi Memorial Fund held on Thursday, the 8th July 1948 at New Delhi', in Birla Papers, Series Miscellaneous, File No. 1, Gandhi Smarak Nidhi.

[42] Birla Papers, Series Miscellaneous, File No. 1, Gandhi Smarak Nidhi.

[43] R.K. Gupta, *25 years with Sri G.D. Birla.*

[44] All appeals were made to units of industrial undertakings and it was left to the unit to allocate the amount to be paid between the company and the managing agents. 'Minutes of meeting of Industrial Committee of the Gandhi Memorial Fund held on Thursday, the 8th July 1948 at New Delhi', in Birla Papers, Series Miscellaneous, File No. 1, Gandhi Smarak Nidhi.

[45] R.K. Gupta, *25 years with Sri G.D. Birla*, p. 16.

[46] *Ibid*, p. 16.

[47] One such occasion was in June 1948 when the textile industry sub-committee faced problems in collections and inspite of all the 'best efforts' of the members, textile magnate Ram Ratan Gupta had to confess his inability to launch collections. Birla was then called to a meeting to persuade mill-owners. 17 June, 1948: Ram Ratan wrote to Birla: 'Inspite of my best effort we could not start collection. The textile industry resisted anything more than its normal due. I am thinking of asking you to attend the next meeting so that you can help me.' Birla Papers, Series I, File No. G–7, Gupta, Ram Ratan.

[48] On 5 February 1949 Birla wrote to Ram Ratan: 'But your Meyer Mills have not yet sent its donation. The various Chairmen have sent a list of the units that have not yet responded to Sardarji and when the name of the Myer Mills came before him he referred the matter to my brother Rameshwardas in Bombay to find out why.' Birla Papers, Series I, File No. G–7, Gupta, Ram Ratan. On 11 February Myers Mill paid its due. Birla tried to convince defaulters. As he told Jalan: 'In fact I have told some colliery-owners who wanted to be a little miserly that I would not accept any donations from them if they are not desirous. Eventually, I fear, all those who do not pay will be approached by govt. and it is not a good thing that they should pay to the govt. rather than to their own organisation.' Birla to K.D. Jalan, 6 August 1948, Birla Papers, Series I, File No. J–8, Jalan.

[49] Thakurdas to Birla: 25 June 1948, Birla Papers, Series I, File No. P–11, P. Thakurdas.

[50] As Birla conducted a review of the collections six months later, he found the position encouraging. The mills in Madras had been especially forthcoming and had already contributed Rs 20 lakhs out of their total contribution of Rs 25 lakhs. UP and Central India were also responding well. Though Ahmedabad had not yet paid up large sums, he was assured by Lalbhai that 'it is as realised as if it were lying in the Bank of England'. The province that was lagging far behind its target was Bombay presidency which still owed the Fund Rs 54 lakhs. The total collections in just six months amounted to Rs 3,80,000 and Birla was hopeful of reaching a target of $4\frac{1}{2}$ crores by February 1949.

[51] For instance, the textile industry had sent in Rs 215.36 lakhs out of its target of 250 lakhs; jute had contributed Rs 49.71 lakhs of its Rs 50 lakh demand; coal had sent in Rs 17.33 lakhs of 25 lakhs due from it; tea gardens from Bengal and Assam had contributed Rs 18.06 lakhs out of 25 lakh due from them; the gardens in the south of the country had sent Rs 4.14 lakhs out of 7 lakh asked from them; steel had paid up

Rs 20.87 lakhs out of its target of Rs 25 lakhs; sugar mills from UP and Bihar had paid up Rs 20.87 lakhs out of 25 lakhs; other sugar mills had sent Rs 20.06 lakhs of the 25 lakhs allotted to them; insurance companies had paid up Rs 15.82 lakh of their 20 lakh target. The industrial committee had already collected Rs 523.19 lakhs. 'Industrial Committee of Gandhi Memorial Fund, New Delhi. Comparative Position as on 25th March 1950', in Birla Papers, Series Miscellaneous, File No. 1, Gandhi Smarak Nidhi.

[52] Birla to Patel, 4 April 1950, in Birla Papers, Series I, File No. P–7, Patel Maniben, Dahyabhai, etc. Murlidhar to G.D. Birla, 24 February 1950, in Birla Papers, Series Miscellaneous, File No. 1, Gandhi Smarak Nidhi. The largest contributions came from Bombay city which donated a total of Rs 73 lakhs. Birla Papers, Series Miscellaneous, Gandhi Smarak Nidhi.

[53] As Birla was priding himself with ensuring the industrialists' show of support to the cause of the Gandhi Memorial Fund, Ramkrishna Dalmia, well-known industrialist who had a controlling interest in the prestigious leading newspaper published from Bombay, the *Times of India*, made a 'public confession' in early May, about his contribution. Dalmia declared that most businessmen and industrialists had contributed sums to the Fund 'not because of our philanthropic bent of mind or because we had real reverence … but because the contributions were asked for by the authorities and because many of us were expecting that by doing so, we would not be dragged in the sphere of action by the (Income Tax) Investigation Commission; either that or we may escape it or that our case may be settled amicably.' This immediately raised an outcry among Birla and fellow industrialists; all his efforts seemed to go to nought. Statements were made protesting Dalmia's allegations that the funds were given in the hope of 'washing away our sins' and business leaders declared that their 'contributions were inspired by the highest respect and reverence for Bapu'. Patel also issued a strongly worded statement: he would, he said, regard it as 'tainted money' if any donor has made the contribution under a belief or in the impression that he could avoid the purview of the Income Tax Investigation Commission. Dalmia was asked to declare his contributions so that he could 'cleanse the fund of the tainted type.' To Dept. of State, 11 May 1950, from Clare H. Timberlake, American Consul General, in US State Department Papers, Reel I. Also in Birla Papers, Series I, File No. P–7, Patel Maniben, Dahyabhai, etc.

[54] Much like Gandhi, Birla had subjected himself to a conscious religious search: he had in his younger days been attracted to the religious writings of Ramakrishna Paramahansa and had then 'decided to stick to Gita and Upanishads'.

[55] Birla to Sohanlalji Pachisia, 13 April 1956, in Birla Papers, Series Foreign Correspondence, File No. 87–P.

[56] Francis Watson and Hallam Tennyson, *Talking of Gandhiji*, p. 47.

11

At the Peak: The *Duumvirate* Years

The years following independence saw Birla was at the peak of his influence as
a public figure. It is perhaps important to remember that free India's first three
years have been characterized by several analysts as a *duumvirate* made up of
Jawaharlal Nehru, the Prime Minister and Vallabhbhai Patel, the Deputy Prime
Minister. It has even been argued that the 'Nehru era' only truly commenced
after 1950 as it was only thereafter that the Prime Minister had the entire
national stage virtually to himself. Birla's close relationship with Patel gave him
extraordinary prestige and influence. During the *duumvirate* years of 1947 to
1950 he emerged as a key player in the political circles of New Delhi and an
influential public figure. It was widely recognized that he was a close and trusted
ally of Patel. Sir Girija Shankar Bajpai, a distinguished diplomat and former civil
servant, even commented to the US Ambassador in Delhi that Birla was an ex-
officio member of Patel's bloc, although he considered him a 'sinister' influence
over the Deputy Prime Minister.[1] In these years Birla's influence stood at its peak
and his confidence knew no bounds. This stemmed not only from his being part
of Patel's inner circle but also from his optimism that the future of the country
was secure with Patel as one of the two helmsmen.

A Shared Vision

In retrospect it can be said that the Birla–Patel relationship was political as well
as personal. The two men shared a close affinity of views on many issues. As seen
earlier, in ideological terms they had been close since the mid-1930s. As a
benefactor and host of Gandhi, Birla had been a perceptive observer of the inner
workings of the Congress high command. He had witnessed from close quarters
the vigorous attempts by Patel and other Congress right-wing leaders to counter
Nehru's efforts to steer the Congress towards a leftist direction. As we have seen
earlier, his own efforts had been directed towards strengthening the hands of
those within the organization who did not belong to the leftist 'Nehru camp',
especially of Patel. Further, Patel's advocacy of free enterprise and championing

of rich peasant landed interests made him a natural ally of Birla. Both shared a similar vision of what an independent India should be: one with a strong centre, an economic system which encouraged free enterprise and opposed the forcible dispossession of propertied groups, and endowed with a polity which guaranteed citizens' rights while balancing them with society's need for law and order. They both believed in a strong military, and saw India's rightful place in the international arena as an ally of the West as opposed to the totalitarian communist regimes in the Cold-War era.[2]

In the turbulent and uncertain years which preceded independence and partition, Birla and Patel found themselves on the same side of the political spectrum. This could be seen most strikingly in the common approach they had to the problem of partition. As seen earlier, Birla had been an early advocate of partition. In the protracted negotiations which had taken place between 1945 and 1947 in the run-up to the transfer of power, he had been a trusted ally of Patel. In the post-independence months, as the new government found itself faced with formidable challenges, Birla and Patel found themselves in agreement over a range of problems. For instance, on the minorities question, they both disagreed with the position taken by Nehru, who was determined to offer equal treatment to the Muslims in India, even though the minorities in Pakistan were being systematically forced out of that country. Patel was less inclined to treat the Indian Muslims with impartiality, given the treatment which had been meted out to the Hindus and Sikhs in Pakistan.[3] Likewise, Birla had an appreciation of the complexity of the refugee crisis, having been invited in September 1947 by Lady Edwina Mountbatten to join the Executive Council and Finance sub-committee of the United Council of Relief and Welfare.[4] His view of the refugee problem was rooted in the conviction that refugee rehabilitation could not be de-linked from economic conditions. The economic disruptions following partition had led to wide-ranging consequences: a worsened trade situation because of acrimonious relations with Pakistan; reluctance of private enterprise to invest; shortages of raw materials; disruption of the normal trade channels and, worst of all, chronic unemployment and under-employment. The unemployment situation was, in his view, further aggravated by the incoming refugees and created widespread discontent among the middle classes.[5] To Birla the immediate imperative was to find gainful employment for the refugees, thereby reducing the large expenditure the government was incurring upon handing out doles and running refugee camps. Unless the refugees were made to contribute to production, they would become a major liability on the country's meagre resources, Birla feared.[6] He was critical of the 'charity feeding' of the refugees, and he made his views known to Patel and other members of the Cabinet with whom he was close.[7]

Further, Birla and Patel both shared what some political observers described as a hard-line position towards Pakistan in the aftermath of partition. He took the view that the Bengal situation, which he knew intimately because of his business connections, was of enormous consequence. He feared a massive exodus from East Bengal and saw a 'bust-up' in the offing. He regularly appraised Patel of the situation in Bengal based upon information he received from the relief centres opened by his firm, Birla Brothers, and other Marwari associates.[8] He impressed upon Patel that the situation was far more serious than the government was prepared to admit. He even predicted that unless the exodus subsided, it could lead to an outbreak of hostilities between the two states.[9] In October 1948 Birla took up this issue with Khawja Nazimuddin, the Governor-General of Pakistan and an old acquaintance. He wrote:

The man-in-the-street today is asking the Government: Why is it that Hindus flee from Pakistan in panic while Muslims who are here are not sent back for making room for the immigrant Hindus? Whatever may be said in the Press of Pakistan, it is a fact as you know and which none can deny that 40 million of Muslims scattered all over the country today can move about peacefully and freely. Not only this. Many Muslims who had gone away to Pakistan are returning to India to settle down in their own homes in peace and comfort. On the other hand, the Hindus are fleeing to India from East Bengal. And the Sindhis and Punjabi Hindus who migrated from Pakistan are finding it impossible to go back.[10]

Patel also believed that the time was ripe for the Government of India to make it clear to Pakistan that if the influx of refugees continued, there would be no alternative but to send Muslims out from free India in equal numbers.[11]

In foreign affairs too, Patel and Birla shared a common approach. They were both sceptical of Nehru's foreign-policy leanings, especially towards Communist countries, and China in particular. They saw that, within Asia, India would be confronted with a Communist threat and genuinely believed that a tilt towards the United States was desirable.[12] Birla believed that the support of the Western bloc was essential for India both in military and in economic terms. In August 1947, a week before independence, Birla had tested the waters to gauge the US attitude to India and had invited Henry Grady, the US Ambassador, to lunch with Patel and himself at Birla House. In their talks Birla raised the question of economic co-operation between India and the US. He asked Grady if the US could supply about $500 million worth of capital goods a year to India in the coming several years to help develop infrastructure, power and machinery needed for rapid industrialization. He was confident that the country would not require a loan to pay for this, but would have a sufficiently favourable trade balance to pay it with.[13]

Birla's long association with Patel extended to their personal and domestic spheres. They shared similar temperaments and personality traits. Unimaginative and practical, blunt in speech, both would not permit the heart to rule the head. Both had a resoluteness in action, clarity in thought and were utterly devoted to duty. Over the years their two families had grown close too. Birla had high regard for Maniben, Patel's daughter, whom he treated as part of his own family.[14] Patel too took an interest in the welfare of Birla's family and was on affectionate terms with its members. After 1946, when Patel took up residence at 1 Aurangzeb Road in Delhi, not far from Birla House, the two went for their morning walk together. Patel was also a frequent guest of Birla's and made no pretence about accepting hospitality from him. Once when asked by Rajajai where he would stay at the time of the Nasik session of the Congress he replied impatiently 'I don't change friends. I will stay at Birla House.'[15] When he had a heart attack a few weeks after Gandhi's assassination in 1948, Birla arranged for him to be moved to his Mussoorie home for convalescence. Birla felt protective towards Patel following the charge of negligence brought against him over Gandhi's assassination. Both men shared a sense of acute loss and perhaps a subconscious sense of responsibility for the tragic event.[16]

Birla clearly held Patel in the highest esteem. He looked upon him as a realist *par excellence*, as the organizer and the doer in the ruling Congress party. In a talk which he gave to the Overseas League in London in 1949, Birla characterized the political leadership of new India in the following terms: 'Pandit Nehru has vision, charm and knowledge of the past and present. His reputation in the international world stands very high. Sardar Patel has a deep knowledge of human psychology, has the capacity to organise and act, and has a heart which infects people with love and activity.'[17]

A VOICE IN THE DUUMVIRATE

Although publicly Birla projected the positive face of India, within political circles it was well known that he was Patel's man. Patel controlled the portfolios of home affairs, states and information and broadcasting and these gave him control over the principal levers of power within domestic affairs. Further, he held great influence within the Congress Party. In these formative years as Patel carried heavy responsibilities on his shoulders he sometimes relied on Birla for advice on sensitive matters. Although Patel did not hold direct responsibility for economic policy-making, Birla was his unofficial adviser on economic issues. An instance of this was when Birla had been asked to help in negotiating the financial settlement between India and Pakistan after partition. The division of assets and liabilities had proved to be quite difficult as the two countries fought in the negotiations over every bit of asset. The main Indian representative was H.M. Patel, Cabinet Secretary, member of the Steering Committee and Secretary to the Partition Committee. He was the final authority in formulating India's stance.[18] Birla gave critical support and advice to H.M. Patel through the course of the protracted negotiations. The latter sent him a rough balance-sheet of assets and liabilities which he hoped could become the basis of a settlement. Birla studied it closely and worked out a revised balance-sheet to be placed before the expert committee. He formulated several principles for the division: first, all immovable assets were to remain as and where they were, as transferring them would mean a reduction of their real value.[19] Second, the Indian union would assume full responsibility for the public debt except for Rs 50 crores which was located in the Pakistan area.[20] Third, that all other liabilities would be taken over according to location.

In setting out these principles, Birla was concerned that India's liability was kept to the minimum and her risks minimized. Of the cash balances of the Reserve Bank and the treasuries, he wanted payment to Pakistan to be a mere Rs 12 crores towards working capital and Rs 31 crores for miscellaneous cash assets.[21] Given this approach, it is hardly surprising that Birla found the arguments put forth by Choudhury Mohammad Ali, the Pakistan representative, that Pakistan take responsibility for only 7 per cent of the total financial liabilities and that it should get a weighted share of the assets to be completely preposterous. Ali wanted an allowance to be made for the fact that the per capita income of Pakistan was 32 per cent less than that of India, and it had the additional responsibility of setting up a new state apparatus. For Birla, this meant that 'Hindustan should accept liabilities and Pakistan should share the assets which means', he told H.M. Patel, 'virtually ... confiscation of Hindu wealth to make gift to Pakistan'. Pakistan's argument for financial division must thus, he asserted, be summarily rejected.

As the two sides haggled over divisions of assets, the deadlock could only be broken in November 1947 when a Pakistani delegation comprising Chowdhury Mohammad Ali and the Pakistan Finance Minister Gulam Mohamad Ali came to Delhi. Meetings were held at Patel's residence and Birla was close at hand to advise. He scrutinized all documents exchanged between the two sides and sent his detailed comments to H.M. Patel before the formal settlement was signed in December 1947. However, the final settlement did not please Birla. He questioned the decision to concede $17\frac{1}{2}$ per cent as Pakistan's share of the cash balances, disputed portion of sterling balances conceded, and the uncovered national debt.[22] Birla advised a cautious approach. To Birla, the settlement of a sum of Rs 7500 lakhs to be paid to Pakistan as its share of cash balances seemed over-generous. An important consideration, he alerted H.M. Patel, was the overall context in which these financial arrangements were being made. If the situation in Kashmir grew worse, the money should be held back and military stores should not be transferred as they would pose a serious danger to India. Further, Birla emphasized that it was not only a financial settlement that should be carried out but a total settlement. Property left behind by Hindu and Sikh refugees, evacuee businesses and factories which the Pakistan authorities had allotted to Muslims, even though the proprietors were willing to operate them, securities of banks left in Pakistan, etc. should all be accounted for. Indian banks should be allowed to function, and evacuee enterprises should be afforded protection. Above all, Birla believed that no settlement should be honoured if war continued. The final settlement which was reached between H.M. Patel and Chowdhury Mohammad Ali did not have Birla's approval. Though he was critical of the financial settlement, Birla's role in enunciating the main principles on which the Indian representatives had made their case must not be underestimated. The principles he put forth in the balance-sheet resonated in the arguments put forth by the Indian negotiators on the Expert Committee on Assets and Liabilities.[23] Sardar Patel and the top Congress leadership greatly appreciated Birla's contribution.

The financial settlement arising out of the partition issue was just one of the many matters on which Birla's expertise was sought by Patel in these years. For instance, in July 1948 Birla was asked to make enquiries in France on behalf of the Indian government in connection with reports that the French were on the verge of producing synthetic petrol. Patel and Birla had detailed discussions over India's oil prospects and the evidence suggests that Birla conducted a systematic investigation of this subject for Patel.[24] Then, in February 1949, Birla reported on the prospects of industrial development in the state of Orissa.[25] In April 1949, they discussed the Industrial Control Bill as well as the question of tariffs on the steel sector. In December 1949 Birla briefed Patel on the state of the cotton and jute industries, and in February 1950 they discussed the question of control over the coal sector. Through these years jute was one issue over which Birla's advice was consistently sought, given his knowledge of the sector and his involvement with the financial negotiations with Pakistan.[26] He often sent notes to Patel on economic conditions in foreign countries which he or his business associates visited, particularly on trade prospects with India.[27] Birla's close reporting over economic policy was an attempt by him to get important members of the Cabinet to take an interest in an economic agenda which he felt was not getting the attention it deserved.[28]

Birla's assistance to Patel was not confined to the economic sphere, but extended to matters in which he had a personal interest. Patel had for long desired an all-embracing rural uplift scheme to be launched in his home province Gujarat which would help raise the social, cultural and educational level of the villagers there. The scheme should in his view take two forms: economic and social uplift which would consist of solving problems such as water supply, sanitation and development of cottage industries and educational development. Much as Birla was doing at Pilani, Patel also had wanted technical educational institutions to be established. Birla helped realize this hope with the establishment of an engineering college known as the Birla Vishwakarma Mahavidyalaya set up at a cost of Rs 25 lakhs. In June 1948 the engineering college was established and Lord and Lady Mountbatten were to perform the opening ceremony.[29] Given such a high profile visit there was much that needed to be done. Patel thought immediately of Birla and asked him to be present on the occasion: 'Apart from intimately associating you with an institution which owes so much to you, I shall personally be assured that, on account of your presence, all the arrangements would go through properly.'[30]

Another instance of such help was on the occasion of Deepawali in 1947 when Patel visited the famous Somnath temple in Saurashtra, reportedly one of the most ancient pilgrimage sites of Hinduism. According to legend, the temple, which reportedly finds mention in the *Rig Veda*, had one of the oldest Shiva deities and a close association with the life of Lord Krishna. The temple was attacked by Mahmud Ghazni in 1063 and later restored by Hindu kings. Several Muslim rulers including Alaudin Khalji and the Mughal Emperor Aurangzeb had subsequently attacked it. The temple thus was unique as a pilgrimage site for Hindus as well as an important landmark in the contentious Hindu-Muslim relations through the centuries. Patel's visit to the temple was full of significance as it came just four days after the annexation of the Muslim princely state of Junagadh on 13 November 1948 in whose territory the temple was located. During the visit Patel was accompanied by N.V. Gadgil, a prominent Maharashtra Congressman, and members of the Arzi Hukumat, the provisional new government, whose armed volunteers had recently marched on Junagadh. He responded to the popular demand for the reconstruction of the temple. According to eyewitness reports, he ceremoniously poured some sea water on the ground at the site and pledged that the temple would be renovated. Patel proclaimed that 'not a single pie would be taken from the treasury of Junagadh' or from the Government of India but would be raised from voluntary donations. Patel's motivation in pledging to reconstruct the temple remains unclear. Was he overcome by feelings of remorse as a devout Hindu at the site of this dilapidated ancient temple? Or was he mobilizing popular support within Junagadh to legitimize government action against their ruler by appealing to majority Hindu sentiments? Or was he taking the wind out of the sails of extreme Hindu right-wing nationalists to pre-empt a campaign for the restoration of temples allegedly destroyed by Muslim leaders? A definite answer can perhaps never be found for these questions.

Once Patel had made the promise, the question remained of finding money for the project. The Jam Saheb of Nawanagar, an important princely ruler from western India, donated Rs 1 lakh on the spot and it was announced that the Arzi Hukumat would give Rs 51,000.[31] A trust was formed, consisting of the Jam Saheb of Jamnagar, Samuldas Gandhi, K.M. Munshi, N.V. Gadgil, D.B. Rege and B.M. Birla.[32] A substantial responsibility for the reconstruction project was taken by the Birla family.[33] The famous architect, Prabhashankar Sompura, designed the new temple on the pattern of Chalukya architecture with a seven-storey *Kailash mahameru prasada*.[34] The new temple constructed at an estimate cost of Rs 3 crores, was 155 feet tall. Unfortunately, Patel did not live to see the consecration ceremony after the first phase of the reconstruction, which was held on 11 May 1951 in the presence of the then President Rajendra Prasad.[35]

Patel's achievements during the *duumvirate* years filled Birla with pride. He regarded the integration of the princely states which had been masterminded by Patel as the greatest triumph of the new nation. He and other big business leaders supported Patel's annexationist policies as they believed that in matters such as tariff, currency and other economic subjects there had to be integration across the country. As he reported to Thakurdas: 'Sardar Patel gave a party to the

Princes and I found that they were as docile and submissive to the new rulers as they have been to the old...I can assure you that in practice the Princes are not going to adopt any different policy from ours.'[36] When the intractable problem of the accession of Hyderabad to the Indian union was solved by Patel following the 'police action' against the Nizam, Birla reacted with immense pride. 'May God be thanked you have performed the job. May Almighty give you more strength to reconstruct the country', he wired Patel.[37] Further, he was satisfied with the manner in which the former princely states were drawn into the process of states reorganization. He was especially pleased about his native Rajputana, which now emerged as the state of Rajasthan. He hoped that this new set-up would be an efficient and democratic one. However, he recognized that due representation would need to be given to the rulers who were too powerful to be ignored.[38] Birla wanted Patel's achievements in the integration of the princely states to be widely propagated. He urged Patel to broadcast to the nation on his success in the integration of the princely states.[39] Similarly, Patel's contributions to the proceedings of the Constituent Assembly were lauded by Birla. His success in evolving a consensus for the abolition of separate electorates for the minorities was seen by Birla as yet another miracle.[40] 'You seem to be solving one after another problem. The integration of the States, Hyderabad, RSS, communism, law and order and now abolition of communal representation.' 'But what of Kashmir? And our economics', he enquired.[41]

PATEL'S EMISSARY

In the summer of 1949 Birla undertook a high-profile tour of the UK and the USA where he had wide-ranging discussions with political and business leaders on the problems faced by India. Although his visit was a private one, his reception in these two countries was indicative of the esteem which he enjoyed. In Britain he was received by Winston Churchill, the Conservative Party leader, Anthony Eden and the Secretary of State for Defence, A.V. Alexander. In these discussions, Birla emphasized that India needed a 'strong military and extensive industrialization', and he urged for British help in both the areas. Birla had especially extensive and fruitful discussions with A.V. Alexander. Military equipment, he stressed, must be supplied extensively to India while Pakistan did not deserve any. 'In fact' he predicted, 'some day India will be called upon to defend her frontiers'. Birla complained to Alexander about India not receiving military equipment in adequate quantities. The Defence Secretary promised to do whatever he could, and asked him to convey to Patel that 'if there is any difficulty, it is not deliberate, but due to circumstances.'[42]

In Washington he met with the Secretary of Commerce, Charles Sawyer and the Defence Secretary, Louis A. Johnson, besides several Department of State officials. However, several of his interviews on Capitol Hill were fixed without any consultation with the Indian mission in Washington D.C. for which he received a 'polite reprimand', which, he agreed, was well deserved.[43] In these talks he once again raised the question of financial and military assistance for India. The Defence Secretary showed great warmth and was very insistent that Birla should make another visit to Washington for further talks along with Nehru who had recently accepted an invitation to visit the USA. On his raising the possibility of getting a loan, Birla perceived it to be closely linked to India's policy on communism. There existed, Birla could sense, a definite perception in the US that, with China turning Red, India was the only country that could stop the spread of communism in Asia. 'If we exploit this feeling,' he told Patel, 'it is possible that under the Economic Administration (EA) Plan, India may be able to get even a gift though I personally do not like a gift.'[44]

At noon of 8 July 1948 Birla was received at the White House by President Harry Truman. He was accompanied by S.K. Patil, veteran Congressman and close supporter of Patel, who was then Mayor of Bombay. The President seemed to Birla to be in 'a very nice mood'. He explored with Truman the possibility of India deriving aid under the Four-Point Plan.[45] Though Truman was encouraging, Birla did not put much weight on this, as he appeared to him to be just a decorative head.

As an emissary of Patel, Birla's message to the British and American leadership was unambiguous: India needed help, economic and technical, for industrialization; further, the country required military supplies in its confrontation with Pakistan over Kashmir. While he was in the US Birla also explored the prospects of financial aid in meetings with the president of the World Bank, officials of the Export–Import (EXIM) Bank and several businessmen. He was hopeful of India securing a loan of about $100 million from the World Bank and getting favourable consideration for specific projects presented before the Exim Bank.[46] Yet large-scale private capital investment did not, however, seem to be forthcoming. This was not surprising to Birla who could understand the thinking of the people in the City who, 'definitely dislike our labour laws, high taxation and regimentation', as he later conveyed to Patel.

Through his weeks abroad, worries about Patel's health weighed heavily on Birla's mind. He received regular reports over the telephone from Vidya Shankar, Patel's secretary, and from members of his own family. He had been anxious about Patel ever since he suffered a heart attack in March 1948.[47] Birla had thereafter insisted that the Deputy Prime Minister should no longer travel in an Air Force aircraft and arranged for the import of a private Dakota plane for him. Arrangements were made for the aircraft to be pressurized, as Birla was told that it would be medically more suitable for Patel, given his heart condition.[48] However, worries about his health had increased and in recent weeks there had been concern not only about his heart but also the trouble he was having with his intestines. Birla had carried some of the relevant X-rays and medical papers with him to consult specialists in England about Patel's health.[49] During his visit

he spent much time on these consultations and even asked for more details to
be sent to him.

BIRLA AND THE PATELITES

When Birla returned to India in the summer of 1949 he found that the breach
between the *duumvirs* had widened. The two men had in the past two years
differed fundamentally over a number of issues, such as the place of the Muslim
minorities in India after partition, the Hindu Code Bill, the election of the
Republic's first President, the question of privy purses to the princes, and even
over day-to-day matters of administration. On many occasions Patel had given
in to Nehru's reasoning, but their differences seemed to have accentuated, and
came out in full view of the party in 1950. The occasion was the election of the
new Congress president. Patel's candidate was Purshottamdas Tandon who
enjoyed the support of the right within the party, and was known for his Hindu
leanings. Tandon had unsuccessfully contested the election two years earlier, and
his campaign had then been financed by none other than Birla.[50] The 1948
campaign was, in a sense, only a 'preliminary to the major bout' which followed
in 1950.[51] The rival candidate now was J.B. Kriplani, a staunch believer in the
secular ideal and the preferred candidate of Nehru, even though he did not
openly say so. The Tandon–Kriplani election soon came to be seen as a Patel–
Nehru contest and every Congress worker knew it.[52] Patel campaigned openly
for Tandon and, given his influence within the party, the result was not
surprising. It was victory for Tandon, although a narrow one, as he secured 1306
votes against Kriplani's 1092 and a third candidate who got 202 votes.[53]

However, just a few months after this show of strength by the Patelites the
entire political configuration changed. On the morning of 15 December 1950
at 9.37 am Patel passed away at Birla's Malabar Hill residence in Bombay. Patel's
son Dahyabhai, his daughter Maniben, and members of the Birla family were
by his side. The spotlight turned on Birla's home once again, reminiscent of
January 1948 when his Delhi residence had become the centre of the world's
attention on the occasion of Gandhi's assassination. Birla was once again not
present at his home at the time of the demise but immediately flew into the city
upon hearing the news. By then, the crowds had surged into the compound,
disrupted the well laid-out police barricades, jumped over the gates and climbed
the garden walls while multitudes stood in the areas surrounding the home to
pay homage to the Sardar. Congress leaders who flew into Bombay on learning
the news—Nehru, Prasad and Tandon—had to force their way through the
crowds to enter the house. Inside, mourners filled the rooms—in one room,
members of the Bombay government stood in silence, in another representatives
of the armed forces, in yet another the women of the family and their friends.
In the outer porch the Sardar's body lay in state, resting on an inclined platform
facing the gardens and bedecked by flowers, and at each side of his head rested

an open copy of the *Gita*. Just below, down a series of steps, a gun-carriage waited to carry him on his last journey through the streets of Bombay. At 5 pm that evening the procession commenced. As the Sardar's body was carried through the gates of Birla House, so great was the onrush by the crowds from inside and outside the house, that they had to be pushed back to allow the pall-bearers to reach the gun-carriage. In the words of an eyewitness: 'Then, once again, the mob closed in from the outside, holding the scene intact for some minutes in a set-picture of riotous and uproarious disorder, a medieval panorama comprised of equal parts of hilarity, sadness, frustration and confusion.' The crowds surging into Birla House and around it were becoming uncontrollable. Nehru 'roughly, vigorously and ruthlessly' pushed his way through the crowds surrounding Patel's body and 'imperiously and urgently' ordered the soldiers who were to pull the gun-carriage to start the procession. The carriage was followed by an open grey jeep which carried Nehru, Tandon, Maniben and other Congress leaders. This was followed by a convoy of cars carrying members of the Birla family, other close associates of Patel, members of the consular corps, officials, while, on foot, followed the residents of Bombay. As the procession moved slowly through the streets, chaos seemed to reign. Nehru soon got down from the jeep, and forced his way through the crowd urging the driver of the gun-carriage to speed up.[54]

That day's event marked a turning point in Birla's life. Patel's death meant a change in Birla's influence in political circles of the capital. Though he enjoyed close personal relations with a number of influential leaders such as Rajendra Prasad, Rajaji and G.B. Pant, his political influence was derived largely from his association with Patel. Birla could see a changing configuration of power within the Congress between the 'Patelites' and Nehru. The Prime Minister was now eager to assert his authority over the Congress party. As factional strife within the party increased, Nehru began to press for the reconstitution of the Working Committee and the Central Election Committee. This move was at first successfully resisted for several months after Patel's demise by the old Patelites— the right-wing elements in the party who were now led by Purshottamdas Tandon. Then, in August 1951, Nehru forced matters to a head by resigning from the Working Committee and the Central Election Committee after an open exchange of letters with Tandon. Nehru would agree to nothing less than a thorough revamping of the Working Committee. As the deadlock continued, all the remaining members of the Working Committee offered their resignations which forced Tandon to resign, leaving the path clear for Nehru who then took over the presidency. As the Patelites closed ranks in the midst of this crisis, Tandon turned to Birla. He phoned Birla asking him to announce his candidature from Rajasthan for the forthcoming parliamentary general election. Birla could see the fate of the 'Patelites' in the Congress and was astute enough to distance himself from their attempts at consolidation. He told Tandon that, though he had no doubt that he could easily win an election from Rajasthan either on a Congress ticket or as an Independent, the suggestion made little sense. His would be merely a voice in the wilderness unless he had the support of the top most leadership of the Congress. Entering the Parliament as a lone figure would only make demands on his time and health, without any corresponding benefits.[55] He confessed that he saw no future in taking the course proposed by Tandon without the directions of Panditji. Birla thus astutely distanced himself from Tandon and the right-wing group, without jeopardizing his personal relations with them. He also continued to remain personally close to the Old Guard, but at the same time he tried hard to build bridges with the new people who now controlled the government and the party.

COMMEMORATING MODERN INDIA'S 'PERICLES'

While Birla refused to join the 'Patelites' in their struggle against Nehru, he felt responsible for ensuring that the Sardar's memory be kept alive and a befitting memorial created. Like many other associates of Patel he believed that not enough effort was being made by the Congress leadership or the government in this direction. Birla took upon himself the responsibility of mobilizing resources to create a befitting memorial for Patel. Nehru took a discouraging stance when proposals in this regard were put to him. But eventually, the Patelites were able to get a resolution passed by the Working Committee (proposed by S.K. Patil), to collect Rs 1 crore for a memorial. To implement this decision Nehru called a meeting of industrialists on 8 May 1951 at his Parliament House office. This meeting decided to raise Rs 50 lakhs for a memorial to Patel to be used for rural uplift all over the country—for building wells, school buildings, approaches to villages, etc. An industrialists' committee was formed and Birla was voted its chairman. This was not surprising, given Birla's success as fund raiser for the Gandhi Memorial Fund just three years earlier.[56]

Birla threw himself into the work of fund-collection with characteristic zeal. His task was much simpler this time. He roped in all associates who had helped him earlier for the Gandhi Memorial Fund and made them responsible for collections from different industries.[57] Birla only kept the overall charge to himself: he set targets for different industries and carried out periodic reviews. As earlier, there were complaints to be dealt with and much follow-up work which was inevitable in a campaign of this nature.

While the target set for Birla's committee for collection from the corporate sector was met in record time, the collections carried out by the Congress Party organization came nowhere close to its target.[58] Then there was the question of how the money was to be used to honour the Sardar. Nehru, as chairman of the Committee, suggested that an appropriate memorial to Patel would be to dig wells in villages and undertake schemes of rural reconstruction. In his view this would be a fitting tribute as Patel was essentially an agriculturist. The Sardar's followers were, however, outraged by what they considered a nonsensical suggestion. 'This was not a National Memorial', they argued. 'Digging wells and constructing roads was the normal responsibility of the government.'[59] They felt that, at the very least, a statue should be erected at a prominent place in the capital. Their suggestion that a statue be raised near Vijay Chowk in front of the Secretariat building in New Delhi was, much to their dismay, rejected. The Patelites now felt compelled to fight the injustice being done to the memory of the Sardar and decided to take the initiative into their own hands so as to ensure that Patel's legacy was honoured in a befitting manner. Renewed pressure was brought to bear upon the members of the Congress Working Committee to find a suitable site for a statue of Patel, and this was finally agreed to. Yet, funds for this were not forthcoming from the Sardar Patel Memorial Fund of which Nehru was the chairman. So a sum of Rs 10 lakhs was raised by loyal Patelites on the initiative of S.K. Patil, and a statue was finally raised in Parliament Street in New Delhi and the spot later became known as Patel Chowk.[60]

These experiences strengthened Birla's view that the Sardar was not being honoured properly. In 1953, the Shree Krishnarpan Charity Trust, controlled by the Birla family, gave Rs 4000 to V.P. Menon towards the writing of a book on the integration of the states.[61] Then, a few years later, in consultation with Morarji Desai, who had been a close supporter of Patel, Birla commissioned D.V. Tahmankar, a London-based journalist who had been associated with the Poona daily, *Kesari* and the *Deccan Herald*, to write a biography of Patel. Tahmankar was paid £1500 for this work by Birla.[62] All the other expenditure incurred by Tahmankar were to be underwritten by his trust.[63] Once the money was paid, Birla was impatient to see the manuscript soon. When Tahmankar failed to deliver the work relations between the two men soured. 'Do you think a biographical work can be produced like a bar of sweet by putting a penny in a slot machine?' Tahmankar asked Birla. He attributed the delay to lack of cooperation from Patel's close associates and alleged that even Birla had refused to be interviewed about his association with Patel and had curtly directed him to see Morarji Desai.[64] Given the fact that Tahmankar's book was to be the first major biographical work published on Patel, one can understand Birla's impatience to see it published. Much like the other Patelites, Birla was perhaps anxious to ensure that the biography was a favourable one and, in some way make up for the lack of public commemoration of Patel's achievements.

When the long-awaited biography finally appeared in 1970, Tahmankar had been able to persuade Lord Mountbatten to write a foreword and have the book published by George Allen and Unwin, a reputed London publisher. Despite past tensions with Birla, Tahmankar acknowledged his generous financial help and even dedicated the book to him: 'In recognition of his life-long friendship with Sardar Patel and his generous help to the Freedom Movement.'[65] The biography created a portrait of Patel much as Tahmankar's patrons had desired. In a highly sympathetic reconstruction of the main events of Patel's life, Tahmankar set out the record for posterity. In a detailed chapter entitled 'Patel, Azad and Nehru' he assessed the record of the leaders of the nation and depicted Patel as the Pericles of Indian history. He credited him with stabilizing the pre-independence Congress movement by making it a disciplined organization, keeping it united despite the Socialist dissidence, and playing a cardinal role in giving the new nation stability, unity and strength. Tahmankar went to some length in countering allegations, which had been made in Maulana Azad's *India Wins Freedom* belittling Patel, which, among other things, had accused him as the main architect of Partition. A large part of the chapter was devoted to comparing the *duumvirs*. Patel was portrayed as the one with an extraordinarily sagacious mind and organizing power, and Nehru was the one with popular appeal. Patel was shown as practical, with a quick grasp of things, decisive in action, a shrewd judge of men, one who knew how to delegate work and had great organizing ability. On the other hand, Nehru was depicted as a graceful person, with wide knowledge, but easily moved by emotion, a poor judge of character, blind to the mistakes and misbehaviour of his friends and susceptible to flattery.

Tahmankar in particular discussed some of the problems which the country faced, such as the Kashmir issue and the strained relations with China, on which Patel had offered the correct advice and issued warnings to Nehru which he had not cared to heed. These were just two instances in which, according to Tahmankar, Nehru had blundered. Nehru, moreover, was depicted as approaching matters of state with diffidence, self-doubt and hesitation in taking decisive action. Tahmankar attributed Nehru's inability to solve problems and his proneness to indecision as stemming from his agnostic philosophy. 'Agnostics seem to suffer,' he wrote, 'from a kind of schizophrenia; there is a wide gulf between their ideas, feelings and actions.' Tahmankar raised too the grudge which the Patelites nursed about a lack of commemoration of the Sardar's life. 'There is hardly a village or town in India,' Tahmankar observed, 'which does not have a "Mahatma Gandhi Road" or a "Jawaharlal Nehru Park"; large pictures and statues of both men dominate the scene wherever you go.' Through the publication of the biography Birla felt satisfied that he had done his bit to ensure that, at last, Patel was portrayed in the light of his achievements for posterity.

NOTES AND REFERENCES

[1] Howard Donovan to Secretary of State, Washington, 13 August 1947, in US State Department Intelligence and Research Reports on India, Reel 14.

[2] For Patel's ideas see Rajmohan Gandhi, *Patel, A Life* (Ahmedabad); also see Rani Dhawan Shankardass, *Vallabhai Patel. Power and Organisation in Indian Politics* (New Delhi, 1988).

[3] Patel made his views public at the 1948 session of the Congress party at Jaipur. Pakistan could, he said, either take back and settle all the refugees, or cede sufficient territory contiguous to West Bengal.

[4] Birla to Lady Mountbatten, 18 September 1947 and Edwina Mountbatten to Birla, 19 September 1947, in Birla Papers, Series II, File No. M–26, Mountbatten, Lady.

Although not a very active member of the Council, Birla did help the Council with the resources at his disposal. Birla to B.N. Bannerjee, Joint Secretary, United Council of Relief and Welfare, 22 November 1947, in Birla Papers, Series II, File No. M–26, Mountbatten, Lady.

[5] All this, he felt, was 'breeding communism' and 'even communalism' and must thus be dealt wih urgently. These views have been gathered from a large number of letters written during this period. See for instance, letter to P. Thakurdas, 2 March 1950, in Birla Papers, Series I, File No. P–11, P. Thakurdas, Sir.

[6] Birla to Shanmukham Chetty, 23 February 1948, in Birla Papers, Series I, File No. S–11, Shanmukham Chetty.

[7] He believed that the government's liability must stop soon, doles must end and the refugees given gainful employment and made to start producing. Birla to Shanmukham Chetty, 23 February 1948, in Birla Papers, Series I, File No. S–11, Shanmukham Chetty.

[8] He estimated that approximately 10,000 displaced persons were entering West Bengal each day, with only 2000 leaving for Pakistan in early 1950.

[9] Also see Birla to Vidyashankar, 9 April 1950. In a meeting with Goold-Adams, Editor of the London *Economist*, Birla explained that 'the best way to avoid a war was a real threat of war.' It was not, he said, that India saw war as a solution but that, given the way the situation was unfolding, Pakistan 'ultimately may invite a war.'

[10] Birla to Nazimuddin Khwaja, 18 October 1948, in Birla Papers, Series I, File No. N–6, Nazimuddin Khwaja.

[11] Rajmohan Gandhi, *Patel*, p. 497.

[12] Birla had begun to believe that Nehru 'had antagonized a great many countries without making any friends.' B.R. Nanda, *Jawaharlal Nehru Rebel and Statesman* (Delhi, 1995), p. 229.

[13] Grady found Birla 'a vain, self-seeking man whose influence on the new government cannot be good. His illusions of grandeur are probably second to only those of Mr. Jinnah.' Grady to Loy W. Henderson, 9 August 1947, in US State Department Intelligence and Research Reports on India, Reel 9.

[14] Birla, 'Maniben', n.d., n.p., in Birla Papers, Series Miscellaneous, File No. 123. Notes and Speeches.

[15] Rajmohan Gandhi, *Patel*, p. 526.

[16] When allegations of lapses by official security agencies were made, Birla put forward a stout defence and publicly took the blame upon himself by making the claim that he had personally resisted increasing the number of security personnel at his residence.

[17] Lecture at joint meeting with the Overseas League held at Overseas House on 3 August 1949 with Sir Kenneth Mealing in the Chair. For text of lecture see G.D. Birla, 'The Economic Condition of India', *The Asiatic Review, The Proceedings of the East India Association*, Vol. XLV, No. 164, October 1949, pp. 733–58.

[18] Birla's formal involvement came as a representative of FICCI, along with A.D. Shroff, the Bombay-based businessman, but it was his informal role as adviser to H.M. Patel which was especially critical.

[19] By this principle, 20 per cent of all assets would go to Pakistan, 15 per cent of Post and Telegraphs, 25 per cent of civil aviation, 20 per cent of civil works, etc. In defence he gave Pakistan 33.1 per cent although in defence stores only 10 per cent. Major assets like the Nasik Security Printing Press, undivided India's contribution to the Bretton Woods agreement, would go entirely to India.

[20] Thus India should assume full responsibility of the public debt and Pakistan should pay it its share of the debt—with the liability of the Pakistan government being not towards individual security holders but towards the Indian government.

[21] On the issue of cash balances, he argued that the figure of Rs 4000 million (calculated as the total worth of cash balances) was an overestimation, as it did not account for inflation and thus needed to be drastically brought down. In his view, no notional figure could be put forth.

[22] Chowdhury Mohammed Ali, *The Emergence of Pakistan* (New York, 1967), pp. 180–3.

[23] The three main principles that the Indian representatives put forth were that all immovable assets remain as and where they were, while their Pakistani counterparts wanted joint control over all property; they wanted the Indian Union to assume full responsibility for the public debt while the Pakistani representatives wanted joint responsibility and they rejected the figure of Rs 4000 million as India's cash balances, saying it was inflationary. For more details see Jalal, Ayesha, *The State of Martial Rule. The Origins of Pakistan's Political Economy of Defence* (Cambridge, 1990), pp. 32–7.

[24] See for instance, Birla to Thakurdas, 25 July 1948 and Thakurdas to Birla, 10 July 1948 in Birla Papers, Series I, File No. P–11, P. Thakurdas.

[25] V. Shankar to Birla, 20 February 1949, in Birla Papers, Series I, File No. P–7, Patel, Maniben, Dahyabhai, etc.

[26] Birla to V. Shankar, 27 September 1950, in Birla Papers, Series I, File No. P–7, Patel, Maniben, Dahyabhai, etc.

[27] For instance, he passed on points in the 'economic condition' of the country and on the potential of trade with Indonesia and Burma.

[28] As he told Patel: 'I do not know why I should bother you about matters which concern partly the External Affairs Ministry and partly the Food Ministry. But as none will care to read these letters ... I am sending these to you for your information.' Birla to V. Shankar, 18 March 1950, in Birla Papers, Series I, File No. P–7, Patel, Maniben, Dahyabhai, etc.

[29] For details on the College see Josselyn Hennessy, *Indian Democracy and Education, A Study of the work of the Birla Education Trust* (Calcutta, 1955), pp. 304–5.

[30] Patel to Birla, 6 June 1948, in Birla Papers, Series I, File No. P–7, Patel Maniben, Dahyabhai, etc.

[31] Rajmohan Gandhi, *Patel*, pp. 437–9.

[32] The Trust was responsible not only for the renovation of the temple but also for maintenance of the Somnath complex, renovation of other temples in the complex and the *pooja vidhis*. The members of the Birla family who have served as trustees are B.M. Birla and his son Gangaprasad Birla.

[33] Takneth, *B.M. Birla*, pp. 65–6.

[34] Sompura's grandson, Chandrakant Pathak was later the architect of a number of temples reconstructed by the Birlas at Gwalior, Nagda and Kalyan and the temple at their Hindustan Aluminum plant at Renukoot. In 1984 Pathak was asked by the Vishwa Hindu Parishad to undertake construction of the Ayodhya temple.

[35] The first phase of reconstruction comprised work on the sanctum sanctorum. The second phase was completed in May 1965 and work on the third phase started in 1979 when Morarji Desai was the Prime Minister and the chairman of the Somnath Trust. It was inaugurated by President Shankar Dayal Sharma on 2 December 1995.

[36] Birla to Purshotamdas Thakurdas, 5 August 1947, in Thakurdas Papers, NMML, File No. 384.

[37] Birla to Patel, 17 September 1948, in Birla Papers, Series Very Very Important Correspondence, File No. 5, Grosvenor House, London, 1945–9.

[38] Wire from Birla to Shankarji, 17 January 1949, in Birla Papers, Series Very Very Important Correspondence, File No. 5, Grosvenor House, London, 1945–9.

[39] Birla to Patel, 17 September 1948, in Birla Papers, Series Very Very Important Correspondence, File No. 5, Grosvenor House, London, 1945–9. On his part, in November 1950, Birla donated a Silver Trophy to the Debating Society of the Miranda House for an Inter-Collegiate Debate on the condition that it be named after Patel. Veda Thakurdas to Birla, 28/30 November 1950 and 1 December 1950, in Birla Papers, Series Important, File No. 47–T, 1950–5.

[40] Birla to Patel, 1 June 1949, in Birla Papers, Series Very Very Important Correspondence, File No. 5, Grosvenor House, London, 1945–9.

[41] Birla to Patel, 9 June 1949, in Birla Papers, Series Very Very Important Correspondence, File No. 5, Grosvenor House, London, 1945–9.

[42] Alexander told him that demands for military supplies came not only from western Europe but also from Iraq and Transjordon and fulfilling them was not easy especially since Cripps (as Chancellor of the Exchequer) did not allow manpower to be diverted to arms manufacture.

[43] Birla to V. Patel, 9 June 1949, in Birla Papers, Series Very Very Important Correspondence, File No. 5, Grosvenor House, London, 1945–9.

[44] Birla to V. Patel, 19 May 1949 and 9 June 1949, in Birla Papers, Series Very Very Important Correspondence, File No. 5, Grosvenor House, London, 1945–9. In his talks with the State Department officials Birla got a 'mild but clear hint' that India would not get help from the World Bank unless the Kashmir issued was settled. Though he tried hard to explain to the officials the Indian perspective of the situation in the Valley, he left with the impression that the State Department officials were in 'definite sympathy' with Pakistan on it. Birla to Patel, 9 June 1949, in Birla Papers, Series Very Very Important Correspondence, File No. 5, Grosvenor House, London, 1945–9.

[45] Birla to V. Patel, 9 June 1949 and Birla to V. Patel, 21 May 1949 and 9 June 1949, in Birla Papers, Series Very Very Important Correspondence, File No. 5, Grosvenor House, London, 1945–9.

[46] Birla to V. Patel, 9 June 1949, in Birla Papers, Series Very Very Important Correspondence, File No. 5, Grosvenor House, London, 1945–9.

[47] Birla to Thakurdas, 18 March 1948, in Birla Papers, Series I, File No. P–!1, P. Thakurdas.

[48] Despite its large size, the plane had a seating capacity of only six since the equipment required to pressurize it took up most of the space. Birla to Rajkumari Amrit Kaur, 11 January 1952, in Birla Papers, Series I, File No. A–5, Rajkumari Amrit Kaur.

[49] Vidyashankar to Birla, 4 July 1949, Birla to Vidyashankar, 11 July 1949, in Birla Papers, Series Very Very Important Correspondence, File No. 5, Grosvenor House, London, 1945–9. Also Birla to Patel, 13 June 1949, in Birla Papers, Series I, File No. P–7, Patel, Maniben, Dahyabhai, etc.

[50] Kochanek, *The Congress Party of India: the dynamics of one-party democracy* (Princeton, 1968), p. 21.

[51] *Ibid*, p. 23.

[52] Rajmohan Gandhi, *Patel*, pp. 523–5.

[53] Nehru did not conceal his dissatisfaction and threatened that he would not join the new Working Committee.

[54] Leslie A. Squires to Department of State, 22 December 1950, in Confidential US State Department files on India. Internal Affairs, 1950–4, Reel 2.

[55] Birla to Purshottamdas Tandon, 12 September 1951, in Birla Papers, Series I, File No. T–12, Tandon, Purshottam.

[56] A Central Committee was constituted under the chairmanship of Nehru to administer and supervise expenditure. The other members of the committee were B.C. Roy, Morarji Desai, K.N. Katju, Kasturbhai Lalbhai, Purshottamdas Tandon, A.N. Sinha and Birla. Birla to R.C. Jall, 8 June 1952, in Birla Papers, Series Miscellaneous, File No. 43 Sardar Patel Memorial Fund.

[57] Birla to Lalchand Hirachand and others, 18 May 1951, in Birla Papers, Series Miscellaneous, File No. 46, Sardar Patel Memorial Fund.

[58] S.K. Patil, *My Years with Congress* (Bombay, 1991), pp. 56–7.

[59] S.K. Patil, p. 57.

[60] *Ibid*, p. 56–7.

[61] Birla to V.P. Menon, 7 May 1953, in Birla Papers, Series I, File No. M–10.

[62] Morarji Desai to Birla, 12 June 1959, in Birla Papers, Series I, File No. D–4, Desai, Morarji.

[63] Birla to Morarji Desai, 26 February 1959, in Birla Papers, Series I, File No. D–4, Desai, Morarji.

[64] He sent drafts of chapters to Birla for comment but they remained unread and Tahmankar claimed to have no response. Tahmankar to Birla, 31 January 1963, in Birla Papers, Series I, File No. T–18, Tahmankar.

[65] See D.V. Tahmankar, *Sardar Patel* (London, 1970).

12

Transition to Nehruvian India

With Patel's passing away, Nehru emerged as the undisputed leader within the Congress and the full flush of the Nehru era came to be experienced. As a result, Birla had to make new adjustments in his public career. Although he had known Nehru for over two decades, Birla always found the Prime Minister to be aloof and lukewarm. Perhaps several factors could account for this lack of warmth. To begin with, there existed a lack of intellectual compatibility: Birla's orthodox background with its 'traditionalist' Indian milieu and his deep attachment to Hinduism stood in contrast to Nehru's westernized upbringing, secular outlook and socialist sympathies. Even when the two men were thrown into each other's company, they found little to talk about. One such occasion was when, on his way to Banaras to see his father in July 1946, Birla's car broke down 15 miles from Allahabad and he was forced to take an *ekka* (horse-drawn carriage) to Anand Bhavan, Nehru's residence. Nehru was most hospitable and immediately made arrangements for a bath and lunch for his unexpected guest. In the two hours they spent together, they had no important talk, leading Birla to report to Patel: 'As is usual with him, he was very nice and charming, but was not interested in shop talk.'[1] Nehru had a reputation of being much more comfortable in the company of civil servants and westernized intelligentsia who had been through the 'same kind of schools and who spoke the same kind of English' as him rather than with traditional businessmen.[2] Then, of course, Birla's deep involvement since the 1920s with Hindu cultural nationalism and his close links with Malaviya could not easily be forgotten. As seen earlier, 'Birla money' had been blamed by Motilal Nehru in 1922 as being behind the attempt to capture the Congress at the time of the crushing defeat which the Swaraja Party had suffered at the hands of Malaviya's Independent Congress Party.[3] To further complicate matters had been the Birlas' close proximity to Patel.

UNCERTAINTIES UNDER THE NEW REGIME

Birla's relations with Nehru in the post-1947 years had been strained by two more issues. The first was the controversy over making Birla House, New Delhi, a national memorial for Gandhi. In May 1948, Nehru first wrote to Birla about a 'strong and persistent agitation' in the Congress party and the Constituent Assembly that Birla House be made a national memorial. Nehru suggested that while the house could remain in the possession of the Birla family the garden where Gandhi had been assassinated should be given over to the government for a memorial, and the spot where the Mahatma had fallen could be indicated by a small pillar or column.[4] Birla vehemently resisted any such suggestion. His Delhi home, he replied to Nehru, had been 'a store-house of memories and recollections which constitute for me a book into which I can delve deep to recall...a past which has gone to build up every fibre in my frail body and every tissue of my mind.'[5] Suggestions that Birla be compensated for the take-over of the property made him indignant. 'There could be no greater insult,' he wrote to Nehru, for someone 'who had served the Great Master for 32 years than to suggest that its value to him could be measured in terms of filthy lucre.' Giving up part of his home and dividing the property offered no solution. It was almost as though 'one might ask one to cut one's child into two and give up one piece and retain the other', Birla said.

A number of important public figures rallied around Birla and they spoke in defence of his claims, including Vinoba Bhave and Kishore Mashruwala, both prominent associates of Gandhi. They even asked Rajendra Prasad, in his capacity as president of the Constituent Assembly to circulate a letter to the Congress members of the Assembly to give up the demand for the take-over of Birla House.[6] Not unexpectedly, the strongest support to Birla had come from Patel, who described the proposal as morally wrong and even blamed Congress members for not rejecting it. The 'public clamour', he told Nehru, 'would never have attained these dimensions if we had been bold enough to give a correct lead by making known our opinion publicly to the people.' Gandhi himself, he said, would never have agreed to the idea. Taking over the property against the wishes of its owner to construct a memorial would 'displease the soul most grievously and affect it most painfully'. Patel confessed that personally it was difficult for him to speak out publicly in defence of Birla in view of their close association. However, he hoped to convince Nehru to reconsider the matter.[7] In a strongly worded letter he told Nehru that the proposal 'involves violence of the worst kind to the feelings of both Ghanshyamdas and Bapu'. Forcing Birla to give up the site was wrong, Patel said, and he told Congress colleagues that the correct way was to give a proper lead to the public and to the party, rather than yield to pressure.[8]

However, the agitation for a memorial could not be subdued, and the pressure to give it up continued. Birla now proposed that he would make a gift of the house to the government for it to serve as the residence of the Prime Minister.[9] Nehru, however, turned down this offer due to 'personal and public reasons'. The demand to give up a part of the house appeared most reasonable to Nehru, as it meant no more than making it easy for visitors to go to that part of the garden. It did not, in his view, even require a formal separation or isolation or involve any legal change. Three months later, Birla agreed to allow people wanting to pay homage to the Mahatma to enter the gardens of his house and the controversy settled down.[10] On 30 January each year, as the nation marked Gandhi's death anniversary, about twenty to thirty people gathered in the gardens of Birla House at dawn, including Nehru and old Congress leaders like Rajendra Prasad. They sat in silence for sometime, lost in their own memories of the Mahatma. Later the older among them chanted the hymns which were dear to Gandhi. Birla's reluctance to hand over his home on the plea of emotional attachment could not be appreciated by Nehru and even though he had agreed to open up the garden at restricted hours, the controversy damaged his relations with the Prime Minister.

Another issue which strained their relations was Birla's involvement in the first Cabinet crisis of the Nehru government. This came about in an unexpected way. In 1947 an investigation had been ordered into allegations of income-tax evasion by several business houses. A Commission of Inquiry had been appointed to investigate cases against these firms. However, the cases against four business houses,—the Birlas, Walchand Hirachand, Kasturbhai Lalbhai and Alagappa Chetty—were withdrawn by the Finance Minister, R.K. Shanmukham Chetty, at his own discretion. While it was within the Finance Minister's discretionary powers to withdraw such cases, the issue was complicated as the controversial decision had been made just at a time when the Legislature was considering curtailing the government's power to withdraw prosecution cases. When Chetty's action came to light in June 1948 the matter was raised before the Union Cabinet. Chetty at this time was in London for negotiations over Sterling balances, and K.C. Neogy was the acting Finance Minister. Chetty defended his withdrawal of cases, and argued that the decision had been taken before the bill's introduction in the Assembly, though the actual order was passed subsequently. However, the Cabinet took the stand that there should have been no withdrawal without reference to the Commission.[11] Nehru saw Chetty's action as a grave error and felt the government's position should display its resolve to everyone to 'maintain high standards in our public life'. Chetty's position now became untenable. He became a target of partisan politics. Sixteen Congress and opposition members of the Assembly who had disliked his appointment in the first place almost set themselves up, as one newspaper reported, 'as an inquisition and refused to permit Mr. Chetty to continue in office under any circumstances'[12] while Nehru took the view that individuals would have to 'occasionally suffer' in the public interest.[13] Amidst allegations of misuse of political power to help business friends, Chetty resigned. His resignation came at a most inopportune time. Not only was he faced with undertaking measures to deal with a deteriorating economic situation, but he was due to pilot two important bills on the Reserve Bank and the Banking Bill, through the very legislative session during which he resigned. Birla was widely rumoured to be behind Chetty's withdrawal of the cases. In business circles Padampat Singhania was blamed for leaking the news and for informing Ambedkar, head of the Commission. Singhania, it was claimed, grudged the withdrawal of the Birla cases as his own income-tax cases remained pending before the Commission.[14]

The *Statesman* saw the resignation as an 'outgrowth of the Congress Party's resentment at the government's partiality and weakness for big business.'[15] Officers in the Ministry of Finance privately indicated that they had advised Chetty against the withdrawal of cases. To B.K. Nehru, then joint secretary of the ministry, there was no doubt that the withdrawal was the 'direct result of pressure exerted by Birla vested interests'.[16] Exactly one year after Nehru had formed his Cabinet,—on 16 August 1948—his first Finance Minister had thus resigned amidst allegations of wrong-doing and scandal. Birla moreover was widely rumoured to have been responsible for the first Cabinet crisis of the Nehru government.

Given this background, it is not surprising that Birla was extremely anxious following Patel's death in December 1950. Birla felt the need to clear the air with Nehru and, soon after Patel's demise, sought an interview with him. During this meeting, he explained that 'though it was true that the Birla family was very close to Patelji, the question of hurting Panditji did not arise at all'. 'If you ever want me to do anything for the country,' he said, 'you have only to let me know'.[17]

THE CREDENTIALS OF A 'NATION-BUILDER'

In view of the changed political circumstances and his strong differences with Nehru, Birla felt the need to enhance his credentials as a public figure. In the rapidly changing political environment he was concerned about finding a public role for himself. He could see that his credentials as a wealthy industrialist would not get him adequate recognition in public affairs, especially when Nehru's socialist rhetoric put businessmen on the defensive. He, accordingly, now turned to asserting his nationalist credentials as one of the elders who had played a credible and constructive role during the freedom struggle, and was now striving hard to advance nation-building enterprise.

In 1950, he brought out a 570-page volume, entitled *Path to Prosperity*, edited by Parasnath Sinha, one of the editors of *Hindustan Times*. It contained his writings and speeches on economic issues since his days in the Central Legislative Assembly in 1927. The foreword of the book was written by Sir George Schuster, former Finance Member to the Government of India and member of the British War Cabinet and long-standing friend of Birla. It included Birla's thinking on vital issues such as the currency question, protection for Indian industry, the need for economic planning, issues involving labour welfare, and post-war reconstruction. It portrayed Birla as an economic nationalist par excellence.[18] Though the book showed Birla as having always been a trenchant critic of the Raj's economic policies, much more was needed to establish his nationalist credentials.

Birla therefore decided to write his memoirs. He wanted to put on record his close association with the 'Master' who, he claimed, had loved him 'as a father would his child'.[19] In November 1953, at the still relatively young age of 59, he published his autobiography, *In the Shadow of the Mahatma*, which contained long extracts of his correspondence with Gandhi.[20] Rajendra Prasad, then President, wrote the foreword. He described the author as 'one of those few who became like a child of Gandhiji and in whom the seed of his teachings found a well-prepared field and his message a ready response.' He warmly acknowledged his own long and intimate association with Birla who had been 'a friend who always stood by us during the days of our struggle with freedom and helped us, whenever required, with contribution.'

Birla's memoirs contained a short narrative account of his childhood in Pilani and a chapter on his early political involvement with Lala Lajpat Rai. It then highlighted the good and great deeds which he had performed in the last three decades to assist Mahatma Gandhi and the nationalist cause. The selection of letters exchanged with the Mahatma which he included established Birla's proximity to the 'Father of the Nation' and showed him as a benefactor of the Congress. In the 300 pages of text he set out to portray the image which he wanted to cast for himself—that of someone who had always stood 'in the shadow of the Mahatma'.

The first letter which he included in the book was dated May 1924. This showed the 'outcast' Birla seeking the advice of 'Bapu' at the height of the Maheshwari–Kolwar controversy. The careful selection of correspondence, thereafter, displayed the personal touches in the relationship between the two men, and portrayed them as ' more in the nature of a family attachment of a father towards a son.' Throughout he showed himself as constantly and unquestioningly meeting the financial demands of the Mahatma. At the same time a large part of the book was devoted to Birla's attempts in the 1930s to establish personal contacts between British political leaders and officials and Gandhi. In his portrayal of himself as Gandhi's emissary, Birla included detailed notes on meetings in Britain and India which showed him determined to pull every string on Gandhiji's behalf. Separate chapters highlighted his efforts to 'dissipate mutual suspicion and arrive at a mutual understanding'. For example, in 1932, just before the launch of the second Civil Disobedience Movement, he tried to 'secure a practical victory for Gandhiji' by influencing the India Franchise Committee; and then at the time of the decisions over the Government of India Act of 1935 when he made 'an attempt at presenting the Indian view' and tried hard to establish personal contacts between the British and Gandhi. Other episodes follow which highlight Birla's involvement as Gandhi's emissary in another respect—soothing the differences which ultimately lead the Congress to accept office in 1937; helping in resolving the 'new minister's difficulties'; intervening in the deadlock when, in 1939, the Congress ministries resigned; and over the Rajkot issue. Here his correspondence with Gandhi revolves around personal issues and as always the Mahatma's financial demands, while the correspondence with the British officials show Birla urging upon them the need for a definite date for independence. Throughout these chapters Birla aspired to show the cardinal role he had played by his personal contact in the 1930s which had 'enabled people to understand each other's sincerity and disseminate mutual suspicion'.[21] He then dealt with the 1940s more hastily.

Other aspects of Birla's public life that merit chapters in the book are his involvement with the Harijan Sevak Sangh, his support to Gandhi's journal, the *Harijan*, his educational philanthropy in his pet project Pilani, and his misunderstanding with Linlithgow in 1940 when he was suspected of funding the Congress' agitations. The book concludes with a chapter on 'After Independence' which brings in exchanges with Patel who had 'now taken the place of Bapu' in his correspondence.[22]

In the Shadow of the Mahatma did not turn out to be quite the personal memoir that its title suggested. All details about his own personal life were assiduously kept out—after a brief mention in the introduction, the family finds no place in the entire text. His personal and inner life are completely ignored, and his business interests do not find mention. His involvement within the Marwari community, his close association with Malaviya, who played an important role in his initiation into public life, his interest in Hindu causes, his philanthropy and varied public activities within business and political circles find scant mention. His differences with Gandhi over economic issues, over labour and trusteeship, over the Hindu–Muslim problem and Congress politics are glossed over. The fact about Birla's aloofness from Gandhi's many agitations are also kept out. The book merely places Birla in the context of anecdotes about Gandhi which reveal his close personal relations and instances of support to the Mahatma.

Once the book was published, Birla tried to ensure publicity both in India and abroad. Complimentary copies were sent to all his influential political friends, and his acquaintances in the press all over the world. Among those associated with the foreign press to whom copies were sent were journalists from the *Times Literary Supplement*, the *New Statesman*, the *Economist*, the *New York Times*, *Newsweek*, *Fortune* magazine and the *Washington Post*.[23] Being one of the earliest Indian accounts of the national movement, the book was extremely well received, and Birla found the reviews heartening. 'All the important papers here', he wrote to his old friend Agatha Harrison, 'with the exception of one or two have given it very flattering reviews'.[24] When the book was put on sale in London even more reviews followed and the British press also welcomed it.[25] Likewise the reception within the country was heartening. Unfortunately, it is not known how far Birla succeeded in impressing Nehru with his nationalist credentials.

While this was a time of transition marked by uncertainties about his future in Indian public life, within Birla's family and personal life there was much satisfaction and happiness. His eldest grandson, Sudarshan Kumar, was in his late teens while the youngest, Aditya, born in 1944, showed much promise even at that young age. While Birla had not been able to spend time with his own children, he greatly enjoyed the company of his grandchildren and became particularly attached to Aditya. Summers were spent in their company in the hills, or in London and Zug, Switzerland, where there were now family homes. A routine of travel evolved, frequently by a DC 10 aircraft which Birla increasingly used. This afforded him mobility to visit his various mills and their offices within India.

Notes and References

[1] Birla to Patel, 3 July 1946, in Birla Papers, Series I, File No. P–7, Patel, Maniben, Dahyabhai, etc.

[2] I.G. Patel, 'Free Enterprise in the Nehru era' in D. Tripathi (ed.), *State and Business in India, A Historical Perspective*, p. 351.

[3] See Motilal Nehru to Jawaharlal Nehru, in J. Nehru, *A Bunch of Old Letters*, p. 52.

[4] Nehru to Birla, 7 May 1948, in Birla Papers, File: no name.

[5] Birla to Nehru, 12 May 1948, in Birla Papers, File: no name. Also in Valmiki Chowdhury (ed.), *Dr. Rajendra Prasad. Correspondence and Select Documents*, Vol. 9 (New Delhi, 1987), pp. 68–70.

[6] Prasad later claimed to have forgotten to send the letter. See Patel to Nehru, 13 May 1948, Birla Papers, File: no name.

[7] Patel to Nehru, 13 May 1948. Also in Valmiki Chowdhury (ed.), *Dr. Rajendra Prasad. Correspondence and Select Documents*, Vol. 9 (New Delhi, 1987), pp. 70–1.

[8] See Patel to Rajendra Prasad, 14 May 1948, in *Ibid*, p. 66.

[9] He suggested this first to Patel who informed him of Nehru's decision to occupy the residence of the former Commander-in-Chief, Birla to Nehru, 1 June 1948.

[10] The pressure for giving up the house, however, continued and a number of politicians continued to press for the house to be converted into a national memorial as later chapters show.

[11] See Nehru to Vardachariar, 25 June 1948, in S. Gopal (ed.), *Selected Works of Jawaharlal Nehru*, Second Series, Vol. 6, pp. 396–7. The approximate amount involved in evasion aggregated to $1,800,000,000. US State Department Intelligence and Research Reports on India.

[12] In explaining his case before Parliament, Chetty made an able defence and many felt that had he done so earlier he could have remained in the Cabinet. See M. Brecher, *Nehru A Political Biography* (London, 1959) for details.

[13] See Nehru to R.K. Shanmukham Chetty, 16 August 1948, Birla Papers, File: no name; See Nehru's statement to the Assembly and Nehru to Premiers of Provinces, 1 September 1948, in S. Gopal (ed.), *Selected Works of Jawaharlal Nehru*, Second Series, Vol. 7, pp. 551–4 and pp. 360–5.

[14] Robert B. Streeper, American Consul General to Secretary of State, 23 August 1948, in US State Department Intelligence and Research Reports on India, Reel 14.

[15] US State Department Intelligence and Research Reports on India.

[16] US State Department Intelligence and Research Reports on India.

[17] B.K. Birla, *A Rare Legacy*, pp. 223–4

[18] See foreword by George Schuster in Parasnath Sinha (ed.), *The Path to Prosperity* (1950).

[19] In mid-1950 he bought the rights to all his correspondence with Gandhi from Navajivan Press. Birla to P.D. Himmatsinghka, 19 July 1950, in Birla Papers, Series I, File No. H–3, P.D. Himmatsinghka and Birla to Lord Halifax, 2 September 1952, in Birla Papers, Series Foreign Correspondence, File No. H–56, 1951–5.

[20] G.D. Birla, *In the Shadow of the Mahatma, a Personal Memoir* (Orient Longman, 1953).

[21] Birla to Lord Halifax, 2 September 1952, in Birla Papers, Series Foreign Correspondence, File No. H–56, 1951–5.

[22] Birla to Lord Halifax, 2 September 1952, in Birla Papers, Series Foreign Correspondence, File No. H–56, 1951–5. The recurring theme which Birla reminiscences about through a large part of the book is just what he had missed most dearly under the premiership of Nehru—the 'personal touch'.

[23] O. Adler of the *New York Times*, Malcolm Muir and Harry F. Kern from *Newsweek*. Ralph D. Paine Jr. from the *Fortune* magazine, John Jessup, *Life*, Arthus Sulzberger, *New York Times* and Ferdinand Kuhn of the *Washington Post*. Birla to Herzberg, 16 February 1954, in Birla Papers, Series Foreign Correspondence, File No. H–56, 1951–5.

[24] Birla to Agatha Harrison, 2 April 1954, in Birla Papers, Series Foreign Correspondence, File No. H–56, 1951–5.

[25] The *Times Literary Supplement* complimented Birla on the book.

13

Socialism, Nehru-Style

Apart from his personal differences with the Prime Minister, Birla was growing apprehensive about the future of big business in an India where Nehru was in complete command. As a businessman, his fears were not entirely unjustified. Since the early 1930s Nehru had been widely perceived as the leading exponent of socialism, someone who made no secret either of his radical leftist ideas or his penchant for radical economic reform. His efforts in 1936 to swerve the Congress towards the left with the proposal to affiliate trade unions and peasant leagues to it had deeply alarmed, not only Birla and business leaders, but the entire right-wing elements within the Congress party.[1] Further, in the 1940s there had been no sign that Nehru had changed his economic views, and it was these impressions of Nehru's doctrinaire socialism that made Birla sceptical about him.

Birla's apprehensions were somewhat ironical, given that in January 1944, he and his fellow businessmen had authored the famous Bombay Plan. Widely acclaimed at that time as a bold plan for national economic reconstruction, it had envisioned a prominent role for private enterprise in independent India. Birla and his co-authors had been optimistic that the private sector would be an equal partner in nation-building, and private enterprise would have a substantial role working in close partnership with the government to rapidly address problems of poverty and economic backwardness. It was ironical, given such bold optimism in the recent past, that Birla and other business leaders were now becoming apprehensive of economic policies under a national government in the post-colonial era.

Like the leaders of big business, Nehru too was committed to planned economic development. However, his conception of the planning diverged quite considerably from theirs, as it emphasized the socialist idea of full employment, equality and welfare. His self-declared mission was that of creating a socialist atmosphere in the country. The Nehruvian vision was of 'economic freedom and uplift of the masses, reduction in disparities of income and wealth and the concentration of economic power .... extension of the public sector and regulation of the private sector and the use of planning for full employment and regional justice.'[2] Although Nehru did not believe in either state ownership for its own sake, or an authoritarian curbing of private enterprise, he did think that the control and regulation of private capital was needed, and the state had a legitimate and predominant role in determining the allocation of economic resources.

UNCERTAINTIES AND APPREHENSIONS

Given such sharply divergent and strongly held views, the first three years of independence were marked for business by uncertainty, fears and apprehensions. In the months following independence, the Nehru government showed itself to be slow in focusing upon economic questions, as it had been preoccupied with pressing problems such as the relief and rehabilitation of the refugees, the integration of the princely states, the conflict over Kashmir and, not the least, the deliberations of the Constituent Assembly. However, all the signs in the sphere of economic policy-making pointed to a poor left-wing orientation. For instance, in January 1948 the Congress, as the ruling party, took the first steps to outline its economic vision when the report of its Economic Programme Committee was published.[3] The report declared the nationalization of public utilities and key industries, public ownership of monopolies and early abolition of the managing-agency system to be the party's stated goals. Further, it recommended that the process of transfer of assets from private to public ownership for existing industries should commence in a period of five years. Not unexpectedly, big business reacted to such proposals with alarm. The Bombay-based businessman, Homi Mody, described it as a veritable bombshell and urged Birla to exert his powerful influence in the capital to stop its implementation as official policy.[4] Mody could foresee nothing but disaster overtaking the country as such economic thinking could damage the entire economic structure.[5] Birla too was perturbed by these proposals and could now see the extent to which Nehru's socialist rhetoric could go. To him, the recommendations of the Committee were especially disconcerting because of Nehru's role in its deliberations as chairman. He feared that the report which went 'far beyond the necessities of the case' was 'likely to substantially influence ... future economic and industrial policy.'[6] Together, Mody and Birla drafted a strong refutation of these proposals on behalf of FICCI. Overall recommendations, they took the view, were disastrous as the Committee had failed to adopt a correct approach. As a result its recommendations could only 'result in frightening away initiative and enterprise.'[7]

However, Birla's fears were somewhat allayed with the announcement of the Government of India's Industrial Policy Resolution in April 1948 which laid down, for the first time, a policy framework for the national economy. It declared that public ownership of assets would be confined to only three industries, which were, munitions, atomic energy and railways. In six other—coal, iron and steel, aircraft manufacturing, shipbuilding, telegraphic and telephonic materials and minerals—the government reserved for itself the exclusive right to start new ventures. However, the existing firms in these areas were to remain free from government control and no redistribution of assets through nationalization was to take place for at least ten years.[8] Moreover, it was significant that the new official policy disavowed the radicalism of the Congress party's Economic Programme Committee. Birla thus found the Industrial Policy Resolution to be quite satisfactory. It was reassuring that the 'government had definitely decided that they want private enterprise.' Nationalization, at least for the time being, had been ruled out, Birla noted with satisfaction to G.B. Pant, the UP Premier.[9]

Though the broad direction signposted by the Industrial Policy Resolution was reassuring, Birla still remained sceptical of the future of private enterprise in what he perceived as a hostile political environment. 'The British have gone and the princes and the zamindars are in the background. The Congress, accustomed to a target for its hatred, is now finding only one target, that is the capitalist,' he lamented to G.B. Pant. He found it curious that even S.P. Mookerjee, the Industry Minister, who was reputed to be sympathetic to business, was catering evidently to the left-wingers and often spoke disparagingly at meetings of chambers of commerce. Some others ministers like N.V. Gadgil hurled abuse at business at the slightest opportunity. Perhaps the most 'incorrigible' was Jagjivan Ram, the Labour Minister, who never failed to remind the public that industry was only wanted for a few more years.[10] In Birla's view the one minister who sympathized with business was Finance Minister, John Mathai. However, though fully alive to the economic situation, he could not be effective as he lacked the support base of a professional politician.[11]

Birla pinned his hopes in these years on Patel who he believed was doing all he could to bring business and government closer. Patel had even recommended to the Cabinet the formation of a committee, with representatives of the government, business and academics, to formulate economic plans for the country. In public declarations the Deputy Prime Minister had repeatedly assured big business that private enterprise would remain an integral part of the economy. He had allayed the fears of businessmen about nationalization by clarifying that it was not a part of the government's agenda, and that any talk of it indulged in by politicians was for the sake of leadership.[12] Though Patel's assurances were helpful, they did not go far enough in the face of government proposals which pointed in the opposite direction.[13] Birla felt that much harm was being done as a result, and the confidence of businessmen was getting eroded. He urged Patel to maintain closer touch with the business centres of Calcutta and Bombay. He requested Patel to visit Calcutta at least once every year and to make two visits to Bombay.[14] In spite of their dissatisfaction with the government, businessmen were full of respect towards him as he held out hope for improvement in economic policy, he proudly assured Patel.[15]

In specific terms, there were a number of issues which caused discontent within business circles. One such long-standing issue was the continuation of wartime price controls. Controls had been a bone of contention between business and the government since the early 1940s when they were imposed on essential items like foodgrains, sugar, cotton and cloth. After independence Gandhi had tipped the scales in favour of de-control by publicly denouncing government agencies for enforcing these. As a result, in December 1947, controls were removed from sugar and foodgrains, and later from cloth. However, as there occurred a sharp rise in the wholesale price index for foodgrains and other consumer goods within six months the control measures were brought back by 1948. This lead to a renewed outcry of protests by business. Birla had, for long, argued against all controls. In his view, the root cause of increase in prices was the scarcity of essential goods and what was needed was, therefore, increased production. He was of the view that, if the government took steps to increase production, shortages and unproductive speculation would end. He urged the new national government to create a favourable climate for investment and abolish the price controls and rationing of essential commodities.[16]

Another long-standing issue behind the discontent was the high taxation structure to which business had been subjected. Though high taxation levels went back to post-World War I years, big business traced the dramatic increase to the Liaquat Ali Budget of February 1947, which increased the level of burden as well as widened the net besides levying a new business profit tax. Business was further alarmed when, in 1948, the government proposed that private companies pay a greater proportion of their profits as dividends, rather than keep them as reserves. Further, companies in which less than 51 per cent of the voting shares were vested in public hands were to be assessed as associations of individuals for which the rates applicable were much higher than those for corporations.[17]

What was, however, especially worrisome to Birla and his colleagues was the Industries (Development and Control) Bill introduced in the Central Assembly in April 1949. The bill heralded the beginning of industrial licensing and a comprehensive system of control of private enterprises. Industry was to be subject to widespread government regulation and control, so much so that it could even take over the management of a company. In addition, it was to give the bureaucracy jurisdiction over the issues of industrial licensing, and existing industries were required to register with the government and apply for a licence before any new facility could be built. In Birla's view, the bill represented the beginning of regimentation and pervasive control by government over industry.[18] If the bill became law, all industrial initiative would end as complicated licensing procedures would subject business to endless regulation by government agencies. As he complained to John Mathai, the Finance Minister: 'It seems as if we businessmen with all our past experience have forgotten all about our art. The order will now come from the Secretariat as to how to produce, when to produce, what to produce, where to produce.' Further, he was cynical about the vast powers which the bill bestowed on the bureaucracy in awarding industrial licences, investigating industries and determining the supply, distribution and prices of products. Such vast powers, he was convinced, were not likely to be exercised with wisdom.[19] Birla likened the bill to 'Damocles' sword permanently hanging on you threatening that Government may take charge of your creation if in their opinion you are not managing your job.'[20] The measure would create an adverse reaction amongst investors and Birla was convinced that it would have to be substantially modified.[21]

By mid-1949, Birla feared that government measures were leading to a crisis of confidence. There was stringency in the money market, and alarming news from Bombay stock exchange meant bad news for the state of the market. Birla alerted Mathai that 'the crisis must be nipped in the bud' before the panic spread and it became uncontrollable.[22] More serious was the problem of the decline of production in major industries. In a note on the economic condition which Birla drafted, he outlined serious problems.[23] The blame for this shortfall lay with the government's 'badly managed production controls, too much interference by government …. and a feeling of despair among businessmen.'[24] Further, there loomed a crisis in the cotton trade which could lead to the closure of mills. Industries such as sugar and *vanaspati* were suffering because of acrimonious relations with Pakistan. Jute had already seen a debilitating setback because of the dislocation in supplies caused by the partition of the country.[25] Such criminal negligence of the economy, Birla warned, would undo all the achievements of the new government, shatter all other structures and shake the 'fragile foundations of independence.'[26]

It was not only the Industrial (Control and Regulation) Bill which was leading to concern but the uncertainty about the idea of economic planning was also causing anxiety. In the early months after independence, the 'Babel of voices' making pronouncements on economic policy had led to apprehensions and Birla alleged that the 'spirit of suspense' was hindering investments and production.[27] The setting up of a six-member Planning Commission in March 1950 did not reassure Birla and his business friends. In many ways, it paved the way for ascent of an intellectual-moral elite consisting of people who were broadly committed to Nehru's 'socialistic ideals, sceptical of the market, suspicious of business and firmly believed in the role of the state in allocating resources.'[28] Such left-leaning intellectuals who came to hold centre-stage in the planning process were hardly people whose ascendancy would instil any measure of confidence in business circles.

Though the 'somewhat chaotic state of piecemeal planning' was given some shape by the publication of a draft outline of the First Five-Year Plan, there remained much uncertainty and apprehension about the Plan proposals.[29] As the principal spokesman of FICCI, Birla put the business point of view before the Planning Commission.[30] He took the view that the Plan as envisaged in the draft outline was incapable of achieving its objective and predicted that 'we will regret after five years that we missed the bus.[31] The uncertainties which characterized government policies were in Birla's view, hindering industrial corporate performance which was being stopped in the tracks. Yet Birla recognized that the government's policies had been neither extreme Left nor extreme Right. Nonetheless, mistakes had been made which he saw as arising from the new ministers' 'lack of knowledge of economics and .... the flush of the assumption of power.'[32]

CORPORATE LOBBYING UNDER THE NEW MASTERS

To face the challenges in the path of private enterprise, Birla felt it was time big business came together to make its voice heard and to effectively lobby the government. This was felt to be necessary as the power structure had changed with the coming of independence. Business needed to find new and influential channels of access. Birla understood that the requirements of lobbying had changed and business would have to assert its claim to show that it was a stakeholder in the economic future of the country. Moreover, business needed to speak in one voice and to show solidarity to survive these difficult days, he told Kasturbhai Lalbhai. Further, there was a need to influence key political leaders and policy-makers by informal meetings, by making representations to ministers and by arranging delegations to call upon the Prime Minister. It was also necessary to improve the image of business by highlighting its contribution to society and to convey at every available opportunity its point of view to the public at large.

The role of FICCI was critical in this regard. It needed to be more proactive to become an efficient instrument of political lobbying. In Birla's view, the Federation needed a more effective organization capable of reacting promptly to government initiatives. He took it upon himself to initiate its organizational restructuring.[33] The Federation had in recent years suffered from decreasing participation by influential businessmen as well as due to a lack of finance.[34] In February 1949, Birla proposed a new organizational structure consisting of 22 new sub-committees to augment the main committee. These bodies were to represent the interest of different sectors such as jute, cotton, sugar and steel, while others were to deal with technical subjects such as taxation, labour welfare and industrial legislation. These sub-committees were meant to constitute a link between industry and government, taking initiatives on matters affecting them and directly contacting ministers and government officials, as and when the need arose. Birla discussed his proposal with key members of the Federation—its president, Tulsidas Kilachand, and founding members Purshotamdas Thakurdas and Kasturbhai Lalbhai. Though Kilachand and Lalbhai approved of his proposal, Thakurdas was not enthusiastic. He felt that the proposed 22 sub-committees would be dominated by ten large firms and lead to even more bickering in the organization.[35]

Disappointed with Thakurdas' response, Birla warned Lalbhai that if he too showed 'no enthusiasm, then from the next election I propose to keep out of the Federation.' His threat worked and the proposal was accepted. G.L. Bansal, then acting secretary of the Federation, was directed to prepare a formal scheme for circulation among the member-bodies and the new structure was adopted by FICCI by late 1949.[36] Further, Birla persuaded influential businessmen to be more active in its deliberations.[37] On his part, he 'promised to attend every meeting without even being a member.'[38] The other problem identified by Birla—lack of finances—was addressed in 1951 by the creation of a new category of associate member under which firms could join the Federation directly, instead of depending upon representation through chambers of business. Till that year only chambers of commerce or trade associations could become direct members of FICCI. In subsequent years the new type of membership became a very important source of the Federation's revenues.[39] To enable the Federation to take a more proactive role, its secretariat was enlarged and a new position of director-general created to be filled by someone who 'could contact the highest authority in the Government of India and place the point of view of the trade and industry.'[40] In keeping with the new role which the Federation envisaged for itself, it began work on an impressive new building at New Delhi's Ferozeshah Road to house the enlarged secretariat.[41]

Another area where big business needed to organize its efforts lay in publicity. Birla understood the need to put across the point of view of business to the larger public through the press. While ensuring that his own newspapers, the *Hindustan Times* and the *Eastern Economist* put forth the business perspective, he argued that sections of the press which were sympathetic to private enterprise needed strengthening. In 1950, for instance, he took up the case of the Bombay-based journal *Bharat*—a 'great supporter of the views held by the industry.' He persuaded business associates to help it as it was in dire financial difficulties.[42] Further, Birla emphasized the need to lobby MPs and state legislators to impress upon them the point of view of the private sector. In April 1950, an industrial tour for MPs was organized by FICCI to 'enable them to have first-hand knowledge of the role of private enterprise in the industrial economy of India'.[43] Thirty-four MPs participated in the extended tour which took them to factories in Delhi, Gwalior, Mithaour, Bombay, Walchandnagar, Cochin, Bangalore, Visakhapatam, Jameshedpur and Calcutta. Birla took a personal interest to ensure the tour's success—six of his mills formed a part of the itinerary and he was present on each occasion to personally welcome the MPs.[44] That the tour was successful was apparent when Punjabrao Deshmukh, one of the MPs, publicly acknowledged that it had led to a 'better appreciation of what has been achieved by private enterprise against no small odds.' He urged the FICCI president to send to each MP a brief statement of the difficulties which private industry faced and the help it expected from the government.[45] FICCI had hoped such tours would become a regular event. However, they were stopped because of reports that Nehru was furious when he heard about it.[46]

With Birla's encouragement FICCI now took it upon itself to publicize its critique of government policies in a systematic manner. It organized representations to ministers on a range of issues such as controls, proposals for state trading and income-tax issues. One of the most significant questions which came up was the Industrial (Development and Control) Bill. Birla orchestrated the Federation's protests on the bill. A special sub-committee was formed to spearhead this and representations were sent to H.K. Mehtab, Minister of Industry and Commerce. FICCI expressed its great misgivings over the bill and declared that the vesting of large-scale, discretionary powers in government officials was highly objectionable. Birla kept Sardar Patel closely informed about the submission made by the Federation before the finance minister and the industry and commerce minister.[47]

THE LIMITS OF NEHRUVIAN SOCIALISM

Although Patel died soon thereafter, the result of the consistent efforts made by FICCI bore fruit by the time the Industrial (Development and Control) Bill was enacted in 1951. A number of changes had been made to it. Its very title had been changed to Industries (Development and Regulation) Act; the term 'controlled industry' had been replaced by 'regulated industry'. The powers of the officials to control and modify licences had been diluted. In cases where take-over of management was considered necessary by the authorities, a limit of five years was specified. Measures to regulate production, raw materials, and pricing were also dropped.[48] On the whole, it was widely acknowledged that the Act which emerged was quite different from the drastic measures of control which had been stipulated in the bill.

Further, there were encouraging signs that the lobbying by big business was yielding results. This was shown in December 1952 when the final draft of the First Five-Year Plan was approved. Its realistic scope and underlining caution led to a sense of satisfaction among Birla and his colleagues. The Plan envisaged a major role for private enterprise: out of a total investment of Rs 3500 crores, Rs 2000 crores was to be in public and Rs1500 crores in private sector. Certain projects could be undertaken only by the state; certain others by both public and private sectors while others were left free for private enterprise. Thus, a very large field was left open to private enterprise, as Birla explained.[49] Further, in his view, these alignments were after all 'not so rigid.' All these were signs, Birla assured his business colleagues that the future of private enterprise was secure at least for the duration of the First Plan.[50] He expressed satisfaction with the Plan in the following terms:

I am glad that the government have confined their task to the undertaking of a few economic programmes of basic and public character...Excepting the branches of basic and public activity, agriculture, irrigation and transport reserved for its work it has left the entire field of economic enterprise to private effort. And this is a right thing they have done.

There were other welcome signs too. Birla was encouraged by the formation of financial institutions such as the Industrial Finance Corporation of India (IFCI) in 1948, the state finance corporations and later the National Industrial Development Corporation (NIDC) in 1954. In 1953–4, on the recommendation of the World Bank, Birla and the leading industrialists Ramaswamy Mudaliar and A.D. Shroff were co-opted onto a steering committee to discuss the setting up of the World Bank for the development, expansion and modernization of private sector units. As a result, in 1955, the Industrial Credit and Investment Corporation of India (ICICI) was established. These financial institutions were meant to extend medium and long-term credit to large-scale industry, act as underwriting institutions and assist private entrepreneurs in obtaining capital, technology, know-how and foreign collaborations.[51] These were now clear signs that the government expected private enterprise to play a part in the industrial development. In addition, there had been taxation reforms such as the abolition of Capital Gains Tax in 1949–50 and Business Profits Tax in 1950–1 and the reduction in the personal income tax, super tax and corporate tax. All these gave Birla grounds for optimism.

Though the essential elements of Nehruvian economics, that is, industrial licensing, regulation of private enterprise and central planning, were in place by 1951 (without the sobering influence of Sardar Patel) Birla was no longer despondent. His anxieties of the early years of independence had been allayed by the concrete policy measures which the government was now implementing. He learnt a valuable lesson which gave him insight into the ways the Nehruvian government worked, especially in the area of the economy. He could see that economic planning under Nehru was part of the democratic process involving discussion and debate in which diverse ideologies and viewpoints were given a voice and different interest groups, reconciled. Through a process of discussion and scrutiny, proposals of an extreme nature tended to get moderated. The Industrial (Development and Regulation) Act, enacted after three years of intense debate, led H.K. Mehtab, the Industry Minister, to concede that it had become 'the most ancient bill' in Parliament and the final form that it took was found to be quite acceptable to business.[52] The story of the First Five-Year Plan was similar. The draft plan was subjected to a similar process of public debate, scrutiny and criticism. Only after months of discussion in the different states and at the centre was the Draft Outline published in July 1952. This was again subjected to prolonged scrutiny and criticism till a final draft emerged in December 1952.

Birla learnt a valuable lesson that in a democratic set-up, business could not be completely ignored. At the same time, he realized that the democratic process also meant a slow-moving machinery in which 'a lot of noise had to be made in order to get them to move.'[53] It reaffirmed his faith in corporate lobbying as he realized that big business must mobilize both at individual and professional levels to lobby influential politicians for their interest to be safeguarded. Although for business the new regime of control and regulation meant delays, expenses and maintaining *liaison* officers in Delhi, business expansion was no longer jeopardized by threats of nationalization, as it had been in the early years of independence.

Further, it was apparent to Birla that Nehru was, after all, not contemplating a socialist revolution, or a wholesale programme of nationalization. The conflict between public and private sectors, which had characterized earlier political rhetoric, appeared to have subsided. 'This is heartening', he told President Rajendra Prasad, that the public sector was being seen as a 'friend and ally of the private sector.' He said that, 'if the present atmosphere continues I hope after 6 or 8 months the momentum in every direction will grow.'[54] Political observers openly talked about the curious dichotomy between the Prime Minister's theory and practice as nobody quite knew what Nehru's socialism meant. Birla's *Eastern Economist* summed up the situation as one which 'covers stringent control as well as complete decontrol, restriction of private enterprise and assistance to private enterprise and increasing nationalization and decreasing nationalization'.[55]

THE MAHALANOBIS MODEL AND RETREAT TO POPULISM

Yet the overall sense of optimism which big business had begun to enjoy by the mid-1950s received a severe set-back as the general elections of 1956 approached. Nehru's increasingly leftist pronouncements from late 1954, exemplified by the adoption by the Congress of the 'socialistic pattern of society' as the declared objective at its annual session held at Avadi in January 1955, inaugurated another torrent of 'vague idealism'.[56] By the middle of the year the Leftists within the ruling party were bent upon going further. Their first intention was the move to amend Article 31 of the Constitution under which compensation for acquisition of property by the state was to become discretionary and non-justifiable. Such an event called into question the basic right to property.[57]

It was in this context of renewed leftist rhetoric that a new framework for planning was introduced by P.C. Mahalanobis, from the Indian Statistical Institute, who soon became Nehru's trusted economic adviser. Mahalanobis' influence with the Planning Commission had been growing in recent years. He believed in promoting greater investment in machine-building in the Second Plan and in the creation of a large capital goods industry to provide the basis for the expansion of secondary industries as well as to encourage the decentralization of cottage industries to generate employment. Mahalanobis' plan inaugurated another period of disquiet for business. At the FICCI annual session, Homi Mody warned the government not to take measures which would mean that 'we will have to be carried in an ambulance'. Many business leaders, especially from Bombay, had been somewhat perturbed by the drift in official policies. The need for lobbying and mobilizing to cause 'speedy action whenever an issue arises' had recently brought them together in a smaller and more manageable organization—the Council of Industry. Its committee was made up of six prominent business leaders who were J.R.D. Tata, Lala Shri Ram, Ramaswamy Mudaliar, D.M. Khatau, Kasturbhai Lalbhai and, of course, Birla. The council saw itself charged with the responsibility of propagating the viewpoint of industry in a sustained and vigorous manner to both the government and the public at large.[58] Business was thus well prepared to react to the new policy directives. Although Birla was critical of the 'reckless' turn the government seemed to be taking, he was not perturbed.[59] His experience of the last few years had shown that in the long-drawn process of review and discussion that would inevitably take place, much would change in the draft plan proposals before they were finally adopted.

Birla was thus not unduly worried by the new plan-frame. When nervous business leaders called upon him to lead a delegation to the Prime Minister, he cautioned them not to over-react but to allow the situation to unfold. Rushing to Nehru in a panic made little sense to him. Through the years of political lobbying, he had learnt the crucial ingredients for a successful meeting with the top leadership. To begin with, it was necessary to 'prepare' the mind of important ministers, those in charge of the commerce, industry and finance portfolios.[60] The way to achieve this was through informal discussions with ministers at which specific issues concerning businessmen could be raised, while emphasizing how the private sector could, in overall terms, advance the objective of the Plan. If a delegation was taken prematurely to Nehru, Birla feared that 'the finance minister may stiffen.'[61] Such a scenario would do more harm than good.[62] Only when business leaders were confident that they had the 'blessings' of the finance, commerce and industry ministers, must the Prime Minister be approached by a small delegation of eight to ten.

Birla went on to demonstrate the efficacy of this 'technique.' In 1955, he took the opportunity to write to important ministers, especially T.T. Krishnamachari and Morarji Desai, conveying his critique of the draft proposals. In March 1955, soon after the budget session, he and Kasturbhai Lalbhai met Nehru and raised specific difficulties with the budget proposals.[63] Also present were B.C. Roy, Morarji Desai, G.B. Pant and Maulana Azad. He and Lalbhai told Nehru that they had no disagreement with his conception of the socialistic pattern of society, and that they especially welcomed his recent statement that both the public and private sectors were common limbs of the national economy. Their problems, they said, arose from the day-to-day working of policies. What they desired was an informal machinery to review and tackle problems as they arose, more informal talk between business and government and more informal meetings between business leaders and Nehru. The realization of Nehru's dream of economic development would be impeded by a lack of co-operation between private enterprise and the government. In his talks with Birla and Lalbhai, Nehru agreed to the principle of joint meetings between government personnel and businessmen.[64] In addition, Birla proposed the setting up of an ad hoc committee of the Cabinet which could meet with business leaders.[65]

On 15 January 1956, Birla led another delegation to Nehru. Also present was G.B. Pant. On this occasion the business leaders vigorously countered the framework of the Second Five-Year Plan. They questioned the overall size of the plan which stood at Rs 4800 crores, in addition to the expenditure expected from the private sector. They believed that such targets were 'utterly beyond the resources of the country' and could only be implemented by increased taxation, drastic controls over consumption and 'deficit running into a figure greatly beyond the margin of safety'.[66] Mahalanobis' plan, in their view, ignored the basic economic criterion of efficiency and performance in favouring the public sector, as compared to the more competitive and efficient private sector.[67] Further, they emphasized that the country's growing foreign exchange needs could not be underestimated.[68] They also pointed out the likely problems that could be accentuated by the plan-frame such as shortages of essential items like cloth, transport bottlenecks and the slow-moving bureaucratic machinery. Further, Birla urged that the private sector could undertake to invest as much as Rs 1000 crores over the next five years and raise this capital if the government did not impose fiscal measures which would dry up its resources for the raising of capital. This could be done through untapped sources, or by ploughing back the profits earned in corporations.[69]

Birla also took his criticism to public fora where he declared that Mahalnobis' plan-frame seemed highly impractical. He argued that there must be a place for all—large, medium and small-scale sectors—in a well-integrated economy, with each sector complementing the other. While the small-scale sector did appear to create more employment, the overall impact of allied employment which the large-scale industries provided, could not be ignored. In his view the restrictions on factory production could lead to a massive shortage of consumer goods and give rise to strong inflationary tendencies. To adopt a path of restricted consumption and higher taxation, would only bring disastrous results.[70] The *Eastern Economist* denounced Mahalanobis as a 'statistician completely devoid of a sense of economic organisation.' It described his plan-frame as no more than a 'theoretical shibboleth which, if enforced, would in one sweep endanger India's future industrialisation.'[71]

Given such a consistent critique of the Mahalanobis model, it is not surprising that Birla and other businessmen found the Second Plan less than satisfactory. It was dangerous, Birla forthrightly declared in a speech, to 'ignore realities and base our hopes on mistaken calculations and emotional approaches'. Higher employment should not be the desired objective, but rather increased production. He urged the government to stop 'toying with ideas likely to take us on a backward march.'[72] In his view the problems which needed to be urgently addressed were different. They were inadequacy of internal resources, shortage of foreign exchange and technical personnel and, above all, the 'dilatory, hide-bound' bureaucratic machinery.[73] A major concern for Birla was the need of securing large loans, as it would be simply impossible to implement the Plan without a substantial amount of foreign exchange. The heavy import requirements of the Plan would, he warned, lead to a foreign exchange crisis, unless precautionary measures were taken. Throughout 1955–6 he repeatedly warned T.T. Krishnamachari and other Cabinet ministers who were close to him that the economy would soon be on the brink of a crisis which would upset the whole apple-cart.[74] He urged them to take the matter seriously and face up to this stark reality.[75] In a letter to Nehru in August 1955, Birla pointed out five impediments to economic success: lack of foreign exchange, shortage of technical personnel (especially acute for the public sector which lacked managerial expertise); transport difficulties to ease the flow of raw materials to the cities and to ease the flow of manufactured goods to the countryside, the need for an equilibrium between heavy, medium and small-scale sectors to achieve a raise in the standards of living, and, not the least, his ' greatest fear'—the machinery of the government.[76]

Though Birla was not pleased with the final form of the Second Five-Year Plan, he could see that many changes had taken place from the plan-frame. The most significant was a drop in the allotment for public-sector industry by Rs 210 crores and a sharp decline in public outlay for industry and mining and an increase for transport and communications by approximately Rs 400 crores. There were reassuring signs too. For the private sector it came in the form of the Industrial Policy Resolution of 30 April 1956. Though it reiterated that industrial policy would be governed by the larger objective of achieving a 'socialist pattern of society' and the state would assume a predominant responsibility for new industrial ventures, it also assured the private sector that it would have 'the opportunity to develop and expand.'[77] The Industrial Policy Resolution was welcomed by big business as it showed that there was enough scope for the private sector.[78] To them the new Industrial Policy Resolution seemed, in some ways, more encouraging and even less inhibiting than the 1948 Industrial Policy Resolution. Birla's *Eastern Economist* declared it 'a splendid piece of ideological tight-rope walking': 'There is nothing that should terrify private enterprise in Socialism. On the other hand, there is nothing in this mixture which enables the public sector to do any job for which it is not otherwise qualified'.

THE CUT AND THRUST OF POLITICS

Birla understood from the first ten years' experience of decision-making under Nehru that a framework for private enterprise was not merely a product of economic rationality but was also shaped, after all, by political considerations.

Through his writings and speeches he had, as we have seen, evolved a systematic critique of government policies. By encouraging personal contact through meetings and delegations to the top leadership he ensured that the viewpoint of big business was effectively conveyed. Yet these were not enough to secure a voice for free enterprise. Birla knew all too well that it was the cut and thrust of politics which shaped economic decision-making. The complexities and uncertainties of Indian politics which he had observed from close quarters over three decades led him to argue for a need to engage more actively with the political process. It was prudent, he realized, to consolidate links with the political machinery of the ruling party and one way of doing this was through the corporate funding of the electoral process. Though there were other opportunities for providing financial support to the Congress such as appeals for relief work and for causes the party espoused and donations at the time of annual sessions, it was on the occasion of national elections that the largest fund-raising drives were launched.

The party needed huge sums during national and provincial election campaigns to solicit support from its complex and carefully crafted 'vote banks' across the length and breadth of the country. Funds were required to sustain party workers and for the vast expenses incurred during such canvassing, especially for travel and printing. At such times, traditional sources of funds such as members' dues and levies on members of Parliament and legislative assemblies needed to be supplemented by donations, purses and fund drives.[79]

The first general election following independence was in 1952 when the Congress party had faced a 173 million-strong electorate. It had put up over 4000 candidates in the national and provincial elections.[80] Given his past experience with fund-raising during the 1946 elections, Birla looked upon the elections as an opportune time to consolidate his links with leaders within the ruling party and to establish his credentials as a supporter of the Prime Minister. In March 1951 he sent a message to Nehru offering him help in fund-raising for the coming elections. The provincial Congress leaders had already launched donation drives and Birla presumed that the central leadership too would be intiating collections.[81] He assured Nehru that he was waiting for his 'command in connection with the elections' and 'was prepared to finance them to a considerable extent'.[82] However, as Birla did not find Nehru forthcoming in asking for help, he thenceforth kept aloof from the central leadership's preparations for the campaign. Though Nehru had indirectly rebuffed him, Birla was approached soon thereafter in December 1951 by N.V. Gadgil, the prominent Maharashtra Congressman, for a contribution to the party's election coffers. Nehru should not have hesitated in asking for his help eight months earlier, Birla told Gadgil, but he promptly sent Rs 50,000 to Nehru.[83] Evidence suggests that this was probably his only major individual contribution to the 1952 elections.

Given the overall popularity and confidence of the Congress party in the first general elections, no major fund-raising drive seems to have been launched.

Though election costs varied, such was the popularity of the party that its candidates in the parliamentary elections often did not need to spend more than Rs 5000, even though the statutory amount laid down by the Election Commission was Rs 25000.[84] Much of the central election expenses were met out of an old election fund which had money left over from a collection conducted by Patel in 1946. It was only for the expenses of PCCs (Provincial Congress Committees) that collections were made in 1952.[85] The Congress rode a wave of popularity as memory of its role as the 'party of independence' as well as the personality of Nehru brought it easy success. It won an overwhelming majority of seats in the Parliament and a working majority in all except four states.[86]

However, by the time the second general election approached in 1957, the situation had changed dramatically. Although there were only three all-India parties besides the Congress—the Praja Socialist Party, the Bharatiya Jana Sangh and the Communist Party of India (CPI)—there were a number of regional parties which had gained strength such as the Ganatantra Parishad in Orissa, the Dravida Munnetra Kazhagam in Tamil Nadu and Akali Dal in Punjab. Moreover, the CPI had by now emerged as a major force, having only recently won the state elections in Kerala. The Congress party's long-standing popular image had begun to fade, and the rise of opposition parties meant that the election campaign would have to be fought differently from the previous election. The necessity for the Congress to mount an effective campaign seemed paramount, and funds were needed for this purpose. Birla was now co-opted into the party's fund-raising drive by T.T. Krishnamachari and came to be involved with all the stages of this effort. In 1955 he was taken by Krishnamachari to see Morarji Desai, the then Congress treasurer, who informed him that it was Nehru's desire that he should 'undertake the responsibility of collecting funds' for the coming election.[87] The entire responsibility for the central fund-raising efforts thereafter came to be placed upon the trio of Desai, Krishnamachari and Birla.

The donation drive was kicked off with Desai calling a meeting of 15 to 20 leading industrialists in the twin business metropolises of Bombay and Calcutta. He candidly informed the business leaders that he was soliciting donations for their support. In his characteristically arrogant manner, Desai made it clear that he would not approach businessmen individually and that those present should submit, on their own initiative, lists of those who wished to contribute, along with the amounts they would give. Many businessmen promised to help straightaway. Others such as J.R.D. Tata informed Desai that they would need the approval of the High Court to alter the articles of associations of their companies to enable them to make political donations.[88] Having made the initial appeal, Desai then withdrew from the scene and left all follow-up work to Krishnamachari and Birla. The two held a series of meetings with industrialists at the Taj Hotel in Bombay and the Calcutta Club as well as the Great Eastern Hotel in Calcutta (sometimes in the presence of the Bengal Chief Minister, B.C. Roy).[89] The details of donations and dates of payment were finalized at such meetings. It was made clear that the collections were for the central funds only, as donations to the provincial congress committees (PCCs) were to be conducted separately. Cheques were made in the names of Nehru and Desai as party president and treasurer respectively and an account maintained in the Birla-controlled United Commercial Bank. Cheques could be sent either to Desai, B.C. Roy, Krishnamachari or Birla. Many industrialists wanted a part of their contribution to go to the central fund and the rest to the PCCs.[90] This was agreed upon as the disbursement of funds was Nehru's prerogative who could allot them to states with a shortfall in their collections.[91]

After these meetings with the industrialists which enabled him to test the ground , Birla estimated that a total of approximately Rs 1 crore 92 lakhs could be raised. He also worked out the province-wise estimates. The largest amount was expected from Bombay at Rs 65 lakhs, to be followed by Calcutta at Rs 32 lakhs. Smaller donations of Rs 10 lakhs each were promised from Delhi, and from Madras and Coimbatore combined. While this was not surprising, Birla was somewhat disappointed with the promise of a mere Rs 15 lakhs from Ahmedabad. A further sum of Rs 40 lakhs was promised by European businessmen who had been bracketed together in one single category.[92]

To realize these targets, Birla roped in his brothers Rameshwardas and Braj Mohan and enlisted the help of close friends such as industrialists K.M.D.Thackersey and Kasturbhai Lalbhai. Rameshwardas and Thackersey were made responsible for collections from Bombay while Lalbhai helped in Ahmedabad. Birla oversaw collections from Calcutta, with help from Braj Mohan. Nonetheless, the overall responsibility for collection of funds from the industrialists rested with him alone. By June 1955, his own companies had given a sum of Rs 7,40,500 out of the total AICC balance of Rs 10,59,708.[93] In overall terms the Birla group had promised a total donation of Rs 20 lakhs. Apart from this, Birla gave large sums for the Congress electoral campaign in Travancore, Cochin and Kerala during 1955–6.[94] Given Birla's skills at fund-raising , the Calcutta collections soon out-paced those from all other cities.

For Birla the work involved in political-fund collection proved to be varied and demanding. The amounts had to be finalized with individual industrialists, collections had to be carried out within a certain time-frame, reminders frequently had to be sent and he often had to intervene to sort out problems when provincial leaders made demands in contravention of the total donations agreed upon or put pressure upon businessmen for extra contributions. Birla's past experience in working for the Gandhi and Sardar Patel memorial funds came in handy in dealing with such problems. He knew that some kind of agreement with the PCCs was needed to avoid the overlapping of demands with central funds.[95] Mangturam Jaipuria, a Marwari industrialist from Calcutta was, for instance, asked for a donation by C.B. Gupta and Sampurnand in UP and also by B.C. Roy.[96] Businessmen often complained about exacting Congress demands.

Birla had to deal with them sympathetically, while ensuring that there was no fall-out in the collection drive.[97]

Despite the demanding nature of work which fund-raising entailed, Birla gave personal attention to all the details. All accounts of donations maintained by his office staff were closely scrutinized by him, monthly estimates prepared and all changes reviewed personally. In addition, the lengthy correspondence with regard to the collections was carried out by Birla himself.[98] His reminders were worded according to the donor and Birla was careful to praise the donor's generosity.[99] All accounts were meticulously maintained and then passed on to the Congress treasurer Desai, who was responsible for showing them to Nehru.[100]

As the fund-raising drive gathered pace, the Congress party was able to secure large donations. The largest single donation came from the Birla and Tata groups, each of which gave Rs 20 lakhs. Other large donations came from the prominent businessmen A.N. Mafatlal, S.P. Jain, Lala Shri Ram and G.L. Bangur, each of whom contributed between Rs 4 and 6 lakhs. The positive response from the business community made Birla hopeful of reaching his target. In February 1957, the central party funds had Rs $97\frac{1}{2}$ lakh and Birla was still hopeful of collecting another 30 lakhs. Contribution continued to pour in till after the election was over and a sum of 20 lakhs came in later. Though the total collection exceeded 1 crore 20 lakhs, it did not, for all Birla's efforts, reach the Rs 1 crore $91\frac{1}{2}$ lakhs mark.[101]

While there was support for the ruling party and a willingness to contribute to the political processes, there was much concern within business circles that there should be transparency in the funding given by big business to political parties. The framework governing corporate and company law, they argued, should be amended to enable companies to make donations and report these in their books of accounts and annual statements, so as to ensure a degree of transparency. Many companies raised this question by appealing to amend their Memoranda of Association. So many were the applications by which companies sought amendment that the judges of Calcutta and Bombay High Courts expressed concern. The contributions by business and industrial houses, they feared, could affect the nascent Indian democracy. For instance, the Calcutta High Court judge recommended legislation to 'keep the springs of democracy and administration reasonably pure and unsullied' and to 'control the dangers and mischief inherent in the situation before it is too late.'[102] The Bombay High Court asked Tata Steel to publish complete statements of donations by it to leading political parties in two leading newspapers at the end of every financial year, and the Calcutta High Court asked TISCO, another Tata enterprise, to publish in its accounts the precise contributions that they made to political parties and to approach the Court again after a period of six years.[103] While the older companies were amending their Memoranda of Association, a large number of new companies incorporated clauses in their Memoranda to allow financial donations to political parties. All these problems signified the attempt by business circles to forge relationships with the new political system, which was taking shape in an evolving democracy.

DEMOCRACY IS OUR BEST INSURANCE

Birla's experience demonstrated that Nehru's socialism was not absolute. Over the first decade of independence, he had seen many instances of a divergence between the radical pronouncements of the top leadership and actual policy outcomes, which were realistic and took cognizance of the complex, multi-faceted nature of the economic problems, which the country faced. For instance, the report of the Economic Programme Committee of the Congress, which professed to be its economic blueprint for the future, was never implemented in full. The same held true for many government and party pronouncements: Five-Year Plans were changed by the time draft outlines became formal plans. So many were the conflicting signals that Birla's *Eastern Economist* likened the government's economic policy to 'Dr Jekyll and Mr Hyde.' Further, there was a vast divergence between policy outcomes and implementation, and businessmen gradually learnt how to find ways of coping with policies which were meant to curtail them. Birla also saw that the larger context of the democratic process in which economic policy-making was conducted ensured that the viewpoint of big business could not be completely ignored. Amongst the diverse ideological groups that were heard, businessmen and their chambers of commerce had ample opportunities to make their points of view known. As he wrote to a business associate soon after the Mahalanobis Draft Plan was announced in 1955:

I take an optimistic view. Because I have great faith in the robust common-sense of the people ... To give an instance, hardly the draft plan by Mahalanobis and a number of leftist economists had come out before a reaction against the same set in from different quarters. As I have said so often to my friends abroad, democracy is our best insurance. In it ... plenty of 'words would flow', but ultimately it must be followed by 'water'. So the 'words' have their value since they do make a helpful contribution![104]

His overall experience of the democratic process heartened his faith that the future of free enterprise was secure and that its voice could never be lost.

NOTES AND REFERENCES

[1] On this issue, see D.A. Low, *Britain and Indian Nationalism, The Imprint of Ambiguity, 1929–1942* (Cambridge, 1997), chapter 6 and Bipan Chandra, Jawarharlal Nehru and the Capitalist Class, 1936, *Economic and Political Weekly*, Vol. X, Nos 33–5, Special No., August 1975.

[2] V.K.R.V. Rao, 'Nehru's economic vision' in Sheila Dikshit, K. Natwar Singh, et al. (eds), *Jawarharlal Nehru Centenary Volume* (Delhi, 1989), pp. 506–13. Also see Sukhamoy Chakravarty, 'The Nehru legacy in planning' in *Ibid*, pp. 116–22.

[3] The Economic Programme Committee consisted of Nehru (chairman), Maulana Azad, J.C. Kumarappa, N.G. Ranga, John Mathai, Shankarrao Deo, Gulzarilal Nanda and Jayaprakash Narayan.

[4] Mody was concerned that Birla intervene before the AICC ratified the report.

[5] Homi Mody to Birla, 28 Jan 1948, in Birla Papers, Series I, File No. M–19, Mody, Sir Homi and Russi.

[6] While Birla had expected some controls on the private sector to be imposed, he had not anticipated the report as it emerged. Yet the bill, he knew, was the 'lesser of two evils' in that it vested powers of industrial control on the centre rather than the provinces. See Birla's lecture at the joint meeting with the Overseas League held at Overseas House on 3 August 1949 with Sir Kenneth Mealing in the Chair. Birla, 'The Economic Condition of India', in the *Asiatic Review*, Vol. XLV, No. 164, October 1949.

[7] The report was found especially disappointing to business after the assurances government had given at the Industries Conference in December 1947 which had declared that a machinery would be constituted of representatives of government, employers and workers to look into matters of the economy. The FICCI complained that the new recommendations were virtually 'short circuiting .... resolutions passed at the Industries Conference.' Telegram sent by Homi Mody to S.P. Mukherjee, n.d., in Birla Papers, Series I, File No. M–19, Mody, H.P. and Homi.

[8] 'The rest of the industrial field will normally be left open to private enterprise' it had declared and stated that 'private enterprise, properly directed and regulated, has a valuable role to play.'

[9] Birla to G.B. Pant, 15 October 1948, in Birla Papers, Series I, File No. P–10, Pant, G.B.

[10] Birla to G.B. Pant, 15 October 1948, in Birla Papers, Series I, File No. P–10, Pant, G.B.

[11] Birla to Purushottamdas Thakurdas, in Birla Papers, Series I, File No. P–11, Thakurdas, P.

[12] In February 1949, Patel declared: 'Take it from me that this government has not got the capacity and means to undertake nationalization of any industry at present' and in December 1949 he reassured businessmen when he said, 'Take it from me—if anyone talks of nationalization, it is only for the sake of leadership.' See M. Kidron, *Foreign Investments in India* (London, 1965), pp. 86–7.

[13] Birla complained so to S.P. Mukherjee. See Birla Papers, Series II, File No. M–30, Mukherjee.

[14] Birla to V. Patel, 26 April 1949, in Birla Papers, Series I, File No. P–7, Patel Maniben, Sahyabhai, etc.

[15] Birla to V. Shankar, 5 August 1950, in Birla Papers, Series I, File No. P–7, Patel Maniben, Dahyabhai, etc.

[16] In a public debate in the early 1940s C.N. Vakil, the renowned economist, and Birla had argued for increasing production, deficit financing and increase in money supply. He put forth a monetarist argument and stated that the rise in prices were not linked to increase in money supply but could be attributed to falls in production. Birla recommended a 'reflationary' policy and an increase in the volume of currency and credit. In his view, a large part of the money supply had gone out of circulation and this needed to be remedied by increasing the supply. Birla believed that the controls were leading to a crisis, and he predicted that 20 lakh businessmen would fail because of the standstill position with regard to distribution.

[17] To compound the problem were 'the present terror technique of the Income-Tax department' which, Birla wrote to Vallabhbhai Patel, 'will have to be changed into mutual co-operation between assessees and the assessor.' Birla, 'Economic Condition', n.d., Birla Papers, Series Very Very Important Correspondence, File No. 5, Grosvenor House, London, 1945–9. In 1950 Tulsidas Kilachand, FICCI president and Birla began collecting 'evidence' of the 'high-handedness' of the Income-Tax officials.

[18] Birla, Notes entitled 'Industrial Co-operation between India and America', 11 November 1949, in Birla Papers, Series Miscellaneous, File No. 124, Notes and Speeches.

[19] Birla to V. Patel, 29 April 1949, in Birla Papers, Series I, File No. P–7, Patel, Maniben, Dahyabhai, etc.

[20] Birla, Notes entitled 'Industrial Co-operation between India and America', 11 November 1949, in Birla Papers, Series Miscellaneous, File No. 124, Notes and Speeches.

[21] As he told John Mathai: 'you can't tie the legs of the man and then ask him to run. So these knots that tie the legs have to be loosened, if not untied'.

[22] G.D. Birla to Mathai, 27 April 1948, in Birla Papers, Series I, File No. M–16, Dr Mathai.

[23] In Birla's estimate, while textile mills could easily produce 5000 million yards a year, they were producing merely 4000 million yards; cement which had the capacity to produce $2\frac{1}{2}$ million tons was only producing 1.7 million tons and steel which could optimally produce 13 lakhs tons, was producing much less.

[24] Birla complained in a note he sent to Patel on the country's economic condition. Birla, 'Economic Condition', n.d., Birla Papers, Series Very Very Important Correspondence, File No. 5, Grosvenor House, London, 1945–9.

[25] Birla recommended barter with Pakistan for both cotton supplies and jute. On his own initiative, he had held talks with Ghulam Mohammad, Pakistan's Finance Minister, in late 1948 and then with G. Faruque and Ispahani and discussed trade conditions between the two countries. Birla argued that irrespective of exchange problems, trading should commence and he felt Pakistan should raise restrictions on unofficial exchange transactions. Birla to V. Shankar, 21 January 1950 and 28 September 1950, in Birla Papers, Series I, File No. P–7, Patel, Maniben, Dahyabhai, etc.

[26] In his talk to the Overseas League in London, in August 1949, Birla posed the question: 'How long, without improving the economic situation can India remain free from Communism?' Policies were needed to encourage both internal and foreign investment and government's attitude to private capital would thus have to change. 'The Government of India will have to realise', he noted, 'that they cannot have Damocles' sword hanging on the investor'. Note by Birla, n.d. There was, he declared, 'too much regimentation and interference from govt. in various stages of production and distribution' which had contributed to the tightness of the money market. 'Controls', he declared, 'should not mean laying down a few hundred "don'ts" hindering all initiatives and incentives as has been the case in India; but they should mean positive encouragement to production, and an invitation for cooperation to that end of all sections of society.' The policies were leading to an end of business initiatives and Birla was convinced that 'as long as this obstruction and interference continues, there is no possibility of increased business.' He blamed government interference for being 'substantially responsible for holding up progress.' Birla to H.K. Mehtab, 29 May 1950, in Birla Papers, Series II, File No. M–37, Mehtab, H.K.

[27] 'All that I ask at this stage is that they ought to declare their policy. If it is their desire that for the next few years they will rely on private enterprise they should say so;

if on the other hand it is their desire to start industries of their own and manage them through their own agencies, they should declare it. All I can say is that the spirit of suspense is hindering production; and when I say this I am not expressing vague fears but only telling you what is today in every businessman's mind.' Birla to FICCI, 1947, cited in Kidron, *Foreign Investment in India*, p. 84.

[28] Khilnani, *The Idea of India*, pp. 81–6.

[29] FICCI, *Silver Jubilee Souvenir*, 1927–51, p. 177.

[30] 'Summary record of the Planning Commission meeting with the office bearers of the Federation of Indian Chambers of Commerce and Industry at 10 a.m.—on the 14th May, 1952', in Birla Papers, Series Important, File No. 44–P, 1950–5. Also see 'Confidential Note' by G.D. Birla, 16 May 1952, in Birla Papers, Series Important, File No. 113, Miscellaneous, 1952.

[31] Note by Birla, no title, n.d., in Birla Papers, Series Important, File No. 113, Miscellaneous, 1952.

[32] Birla, 'The Economic Condition of India', in the *Asiatic Review*, Vol. XLV, No. 164, October 1949.

[33] He began to estimate how much FICCI needed for its monthly expense and for it to move into a new site.

[34] 'Things are getting from bad to worse .... There is no finance. Nobody pays. Nobody takes any interest and everybody is getting demoralized', complained Birla to Lalbhai, 8 February 1949, in Birla Papers, Series I, File No. K–9, Kasturbhai Lalbhai.

[35] This was the second scheme prepared by Birla for the reorganization of FICCI. The details of the first proposal he put forth are not known; we do know that it had been informally circulated among leading industrialists from different member bodies. Calcutta and north Indian organizations had supported his ideas whole-heartedly but Bombay and Ahmedabad member bodies showed reluctance in bringing about changes on the lines suggested by him and thus the scheme was dropped.

[36] The scheme was implemented in late 1949 and for part of 1950 after which it was substituted by Advisory Committees. Tulsidas Kilachand, 'Reorganizing the Federation', in FICCI, Silver Jubilee Souvenir, 1927–51, pp. 227–30.

[37] He wanted Kasturbhai Lalbhai to take more interest and on Birla's persuasion, a reluctant Lalbhai was co-opted as a committee member for 1949–50.

[38] Birla to K. Lalbhai, 9 March 1949, in Birla Papers, Series I, File No. K–9, Kasturbhai Lalbhai.

[39] According to Kochanek, this led ultimately to the dominance of the Birla group within the Federation. For details see, Kochanek, *Business and Politics in India*, pp. 170–85.

[40] Tulsidas Kilachand, 'Reorganising the Federation', in FICCI, *Silver Jubilee Souvenir*, 1927–51, p. 227.

[41] FICCI officials asked Birla to intervene with Patel, Gadgil and Shankar Prasad, the Chief Commissioner, to negotiate a plot with the New Delhi Administration for the FICCI building. G.L. Bansal, secretary of FICCI to the president, FICCI, 22 March 1950, in Birla Papers, Series I, File No. T–3, Kilachand Tulsidas. The foundation stone of the new building was laid by Rajendra Prasad on 2 April 1951. Along with strengthening FICCI, Birla and other prominent business leaders formed new pressure groups. In 1950 the Association of Indian Trade and Industry was established in Bombay. Sponsored by Birla, Hirachand, Kilachand, Ruia and Khatau its primary function was economic research and it started a monthly journal called *Economic Trends*.

[42] On Birla's solicitation, a number of businessmen came forward to subsidize the paper through advertisements or other means, for a period of one year in the first instance, to the extent of Rs 25,000 each per month. Among those who supported it were J.R.D. Tata, Kasturbhai Lalbhai, Tulsidas Kilachand and Ambalal Sarabhai along with some business associations such as the Vanaspathi Association. J.R.D. Tata to Tulsidas Kilachand, 30 May 1950, in Birla Papers, Series I, Tulsidas Kilachand to Birla, 29 May 1950, in Birla Papers, Series I, File No. T–3, Tulsidas Kilachand. The paper was owned by a company called the Hindustan which was managed by the Akhil Bharat which had a capital of nearly 32 lakhs. Many important businessmen of Bombay had leading shares in the company. Birla to Ambalal Sarabhai, 29 June 1950, in Birla Papers, Series I, File No. A–4, Ambalal Sarabhai.

[43] Tulsidas Kilachand, 'Reorganising the Federation', in FICCI, *Silver Jubilee Souvenir,* 1927–51, p. 230.

[44] The Birla factories they visited were Jiyajeerao Cotton Mills, Gwalior; Textile Machinery Cooperation, Gwalior; Birla Hosiery, Gwalior; Hind Cycles, Bombay; Hindustan Motors, Calcutta and Textile Machinery Corporation, Calcutta. The expenses incurred during the visit were borne by the mills; the total expenses were estimated to be Rs 75,000–80,000; the Birla mills together paid Rs 20,000 as their share of the expenses. Tulsidas Kilachand to Birla, 6 May 1950, in Birla Papers, Series I, File No. T–3, Kilachand Tulsidas.

[45] Tulsidas Kilachand to Birla, 6 May 1950, in Birla Papers, Series I, File No. T–3, Kilachand Tulsidas; also see Tulsidas Kilachand, 'Reorganising the Federation', in FICCI, *Silver Jubilee Souvenir,* 1927–51, p. 230. In response FICCI brought out a booklet 'Impediments in the way of increasing Industrial Production'. See *Ibid,* p. 174.

[46] Kochanek, *Business and Politics in India,* p. 241.

[47] Birla to V. Shankar, 20 March 1949 and 11 June 1950, in Birla Papers, Series I, File No. P–7, Patel, Maniben, Dahyabhai, etc. Birla assured his American business associates that he was doing his best to modify the bill and that the Sardar is a 'very practical man' and they could hope for improvements in economic policy from him.

[48] Kidron, *Foreign Investment in India,* p. 241.

[49] The boundaries of which, according to him, were dictated only by considerations of the capital it could command.

[50] As B.M. Birla said at the meeting of FICCI: 'Today the most valuable gift that the Planning Commission has made to this country, particularly to the industrial and commercial community, is the recognition that there is a great and legitimate part for them to play, that there is such a thing as a private sector, that it has been given certain duties to fulfil, that it is necessary for the economy of the country as a whole that it should also play its part along with that field which is called public sector.' Venkatsubbiah, *Enterprise and Economic Change,* p. 100.

[51] For details see Government of India, *Report of the Industrial Licensing Policy Enquiry Committee,* Appendices, Vol. IV.

[52] K.M. Chenoy, Industrial Policy and Big Business in India (unpublished PhD thesis, JNU, 1983), pp. 320–1. Birla's *Eastern Economist* declared with satisfaction that ' what was regarded as a grand instrument of industrial policy in 1949, namely the Industries (Development and Control) Bill, was never put into full use even after its belated enactment in 1951 and its amendment last year. The law is still on display on the shelf–except for some action on the more routine and less objectionable sections like registration, licensing and the establishment of development councils'. *Eastern Economist,* 13 August 1954.

[53] Birla, 'The Economic Condition of India', in the *Asiatic Review*, Vol. XLV, No. 164.

[54] Birla to Rajendra Prasad, 2 August 1954.

[55] As the *Eastern Economist* put it in an editorial in 1954: 'Thus the Congress party stands "for private enterprise for which too, there is greater scope" and yet, in terms of the Prime Minister's address to the National Development Council on Tuesday, the goal is definitely "a socialist pattern of society". Then, the GOI is developing large scale industries, but there is a constant cry that the emphasis should be on small scale industries.'

[56] Yet, as always, according to the *Eastern Economist*, this was followed by a multitude of contradictory statements. In one week, while Khandubhai Desai, Union Labour Minister defined 'socialistic pattern' in one way the Union Minister of Revenue and Civil Expenditure—Shah—defined it differently and reassured private business. *Eastern Economist*, 28 January 1955.

[57] This had originally been given notice by Nehru in December 1954.

[58] Birla to Homi Mody, 18 January 1954, Homi Mody to Birla, 30 January 1954, Homi Mody to Birla, 31 March 1954, in Birla Papers, Series I, File No. M–19, Mody, Sir Homi and Russi. Also see *Eastern Economist*, 30 April 1954. In December 1953 a conference of leading industrialists was called in Bombay at the initiative of Homi Mody to discuss the situation 'confronting industrial interest and to formulate a plan of action'. It appeared imperative to Mody for business to come together urgently to 'save the private sector from the dangers which are gathering around it'. Though Birla did not attend the conference, he assured Mody of his 'fullest support' and gave him proxy for the meeting. He also agreed to contribute towards the cost of hosting the conference along with the Tatas. The businessmen felt that: 'in view of the various legislative and administrative acts of the government, the burdens being piled on industry, the interference in the operations of industry by the acts of the government, the award of the industrial courts and Labour tribunals and the way in which the effective functioning of the private sector was being "hamstrung", business leaders felt the need for a "sustained and vigorous" presentation of the viewpoint of industry to government and to the public'. It was thus decided to set up a council of industrial interests and to immediately constitute a small committee of influential business leaders composed of Birla, J.R.D. Tata, Lala Shri Ram, Ramaswami Mudaliar, D.M. Khatau and Kasturbhai Lalbhai with a 'view of ensuring speedy action whenever an issue arises calling for it.'

[59] The *Eastern Economist* commented that 'no one need deny the determination with which action is being taken or suggest now that the bark of the Congress leaders in this mood is worse then their bite.'

[60] It was important that 'the mind of all the ministers (be) … prepared beforehand and a sympathetic atmosphere created' as without this 'nothing would be gained.'

[61] Note by Birla, no title in Birla papers, Series I, C–27, Ceylon high commissioner.

[62] Birla to Babubhai M. Chinai, 27 December 1957, in Birla Papers, Series I, File No. C–27, Ceylon High Commissioner. Birla decided to make a trip to Delhi to gather feedback on the reaction of the ministers to the businessmen's views and he asked Chinai to keep 'things in suspense' till then.

[63] The budget of 1955–6 raised and revised a number of taxes; levied special taxes on salaries of business executives, imposed new and increased excise duties, gave preferential rates to cottage industries and spelt a rise in personal taxation above the Rs 20,000 mark. Birla declared that there was nothing positive in the budget; 'they seek to control expenditure and in this process they also curb production', he declared. *Eastern Economist*,

5 March 1955.

[64] He suggested that cabinet ministers such as Maulana Azad, G.B. Pant, the Finance Minister, B.C. Roy, Minister for Commerce and Industry, and Morarji Desai and the Congress president could be a part of the committee. In addition, a member of the Planning Commission could be invited to these meetings which could be held once a quarter. Nehru supposedly assured Birla and Lalbhai that they, as well as other businessmen such as J.R.D. Tata, could see him or his ministers whenever they felt an important issue needed to be discussed. Nehru to Birla, 3 April 1955, in Birla Papers, Series I, File No. N–24, Nehru, Jawaharlal and Indira Gandhi.

[65] After returning from the meeting, Birla wrote a one-page note suggesting ways in which businessmen could approach the proposed committee of Cabinet which was to be sent to close business colleagues, G.D. Birla, Note, n.d., no title in Birla Papers, Series Important, File No. 158, Miscellaneous, 1955–6. If an 'ad hoc' Committee of Cabinet was constituted, various ways of solving problems that business faced could be found. Calcutta and Bombay businessmen, he said, could approach B.C. Roy and Morarji Desai who could then take up the issue with the Prime Minister. On more important matters, notes could be sent either to Roy, Desai or the ministers concerned who could then hold discussions with the Prime Minister and the committee if necessary. In addition, meetings should be held with the ad hoc committee from time to time. Birla stressed the need to keep the discussions informal and saw the usefulness of the committee in that it would 'have combined wisdom at its disposal and thus will be in a position to take a wider view and a quick decision. The danger of taking a narrow view will thus be eliminated.' However, nothing seems to have eventually come out of this proposal to form a committee and it remained a recurrent theme in meetings that were held with Nehru through these years.

[66] Birla, 'Agenda for discussion with the Prime Minister' (2-page note containing points for discussion suggested by Birla, Kasturbhai Lalbhai and H.P. Mody), n.d., Birla Papers, Series Important, File No. 158, Miscellaneous, 1955–6.

[67] There is also no information about which industrialist accompanied Birla to the meeting but they seem to have been both from Bombay and Calcutta. Mody wanted the recommendations of the Mathai Commission regarding putting a ceiling on personal incomes to be taken up to the Prime Minister. The Planning Commission, he said to Birla, had recently in a memorandum before a panel of economists proposed that this would be begun in the public sector and then extended to the private sector. According to the memorandum the ceiling would be on a gross income of Rs 20,000. See Homi Mody to G.D. Birla, 27 December 1955, in Birla Papers, Series I, File No. M–19, Mody, Sir H.P. and Russi. It is not known if this was discussed at the meeting held with Nehru.

[68] Birla, 'Agenda for discussion with the Prime Minister' (2-page note containing points for discussion suggested by G.D. Birla, Kasturbhai Lalbhai and H.P. Mody) n.d., Birla Papers, Series Important, File No. 158, Miscellaneous, 1955–6. The business delegation's critique of the Plan was later encapsulated by FICCI in a publication.

[69] Birla to Pant, 20 March 1956, in Birla Papers, Series Foreign Correspondence, File No. 87–P, 1955–6. Also in Birla Papers, File No. P–10, G.B. Pant.

[70] Birla to Morarji Desai, 27 June 1955, in Birla Papers, Series I, File No. D–4, Desai, Morarji.

[71] FICCI responded to the Mahanalobis Plan-frame by arguing that the planners had ignored the basic economic criteria in favouring the public sector. For the private sector they said, the high taxation would weaken initiative and the restrictions on factory production in favour of cottage and small-scale industries would lead to a huge shortage

of consumer goods. The whole plan would collapse, they warned, with strong inflationary pressure and rising prices. Though they agreed with the emphasis on larger investment outlays and higher allocation to basic and heavy industries they countered all else in the Plan. The sphere of the public sector, they said, should lie in the formation and maintenance of social capital. Francine Frankel, *India's Political Economy, 1947–1977: The Gradual Revolution* (Princeton, 1978), p. 129. They agreed though, with the emphasis on larger investment outlays and higher allocation to basic and the formation and maintenance of social capital.

[72] He likened the restrictions on factory production in favour of cottage industries to a plan the railways should progress through the bullock cart.

[73] Birla to UCO Bank on 28 March 1956, reported in *Eastern Economist*, 30 March 1956. The first problem, in Birla's view, was the question of foreign exchange. Given the greater emphasis that the Plan laid on industrialization as compared to the first Plan, the need for importing capital goods was large. Expanding transport facilities and importing personnel to provide expertise would also add to the requirements of foreign exchange making it a 'serious headache'. The foreign exchange requirement, in Birla's estimate, was Rs 1500 crores in five years. A way had to be found to meet this need. One possibility was to procedure large loans, possibly from United States. Apart from borrowed money, Birla pointed out ways to secure foreign exchange in an article he wrote for the *Hindustan Times* in October 1955. Producing good and larger quantity of steel to meet the demands of the railways and heavy engineering industries would lighten the dependence on foreign supplies. However the need to import equipment would continue as the economy was still in the expanding phase. Another way to meet the demand for foreign exchange was to rely on supplier's credit institutions abroad for the next 10 to 15 years. This could be fully exploited and would not be difficult because, in Birla's view, most countries were willing to grant credit facilities for purchases. Promoting foreign exchange would also alleviate the foreign-exchange problem. Birla pointed out that a number of industrialized nations such as the United States, Japan and Australia had benefited from foreign investments. Another step to meet the problem was to promote exports and maintain the position of the Indian rupee. Alongside the traditional export of cloth, jute and tea, new exports should be promoted such as engineering goods and new markets should be explored. G.D. Birla, 'Foreign Exchange for Second Plan', *Hindustan Times*, 29 October 1955. Later reprinted in the *New York Times*. Draft of the article is in Birla Papers, Series Miscellaneous, File No. 123, Notes and Speeches.

[74] Birla to T.T. Krishnamachari, 20 August 1956, in Birla Papers, Series Foreign Correspondence, File No. 82–K, 1955–6.

[75] Birla to G.B. Pant, 20 August 1956, in Birla Papers, Series Foreign Correspondence, File No. 87–P, 1955–6.

[76] While cottage industry could, no doubt, provide larger employment, it was not only the target of 10 million jobs which was important in the Plan but also raising the standard of living. This could be achieved only with ample production wealth. 'But if we only had the jobs and no substantial increase in wealth then 25 per cent rise in standard would remain a mere dream', Birla wrote to Nehru. He also spoke of the lack of collaboration between producers and the administration, and 'brakes' which administration put to production, which 'could lead to a traffic jam'. What was required was that the whole administrative machinery, the administration of the financial institutions like the Reserve Bank, the State Bank, and the various financial corporations move with a common object and in a common rhythm. Birla to Nehru, 25 August 1955, in Birla Papers, Series I, File

No. N–24, Nehru, Jawaharlal and Indira Gandhi.

[77] The number of industries reserved for the private sector expanded from 6 to 17. This included all basic and strategic industries, public utilities and industries requiring large investments. These constituted Schedule 'A'. The second category was 'Schedule B' which consisted of 12 'essential' industries which were left to the public sector, but the private sector was to have the 'opportunity to develop either on its own or with state participation'. This category was described as 'industries which will be progressively state-owned and which the state will therefore generally take the initiative in establishing new undertakings.' This was, however, qualified by adding, 'but in which private enterprise will also be expected to supplement the efforts of the state. This concurrent list included machine tools production, aluminum, essential drugs, basic chemicals, sea and road transport. All other industries were left to the private sector. Existing private industrial concerns were guaranteed that they would not be nationalized, private capital could enter industries reserved for the state and joint state private undertakings could be undertaken in the name of the reserved sector. For a study of the resolution see I.G. Patel, 'Free Enterprise in the Nehru Era', in I.G. Patel, *Essays in Economic Policy and Economic Growth* (London, 1986), pp. 165–81.

[78] While classifying industry into three categories 'having regard to the part which the State would play in each of them,' it carefully added qualification that 'these categories will inevitably overlap to some extent and too great a rigidity might defeat the purpose in view.' Thus it dropped the category of exclusive monopoly of the central government.

[79] See Somejee, A.H. and Geeta, 'India' in *The Journal of Politics*, 1963, Vol. 25, pp. 686–737.

[80] The total number of parties that were contesting was 59 and independent candidates. The main all-India parties were the Congress, the KMPP, the Socialist Party, the Communist Party and the Jana Sangh.

[81] Birla to N.V. Gadgil, 30 December 1951, in Birla Papers, Series I, File No. G–9, Gadgil, N.V.

[82] Nehru to V.K. Krishna Menon, 30 November 1951, in S. Gopal (ed.), *Selected Works of Jawarharlal Nehru*, Second Series, Vol. 17, p. 497.

[83] Birla to N.V. Gadgil, 30 December 1951, in Birla Papers, Series I, File No. G–9, Gadgil, N.V. For a study of the elections see Norman D. Palmer, *Elections and Political Development. The South Asian Experience* (North Carolina, 1975).

[84] See S.K. Patil, *My Years with Congress*, p. 130.

[85] See Nehru to V.K. Krishna Menon, 30 November 1951, in S. Gopal (ed.), *Selected Works of Jawarharlal Nehru*, Second Series, Vol. 17, p. 497.

[86] Only in Tripura did it suffer defeat at the hands of the Communists.

[87] Morarji Desai, *The Story of my Life*, Vol. II, p. 88.

[88] *Ibid*, p. 88.

[89] M.C. Dahanukar to Birla, 13 Februrary 1957, in Birla Papers, Series I, File No. D–2, Dahanukar, M.L. Also Birla to H.D. Mundhra, 5 January 1956, in Birla Papers, Series I, File No. 52, Mundhra, Haridas.

[90] Birla to K.C. Thapar, 24 July 1956, in Birla Papers, Series I, File No. T–1, Thapar, K.C.

[91] Morarji Desai, *The Story of my Life*, Vol. II, p. 89.

[92] Birla, 'Summary', 11 December 1956, in Birla Papers, Series Miscellaneous, File No. 116, Donations.

[93] Birla to Desai, 25 June 1955, in Birla Papers, Series I, File No. D–4, Desai, Morarji.

[94] In December 1955, he sent Rs 50,000 for Travancore Cochin and in 1956 he gave another Rs 1 lakh, in two separate instalments, for 'Congress work in Kerala.' K.P. Madhav Nair to Birla, 1 November 1956, and Birla to K.P. Madhav Nair, 12 December 1955, and Madhav Nair to Birla, 26 June 1956, in Birla Papers, Series I, File No. A–17, AICC.

[95] Birla persuaded Krishnamachari to discuss the problem with Pant who would be able to wield his influence with UP and Bihar. No decision seems to have been reached on the matter and problems of overlapping demands continued to crop up through the months of fund collection.

[96] S. Jaipuria to Birla, 11 February 1956, Birla to Mangutaram Jaipuria, 28 July 1956, in Birla Papers, Series I, File No. J–5, Jaipuria, M.R.

[97] Birla to K.C. Thapar, 2 August 1956, Thapar to Birla, 7 February 1957 and Birla to Thapar, 19 February 1957. Complaints about exorbitant demands of provincial leaders and 'harassment' of merchants continued to pour in till much after the election and Birla had to deal with them. Parmanand Kejriwal to Birla, 20 March 1958, in Birla Papers, Series Important, File No. 64–K.

[98] See for instance, Birla to Kantilal Nihalchand, 6 February 1957, reminding him to send the sum of Rs 17,500 which was due for the Congress; Birla to M.L. Kanoi, 20 January 1956, in Birla Papers, Series Important, File No. 64–K.

[99] Birla to M.L. Dahanukar, 25 February 1957, in Birla Papers, Series I, File No. D–2, Dahanukar, M.L.

[100] S.K. Patil, *My Years with Congress*, pp. 130–1

[101] Morarji Desai, *The Story of my Life*, Vol. II, p. 89. Desai states that the target was 1 crore 20 lakhs but Birla estimated it to be 1 crore $91\frac{1}{2}$ lakhs.

[102] Justice P.B. Mukherji of Calcutta High Court declared that 'having regard to the dangers of power of money to purchase views, it will be highly undesirable to encourage any kind of secrecy in respect of such payments.'

[103] 'The Week's Notes' and 'Company Contributions to Party Coffers' in the *Eastern Economist*, 12 July 1957.

[104] Birla to Francis Watson, 5 July 1955, Birla Papers, Series Foreign Correspondence, File No. W–94, 1955–6.

14

Business Fortunes in Nehru's India

It appears somewhat ironical that in the first decade of independence when Nehru's rhetoric of state enterprise and socialism was at its peak, Birla's business empire expanded vigorously. At the time of independence the traditional business strength had been in jute, textiles, banking and publishing. Recent diversifications had been in insurance, textile machinery, automobiles, bicycles and plastics. The decade following independence proved to be critical as it was marked by expansion into several key sectors of the economy such as engineering, tea, chemicals, cement, non-ferrous metals, glass, aluminium, shipping and aviation.

Let us look at the direction of this business expansion to appreciate the strategic vision which underlay it. Independence in 1947 involved not simply a political transfer of power; it also involved critical changes in the nature of control over the Indian economy. The withdrawal of European managing agencies and the exodus of capital opened up extraordinary take-over opportunities.[1] As the most prominent Indian business house in Calcutta, the bastion of European capital, the Birlas were particularly well positioned to benefit from such opportunities. In particular, their strength in jute enabled them to acquire several jute companies such as Bally Jute, Rameshwara Jute and Soorah Jute. It also led the Birla group into tea, till then a European monopoly. The Birlas were able to acquire tea estates which were then consolidated under the firm Jayshree Tea Industries. A raft of other acquisitions further added to the Birla stable of companies: Century Spinning and Weaving, Sirpur Paper, Hyderabad Asbestos (Hyderabad Allwyn), and Shree Digvijaya Woollen Mills in Saurashtra. The years following independence and partition were marked by this spate of acquisitions and take-overs.

Older concerns were expanded. For example there was substantial expansion in the capacity of the textile firms. Several of these diversified into newer technologically advanced areas. For example, Kesoram diversified into rayon and steel tubes. Birla Jute expanded into cement and chemicals. Likewise, Jiyajeerao Cotton Mill in Gwalior diversified into chemicals. Many of the older firms were able to acquire new technology to enhance their competitiveness and market

share. Hindustan Motors, for instance, tied up with the British tycoon, Lord
Nuffield, to manufacture the legendary Morris Minor. It achieved self-sufficiency
in the manufacture of iron casting, forgings and tools required to manufacture
the new V-8 engine which powered the automobile.[2]

A further impetus to the extraordinary growth seen in these years came from
the initiatives taken by the younger generation of the Birlas. We have noted that
by the early 1940s all the sons of the three Birla brothers had joined the family
business. Several of their key initiatives, which had been stalled due to wartime
delays and scarcities of plant and equipment came to fruition following
independence. For example, the India Steamship Company, steered by Krishna
Kumar began its liner services. Bharat Airways, an initiative of Basant Kumar
launched its inaugural flight six weeks after independence.[3] Thus the Birla
presence came to be established in the key areas of shipping and aviation.

The new initiatives for diversification reflected Birla's strategic vision of
moving away from consumer products and low-technology areas into basic
industry. This is illustrated by his entry into staple fibres. In 1949 Birla visited
several staple fibre factories in the USA and came back determined to put up
a plant. He envisaged an ambitious project outlay of Rs 2.5 crores in the initial
stages and Rs 4 crores later. He tried to interest the Maharajas of Gwalior,
Travancore and Mysore to participate as investors.[4] When the Maharaja of
Gwalior agreed, he located the staple fibre manufacturing unit in Nagda,
Madhya Pradesh and made it a division of Gwalior Rayon Silk Manufacturing
(Weaving) Co. Ltd. (MP).[5] He kept a close eye on new technological developments
in this field.[6]

Likewise, he grew interested in rayon pulp. Since India did not have a large
supply of pinewood that was used as raw material for its manufacture, he
experimented with eucalyptus cultivation and sugar-cane. He was able to obtain
a large agricultural plot of 15,000 acres in Mysore and vigorously exploited
technical collaboration from manufacturers in America and Europe. His efforts
were finally successful in the late 1950s when Century established a rayon pulp
plant with a substantial production capacity.[7]

For long Birla had been eyeing the highly lucrative steel industry, till now the
preserve of the Tatas. It had been his ambition to establish a steel plant as he
hoped the industry would see rapid expansion after independence. This was
confirmed by a Planning Commission report which projected a great shortage
of steel, so severe that even the replacement of rails would be affected.[8] Birla was
emboldened to draw up detailed plans of setting up a pig-iron plant initially,
which would be expanded into a full-fledged steel mill where he ultimately
hoped to develop the capacity to produce steel machine goods. As Birla developed
his plans, in 1951, the Bengal Chief Minister Bidhan Chandra Roy suggested
that he should locate his plant at Durgapur, where the West Bengal government
proposed to set up a coke oven and gas production plant. Birla's steel mill could
complement these facilities.[9]

Encouraged by Roy, Birla proceeded to make enquiries with the Government of India. He learnt that a licence needed to be obtained. However, the government seemed uncertain to open up steel to the private sector at a time when it was contemplating foreign participation in a public-sector steel project. Birla tried to get informal approval of his project, so that he could develop his plans. He had talks with H.K. Mehtab, Minister for Industry, who encouraged him in these early stages to pursue the project.[10] Likewise, T.T. Krishnamachari too was optimistic that the project would be approved. Other leaders whom he kept in the picture by informing them regularly about the progress of his plans were G.L. Nanda and G.B. Pant. As the overall signs were encouraging, Birla went ahead to put in place detailed plans of a facility with an annual capacity of 250,000 ton pig-iron and one million ton steel. He and Braj Mohan entered into negotiations with British firms for financial and technical assistance[11]. They succeeded in obtaining approval of the Licensing Committee, and a company, the Durgapur Iron and Steel Co., was registered with an authorized capital of Rs 50 crores.[12]

Thus, things appeared to be moving quite smoothly till the autumn of 1954 when the West Bengal Government's proposal of the coke oven project was turned down by the Planning Commission.[13] Soon thereafter, upon returning from a trip to China, Nehru himself turned down Birla's proposal at a Cabinet meeting on the ground that it went against the 1948 Industrial Policy Resolution which had laid down that future expansion in steel should be in the public sector. Birla was indignant. The 1948 Industrial Policy Resolution could not, he believed, be interpreted in such a rigid and unimaginative manner. He was merely trying to be of 'service' to the nation and had taken the risk to undertake a 'serious headache and a risky business' to be able to make a 'definite contribution to the country'. Yet, the government had turned his proposal down.[14] This was not, he protested to T.T. Krishnamachari, what Nehru's socialistic pattern of society was supposed to be all about. For him it meant a 'better way of life, viz. greater consumption of consumer goods, better health, more houses and so on and so forth.' Only rapid industrialization could achieve this goal and anyone promoting it should be encouraged, rather than stopped.

On his part, T.T. Krishnamachari was incensed. To allegations that he had been soft on the Birlas in particular and big business in general, he is said to have retorted that he was merely doing his job: 'You cannot ask a Jail Superintendent not to speak to a convict.'[15] Krishnamachari protested to Nehru that the rejection was inconsistent with the government's policy which relied to a great extent on private enterprise in complementing the goals of planned development. In late 1954, when Krishnamachari submitted his resignation from the Union Cabinet, this was apparently one of his main reasons, the other being his demand for the abolition of the Ministry of Production.[16] However, Nehru worked out a compromise and called back Krishnamachari. To assuage him, the charge of Iron and Steel was placed under him, and Nehru retained the Ministry of

Production on the understanding that it would solely be concerned with the public sector, while the Commerce and Industry Ministries would deal with the private sector.[17] It was widely believed in business circles that, had the Birlas demanded less control and agreed to a 51–49 ownership with the government, their steel project may have been approved.[18] In 1955 Birla made one last attempt to revive the project with T.T. Krishnamachari after J.R.D. Tata's TISCO was given the permission to double its capacity. However, nothing came out of his attempts, and in 1958 the company he had set up for a plant in Durgapur was liquidated.[19]

Another challenging area which Birla began exploring in the mid-1950s was aluminum. It appeared an attractive proposition, given India's large bauxite deposits and coal reserves. However, he knew that foreign technical collaboration was necessary to make a success of such an ambitious project, given India's lack of expertise in this area. Before making any plans, Birla asked the finance minister for his 'informal blessings' and Manubhai Shah and T. T. Krishnamachari for their 'go-ahead' signal.[20] His experience with the aborted steel project had made him cautious and he wished to obtain explicit approval from as many influential ministers as he possibly could before investing his time and energy in the scheme. He then did the preliminary work of drawing up the terms for collaboration, exploring foreign exchange loans and drafting of production details. Birla became so enthusiastic about the project that he planned each detail personally. In 1957 he visited the USA in search of collaborators. Through the mediation of George Woods, President of the World Bank, he established contact with Edgar Kaiser, the American industrialist who headed the huge conglomerate, Kaiser Corporations, which was well known for its strength in the metallurgical field.[21]

Kaiser was impressed with Birla's meticulous plans. On 16 December 1957 they signed a collaboration agreement, which was publicly announced only in October 1958. According to its terms, Kaiser Aluminum and Chemical Corporation were to participate in the capital structure and provide technical services.[22] Kaiser recommended a 20,000 ton plant with an estimated cost of Rs 15 crores. A market study undertaken prior to this agreement showed considerable potential for aluminum.[23] As much of the plant and equipment had to be bought from foreign suppliers, Birla decided that half the capital also be raised overseas. It was agreed that the Kaiser Corporation would become an equity-holder with a 26 per cent stake in the company, the Birlas would retain 25 per cent and 49 per cent would be offered to the public. Birla also negotiated with the Export–Import Bank which promised to grant long-term credit.[24] Once the technical and financial arrangements were in place, the question of location came up. When C.B. Gupta, one of the most influential Congress leaders of Uttar Pradesh and later its chief minister, suggested that the plant be located in his state near the upcoming Rihand dam, Birla jumped at the idea. Gupta was concerned about ensuring full utilization of the dam's power-generation capacity and believed that the Birla venture, expected to require about 48,000 kilowatts, would help the situation.[25] Birla, on his part, was assured of captive power-supply. Thus Rihand was chosen as the site for the plant and an agreement signed with the UP Government for the supply of electricity.[26] However, the agreement raised some public criticism as the Rihand project had largely been conceived to energize the state's tube wells and river pumping-stations.[27] The agreement stipulated supply of electricity at the rate of 1.99 paisa per unit and was to be in force for 25 years, with a provision for upward revision by 10 per cent after 16 years.[28] Birla also signed a mining lease with the Madhya Pradesh Government. The Hindustan Aluminum Corporation Ltd. (HINDALCO), the new company, was commissioned in a record time of 18 months and began commercial production in October 1962 with a plant that had an annual capacity of 20,000 tons. Unfortunately, the agreement with the UP government ran into controversy when the company wanted to expand its capacity to 40,000 tons and then to 60,000 tons. Unable to meet these, the UP authorities asked HINDALCO to install a captive power plant. Birla then set up the Renusagar Power Plant, a pioneering move to establish captive power facility, with a capacity of 67.5 MW each of turbo-generators.[29]

Birla's entry into fertilizers in the 1950s gives yet another example of his strategic vision for business in post-independence India. His persistent attempt to move into basic industries involving the adoption of high technology was exemplified by his diversification into the production of ammonium sulphate, urea and other nitrogenous products. All these were badly needed for transforming the agricultural sector, which was undergoing land reforms. His discussion with George Woods, further encouraged him. He drew up an ambitious plan, with a projected investment of approximately Rs 20 crores, half of which was to be raised in foreign exchange. Birla approached business associates in America and Germany for collaboration.[30] These plans only fructified much later in the 1960s when Zuari Agro Chemicals was set up in Goa to produce urea and ammonia.

So enthusiastic and confident was Birla about diversification that he did not hesitate when, in 1957, he was invited by the communist leader E.M.S. Namboodaripad to set up industries in Kerala where the Leftists had wrested power. Birla and Namboodaripad were able to frankly discuss the state's industrial needs, notwithstanding their ideological differences. Birla proposed to set up a rayon pulp plant, with a production capacity of 100 tons per day. Birla succeeded in obtaining a licence by making the case that his mill would lead to a saving of Rs 1 lakh in foreign exchange. He was able to show that the outflow involved in obtaining plant and equipment would be offset by the huge savings in foreign exchange and the costs would be recovered in less than a year.[31] When some of his business associates questioned his wisdom in investing in a communist-ruled state, Birla brushed aside their fears: 'It's in the interest of the Keralites as well as ours ... If there is communist rule today, it does not follow that it will last forever'.[32] Thus Grasim Industries came to establish a plant using innovative technology which produced rayon grade pulp made from bamboo and other hardwoods at Mavoor in Kozhikode district.

Thus in overall terms, the expansion plans charted after independence were successful in propelling the Birla group to new heights, and second only to the Tatas in terms of assets, turnover and profits. However, there had been three set-backs. First, in August 1953, at the time of the nationalization of the civil aviation sector, Birla's Bharat Airways came to be nationalized, and the compensation offered was a mere pittance. The company was later renamed Bharat Commerce and Industries Ltd and moved into cotton spinning.[33] The second set-back was the Durgapur steel plant episode, and the third came in 1956 when life insurance was nationalized.

The Birla group had found ways of dealing with the 'Licence Raj'. Like other business houses, they had perfected the art of working the system of industrial licensing to their advantage by making multiple applications and pre-emptive bids. Applications were made in the name of various firms controlled by the group and, once a licence was secured, one firm only would implement it. Such applications 'foreclosed' licensable capacity to other potential entrepreneurs.[34] Licence and permit regimes also encouraged corruption among businessmen and bureaucrats.[35] Like others, the Birlas too depended upon contact men to expedite the progress of applications through the relevant divisions of the Ministries of Industry and Commerce. Finally, personal contact with functionaries in New Delhi went a long way in making the system work.

In retrospect, the Nehru years had seen a major business expansion for the Birlas. Notwithstanding the socialist rhetoric of planned economic development, the Birla business empire had continued to flourish. This was due to Birla's strategic vision in which he was fully supported by his brothers and the younger generation. Before independence, the Birla group's share capital stood at Rs 24.8 crores; in 1958 it stood at Rs 68.6 crores. The book value of gross capital stock of public companies more than doubled in these years from 65.26 crores in 1951 to 152.14 crores in 1958 and the number of private companies controlled by them increased from 61 in 1951 to 105 in 1958.[36] Together with the Tatas, the Birla group accounted for approximately one-fifth of the physical assets of the corporate private sector by 1958.

Notes and References

[1] See Anna Maria Misra, *Business, Race and Politics in British India, 1850–1960* (Oxford, Clarendon Press, 1999), for a discussion of these issues.

[2] In its annual report released in June 1954 it showed a total credit balance of Rs 454,000. It also began to produce body parts. See J. Wesley Adams to Secretary of State, 'Weekly Report, July 29, 1954', in CIA Papers, Reel 23.

[3] For details of the company see *Eastern Economist*, 16 January 1953.

[4] Birla to His Highness Rajpramukh Sahib of Travancore, 26 May 1950, in Birla Papers, Series I, File No. T–6, Travancore Maharaja.

[5] *Modern India. Heritage and Achievement,* G.D. Birla, Eightieth Birthday Commemoration Volume (Pilani, 1977)

[6] Birla to T.T. Krishnamachari, 7 April 1956, in Birla Papers, Series Foreign Correspondence, File No. 82–K, 1955–8.

[7] Birla to T.T. Krishnamachari, 7 April 1956, in Birla Papers, Series Foreign Correspondence, File No. 82–K, 1955–8. Birla to Escott Reid, 25 November 1955, in Birla Papers, Series I, File No. C–18, Canadian High Commissioner and Trade Commissioner.

[8] Birla to T.T. Krishnamachari, 4 August 1954, in Birla Papers, also see Birla to T.T. Krishnamachari, 31 July 1954, in Birla Papers, Series I, File No. K–13, T.T. Krishnamachari.

[9] Birla to T.T. Krishnamachari, 4 August 1954, in Birla Papers, Series I, File No. K–13, T.T. Krishnamachari.

[10] Birla to G.L. Nanda, 10 October 1951, in Birla Papers, Series I, File No. N–11, Nanda, G.L.

[11] Birla on his trip to UK met members of the Treasury, Board of Trade, and Commonwealth Relations' Office, Birla to T.T. Krishnamachari, 31 July 1954, in Birla Papers, Series I. Also see Fredrick P. Bartlett to Secretary of State, 'Weekly Report', 30 September 1954 and Fredrick P. Bartlett to Secretary of State, 23 September 1954 and 14 October 1954, in CIA Papers.

[12] *The Economist* (London), 4 December 1954, p. 815.

[13] 'All About Durgapur', in *The Economic Weekly,* 4 December 1954.

[14] Birla to T.T. Krishnamachari, 24 July 1955, in Birla Papers, Series I, File No. K–13, T.T. Krishnamachari.

[15] Gita Piramal, *Business Maharajas,* p. 126.

[16] *The Economist* (London), 4 December 1954, p. 815 and see M. Brecher, *Jawaharlal Nehru, A Political Biography,* pp. 455–6 for details about this story.

[17] See M. Brecher, *Jawaharlal Nehru, A Political Biography,* pp. 455–6.

[18] 'All About Durgapur', in *The Economic Weekly,* 4 December 1954.

[19] Birla to T.T. Krishnamachari, 24 July 1955, in Birla Papers, Series I, File No. K–13, T.T. Krishnamachari.

[20] Birla to Manubhai Shah, 17 August 1956, in Birla Papers, Foreign Correspondence, S–90, 1955–6.

[21] Woods was well known to Birla and a number of businessmen in India having had a long association with India. He had first come to India in 1952 as a consultant to West Bengal to advise on the merger of Tata Iron and Steel and the Steel Company of Bengal. In 1954 he returned to help the Industrial Credit and Investment Corporation of India.

[22] Birla to George Woods, 9 February 1958, in Birla Papers, Series Foreign Correspondence, File No. 137–S, 1958–60.

[23] Birla to Manubhai Shah, 11 August 1958, in Birla Papers, Foreign Correspondence, File No. 137–S, 1958–60.

[24] Birla to George Woods, 9 February 1958, in Birla Papers, Foreign Correspondence, File No. W–116, 1956–58.

[25] Piramal, *Business Maharajas,* p. 129.

[26] See Birla to Sampurnanandji, 13 August 1958, in **Birla** Papers, Foreign Correspondence, File No. S–137, 1958–60; Birla to G.B. Pant, 13 **August** 1958, in Birla Papers, Foreign Correspondence, File No. P–135, 1959–60; G.B. Pant to Birla,

2 September 1958 and Birla to G.B. Pant, 8 September 1958, in Birla Papers, Foreign Correspondence, File No. P–135, 1959–60.

[27] Kidron, *Foreign Investments in India* (London, Oxford University Press, 1965), p. 147.

[28] Piramal, *Business Maharajas*, pp. 130–1.

[29] Piramal, *Business Maharajas*, pp 130–1.

[30] Birla to George Woods, 9 February 1958, in Birla Papers, Series Foreign Correspondence, File No. 116–W, 1956–8.

[31] Birla to S. Ranganathan, ICS, 20 August 1958, in Birla Papers, Foreign Correspondence, File No. S–137, 1958–60.

[32] Pirmal, *Business Maharajas*, p. 91.

[33] B.K. Birla, *A Rare Legacy*, p. 58.

[34] Frankel, Francine, *India's Political Economy, 1947–1977: The Gradual Revolution* (Princeton, Princeton University Press, 1978), p. 335.

[35] Tomlinson, B.R., *The Political Economy of the Raj, 1914–1947: the Economics of Decolonisation in India* (London, Macmillan, 1979), p. 185.

[36] See R.K. Hazari, *The Structure of the Corporate Private Sector: a Study of Concentration, Ownership and Control* (Bombay, Asia Publishing House, 1966).

15

'Reforms by Stealth': The Promise of the Shastri Years

With the passing away of Jawaharlal Nehru on 27 May 1964, an era ended in the twentieth-century history of India. Speculation had been rife about who would succeed Nehru and what direction the new leader would chart for India. Birla was greatly heartened when Lal Bahadur Shastri emerged as Nehru's successor. Shastri and he had many common associations which, by a remarkable coincidence, had shaped their respective careers in their formative stages. Lal Bahadur was a graduate of the Kashi Vidya Peeth (which later developed into the BHU, of which the Birlas had been the largest benefactors) and the title Shastri in his name originated from the degree which he had earned in 1925 from that institution. Further, the new Prime Minister had been initiated into public life by none other than Lala Lajpat Rai through his Servants of the People Society. As mentioned earlier, Lajpat Rai had founded this body to prepare a cadre of future leaders and had approached the Birlas for financial assistance for its work. The Society, inaugurated at Lahore in 1921 by Gandhi, had been established as 'a life order'. It accepted only those young men who resolved to dedicate their whole life to the service of the people of the country. Shastri had been drafted into the Society and persuaded to take its pledge of dedication by Purshottamdas Tandon, the well-known Congress leader from Allahabad.[1] Members of the Society formed a committed band of volunteers hand-picked by Lajpat Rai himself. They undertook a pledge to serve for at least 20 years and agreed to be bound by the Society's strict rules and discipline.[2]

Within this closely-knit political group, the Birla family had been widely acknowledged even in the 1920s as valued patrons whose support was critical in making the mission of the Society successful. Shastri's first task at the Society had involved *Acchut Uddhar*, an anti-untouchability campaign which Lajpat Rai had started in Punjab and the UP. This project had been undertaken because none other than Jugalkishore had undertaken to give the Society Rs 5000 a month for this.[3] It can thus be said that, when Lal Bahadur Shastri was trying to find his feet in public affairs, the Birlas were already well established in their role as patrons. In any case, they belonged to the same political world, and shared close personal ties with important political leaders like Lajpat Rai and Purshottamdas Tandon.[4] Soon after Shastri became the Prime Minister the occasion arose for the two men to come together to pay tribute to their common mentor. Shastri co-opted Birla onto a committee to celebrate the birth centenary of Lajpat Rai. Birla was also invited to become a trustee of the Servants of the People Society whose presidentship Shastri had recently assumed, and Birla soon plunged wholeheartedly into the work of the Centenary Committee to make it a success.[5]

Given such long-standing associations, Birla personally enjoyed an excellent rapport with Shastri. He believed the new Prime Minister was endowed with a 'robust common-sense', while having no socialist illusions. He was also a prudent leader who could be expected to adopt a pragmatic approach to the problems confronting the nation. He was hopeful too that the change in political leadership would create an environment conducive for private enterprise to play a meaningful and direct role in economic development by breaking the shackles of the Nehru era.

The Cabinet which Shastri assembled further raised Birla's hopes. The erstwhile Leftists, V.K. Krishna Menon and K.D. Malaviya had been dropped. T.T. Krishnamachari, well known for his sympathy with business, was once again placed in charge of Finance; C. Subramaniam held the portfolio of Agriculture while Asoka Mehta was placed in charge of Planning. These three influential ministers were responsible for formulating the economic policy. They did not believe in licences and control and advocated greater reliance on the market. Though some ministers were perceived to be Left-of-Centre like Gulzarilal Nanda and Y.B. Chavan, they were not known to be ideologically committed to the Left. In such a Cabinet, Birla hoped that many of its top leaders would now be in a better position to speak openly in favour of private enterprise than they could have been under Nehru. Further, outside the Cabinet there were many political figures who were influential in the new dispensation whom Birla could count upon as his friends. S.K. Patil, with whom he shared a close personal association, was extremely powerful, having played a critical role in rallying Congress MPs from Maharashtra and Gujarat in favour of Shastri. He was known to be an open and articulate champion of the private sector.[6] There were many regional Congress party bosses too with whom Birla enjoyed a close personal rapport, such as C.B. Gupta in UP and Atulya Ghosh in West Bengal. Yet another ground for Birla's optimism was the new Prime Minister's dependence upon civil servants for advice on economic policy. Shastri appointed L.K. Jha, his principal private secretary, with a special brief for economic affairs.[7] Shastri's cabinet secretary was Dharma Vira, a respected civil servant, who himself came from a family background in business. Birla was on good terms with both, and he had had close dealings with Jha since the early 1940s.[8]

HOPES IN THE NEW DISPENSATION

All around there were signs of change. It seemed to Birla that the time was therefore ripe to give a new economic direction to the country and to pull it out of the confusions and ambivalences which had filled the 17 years since independence. Birla was full of ideas about what needed to be done. It was uncharacteristic of him to give unsolicited advice, even more so in writing. Yet, so enthused was he at the prospect of real change, that he set out his ideas for policy changes in the economic sphere in a 16-page note which he drafted for the new Prime Minister.

Have we been too dogmatic—just running after fancies and less practical about our aims and the methods to achieve them? ... Unfortunately we have never shed the complex of the doctrinaire way of thinking. We have been running not after production, but after giving political slogans to the people. Production, all admit is the pivot—the key to eliminate poverty. But we have devoted precious little energy, thought and efforts towards increased production. All the time we have continued to emphasise socialism, control, regimentation and all this is to divert people's attention from our failure and have done everything possible to disturb production, the very thing needed to improve the economic condition ...

If then these so-called capitalist countries wedded to a system of free enterprise have done better and are more efficient, more prosperous and have better standard than the so called socialist countries like Russia, then, are they the better model for us to imitate? Should we not follow these successful countries and copy their methods than continue to beat the tom-tom of Avadi and Bhubaneswar ... It is clear that Socialism, the controlled economy and planning have not brought their rewards to these so-called socialist countries or to us...

... We worship austerity which leads to the worshipping of scarcity. Less consumption leads to less production and greater poverty. This thinking has now to be reversed. The virtue of a man should not be measured by his economic suffering but by the contribution that he makes in creating more goods. If this dangerous psychology is to be changed, the first change should be in the Planning Commission so that it may recast its policy to create affluence of consumer goods. The Planning Commission is a Commission of negatives. It advocates 'don'ts, not 'dos'. They have in their armoury a thousand devices to stop people doing things, but not one positive policy to encourage production. ... If we do not take a positive view and replace the policy of austerity by greater consumption and greater production and replace the policy of negation by a positive policy of action, a policy of 'don't' by a policy of 'do', India will be doomed.[9]

Although Shastri's response to the note is not known, Birla at least had the satisfaction of conveying his ideas frankly and boldly to the top leadership—something no businessman could have dared to do to Nehru. Even J.R.D. Tata, with whom Nehru shared a warm personal friendship, could not think about giving advice with any seriousness about the economy. 'He always looked out of the window or asked me to look at the panda in the garden whenever I wanted to talk seriously about the economy,' Tata later recalled.[10] Now it seemed like the wind was blowing to bring about the changes that Birla and other proponents of private enterprise had long been advocating. Economic conditions prevalent at the time also favoured drastic measures of reform. The optimism that had marked the first decade of economic planning had evaporated.[11] The country was faced with pressing economic challenges: agriculture was stagnant, industrial growth had slowed down, foreign exchange reserves were at their lowest, unemployment was rampant and acute shortage of commodities led to black marketing. From the reports and advice he received from various quarters, Shastri could see the 'facts as they were in all their starkness'.

Within three months of his coming to power, Shastri showed signs of taking radical steps which seemed to mark a clear departure from the old Nehruvian framework. To begin with, in the summer of 1964, Shastri committed himself to reviewing controls: G.L. Nanda, the Home Minister, assured FICCI that changes would be forthcoming and even asked the Federation for recommendations in this regard. In August 1965 Shastri announced on the floor of Parliament that controls in general were going to be reconsidered. This was followed by decontrol in the specific sectors of steel and cement.[12] Industries in which controls did not serve any useful purpose were also to be decontrolled, and it was by now well known in business circles that the government was looking for more 'candidates' for decontrol. Further, the status of the public sector came to be questioned at the highest level. Shastri ordered all major projects in the public sector which had not taken off to be reviewed. The Finance Minister and the Deputy Chairman of the Planning Commission were directed to make a fresh assessment of projects for which funds were being allocated. Then in a series of measures closely analysed by Francine Frankel, Shastri attempted economic decentralization by trying to shift decision-making from the Planning Commission to the ministries as well as from the centre to the states. The hold which the Planning Commission under Nehru had enjoyed was drastically reduced when in February 1965 the National Planning Council was set up. This was a 17-member body which included industrialists, scientists, economists, trade unionists and rural workers. The Council—which many saw as a rival to the Planning Commission—was meant to advise the government on policy issues and to look into developmental priorities.

Alongside, a vigorous debate took place on the upcoming Fourth Five-Year Plan: its size, the division of resources between industry and agriculture, and the distribution of investment funds between the public and the private sectors. Cabinet ministers were now publicly questioning the wisdom of past policies such as the Industrial Policy Resolution, and influential civil servants like L.K. Jha openly favoured a greater role for the private sector.[13] Jha had even gone on record to say that the Prime Minister himself felt that 'there is something wrong with planning if it has achieved so little for the common man.'

There also seemed a willingness to consider the role which foreign capital could play in economic development and some loosening of restrictions on collaboration ventures. This became clear to Birla when he attended the 20th

Congress of the International Chamber of Commerce which was hosted by FICCI in Delhi in February 1965.[14] The Congress was inaugurated by the Prime Minister who referred to the role of foreign capital as 'filling the gap between requirements and availability of industrial capital, for exchange and technical know-how.' Addressing the concerns of foreign investors, he called upon them to empathize with the constraints of developing countries like India. The International Chamber of Commerce, in turn, emphasized that if the government wanted more foreign capital it would have to reconcile itself to less 'statism,' and would need to establish a more liberal system of taxation which would encourage capital formation through personal savings or corporate reserves.[15] Following this event there was optimism in business circles that there would be more openness towards foreign private investment and that the benefits would spill over to the indigenous private sector.

Although many hopes had been raised, big business leaders were anxious that real change should be manifested in policy outcomes. Krishnamachari's first budget seemed promising: he could see that 'in the corporate sector the primary need of the hour is to infuse some confidence'.[16] Birla declared that he was very happy to finally see an export and production-oriented budget. In his view Krishnamachari had in a 'really very good move' granted tax-free facilities to exporters and to export-oriented manufacturers. Excise duty was, moreover, reduced for several basic consumer items, tax relief was extended to a larger brand of industries and the rate of personal tax was reduced for individuals across the board. Important concessions were also granted with regard to the Compulsory Deposit Scheme for taxpayers. In overall terms the budget, in Birla's view, was creating a new psychology and a new hope. 'You have brought sunshine in the hearts of people', he congratulated the Finance Minister.[17]

Although the chambers of commerce and the stock exchange did not by contrast react favourably to the budget, Birla attributed their reaction to their unrealistic expectations. He stoutly defended Krishnamachari, who had to 'steer through crowded traffic and act within limitation' and thus could not have done better. Birla complimented the Finance Minister for his brilliant effort, though he did seek a more 'generous' interpretation of the budgetary provisions.[18]

BRIDGING THE GULF BETWEEN BUSINESS AND GOVERNMENT

Yet, before long, Birla's big business colleagues were becoming restive with the painfully slow pace of change. Many expected a paradigm shift with the coming of Shastri to power and hoped that the Nehruvian controls would simply be dismantled overnight. Further, they hoped that, at the very least, their applications for licences to set up new industries would be expeditiously granted. Shastri's earlier stint as Minister for Commerce and Industry between 1958 and 1961 had led to this optimism, as he had then granted a large number of industrial licences and approved several foreign and technical collaborations.[19] Nonetheless, due to a mismatch between business expectations and official performance, differences between the two persisted. Such disenchantment was probably accentuated by the accumulated frustrations which big business had experienced in the aftermath of the 1962 war. In that hour of national crisis business had rallied solidly behind Nehru by contributing money and materials for national defence and had justifiably hoped that it would be recognized as a legitimate stake-holder in the country's economic fortunes. However, in managing the economic difficulties which inevitably followed the war, business continued to be disregarded in all policy-making.

Such long-standing frustrations probably influenced business leaders when they gathered to hear the new Prime Minister at the annual session of FICCI in 1965. In his presidential address, K.P. Goenka spoke of business' dissatisfaction with the tempo of economic reform and the deepening gloom in which it functioned. He outlined a bold agenda of economic reform which included a production and investment-oriented tax structure, a realistic approach to the Fourth Five-Year Plan and a radical change in the government's food policy. In an aggressive rejoinder, Shastri blamed the business community for spreading gloom and alluded to the troubles the government had with traders in foodgrains when they had exercised a veto over a statist-oriented food policy and had rejected his plea to disgorge hoarded stocks in August 1964.[20] Shastri had been faced with a serious food situation. Fears of food shortages had loomed on the horizon. Speculation and hoarding had been rampant and the public distribution system had turned out to be ineffective. It had proved impossible to hold the price-line for basic commodities. Such thoughts were probably uppermost in Shastri's mind when he accused the business community of spreading gloom, and for not playing its role of giving 'proper advice to the trading community.' However, FICCI, in its resolution, stuck to its position in holding the government responsible for the alarming food situation. It blamed rising prices on official policies which failed to address problems of low productivity and production, inadequate and ill-spaced imports, controls imposed on price, procurement, transport and distribution, and the tardy implementation of agricultural programmes. It blamed the government for trying to create a scapegoat for its own failure, and for unfairly 'maligning the traders and attempting to mar the image of a specific section of society.'[21]

Such exchanges came as a shocking departure from the traditional conviviality which usually marked the FICCI annual sessions which had by convention been addressed by the Prime Minister. Birla had cause to be dissatisfied with the way the proceedings had been conducted.[22] Beyond the formal FICCI session, he informally took upon himself the task of easing tensions between the Prime Minister and business leaders. He tried to convince his close colleagues that, though tensions persisted, there was much ground for optimism.[23] Here was an opportune time for securing a new policy direction which business leaders must seize. The old ideological antipathy to business, which formed an element in the mindset of the top political leadership, was no more. Business now had a unique opportunity to overcome its subordinate status and renew its legitimacy by forging a constructive relationship with leaders who were themselves anxious to make a break from the past. There were many helpful signs: both Nanda and Krishnamachari were 'in a constructive mood'[24]; Krishnamachari had even proposed the formation of an informal consultative group of businessmen to discuss economic policy.[25] The Finance Minister had admitted that the fundamental need was to increase production. This realization, in Birla's view, was in itself fifty per cent of the solution.[26] Birla urged his colleagues like J.R.D. Tata and S.L. Kirloskar to take advantage of this.[27]

Though Birla reassured his friends in the business world about a marked improvement in economic policies, he had also begun to feel that there was still much that needed to be remedied. In his view, the Shastri administration had only just begun the large task which lay ahead to bring the economy back on the rails. As he told Krishnamachari: 'Lots of loose ends have still to be tied up and plenty of garbage to be cleared. But hope is inspired that it will be done.'[28] As the Shastri administration tried hard by the middle of 1965 to cope with a worsening economic situation and a potential conflict with Pakistan, Birla was anxious for more concrete measures on the economic front. 'You are not making vigorous efforts,' he complained to Krishnamachari and urged him to take more energetic action. The desperate need was to increase production, to strive hard to curtail imports and to ensure co-operation between his colleagues in the different ministries and the leaders in industry. He urged him to call a conference of industrialists and use the personal touch.[29] He cautioned Krishnamachari, that 'if the present conditions do not improve, I fear it is going to give you a bad name.'[30]

'AID TO INDIA' MISSION

An element that could play a critical role in bringing about the transformation which Birla was seeking lay in the external pressures upon the Shastri administration. In international circles there had been growing concern at the country's perfunctory economic performance and India's reputation as a development model was on the wane. By the early 1960s the World Bank and the International Monetary Fund (IMF) were becoming concerned at the 'mismanagement' of the Indian economy. Several reports sponsored by the World Bank, as well as studies by several leading international economists, increasingly pointed to the need for a radical shift in macro-economic policies.[31] Their influence was considerably heightened by the impending food crisis which faced India, aggravated by the serious drought of 1965. This forced the Indian leaders to urgently seek aid from international donor institutions as well as the US administration.

As an astute player in the economic arena, Birla realized how desperately the country needed aid. As one who had, since the late 1950s, propounded the benefits of foreign aid, he believed that he could play a useful role in bringing about an understanding between the top leaders in New Delhi as well as the prospective donor agencies in Washington and New York. He had close contacts with George Woods of the World Bank, and had taken an active interest in the work of the Aid India Consortium which had been formed in 1958 with the support of Eugene Black, the then president of the World Bank.[32] In April 1965, Birla visited New York and Washington in what was a timely visit, as a team of experts from the World Bank was about to submit an in-depth report to George Woods, which was then to form the basis for further discussions about conditions for aid.[33] Birla's specific aim was to meet Woods, and he held a series of meetings with him. After each meeting he sent detailed reports to Krishnamachari and L.K. Jha. Birla found Woods sympathetic and appreciative. However, Woods expressed deep dissatisfaction with India's economic conditions and was frank in expressing the concerns of the Bank as a financing institution. These related to the prevalence of extensive and continuing controls, a rural sector sorely in need of incentives and investments for production and a family planning effort that was having minimal impact.[34] In specific terms, the main worry related to the Fourth Five-Year Plan, the need for realism in calculations with regard to its economic estimates, 'complacency and too much red-tapism,' and overall slow results and slow progress.[35]

Birla also held important meetings with Pierre Paul Schweitzer, Managing Director of the IMF. These discussions also revolved around India's needs for increased allocations of aid.[36] In Schweitzer's view, three main problems needed to be addressed: holding the price line, giving incentives for increase in agriculture and expanding production, and maintaining stable balance of payments.[37] Birla agreed that unless the errors of past economic policies were rectified, aid would not be forthcoming. He kept Krishnamachari closely informed about his meetings. In these meetings Birla was also questioned about the growing tensions between India and Pakistan, which were to escalate into a full-blown war later that year. George Woods even remarked on the 'stupidity' of both the countries and 'expressed his unconscious doubts' about the wisdom of World Bank aid while the two countries spent time and energies in fighting each other.[38] Birla was cautious not to be drawn into making any comment on this issue and reassured Krishnamachari: 'As I have said before, I did not make any comment. It would have been presumptuous on my part to do so since I represent none but myself.'[39]

Soon after Birla's return to India, the border skirmishes with Pakistan flared into a full-fledged war in September 1965.[40] Birla, who was in Delhi, immediately flew back to Washington, and renewed his efforts to ensure that the prospects of aid were not jeopardized. He re-established contact with official circles as well as the press, spending his time and money in meeting influential friends and acquaintances on Capitol Hill. He held detailed discussions with George Woods as well as Anthony Solomon, the Assistant Secretary of State for Economic

Affairs in the US State Department. He also met the noted columnists, Walter Lippman, Averell Harriman and Joseph Kraft.[41] He left instructions with his staff in Delhi to send one or two telexes everyday giving the latest war news. On his part he sent daily reports of his meetings to L.K. Jha for the Prime Minister. In these reports he conveyed the hectic lobbying being carried out in Washington by both pro-India and pro-Pakistani groups. He noted that Pakistan was increasingly being seen as the aggressor by all officials. However, he was forthright in conceding that there existed little sympathy for India on the Kashmir question. He suggested that India should capitalize on American sympathy and use the opportunity to 'explain our case on Kashmir'.[42] He encouraged Shastri to remain tactful, thoughtful and practical. Yet, he also urged the Indian leadership to use their utmost diplomatic skill to 'show that we are not rigid'.[43] In these weeks he remained closely attuned to the undercurrents on Capitol Hill. For instance, on 16 September 1965, he telexed the Prime Minister's office that 'extreme pressure has been put on Ayub by US during last twenty-four hours to accept unconditional cease-fire.'[44]

In these tense weeks Birla's concern had been to ensure that foreign aid to India was not cut—an outcome he could not prevent. Soon after the war broke out, the US cut off military aid, and USAID announced a suspension of its consideration of future economic aid to both countries. However, he conveyed to the officials concerned that the stopping of aid would not be an effective deterrent upon the Indians.[45] Fortunately, the hostilities between India and Pakistan soon stopped. The news of the cease-fire delighted Birla: 'God is gracious,' he telexed Shastri. He looked upon the war only as a temporary set-back in his efforts to procure aid for India, and remained confident that Washington would offer enhanced aid following a dialogue between Shastri and the US President.[46]

As Birla had expected, the cessation of the war was followed by renewed consultations between top Indian officials and economists such as S. Bhoothalingham, I.G. Patel, L.K. Jha, and V.K. Ramaswamy, and World Bank officials, Bell and De Lattre. They worked out the details for the increased aid allocations, and also discussed a number of issues such as decontrol over imports and the likely changes in agricultural and industrial policies as incentives for higher levels of aid.[47] While top Indian policy-makers moved closer to accepting World Bank terms and its associated recommendation for currency devaluation, the only hurdle that stood in the way was the opposition of M. Krishnamachari who as Finance Minister saw personal defeat in devaluation. Convinced by his advisers and having made up his mind that there was no other alternative than to agree with the World Bank terms, Shastri used the excuse of a minor corruption scandal to ease Krishnamachari out of office just before he left for Tashkent.[48] The decision to devalue in principle was then communicated informally to the IMF at the end of 1965.[49]

'THE NEW DESTINY'

Birla knew that the decision would be implemented following personal dialogue only during Shastri's forthcoming visit to Washington. Then the renewal of aid and the accompanying economic reforms would merely be a matter of time. He was particularly optimistic about the outcome of such a meeting after Woods had commented that US President Johnson was 'a Texan, uncultured, uneducated, and therefore when he takes an abrupt action, he can be excused for his background.' This statement made Birla optimistic as he felt that he could be 'compared with our Sardar Patel'. Birla gathered that policy-makers in the US had a high opinion of Shastri as a 'shrewd, deliberate, honest and humble' person. Thus, in his view, the ground was well laid for a successful meeting between the two leaders.[50] However, he was anxious to leave no stone unturned to ensure its success. He sent S. Mulgaonkar, the editor of *Hindustan Times* on a cross-country visit to meet US editors to ensure suitable pre-visit publicity for the prime ministerial visit. Keen to 'be of what help he can in ensuring that the Prime Minister's visit with the President goes well', he himself planned a visit to Washington in November with the express objective of meeting persons who were likely to play a part in making the visit successful. He had meetings fixed with Robert Komer, special assistant to the President, and the Assistant Secretary of Defence. He also decided to sponsor a special advertisement supplement on India in the *New York Times* whose publication was to coincide with Shastri's visit. He personally instructed the top editorial staff of *Hindustan Times* and *Eastern Economist*, to work on the issue. He himself wrote a piece for it, entitled 'New Destiny'. In this article, he lauded the achievements of the Shastri government. The war, he wrote, had after all not been an unmixed blessing. The entire atmosphere in the country, he continued, had been completely transformed, and it had almost been like an awakening. In the electrifying atmosphere which gripped the country, the many problems which Shastri had faced such as inter-state rivalry over Fourth-Plan allocations, the controversy over language and the demand for a more homogeneous Punjabi state had submerged overnight. Under Shastri the country had emerged as 'a nation of self confidence, solidarity, political stability, conscious of a new destiny and with the will to chart a new course on broader horizons'. 'Tomorrow for India will never be the same after this experience', he declared confidently.

Birla at the same time made a case for increased aid to this new India and promised that 'when it is resumed it has a better chance of being more productively and effectively used.'[51] The stoppage of aid had led to a 'new thinking' as it had shown how vulnerable India was. It had also led to an urgent resolve to address the problems of food production and increased production, both to replace avoidable imports and to promote exports. There were signs of an entirely new way of thinking towards economic problems. Even controls and beauracratic delays were going to be looked into. Shastri was giving a 'more practical bias to economic thinking'.[52]

Birla was ready to send his article to press just when Shastri's unexpected death in January 1966 at Tashkent within hours of signing a peace treaty between India and Pakistan changed the entire political scenario. Birla was stunned by the news. As well as the feeling of personal loss which he had towards the departed Prime Minister, he knew that an invaluable opportunity had been lost to bring about fundamental changes in the direction of economic policy. It was particularly frustrating that his strenuous efforts for foreign aid now seemed likely to come to nought. Even more disappointing was the halting of the process of economic reforms which Shastri had showed a willingness to consider. Birla could see that a precious opportunity had been lost. It remains a matter of speculation what would have been India's economic destiny if the process of economic reforms initiated belatedly in 1991 had been embraced by the political leadership in the mid-1960s as Birla had envisioned.

NOTES AND REFERENCES

[1] Shastri joined the Society on 1 April 1927 and was first placed on probation. In 1928 he commenced his 'training' work and was then confirmed as a life member in 1932. See *70 Years. Servants of the People Society, Report 1981–1992* (New Delhi, 1992), p. 40.

[2] *Constitution, Servants of the People Society* (New Delhi, n.d.).

[3] On Jugalkishore's support, see Feroz Chand, *Lajpat Rai: Life and Work* (New Delhi, 1978), p. 435.

[4] Over the years Shastri grew close not only to Birla but also to the younger generation of the family. He often co-opted them to serve causes which were dear to him. For instance, in 1961, when he was Minister for Commerce and Industry, he asked Krishna Kumar to become a trustee of the Vishwayatan Yogashram Trust which had been set up by Dhirendra Brahmachari, and in which he was also a trustee. Shastri got Krishna Kumar involved with the work of the Trust and he was later even invited to be its chairman, a post which he refused. For details see K.K. Birla, *Indira Gandhi: Reminiscences* (New Delhi), pp. 8–14.

[5] The major centres for collection were Delhi, Bombay, Calcutta and Kanpur. As on previous occasions, Birla kept overall charge of collections but asked both Braj Mohan and Rameshwardas to help with Bombay and Calcutta while he personally co-ordinated the Delhi and Kanpur collections. Fellow businessmen whom he was personally close to such as Shriyans Prasad Jain were roped in to help. Given his personal connection with the Fund, Birla ensured that his group was the largest single donor to the Fund giving the substantial sum of Rs 4,50,000. 'Lajpat Rai Centenary Committee', 14 April 1965, in Birla Papers, Series Miscellaneous, File No. 66, Lajpat Rai Centenary Celebrations.

[6] Patil openly questioned government policy on the economy. As the *Eastern Economist* reported in December 1964: 'The other day, for instance, Mr. S.K. Patil found it necessary to examine in public the alleged virtues of one of those sacred cows of Congress socialism—the Industrial Policy Resolution. Purists and pedants might question, if they like, the propriety of a cabinet minister challenging what is claimed to be a fundamental policy of the government, but a more realistic reaction would surely be to attempt to realise the implications of a situation in which the government's major policies are proving so demonstrably restrictive or sterile that even a member of government is compelled to

protest against them in public.' See 'We are not impressed', in *Eastern Economist*, 11 December 1964.

[7] For Jha's views on the economy see L.K. Jha, *India's Economic Development* (New Delhi, 1991).

[8] The Birlas had been close to Jha since he was posted to Calcutta in the 1940s and through the 1950s while he was secretary, Ministry of Commerce and Industry. The Birla brothers had often discussed their personal business matters and larger issues of economic policy with him.

[9] Birla's notes, Birla Papers, Series Miscellaneous, File No. 120. Notes and Speeches.

[10] R.M. Lala, *The Joy of Achievement. Conversations with J.R.D. Tata* (New Delhi, 1995), p. 99.

[11] P.N. Dhar, *Indira Gandhi, the 'Emergency' and Indian Democracy* (New Delhi, 1999), p. 68.

[12] Kochanek, *Business and Politics in India*, p. 190 and pp. 253–5.

[13] On these initiatives see Francine Frankel, *India's Political Economy, 1947–77. The Gradual Revolution*. 'We are not impressed', *Eastern Economist*, 11 December 1964.

[14] The theme of the conference was 'World Progress through Partnership' and the underlying concerns that went towards hosting it were the country's need for development capital and foreign private investment.

[15] *Eastern Economist*, 19 February 1965.

[16] Birla told his business colleagues that a finance minister had finally agreed with the private sector's long-standing case that resources 'have to be augmented from within as well as from without, and it is therefore necessary to provide incentives for the existing companies to plough back a larger share of their profits and also diminish the disincentive for inter-corporate investment.'

[17] On Krishnamachari's tenure see R. Tirumalai, *T.T.K. The Dynamic Innovator*. For a study of the previous budgets see Indian Merchants' Chamber, Economic Research and Training Foundation, *Union Budgets. A Factual Study of Finances of Government of India* (Bombay, n.d.).

[18] Birla to T.T. Krishnamachari, 28 February 1965, in Birla Papers, Series Important, File No. 91–K, 1963–6.

[19] It was believed that the number of new companies floated in just the first nine months of 1961 was 1252 and a large number of deals for technical and foreign collaboration were approved by the ministry. Shastri had then made clear that the field for expansion for private capital was open and that the state entered production only when the investment was too large or complex for the private sector or 'because the government were able to get more reasonable terms than the private sector could manage.' See Mankekar, *Lal Bahadur, A Political Biography* (Bombay, 1964). Also see Kidron, *Foreign Investment in India*, p. 148.

[20] The traders had successfully fought against monopoly procurement and statutory rationing and the centre had to grant concessions on statutory rationing, rice zones and could only put forth a diluted Food Grains Policy in November 1964.

[21] See Vankatsubbiah, *Enterprise and Economic Change*, pp. 125–6. Also see *Eastern Economist*, 26 March 1965.

[22] For details see *Eastern Economist*, 26 March 1965. The *Eastern Economist*, reflected Birla's critique when it called Goenka's address 'a tactless and tasteless indictment of the government and all its works. Shuttling as it did, between an unlovely querulousness and a clumsy aggressiveness, it breathed neither restraint nor dignity. Its matter, moreover,

was not improved by its manner. The drafting was incredibly poor, riddled with clichés and marred by faults of idiom or grammar.'

[23] Within FICCI, Birla personally intervened with business leaders to water down their official critique of the budget. Birla had never believed in publicly expressing dissatisfaction with economic policy because he felt that hardened the official stand and not much could then be achieved. In keeping with this policy, he intervened with members of the FICCI committee and was able to ensure that a rather aggressive draft resolution on the budget was toned down substantially. The original resolution which had said that 'the Federation cannot help expressing its disappointment that the latest budget' was changed to state that 'the Federation is happy to note that there is a welcome trend in the direction of simplification of the tax structure.' A much 'milder version' was thus adopted which urged for further reforms while 'judicially appreciating' concessions provided. For both resolutions, see *Eastern Economist*, 26 March 1965.

[24] Birla to H.V.R. Iyengar, 14 April 1965, in Birla Papers, Series Important, File No. 89–I, 1964–7.

[25] H.V.R. Iyengar to Birla, 9 April 1965, in Birla Papers, Series Important, File No. 89–I, 1964–7.

[26] Birla tried to convince them of the changed environment which had been apparent, he claimed, at a meeting which he had organized in December 1964 between prominent industrialists and the new Prime Minister, along with Krishnamachari and Gulzarilal Nanda, the Industry Minister. At this meeting, there had been overall agreement that production must rise and the price-line must be held. Birla had drawn attention to what he considered as the two main hurdles, which were 'capital formation and the processing'. Birla to T.T. Krishnamachari, 4 January 1965, in Birla Papers, Series Important, File No. 91–K, 1963–6. He wrote after the meeting to Krishnamachari: 'I am hoping you will act with vigour, understanding and co-operation of all concerned to lead the country on the right track'. For this correspondence see T.T. Krishnamachari to Birla, 13 January 1965 and Birla to T.T. Krishnamachari, 17 January 1965, in Birla Papers, Series Important, File No. 91–K, 1963–6.

[27] H.V.R. Iyengar to Birla, 12 April 1965, Birla to H.V.R. Iyengar, 14 April 1965, in Birla Papers, Series Important, File No. 89–I, 1964–7.

[28] Birla to T.T. Krishnamachari, 28 February 1965, in Birla Papers, Series Important, File No. 91–K, 1963–6.

[29] No doubt the overall atmosphere was an improvement, but there was, he complained, 'no positive and vigorous policy' that was being pursued by the Prime Minister or by him. It was time, he said, that the Finance Minister took a 'personal and kind of moral interest' to push private-sector projects through as otherwise 'the caravan will not move.' Birla to T.T. Krishnamachari, 10 December 1964, in Birla Papers, Series Important, File No. 91–K, 1963–6.

[30] Birla to T.T. Krishnamachari, 15 June 1965, in Birla Papers, Series Important, File No. 91–K, 1963–6.

[31] In 1960, a World Bank team led by Michael Hopman came to evaluate the strategy and status of the Indian economic growth; then there was a comprehensive review of Indian economic policy commissioned by World Bank President, George Woods and directed by Bernard Bell. Among economists, Jagdish Bhagwati, then based in the Delhi School of Economics and John P. Lewis were pointing to problems in economic policy. See for instance, John P. Lewis, *Quiet Crisis in India* (1962).

[32] On Wood's involvement with India, see Robert W. Oliver, *George Woods and the World Bank* (London, 1995), pp. 127–51. Also see Bachi J. Karkaria, *Dare to Dream, A Life of M.S. Oberoi* (New Delhi, 1993), p. 116.

[33] On the basis of this further discussions were to take place with, on the one hand, the Indian ministers and on the other, with the World Bank. The team was then scheduled to go back to India.

[34] Birla to T.T. Krishnamachari, 9 May 1965, in Birla Papers, Series Important, File No. 91–K, 1963–6.

[35] According to Woods, many governments which were participating in finance felt that the Plan should be discussed with them but on this score, he had been firm that it was the Indian government's business to formulate the Plan and the Consortium's business to only see that it was realistic and implemented.

[36] See Birla to T.T. Krishnamachari, 1 May 1965, in Birla Papers, Series Important, File No. 91–K, 1963–6. Also see Birla, 'Note', in Birla Papers, Series Miscellaneous, File No. 164, Notes and Speeches.

[37] The price-line could be held, he told Birla, by increasing production of agricultural goods which could be achieved with 'providing fertilizers, more irrigation and good production'; the problems of industrial production could be met by removing the regimentation of the economy which had 'gone too far' and the balance of payments problem could be resolved with 'foreign capital and investment'. Birla, 'Note', 18 May 1965, in Birla Papers, Series Miscellaneous, File No. 164. Notes and Speeches.

[38] Birla's discussions made one thing clear, he told his contacts in New Delhi: 'If we attack Pakistan, whether in East Bengal or in the Punjab, we would be misunderstood. So far our position has been appreciated. The aggressor has been Pakistan ... But if we attack, then, according to them, Pakistan would be justified in using American equipment.' The issue of Kashmir, Woods thought, could for the time being be put in the 'freezing pot'.

[39] Birla to T.T. Krishnamachari, 9 May 1965, in Birla Papers, Series Important, File No. 91–K, 1963–6.

[40] On his return to Delhi, encouraged by his meetings, Birla tried hard to impress upon the political leadership that it should change its foreign-policy leanings. It will be a 'mistake', he wrote to Krishnamachari, to rely too much upon Russia. 'They are drifting away gradually from us which perhaps is not realized.' They had 'not said a word about China or Kutch' but had merely asked the two countries to resolve their differences amicably. Birla was firmly of the view that 'we should not exaggerate the help by Russia and belittle that of America.' Birla to H.V.R. Iyengar, 25 May 1965, in Birla Papers, Series Important, File No. 89–I, 1964–7.

[41] He sent almost daily reports of his meetings to Shastri and to L.K. Jha.

[42] Birla Telex to Saxsena, 13 September 1965, in Birla Papers, File No. 106. Letters to P.M. etc. from abroad, 1965.

[43] To say that there was no Kashmir problem 'sounds unrealistic' to people in the US and he told the leadership at home that to refuse to talk with Pakistan would look 'rigid' and must not be indulged in. Birla to Saxsena, telex, 18 September 1965, in Birla Papers, File No. 106. Letters to P.M. etc. from abroad, 1965.

[44] Ayub Khan had partly 'rehabilitated his position' by promising the US President cooperation on the phone, reported Birla in mid-September. Birla to Saxsena, telex, 16 September 1965, in Birla Papers, File No. 106. Letters to P.M. etc. from abroad, 1965.

[45] 'They are highly sensitive people. They have lived for centuries in poverty. They would be prepared to go on starvation diet and on a lower standard of living if it comes to that ... Only emotional approach can get a response.'

[46] He suggested that Shastri attend the UNO meeting. In a telex sent on 25 September 1965 Birla wrote: 'Greatest casualty is aid which will not be resumed either to us or to our neighbour until personal meetings. Subsequent procedures of Security Council Resolution specially political settlement will not come in way of aid. This latter negotiation will be a long-term process which may take years. But many things including economic aid held up until personal meeting. Congress here highly critical. Urgency of meeting should be fully realised because an atmosphere should be created. Why not Shastriji attend UNO meeting for which ample precedent in past.'

[47] See B.H. David Denoon, *Devaluation under pressure: India, Indonesia and Ghana* (MIT, 1986), pp. 63–5.

[48] T.T. Krishnamachari rebutted stories about the malfeasance of his son and asked Shastri to clear him of charges. Shastri refused to do so without an investigation and instead offered Krishnamachari the option of having a Supreme Court justice do an enquiry during which he would have to step out of office. Not surprisingly, Krishnamachari considered this an insult and submitted his resignation, expecting Shastri not to accept it. It was, however, accepted and Shastri soon thereafter appointed Sachin Chowdhury as his successor.

[49] I.G. Patel, 'The Landscape of Economics', in *The Indian Economic Journal*, Vol. 45, No. 1, pp. 19–35.

[50] Birla note on meeting with G. Woods, 9 May 1965, in Birla Papers, Series Miscellaneous, File No. 164, Notes and Speeches.

[51] He refuted the American contention that aid would be resumed only after India established peaceful relations with Pakistan. 'Could England be told in the midst of the Second War', he asked, 'that she must establish peace with Hitler before claiming world sympathy?' He claimed India 'feels hurt that the US has not recognised that India has all along wanted peace and that aid should have been stopped when it was most needed.'

[52] Birla, 'New Destiny', text of article which was published in the *New York Times*, 20 March 1966. It was drafted before Shastri's demise and then rewritten by Birla. It was finally published on 20 March as 'The Search for a New Destiny'. Birla Papers, Series Miscellaneous, File No. 162, Notes and Speeches. Also see *New York Times*, 20 March 1966.

16

Out of Tune with the New Politics

Within hours of Shastri's death, the Congress party was embroiled in an internal factional struggle over choosing his successor. As the party leadership was torn between Morarji Desai and Indira Gandhi, Birla came to be involved in this struggle in a rather unexpected way. Indira Gandhi approached the Birla family through Krishna Kumar for help in garnering support within the ranks of the party.[1] Indira Gandhi had come to know the Birlas personally over the years. She had first visited Pilani in the early 1950s with her father and had since then grown to know the family. She was especially close to Krishna Kumar whom she had co-opted in the early 1960s to help in fund collection for the Vishwayatan Yogashram Trust of which she was the patron. The Trust had been set up by Dhirendra Brahmachari, a yoga teacher known to be close to her personally.[2] Krishna Kumar was made a trustee and in September 1961 Indira Gandhi had visited the Birla residence in Calcutta to meet with the city's prominent industrialists. Uncertain about her political support within the party, she now looked to the Birlas for help from 'friends amongst Congress MPs'. The prospect of Indira Gandhi taking on the leadership of the party enthused both Krishna Kumar and Birla—Krishna Kumar because it meant he could further his own latent hopes of a political career and Birla because he 'could not stand Morarji Bhai's didactic attitude and sermonising demeanour' and much preferred power to pass to an inexperienced Indira Gandhi.[3]

Birla's dislike of Desai had much to do with his disastrous tenure as Finance Minister in Nehru's Cabinet. Many industrialists, though personally close to Desai, found him unimaginative. Their differences had come to a head over the budget of 1963, which proposed a stiff dose of taxation with a super profits tax on company profits.[4] Taking up cudgels on behalf of the industrial community, Birla accused Desai of producing the worst budget since independence and likened it to the 'Liaquat Ali budget with the exception that your rates are higher than his'.[5] He accused Desai of trying to kill production and of curbing the private sector for his selfish political ends.[6] Many businessmen felt that Morarji 'thought in categories too simplistic for comprehending the complex problems of India's economic growth.'[7] Perhaps another reason for Birla's preference for Indira Gandhi was his intrinsic trust in the wisdom of the Syndicate. By propping up Indira Gandhi, who had a natural constituency as Nehru's daughter, Birla saw that the Congress could once again portray a good public image in the approaching elections. Moreover, an inexperienced leader like her would let consensus prevail and could be amenable to influence from different quarters. He took close interest in the succession drama and his stance reflected the calculations of the inner circle of the Syndicate.[8]

THE UNFINISHED AGENDA

Not surprisingly, Indira Gandhi's succession was ensured by the coming together of the leadership in an anti-Morarji stand. In the Working Committee election she successfully overwhelmed Desai by winning 355 votes to his 169. The news pleased Birla immensely and he lost no time in expressing his feelings to the new Prime Minister.

My congratulations to you on your most inspiring broadcast which I heard with great enthusiasm. May God bless you in implementing the ideas and sentiments which you have given to the Nation. I have no doubt that you will get support from all sides. My services for what they are worth, are at your disposal.[9]

He also took the trouble to meet with her personally to give her his 'blessings.' Indira Gandhi responded warmly.

I am sorry I have been unable to acknowledge your kind letter of congratulations and good wishes earlier .... As an elder statesman of the Indian business community, I shall always value your advice.[10]

With Indira Gandhi installed in the Prime Ministerial office, Birla saw the time as opportune for turning his attention to the unfinished business of securing enhanced international aid. As seen earlier, his efforts in this area had met with considerable success under the Shastri administration but had remained unconsummated due to the unexpected circumstances of the last phase of his premiership. Eager to carry forward his unfinished agenda Birla now renewed his efforts. As soon as political conditions seemed somewhat settled in New Delhi, Birla flew to Washington in March 1966. The time was opportune, as Indira Gandhi's own visit to the US was scheduled for later in the month. In Washington, Birla met with 'all the important persons who count and who were in the confidence of the President' in political and White House circles.[11] The meetings with Dean Rusk—special adviser to the President—were especially significant as Rusk briefed him about the concerns of the President and outlined the main points which the President hoped to discuss with Indira Gandhi during her impending visit. He also renewed contacts with important officials at the World Bank such as George Woods. In all these meetings Birla's message was unambiguous—though the political leadership had changed there remained a commitment to accept the conditions of the donor agencies which the Shastri regime had agreed to. The new leadership of Indira Gandhi, he emphasized in his meetings, was quite strong, there was no question of instability, and the White House needed to show its support to it with massive help.[12]

After almost two hectic weeks filled with meetings, Birla went to Paris where he was scheduled to meet Indira Gandhi who had stopped *en route* to Washington. In a long meeting with her he reported his talks in Capitol Hill. He conveyed that there was 'plenty of sympathy in Washington' and the mood was encouraging.[13] He urged her to be forthcoming in giving assurances on four counts: food and fertilizer production, seriousness about family planning, improved relations with Pakistan and economic liberalization. The American conditions and the proposals of the World Bank 'were reasonable' and should, he emphasized, be 'empathized with'.[14] Though Birla was not present in Washington during the Prime Minister's visit, he made public his commitment to it by sponsoring the *New York Times* advertisement supplement which had been put in cold storage. It coincided with Indira Gandhi's visit. Entitled *India: Today and Tomorrow* the supplement prominently carried a photograph of the young Prime Minister and a message from her. The editorial staff of the *Hindustan Times* and the *Eastern Economist* had carefully crafted an image portraying India and 'the future of Indo-American relations'.[15] Birla edited his own piece, which was now entitled 'In Search of a New Destiny', in keeping with the changed context. He pushed for an even stronger case for American aid which would have a 'better chance of being more productively and effectively used' because of the 'new thinking' in the country.[16]

As is well known, Indira Gandhi's US trip appeared, on the face of it, to be a tremendous success. She struck an immediate rapport with President Lyndon Johnson and agreements were reached on a number of pending issues. She is known to have agreed to currency devaluation, to encourage American collaboration in Indian industry especially in fertilizer production and to reduce state controls on industry.[17] In return Johnson promised over three million tons of food and $900 million as aid and the World Bank agreed to be more responsive to India's needs. Birla kept himself closely attuned to the Prime Minister's visit through his contacts in Washington. As he heard reports of Johnson's praise for Indira Gandhi and the success of the trip a pleased Birla wrote to the Prime Minister:

My congratulations on your successful trip, and all good wishes! I understand from my friends in Washington that the President was highly pleased with your talk and was very much impressed by the way in which you handled him. I hope that we shall now pursue the matter in order to finalise our plans for aid.[18]

By all accounts the visit seemed to have gone exactly as Birla had hoped. He saw in Indira Gandhi's warm meeting with President Johnson a fruition of his efforts. This was just what Birla had been working for through the Shastri years during his many trips to Washington, which were undertaken specifically to achieve these aims.[19]

Even more encouraging news followed for Birla in the following months. Asoka Mehta, an important member of Indira Gandhi's Cabinet, was sent to Washington to follow up on the Prime Minister's visit and see what exactly the international donors were offering in return for devaluation and decontrol. To Birla's satisfaction the Asoka Mehta–George Woods meetings turned out to be much as expected: Woods pledged to raise the aid level and Mehta committed the Indian government to replace import control with tariffs, simplify procedures in industrial licensing and to make no new commitment in the public sector unless the expected rate of return was equal to that of the private sector.[20] He is also known to have agreed, following discussions with the IMF, to devalue the rupee. A delighted Birla wrote to Asoka Mehta:

My congratulations on your success in Washington and double congratulations on your hitting hard the communists and the fellow travellers!! They and their press have been all this time creating a feeling in the country that you have returned empty-handed and that USA except expressing lip sympathy are not going to help. Now that they discover that the aid is coming in a most generous fashion they are greatly disappointed. They would have been pleased had no aid come and consequently production went down, unemployment increased, no food came and there was starvation. Then only they would have been happy because of dissatisfaction all round. They want chaos in the country. I am surprised why the Congressmen are taking all this lying down, If only they too hit hard as you did, the communists and fellow travellers will be completely silenced. I hope this shall be done.[21]

On the night of 5 June the All India Radio announced that the rupee had been devalued by 35 per cent—a news which shocked the nation but which Birla was waiting for with much anticipation.[22] He heard the official announcement the following morning in Boston where he had just undergone a long overdue prostate operation. As he lay convalescing at his hotel room in the Ritz Carlton he kept in touch with events in India, both through correspondence with family and friends and through the Indian newspapers which were delivered to him regularly.

The news of devaluation was received with widespread criticism within India. This snowballed into an attack on the Prime Minister herself by dissidents within the Congress parliamentary party. Senior leaders were opposed to it as they had feared that the inflationary impact of increased import costs would undermine the ruling Congress' electoral prospects in the forthcoming elections.[23] Making history, the Congress Working Committee passed a resolution denouncing the government for the decision on devaluation. The dissent within Congress circles over devaluation and the growing attack on Indira Gandhi much disappointed Birla. He was alarmed at the attitude of the top leadership, none of whom came to the support of the Prime Minister. Writing to Satyanarain Sinha from his Grosvenor House residence in London he expressed his disenchantment with the political undercurrents in the party:

I was reading the Indian newspapers and I am very much depressed that Indiraji is not getting full support from the party. This will weaken her hands and strengthen the position of the opposition. In the Working Committee it appears that the supporters keep mum and the opposition has a free field. The Parliamentary Party showed greater responsibility. But I was sorry to note that Tantia said that he was ashamed and would rather starve than get any aid from America under pressure. It is all bravado to talk of starvation. But neither he nor I would starve. Starvation will be confined to the poor people. Therefore for a man like him to talk of starvation is not very helpful. He also indirectly helped the opposition. The country seems to have gone mad not realising that before elections everybody should be united.

In the next election you have to select people who would be more reliable and responsible. C.D. Pande was bold enough to come out frankly. I do not know what Raja Pant has been doing. The next election is going to be a very difficult task for all of you. But nobody seems to have realised this. There is a talk, it appears, that Sachin Choudhuri will resign and in the next elections T.T.K. will come back. Perhaps Kamaraj is having his way. But you know better how the things are shaping.[24]

To make matters worse, opposition parties from the extreme Left to the far Right damned devaluation as a sell-out to the US. Within leftist circles, devaluation was seen as the ultimate step in national humiliation.[25] Even the right-wing Swatantra Party, which brought together aristocrats and businessmen, despite its support to liberalization, argued that devaluation had been brought about because of the poor past economic policies. The only group to come out openly in favour of the devaluation was big business. Corporate circles were forthright in their support. The Federation sponsored a series of advertisements in the major newspapers supporting Indira Gandhi.[26] Lakshmi Niwas, then president of FICCI, gave a radio speech in favour of devaluation and added that the export duties that were imposed were thwarting the directions of the move.[27] Of course, FICCI saw it as only the first step in the liberalization of the economy and expected a drastic revision of policies to follow. Birla himself made no public statements, not being in the country at the time, but Rameshwardas declared his support when he asserted that the Finance Minister had done 'the right thing in the prevailing circumstances'.[28]

RETREAT FROM POLITICAL INVOLVEMENTS

Through these months Birla looked for opportune moments to meet Indira Gandhi to show his support and in the hope of adding a personal touch to their relations. It was not, however, easy to meet the Prime Minister and there were few occasions when he could meet with her easily. He met her, as always, on her birthday, sent flowers on important occasions and responded generously to public appeals from the PMO (Prime Minister's Office).[29] In her early months in office it had appeared to Birla that he might continue to play the role of unofficial adviser as he had done during the Shastri regime but in the post-devaluation scenario things changed rapidly. It proved difficult to add a personal

touch to their relations and they increasingly came under strain. This had little
to do with Birla, but more with Indira Gandhi's changing political circumstances
and her deep personal biases.

A major issue which affected their relations was the fall-out of Indira Gandhi's
US visit and the failure of US aid to materialize. While Indira Gandhi was being
unequivocally condemned over devaluation within the country, the aid-givers,
especially the Johnson administration, also let her down. The non-project aid
never materialized and even the food aid was handed out insultingly. To make
matters worse, the country desperately needed aid since devaluation was followed
by successive bad monsoons. A 'proud and patriotic' Indira Gandhi felt deeply
let down and the whole episode left a deep impact on her psyche. She saw this
as a personal affront. This attitude of the American administration stung her and
the unfortunate experience over aid not only conditioned her subsequent
economic policies but also flawed her relations with her advisers. As Indira
Gandhi faced her first serious political crisis, her relations with all those who had
led her up what now seemed to be the wrong path underwent a dramatic change.
She started to distrust many former advisers: both C. Subrahmaniam and Asoka
Mehta began to bear the brunt of her distrust and were soon eased out.[30] As her
confidence in these former advisers eroded, her relations with Birla were also
strained as he was seen to be one of the most prominent protagonists of the 'aid
to India' lobby since the 1950s.

Further, her relations with Birla also deteriorated as she faced trouble from
the Syndicate leadership in the months following devaluation. Within political
circles, Birla was seen to be close to a number of leaders of the Syndicate,
especially S.K. Patil who made no secret of his links with big business. Patil had
been a long-time critic of Indira Gandhi and had, in the first instance, opposed
her candidature to the prime ministership in 1966. As Indira Gandhi distanced
herself from the old leaders, she clubbed Birla with them and ensured that a
distance was maintained.

Things became worse because of her instinctive distrust of big business which
she had inherited from her father. Her disdain for business was often apparent in
statements such as: 'Our private enterprise is more private than enterprising.' Her
unfriendly attitude towards business could barely be concealed when, soon after
she entered office, she was invited by FICCI to inaugurate its 38th Annual session.
To begin with, she was reluctant to come, on the ground that its inauguration by
the Prime Minister was no more than a ritual and she was 'not much of a believer
in rituals'. When she was finally persuaded to come, she described the Federation
as an 'ageing' group which was getting behind the times.[31] She made a conscious
attempt to distance herself from the ranks of the older business leadership when
she declared that it would be the younger generation which she would prefer to
deal with.[32] Her relations with business deteriorated further when, the following
year, she refused point-blank to attend the FICCI session, leaving business to
lament the break in a '20-year-old tradition'.

There was little Birla could do to ease the growing tensions with the top leadership. The attitude of the top leadership towards him and the workings of the new regime forced him to retreat from his self-found role of unofficial adviser. His trip to the US in March 1966 proved to his last mission in that role. Meanwhile, he found himself a lone voice within business circles where he was perceived as being close to the ruling establishment.

A LONE VOICE: BIRLA, BIG BUSINESS AND THE 1967 ELECTIONS

By the later months of the year, at the national level, the electoral clock was ticking away. Let down by aid-givers and in trouble with the older Congress leadership, an insecure Indira Gandhi began to believe that her survival depended on a reversion to left-leaning politics and a revival of her mildly radical image.[33] Her changed political stance, which would undoubtedly affect her economic agenda, became apparent when, in July 1966, just a month after devaluation, she issued a joint communiqué with Brezhnev, the Russian Premier, condemning 'American bombing in Asia'. The devaluation experience conditioned the economic policies that she promoted in the future. There occurred a change in economic orientation and a withdrawal of support from growth-oriented economic policies to a leftist position with a more populist appeal. Determined not to be insulted by foreign powers, she made self-reliance in food a national pursuit and did all she could to usher in the Green Revolution. While this was commendable, there was a flip side to this about-turn: on the industrial front, she returned to pervasive control systems. As she turned Left, the party began to talk of nationalization of private-sector banks and warned about the dangers of concentration of economic power in the hands of some business houses, and increased government controls through state-trading in a variety of commodities.

An influential section of the business community was beginning to get restive at the economic situation. Not only had their frustrations accumulated over the years but they could see that devaluation was not leading to the economic changes that they had expected. No doubt there had been a partial decontrol of 48 industries but it was clear that Indira Gandhi was moving towards the Left both because she saw it as the way to establish her dominance and face the critique within the party, and because of fears of a worsening food situation. Business had much awaited follow-up action and had expected 'new freedoms' to follow devaluation. In their view the limited liberalization of imports was not enough and devaluation had, much to their disappointment, 'proved to be no tonic'.[34]

In such an atmosphere, business leaders felt that they needed to take a more proactive role in the political process rather than merely depend upon the right-wing leadership of the ruling Congress party to safeguard their interests. This was the strategy which big business had consistently followed since the 1930s under Birla's direction and it now came to be aggressively challenged. In private business circles, Birla's colleagues alleged that the contempt with which business was treated under Nehru's regime had 'grown larger and not diminished as the years have gone by'. Business leaders began to be infuriated with their subordinate status and accused Indira Gandhi of trying to 'liquidate the private sector'. This view was strengthened by Indira Gandhi's attitude towards the Federation and then by the Draft Election Manifesto of the party.[35] The frustration that engulfed business became apparent at a meeting of the FICCI Executive Committee in September 1966. Though the Committee met to study the Fourth Five-Year Plan, the Congress Draft Election Manifesto took up its entire deliberations. Allegations rent the air that business had been treated with utter disregard by the government. The 1966 Election Manifesto was compared with those of 1956 and 1961 and members commented on the vast difference in the attitude towards business. They indicted the Congress Party for not even acknowledging the private sector in the new manifesto. This, they said, only went to show the worsened position of the private sector. Business leaders complained that the exclusion was a 'deliberate step towards a further diminution of the Private Sector into insignificance.' If this were not amended, they needed to warn leaders that they would consider 'withdrawing… support to the Congress party as such.' Senior members of FICCI expressed 'a strong feeling of having been taken for granted by the party in power' which, to make matters worse, was quite confident that for all their 'disagreements and dissatisfactions … the industrial and mercantile community and the big business is going to finance it to win the elections'[36] Both within FICCI and in private business circles, there was, for the first time, open talk of withdrawing support from the Congress party. As the 1967 elections drew closer a number of Birla's friends from the business world vociferously challenged and even blamed his strategy for the subservient position in which business found itself.

The obvious political alternative for big business seemed the right-wing Swatantra party which had rallied around the personality of Rajaji.[37] As an avowedly right-wing party it was naturally attractive to business: its manifesto promised protection for industry with minimal controls, balanced development of capital goods industry and a minimal role of the public sector in industrialization and an aversion to Soviet-style planning.[38] The party had enjoyed support especially from Bombay-based business and in the parliamentary election of 1962 influential business leaders such as J.R.D. Tata and Dharamsey Khatau had supported it financially.

Birla too shared the sense of loss of confidence which business leaders experienced towards the Congress. He had, over the past few months, found it difficult to hide his dissatisfaction with the government's policies and had become a vocal critic of the ruling party at various public forums. For instance, in February 1965, while addressing the Indian Merchants' Chamber he claimed that all government plans had remained on paper, its slogan of democratic socialism was outmoded, politicians were 'ignorant about economic affairs' and that the mess that the country was in could be blamed largely on the government's economic policies. It was high time, he told fellow businessmen, that there was a dialogue between business and the government and he urged the business community to take steps that would 'compel the government to take action'.[39] A few weeks later, on 2 April 1965, while presiding over the Golden Jubilee celebration of the Marwari Relief Society, which he and Jugalkishore had been instrumental in forming in their early days in Bara Bazaar, Birla found it difficult to check his emotions when he referred to the problems his fellow Marwari businessmen were facing. He warned that 'the Government must understand that if it throws away the "Pagree" (head-gear) of businessmen, a time would soon come when the Gandhi caps of the leaders would be thrown away by the public'.[40] Likewise, while addressing the Engineering Association of India he asked:

How can you depend on this government? Just now if you go to Delhi you will find that everybody is running after tickets. Where do they have the time to think about your problems? They do not have time to produce your balance sheets. They have to produce their own balance sheets.

There had, he declared, occurred a collapse in the country's economy leaving the 'establishment, the administration in Delhi bewildered. Delhi has been paralysed.' It was, he said, all thanks to bad planning, bad fiscal policy, bad monetary policy and too much regimentation and interference by the bureaucracy. Birla had never been as lucid as when he called the Plans stupid, the planners amateurs, planning a most dangerous thing and the Fourth Plan insane and prepared mostly for the purpose of election.[41]

Such forthright public criticism was completely uncharacteristic of Birla. Friends and colleagues who had known him over the years were taken by surprise at his outspokenness and some even congratulated him on his new, candid stance. J.R.D. Tata wrote: 'I am glad to find that you no longer hesitate to express in public constructive criticism of official economic policy and I congratulate you on it.'[42] In private Birla was even more openly sceptical of the government's suspiciousness of business which he said, 'even the Prime Minister has not escaped'.[43]

Encouraged by his new public critique, Birla was approached by business friends as they thought of ways of dealing with the political leadership of Indira Gandhi. Soon after the FICCI Executive Committee meeting of September 1966, Bombay industrialist Viren J. Shah (Mukund Steel) urged Birla to openly and fearlessly speak out against the Congress party.[44] Despite his critique of the economic policies and even acknowledgement of the need to 'adopt democratic methods to set things right', Birla ruled out any possibility of breaking with the Congress Party. Explaining his stand to Shah, he wrote:

As far as I am concerned my loyalty is still with the Congress although I know they have bungled. But one does not change the party so swiftly. I would rather try and improve the party. But I may fail.[45]

Eager to elicit Birla's support, Shah persisted. A few days later, he sent him the draft election manifesto of the Swatantra Party for his comments. Birla again refused to be drawn into these political moves and replied briefly: 'Your election manifesto is good and I agree with the views.'[46] On the eve of the elections he publicly confessed that he was 'wedded to Congress people' and for all their blunders, he told fellow businessmen, he was unwilling to break with them.

Birla's refusal to join the dissenting ranks was characteristic and quite in keeping with his overall view of Indian politics. He had, as we have seen, for long understood the importance of centrist parties in the Indian political context. He believed that a party like the Swatantra could make no dent in the political scene given its dominant composition of princes and business interests. Representing a narrow group he did not see them as a viable alternative. His *Eastern Economist* encapsulated Birla's argument when it wrote that the Swatantra Party 'lacks the killer instinct which is so necessary for political effectiveness'. It suggested that Masani and his party colleagues 'would do well to give serious thought to strengthening this soft stuffing of the political framework of their party before they venture to point a finger of scorn at those businessmen who may be willing to deny themselves the safeguard of an insurance policy against the political hazards of the day.'[47] In Birla's eyes, the Swatantra Party did not pose an alternative to the Congress and thus it made little sense to back the party. As he told fellow businessmen at the Indian Chamber of Commerce:

You can break the Congress—but it is not going to help. You will be replacing this government by a communist government and they will be the first to cut your throat. Do not make that mistake ... It is a question of self-interest.[48]

Given that he saw the lack of a real opposition alternative he believed it was inadvisable to disturb the stability of the government. He warned the Indian Merchants' Chamber not to play into the hands of the Communists. As he put it, 'It is the game of the Communists to disturb this government in the expectation that they can be the alternative and you can realise what that alternative would be. It would be something worse.'[49]

Yet while he refused to break with the Congress party he wanted its leadership to realize that the party was not invincible. He wanted it to be humbled, to realize how it had blundered and to lose some of its 'unabashed confidence' in the polls. He wanted it to come back only with a highly reduced majority. It was time, he felt, much like his business colleagues, that the Congress needed to learn a lesson.[50] This would, he hoped, lead to 'a lot of frank talk' within the party once the election was over and would, he hoped, lead to the realization that 'if they do not correct their position' it 'will be impossible for them to face any more election. In their own interest, I hope they will be more amenable to reason', Birla told J.R.D. Tata.[51] As important sections of business extended much of their support to the right-wing Swatantra Party, Birla personally advised caution. He continued to propagate the view that weakening the Congress would merely create a vacuum from which only the Communists would benefit.[52]

While Birla did not find it difficult to cope with the pressure from his friends in Bombay, he faced a much more difficult position at home. Many members of the family had been converted to the cause of the Swatantra Party and were quite willing to openly support the opposition. There was pressure on Birla to change track from both his brothers and from the younger members of the family. Braj Mohan had been an early convert to the philosophy of the Swatantra Party and had been one of its main financiers since 1962. For the forthcoming election, he had already committed himself to financially supporting a number of its candidates such as D.N. Patodia, S.K. Taparia and N.K. Somany.[53] Rameshwardas, in Bombay, empathized with the position held by the city's industrialists and openly sympathized with the Swatantra Party. He had committed his support to Viren Shah soon after the FICCI Executive Committee meeting of September 1966. That left Jugalkishore who was now in his nineties and generally kept out of political matters. Within the younger generation, Madhav Prasad had agreed to support the Swatantra Party and Krishna Kumar too had begun to sympathize with the opposition. Lakshmi Niwas, as FICCI president for that year, held an ambiguous position towards the Congress as a number of prominent FICCI leaders stood for the election as opposition candidates. Birla increasingly found himself a lone voice in discussions at home when he tried to convince the family of the futility of breaking with the Congress. For all his warnings, Birla found it impossible to stem the tide at home and in his circle of business friends.

As the elections approached, Birla's old associates from the Congress, such as Atulya Ghosh, C.B. Gupta and S.K. Patil once more canvassed his help with 'donations for the election fund for the centre'. This appeared a good opportunity to Birla to mend bridges with the top leadership. In the expectation that he may be involved by the Congress high command in fund raising Birla began to test the waters with his business friends. Not unexpectedly, he discovered that many of them were anxious to hedge their bets and were quite happy to support the Congress along with the opposition. In December 1966 he offered his support to Indira Gandhi and indicated that businessmen like himself and J.R.D. Tata were:

all anxious to do our bit. But the question is to whom should we send our contribution. In the past when I had collected such funds, I had sent the money to the Prime Minister. I believe it would be appropriate this time also if the cheques are sent to the Prime Minister drawn in favour of the AICC. If you kindly give me direction, we will take immediate action.[54]

When he did not receive a positive response to his letter from the PMO, Birla decided not to take upon himself the responsibility of collecting funds from business colleagues but only make a personal contribution. In January 1967 he sent his first instalment of Rs 2,50,000 to Indira Gandhi from the account of his Century Mills with the promise to send some more money from time to time.[55] He later contributed Rs 3,00,000 for the Central Fund (through C.B. Gupta) and then another 2,00,000. A separate cheque of Rs 1,00,000 was sent by Mandelia to the Central Fund (through S.K. Patil).[56] Separate donations were made to city and district Congress committees with the largest sum going to Gupta's constituency of Lucknow City.[57]

CAMPAIGNING IN JHUNJHUNU

Though Birla could shun the appeal of his business colleagues to support the opposition, he could not keep completely aloof from the elections and got involved in a rather indirect way when his close kinsman Radha Krishen Birla, decided to stand for the election as a Swatantra Party candidate from the Jhunjhunu constituency.[58] Radha Krishen's association with the Birla family went back several generations—they were neighbours in Pilani—and Radha Krishen had himself spent his entire career in different Birla enterprises. Given such a close family association, Birla found it difficult to keep aloof from Radha Krishen's campaign. Perhaps an even more compelling reason for his interest in the election was his desire to nurture his home village Pilani which lay within Radha Krishen's constituency. Birla took upon himself the responsibility of planning the strategy and logistics for this campaign.

Radha Krishen's campaign brought back memories of his own election 43 years earlier in 1924. Birla had then learnt the ground rules about successful canvassing from Lajpat Rai and Malaviya and he applied them to Radha Krishen's election campaign. He started with preparing a two-page note on how the campaign should proceed. At least a hundred key reliable employees from the Birla mills were carefully selected for canvassing amongst the 5,00,000 strong electorate in the area. A provision was made for 100 vehicles for a start.[59] Then the voters' list was divided into 100 sections for each of the reliable employees to approach. They were instructed to start door-to-door campaigning with 5000 voters and to contact each voter personally. After the voters were met, on Birla's advice, a 'green sign' was put against the names of those who were in favour and a 'red sign' against those who were against and perhaps needed further convincing. Detailed procedures were laid down by Birla for keeping accounts of election expenses.[60] A strategy was laid down for dealing with the press—especially the local press, which Birla considered more influential in the area.

Radha Krishen's campaign proceeded as planned. Finding key men did not pose any difficulties with over 18,000 Birla employees in the district. Moreover, the reputation of the House of Birlas easily attracted helpers: many came readily to help in the hope that it might give them a break with the Birla Group. The Birla name became Radha Krishen's main campaign platform and his claim to the district.[61] Rumours spread that electricity had come to the area thanks to a Rs 15 crores contribution that the Birlas had made to the state exchequer. Voters were told that prosperity would come to the area if they voted for Radha Krishen as the Birlas would locate an industrial venture there. 'You all know', stated Radha Krishen's election manifesto, 'what the Birla family has done in this direction and will keep on doing.'[62] The campaign was much like Birla's own campaign of 1924. Radha Krishen invoked his Hindu credentials and the emotional appeal of the cow to his largely Hindu constituency. Caste considerations also came into play. On Birla's advice the prominent Jat leader, Kumbharam Arya, a dissident Congressman who now headed the newly formed Janata Party, was drafted into the campaign to influence the large local Jat population. Influential political leaders such as the Rajmata of Gwalior, Rawal Madansingh of Nawalgarh as well as top Birla men such as D.P. Mandelia, who were locally influential, were roped in. Reminiscent of Birla's own campaign, some preachers from the Arya Samaj were also involved.[63] Not unexpectedly, the campaign proved to be a high-pitched one. Left-wing Congressmen alleged that more than Rs 70 lakhs were spent by the Birlas on Radha Krishen's election.[64] The campaign was not an easy one. There were nine other candidates in the fray—the most influential one was R.R. Morarka, a fellow Marwari, who belonged to a local family and had been a prominent parliamentarian and the Congress candidate who represented the constituency since 1952.[65] The others in the fray were Ghasi Ram, a peasant leader with communist affiliation and there were seven Independents.

However, Birla's meticulous planning and the support extended by the House of Birlas ensured Radha Krishen's success. It also displayed Birla's ambition to be closely involved with the politics of his home-town, Pilani. He looked upon himself as a patron and assured its residents that 'as far as the nursing of the constituency is concerned, there would not be any negligence'.[66]

Meanwhile, at the national level, the elections were conducted in an atmosphere of uncertainty and frustration with rising prices, food scarcities, near famine in Bihar and mass agitations.[67] However, as Birla had expected, the Congress returned to power, though with reduced parliamentary support. In the Lok Sabha it ended up with 283 seats out of a total of 520. What was worse was that many of the Old Guard such as S.K. Patil, Atulya Ghosh and Kamaraj lost their seats. As his *Eastern Economist* put it, 'the prestige of the Congress has been humbled more than its power'.[68] The Swatantra Party won an impressive 44 seats in Parliament. It was well known in political circles that for the first time opposition parties like the Swatantra Party had enjoyed generous funding from big business, and the Congress' monopoly over business funds had been broken. Even Indira Gandhi complained to Lakshmi Niwas that business support had contributed to her party's political instability.[69]

POLITICAL BACKLASH

The overall picture which emerged after the election led to greater political uncertainty and the fall-out of the 1967 election proved to be serious for Birla personally and for his business friends. The sensational electoral set-back of the Congress inaugurated a phase of bitter infighting within the party. Indira Gandhi was anxious to establish her personal authority and was determined to break with the Syndicate and not to allow herself to become its puppet. One way was to promote a more populist stance towards economic policy and she began to move aggressively to the Left. She also began to distance herself from the earlier position on the US. The government's attitude towards foreign investment and collaboration in fertilizer projects which had been favoured by the World Bank became negative. Asoka Mehta's proposals for joint ventures between foreign investors and Indian firms were 'shot down one by one' at Indira Gandhi's behest leading ultimately to his resignation in August 1968.[70]

Alongside, she encouraged a group of radicals known as the Congress Forum for Socialist Action and especially the 'Young Turks' who seized the slogan of the re-dedicating of the party to its old socialistic objectives. They called for a left-wing re-orientation of the party and a purge of the old discredited leaders. The Young Turks especially resented business support to the Syndicate and wanted to expose the nexus between big business and right-wing Congressmen. They also demanded strong measures to curb the economic power of the top business houses through monopoly legislation and a variety of other demands such as nationalization of private-sector banks.

To consolidate her position, Indira Gandhi began to use economic policy as an active instrument for popularizing her party and stamping her own authority. As part of this strategy came several commissions of enquiry whose findings were used as a basis for anti-business policies which served to boost her leftist credentials and to isolate the right-wing Syndicate within the Congress. The work of the Monopolies Inquiry Commission, which reported in December 1965, proved to be handy.[71] Though the Commission had not been appointed by her, Indira Gandhi used it to her political advantage. The Commission had been charged with the task of enquiring into the 'extent and effect of concentration of economic power in private hands and the prevalence of monopolistic and restrictive practices in economic activity and was to suggest legislative or other measures which might be required to protect public interest'.[72] It identified 20 business houses as large industrial houses. While it conceded that pure monopoly was almost nonexistent, it warned that monopolistic trade practices are definitely prejudicial to the interests of the public as they increased costs of goods and services and gave higher profits to big business. Its most significant finding was that in the use of bank credit the main beneficiary had been the big and medium enterprises of the private sector which had monopolized industrial licensing either for expanding new industries or for expanding existing capacity.[73] Pointing to the House of Birlas it claimed that it had managed to get the lion's share of loans from financial institutions. While 56 per cent of the total financial assistance had gone to the large business houses, one-fourth of this went to the Birlas alone. This marked the Birlas as the major beneficiaries of easy long-term credit provided by financial institutions controlled by the government.

Birla, on his part, tried to maintain personal contact with Indira Gandhi but increasingly found himself being rebuffed by her. In early 1968 he sent a silver tea set and tray to her on the occasion of the wedding of her elder son, Rajiv. Indira Gandhi returned it a few days later with a short terse note in which she explained: 'When your representative came with the present for Rajiv, I had told him how much I was touched by your thought but that, as mentioned in my card, I was not accepting presents. Hence it would not be proper to keep yours. I did not want to do anything in a hurry or without mentioning it to you. So I took the opportunity of talking to L.K. Jha when he was here the other day. He agreed with my point of view and advised me to send the tea set and tray back to you. I am sure you will understand.'[74]

Close on the heels of the report of the Monopolies Commission Inquiry came the Industrial Licensing Policy Committee which reported in 1969. Chaired by Subimal Dutt, it concluded that the working of the system of industrial licensing had failed to enforce the objectives of the Industrial Policy Resolution of 1956 and that concentration of wealth and economic power had been accentuated. The Committee found evidence that the licensing policy had resulted in growing disparities in income and property and the emergence of monopolistic situations. It concluded that industrial licensing as well as credit policies of financial institutions had helped the growth of large industrial houses and it recommended a thorough revamping of the licensing policy.[75] It was very critical of large business houses which it said followed unethical practices such as multiple applications in different names for the same item and deliberate pre-emption of capacity. The Committee recommended the joint sector as the main policy instrument against concentration.[76] It proposed a ban on the entry of the 20 leading big business houses into certain areas of industry which would, in other respects, be free of licensing restrictions.

What all this meant for Birla and his circle of business associates was not only a change in economic policy but also a personal, vicious attack on them. These findings were used by the Young Turks in parliamentary proceedings to launch scathing attacks upon the so-called monopoly houses, particularly the Birlas. A key issue which arose from these controversies related to the structure of the banking industry. The Young Turks took it up in a vigorous campaign to argue that credit policies of the larger banks should promote integrated social development.[77] As Indira Gandhi's troubles with the Syndicate grew worse and her frustrations with Morarji Desai, her Finance Minister and rival, worsened, this issue came to be politically charged.[78] Though Desai believed in strict social control of banking he was opposed to outright nationalization.[79] Indira Gandhi now used the bank nationalization issue as a means of hitting out at Desai.[80] In an unexpected move carried out with great secrecy, Indira Gandhi nationalized 14 top banks on 19 July 1969.[81]

Birla's business empire came to be directly affected as it meant the take-over of his United Commercial Bank (UCO Bank) which stood among the five largest banks in the country. Established in 1942, UCO Bank had been nurtured by Birla personally. It provided the nerve-centre by which complex financial transactions were carried out by several hundred Birla companies on a daily basis. As a financial institution UCO Bank enjoyed considerable stature with a branch network extending to 314 locations within India and an overseas presence in eight countries including London, Malaysia, Singapore and Hong Kong. Its credit advances stood at Rs 14,399.91 lakhs and its deposits exceeded Rs 21,794.35 lakh in 1968.[82] Business leaders were outraged by this sudden move.[83] Birla was shocked at the populism and sloganeering which accompanied the move and he was dismayed by the inability of the Congress Right to oppose Indira Gandhi. In a piece entitled, 'Hell hath no fury', his *Eastern Economist* caricatured the Prime Minister 'like a woman scorned' whose actions were her private and 'very personal moon-shot' and had sent 'the country into a lunar wilderness of her making'. It characterized nationalization as 'a simple act of political aggrandizement' which had 'certainly been dictated by the confrontation between Indira Gandhi and the rest of the high command'.[84]

The nationalization of banks inaugurated the policy of hitting out at big business. It was as Indira Gandhi declared, 'only the beginning of a bitter struggle between the common people and the vested interests in the country.'[85] The Birlas in particular were subjected to repeated criticisms both by the Commissions which Indira Gandhi patronized and in the press. In a series of articles which the economist R.K. Hazari published, he showed how large and medium-sized firms enjoyed a higher ratio of approval of licensing applications as compared to the others. He proved that influential business houses such as the Birlas had utilized the system of industrial licensing to gain a disproportionately large share of the increase in the country's industrial capacity. He also showed the controls which big business groups exercised over diverse industries through interlocking directorships and how licences benefited them. This argument was taken further by B. Dutt of the Company Law Department who put forth data proving that the assets of the 20 large industrial houses had increased by more than 54 per cent in just four years. Singling out the House of Birlas, Dutt showed an increase in their assets by 96.6 per cent between 1963–4 and 1967–8.

The unrelenting criticism of big business and of the Birlas in particular, helped Indira Gandhi in her political aims. The commissions created the framework for anti-monopoly legislation which she was now determined to use against business. In 1969 she enacted the Monopolies & Restricted Trade Practices Act (MRTP). The MRTP meant a more tight investment regime for the larger houses; tightening of licensing and controls over interlocking directorships. All firms above a certain asset base were restricted from entry into almost all sections of industry and even expanding the existing plant required permission from the government on a 'case-by-case' method.

Indira Gandhi's attack on business continued unabated. In 1969, she abolished the managing agencies.[86] Both the Birlas' managing agencies—Birla Brothers (which had been founded in 1919) and Birla Trust which were estimated to be worth 300 million pounds and which spearheaded the growth of Birla's industrial empire and controlled more than 200 companies were abolished.[87] In the following year industrial policy was revised extensively to target the larger houses. Large industrial houses controlling a capital of over Rs 35 crores were almost completely confined by various regulations. Regulations covering foreign exchange controls followed. The imposition of FERA (Foreign Exchange Regulation Act), forced foreign entities to reduce their shareholding to 40 per cent. All these regulations were supplemented by revenue laws which provided for high taxation on incomes of the highest slabs, gift and wealth taxes, and a levy of high estate duty. Taxation laws discriminated against companies which had a few shareholders as well as against inter-corporate investment.

Along with the politicization of economic policy which affected business interests, personal attacks were made on Birla's business empire. Though a number of business houses were targeted by the Young Turks, the Birlas were in particular singled out. From 1967, Chandrashekhar, then a young Congress radical, Rajya Sabha member and a leading Young Turk, submitted a series of memoranda to Indira Gandhi which were subsequently laid on the table of both Houses of Parliament. Addressing the Prime Minister, Chandrashekhar made wide-ranging charges against the Birlas. As he put it:

The charges against the Birlas range from the issue of duplicate shares to the employment of fictitious persons. They have been systematically cheating the public and defrauding the revenue authorities in various ways over a long period of time. ... They have amassed wealth at the cost of the suffering, the anguish, the starvation and degradation of the people ... Industrial empires founded on systematic tax evasions and public cheating have no right, much less justification to exist.

Chandrashekhar claimed that he had evidence to show large-scale corrupt practices and tax evasion in the Birla empire. Citing a number of companies he showed discrepancies that indicated defraud of capital revenues. He alleged that companies made import-duty claims which were realized far in excess of the actuals. Further, loans were taken even when companies did not require them and prices were increased arbitrarily in areas where the Birlas enjoyed a monopoly. He accused them of deliberately undervaluing stock and using other methods of frittering away profits of companies to reduce tax liability. Firms such as Hyderabad Asbestos Cement Products Ltd, he claimed, had expanded capacity without industrial licences being granted. He showed how licences were worked to unfairly keep out potential competitors.[88] Amongst the many accusations alleged by Chandrashekhar were falsifying account books, evading excise taxes and income tax. Chandrashekhar indicted the government for favouring the Birlas by overlooking these faults; for giving over companies to them in states such as Andhra Pradesh and Gujarat and for showing preference to them whenever proposals were put up to the government for transfer of shares. He claimed that the Birlas had highly-placed government officers on their pay-roll as their contact men to move files in government offices. Birla's UCO Bank office, he said, was 'the real den of Birla Brothers' which orchestrated 'all the mischievous work of corruption and under-hand dealings with the ministries'.[89] Chandrashekhar challenged the Prime Minister to take matters in hand.

The Birlas because of their all-pervading influence, have been indulging in these activities on a large scale with perfect sense of immunity. This has created an impression in the country that they are invincible. It is imperative that this immunity is broken and this impression removed, Under the circumstances, a vigorous onslaught on their infinite crimes is essential...At this momentous and difficult turn in our political life you have heavy responsibilities to discharge. I am fully aware of the pressure of work upon you. I would not have added to your worries had I not been convinced that a decisive stage has come where we are called upon to take a certain amount of risk in dealing with such people who have neither any respect for social values nor any regard for human dignity.[90]

In a passionate tone he avowed that: 'This behaviour to smash the very fundamentals of our social and political life cannot be tolerated' and he demanded 'a comprehensive enquiry into their affairs by a specially constituted commission, somewhat on the lines of the Vivian Bose Commission.'

The charges created a storm in Parliament[91]. So pervasive were the allegations that the matter was raised in the Cabinet on two or three occasions by President Fakhruddin Ali Ahmed. The Prime Minister is known to have discussed the matter with Morarji Desai, then Deputy Prime Minister, who recommended a detailed enquiry into the House of Birlas.[92] In December 1968 Chandrashekhar took the attacks further when he joined with the Communist Party of India (CPI) in Parliament to accuse Morarji Desai, in his capacity as Finance Minister, of partiality to the Birlas and of hindering an enquiry against them.[93] All this fitted in well with Indira Gandhi's larger political agenda of hitting out at Desai and the Syndicate leadership. Not surprisingly, she refused to come to the defence of her deputy and chose to stay neutral amid the storm of accusations and counter accusations. As she condoned these attacks to further her factional aims, questions continued to be raised about the Birlas. George Fernandes, the Socialist trade unionist, described them as speculators who had migrated into industry and accused 'Birla's association with Gandhiji' for having given the group 'tremendous economic and political muscle with which to manipulate the levers of power'.[94] All this resulted in the appointment of the Sarkaria Commission in 1970 to inquire into the alleged malpractices which had enabled the Birlas to increase their assets and sales. It was wound up eight years later by George Fernandes with nothing to show for its labours after an expenditure of Rs 7 crores.[95]

As the Communists joined in the attacks on the Birlas and big business in general, many cadres of the CPI in West Bengal made the Marwaris the targets of their attacks as outsiders with vested interests. Calcutta witnessed an increasing frequency of strikes and demonstrations against business houses.[96] One of the issues which was taken up with a vengeance was the controversy over Birla House, New Delhi. In late 1969, the Communist leader Shashi Bhushan went on an indefinite fast on the grounds of Birla House. Then S.A. Dange, the CPI leader, declared that 1 October 1970 would be observed as 'anti-monopoly anti-Birla day'. It was to be marked by a *gherao* of the managers of the Birla concerns and by demonstrations. Dange challenged Birla that if his Delhi home was not given over to the public within six months it would be taken over by the working class of Delhi.

Birla's strategy was to maintain an assiduous silence and furnish as little provocation as possible.[97] He did, however, let his *Eastern Economist* speak occasionally on his behalf. It termed Dange's challenge the 'grossest expression of the politics of persecution'. Quite reminiscent of Birla's emotional appeal to Nehru in 1950, for not to press for the house, the journal said the house was 'a place which was being regularly lived in and which, in the course of that process, had come to acquire intimate and even sacred meaning for its owners.'[98] The old controversy had been made alive once again by the Young Turks and the Communists.

GIVING UP BIRLA HOUSE

Undoubtedly the glare of publicity deeply upset Birla who had so assiduously maintained a low public profile throughout his life. To Birla the allegations in Parliament and the agitation over Birla House portended the tone of the new politics which was becoming dominant under Indira Gandhi. He was aware that she was gaining political mileage by unabashedly attacking his business empire. Disenchanted with the new style of politics he could see no way out but to withdraw from the public arena. He realized that there was only one way out of the public glare and that was to give up his house. When the issue had been raised on earlier occasions he had found a solution by opening up a part of the garden, which included the spot where Gandhi had been assassinated, to the public. However, it saddened him that the controversy had been reopened. As the Communists' pressure continued, a saddened Birla agreed to give up a larger part of the house. In a quiet ceremony held on 2 October 1971, a portion of Birla House was renamed Gandhi Sadan and dedicated to the nation by the President V.V. Giri. An ageing Birla himself moved hastily into a rented house in Vasant Vihar while construction was begun on a new plot of land, a few kilometers away from the old Birla House, on Amrita Shergill Marg. This house did not bear the family title and was called 'Mangalam'.

Meanwhile, outrage at the unfortunate turn of events provoked Krishna Kumar to run for the 1971 election as an independent opposition candidate in the parliamentary elections. As in 1967, there was much discussion over the sagacity of the decision and Birla canvassed the view that it would be futile to oppose the ruling party openly. Though Birla shared the family's disenchantment with Indira Gandhi's regime, he saw that opposition candidates could only make limited inroads into the Congress' regional support. He had always emphasized the importance of working through centrist parties, while ignoring their leftist rhetoric. He was convinced that only centrist parties like the Congress could keep the

Communists at bay. This was a time-tested strategy which big business had followed from the pre-independence years.[99] It was not just on political grounds that he objected to his son's decision. He also believed that his primary commitment must remain the expansion of the business empire and political involvements must be kept as secondary, much as he had himself done in his younger days. Birla's arguments fell on deaf ears and Krishna Kumar remained unconvinced. His decision was supported by Braj Mohan and the younger men in the house. A determined Krishna Kumar disobeyed his father and stood for the election. A distraught Birla is said to have not spoken to his son for two weeks.

These circumstances hastened Birla's withdrawal from public activities. As he became detached from political affairs, he got succour from his spiritual vision of life. As always, he derived consolation and guidance from the *Bhagwad Gita*. Increasingly, he found great satisfaction from undertaking *tirtha-yatras* (pilgrimages). Between 1969 and 1972 Birla visited four of the holiest abodes of Hinduism. On these pilgrimages he was accompanied by Basant Kumar and Sarala, his wife. He started with Badrinath, considered the abode of Lord Vishnu and one of the most sacred centres of Hindu pilgrimage. The trek to the temple shrine at an altitude of more than 3000 metres is known to be one of the most arduous climbs in the Garhwal hills because of the hilly terrain and cliffs. Birla and his fellow pilgrims performed the trek quite comfortably. An emboldened Birla then undertook a pilgrimage to Kedarnath, one of the twelve 'Jyotirlingas' of Shiva. Legend has it that the shrine was built by the Pandavas to atone for their sins after the battle of Kurukshetra. Lying, as it does, at an altitude of 3584 metres in the Garhwal hills the trek to Kedarnath meant an ascent of 5000 feet. Birla and his family started the trek from Gaurikund and walked 16 kilometres in a single day. This was followed by a pilgrimage to Gangotri, the source of the river Ganga and then to Yamunotri, the source of the river Yamuna. According to myth, Yamuna was the daughter of Surya, the sun god, and the twin sister of Yama, the god of death, and a dip in the water would guarantee an easy end and would lead to *moksha*. The trip to Yamunotri gave him the most spiritual satisfaction. He reflected on the legends and epics connected with the holy places. He often thought of Gandhi and reminisced about their discussions on Hinduism. He recalled an especially interesting discussion on birth and reincarnation in which Gandhi advised him not to think about irrelevant philosophical questions but to pursue his duty and fulfil his *karma*. The pristine beauty of the landscapes he encountered during his pilgrimages gave him glimpses of God.[100]

Notes and References

[1] For details see Krishna Kumar Birla, *Indira Gandhi Reminiscences* (New Delhi, n.d.).

[2] Details on Indira Gandhi's association with the Trust are not available. See Inder Malhotra, *Indira Gandhi, A Personal and Political Biography* (London, 1989), pp. 187–9.

[3] *Ibid*, pp. 20–1.

[4] The 1963 budget was presented in the backdrop of the China war of 1962 which saw an enormous increase in defence expenditure from Rs 395 crores in the previous year to Rs 868 crores. The taxes imposed were on a large scale amounting to Rs 280 crores. Amongst the taxed items were shares and in direct taxation the surcharge was increased from 4 to 10 per cent. For details see Morarji Desai, *The Story of my Life* (New Delhi, 1979), Vol. 2, pp. 206–14.

[5] Birla to Morarji Desai, 2 March 1963, in Birla Papers, Important Files, Series I, File No. J–11, L.K. Jha. It appeared almost impossible to Birla to make any headway with the finance minister leading him to appeal to L.K. Jha to intervene to halt the 'worsening situation' which Desai had brought about. 'The people are losing confidence in the estimates of the Finance Ministry. This is really bad especially under the stewardship of Morarjibhai ... At any rate after this budget, it would be futile for anyone to expect expansion of industry' he told him. Birla to L.K. Jha, 3 March 1963, in Birla Papers, Important Files, Series I, File No. J–11, L.K. Jha.

[6] Birla wrote an argumentative letter to the Finance Minister, copies of which were sent to close business friends and to L.K. Jha.

[7] To many of them even 'the radicalism of Nehru and T.T.K. was perhaps more useful' than 'Morarji Desai's vague generalizations'. Venkatsubbiah, *Enterprise and Economic Change*, p. 110.

[8] As 19 January, the date for the election of a new leader, came closer, Birla could see that though Morarji Desai was 'fighting' hard to be elected the new leader there was no way he would succeed. It would be Indira Gandhi, he told his friends overseas, who would come to be the next Prime Minister. Birla to Louise S. Ansberry, 17 January 1966, in Birla Papers, Series Foreign Correspondence, File No. 144–A, 1960–6.

[9] Birla to Indira Gandhi, 27 January 1966, in *Nehru Family and Ghanshyamdas Birla*, p. 154.

[10] Indira Gandhi to Birla, 11 February 1966, in *Nehru Family and Ghanshyamdas Birla*, p. 154.

[11] Amongst those he held meetings with were Hubert Humphrey, Vice-President, Jack J. Valenti, special adviser to the President, Robert Kromer, special assistant to the President for National Security Affairs, Dean Rusk, Secretary of State, Arthur Dean, the unofficial adviser to the President, George Woods, Ambassador Arthur Goldberg, Thomas Mann, Under Secretary of State for Economic Affairs, Philip Potter of Baltimore 'Sun' who was supposed to be 'closely in the confidence of the President'. The main discussions were over economic aid to India. Birla sensed that the atmosphere was full of sympathy for India and her ratings had jumped as a result of the war with Pakistan, and that there seemed to be a desire for India to be 'strong and influential' and with Japan to be the stabilizing force in Asia. Yet he, believed that it was necessary to convince the US President that 'we are serious about our intentions and are determined to translate them into action.' Arthur Dean told Birla that the most important points for President Johnson were 'food', 'fertilisers', 'family planning' and 'good economy'.

[12] Birla, Note, dated 16.3.66 about talk with Jack Valenti; Note, 22.3.66 on summary of talks; Note, 14.3.66 on talk with Arthur Dean and Lloyd Cutler; Note, 18.3.66 on talk with Dean Rusk; Note, 15.3.66 on talk with George Woods; Note, 19.3.66 on talk with Arthur Goldberg and Freeman; Note, 21.3.66 on talk with Arthur Goldberg; Note, 21.3.66 on talk with Robert Komer; Note, 21.3.66 on talk with Thomas Mann; Note, 21.3.66 on talk with William Gaud; Note, 15.3.66 on talk with Philip Potter; Note,

17.3.66 on talk with George Woods. In Birla Papers, Series Miscellaneous, File No. 164, Notes and Speeches.

[13] Birla to Chester Bowles, 20 April 1966, in Birla Papers, Series Important, File No. 81–B, 1965–7.

[14] For details of his meeting see Birla to P.C. Bhattacharyya, 16 March 1966, in Birla Papers, Series Important, File No. 81–B, 1965–7.

[15] There were also articles on, 'Basic facts about India and its people'; on 'India's economic development goes ahead'; a short article by Edgar Kaiser, well-known American businessman and Birla's collaborator in his aluminum project, on 'American business and India'; one on 'Agriculture' and others on 'Secular Democracy and the Minorities'; the 'Population Problem'; 'Education as the key to Prosperity and Welfare'; 'Investment Opportunities in India' by G.L. Mehta and on 'Developing Industrial Structure' by V. Balasubramanian, editor of the *Eastern Economist.*

[16] In his article he said that 'India fully appreciated US arguments that wheat shipments could not be expected forever'; that she was trying to be self-sufficient but that aid was needed to 'give us the capacity to stand on our own legs'. The leadership he claimed was 'giving a more practical bias to economic thinking such as is evident in the searching look at controls and bureaucratic delays'.

[17] Addressing a gathering of American businessmen in New York she even promised to treat foreign investors 'completely on a par with national investors'. She also agreed to an American proposal to use the large rupee funds the US had built up because of the massive shipments of PL 480 wheat, to set up an Indo-American Educational Foundation. For details, see Inder Malhotra, *Indira Gandhi, A Personal and Political Biography* (London, 1989).

[18] Birla to Indira Gandhi, 2 April 1966, in *Ghanshyamdas Birla and Nehru Family*, p. 156.

[19] For debates on devaluation and its impact, see Jayati Ghosh, 'Liberalisation Debates' in Terence J. Byres (ed.), *The Indian Economy, Major Debates since independence*, pp. 295–334 (Delhi, 1998).

[20] For details, see David B.H. Denoon, *Devaluation under pressure: India, Indonesia and Ghana* (Massachusetts, 1986), pp. 25–85. Also see Robert W. Oliver, *George Woods and the World Bank* (Boulder, 1995), pp. 140–3.

[21] Birla to Asoka Mehta, 14 May 1966, in Birla Papers, Series Important, File No. 94–M, 1966–7.

[22] Undoubtedly a variety of factors favoured a change in economic policy and a number of advisers were propelling the government to accept devaluation. The balance of payments problem had worsened because of the increased government expenditure on the military during the 1962 and the 1965 war. The 1965 drought meant additional foreign exchange requirements for food and it precipitated the balance of payments crunch.

[23] Some of them, especially Kamaraj, were upset for having been kept in the dark and they retaliated over her non-consultative style of functioning. See Inder Malhotra, *Indira Gandhi, A Personal and Political Biography.*

[24] Birla to S.N. Sinha, 27 July 1966, in Birla Papers, Series Important, File No. 100–S, 1966–7, Satyanarain Sinha.

[25] Meeting in June 1966, the National Council of the Communist Party of India asked for the 'immediate resignation of the Central Government headed by Indira Gandhi because it had proved itself wholly unworthy of any national trust and thereby forfeited

its moral and political right to be placed at the helm of national affairs.' Francine Frankel, *India's Political Economy*, p. 392.

[26] See David B.H. Denoon, *Devaluation under pressure: India, Indonesia and Ghana*, pp. 25–85.

[27] For the views of L.N. Birla, then president of FICCI, see his article, 'Make Devaluation Work' in *Eastern Economist*, 15 July 1966. FICCI took the view that devaluation was an admission of the failure of the financial and fiscal policies of the preceding 15 years and therefore a 'drastic revision' of policies was required. According to them the purpose of devaluation would be defeated if the economy was not freed from controls and regulations.

[28] Rameshwardas welcomed it in his speech as Chairman to the 68th Annual Meeting of the Birla Century Spinning and Manufacturing Company on 10 June 1966. He claimed that he 'too had been advocating devaluation' but said that 'devaluation alone will not solve our problems. It will have to be accompanied by other measures to become effective. The economy should be freed from regimentation and controls and production should be encouraged. The level of taxation, both personal and corporate, should also be brought down. Unless this is done, devaluation by itself will not produce miracles.' He felt that the Finance Minister had done 'the right thing in the prevailing circumstances'. In his view, 'devaluation was the only practical and wise remedy as, besides encouraging exports and discouraging imports it would open the way for larger aid and private investment from abroad.' For the text of his speech, see *Eastern Economist*, 17 June 1966.

[29] For instance, he visited her on her birthday in 1968. See Jaju, *G.D. Birla, A Biography*, p. 160. Also see Birla to Indira Gandhi, 19 November 1966, in *Nehru Family and Ghanshyamdas Birla*, p. 157.

[30] Later, L.K. Jha became Governor of the Reserve Bank.

[31] She complained that although the older generation's 'experience will always be useful,' the younger generation had not played its part and urged it to take a constructive lead. Indira Gandhi declared that she would 'keep in touch with the younger generation'. On hindsight this probably had something to do with her attempts to assert herself within the Congress which was dominated by the older figures.

[32] She announced her intention to convene 'Round Tables' with younger industrialists to discuss economic issues. For Indira Gandhi's speech and details of the session, see *Eastern Economist*, 18 March 1966. Keeping her word, two months later she convened a two-day Round Table to which FICCI was invited. Taking the clue from her inauguration address, FICCI sent Krishna Kumar Birla, Charat Ram, Arvind Mafatlal, Madanmohan Mangaldas, Gautam Sarabhai and Keshub Mahindra to the conference—all representing the up-coming generation, who were yet to make a mark in either business or political circles of the corporate world.

[33] Inder Malhotra, *Indira Gandhi, A Personal and Political Biography*, p. 100.

[34] Reflecting this view the *Eastern Economist* wrote that there has been 'Too little too late.' In a lead article it declared that the 'much awaited follow up action consequent upon devaluation has emerged in a hesitant manner ... As days go by, the frustration of industry continues to rise. The bureaucratic machinery in the Capital seems to be moving at a snail's pace ... The files seem to be moving from Ministry to Ministry ...' See *Eastern Economist*, 19 August 1966. On 30 September it asked, 'Why then should there be any political uncertainty clouding our economic horizon? The answer evidently is that it is not the return of the Congress to power which is in doubt, but rather the intentions of the party in the field of economic policy. The prevailing uncertainty in other words, is

to be blamed on the obstructionist and negative attitudes of the ruling party in the government where the economic development of the country is concerned.' See 'Waiting for 1967', *Eastern Economist*, 30 September 1966.

[35] Many business leaders had expected the Draft Election Manifesto to take up economic issues.

[36] Viren J. Shah to Birla, 31 October 1966, in Birla Papers, Series Important, File No. 100–S, 1966–7. It was time, the leaders asserted, that action be taken 'to get its views not only heard but also acted upon.' Many leaders felt that the old strategy needed to be discarded and 'the time has come now when some sort of hard bargaining ... may be necessary.' The prevalent view among the FICCI Executive was that their views had 'failed to gain ground because we have been trying to propagate an economic policy in a political vacuum'. They were determined to take a 'firm stand and support the democratic opposition.' Ramakrishna Bajaj to Birla, 24 September 1966, in Birla Papers, Series Important, File No. 81–B, 1965–7.

[37] See Rajmohan Gandhi, *Rajaji: A Life* (Penguin, 1997). As is well known Bombay business had played an important role in the formation of the party.

[38] See H.L. Erdman, *The Swatantra Party and Indian Conservatism* (Cambridge, 1967).

[39] He said that the many interpretations to which it had been put was much like the '*Gita* had many *Bhasyas*'—it could be interpreted in a hundred ways. Birla's speech at the 58th Annual Meeting of the Indian Merchants' Chamber, 25 February 1966, in Birla Papers, Series Miscellaneous, File No. 120, Notes and Speeches.

[40] S.P. Shrivastava (ed.), *Greatness Personified, Vaishyarshi G.D. Birla* (Calcutta, n.d.), pp. 235–6.

[41] He credited the success of the first three Plans substantially to the private sector whose production figures had gone up enough to change the index. The Fourth Plan, he was sure, could not be implemented—that was known to the planners who had begun to realize they were in a 'leaky boat which might sink.' Birla, 'Inaugural Speech at the 24th Annual Session of the Engineering Association of India, 2 January 1967', in Birla Papers, Series Miscellaneous, File No. 120, Notes and Speeches.

[42] J.R.D. Tata to Birla, 3 February 1967, in Birla Papers, Series Important, File No. 101–T, 1966–7.

[43] Birla to Nawab Chhatari Ahmad Said, 7 June 1967, in Birla Papers, Series Important, File No. 95–N, 1966–7.

[44] Shah was himself standing on a Swatantra Party ticket along with Bombay industrialist Manu Amersey and Pashabhai Patel, Baroda industrialist and relative of Sardar Patel.

[45] Birla to Viren J. Shah, 5 November 1966 and Birla to Viren J. Shah, 13 November 1966, in Birla Papers, Series Important, File No. 100–S, 1966–7.

[46] Viren J. Shah to Birla, 26 November 1966 and Birla to Shah, 27 November 1966, in Birla Papers, Series Important, File No. 100–S, 1966–7.

[47] See 'The Moving Finger Writes', *Eastern Economist*, 12 September 1969.

[48] Birla, *Government and Business*, pp. 8–9.

[49] Birla, Speech at the 58th Annual General Meeting of the Indian Merchants' Chamber, 25 February 1966. Printed by the *Indian Merchants' Chamber* (Bombay, 1966).

[50] Birla, 'Inaugural Speech at the 24th Annual Session of the Engineering Association of India, 2 January 1967', in Birla Papers, Series Miscellaneous, File No. 120, Notes and Speeches.

[51] Birla to J.R.D. Tata, 13 February 1967, in Birla Papers, Series Important, File No. 100–S, 1966–7.

[52] The *Eastern Economist* attacked journalists such as Inder Malhotra of the *Statesman* who wrote about the failure of the opposition to form a united front against the Congress as 'doing the country no good' in its columns. According to it: 'An anti-Congress alliance which comprehends within itself, either directly or through the permutations and combinations of electoral arrangements, such disparate political groups as the Communists (whether Right or Left), Swatantra, Jan Sangh, DMK and Muslim league would certainly not make democratic sense to me even if such a front were to succeed to make inroads into the Congress domination of government at the Centre and in the States'. See 'The Moving Finger Writes,' *Eastern Economist*, 2 December 1966.

[53] Takneth, *B.M. Birla*, pp. 90–1.

[54] Birla to Indira Gandhi, 28 December 1966, in Birla Papers, Series Miscellaneous, File No. 68, Donation to Congress Election Fund, 1967.

[55] Birla to Indira Gandhi, 2 January 1967 and 'Contribution sent to Congress Election Fund', in Birla Papers, Series Miscellaneous, File No. 68, Donation to Congress Election Fund, 1967.

[56] See 'Contributions sent to Congress Election Fund', in Birla Papers, Series Miscellaneous, File No. 68, Donation to Congress Election Fund, 1967.

[57] At the personal level, he supported old friends in the party such as Sushila Nayar and Baburao Patel. Birla to Baburao Patel, 2 February 1967, in Birla Papers, Series Important, File No. P, 1966–7.

[58] Radha Krishen had worked with Digvijay Woollen Mills and Saurashtra Chemicals, Porbander, See R.K Birla, *'Bhuli Baatein Yaad Karoon'*, published by Harshvardhan Birla (n.d., Amritsar, Punjab). Radha Krishen had been given a ticket from the Swatantra Party and in return, agreed to financially support the party's MLA candidates from his district. He stood as an Independent with a Swatantra Party ticket.

[59] So high-pitched was the campaign that local businessmen feared that it would raise the level of financial expenses during future elections in the area. *Statesman*, 5 February 1967.

[60] He issued instructions that all accounts should be kept meticulously; the salaries of mill officers who were involved with the campaigning was to be paid by the mills only; conveyance would be the property of the mills; a detailed budget of the expenses was to be maintained and the Birla mills in the area were to 'pass a resolution at their Board meeting that it is in their own interests that a man who is pro-business is promoted and supported and that there is full justification why they are sending their conveyances with driver and fuel and all that.'

[61] Birla's involvement with the campaign was well known and his close association with the ruling Congress party sparked rumours in the national press that Radha Krishen had clandestinely been asked to contest by the Prime Minister herself as a way of keeping out the Congress candidate R.R. Morarka (chairman of the Public Accounts Committee). So strong were the rumours that Indira Gandhi was forced to intervene. She stated that she was 'surprised at the propaganda ... that a leading business house had decided to put up a candidate against Mr Morarka because Mrs Gandhi did not want the PAC chairman to stand from this constituency.' See the *Times of India*, 10 November 1966. For details of the campaign also see 'Electioneering in Basic Terms', the *Statesman*, 5 February 1967.

[62] *Hindustan Times*, 17 February 1967.

[63] 'Note', 16 November 1966, in Birla Papers, Series Miscellaneous, File No. 164, Notes and Speeches.

[64] Chandrashekhar, *A Peep into Birla House* (New Delhi, 1969), pp. 44–5.

[65] Fellow Calcutta Marwari and Rajya Sabha MP, Ram Kumar Bhuwalka reported to Birla that amongst the Calcutta Marwari community: 'All eyes are focused on the election front this time in Rajasthan which has, by the way, become the talk of the town whereas the election campaign in the city itself has not caught the full tempo.' Ram Kumar Bhuwalka to Birla, 6 February 1967, in Birla papers, Series Important, File No. 81–B, 1965–7.

[66] Birla to Rawal Madansingh of Nawalgarh, 28 February 1967, in Birla Papers, Series Important, File No. 100–S, 1966–7.

[67] Norman D. Palmer, 'India's Fourth General Elections', in *Asian Survey*, 7 May 1967, p. 277.

[68] As the *Eastern Economist* put it: 'There can be no doubt at all that the wind of change now blowing through our political landscape will, on balance, be for the good of the country and let us add, for the good of the Congress also .... By proving that office can be made to change hands with the help of the ballot box, the verdict of the fourth general election should have a soothing, sobering and steadying effect on our politics.' See 'The People have Spoken,' *Eastern Economist*, 24 February 1967.

[69] Lakshmi Niwas claimed that economic distress had contributed to the rout of the ruling party. He said that the high prices, penal taxation and shortages along with corruption and inefficiency had contributed to the widespread dissatisfaction. He wrote: 'One unmistakable lesson is that the difficulties of the people should not be ignored or minimised. The country cannot move from "vanity to vanity" in the economic field, as anywhere else with success ... Many changes in policy are, therefore, called for if the economy is to be repaired and not broken away. No better beginning can be made than by sweeping away the dry husks and restraints which are choking the economy. In the formulation of new measures the accent must be on giving a wider scope for all to produce more. The authorities, both at the centre and in all the states, should do well by eschewing experimental and ideological policies, also pomposity and smugness.' For details see 'Economic distress and the Election', *Eastern Economist*, 24 March 1967.

[70] Francine Frankel, *India's Political Economy*, p. 393.

[71] It had been appointed in May 1964.

[72] Chaired by Justice K.C. Das Gupta of the Supreme Court, the panel consisted of G.R. Rajagopal (Legal Draftsman), K.R.P. Aiyangar (former chairman of the Tariff Commission), R.C. Dutt (chairman of Company Law Board) and I.G. Patel (chief economic adviser of the Government of India).

[73] The Commission looked into the concentration of economic power and concluded that it had 'helped the economic betterment of the country' but it felt that a 'constant watch must be kept by a body independent of Government to see that big business does not misuse its power'. It studied the reasons behind the increase in concentration and recommended ways in which concentration could be monitored. R.C. Dutt dissented from the majority recommendations since he felt that the harmful effects of concentration had been underestimated by the Report. For a critique of the report see R.K. Hazari, 'The Great Escape. Concentration good. monopoly justifiable.' *The Economic Weekly*, 18 December 1965, pp. 1843–8.

[74] Indira Gandhi to Birla, 11 March 1968, in Birla Papers, Series Very Very Important Correspondence, File No. 14, Indira Gandhi, 1966–8.

[75] For details on the various commissions, see N.K. Sengupta, *Government and Business* (New Delhi, 1987), pp. 111–23.

[76] For details, see N.K. Sengupta, *Government and Business*, pp. 58–9.

[77] This was not a new idea—it had been first discussed in the Nehru Cabinet in 1948, and then revived by Kamaraj in the early 1960s. However, nationalization had not been considered necessary since it was felt that the Reserve Bank could regulate the scheduled banks.

[78] For Desai's views, see his *The Story of my Life*, Vol. 2, pp. 264–70.

[79] He had favoured 'social control' of banking which had legally come into force on 1 February 1969. It meant appointing watchdog committees to monitor credit policies and other operations of privately owned banks. It was intended to reduce the dominance of industrialists on bank management. Birla's UCO bank was also subjected to it and its Board of Directors was reconstituted.

[80] As Indira Gandhi herself admitted it was the Congress opposition to her that led her to such a measure. 'They drove me up the wall and left me with no other option', she wrote to a friend. For details, see Inder Malhotra, *Indira Gandhi, A Personal and Political Biography*, p. 120.

[81] Banks which had deposits of more than 50 crores were nationalized. Birla's UCO Bank qualified along with 13 other commercial banks. Birla had taken a keen personal interest in his bank and held its chairmanship which ensured that it became one of the five largest banks. UCO stood third after Central Bank, and the Punjab National Bank. The other big banks were Bank of India and the Bank of Baroda. Like other banks it had expanded vigorously since 1951 when, with the inauguration of planning, a promotional banking policy was followed whose objective was the 'building of a geographically wide and functionally diverse financial infrastructure'. See M. Narasimhan, 'The Indian Financial System', in FICCI, *Indian Business through the Ages*, p. 199.

[82] See Birla Institute of Scientific Research's *Banks since nationalisation* (New Delhi, 1981), pp. 7–11.

[83] Nationalization was vehemently denounced by a number of prominent businessmen. J.R.D. Tata denounced the 'illiberal and authoritarian tendencies', in the government. See for instance, *Eastern Economist*, 8 August.

[84] *Eastern Economist*, 25 July 1969. The nationalization of insurance and coal industries soon followed.

[85] Robert L. Hardgrave, Jr., 'The Congress in India—Crisis and Split', in *Asian Survey*, March 1970, Vol. X, No. 3, pp. 256–62.

[86] These were forms of corporate organization where one holding company controlled the equity and administration of a large number of enterprises which could be unrelated.

[87] See Ross, *The Emissary*, p. 198.

[88] Birla's most prestigious plants such as HINDALCO were accused of using electric power below costs and others such as Hindustan Motors of 'all sorts of malpractices' such as over-invoicing, tampering with import licences and importing goods without authorization.

[89] See Chandrashekhar, *A Peep into Birla House* (New Delhi, 1969).

[90] Chandrashekhar to Indira Gandhi, 5 July 1967, in Chandrashekhar, *A Peep into Birla House*.

[91] Shashi Bhushan, M.P., 'Introduction', in Chandrashekhar, *A Peep into Birla House*.

[92] Morarji Desai, *The Story of my Life*, Vol. II, pp. 297–9.

[93] Morarji Desai, *The Story of my Life*, Vol. II, pp. 297–9.

[94] Gita Piramal, *Business Legends*, p. 120.

[95] Gita Piramal, *Business Legends*, p. 121.

[96] The family maintained a low profile through all this and made no public pronouncements except for B.M. Birla who spoke to a group of demonstrators once to tell them that they were barking up the wrong tree. Commenting on the incident, the *Eastern Economist* said, ' It follows that businessmen have a clear stake in dynamic economic expansion, while politicians may have a stake, equally clearly, in retarded economic development out of which arises popular frustration which it is politically profitable to exploit. It is no doubt appropriate to the lopsided times in which we live that those who claim to be protesting against employment should be directing their demonstrations against industrialists (who are being told by politicians that they cannot expand their business activities), instead of against ministers and bureaucrats who seem to be committed to preventing growth in some of the more enterprising and efficient sectors of our industry and commerce.' See 'The Moving Finger Writes', in *Eastern Economist*, 4 December 1970.

[97] The only response of the Birlas was from D.P. Mandelia, then chief executive of Birla Brothers who responded to some of the allegations raised by Chandrashekhar and others in Parliament. See 'An Explanation' in 'Company Affairs' in *Eastern Economist*, 25 August 1967.

[98] See lead article, 'The Politics of Persecution', in *Eastern Economist*, 12 June 1970.

[99] A number of industrialists ran for office in the 1971 mid-term elections such as Naval Tata, Piloo Mody and Ramnath Goenka.

[100] For details of his pilgrimages see Birla, *Yamunotri* (n.d., n.p.).

17

Twilight Years

Following his disappointment at the turn politics had taken under Indira Gandhi, Birla increasingly retreated from public life. However, this did not prove to be easy. He missed the bustle of an active life, and the isolation from the corridors of power was not easy to take. The attacks by Communists and Young Turks within the ruling Congress continued through the 1970s and even the early 1980s, both on him as an individual and on his business empire. For example, Jyoti Basu, the Communist Chief Minister of West Bengal, openly attacked him on the eve of his eighty-first birthday by declaring: 'All the activities of the Birlas are aimed at personal enrichment. Even the educational and religious trusts set up by Birla were established merely to evade taxes. Profit is the Birlas' primary objective, they won't touch anything that is not profitable.'[1] In such an unfriendly atmosphere, Birla decided that it was wise to keep out of the public glare as much as he could. He was content to see his son Krishna Kumar take an increasing interest in political matters, although he often grew anxious on this score. Krishna Kumar, however, managed to establish a close rapport with Indira Gandhi and her younger son, Sanjay. In the early 1970s he even financed Sanjay when he was establishing Maruti, his automobile venture.

Birla's public activities came to be restricted to the occasional address to a chamber of commerce, or a rare interview to the press, or speeches at functions of family-run institutions in Pilani or the Kala Mandir in Calcutta. However, his eightieth birthday was celebrated with much fanfare. The initiative in organizing the celebrations was taken by C.R. Mitra, Director of Birla Institute of Technology and Science, Pilani, when he decided to set up a Commemoration Volume Committee, which consisted mainly of faculty members and other prominent persons associated with educational institutions in Pilani. The fruit of their endeavours was a 944-page volume entitled, *Modern India, Heritage and Achievement*. Its first section consisted of commemorative messages from prominent public figures, a veritable 'Who's Who': religious luminaries, dignitaries like the President, Vice-President, and Governors, Union ministers and others. Then followed an elaborate section of tributes and reminiscences. Some talked of 'G.D. Birla: the Man'; others of 'G.D. Birla and Education' and yet others of 'G.D. Birla and Industry'. Part two of the volume explored the theme of 'Modern India: Heritage and Achievement', with articles on heritage, polity, economic development, Gandhian thought, education, literature and the arts. In each section, alongside some general essays, there were articles highlighting the role Birla had played as one of the makers of modern India. Besides illustrations, the volume also contained a vinyl audio disc, which had on one side a prayer hymn by M.S. Subbulakshmi, the doyen of Indian classical music singing *'Piba Re Ramarasam'* by Adi Shankaracharya. On the other side it had Birla's speech at the inauguration of BITS in August 1964.[2]

This was the last occasion when Birla's birthday was celebrated in an elaborate public manner. From that year onwards it came to be marked unostentatiously and was spent quietly with family members and a few close associates. Over the last decade or so it had been marked by prayers at the Lakshmi Narayan Temple, in Delhi as his birthday coincided with the festival of *Ramnavami*. The well-known preacher Pandit Ram Kinkar gave a series of talks on the epic *Ramayana* which were attended by members of the Birla family.

Another step in the withdrawal from public involvements was his giving up the chairmanship of the *Hindustan Times* in 1970, a post he had occupied since the death of Malaviya in 1946. For over 40 years since he had gained a controlling interest in it, Birla had taken a keen interest in the paper. His interest extended to appointing top-level managerial staff and editors. These had included luminaries from the world of journalism such as Pothan Joseph, Devdas Gandhi, Durga Das and S. Mulgaonkar. When he stepped down as chairman, his son Krishna Kumar took up this responsibility.

Although he declared himself to be retired from public life, Birla did spend time looking into the affairs of the business empire, though his role came to be well defined. As we have seen, the next two generations had by then taken charge of different branches of the business. Sons, nephews and grandsons came to Birla or Braj Mohan for advice but any interference in the running of their companies was rare. Birla's concern with the business came to be limited to two areas: first, looking at the performance of companies which came under his purview, and second, overseeing the overseas expansion of the business spearheaded by his grandson Aditya. The companies in which Birla continued to take interest were Gwalior Rayon, HINDALCO and Mysore Cement. These had been his favourite ventures and he continued to run them personally. This involved paying visits to their factories two or three times a year, as had become customary for all his enterprises. These visits were made by air in his 13-seater Dakota DC-3 plane which he had been using for the past 25 years. He thus indulged in his old passion for air travel. During these visits he looked into the managerial and administrative issues and renewed contact with managers and workers. He insisted on looking at the daily production results of each of the companies to be able to monitor progress. While he kept overall control, he increasingly involved younger family members.[3] Thus Aditya helped with Hindalco and Gwalior Rayon, while Sudarshan Kumar did so with Mysore Cements.[4]

Birla's experience of observing Aditya closely in helping manage Hindalco and Gwalior Rayon led him to develop great confidence in the abilities of Aditya. An engineering graduate from the prestigious Massachusetts Institute of Technology (MIT), he had shown the ability to move the business into uncharted areas. When he showed an interest in expanding overseas Birla gave him all the encouragement that he needed. Till the 1970s the only major overseas business interests had been in Africa. These were a textile mill established in 1959 in Ethiopia and an engineering unit set up in Nigeria in 1964 by Braj Mohan.[5] Aditya was keen on expanding into South-east Asia. At a time when the dominant political leadership was bent on restricting the growth of 'monopoly houses', South-east Asian countries provided a marked contrast as they were opening up their economies and attracting foreign capital. With his grandfather's encouragement, Aditya ventured into Thailand in 1969 to set up Indo-Thai Synthetics Limited, with a capacity of 12,000 spindles. He then set up a rayon manufacturing unit in that country with a capacity of 24 tons. Thereafter, much of his energies came to be focused on expansion of the Birla business in South-east Asia. He established joint ventures for textiles in the Philippines and then expanded his operations to Malaysia and Indonesia.[6] As the investment climate within India grew more restrictive, Birla whole-heartedly encouraged such a strategy of overseas expansion. For instance, in 1978, when his application to raise the capacity of the viscose fibre plant of Gwalior Rayon was held up for 18 months, Aditya decided that it made better sense to establish such a facility in Thailand rather than in Gwalior.

In December 1976, Birla personally visited several South-east Asian countries. He made a specially momentous visit to the Philippines where he had been invited as the guest of honour to mark the twenty-fifth anniversary of the Indian Chamber of Commerce in the Philippines. So successful had their business ventures been in that country that Birla was a personal guest of the President and stayed at Malacanang, the presidential palace[7]. President Ferdinand Marcos complimented the business vision of Birla in glowing terms: 'We in the Philippines regard Mr Birla as a man of immense stature and vision, a Pillar of Asia, the unofficial ambassador and statesman of a great country.' Though he took a close interest in the overseas expansion spearheaded by Aditya, Birla was acutely conscious that he could now play only a limited role. On his trip to Manila when he was asked by the press about his future plans, he retorted: 'What plans can a man of 82 have?'[8] It appeared to him that 'whatever mission was cast for me is almost over. I should learn to live the rest of the years of my old age intelligently and with great understanding.'

One way of acceptance was by reminding himself of tales and teachings from religious texts. Birla compared himself with Arjuna in the epic *Mahabharata*, who, after the victory of the battle of Kurukshetra had to spend one night in the camp of the vanquished without any rancour. Just as Arjuna got off his chariot which had driven him to victory it burnt down with all his weapons. Arjuna was taken by surprise till an explanation was provided by Krishna : 'Arjuna, your mission in life is over. This you should understand'.[9]

Although he found comfort in such religious teachings and discourse, Birla felt lonely, even depressed. His older siblings were no more: Jugalkishore had died in 1967 and Rameshwardas had passed away in 1973. A distraught Birla had then performed an arduous pilgrimage in the memory of Rameshwardas to Jamnotri, in the UP hills, at an altitude of 4421 metres.[10] The younger generation was preoccupied with their business and families. Amongst his sons Birla had drawn closer to Basant Kumar and his wife Sarala with whom he spent much time in his later years. One reason may have been that Basant Kumar had lost his mother at a very young age and that had led to a special bonding. Close family members noticed that in these years Birla's 'mental make-up had changed considerably.' He grew more sentimental and missed Mahadevi. Much to the surprise of his children, Birla spoke openly of her and of their times together. The children saw a changed father who was finally willing to share his most intimate thoughts with them and even treat them as equals. The other person whom Birla missed was Gandhi and he often reflected upon his close association with the Mahatma. In overall terms, there occurred a marked change in Birla's temperament. Basant Kumar noticed that his father's 'anger and pride ... vanished completely. He was kind to everyone, spoke sweetly and saw to it that all were happy and pleased'.[11]

What gave Birla sustenance was a spiritual feeling of proximity to God. He had for the last 40 years regularly read the *Bhagwad Gita* and he grew reflective about its teachings. Thoughts of self-effacement, self-realization and merger of the self with the cosmic soul preoccupied him. Such feelings became even more pronounced after December 1977 when he suffered a severe heart-attack while on a visit to Aditya in Bombay. He was cared for by Basant Kumar and Sarala as well as Braj Mohan who moved to Bombay during those anxious weeks. For someone who had enjoyed excellent health for the most part of his life, this came as a severe set-back.

Following the heart-attack, Birla began to seriously think about the question of succession and the possible division of family assets. Most of the businesses were already under the charge of the younger generation much as Birla and his brothers had planned. There was no interference in each other's companies except by the patriarchs, Birla and Braj Mohan. Yet the lines of division were blurred and the companies existed as part of a large group, with Birla seen as the cementing factor. Accepting the need for actually working out a succession plan involving the division of the empire was not easy for Birla. Division negated the fundamental principle of family solidarity, which the three Birla brothers had practised throughout their active working lives and had striven so hard to inculcate in the next generation. It was the solidarity and the strength of the family as well as its community networks which had kept the group together. A formal division negated this. As with other such family businesses, 'to agree to divide is an admission of a weakness in the family and a reflection of its reputation in the community.'[12] Yet, Birla realized that the bonding which he and his brothers had cherished, had not been transmitted to the younger generation. 'Young people,' he said in an interview, 'find it more difficult to work in harmony than those of my generation do.' Companies floated by different members of the family often found themselves in competition in the market-place. One such instance was of two Birla-run enterprises—Universal Electric and Electronic Construction and Equipment (ECE) Company—which battled in the market-place in the area of electric metres. When faced with questions about rivalries among the cousins, Birla's eldest grandson, Sudarshan Kumar, spoke up in defence: 'It is this mutual competition which has been our strength. Each company has to stand on its own feet.'[13] Such forthright style stood in contrast to the family values which the Birla brothers had imbibed. Birla was aware that areas of responsibility needed to be worked out in more concrete terms to hold the younger generation together.

Although it is impossible to get the details, the first division appears to have been made by Birla after his heart-attack in 1977. It was based on the principle that the status quo would prevail and the 'line of actual control'—that is the person who ran a company—was to inherit it. While it was easy to lay down the principle in abstract, the implementation was a hugely challenging and complex exercise. At stake was direct control over 200 companies and indirect control over 70. Not only did the Birlas control the country's biggest jute mills, they also produced 45 per cent of its aluminum, owned the largest tea gardens, the second largest paper mill, the biggest car manufacturing unit and produced 3 per cent of the country's sugar. The business operations spanned nearly a dozen countries. Then there were the large educational and charitable trusts, hospitals, about 40 temples, dharamshalas and a planetarium.[14]

Birla had already given ample indications about who would inherit the companies which were directly under him. Aditya was to inherit Gwalior Rayon and HINDALCO while Sudarshan Kumar was to get Mysore Chemicals. Whether Birla consulted Braj Mohan and how the younger generation responded to this principle of division is unknown. However, what is clear is that these arrangements could not be completely satisfactory. One intractable difficulty was due to the intricate pattern of inter-corporate investments which ran through the business empire. For example, Basant Kumar who was supposed to inherit Century Textiles, then a Rs 1400 crores enterprise, did not control its majority shareholding. The family's control over Century came from ownership of its 36.4 per cent of the stock, (which came to over $4040 million), which was held by the firm Pilani Investments. Pilani Investments, in turn, had been set up by the Birla brothers together with an equity base of Rs 8 crores and had grown to become a Rs 800 crores company.[15] Century, in turn, held substantial shares in other companies such as Zuari Agro Chemicals which was controlled by Krishna Kumar. Century also owned shares of Gwalior Rayon run by Aditya and Mysore Cement—to be passed on to Sudarshan Kumar. Cross-holdings had arisen because of the closely knit nature of the early expansion which the Birla brothers had carried out in a context in which division could not be envisaged. Another reason was that companies floating new ventures could turn to sister companies for finance and the family could thus maintain close control. Thus control of companies was not linked to share ownership which made a clean division hugely complicated.[16]

These complicated cross-holding patterns militated against an amicable settlement. While Birla seems to have worked out the principle of division in his last years, the details thus remained blurred. It was probably fear of discontentment over the division of the spoils and a feeling of inability to handle such a situation, that led Birla to avoid spending much time in Calcutta in these years where the larger family was based.[17]

It was spiritual interests that enabled him to find a way out of family differences. Birla was acutely conscious that in his eighties, life was ebbing. After 1977, he spoke on six different occasions on mainly spiritual topics at the Birla Academy (which had been set up in 1962 by Basant Kumar and Sarala) and at the Sangeet Kala Mandir. As he explained in one of his talks

When you arrive at the ashram of Adi-Shankara then you see Brahma everywhere, you are made sublime by meditation—the distinction between the individual soul, the *atman*, and the cosmic soul, *paramatman*, disappears. Only pure devotion remains—devotee, devotion and Deity become one.[18]

In 1978, Birla published some of his religious thoughts in a book entitled *Krishnam Vande Jagatguru*.[19] The book looked at Krishna and the teachings of the *Bhagwad Gita*. He also began work on another favourite subject of his—the life of Rama—and began collecting whatever material he could get. He grew close to Swami Akhandanandji Saraswati and 'whenever he had any philosophical problem or query, he would personally get it explained or resolved by ringing him or sending someone to get clarification from him', recalls Basant Kumar.[20]

In 1978, he published *Bapu: A Unique Association*, a four-volume collection of his correspondence with Gandhi. Its preface was written by Kaka Kalelkar, one of the few surviving close associates of Gandhi. Birla stated that the purpose behind the publication was to help people understand Bapu's heart. In the preface he did not hide his own mental and physical frailty when he wrote:

The spotless standard of Yama's troops
Comes before my eyes be-dimmed by age
And fighting a losing battle with diseases
This mortal frame doth droop day by day.[21]

What provided sustenance in these later years was the deep sense that there existed a divine purpose and pattern in his life. Birla felt a sense of contentment which was derived from his faith in religion. In January 1982 he lost his only surviving brother Braj Mohan. Birla grew even more withdrawn with the only surviving member of his generation in the family gone. He undertook a pilgrimage to the holy site of Kedarnath. He spent the summer of 1983, as he often did, at the family home in Zug, Switzerland. After spending May there he moved to London where he stayed at his Park Towers apartment in Central London. On the morning of 11 June 1983, Birla went on his morning walk with two business associates: Nandlal Hamirwasia, president of Mysore Cement and Sushil Kumar Sabu, vice-president of Gwalior Rayon. As they passed Piccadilly Circus and entered Regent Street Birla felt uncomfortable. He was rushed into a taxi and they headed back to his apartment. As they entered the apartment block Birla's frail body slumped into a sofa and he soon breathed his last.

The news was received with shock throughout India and abroad. Almost the entire family arrived in London within the next 24 hours. On 13 June 1983, in deference to his wishes, he was cremated at the Golders Green crematorium at 4.45 pm. There were about 300 people present to pay homage. Birla's last rites were performed according to traditional Sanatan dharma practices by Pandit Mathoor Krishnamurty of the Bharatiya Vidya Bhawan. Mantras were read out and portions of chapter XVIII of the *Bhagwad Gita*, the holy text which he had read since early childhood, were recited. Family and friends sang *Raghupati Raghav Raja Ram*, the bhajan which the Mahatma had popularized. His ashes were brought to India and taken to Bombay, Delhi, Pilani and Calcutta to enable people to pay their respects. The ashes were then immersed in the Ganges at Haridwar and at Gangotri.

Notes and References

[1] Basu declared that: 'The association which men such as Birla had with political leaders such as Gandhi and Sardar Patel was an investment. Those leaders were naive in associating themselves with Birla.' See Dilip Thakore, 'A legend in his lifetime', in *BusinessWorld*, 30 March–12 April, 1981.

[2] *Modern India. Heritage and Achievement. Shri Ghanshyamdas Birla Eightieth Birthday Commemoration Volume* (Shri Ghanshyamdas Birla Eightieth Birthday Commemoration Volume Committee, Pilani), n.d.

[3] Minhaz Merchant, *Aditya Vikram Birla: A Biography* (New Delhi, 1977), p. 142.

[4] T.N. Ninan and B.M. Birla, *A Great Visionary* (New Delhi, 1996).

[5] B.M. Takneth, pp. 50–1.

[6] Minhaz Merchant, *Aditya Vikram Birla: A Biography* (New Delhi, 1977), pp. 130 and 144–8.

[7] Anonymous, *A Pillar of Asia* (n.d., n.p.).

[8] 'Investment. Birlas Expansion', in Anonymous, *A Pillar of Asia* (n.d., n.p.).

[9] Ramanuja, *G.D. Birla*, p. 130.

[10] Ramanujan, *G.D. Birla*, pp. 55–65.

[11] B.K. Birla, *A Rare Legacy*, p. 233.

[12] Sudip Dutta, *Family Business*, p. 115.

[13] T.N. Ninan, 'Empire in Transition', in *India Today*, 15 July 1983.

[14] T.N. Ninan, 'Empire in Transition', in *India Today*, 15 July 1983.

[15] Sudip Dutta, *Family Business*, p. 141.

[16] T.N. Ninan, 'Empire in Transition', in *India Today*, 15 July 1983.

[17] *Ibid.*

[18] B.K. Birla, *A Rare Legacy*, p. 225.

[19] G.D. Birla, *Krishnam Vande Jagatguru* (n.d., n.p.).

[20] B.K. Birla, *A Rare Legacy*, p. 228.

[21] G.D. Birla, *Bapu, A Unique Association* (Bombay, 1977), p. xii.

Legacies

As word about the passing away of Birla spread by radio and television, tributes began to pour in from around the world. A number of prominent persons, both within India and abroad, expressed their condolences. Giani Zail Singh, then President of India, phoned the family in London; Prime Minister Indira Gandhi, then in Copenhagen, told the press that the country had lost a veteran who would be missed in public life. In the UK, Margaret Thatcher, then Prime Minister of Britain, called Birla 'a most distinguished son of India'. Former British Prime Ministers Harold Macmillan and James Callaghan also expressed their condolences, as did many other public figures such as Lord Listowal and Lord Fenner Brockway.[1] Chambers of commerce and organizations with which Birla had been associated closed down as a mark of respect.[2] Leaders of industry recalled their close association with Birla. Ramakrishna Bajaj, the Bombay businessman, saw in the passing away of Birla the end of the 'golden age of pioneering entrepreneurship' in India's history. He called him a 'great karmayogi' who strove to achieve his visions without expectation of reward.[3]

Obituaries and tributes dwelt on the many facets of Birla's long life. For example, the Bombay-based *Commere* acknowledged his dominance of the Indian economic scene 'as a veritable colossus for well over seven decades.'[4] The *Economic Times*, the *Financial Express* and other newspapers highlighted the role Birla had played as 'guide, chief protagonist and authentic spokesman' of business. 'Half the story of Indian industry in the last half century is the story of G.D. Birla and his accomplishments', wrote the *Economic Times*.[5] *Business India* lauded Birla as the father of Indian industry.[6] The *Commerce* declared him 'a maker of modern industrial India' and 'dazzling symbol of India's economic independence'.[7] The *Times*, London described him as 'one of the most influential of Indian businessmen who also played a role in the financing of Gandhi's movement for Indian independence'.[8] The *Times of India* called him 'one of the pioneers of Indian industry, the patriarch of one of India's wealthiest families, a patron of religious and cultural activities and promoter of education and temples.'[9] It described him both as a visionary and as a practical man, as not only a builder of Indian capitalism but also as a significant political entity with a keen political sense.[10] Of all the tributes that poured in, perhaps the most laudatory was from Ian Jack of the *Sunday* magazine who declared, in a cover story, 'The king is dead.'[11]

In retrospect, it can be said that perhaps Birla's most important legacy was that his unswerving efforts, from the 1920s, established a recognized role for private enterprise in modern India. As one of the most influential spokesmen for Indian big business as well as its chief strategist for at least four decades, between the 1920s and 1950s, Birla had played a cardinal role. His dogged fight against foreign capital in the colonial period, his successful attempts at forging unity within Indian business from 1920s onwards, his efforts at establishing chambers of commerce, his attempts within Congress organizational circles to bring about right-wing solidarity, and within wider nationalist politics his promotion of the Constitutionalist viewpoint in the 1930s and 1940s, all played a role in ensuring that private enterprise had an important voice within India. When India became free in 1947, Birla's vision of an independent India with a strong centre firmly implanted on the road of rapid industrialization, with private enterprise playing a pivotal role, had been substantially realized. This vision of an independent 'Hindustan'—and a capitalist one too—is perhaps best epitomized in the names of two of the newspapers which he owned—the *Hindustan Times* and the *Eastern Economist.* In a sense the modern Indian nation, as it was established in 1947, represented a vision of an independent India that was closer to Birla's than Mahatma Gandhi's or even Jawaharlal Nehru's.

Though in the years following independence this vision was somewhat challenged, during the premiership of Jawaharlal Nehru and then Indira Gandhi, it could never be dislodged. Till the early 1960s Birla continued to play a watchdog role for private enterprise which he had taken on during the years of the British Raj and his advice continued to be heard in corporate circles with respect. His abiding concern was that economic policies in free India must remain on a track that favoured private enterprise. Despite his lukewarm relations with Nehru, he maintained close contact with Congress provincial bigwigs. In 1957, at the height of Nehru's socialist rhetoric, he was awarded the *Padma Vibhushan*, one of the country's highest awards. In these years many businessmen showed a crisis of confidence with Nehru's economic philosophy, with the restrictive legislation they faced, with repeated threats of nationalization. In the face of these many wavered from their traditional support of the Congress party in favour of alternatives like the avowedly right-wing Swatantra Party. But Birla warned business colleagues that their support to right-wing forces would merely benefit the Communists and that they had no choice but to work through centrist parties like the Congress. Likewise, he advocated a flexible and broad approach which could accommodate diverse political interests, including the Communists who were making important gains in Kerala and West Bengal. For example, when a Communist government came to power in Kerala in 1957, he was the first businessman to invest in the state. Likewise, he offered, in a meeting with the Soviet premier Krushchev, to set up factories in the USSR. He evolved a deep understanding of the dilemmas and limitations of the Indian Left and advocated a policy of accommodation and reconciliation with them. Even though business' role was challenged and it held a subordinate political status, the astute political sense of Birla and other business leaders, enabled it not only to survive Nehru's socialist era and the turbulent years of Indira Gandhi's premiership, but it ensured that it could re-emerge as an important player when political conditions were favourable. This was most apparent in the Lal Bahadur Shastri interregnum when business emerged once again as an influential voice and as a powerful interest group. In the 1980s, when Rajiv Gandhi became India's Prime Minister, he initiated by piece-meal measures economic reforms which Birla had been advocating for decades. Thereafter, in 1991, P.V. Narasimha Rao, initiated dramatic economic reforms marking a decisive shift towards a market-based economy and minimal state control. With these reforms India's political leadership signalled that the country would open up its economy to exploit opportunities which would enable it to emerge as a global economic superpower. Private enterprise was well positioned to take advantage of the new reforms. Birla's vision had, at last, been embraced by the country's political leadership.

Whether Birla's vision of a capitalist India with private enterprise playing a pivotal role has been the appropriate route for India since 1947 is open to debate. He had an almost sanguine faith in private enterprise and in the 'redeeming power of capitalism' to provide solutions to India's problems of economic underdevelopment.[12] While there could be differences of opinion about the relevance of the capitalist alternative of development for a poor country like India, there can be no doubt about the sincerity of Birla's beliefs. It was not merely the pursuit of profit that led him to propound his views, but his vision was to see India emerge as an economically powerful, industrialized nation.

Yet, there were limitations. For example, Birla was blinded to alternative paths of development. His faith in capitalism led him to view large-industrialization as the panacea to improve people's lives and he saw his own role as a protagonist of private enterprise. He did not regard the redistribution of wealth as a responsibily of either private enterprise or the state. Expansion of industry was, in his view, the way to national economic well-being and benefits would follow as a natural consequence of 'trickle-down'. The charge could even be made that questions of redistribution of wealth did not interest Birla. It is somewhat ironic that Birla saw a rather limited role for himself in this regard in the post-1947 context even though he had been lauded by Mahatma Gandhi as an upholder of his doctrine of 'trusteeship' under which those who possessed capital would use it for the common weal.

In addition to his role as a champion of enterprise, one of Birla's most important legacies lies in the educational endowments which he and his brothers made in the modern Indian state of Rajasthan. Birla's support to education had started in the 1920s with the endowment of the Birla Education Trust under Madan Mohan Malaviya's inspiration. A large number of educational institutions committed mainly to primary education were patronized in the Shekhawati region.[13] In less than two decades, by the 1940s, the Birla Education Trust ran no less than 400 primary schools, a girls' school, an intermediate arts college and an engineering college.

Then, in the 1950s and 1960s higher technical education became the focus of Birla's philanthropic agenda. Amongst the institutions he supported was the well-known Central Electronics Research Institute. He endowed the Birla Museum of Industry and Technology in Pilani and extended generous support to institutions of higher learning.[14] Alongside, the Birla Institute of Technology and Science (BITS) was established at Pilani which was envisaged as a 'privately endowed and independent Massachusetts Institute of Technology (MIT) of India' and was seen as an institution of national importance. In its early years of planning, BITS had a tie up with MIT. It took in its first batch of students in July 1964. Over the years BITS has grown to compete with the esteemed Indian Institutes of Technology (IITs) which were established at Kanpur, Bombay, Delhi, Kharagpur and Madras.[15] Pilani as an educational hub showcased Birla's contributions to the new nation. Through Pilani, he showed himself to be an enthusiastic participant in Nehru's project of nation-building with its emphasis on science, technology and modernization.[16]

Birla's educational philanthropy, especially his support to primary education in Rajasthan, has few parallels in the country. By the 1980s the Birla Education Trust claimed to be the largest private educational foundation in the country, with assets worth Rs 1147.11 lakhs.[17] The sleepy desert village of Pilani had been transformed into a major university town, with over 10,000 students.

Perhaps the most visible legacy of Birla and his brothers are the temples they have built all over India. Many of these stand out as examples of architectural excellence and are popularly known as 'Birla *Mandir*' (temple). The inspiration for endowment of temples came from Jugalkishore, but he always had the consent of the other brothers. Although there is no evidence that Birla actively partook in decisions on matters of temple-building, he did believe in their necessity. As he himself admitted, the desire to 'spread a kind of religious mentality' lay behind the family's temple-building endeavours.[18] By the time of his demise, the family had endowed more than 40 large temples in almost all the major cities of India as well as dharamshalas and many religious institutions and sites.

Birla's familial legacies have been somewhat mixed and are marked by both successes and failures. His great success was in the grooming of the next generation for the family business. Not only were his sons and nephews inducted and groomed to head companies that made up the large empire but even the next generation of grandsons and grand-nephews were trained during his lifetime to take over the reins of the empire. As we have seen, Birla had meticulously planned the training, apprenticeship and induction of the younger generation into the business. The same was done for the grandchildren once they came of age. Birla was thus able to ensure that the family business empire continued to grow. On his demise there was no crisis in terms of day-to-day management and the family members continued to manage the companies they had controlled in the past.

While this was a great achievement, Birla failed to ensure an amicable division of assets within the large family. The lines of legal, individual ownership were blurred and the principle of succession which Birla had laid out eventually proved to be unworkable in practice. The principle of 'line of actual control' could not satisfy all the heirs. The charge was levelled that it worked most in favour of Basant Kumar and his son Aditya who together ended up with control of 16 of the 23 most profitable companies which had an estimated combined asset of Rs 930 crores and a turnover of Rs 1300 crores. Discontent had been simmering even in Birla's last years; one of his last actions had been to pass on the control of Jiyajeerao Cotton to Sudarshan Kumar, rather than Aditya, in an attempt to be fair.[19]

The principle of 'line of actual control' eventually became complicated because it could not ensure legal control to individuals. This was due to the maze of cross-holdings and interlocking directorships which connected different Birla firms and which proved impossible to disentangle. In the absence of the domineering personality and moral force of Birla, individual heirs wanted complete control over their share of the inheritance. The complicated structure of cross-holdings of shares and interlocking directorships had come about because the family business had grown in a legal framework of the colonial Managing Agency system which had continued after 1947 and upon which restrictive controls had been superimposed such as the MRTP Act and FERA.

The failure to work out legal control led to discord within the family. As soon as Birla passed away, disputes surfaced. It was clear that the only way to disentangle the ownership of business was by selling shares or buying each other out both of which would involve substantial capital gains tax and other legal complications. Krishna Kumar could see the problems this could pose when he commented: 'It is not easy, even if someone wants to, and I don't think is going to happen.' Attempts were finally made to settle the dispute three years later when on 15 August 1986 the entire clan met to press their claims and to seek a solution. Over the next four months numerous inconclusive meetings were held. 'Everyone was dissatisfied, restless and upset' and there were 'arguments, wranglings and antagonisms.' It took over a year of discussions to resolve the question of ownership of most units but there were companies such as Century Spinning (one of the most profitable units of the Group) and Pilani Investments (which had been one of the main promoters and sources of investment for many of the Birla firms) whose ownership remained unresolved till the 1990s.[20]

Though Birla had managed to build up a business which rivalled the Tatas, his failure at ensuring an equitable division led to the breaking up of the Group within the next generation.

Within the business world, too, the legacy remains mixed. While there is no doubt that Birla's achievements were path-breaking in many areas such as the breaking of the European monopoly of the jute industry, overseas expansion in the 1960s when business within the country was faced with repressive legislation, and the creation of a truly Indian multinational presence, in terms of corporate values the Birla Group continued to hold on to conservatism and a reluctance to change in areas of corporate governance. For example, in the style of management within Birla businesses kin-based affinity and loyalty have always remained the byword. It has been well recognized that top managerial positions were held by Marwaris and only by those close to the Birla clan. This has delayed the professionalization of management of many of their firms.

Besides, the charge has been made that the Birla groups showed an obsessive concern with profits. Also, Birla companies had a reputation of being inattentive to the consumer. Further, in terms of expansion, the Group avoided high-risk sectors and preferred low-risk areas. Thus, the Group kept out of both infrastructure and consumer goods sectors and preferred 'lower risk, intermediate businesses such as textiles, jute, synthetics, engineering and capital goods.'[21] Critics have suggested these characteristics of the Birla business empire are epitomized by their Ambassador car which was the first car to be manufactured on a large scale in the country and between the 1950s and 1970s enjoyed the reputation of being 'the Indian Warhorse'. From the production of its first model based upon the legendary Morris prototype popularized by Lord Nuffield, the Birlas' Ambassador did not see any change in its basic product specifications. It has been described somewhat uncharitably as having a 'steering mechanism with the subtlety of an oxcart, guzzled gas like a sheik, and shook like a guzzler'.[22]

Yet, these criticisms appear minor when one considers the scale of Birla's achievements. His was a life which was shaped by some of the most momentous events of the twentieth century. As he himself said, he had been born in the Victorian age and lived on to see India progress into the nuclear age. Undoubtedly, he must be regarded as one of the greatest Indians of the twentieth century, for his outstanding leadership of business, his political sagacity, his multi-faceted philanthropy and, above all, his vision of India for which he worked tirelessly.

NOTES AND REFERENCES

[1] *Bhavan's Journal*, Vol. 29, No. 24, 16–31 July (Bharatiya Vidya Bhavan, Bombay), 1983.

[2] For instance, in London, a meeting was held at the UK Centre of the Bharatiya Vidya Bhawan; in Bombay, a meeting was attended by prominent businessmen, political leaders like Morarji Desai and well-known persons such as Nana Palkhivala to condole the passing away of Birla.

[3] The *Economic Times*, Bombay, 26 June 1983.

[4] *Commerce*, 25 June 1983.

[5] The *Economic Times*, 14 June 1983. The *Financial Express* called Birla a 'visionary who continuously and ceaselessly, strived to build a modern India firmly rooted in its tradition and culture'. *Financial Express*, 14 June 1983.

[6] *Business India*, 20 June–3 July 1983.

[7] *Commerce*, Bombay, 25 June 1983.

[8] The *Times*, London, 13 June 1983.

[9] The *Times of India*, New Delhi, 12 June 1983.

[10] The *Times of India*, Bombay, 14 June 1983.

[11] Birla's close business associates recalled their own personal associations with him. D.P. Mandelia, called him 'the superb master sculptor' who 'sculpted young men' in the ways of the business world.

[12] Ian Jack, 'The King is Dead', *Sunday*, 26 June–2 July 1983.

[13] The institutions which Birla supported were mainly primary schools, since the fundamental tenet of the Trust was in 'higher education for the few and lower for the many.' *The Birla Education Trust and its institutions* (Pilani, 1944), pp. 5–6.

[14] For instance, the Hindu College of the University of Delhi received Rs 10,000; Rs 14,00,000 was donated to the Chief Minister of West Bengal for an agricultural college and hostel in the state and finally the most significant donation was to the emerging intellectual powerhouse of Nehru's India—the Delhi School of Economics—which received Rs 6 lakhs for a new building. A large bronze plaque proclaiming Birla's name was placed at the door of the building. Ironically, the building was almost never called Birla Bhawan by the faculty and students of the School while, by contrast, the donation of Rs 1 lakh by Lady Ratan Tata to the library resulted in it always being called the Ratan Tata Library. In a sense this reflects the different perceptions in Delhi's intellectual circles about the two donors. M.N. Srinivas, then professor at the School, recalls that 'There seems to have been an almost unspoken taboo on using the title 'Birla Bhawan', for during all my years at the DSE, I never once heard anyone refer to it by that name.' M.N. Srinivas, 'Sociology in Delhi' in Dharma Kumar and D. Mookerjee (eds), *Delhi School, Reflections on the Delhi School of Economics* (Delhi, 1995), p. 39. As P.N. Dhar, also then professor at the School, recalls: 'In fact the impression one gets is that no one, not even the faculty, seems to have noticed the plaque. I have often wondered about the difference in the general attitude to the two main donors to the School.' P.N. Dhar, 'Early Years', in *Ibid*, pp. 18–19.

[15] Birla Papers, Series BITS, File No. 12.

[16] Birla Papers, Series BITS, File No. 12, Correspondence with Jawaharlal Nehru on BITS.

[17] *Modern India, Heritage and Achievement* (Sri Ghanshyamdas Birla Eightieth Birthday Commemoration Volume Committee, Pilani, 1977), p. 305. Also see B.K. Birla, *A Rare Legacy*, p. 224.

[18] Bourke White, *Halfway to Freedom* (Asia Publishing House, Bombay, 1950), p. 71.

[19] Ian Jack, 'The King is Dead', *Sunday*, 26 June–2 July 1983.

[20] B.K. Birla, *A Rare Legacy*, pp. 72–4.

[21] Gita Piramal, *Business Maharajas*, p. 142.

[22] Shashi Tharoor, *India From Midnight to Millennium* (Delhi, Penguin, 1999), pp. 162–3.

Bibliography

Private Papers

G.D. Birla Papers, New Delhi and Calcutta, In private custody of the Birla family
Churchill College Archives Centre, Cambridge
    Papers of Sir P.J. Grigg
India Office Library and Records, London
    Earl of Halifax (then Lord Irwin), Mss. Eur. C. 152
    Linlithgow Papers, Mss. Eur. 125
    Zetland Papers, Mss. Eur. D. 609
Nehru Memorial Museum and Library, New Delhi
    All India Congress Committee Papers
    Brijlal Biyani Papers
    B.S. Moonje Papers
    Hiralal Shastri Papers
    H.P. Mody Papers
    Jamnalal Bajaj Papers
    Jawaharlal Nehru Papers
    Kasturbhai Lalbhai Papers
    K.M. Munshi Papers
    M.S. Aney Papers
    Purshotamdas Thakurdas Papers
    Walchand Hirachand Papers
National Archives of India, New Delhi
    Rajendra Prasad Papers
Centre of South Asian Studies, Cambridge
    Benthall Papers
Central Library, National University of Singapore
    U.S. State Department Confidential Papers of India (microfilm)

FICCI Records Room and Library, New Delhi

Proceedings of the Executive Committee, 1927–65 (annual).
Correspondence and Relevant Documents for the year, 1927–66 (annual).
Proceedings of the Annual Meetings, 1927–66 (annual).
Representation Submitted to the Viceroy by the Committee of the Federation on the Present Political Situation in India in 1930 (Delhi, 1930).
A Statement on behalf of the Federation of Indian Chambers of Commerce and industry in reply to the circular letter dated the 27th July 1929 issued by the Associated Chambers of Commerce of India and Ceylon to influence opinion in England against India's right to adapt her economic policy to her own needs, 1929.

Proceedings of the Third Annual Meeting held on 14, 15 and 16 February, 1930 relating to the resolutions on: Exchange Ratio and Gold Standard and Sale of Silver (FICCI, 1930).
Report of the Representatives of the Federation on the Round Table Conference 1932 (Bombay, 1932).
Note on the Ottawa Scheme of Preferences (Delhi, 1936).
Federation of Indian Chambers of Commerce and Industry Silver Souvenir 1927–1951 (New Delhi, 1952).
Men of FICCI (New Delhi, 1966).
Five Decades of Progress (New Delhi, 1976).

Official Publications

Report of the Indian Industrial Commission, 1916–18, Cmd 51.
Report of the Indian Fiscal Commission 1921–2 and Minute of Dissent, Cmd 1764.
Minutes of the Evidence Recorded by the Indian Fiscal Commission, Vol. II (Calcutta, 1923).
International Labour Conference, Geneva 1927, Record of Proceedings.
Report of Sedition Committee 1918 (Calcutta, 1918).
Central Legislative Assembly Debates (LAD) Annual Volumes 1926–31.
Bengal Legislative Council Debates, 1920–2.

Unofficial Publications

Constitutional Proposals of the Sapru Committee (Bombay, 1946).
Economist Intelligence Unit *India to 1900 How Far Will Reform Go?* EIU Economic Prospects Series Special Report No. 1054 (London, 1988).
History of the Reserve Bank of India 1935–57 (Bombay, 1970).
Indian Chamber of Commerce, Calcutta, *Diamond Jubilee 1925–1985*, Commemorative Volume.
Indian Chamber of Commerce, Calcutta, *Silver Jubilee Souvenir*, 1925–1950.
Indian Merchants' Chamber 50 Years 1907–50 (Bombay, 1958).
Indian Year Book and Who's Who 1941–2 (Bombay, 1942).
Report of the Indian Chamber of Commerce, Calcutta, annual 1927–30.
Report of the Marwari Association, Calcutta, 1920–5.
Tata Sons Ltd., *Statistical Outline of India 1989–90* (Bombay, 1990).
The Indian Annual Register, N. Mitra (ed.), Calcutta, annual, 1927–35.
The Investors' Indian Yearbook, Calcutta, 1927–47.

Newspapers and Periodicals

Birla Park Annual, Calcutta, yearly, 1928.
Capital, Calcutta, weekly, 1927–47.
Commerce, Bombay, weekly, 1920–30.
Eastern Economist, New Delhi, weekly, 1943–69.
Empire (later *New Empire*) evening daily, Calcutta, 1920.
Friend, London, weekly, 1938.
Hindustan Times, New Delhi, daily, 1927–50.
Maheshwari Bandhu, Calcutta, weekly, 1926–31.
Maheshwari, Calcutta, weekly, 1925.
Shri Marwari Agarwal, monthly, 1923–32.
Tyagbhumi, monthly, 1928.

Writings of G.D. Birla

'Ham Paradhin Kyon Hai?', *Tyagbhumi*, 1928.
'Quo Vadis', *Birla Park Annual*, L.N. Birla (ed.) (Calcutta, 1928).
The Present Depression and Monetary Reform (Calcutta, 1931).
Indian Prosperity (New Delhi, 1934).
Bapu (New Delhi, 1940).
Bikhre Vichar (Delhi, 1941). Also in Birla, G.D., *Bikhre Vicharon ki Bharoti* (New Delhi, Sasta Sahitya Mandal Prakashan, 1978).
India's Sterling Balances (New Delhi, 1943).

India's War Finance (New Delhi, 1943).

Rupiye Ki Kahani (New Delhi, 1943). Also in *Bikhre Vicharon ki Bharoti* (New Delhi, Sasta Sahitya Mandal Prakashan, 1978).

Inflation or Scarcity? (n.p., 1943).

Birla, Thakurdas, Tata, *et al.*, *A Plan for Economic Development of India* (Bombay, 1944).

Indian Currency in Retrospect (Kitabistan, Allahabad, 1944).

'War Finance under National Government', *Eastern Economist*, 14 April 1944.

Kardar Se Sahujar (New Delhi, 1945).

Basic facts Relating to India and Pakistan, *Eastern Economist Pamphlets 5* (New Delhi, Eastern Economist, 1947).

Lecture at Joint Meeting with the Overseas League, 3 August 1949, *The Asiatic Review*, Vol. XLV. No. 164. (London, October 1949).

Roop Aur Swaroop (New Delhi, Sasta Sahitya Mandal Prakashan, 1950).

Path to Prosperity, A Collection of Speeches and Writings of G.D. Birla (Allahabad, 1950).

In the Shadow of the Mahatma: A Personal Memoir (Bombay, Orient Longman, 1953).

Kuch Dekha Kuch Suna (New Delhi, 1962).

Dhruvopakhyaan (New Delhi, 1960).

A Question of Madness, Inaugural address at the 48th Annual Meeting of the Indian Chamber of Commerce, 18 April 1974 (Calcutta, Indian Chamber of Commerce, 1974).

Bapu: A Unique Association, Vols. I–IV, (Bombay, 1977).

Bikhre Vicharon Ki Bharoti (New Delhi, Sastra Sahitya Mandal Prakashan).

Krishnam Vande Jotatguru (Bombay, 1979).

Jamunotri (n.d., n.p.).

Towards Swadeshi (Bombay, Bharatiya Vidya Bhavan, 1980).

'Bhagwan Ki Dharohar', *Jivan Sahitya*. Vol. 44, No. 7, July 1983.

'Gandhiji Ka Pratham Darshan', *Jeevan Sahitya*.

Shri Jamanalalji (n.d., n. p.). Also in Birla, G.D., *Bikhre Vicharon ki Bharoti* (New Delhi, Sasta Sahitya Mandal Prakashan, 1978).

Ve Din (n.d., n.p.). Also in Birla G.D., *Bikhre Vicharon Ki Bharoti* (New Delhi, Sasta Sahitya Mandal Prakashan, 1978).

A Bridge of Words: Selected Correspondence of G.D. Birla (Calcutta, G.D. Birla Memorial Foundation, 1994).

Published Collections of Source Material

Chopra, P.N. (ed.), *Towards Freedom: January–December 1937* (New Delhi, 1985).

Choudhory Valmiki (ed.), *Dr Rajendra Prasad: Correspondence and Select Documents*, Vol. III, January–July 1939 (New Delhi, Allied Publishers 1984).

Das Durga (ed.), *Sardar Patel's Correspondence, 1945–50*, Vols I–X (Ahmedabad, Navjivan Publishing House, 1971–4).

Nehru Family and Ghanshyamdas Birla (New Delhi, Vision Books, 1986).

Speeches and Writings of Pandit Madan Mohan Malaviya (n.d. n.p.).

The Collected Works of Mahatma Gandhi (Ahmedabad, Navajivan Press, 1958–84).

Mansergh, Nicolas (ed.), *The Transfer of Power: Constitutional Relations Between Britain and India 1942–47*, Vols. 1–4 (London, Her Majesty's Stationery Offices, 1970–83)

Gopal, S. (ed.). *Selected Works of Jawaharlal Nehru*, Vols. 1–5 (New Delhi, Orient Longman 1972–82).

Unpublished Dissertations

Chenoy, Kamal A. Mitra, 'Industrial Policy and Big Business in India: A Case Study of FICCI, 1947–1966', unpublished PhD thesis, Jawaharlal Nehru University, 1983.

Kaviraj, Sudipto, 'The Ideological Origins of the Split in the Indian Communist Movement', unpublished PhD thesis, Jawaharlal Nehru University, 1979.

Secondary Sources

Anon., *A Pillar of Asia* (n.d., n.p.).

———, *Basantlal Morarka Smriti Granth* (Calcutta, n.d.).

Anon., *Bhagirath Kanoria Smriti Granth* (Calcutta, n.d.).

———, *Birla Bandhuon Ki Desh Seva* (n.n., n.d., n.p.).

———, *Padma Vibushan Dr. Ghanshyamdasji Birla Ek Jivan Jhanki* (Pilani, 1983).

———, *Rashtrasevak Shri Hanumanbaksh Kanoi Abhinandan Granth* (Dibrugarh, Kanoi Abhinandan Samiti 1969).

———, *Sitaram Seksaria Smriti Ka* (Calcutta, 1950).

Adarkar, B.N., 'The Ottawa Pact' in Radhakamal Mukherjee (ed.), *Economic Problems of Modern India*, Vol. 11 (London, 1939).

Ahmed, N., *An Economic Geography of East Pakistan* (London, Oxford University Press, 1956).

Ali, Chowdhury Mohammed, *The Emergence of Pakistan* (London, Columbia University Press, 1967).

Alter, Joseph S., *The Wrestler's Body: Identity and Ideology in North India* (California, University of California Press, 1992).

Amar Chitra Katha, *G.D. Birla*, Illustrated Series.

Aziz, K.K., *The Making of Pakistan: A Study in Nationalism* (London, Chatto & Windus, 1967).

Bagchi, A.K., *Private Investment in India 1900–39* (Cambridge, Cambridge University Press 1972).

———, 'Reflections on Patterns of Regional Growth in India during the Period of British Rule', *Bengal Past and Present*, XCV, (I), 180, 1976.

Bajaj, *Hindustan Sugar Mills Golden Jubilee 1932–82*, Pamphlet (Bombay, Hindustan Sugar Mills, 1982).

Bajaj, Kamalnayan, *Kakaji, Bapu, Vinoba* (Delhi, n.d.).

Bajaj, Ramkrishna (ed.), *Rachnatmak Rajneeti* (New Delhi, 1965).

———, *Patravyayahor*, Vol. VII, Correspondence With Social Reformers and Businessmen.

Bakshi, S.R., *Swaraj Party and the Indian National Congress* (New Delhi, 1985).

Barua, Rishi Gemini Kaushik, *Mai Apni Marwari Jati (Samaj) Ko Pyar Karta Hun*, Vols I–VIII (Calcutta, 1970).

———, *Raja Baldeodas Birla* (Calcutta, Gemini Prakashan, n.d.).

———, *Shri Surajmal Jalan Madhumangal Shri* (Calcutta, n.d.).

Basu, S.K., *Industrial Finance in India* (Calcutta, 1939).

Bayly, C.A., *Indian Society and the Making of the British Empire* (Cambridge, Cambridge University Press, 1988).

———, *Local Roots of Indian Politics Allahabad 1880–1920* (Oxford, Oxford University Press, 1975).

———, 'Indian Merchants in a "Traditional" Setting. Benaras, 1780–1830' in C.J. Dewey, and A.G. (eds), *The Imperial Impact: Studies in the Economic History of Africa and India* (London, Athlone Press for the Institute of Commonwealth Studies, 1979).

———, 'Patrons and Politics in Northern India' in *Modern Asian Studies*, Vol. VII, No. 3 (1973).

———, 'The Age of Hiatus: The North Indian Economy and Society, 1830–50' in Asiya Siddiqi (ed.), *Trade and Finance in Colonial India 1750–1860* (Delhi, Oxford University Press 1995).

Behn, Mira, *The Spirit's Pilgrimage* (London, Coward-McCann, 1960).

Beloff, Max, 'The Political Blind Spot of Economists', *Government and Opposition*, Vol. 10, No. 1 (1975).

Berry, Mary Elisabeth, 'Introduction' to 'Giving in Asia: A Symposium', *Journal of Asian Studies*, Vol. 46, No. 2 (1987).

Bhandari S.R., *Agarwal Jati Ka Itihas* (Bhanpura, 1937).

———, *Maheshwari Jati Ka Itihas* (Bhanpura, Maheshwari History Office 1940).

———, *Oswal Jati Ka Itihas* (Bhanpura, 1934).

Bharat Ram, *Reminiscences and Reflections* (New Delhi, Vikas Publishing, 1990).

Bharatiya Vidya Bhavan, *Special Issue on G.D. Birla*, Vol. 29, No. 24 (16–31 July 1983).

Bhattacharya, S., 'Cotton Mills and Spinning Wheels: Swadeshi and the Indian Capitalist Class, 1920–22', *Economic and Political Weekly*, Vol. XI, No. 47 (1976).

Bhatia, S., *Social Change and Politics in Punjab 1898–1970* (New Delhi, 1987).

Birla, B.K., *A Rare Legacy. Memoirs of B.K. Birla* (Bombay, 1994).

Birla, Krishna Kumar, *Indira Gandhi Reminiscences* (New Delhi, n.d.).

Birla, L.N. and P.P. Pillai, *India and the ILO* (n.p., 1946).

Birla, Radhakrishan, *Bhuli Baaten Yaad Karon* (Harshwardhan Birla, Amritsar, n.d.).

Birla Education Trust, *The Birla Education Trust and Its Institutions* (Pilani, Birla Education Trust, 1944).

———, *The Birla Education Trust Golden Jubilee Volume* (Pilani, Birla Education Trust, 1951).

Birla Education Trust, *The Changing Face of Pilani. Diamond Jubilee of the Birla Education Trust, 1907–1967* (Pilani, Birla Education Trust, 1961).

Birla Institute of Scientific Research, *Banks Since Nationalisation* (New Delhi, Allied Publishers, 1981).

Birla, Sarala, *Amhad Ki Jhankaren* (Calcutta, S.S. Printers, n.d.).

Bolitho, Hector, *Jinnah: Creator of Pakistan* (London, J. Murray, 1954).

Bourke-White, Margaret, *Halfway to Freedom* (New York, Simon and Schuster, 1949).

Brecher, Michael, *Nehru: A Political Biography* (Delhi, Oxford University Press 1966).

———. *Succession in India. A Study in Decision-Making* (West Port, Connecticut, Greenwood, 1976).

Bridge, Carl, *Holding India to the Empire* (London, Envoy Press, 1986).

Broomfield, J.H., *Elite Conflict in a Plural Society: Twentieth Century Bengal* (Berkeley, University of California Press, 1968).

Brown, Judith M., *Gandhi and Civil Disobedience. The Mahatma in Indian Politics 1929–34* (Cambridge, Cambridge University Press, 1977).

———, *Gandhi: Prisoner of Hope* (London, Yale University Press, 1989).

———, *Gandhi's Rise to Power. Indian Politics 1915–1922* (Cambridge, Cambridge University Press, 1972).

———, *Modern India: The Origins of an Asian Democracy* (Oxford, Oxford University Press, 1985).

Buchanan, D.H., *The Development of Capitalist Enterprise in India* (New York, Macmillan, 1934).

Burman, Debajyoti, *The Mystery of Birla House* (Calcutta, Jugabari Sahitya Chakra, 1950).

——— , *T.T.K. and Birla House* (Calcutta, 1957).

Byres, Terence J. (ed.), *The Indian Economy. Major Debates since Independence* (Delhi, Oxford University Press, 1998).

Chablani, H.I., *Studies in Indian Currency and Exchange* (Bombay, 1931).

Chakrabarti, Atulnanda, *The Mahatma and His Men: G.D. Birla* (Calcutta, 1970).

Chand, Feroz, *Lajpat Rai: Life and Work* (New Delhi, 1978).

Chandavarkar, Anand, *Keynes and India: A Study in Economics and Biography* (London, Macmillan, 1989).

Chandavarkar, R., 'Workers Politics and the Mill Districts of Bombay between the Wars', *Modern Asian Studies*, Vol. 15, No. 3 (1981).

———, *The Origins of Industrial Capitalism in India: Business Strategies and the Working Classes in Bombay, 1900–1940* (Cambridge, Cambridge University Press, 1994).

Imperial Power and Popular Politics: Class, Resistance and the State in India 1850–1950 (New York, 1998).

Chandra, Bipan, 'Jawaharlal Nehru and the Capitalist Class in 1936' in *Economic and Political Weekly*, Vol. X, Nos. 33–35 (1975).

———, (ed.), *The Indian Left Critical Appraisals* (New Delhi, Vikas Publishing, 1983).

———, *et al.*, *India's Struggle for Independence* (New Delhi, Viking, 1988).

———, 'The Indian Capitalist Class and Imperialism before 1947' in Bipan Chandra (ed.), *Colonialism and Nationalism in India* (New Delhi, 1979).

———, *Communalism in Modern India* (New Delhi, Vani Educational Books 1983).

Chatterjee, B., 'Business and Politics in the 1930s, Lancashire and the Making of the Indo-British Trade Agreement, 1939', *Modern Asian Studies*, Vol. 15, No. 3 (1981).

———, *Trade, Tariffs and Empire: Lancashire and British Policy in India 1919–1939* (Delhi, Oxford University Press, 1922).

Chatterji, Joya, *Bengal Divided: Hindu Communalism and Partition, 1932–1947* (Cambridge, Cambridge University Press, 1994).

Chattopadhyaya, R., 'Attitude of Big Business Towards Economic Planning, 1930–1956, paper presented at the seminar on 'Business and Politics in India: A Historical Perspective' at the Indian Institute of Management, Ahmedabad, March 1989 (mimeograph).

Chattopadhyaya, R., 'Liaquat Ali's Budget of 1947–8, The Tryst with Destiny', *Social Scientist* (181–2), Vol. 16, No. 6–7 (1988).

Chaudhury, K.N., 'Economic Problems of Indian Independence' in C.H. Philips and M.D. Wainright (eds), *The Partition of India Policies and Perspectives 1935–1947* (London, Allen and Unwin, 1970).

Cheong, W.E., *Mandarins and Merchants, Jardine Matheson & Co., China Agency of the Early 19th Century* (London, 1979).

Chinoy, Sultan, *Pioneering in Indian Business* (Bombay, Asia Publishing House, 1962).

Chowdhury, S. (ed.), *Calcutta. The Living City*, Vol. II (Calcutta, Oxford University Press, 1990).

Chowdhury, Ram Narayan, *Bapu As I Saw Him* (Ahmedabad, Navjivan Press, 1958).

Cooper, Ilay, *Rajasthan: The Guide to Painted Towns of Shekhawati and Churu* (Churu, 1988).

Coupland, R., *The Future of India: Report on the Constitutional Problem in India*, Part III (Oxford, Oxford University Press, 1943).

Daga, Rampratap, 'Vartman Andolan Par Spasht Vichar', in *Maheshwari Bandhu*, 21 February 1926.

Dagli, Vadilal, 'A Maker of Modern Industrial India', *Commerce*, 25 June 1983.

Dalmia, Ramkrishna, *A Short Sketch of the Beginning of my Life and a Guide to Bliss* (New Delhi, 1962).

——, *Some Notes and Reminiscences* (Bombay, 1948).

Dalmia, Vasudha and Heinrich von Stietencron (eds), *Representing Hinduism, The Construction of Religious Traditions and National Identity* (New Delhi, Sage Publications, 1995).

Dantawala, M.L., *A Hundred Years of Indian Cotton* (Bombay, 1948).

Dar, S.L. and S. Somaskandan, *History of the Benaras Hindu University* (Banaras, 1966).

Daruwala, Rusi J., *The Bombay Chamber Story* (Bombay, 1986).

Das, Durga, *India from Curzon to Nehru and After* (London, Rupa & Co., 1969).

Das, Gurcharan, *India Unbound* (New York, A.A. Knopf, 2001).

Das, N., *Industrial Enterprise in India* (London, 1938).

Das, Suranjan, *Communal Riots in Bengal 1905–1947* (Delhi, Oxford University Press, 1991).

Datta, Kali Kinkar, *Rajendra Prasad* (New Delhi, 1970).

Denoon, Davi B.H., *Devaluation Under Pressure: India, Indonesia and Ghana* (Cambridge, MA, MIT Press, 1986).

Desai, A.V., 'Origins of Parsi Enterprise', *IESHR*, Vol. V, No. 4 (1968).

Desai, Morarji, *The Story of My Life*, Vol. 1& 2 (New Delhi, Macmillan, New York, 1979).

Dewey, C.J., 'The Government of India's "New Industrial Policy", 1900–25: Formation and Failure' in K. N. Chaudhuri and C.J. Dewey, (eds), *Economy and Society; Essay in Indian Economic and Social History* (New Delhi, 1979).

——, 'The End of Imperialism of Free Trade. The Eclipse of the Lancashire Lobby and the Concession of Fiscal Autonomy to India' in C.J. Dewey and A.G. Hopkins, (eds), *The Imperial Impact. Studies in the Economic History of Africa and India* (London, 1979).

Dhanki, P.N., *Indira Gandhi, the 'Emergency' and Indian Democracy* (New Delhi, Oxford University Press, 1999).

Dhyani, S.N. *International Labour Organisation and India: In pursuit of Social Justice* (New Delhi, 1977).

Dikshit, Sheila, K. Natwar Singh, et al. (eds), *Jawaharlal Nehru Centenary Volume* (Delhi, Oxford University Press).

Dixit, Prabha, *Communalism: A Struggle for Power* (New Delhi, 1974).

Dobbin, Christine, *Urban Leadership in Western India. Politics and Communities in Bombay City, 1840–1885* (Oxford, Oxford University Press, 1972).

——, *Asian Entrepreneurial Minorities: Cojoint Communities in the Making of the World Economy, 1570–1940* (Surrey, Curzon Press, 1996).

Drummond, I.M., *British Economic Policy and the Empire 1919–1939* (London, Allen & Unwin, 1972).

Dutt, R.P., *India Today* (Bombay, 1949).

Dutta, Sudipto, *Family Business in India* (New Delhi, Sage Publications, 1997).

Eck, Diana L., *Banaras: The City of Light* (Princeton, A.A. Knopf, 1984).

Erdman, Howard, L, *Political Attitudes of India Industry. A Case Study of the Baroda Business Elite*, Institute of Commonwealth Studies Papers, No. 14, (London, 1971).

——, *The Swatantra Party and Indian Conservatism* (Cambridge, Cambridge University Press. 1967).

Evenson, Norma, *The Indian Metropolis; A View Towards the West* (Yale, Yale University Press, 1989).

Fox, Richard, 'Pariah Capitalism and Traditional Merchants' in Milton Singer (ed.), *Entrepreneurship and Modernization of Occupational Cultures in South Asia* (Duke, 1973).

Frank, Katherine, *Indira: The Life of Indira Nehru Gandhi* (London: Harper Collins, 2001).

Frankel, R. Francine, *India's Political Economy, 1947–1977: The Gradual Revolution* (Princeton, Princeton University Press, 1978).

Fischer, Louis, *The Life of Mahatma Gandhi* (London, J. Cape, 1951).

Fukazawa, H., 'The Cotton Mill Industry', V.B. Singh (ed.), *Economic History of India 1857–1956* (Bombay, 1965).

Gadgil, D.R., *Origins of the Indian Business Class* (Poona, 1951).

——, *The Industrial Evolution of India in Recent Times* (Delhi, Oxford University Press, 1971).

Gallagher, J., G. Johnson and A. Seal, *Locality, Province and Notion. Essays on Indian Politics, 1870–1940* (Cambridge, Cambridge University Press, 1970).

Gandhi, M.K., *Delhi Diary* (Ahmedabad, Navajivan, 1948).

Gandhi, Rajmohan, *Rajaji: A Life* (Delhi, Penguin, 1997).

——, *Patel: A Life* (Ahmedabad, Navajivan, 1990).

——, *The Good Boatman: A Portrait of Gandhi* (New Delhi, Viking, 1995).

Giri, V.V., *My life and Times*, Vol. 1 (Madras, 1976).

Goenka, B.D., *Mere Sansmaran* (Calcutta, n.d.).

Gopal, S., *Jawaharlal Nehru A Biography*, Vol. I, 1889–1947 (London, 1975), Vol. II, 1947–1956 (London, 1979), Vol. III, 1956–1964 (London, Harvard University Press, 1983).

Gopal, S, *Radhakrishnan: A Biography* (Delhi, Oxford University Press, 1989).

Gordon, A.D.D., *Businessmen and Politics. Rising Nationalism and a Modernising Economy in Bombay 1933–1978* (New Delhi, Manohar, 1978).

Gordon, Leonard A., *Bengal: The Nationalist Movement 1876–1940* (New York, Columbia University Press, 1974).

Gordon, Richard, 'The Hindu Mahasabha and the Indian National Congress, 1915 to 1926' in *Modern Asian Studies*, Vol. 9, No. 2 (1975).

Goswami, Onkar, 'Collaboration and Conflict. European and Indian Capitalists and the Jute Economy of Bengal 1919–39', *Indian Economic and Social History Review*, Vol. XIX, No. 2, 1982.

——, 'Then Came the Marwaris: Some Aspects of the Changes in the Pattern of Industrial Control in Eastern India', *Indian Economic and Social History Review*, Vol. 22, No. 3 (1985).

Graham, Bruce, *Hindu Nationalism and Indian Politics: The Origins and Development of the Bharatiya Jana Sangh* (Cambridge, Cambridge University Press, 1990).

Greenough, Paul, *Prosperity and Misery in Modern Bengal: The Famine of 1943–44* (New York, Oxford University Press, 1982).

Guha, Ramchandra, *Savaging the Civilized. Elwin Verrier, His Tribals and India* (Delhi, Oxford University Press, 1999).

Gupta, Fatehchand, *Marwari Gaurav* (Delhi, 1960).

Gupta, G.P., *The Reserve Bank of India and Monetary Management* (Bombay, Asia Publishing House, 1962).

Gupta, Moti Lal, *Braj: The Centrum of Indian Culture* (Delhi, Agam Kala Prakashan, 1982).

Gupta, Rajkumar, *Twenty-Five Years with Shri G.D. Birla* (n.d., n.p.).

Gupta, S.L., *Pandit Madan Mohan Malaviya: A Socio-Political Study* (Allahabad, 1978).

Hanson, A.H., *The Process of Planning: A Study of India's Five Year Plans 1950–64* (London, Issued under the auspices of the Royal Institute of International Affairs by Oxford University Press, 1966).

Hardgrave Jr., Robert L., 'The Congress in India—Crisis and Split' in *Asian Survey*, March 1970, Vol. X, No. 3, pp. 256–62.

Hardiman, David, *Feeding the Bania: Peasants and Usurers in Western India* (New Delhi, Oxford University Press, 1996).

Harris, F.R., *Jamsetji Nuserwanji Tata. A Chronicle of his Life* (Bombay, Blackie, 1958).

Hasan, Mushirul (ed.), *Communal and Pan Islamic Trends in Colonial India* (New Delhi, Manohar, 1985).

Haynes, Douglas E., *Rhetoric and Ritual in Colonial India: The Shaping of a Public Culture in Surat city 1850–1928* (Berkeley, University of California Press, 1991).

——, 'From Tribute to Philanthropy. The Politics of Gift Giving in a Western Indian city' in *Journal of Asian Studies*, Vol. 46, No. 2, May 1987, pp. 339–60.

Hindustan Times Press, *Hindustan Times Contempt Case* (New Delhi, Hindustan Times Press, n.d.).

Husain, Aziz, *Fazl-i-Husain: A Political Biography* (Bombay, Longmans, Green, 1946).

Hazari, R.K., *The Corporate Private Sector: Concentration, Ownership and Control* (Bombay, Asia Publishing House).

——, *The Structure of the Corporate Private Sector: A Study of Concentration, Ownership and Control* (Bombay, 1966).

——, 'The Great Escape. Concentration good, monopoly justifiable', *The Economic Weekly*, 18 December 1965, pp. 1843–48.

Hennessy, Josselyn, *India Democracy and Education: A Study of the work of the Birla Education Trust* (Calcutta, Orient Longman, 1955).

Ikramullah, Begum Shaista Suhrawardy, *Huseyn Shaheed Suhrawardy: A Biography* (Karachi, 1992).

Ispahani, M.A.H., *Quaid-e-Azam Jinnah As I Knew Him* (Karachi, 1966).

Ispahani, M.A.H., 'Factors Leading to the Partition of British India', C.H. Philips and M.D. Wainright (eds), *The Partition of India Policies and Perspectives 1935–1947* (London, Allen & Unwin, 1970).

Jack, Ian, 'The King is Dead', *Sunday*, Calcutta, 26 June–2 July 1983.

Jackson, Stanley, *The Sassoons. Portrait of a Dynasty* (London, 1989).

Jaffrelot, Christopher, *The Hindu Nationalist Movement in India* (Delhi, Viking, 1993).

Jain, L.C., *Indian Economy During the War* (Lahore, 1944).

———, *Indigenous Banking in India* (London, Macmillan, 1929).

Jain, Yashpal, *Jivan Sahitya G.D. Birla Smriti Ank* (Delhi, Sasta Sahitya Mandal Prakashan, 1983).

Jaju, Ram Niwas, *G.D. Birla: A Biography* (New Delhi, Vikas, 1986).

Jalal, Ayesha, *The Sole Spokesman: Jinnah, the Muslim League and the Demand for Pakistan* (Cambridge, Cambridge University Press, 1985).

———, *The State of Martial Law, the Origins of Pakistan's Political Economy of Defence* (Cambridge, Cambridge University Press, 1990).

Jalan, Nandkishore, *Shri Ishwardas Jalan Abhinandan Granth* (Calcutta, 1977).

Jha, L.K. *India's Economic Development* (New Delhi, Har-Anand Publications in association with Vikas Publishing House ,1991).

Jha, Manoranjan, *Role of Central Legislature in the Freedom Struggle* (New Delhi, 1972).

Jha, Prem Shankar (ed.), *History in the Making. 75 Years of the Hindustan Times* (New Delhi, The Hindustan Times, 2000).

Jones, Kenneth, *Arya Dharma Hindu Consciousness in 19th Century Punjab* (California, University of California Press, 1976).

Jordens, J.T.F., *Swami Shradhanand: His Life and Causes* (Delhi, Oxford University Press, 1981).

Joshi, Arun, *Shri Ram. A Study in Entrepreneurship and Business Management* (Delhi, 1975).

Juneja, M.M., *G.D. Birla. Life and Legacy* (Delhi, Modern Publishers, 1999).

———. *The Mahatma and the Millionaire* (Hissar, Modern Pubishers, 1993).

Kalelkar, Kaka (ed.), *To A Gandhian Capitalist* (Bangalore, U.S. Mohan Rao, 1951).

Kannamgara, A.P., 'Indian Millowners and Indian Nationalism Before 1914', *Past and Present*, 40, 1968.

Karkaria, Bachi J., *Dare to Dream: A Life of M.S. Oberoi* (New Delhi, Penguin, 1993).

Karnik, V.B., *The Indian Trade Unions. A Survey* (Bombay, Manaktalas, 1966).

Kaura, Uma, *Muslims and Indian Nationalism: The Emergence of the Demand for India's Partition 1928–40* (New Delhi, 1977).

Kedia, Bhimsen, *Bharat Mein Marwari Samaj* (Calcutta, 1947).

Kerr, J.C., *Political Trouble in India 1907–77* (Calcutta, 1917).

Khanolkar, G.D., *Walchand Hirachand: Man, His Times and Achievements* (Bombay, 1969).

Khilnani, Sunil, *The Idea of India* (London, Hamish Hamilton, 1997).

Kidron, Michael, *Foreign Investments in India* (London, Oxford University Press, 1965).

Kling, B., 'Origins of the Managing Agency System in India', *Journal of Asian Studies*, Vol. XXVI, No. 1, 1966.

Kochanek, Stanley R., *Business and Politics in India* (Berkeley, University of California Press, 1974).

———, *The Congress Party of India: the Dynamics of One-Party Democracy* (Princeton, Princeton University Press, 1968).

Krishna, G., 'The Development of the Indian National Congress as a Mass Organisation', *Journal of Asian Studies*, Vol. XXV, No. 3, 1966.

Kudaisya, G., 'Foreshadowing "Quit India": The Congress in Uttar Pradesh 1939–1941' in Neera Chandoke (ed.), *Mapping Histories. Essays presented to Ravinder Kumar* (Delhi, Tulika, 2000).

Kulkarni, V.A., *Family of Patriots: The Bajaj family* (Bombay, 1951).

Kulke, E., *The Parsees in India, A Minority as Agent of Social Change* (Bombay, Vikas Publishing House, 1974).

Kumar, R. (ed.), *Essays on Gandhian Politics. The Rowlatt Satyagraha of 1919* (Oxford, Oxford University Press, 1971).

Lamb, Helen B., 'The Indian Merchant' in M. Singer (ed.), *Traditional India, Structure and Change* (Philadelphia, American Folklore Society, 1959).

La Motte, Ellen N., *The Opium Monopoly* (New York, Macmillan, 1920).

Lala, R.M., *Beyond the Lost Blue Mountain: A Life of J.R.D. Tata* (New Delhi, Viking, 1992).

——, *The Joy of Achievement. Conversations with J.R.D. Tata* (New Delhi, Penguin, 1995).

Levkovsky, A.I., *Capitalism in India. Basic Trends in its Development* (Bombay, 1966).

Lewis, John P., *Quiet Crisis in India* (1962).

Lipton, Michael and John Firn, *The Erosion of a Relationship: India and Britain since 1960* (London, Oxford University Press for the Royal Institute of International Affairs, 1975).

Lokanathan, P.S., *Industrial organisation in India* (London, Allen & Unwin, 1935).

Low, D.A., *Rearguard Action: Britain and India: Selected Essays* (New Delhi, Sterling Publishers, 1996).

——, *Britain and Indian Nationalism, The Imprint of Ambiguity 1929–1942* (Cambridge, Cambridge University Press, 1997).

——, 'Peasants and Political Power: Asia, Africa and the Pacific', The Australian National University, 1980, University Lectures (mimeographed).

——, 'The Forgotten Bania Merchant Communities and the Indian National Congress' in D.A. Low (ed.), *Indian National Congress Centenary Hindsights* (Oxford, Oxford University Press, 1988).

——, 'Introduction' to D.A. Low (ed.), *The Political Inheritance of Pakistan* (London, Macmillan, 1990).

——, (ed.), *Congress and the Raj: Facets of the Indian Struggle* (London, Heinemann, 1977).

——, 'Peace With Conflict: The Gandhi–Emerson Talks, March–August 1931' in D.A. Low, *The Imprint of Ambiguity: India and Britain in the 1930s* (forthcoming).

Lubbock, Basil, *The Opium Clippers* (Glasgow, Brown, Son & Ferguson, 1933).

Ludden, David (ed.), *Making India Hindu: Religion, Community and the Politics of Democracy in India* (Delhi, Oxford University Press, 1996).

McPherson, Kenneth, *The Muslim Microcosm, Calcutta 1918 to 1935* (Wiesbaden, Steiner, 1974).

Mahindra, K.C., *Sir Rajendranath Mukherjee* (Calcutta, 1933).

Malhotra, Inder, *Indira Gandhi: A Personal and Political Biography* (London, Hodder & Stoughton, 1989).

Mandelia, D.P., *G.D. Birla: A Superb Master Sculptor* (n.d.; n.p.).

——, *Financial Aspects of Pakistan* (Bombay 1945).

Manekar, D.R., *Lal Bahadur: A Political Biography* (Bombay, Popular Prakashan, 1964).

Malgaonkar, Manohar, *The Men who killed Gandhi* (Delhi, Macmillan, 1978).

Markovits, Claude, *Indian business and nationalist politics, 1931–1939: the indigenous capitalist class and the rise of the Congress Party* (Cambridge, Cambridge University Press, 1985).

——, *The global world of Indian merchants, 1750–1947: traders of Sind from Bukhara to Panama* (Cambridge, Cambridge University Press, 2000).

Merchant Minhaz, *Aditya Vikram Birla: A Biography* (New Delhi, Penguin, 1977).

Misra, Anna Maria, *Business, Race and Politics in British India, 1850–1960* (Oxford, Clarendon Press, 1999).

Moggridge, D.E., *British Monetary Policy, 1924–31* (Cambridge, 1972).

Molesworth, G.N., *Curfew on Olympus* (London, Asia Publishing House, 1965).

Moon, P. (ed.), *Wavell, The Viceroy's Journal* (London, Oxford University Press, 1973).

Moore, R.J., *Churchill, Cripps and India, 1939–1945* (New York, Clarendon Press, 1979).

——, *The Crisis of Indian Unity, 1917–1940* (Oxford, Clarendon Press, 1974).

Moraes, Frank, *Sir Purshotamdas Thakurdas* (Bombay, 1957).

Morris, D., *The Emergence of an Industrial Labour Force in India: Study of the Bombay Cotton Mills, 1854–1954* (Berkeley, University of California Press, 1965).

——, 'The Growth of Large-Scale Industry to 1947', D. Kumar (ed.), *The Cambridge Economic History of India, Volume 2: c. 1757–c. 1970* (Cambridge, Cambridge University Press, 1983).

Mukherjee, A., 'The Indian Capitalist Class Aspects of its Politics 1920–1947' in S. Bhattacharya and R. Thapar (ed.), *Situating Indian History* (New Delhi, Oxford University Press, 1985).

——, 'The Rupee Question, 1926–28 Rupee–Sterling Ratio and the Gold Standard' in *Studies in History*, 5, 1 n.s. (1989).

——, 'Indian Capitalist Class and the Public Sector' in *Economic and Political Weekly*, Vol. 2, No. 3, 1976.

——, 'Indian Capitalist Class and Congress on Planning and Public Sector, 1930–47' in K.N. Panikkar (ed.), *National and Left Movements in India* (New Delhi, Vikas Publishing, 1980).

——, 'The Indian Capitalist Class and Foreign Capital, 1927–47', *Studies in History, I* (D, 1979).

Nanda, B.R., *Gokhale: The Indian Moderates and the British Raj* (Princeton, Princeton University Press, 1977).

——, *Jawaharlal Nehru: Rebel and Statesman* (Delhi, Oxford University Press, 1995).

——, *In Gandhi's Footsteps: The Life and Times of Jamnalal Bajaj* (New Delhi, Oxford University Press, 1990).

——, *Mahatma Gandhi, A Biography* (London, G. Allen & Unwin, 1958).

——, *The Nehrus* (London, G. Allen & Unwin, 1962).

——, 'The Swarajist Interlude', B.N. Pandey (ed.), *A Centenary History of the Indian National Congress*, Vols I–III (New Delhi, Vikas Publishing, 1985).

Nath, Kedar (ed.), *Shreysadhak Jamnalal Bajaj* (Delhi, 1968).

Nehru, Jawaharlal, *A Bunch of Old Letters written mostly to Jawaharlal Nehru and some written by him* (New York , Asia Publishing House, 1958).

Nevatia, Radhakrishna (ed.), *Bara Bazaar Ke Karyakarta Sansmaran Avam Abhinandan* (Calcutta, Bara Bazaar Kumarsabha Pustakalya, 1982).

——, *Shri Ramdev Chokhany* (Calcutta, n.d.).

Nevatia, Ramkrishna, *Rajnaitak Kshetra Mein Marwari Samaj Ki Ahutiyan* (Calcutta, Akhil Bharatiya Marwari Sammelan, 1948).

Nigam, R.K., *Managing Agencies in India* (New Delhi, 1957).

Oliver, Robert W., *George Woods and the World Bank* (London, Boulder, 1995).

Ostergaard, G. and M. Currell, *Gentle Anarchists* (Oxford, 1971).

Owen, David Edward, *British Opium Policy in China and India* (Yale, Yale University Press, 1934).

Palmer, Norman D., *Elections and Political Development, The South Asian Experience* (North Carolina, 1975).

——, 'India's Fourth General Elections' in *Asian Survey*, 7 (May 1967).

Parekh, Kishore *et.al*, *Words to Remember* (n.d., n.p.).

Pandey, B.N. (ed.) *A Centenary History of the Indian National Congress*, Vol. III (New Delhi, Vikas Publishing, 1985).

Pandey, Gyanendra, *The Construction of Communalism in North India* (New Delhi, Oxford University Press, 1990).

Pandey, Sukhdeo, *Mere Pilani Ke Sansmaran* (Pilani, Hindi Bhavan, Samvat 2029).

Papanek, H., 'Pakistan's Big Businessmen: Muslim Separatism, Enterpreneurship and Partial Modernisation', in Mary B. Rose (ed.), *Family Business* (Aldershot, E. Elgar, 1995).

Parvate, T.V., *Jamnalal Bajaj* (Ahmedabad, 1962).

Patel, I.G., *Essays in Economic Policy and Economic Growth* (Basingstoke, Macmillan, 1986).

Patel, Maniben Vallabhbhai, 'Shri Ghanshyamdas Birla' in *Words to Remember* (n.d., n.p.).

Patil, S.K., *My Years with Congress* (Bombay, Prachure Prakashan Mandir, 1991).

Patodia, Rameshwar Prasad, *Anandilal Poddar Smriti Pushpa* (Calcutta, n.p., n.d.).

Pavlov, V.I., *The Indian Capitalist Class* (Delhi, 1964).

Payne Robert, *The life and death of Mahatma Gandhi* (London, Bodley Head, 1969).

Perti, R.K., 'Cabinet Mission', in B.N. Pandey (ed.), A *Centenary History of the Indian National Congress*, Vol. III (New Delhi, Vikas Publishing, 1985).

Piramal, Gita, *Business Maharajas*, p. 126 (New Delhi, Viking, 1996).

——, *Business Legends* (New Delhi, Viking, 1998).

Poddar, A., *A Short Life Sketch of Seth Anandilal Poddar* (Calcutta, n.d.).

Puri, Nina, *Political Elite and Society in the Punjab* (Delhi, 1985).

Qanungo, Bhupen, 'The Quit India Movement, 1942' in B.N. Pandey (ed.), *A Centenary History of the Indian National Congress*, Vol. III (New Delhi, Vikas Publishing, 1985).

Rai, Satya M., *Legislative Politics and Freedom Struggle in Punjab 1897–1947* (New Delhi, 1984).

Ramanujam, K.S., 'The Passing Away of a Titan', *Commerce*, 25 June 1983.

Rao, P. Chentsal, *B.M. Birla: His Deeds and Dreams* (New Delhi, 1983).

Rao, V.K.R.V., *War and the Indian Economy* (Delhi, 1943).

Ray, Rajat K., *Industrialization in India, 1914–1947 Growth and Conflict in the Private Corporate Sector* (Delhi, Oxford University Press, 1982).

——, *Social Conflict and Political Unrest in Bengal 1875–1922* (Delhi, Oxford University Press, 1984).

——, *Urban Roots of Indian Nationalism* (New Delhi, Vikas Publishing, 1979).

——, '"The Bazaar": Changing Structural characteristics of the indigenous section of the Indian economy before and after the Great Depression' in *Indian Economic and Social History Review*, Vol. 25, No. 3 (1988).

Reeves, P.D., B.D. Graham, J.M. Goodman (eds), *A Handbook of Elections in Uttar Pradesh*, 1920–57 (New Delhi, Oxford University Press, 1975).

Relief Co-ordination Committee, *Relief Organisations Fight Bengal Famine* (Calcutta, Relief Co-ordination Committee, 1943).

Renford, Raymond K., *The Non-Official British in India Till 1920* (New Delhi, Oxford University Press, 1987).

Ross, Alan, *The Emissary G.D. Birla, Gandhi and Independence* (London, Collins Harvill, 1986).

Rothermund, D., *An Economic History of India* (London, Croom Helm, 1988).

———, *India in the Great Depression 1929–36* (New Delhi, 1992).

Rudner, David West, *Caste and Capitalism in Colonial India, The Nattukottai Chettiars* (Berkeley, University of California Press, 1994).

Rungta, R.S., *The Rise of Business Corporations in India and their development during 1857–1900* (London, 1965).

Sabade, B.R. and M.V. Namjoshi, *Chamber of Commerce and Trade Associations in India* (Poona, 1977).

Sarkar, J., 'The Beginnings in Calcutta' in *Economic Times*, 26 June 1983.

Sarkar, N.R., 'My Days in the Federation' in *FICCI Silver Jubilee Souvenir* 1927–1957 (New Delhi, FICCI, 1951).

Sarkar, S.C., 'G.D. Birla, Industrialisation and Culture', *Commerce*, 25 June 1983.

Sarkar, Sumit, *Swadeshi Movement in Bengal, 1903–8* (New Delhi, People's Publishing House, 1973).

———, 'The Logic of Gandhian Nationalism: Civil Disobedience and the Gandhi–Irwin Pact (1930–31)' in *Indian Historical Review*, Vol. III, No. 1, July 1976.

———, *Modern India, 1885–1947* (Delhi, Macmillan, 1983).

Schomer, Karine, Joan L. Erdman et al. (eds), *The idea of Rajasthan. Explorations in Regional Identity* Vol. I & II (Delhi, Manohar, 1994).

Seksaria, Sitaram, *Beeta Yug Nai Yad* (Sasta Sahitya Mandal, n.p., 1970).

Sen, S.K., *Studies in Economic Policy and Development of India, 1848–1939* (Calcutta, Progressive Publishers, 1972).

———, *The House of Tatas* (Calcutta, 1975).

Sengupta, N.K., *Government and Business* (New Delhi, Vikas Publishing, 1987).

Servants of the People Society, *Constitution* (New Delhi, Lajpat Bhawan, n.d.).

———, *70 Years. Report 1981–1992* (New Delhi, Lajpat Bhawan, 1992).

Shah, K.T. (ed.), *Report of the National Planning Committee* (Bombay, 1949).

Shah, Kantilal, *Thakkar Bapa* (New Delhi, 1955).

Shankar, V., *My Reminiscences of Sardar Patel*, Vol. I and II (Delhi, Macmillan, 1974).

Shankardass, Rani Dhawan, *Vallabhai Patel, Power and Organisation in Indian Politics* (New Delhi, 1988).

Sharma, Daryao Prasad, *Deshbhakt Udyog Pravartak Ghanshyamdas Birla Sansmaranatmak Jivanvjit* (Delhi, Keshav Kumar Sharma, 1978).

Sharma, G.D., 'The Marwaris Economic Foundations of an Indian Capitalist Class' in Dwijendra Tripathi (ed.), *Business Communities of India: A Historical Perspective* (New Delhi, Manohar, 1984).

Sharma, K.L., 'Changing aspects of merchants, markets, moneylending and migration: reflections based on field notes from a village in Rajasthan' in Philippe Cadène, Denis Vidal (eds), *Webs of trade: dynamics of business communities in Western India* (New Delhi, 1997).

Sharma, R.C. (ed.), *Modern India. Heritage and Achievement. Shri Ghanshyamdas Birla. Eightieth Birthday Commemoration Volume* (Pilani, Eightieth Birthday Commemoration Volume Committee, 1977).

Sharma, Udayvir, *Shekhawati Ka Itihas* (Lakshmangarh, 1980).

Sharma, Vishembar Prasad, *Maheshwari Jan-Jagriti Darshan* (Nagpur, 1956).

Shastri, D.D. (ed.), *Ek Bindu Ek Sindhu* (Mathura, 1948).

Shekhar, Chandra, *A Peep into Birla House* (New Delhi, Shashi Bhushan, MP, 1969).

Shenoy, B.R., 'The Rupee–Sterling Ratio and the Exports of Gold' in Radha Kamal Mukherjee and H.L. Dey (ed.), *Economic Problems of Modern India* (London, 1941).

Shirokov, G.K., *Industrialisation in India* (Moscow, 1973).

Shrivastava, S.P. (ed.), *Greatness Personified. Vaishyarshi G.D. Birla* (Calcutta, Birla Academy of Art and Culture, n.d.).

Siddiqi, Asiya (ed.), *Trade and Finance in Colonial India 1750–1860* (Delhi, Oxford University Press, 1995).

Singh, Anita Inder, *The Origins of the Partition of India* (New Delhi, Oxford University Press, 1986).

Singh, Mohan, *Shekhawati Main Swatantra Andolan Ka Itihas* (Jhunjhunun, Ravindra Prakashan, 1990).

Singh, Mohinder, 'The Congress and Nationalist Sikh Politics', in B.N. Pandey (ed.), *A Centenary History of the Indian National Congress* (New Delhi, Vikas Publishing, 1985).

Singhi, Bhawarmal (ed.), *Padam Bhushan Shri Sitaram Seksaria Abhinandan Granth* (Calcutta, 1974).
Sinha, N.K., *The Economic History of Bengal*, Vol. III (Calcutta, K.L. Mukhopadhyay, 1965).
Sinha, S.L.N., *The History of the Reserve Bank of India, 1935–57* (Bombay, 1970).
Shradhanjali Swaragiya Jugalkishore Birla (n.n., 1974, Sanskriti Sansthan, Pilani).
Somejee, A.H. & G., 'India' in *The Journal of Politics*, 1963, Vol. 25, pp. 686–737.
Srinivas, M.N., 'Sociology in Delhi' in Dharma Kumar and D. Mookherjee (eds), *Delhi School. Reflections on the Delhi School of Economics* (Delhi, Oxford University Press, 1995).
Srivastava, B.K. and Venkatramani, *The Quit India Movement: The American Response* (New Delhi, Vikas Publishing, 1979).
Srivastava, C.P., *Lal Bahadur Shastri: a life of truth in politics* (Delhi, Oxford University Press, 1996).
Subramanayam, M., *Why Cripps Failed* (New Delhi, The Hindustan Times Press, 1943).
Sullivan, R.J.F., *One Hundred Years of Bombay, History of the Bombay Chamber of Commerce 1836–1936* (Bombay, The Times of India Press, 1937).
Sundaram, V.A. (ed.), *Benaras Hindu University 1905–35* (Banaras, 1936).
Tahmankar, D.V., *Sardar Patel* (London, Allen & Unwin, 1970).
Taknet, D.K., *Industrial Entreprenuership among Shekhawati Marwaris* (Jaipur, Manohar, 1986).
——, *Marwari Samaj* (Jaipur, 1989).
——, *B.M. Birla. A Great Visionary* (New Delhi, Indus, 1996).
Tan, Tai Yong and Gyanesh Kudaisya, *The Aftermath of Partition in South Asia* (London, Routledge, 2000).
Tantia, Rameshwar, *Kuch Apni Kuch Jagki* (Calcutta, 1967).
——, *Kuch Ghatnain, Kuch Sansmaran* (Calcutta, 1969).
Tayyeb, A., *Pakistan: A Political Geography* (London, Oxford University Press, 1966).
Tendulkar, D.G., *Mahatma. A Life of Mahatma Gandhi*, Vol. 11 (New Delhi, Publications Division of the Government of India, 1951–54).
——, *Mahatma: Life of Mohandas Karamchand Gandhi* (Bombay, 1954).
Thakore, Dilip, 'A Legend in his Lifetime' in *Business India*, 30 March–12 April 1981.
——, 'G.D. Birla: A Patriarch Passes Away', *Business World*, 20 June–3 July 1983.
The Birla Education Trust and its Institutions (Pilani, Birla Education Trust, 1944).
The House of Birla—1862–1962 A Centenary Souvenir (n.d., n.p.).
The Imperial Gazetteer of India, Vol. VIII (Oxford, Clarendon Press, 1908).
Tharoor, Shashi, *India From Midnight to Millenium* (London, Arcade Publications, 1997).
Timberg, Thomas A., *The Marwaris From Traders to Industrialists* (New Delhi, Vikas Publishing, 1978).
——, 'Hiatus and Incubator: Indigenous Trade and Traders, 1837–1857' in Asiya Siddiqi (ed.), *Trade and Finance in Colonial India 1750–1860* (Delhi, Oxford University Press, 1995).
——, 'A North Indian Firm as seen through its Business Records, 1860–1914 Tarachand Ghanshyamdas, A Great Marwari Firm', *Indian Economic and Social History Review*, Vol. 8, No. 3 (1971).
——, 'Three types of the Marwari Firm', *Indian Economic and Social History Review*, Vol. 10, January 1973.
Tinker, Hugh, *The Ordeal of Love: C.F. Andrews and India* (New Delhi, Oxford University Press, 1979).
Tirumalai, R., *T.T.K. The Dynamic Innovator* (Madras, TT. Maps & Publications Private Ltd., 1988).
Todd, Col., *Annals and Antiquities of Rajasthan or the Central and Rajpoot States of India*, 3 Volumes, (London, Oxford University Press, 1920).
Tomlinson, B.R., *The Political Economy of the Raj 1974–47 The Economics of Decolonization in India* (London, Macmillan, 1979).
——, 'India and the British Empire, 1880–1935', *Indian Economic and Social History Review*, Vol. 11, No. 4, 1975.
——, 'Foreign Private Investment in India, 1920–1950', *Modern Asian Studies*, Vol. 12, No. 4, 1978.
——, 'Britain and the Indian Currency Crisis 1930–1932', *Economic History Review*, Vol. II, No. 1, 1979.
——, 'Colonial Firms and the decline of Colonialism in Eastern India 1914–1947', *Modern Asian Studies*, Vol. 15, No. 3, 1981.
——, *The Economy of Modern India, 1860–1970* (Cambridge, Cambridge University Press, 1993).
Tripathi, Dwijendra, 'Indian Entrepreneurship in Historical Perspective: A Reinterpretation', *Economic and Political Weekly*, 29 May 1971.
——, (ed.), *State and Business in India: A Historical Perspective* (New Delhi, Manohar, 1987).

——, 'Congress and the Indian Industrialists (1885–1947)' in Indian Institute of Management, Ahmedabad (IIMA), Seminar Series in Business History (IV), 'Business and Politics in India'.

——, *Business Communities of India: A Historical Perspective* (New Delhi, Manohar, 1984).

——, The Dynamics of a Tradition. Kasturbhai Lalbhai and his Entrepreneurship (Delhi, Manohar, 1981).

——, 'The Congress and the Industrial Question 1919–35' in B.N. Pande (ed.), A *Centenary History of the Indian National Congress, 1885–1985*, Vol. 11 (New Delhi, Vikas Publishing, 1985).

——, and Markand Mehta, *Business Houses in Western India: A Study in Entrepreneurial Response, 1850–1957* (London, 1989).

——, (ed.), *Business and Politics in India, A Historical Perspective* (Delhi, Manohar, 1991).

Tyabji, Nasir, *Industrialization and Innovation: the Indian Experience* (New Delhi, Sage Publications, 2000).

——, *The Small Industries Policy in India* (Calcutta, Oxford University Press, 1989).

Tyson, G.W., *The Bengal Chamber of Commerce and Industry 1853–1953, A Centenary Survey* (Calcutta, Published for the Bengal Chamber of Commerce and Industry by D.A. Lakin at The Statesman, 1953).

Upadhyaya, Haribhau, *Shreyarthi Jamnalalji* (New Delhi, 1951).

Vakil, C.N., *Economic Consequences of Divided India: A Study of the Economy of India and Pakistan* (Bombay, Vora & Co. Publishers, 1950).

Venkatsubbiah, H., *Enterprise and Economic Change. 50 Years of FICCI* (New Delhi, FICCI, 1977).

Vicziany, Marika, 'Bombay merchants and structural changes in the export community 1850 to 1880', in Asiya Siddiqi (ed.), *Trade and Finance in Colonial India 1750–1860* (Delhi, Oxford University Press, 1995).

Vidyalankar, Satyaketu, *Agrawal Jati Ka Pracheen Itihas* (New Delhi, 1938).

Visharad, Vishambar Prasad Sharma, *Swargiya Ramkrishnaji Mohta Jiwan Charitra Aur Sansmaran* (Calcutta, 1941).

Voight, J., *India In the Second World War* (New Delhi, Arnold-Heinemann, 1987).

Wade, Robert, *Governing the Market, Economic Theory and the Role of Government in East Asian Industrialisation* (Princeton, Princeton University Press, 1990).

Watson, Francis and Hallam Tennyson, *Talking of Gandhiji: four programmes for radio, first broadcast for the British Broadcasting Corporation* (Calcutta, Orient Longman, 1957).

Wolpert, Stanley, *Jinnah of Pakistan* (Oxford, Oxford University Press, 1984).

Glossary

Ahimsa	the philosophy of not harming any animal life; non-violence
Akhara	meeting place for the practice of a specific art or hobby, often used for wrestling
Angrakhan	garment worn by men around the shoulder
Arhatiya	commission agent
Artha	material prosperity; money
Ashram	a hermitage; a community residence usually of small cottages
Ayurvedic	pertaining to the Hindu science of medicine as taught in the Atharvaveda
Bahi-khata	account book of merchants containing separate accounts for each head and class of business
Bania	trader; money-lender
Bassa	dormitory; communal home of immigrant trader
Bhajan	devotional songs
Bhakti	devotion
Bigha	a measure of land in north India
Biradari	community; brotherhood; kinsfolk
Brahman	a member of the highest or priestly caste among the Hindus
Brahman bari	home for brahmans
Chaddar	sheet
Chapkan	a long loose robe chiefly used as a part of official dress
Charkha	hand-operated spinning wheel
Chhatravaas	hostel for students
Crore	unit of ten million
Daan	charity; donation; alms-giving
Daanveer	prince among donors
Dalal	agent between buyer and seller
Dangal	wrestling tournament
Darshan	act of seeing or visiting in order to pay homage
Dharamshala	rest-house for pilgrims; tavern for Hindus
Dharma	religion, moral order, duty, obligation
Dhoti	garment for the lower body
Diwali	Hindu festival of light
Dupatta	a long piece of cloth draped around the shoulders
Fataka	speculation
Gadda	pillow or backrest
Gaddi	a large sitting pad or a cloth throne; in the Marwari context a euphemism for a business firm
Ganesh	elephant-headed god of auspicious beginnings
Ganesh Chaturthi	the day when Lord Ganesh is worshipped
Ghani	a large circular block of wood for grinding oil seeds to extract oil from them

Ghat	landing steps on a river bank used for bathing or ritual performance of death ceremonies
Ghee	clarified butter
Gherao	a form of protest; refers to the act of surrounding a person in order to compel him to meet the demands of the surrounders
Gita	Hindu ethical text
Gomashta	commercial agent; sub-clerk
Goshala	shelter for cows; cowshed
Gur	hard molasses
Guru	teacher; spiritual guide
Hartal	closure of market in protest
Havan	a ceremonial offering to God made through a holy fire signifying the purity of the offering
Haveli	north-Indian-style mansion
Holi	Hindu festival of colour held in spring
Hundi	mercantile notes of credit or written orders for payment
Hundi mukl	ledger into which all copies of the hundis are entered
Jama-bahi	physical inventory of a firm
Jat	rural caste group from Uttar Pradesh, Haryana and Punjab region
Jati	basic unit of Hindu caste
Jati shakti	refers to the social and moral strength of a united community
Karma	a person's actions in one of his incarnations that determine his fate in the next one
Katha	recitation of religious texts at prayer meetings
Khadi	a coarse fabric woven with hand-spun yarn
Khaki	a light cloth of dull brown colour used specially for making military uniform
Khata-bahi	account ledger with separate accounts for each head and class of business
Khattri	north Indian mercantile caste
Kirtan	songs in praise of God
Kuchcha	raw
Kumbh	major Hindu fair held every twelve years
Lakh	unit of 100,000
Lakshmi	Hindu goddess of wealth
Lathi	staff, usually with a metal tip
Mahajani shiksha	education befitting a trader
Mahavidyalaya	high school
Mela	fair
Mistry	mason; labourer
Moksha	salvation of the soul
Mufossil	country stations as opposed to principal towns
Muladhaar	the real cause; convenor
Mukaddam	agent
Munim	factor, agent, head clerk
Nag Panchami	the day when the snake is worshipped
Pagri	headgear which symbolized honour
Paisa	small coin
Pan	betel-leaf served together with betel-nut, lime and spice
Panch	the five members of the Panchayat
Panchayat	court of arbitration usually made up of five members
Pandit	learned man; often used for brahman
Parta	Marwari system of book-keeping
Pathshala	primary school
Patti pahara	multiplication tables and formulas for computing interest
Prachar	to propagate
Puja	Hindu prayer, worship

Purdah	observance of the veil by women
Purna Swaraj	total self-rule
Pustakalaya	library
Qasba	country town
Ramayana	Hindu epic
Ramnavami	birthday of the Hindu god, Rama
Rishi	an ascetic
Rokad khata	daily cash book of a merchant house
Rokara	cash; cash box
Rokarbahi	cash ledger or book
Sabha	assembly, organization
Sadhu	holy man
Sakh	credit worthiness; incorporates a moral dimension
Samvat	Hindu calendar roughly 57 years ahead of the Christian calendar.
Sanad	grant; honour; title deed
Sanatan Dharma	a very conservative form of Hindu religion and tradition
Sanatani	a follower of the conservative form of Hindu religion
Sangathan	organization; unity
Sangh	group; caravan
Sanyasin	female ascetic
Sarai	tavern
Saraswati	Hindu goddess of learning
Sarraf	money changer
Satta	speculation
Satyagraha	passive resistance, picketing or strike
Seth	wealthy merchant
Shastra	Hindu scriptures
Shiva	the Destroyer; one of the three gods of the Hindu Trinity
Shroff	banker
Shuddhi	act of purification; movement for re-conversion of converted Hindu untouchables
Swadeshi	of one's own country; an Indian nationalist movement to encourage the use of indigenous goods and boycott of foreign goods
Swaraj	Self-rule
Tilak	a mark painted or impressed on the forehead
Tirtha-yatra	pilgrimage
Tulsi	basil, considered holy by Hindus
Vaishnavite	pertaining to the worship of Lord Vishnu
Vaishya	member of caste group traditionally associated with commerce
Vanaspati	a commercial name given to the oil extracted from a plant source and used for cooking
Vidyalaya	educational institution
Vishnu	the Preserver; one of the three gods of the Hindu Trinity
Vyayamshala	gymnasium; meant more for exercise
Yagna	Hindu ritual of offering to the Gods through a holy fire
Zamindar	landowner

Biographical Notes

Ali, Chaudhury Mohammad (1905–80) Secretary General to Government of Pakistan; subsequently Finance Minister and Prime Minister of Pakistan.

Bajaj, Jamnalal (1889–1942) Marwari trader, industrialist and nationalist with major interests in cotton and sugar; founder of several Marwari organizations; close associate of Gandhi; treasurer, Indian National Congress 1920–42.

Benthall, Sir Edward Charles (1893–1961) British businessman in Calcutta; Chairman, Bird & Co; Governor, Imperial Bank of India 1928–3; President, Associated Chamber of Commerce of India 1932; member, Governor-General's Executive Council 1942–6.

Bharatiya, Shobhana (b. 1956) granddaughter of G.D. Birla; daughter of Krishna Kumar and Manorama Devi; married Shyamsunder Bharatiya in 1973; Executive Director of the *Hindustan Times*.

Birla, Aditya (1943–95) grandson of G.D. Birla; son of Basant Kumar and Sarala; educated at Massachusetts Institute of Technology; married Rajshree in 1965; inducted into Hindustan Aluminum and Grasim Industries by G.D. Birla; responsible for overseas expansion of business.

Birla, Anasuiya (b. 1923) daughter of G.D. Birla and Mahadevi; married Narendra Singh Taparia in 1941.

Birla, Ashok Vardhan (1939–90) son of Gajanan and Gopi Devi; trained by Basant Kumar in business; married Sunanda in 1958; died in air crash in 1990.

Birla, Baldeodas (1863–1956) father of G.D. Birla; married to Yogeshwari Devi of Churu; established the firm 'Baldeodas Shivnarain'; trader and philanthropist.

Birla, Basant Kumar (b. 1921) son of G.D. Birla and Mahadevi; trained in business by Braj Mohan; married Sarala Biyani in 1942; major interests in textile, rayon, cement, telecom; philanthropist and patron of arts.

Birla, Bhagwani Devi sister of G.D. Birla; married Krishnagopal Mahata of Rajgarh.

Birla, Braj Mohan (1904–82) younger brother of G.D. Birla; married Rukmani Devi of Taparia family; trained in business by Baldeodas; headed Bombay business of Birla Brothers; Founder-President, Indian Sugar Mills Association and Indian Paper Mills Association; President, Indian Chamber of Commerce (1936, 1944); President, FICCI 1954.

Birla. Chandra Kant (b. 1955) son of Ganga Prasad and Nirmala Devi; trained in business by Braj Mohan; heads Hindustan Motors, Hyderabad Asbestos, Orient Cement and other firms.

Birla, Chandrakala (b. 1914) daughter of G.D. Birla; married Banshi Dhar Daga of Jalpaiguri in 1931.

Birla, Durgadevi daughter of Mahadev Somany of Chirawa; married G.D. Birla in 1906; died in 1910.

Birla, Gajanan (1910–61) elder son of Rameshwar Das; married Gopi Devi of Malpani family of Jabalpur in 1929; subsequently married Sumitra Devi in 1946; was disinherited from family business.

Birla, Ganga Prasad (1922) only son of Braj Mohan and Rukmani Devi; first graduate in Birla family; trained by Braj Mohan in business; married Vimala Devi of Jhawar in 1945; subsequently married Nirmala Devi Daga in 1952; started a number of enterprises such as Sirpur Paper Mill, Sirsilk, Asbestos Cement; started overseas ventures in Kenya and Nigeria.

Birla, Jayashree (b. 1951) daughter of Basant Kumar and Sarala; married Prakash Mehta in 1969; Vice-Chairperson, Birla Academy of Art and Culture. Calcutta.

Birla, Jugalkishore (1883–1966) eldest brother of G.D. Birla; married to Jwahari Devi of Biyani family; retired early from business to engage in philanthropy.

Birla, Krishna Kumar (b. 1918) second son of G.D. Birla and Mahadevi; trained in business by Braj Mohan; married Manorma Devi in 1941; elected to Rajya Sabha, 1984 and 1990.

Birla, Kumar Mangalam (b. 1967) son of Aditya and Rajshree; educated at London Business School; trained in business by Aditya Birla; married Neerja Kasliwal in 1989; inherited the Aditya Birla Group of Companies in 1995; member, Prime Minister's Advisory Council on Trade and Industry 1998.

Birla, Lakshmi Niwas (1909–94) son of G.D Birla and Durga Devi; married Sushila Devi, daughter of Diwan of Kishangarh; trained in business by G.D. Birla and Braj Mohan; adopted as son by Jugalkishore; President of FICCI; author and philanthropist.

Birla, Madhav Prasad (1918–90) son of Rameshwardas and Gulab Devi; trained by G.D. Birla in business; married Sumitra Mohta; subsequently married Sushila Taparia (Priyamvada) in 1943; President, Indian Jute Mills Association, 1947.

Birla, Mahadevi daughter of Premsukhdas Karwa; married G.D. Bila upon the demise of his first wife; died in 1926.

Birla, Manjushree (b. 1957) daughter of Basant Kumar and Sarala; married Shailesh Khaitan in 1975; active in educational philanthropy and patronage of the arts.

Birla, Priyamvada widow of Madhav Prasad; head of M.P. Birla Group of Industries.

Birla, Radha Krishen (b. 1913) native of Pilani; joined Birla Cotton Mills, Delhi at young age; served as manager in several Birla companies; later set up independent business with major interests in woollen industry; elected to Lok Sabha in 1967.

Birla, Rajshree (b. 1947) first graduate daughter-in-law in Birla family; married Aditya Birla in 1965; philanthropist.

Birla, Rameshwardas (1892–1973) elder brother of G.D. Birla; trained in family business by Baldeodas; married Gulab Devi of Mundhra family; subsequently married Sharada Devi Jhawar in 1925; looked after Bombay business of the family.

Birla, Sarala (b. 1923) daughter of prominent nationalist leader from Berar, Brijlal Biyani and Savitri Devi; educated at Fergusson College; introduced to Birla family by Jamnalal Bajaj and Mahatma Gandhi; married Basant Kumar in 1942 at Gandhi's ashram; helped G.D. Birla in publishing his memoirs and correspondence; patron of arts and educational philanthropist.

Birla, Shanti (b. 1924) youngest child of G.D. Birla and Mahadevi; married Krishnagopal Maheshwari in 1941.

Birla, Shivnarain (1840–1955) grandfather of G.D. Birla; first member of Birla family to migrate from Rajasthan; trader in silver, gold, cotton and opium.

Birla, Siddharth (b. 1957) son of Sudarshan Kumar and Sumangala; married Anushree Maheswari in 1977.

Birla, Sudarshan Kumar (b. 1934) son of Lakshmi Niwas and Sushila Devi; trained in business by Madhav Prasad; married Sumangala Jhawar in 1955; President, FICCI, 1990.

Birla, Yashowardhan (b. 1967) son of Ashok Vardhan and Sunanda.

Biyani Brijlal (1896–1968) prominent Congress leader from Central provinces; businessman of Maheshwari caste; member, C.P. and Berar Legislature, 1926–9; member, Council of State, 1937; President, All-India Marwari Federation, 1947; member of Parliament, 1952; Minister of Finance, Madhya Pradesh; founder, Berar Chamber of Commerce.

Chandrashekhar socialist leader; member of 'Young Turks' within the Congress in 1960s; President, Janata Party, 1977; Prime Minister, 1990–1.

Chetty, Shanmugam R.K. Finance Minister from 1947 till his resignation in 1948.

Churchill, Sir Winston (1874–1965) Chancellor of the Exchequer, 1924–9; Prime Minister of Britain, 1940–5 and 1951–5.

Cripps, Sir Richard Stafford (1889–1952) British politician; carried constitutional proposals to India in 1942; member of Cabinet Mission in 1946; Chancellor of the Exchequer, 1947–50.

Dalmia, Ramkrishna (1893) bania from Punjab; trader, speculator and industrialist with major interests in cement, sugar, paper, chemicals; controlled the *Times of India.*

Dalmia, Murlidhar Marwari from Shekhawati; joined Birla business at a young age; subsequently Executive President, Birla Jute Mill; key member of Birla Group; responsible for initiating Basant Kumar into the family business.

Desai, Bhulabhai (1877–1946) lawyer in Bombay High Court; nationalist leader; member, Central Legislative Assembly, 1934–9.

Desai, Mahadev (1892–1942) secretary to Gandhi.

Desai, Morarji (1896–1995) nationalist leader from Bombay; Chief Minister of Bombay, 1946–52; Minister for Commerce and Industry, Government of India, 1956–8; treasurer, All India Congress Committee, 1950–8; Deputy Prime Minister and Minister of Finance, 1967–9; Prime Minister, 1977–9.

Deshmukh, C.D. (1896–1982) Governor of Reserve Bank of India, 1943–9; Minister of Finance, 1950–6; Chairman, University Grants Commission, 1956–61.

Fernandes, George (1930) founder of Samyukta Socialist Party; Union Cabinet Minister, 1977–9, 1989–90; President, Samata Party, 1994 onwards; Minister of Defence, 1998.

Gandhi, Devdas (1900–62) son of Mahatma Gandhi; President, All India Newspaper Editors' Conference, 1947–8; Managing Editor of *Hindustan Times*, 1937–57.

Gandhi, Indira (1917–84) only child of Jawaharlal and Kamala Nehru; Minister of Information and Broadcasting, 1964–6; Prime Minister of India, 1966–77; and 1980–4.

Gandhi, M.K. (1869–1948) Gujarati of bania caste; barrister; fought for rights of Indians in South Africa; returned to India in 1915 and resisted British rule with non-violent methods; assassinated by Hindu fanatic.

Ghosh, Atulya (1904–86) Bengal Congress leader; well known for fund-raising skills; prominent member of the 'Syndicate'.

Goenka, Rai Badridas (1883–1973) Marwari merchant, banker and industrialist; major interests in jute, insurance, investment; President, Marwari Association, 1928–30; member, Bengal Legislative Council, 1923–35; Sheriff of Calcutta, 1932–3; Director, Reserve Bank of India, 1935–41; President of FICCI, 1945–6.

Grady, Henry (1882–1957) Chief Trade Negotiator for US President F.D. Roosevelt; Head of Trade Mission to India, 1942; American Ambassador in India, 1947–8.

Gupta, C.B. (1902–80) Congress leader from Uttar Pradesh; Chief Minister, UP, 1960–3, 1967.

Guru Hanuman (1901–99) native of Chirawa village, Rajasthan; legendary wrestler; established akhara at Birla Mill, 1925; recipient of Padma Shree from Government of India, 1983; Dronacharya Award, 1991.

Haq, Fazlul (1873–1962) lawyer; member, Bengal Legislative Council, 1913–20; President of Muslim League 1916–21; Chief Minister of Bengal, 1937–43.

Himmatsinghka, P.D. (1889–1993) prominent Calcutta Marwari and associate of G.D. Birla; solicitor; founder of several Marwari organizations in Calcutta; elected thrice to Bengal Council between 1927 and 1948; Treasurer, Congress Parliamentary Party, 1949–51; member, Rajya Sabha, 1956–62; member, Lok Sabha, 1962–7.

Hirachand, Walchand (1883–1953) Digambar Jain businessman from Sholapur; trader, moneylender, industrialist; major interests in construction, sugar, shipping; President, Indian Merchants Chamber, 1927; President of FICCI, 1933.

Hoare, Sir Samuel (1880–1959) Conservative MP, 1910–44; Secretary of State for India, 1931–5; Foreign Secretary, 1935; Home Secretary, 1937–9; Lord Privy Seal, 1939–40.

Irwin, Lord (1881–1959) Under-secretary for Colonies, 1921–2; Viceroy of India, 1926–31; Foreign Secretary, 1938–40; British Ambassador to Washington, 1941–6.

Ismail, Sir Mirza Prime Minister, Jaipur, 1942.

Ispahani, M.A.H (1902–81) businessman from Calcutta; member Working Committee, Muslim League; Pakistan's Ambassador to the USA, 1947–52; Pakistan's High Commissioner to London, 1952–4; Minister, Industries and Commerce, Pakistan, 1954–5.

Jalan, Ishwardas (1895–1979) Marwari lawyer; Speaker, West Bengal Legislative Assembly, 1947; member, Bengal Legislative Assembly, 1938–58.

Jha, Lakshmi Kant (1913–?) member of Indian Civil Service; secretary to Prime Minister, 1964–7; Governor of the Reserve Bank of India, 1967–70.

Jinnah, Mohammad Ali (1976–1948) President of All India Muslim League, 1934–48; leader of Pakistan movement from 1940; Governor General of Pakistan, 1947–8.

Kamaraj, K. (1903–75) Congressman from Madras; Chief Minister of Tamil Nadu, 1954–63; President of Indian National Congress, 1963–7; key member of the 'Syndicate'.

Khaitan, Devi Prasad first Marwari attorney; General Manager, Birla Brothers, 1911 onwards; President, Marwari Association, 1921; member, Bengal Legislative Assembly, 1922–6; President, Indian Chamber of Commerce, 1930; President, FICCI, 1936.

Khan, Liaquat Ali (1895–1951) General Secretary of Muslim League from 1936; member of the Interim Government, 1946–7; Prime Minister of Pakistan from 1947 till 1951.

Khemka, Sitaram Marwari from Bikaner; joined Birla Brothers Limited, 1918; subsequently responsible for running of Birla firms in the textile business; helped initiate Basant Kumar into family business.

Kripalani, J.B. (1899–1979) President, Indian National Congress, 1946–7; member, Constituent Assembly and Indian Parliament; subsequently active as an oppostition leader.

Krishnamachari, T.T. (1899–1964) businessman from Madras; joined Congress, 1942; elected to Lok Sabha and Union Minister, 1952–65.

Lalbhai, Kasturbhai (1894–1980) Jain businessman; major interests in cotton and textiles; President, Ahmedabad Mills Association, 1936–7; President of FICCI, 1934–5.

Linlithgow, Lord (1887–1952) Chairman of Royal Commission on Indian Agriculture, 1926–8; Chairman of Joint Select Committee on Indian Constitutional Reform, 1933; Viceroy of India, 1936–43.

Lokanathan, P.S. (1894–1972) professor of Economics, Madras University; Executive Secretary of United Nations Economic Commission for Asia and the Far East (ECAFE) 1947–56; editor, *Eastern Economist*.

Mahalanobis, Prasanta Chandra (1893–1972) scientist and statistician; member, Planning Commission, 1955–67.

Malaviya, Madan Mohan (1861–1946) President of Indian National Congress, 1909 and 1918; founder of Independent Congress Party; founder of Banaras Hindu University.

Malaviya, K.D. (1904–81) Congress leader from Uttar Pradesh; Union Minister, 1957–63 and 1973–7.

Mandelia, Durga Prasad (b. 1907) Marwari from Pilani; joined Birla Jute Mills as clerk; subsequently played an important part in companies such as Century Mills, Jiyajeerao Cotton Mills, Grasim, Cimmco, and Hindalco; confidante of G.D. Birla for over 50 years.

Mathai, John (1886–1959) professor of Economics, Madras University, 1920–5; member, Madras Legislative Council, 1922–5; Director-General, Commercial Intelligence and Statistics, 1935–40; subsequently Director, Tata Sons Ltd; Minister of Railways and Transport, 1947–8; Minister of Finance, 1948–50, resigned from Government, June 1950 and rejoined Tata Sons.

Mehta, Asoka (b. 1911) Founder-President, Congress Socialist Party and member, National Executive of Party, 1934–48; leader of Praja Socialist Party in 1950s and 1960s; Deputy Chairman, Planning Commission; Union Minister of Planning; Union Minister of Planning Petroleum and Chemicals and Social Welfare, 1967.

Mehta, G.L. (1900–74) businessman; President of FICCI, 1942–3; President, Indian Tariff Board, 1947–50; member, Planning Commission, 1950–2; Ambassador to the USA and Mexico, 1952–8.

Mitra, C.R. first Director of Birla Institute of Technology and Science, Pilani.

Mody, Sir Homy (1881–1969) Parsi lawyer; Chairman, Bombay Millowners' Association, 1927 and 1929–34; President, Indian Merchants' Chamber, 1928; member, Legislative Assembly 1929–43; Governor of Bombay, 1947; Chairman, Associated Cement Company and Central Bank of India.

Mohta, Ramkrishna prominent trader and philanthropist; close associate of Birla Brothers in Bara Bazaar from the 1900s.

Morarka, Basantlal Marwari businessman in Calcutta; close associate of Birla Brothers from 1900s; Secretary, Bara Bazaar Congress Commmittee, 1920; President, Akhil Bharadiya Agarwal Mahasabha, 1926; later West Bengal politician.

Mountbatten, Lady Edwina (1901–60) wife of Lord Mountbatten.

Mountbatten, Viscount Louis (1900–79) Viceroy of India, March–August, 1947; created Earl Mountbatten of Burma in 1947; Admiral of the Fleet in 1956.

Munshi, K.M. (1891–1971) lawyer; Congress leader from Bombay; founded Bharatiya Vidya Bhavan, 1938; Home Minister of Bombay, 1937–9; later Union Minister of Agriculture and Food; subsequently important member of the Swatantra Party.

Namboodaripad, E.M.S. (1909–98) socialist leader; General Secretary of Communist Party of India; Chief Minister of Kerala, 1957–9; CPI(M) General-Secretary, 1977–92.

Nanda, Gulzarilal (1898–1998) Union Minister, 1951–66; Acting Prime Minister, 1964, 1966.

Narayan, Jayaprakash (1902–79) one of the founders of the Congress Socialist Party, 1934; member of Working Committee of Congress, 1936; after 1947 leading member of Socialist Party.

Nayar, Sushila (1914–2001) personal physician of Gandhi.

Nazimuddin, Khwaja (1894–1973) Bengal Muslim League politician; Prime Minister of East Pakistan, 1947; subsequently Governor-General of Pakistan.

Nehru, Jawaharlal (1889–1964) lawyer from Allahabad; prominent leader of the Indian nationalist movement; President of Indian National Congress, 1929–30, 1936, 1937, 1946. Prime Minister of India, 1947–64.

Nehru, Motilal (1861–1931) lawyer from Allahabad; President, Indian National Congress, 1919 and 1928; founder of the Swarajya Party within the Congress and its leader in the Central Assembly, 1924–6.

Neogy, K.C. (1888–1977) member of Central Assembly, 1921–34 and 1942–7; Union Minister for Commerce, 1948–50.

Pande, Sukhdev (1893–) brahman from UP; Assistant Professor, Banaras Hindu University from 1918; Principal, Birla College, Pilani for 17 years; Secretary of Birla Education Trust.

Pant, G.B. (1887–1961) leading Congress leader from UP; Chief Minister of UP, 1937–9 and 1946–55; Union Home Minister, 1955–61.

Patel, Vallabhbhai (1875–1950) Congress leader from Gujarat; President of Indian National Congress, 1931; member, Interim Government, 1946–7; Deputy Prime Minister of India and Minister for Home, States, Information and Broadcasting, 1947–50.

Patil, S.K. (1900–) journalist; Congress leader from Maharashtra; member, Bombay Municipal Corporation for 17 years; member of Parliament four times; well known for his skills as fund collector for the Congress Party; member of the 'Syndicate'.

Poddar, Anandilal (1874–1940) Marwari trader and industrialist; major interests in cotton and silk; involved for the Congress politics; Mayor of Calcutta, 1944–5.

Poddar, Hanuman Prasad (1892–1971) Marwari; implicated in Rodda case, 1916; along with Jamnalal Bajaj, set up the Akhil Bharatiya Marwari Agarwal Sabha, 1921; proprietor of Gita Press which brought out the monthly *Kalyan*, a popular Hindu journal propagating *Hindutva*.

Prasad, Rajendra (1884–1963) lawyer and politician from Bihar; President of the Indian National Congress 1934, 1939 and 1947–8; President of the Constituent Assembly of India, 1946–9; President of India, 1950–6.

Pyarelal (1899–1982) secretary to Gandhi in his later years.

Rai, Lala Lajpat (1865–1928) lawyer from Punjab; prominent leader of the early Indian National Congress; important protagonist of Arya Samaj in north India; founded the Independent Congress Party with Madan Mohan Malaviya; founded DAV educational institutions.

Rajagopalachari, Chakravarty (1878–1972) lawyer and politician from Madras; Prime Minister, Madras 1937–9; Member of Interim Government, 1946–7; Governor of West Bengal, 1947–8; Governor General of India, 1948–50.

Roy, Bidhan Chandra (1882–1962) physician; Chief Minister of West Bengal, 1948–62.

Saboo, Tarachand Marwari from Pilani; joined Birla business at young age; subsequently key member of Birla group; endowed Saboo Commerce College in Pilani.

Sahni, J.N., editor of *Hindustan Times*, 1926–30.

Santhanam, L. (b. 1895), lawyer of Madras; member, Legislative Assembly, 1937–42; joint editor of *Hindustan Times*, 1943–8.

Sarabhai, Ambalal (b. 1890), Ahmedabad mill-owner with major interests in textiles; close associate of Gandhi.

Sarkar, Nalini Ranjan (1888–1953) President, FICCI, 1935, Mayor of Calcutta, 1934–5; member, Governor General's Executive Council, 1941–2.

Savarkar, V.D. (1883–1966) President, All India Hindu Mahasabha, 1937–44; ideologue of *Hindutva*.

Schweitzer, Pierre-Paul (1912) Managing Director, International Monetary Fund, 1963–73.

Shastri, Lal Bahadur (1904–66) Congressman from UP; Union Minister, 1952–64; Prime Minister, 1964–6.

Shri Ram, Lala (1884–1962) Punjabi of Agarwal caste; businessman with major interests in cotton; President, FICCI, 1930; member of Board of Reserve Bank from 1935; philanthropist.

Shroff, A.D. (1899–1965) Parsi stockbroker, industrialist and financial expert; director of several Tata concerns; Vice-President of Indian Merchants' Chamber; non-official delegate to the Bretton Woods Conference, 1944; founder of Forum of Free Enterprise, 1956.

Singhanai, Lala Padampat Sir (1905–79) Marwari businessman from Kanpur; major interest in cotton; President, FICCI, 1935.

Sinha, Parasnath tutor to Lakshmi Niwas Birla; Managing editor of *Hindustan Times*.

Sri Prakasa (1890–1971) Secretary of Indian National Congress, 1927 and 1931; subsequently High Commissioner for India in Pakistan; Cabinet Minister, Governor of Assam, Madras, and Maharashtra.

Subramaniam, C. (1910) Minister for Steel and Heavy Industry, 1962–3; for Food and Agriculture, 1964–7; for Community Development and Cooperation, 1966–7.

Tandon, Purshottamdas (1892–1962) Congressman from Allahabad; Speaker of Uttar Pradesh Assembly, 1937–9 and 1946–50; President of Indian National Congress until 1950; resigned due to differences with Nehru.

Tata, J.R.D. (1904–93) Parsi industrialist and philanthropist; head of House of Tatas; member of Anti-Non-Cooperation League, 1919; signatory to Bombay Plan of 1944; Indian delegate to the UN General Assembly, 1948; awarded 'Legion of Honour' by Government of France, 1954; awarded Bharat Ratna, 1991, United Nations Population Award, 1992.

Thakkar, A.V. Bapa (1869–1951) Gandhian leader; General Secretary of Harijan Sevak Sangh.

Thakurdas, Purshotamdas (1879–1961) Gujarati of *Kapol Bania* caste; Bombay businessman and philanthropist; major interests in cotton; Vice-President, Indian Merchants' Chamber, 1907; member of Central Legislature; President, Federation of Indian Chambers of Commerce and Industry, 1927–8; unofficial adviser to Government of India for the Indo-British trade negotiations in 1936–8; one of the closest business associates of G.D. Birla; signatory to the Bombay Plan of 1944.

Woods, George Donald (1901–82) President of the World Bank, 1963–8.

Zetland, Second Marquis (1876–1961) Governor of Bengal, 1917–22; Secretary of State for India, 1935–40.

Index

186n, 202, 205, 213, 23n, 231, 235, 272, 284, 309, 310
member of, Central Legislative Assembly 123
  Indian Merchants' Chamber 143n
  Indian Retrenchment Committee 143n
  Royal Commission on Indian Currency and Finance 143n
  representing at Round Table Conference 129, 138, 143n
Thatcher, Margaret 390
Tilak, B.G. 39, 51n, 52n, 53n
Tilak School of Politics 74
Tilak Swaraj Fund 64, 82n
  Birla's contribution to 89
Tiwari, Shivanandrai 49n
Trade Disputes Bill of 1929 121
trade unions 169, 174
Truman, Harry 286

United Commercial Bank (UCO Bank), nationalization of 380n
  riots in Punjab, and impact on 244
  takeover of 368–9
United Council for Relief and Welfare, Birla's contribution to 243
United nations 202, 203, 215n, 216n
United States, aid to India 280, 356
  failure/suspension of 347, 359
Universal Electric and Electronic Construction and Equipment (ECE) Company 386
Uttar Pradesh Congress, threat to 175
Uttar Pradesh, government's agreement with Birla Group for aluminium plant 334–5
Uttar Pradesh Labour Enquiry Committee's report 174

Vaishya caste 69
Vaishya Sabha 30, 50n
  Marawari Association and 30
Vakil, C.N. 222n, 322n

Viceroy's Executive Council 118, 197
  Congress' participation in 231
  control over currency/budget matters 134, 136
  Jinnah's nomination of Muslim members 233
  resignation of Indian members from 205
Vidya Shankar 286
Vishudanand Saraswati Vidyalaya, G.D. Birla's school
  in Calcutta 16, 17, 41, 51n

Wacha, Dinshaw 63
Wadia, C.N. 145n
War years 43–9, 197–213
  and economy 209, 210, 212–13
  distribution of essential commodities during 211
  and political deadlock 197–9
  and price control 307
Watson, J.C. 106n
Wedgewood, Lord 249n
Whitehall, power structure in 140
White Paper of 1933 139, 166, 167
Willingdon, Lord, Viceroy 130, 138, 153n, 172
Wilson, H. Gavin 47
Woods, George 334, 335, 337n, 346, 351n, 352n, 355n, 374n
World Bank 286, 345, 346
  on India's economy 351n
  recommendations of 312
  terms for loans 347

Young India, ban on 74
'Young Turks' 367, 368
Yugantar Samiti 37
Yule, Andrew 47

zamindari, abolition issue of 173
Zetland, Lord 168, 171, 180n, 183n, 184n
Zuary Agro Chemicals, in Goa 335, 387